# HANDBOOK OF
# ORGANIZATIONAL
# CULTURE &
# CLIMATE

# HANDBOOK OF
# ORGANIZATIONAL CULTURE & CLIMATE

## Neal M. Ashkanasy
## Celeste P. M. Wilderom
## Mark F. Peterson
### Editors

Sage Publications, Inc.
*International Educational and Professional Publisher*
Thousand Oaks ▪ London ▪ New Delhi

*For information:*

Sage Publications, Inc.
2455 Teller Road
Thousand Oaks, California 91320
E-mail: order@sagepub.com

Sage Publications Ltd.
6 Bonhill Street
London EC2A 4PU
United Kingdom

Sage Publications India Pvt. Ltd.
M-32 Market
Greater Kailash I
New Delhi 110 048 India

Printed in the United States of America

**Library of Congress Cataloging-in-Publication Data**

Main entry under title:

   Handbook of organizational culture and climate / edited by Neal M.
Ashkanasy, Celeste P. M. Wilderom, and Mark F. Peterson.
      p.   cm.
   Includes bibliographical references and index.
   ISBN 0-7619-1602-4 (acid-free paper)
   1. Organizational behavior.   2. Corporate culture.
I. Ashkanasy, Neal M., 1945-    II. Wilderom, Celeste P. M.
III. Peterson, Mark F.   IV. Title.
   HD58.7 .H363   2000
   658.4–dc21                                00-008367

Printed on acid-free paper.

00   01   02   03   04   05   06   07   7   6   5   4   3   2   1

| | |
|---|---|
| *Acquisition Editor:* | Marquita Flemming |
| *Editorial Assistant:* | Mary Ann Vail |
| *Production Editor:* | Astrid Virding |
| *Editorial Assistant:* | Nevair Kabakian |
| *Typesetters:* | Marion Warren/Janelle Lemaster/Lynn Miyata |
| *Indexer:* | Will Ragsdale |
| *Cover Designer:* | Candice Harman |

To Linda, Zac, Shawn, and David
—N. M. A.


To Usama, Noor, and Senna
—C. D. M. W.


To June and Eugene, Agnes and Tom
—M. F. P.

# Contents

# Viewpoints From Eminent Scholars of Culture and Climate

few scholars have had particularly long and influential roles in developing the ideas of organizational climate and culture. Among these are Andrew Pettigrew, Edgar Schein, and Benjamin Schneider. These three eminent scholars have consented to provide brief but incisive commentaries based on their own perspectives on the field. The first, by Andrew Pettigrew, appears as the foreword to this volume. Pettigrew makes the point that culture and climate continue to have legitimacy in organization science, but that we need to continue to stress the virtue of simplicity. He notes that many of the models of culture and climate come in threes, and he looks forward to a future handbook on the trinity of culture, climate, and change.

The contributions by Schneider and Schein are positioned as introductory commentaries. In the first of these, Schneider uses the metaphor of sibling rivalry to describe the relationship between climate and culture, and he suggests ways in which these children can play together constructively. In the second, Schein suggests ways in which climate and culture differ and discusses his experiences and views about the way each is best understood, represented, and used in work with organizations.

The three contributions by these eminent scholars strike the first notes of chords and phrases that other authors embellish throughout the volume. The directions the various authors take are by no means entirely consistent with one another, nor are they necessarily related to the specific issues raised in the three introductory essays. Nonetheless, frequent references throughout the *Handbook* to earlier publications by key scholars such as Pettigrew, Schneider, and Schein, and to the themes they introduce here, provide a basic coherence to this volume. They remind us that, ultimately, culture and climate reflect the melody, disharmony, and occasional cacophony not just in this field of study, but in organizational life in general.

# Foreword

*—— Andrew M. Pettigrew*

It is a pleasure to write this foreword and an honor to be asked to do so. This *Handbook* appears at a timely moment. We enter this new century challenged not by the natural occurrence of a new date, but by a world variously coping with political, economic, technological, and organizational change. As ever, each generation considers its pressure points uniquely demanding, but we know one of the lessons from history is that history repeats itself. This repetitive character of history is wrapped up in the strengths and weaknesses of the human beings who make history. For all the many explanations of history, we have to return to human conduct as one of the central drivers of our condition. In addressing what is known and not known about organizational climate and culture, this *Handbook* touches on many of the big issues about human conduct in organizational settings: how to understand and explain patterns and divergences in attitudes, perceptions, and values; how to make sense of language and symbols; how to balance continuity and change; how to intervene in organizations to deliver cultural change, improve climates for service and innovation, influence career development, and manage mergers and acquisitions. Appropriately, the contributors to this volume also engage in debates about the strengths and weaknesses of the conceptual language for analyzing, studying, and measuring organizational climate and culture. In all these ways and more, the *Handbook* offers intellectual challenge, reflection, and synthesis in two very important areas of organizational analysis and practice.

In writing a foreword, it is tempting to be forward. Controversial and contested intellectual areas open the gate for boldness. Where are the related fields of organizational climate and culture as I write in 1999? Their different intellectual heritage in the disciplines of psychology, sociology, and social anthropology ensure their different theoretical, epistemological, and methodological biases are still sharply visible. And what of the life cycles of these two important constructs? Climate research started earlier, peaked earlier, and probably has waned earlier. Why? Possibly because of the problems of levels of analysis, aggregation, and measurement so clearly expounded in this volume. Climate studies may also have been boxed in, even marginalized, by the appearance in the intellectual nest in the late 1970s and 1980s of the overnourished, noisy, and enigmatic cuckoo called organizational culture.

Sociologists of knowledge tell us that ideas arise propitiously out of receptive social contexts. In the introduction to this *Handbook,* Ashkanasy, Wilderom, and Peterson remind us that climate research arose from a confluence of field theory and the quantitative study of attitudes. Central to this marriage was Kurt Lewin's 1930s work on climate and leadership. Driving Lewin were the horrors in Germany from which he had escaped. Many authors have speculated on organizational culture's rise to prominence in the late 1970s and 1980s (see, e.g., Martin & Frost, 1996). Big questions rarely have single answers. The failing performance levels of big business in the United States and Europe, and the visibly rising economic power of Japan, and with it the celebration of Japanese management methods and practices, undoubtedly created a receptive context for the famous Peters and Waterman book *In Search of Excellence* (1982). The managerial anxieties in the West in the early 1980s and the feeling that practiced methods of employee commitment building, control, and change were not working undoubtedly propelled the language of culture and change into the managerial consciousness. But if organizational culture rose on a bow wave of managerialism, and the fads and fashions of management have now moved on, why does culture also seem to have peaked as a working construct in the various communities of organizational researchers?

Culture's one big advantage over climate was that it could not be dismissed as simply a variable. Indeed, organizational culture was not just a concept, but the source of a family of concepts and potentially even a generic form of organizational analysis. But the very excitement that brought culture onto the intellectual agenda attracted a scale and diversity of camp followers that eventually created a range and intensity of tribal disputes that undermined the potential of organizational culture. So culture was not so much hijacked for managerial purposes as lost in its own definitional, theoretical, and methodological disputes. In the meantime, organizational culture's probably overstated power as a source of holistic understanding of organizational life was not realized. The big empirical studies using culture concepts as a generic source of organizational analysis by and large did not happen.

This *Handbook* demonstrates that the two constructs of climate and culture have adapted and are still adapting to the threats to their intellectual potential. If culture and climate are still two constructs in search of a role (Pettigrew, 1990), what is their role to be? The role and character of climate studies is undoubtedly changing. Indeed, one interpretation of a shared response from both climate and culture studies is that they are increasingly less likely to be treated as objects of study in their own right; instead they are treated as crucial stepping-stones to the appreciation of wider related phenomena. Thus in this volume the contributions by Schneider and colleagues (Chapter 1), Michela and Burke (Chapter 14), Sathe and Davidson (Chapter 17), Weber (Chapter 19), and Gunz (Chapter 23) all link one or other of the two constructs to the understanding and management of service, innovation, change, mergers and acquisitions, and career development and management.

Other examples of boundary crossing and linkage are also evident in this volume. Kilduff and Corley (Chapter 13) profitably link the structural analysis and methods of network theory with culture, and in so doing begin to pose a novel set of researchable questions. Several authors also attempt to bridge the different intellectual heritages of culture and climate, and in so doing open up either new questions or methods of investigation. To different degrees, the chapters in Part V grapple with the big theoretical and methodological problems of analyzing national and organizational cultures—surely a crucial issue with the currently increasing demands for empirical studies involving international comparisons.

One lesson for the future must lie in the virtues of simplicity of expression in dealing with complex issues of human and organizational behavior. Reading the entire manuscript, I was struck by how often the authors use Edgar Schein's three-level definition of culture and Joanne Martin's triple perspective on culture in terms of integration, differentiation, and fragmentation. Some of the most influential leaders in history have been trinitarians—often using the oratorical device of presenting complex ideas in threes. If the future of organization climate and culture research does rest with connectedness, perhaps the next edition of this *Handbook* will feature climate, culture, and change.

# The Psychological Life of Organizations

## -- *Benjamin Schneider*

Most social and behavioral scientists reason, either implicitly or explicitly, that observed behavior is a function of the salience or meaning of situations for people. Except for extreme behaviorists, behavior is conceptualized as the outcome of a sensemaking process wherein stimuli are processed by humans who then behave in, or perhaps even construct (Weick, 1995), the situations to which they respond. Organizational climate and organizational culture scholars have been concerned with how this sensemaking—filtering, processing, and attachment of meaning—in and to organizations happens and the consequences associated with this process.

In what follows, I present a somewhat random walk through some of the issues and accomplishments of the climate and culture perspectives. In doing so, I make no claims to inclusiveness, exhaustiveness, or lack of bias; I present a set of issues as they exist for me about culture and climate that is biased by my own filtering, processing, and attachment

of meaning. To preface the following discussion, I note that it is clear to me that whereas all manner of scholars, from economists to financial and marketing experts, attempt to understand organizations, climate and culture scholars attempt to understand the ways organizational participants *experience* organizations.

Lewin (1935) called this notion of the experienced situation the "life space." By "life space" he meant the total situation as experienced by individuals. In his early writings, Lewin clearly emphasized the individual notion of life space, but later he explored the degree to which individuals in a situation experience it, and behave in it, similarly (Lewin, Lippitt, & White, 1939). When people come to share the meaning of a situation, I will call this the *psychological life* of the situation. For me, when there is sharedness of the psychological life of organizations, that psychological life is a property *of* the organization.

In what follows, I will explore a number of issues that illuminate the current status of organizational culture and organizational climate scholarship. My discussion will include some observations on the current relationship between the two constructs and the potential usefulness of combining the strengths of the two perspectives for a more comprehensive and powerful future construct domain for research and theory.

I will show that organizational climate, although the elder child in the organizational sciences, has become the ignored child for reasons that can be difficult to understand. The reasons are difficult to understand because the two ideas, although from different scholarly traditions, facilitate complementary understanding of similar psychological phenomena in organizations. I will argue, as I have previously (Reichers & Schneider, 1990; Schneider, 1985), that the two constructs are usefully linked, conceptually and practically. In other words, the siblings have perhaps overdone their need to be independent and should look to their own shared perspectives to find common ground on which they might build a new paradigm for organizational research (Smircich, 1985).

## ORGANIZATIONAL CLIMATE AND ORGANIZATIONAL CULTURE: CURRENT STATUS OF THE RELATIONSHIP

The issue in the literature that most perplexes me is the denial of the contributions of climate research by many culture scholars. For example, Trice and Beyer (1993), in their otherwise wonderfully complete book on organizational culture, have a section on what culture is not; the first item (p. 19) states that culture is not climate. They say that culture is not climate because (a) climate researchers use survey measurement (although they acknowledge that some culture researchers also use surveys), and (b) climate is individually perceived and experienced (although they do

not explain how culture can have an effect without individuals' sensing it).

Other writers on organizational culture dismiss organizational climate as a transient tone or transient mood of a setting, disregarding any connection between the two (Ott, 1989, p. 47). I am unable to find a single researcher who studies climate who thinks it is transient. Ott (1989, p. 47) makes the claim that there is little agreement about the definition of organizational climate compared to the agreement there is about organizational culture. Contrast this view of agreement about the definition of culture with Martin's (1992) view: "Organizational culture researchers disagree vehemently" (p. 4) about many issues, including the role of culture in organizations, the sharedness of culture experiences in organizations, the boundaries around cultures in organizations, and issues involved in organizational change. Martin does not index the word *climate*. Schein (1992) dismisses climate as solely having to do with the meaning of the built/physical environment of organizations for members. In his very interesting book on culture, listings under "climate" in the index send one only to discussions of the built/physical environment. Perhaps this is why Schein equates climate with what he calls "artifacts." Except for early work on the climate connotations of physical space as a variable in understanding organizational development (Steele, 1973, 1981), I am unfamiliar with researchers in the climate tradition who have focused on the built/physical environment as a central issue in their theory and research.

From my vantage point, it seems to me that some culture researchers protest too much about the relevance and importance of climate theory and research for their own thinking and research. Pettigrew's (1979) enlightening early paper on the possible contributions of a culture perspective to our understanding of organizations provided additional insight into the social and behavioral life of organizations, not a denial of the research and theory that had emerged from the climate perspective. Pettigrew's documentation of the ways that myths, stories, rituals, and dress norms reveal insights into organizations in no way denied the importance climate researchers had attached to supervisor-subordinate relationships (McGregor, 1960), the role of reward systems in directing employees' energies and competencies (Litwin & Stringer, 1968), or the centrality of values and belief systems to an understanding of behavior in the workplace (Katz & Kahn, 1978).

Katz and Kahn (1978) use the terms *climate* and *culture* interchangeably in their total systems perspective on the social psychology of organizations. In fact, just to further muddy the waters, on the same page (p. 50) they use these terms interchangeably with a host of other terms familiar to climate and especially culture scholars: *norms, values, folkways, taboos, mores, the history of internal and external struggles, work processes, modes of communication,* and *the exercise of authority.* Researchers, primarily from the climate perspective (e.g., Denison, 1996; James, James, & Ashe, 1990; Reichers & Schneider, 1990; Schneider, 1985), have been more prone to see potential overlap in the two concepts or, at a minimum, less denial of the other's contributions. On this point, Reichers and Schneider (1990) saw two parallel, nonoverlapping tracks of research for the most part, the situation that still exists at this writing. If this is all true—that is, that climate is an important construct, and that it can complement culture thinking and research—why has culture come to dominate thinking and research? My own opinion is that a failure by climate researchers to adopt a more observational methodology, as well as their usual survey methodology, for the study of these more anthropological issues of norms, mores, taboos, myths, and stories opened the door for an invasion by the younger sibling. Climate researchers (e.g., Schneider, 1975) literally ignored the deeper psychology of situations for the people in them, focusing more on their experiences of organizational policies, practices, and procedures. Early climate researchers, trained in psychol-

ogy, took a group-level conceptualization, climate, and unfortunately studied it as an individual-level phenomenon, using all of their psychometric methods to attack the construct. This was unfortunate because much of the early effort on measuring organizational climate at the individual level of analysis was discounted early by climate researchers themselves (Hellriegel & Slocum, 1974; Schneider, 1975).

Pettigrew (1990) has noted that culture researchers have been absorbed in trying to decide what organizational culture is, while climate researchers have gone out and measured it. Perhaps there is something to be gained for a more complete understanding of the psychological life of organizations from combining the measurement accomplishments of climate researchers with the conceptual advances of culture researchers to provide a complementary and useful conceptual and practical sibling rapprochement.

## MUTUAL LEARNING AS A PALLIATIVE FOR SIBLING RIVALRY

Sibling rivalry can be resolved through mutual awareness and the perception of common goals and possible mutual gains. Let me elaborate on these briefly, summarizing what I see as the strengths and weaknesses of climate and culture thinking and research.

The two main strengths of the research and thinking on climate are (a) the strategic focus of climate research on identifiable organizational imperatives (e.g., safety, service) and (b) the measurement and statistical documentation of the degree to which climate is shared by organizational members. The two main strengths of the research and thinking on organizational culture are (a) relatively complete specification of the deep psychological attributes (values, beliefs, meanings) that can be used to characterize culture and (b) a focus on the development or etiology of culture over time, especially through socialization processes. As will become clear, the strengths of each can compensate for the weaknesses of the other.

*Climate's strategic focus.* Climate research languished as an increasingly large number of dimensions were added to its conceptualization, with new facets added each time a researcher thought climate might be useful for understanding some interesting phenomenon. I have argued that climate, to be useful, has to be strategically focused—a climate *for something,* like service or safety or innovation (Schneider, 1975). For example, there is good evidence now to support the idea that the service climate experienced by employees in organizations is shared also by the customers those employees serve (see Schneider, White, & Paul, 1998); one might say there is a shared psychological life for *parties* to an organization, not just the *members* of an organization. Culture has a problem, being almost anything and thus being everything, depending on who is conducting a specific piece of research (Martin, 1992). Organizational culture research needs a strategic focus if it is to be more than a description of one organization at a time (Kotter & Heskett, 1992). Some think a strategic focus for culture research debases the culture construct in that the focus changes from process and internal meaning to outcome (Siehl & Martin, 1990; Trice & Beyer, 1993). My own perspective is that an understanding of the process-outcome relationship enhances understanding *and* predictive usefulness.

*Climate's concern for measurement and statistics.* Climate researchers have resolved many of the measurement problems associated with the documentation of what it means to *share* experiences in organizations (Dansereau & Alutto, 1990; James, Demaree, & Wolf, 1984; Shrout & Fleiss, 1979). The problem is that it took climate researchers long enough to solve these measurement problems that the sexier and more interesting culture construct, with no such obvious measurement hang-ups, looked very appealing. But culture researchers have for too long avoided documentation of a central culture concept: *shared.* Every definition of culture includes the word, but there is little documentation of it. Ideas such as culture strength, for example, are conceptually very important but lose their value in the absence of information about the degree of sharedness that exists in a setting. For example, using Martin's (1992) ideas, one may have either a culture that is integrated or a culture that is fragmented as a function of where and for whom beliefs, values, norms, and so forth are shared.

*The deep psychology of organizational culture.* Culture scholars have written passionately about the many ways culture becomes embedded in organizations (e.g., Schein, 1992)—myths, stories, taboos, the unspeakables, and so forth—and these ideas ring true not only for scholars but for managers. Whereas culture has been the passionate, emotional sibling, climate has been unsmiling and straightforward. Climate scholars have allowed the perceived mechanical/technical demands of measurement purity to eliminate the passion and excitement associated with the early work of Lewin et al. (1939) and McGregor (1960).

*The etiology of culture.* Culture scholars have pursued the issue of how culture emerges in organizations (Schein, 1992; Schneider, 1987) and how newcomers come to learn the ropes through acculturation (Louis, 1990). In contrast, there has been virtually no research on the development of climate, either for individuals or for organizations. This failure has been a major deficit in climate research, for if we do not know how it comes to be or how it changes, we simply do not understand it. It seems quite clear to me, however, that a focus on deep values and norms as the basis for culture also does not make clear the avenues for change. Organizational change is an arena in which the strengths of both approaches might be most usefully merged—more on this point later.

## CONCLUSION

In my own research and consulting, I have interviewed perhaps a thousand employees who worked in more than 20 organizations about how they experience their work organizations. Employees discuss their experiences using terms such as *cheap, adventurous, innovative, service oriented,* and *employee centered.* I then ask them to describe the kinds of things that happen to them and around them that make them describe their organization using words like *cheap,* or *adventurous,* or *service-oriented.* The terms people use to describe the setting are what I call climate; the things that they report happen to them and around them are the stimuli that yield the climate. In more recent times I have also asked employees to tell me *why* they think these things happen in their organizations. When I do this, more of the stories, myths, and attributions about management beliefs and values emerge. This has led me to now think about organizational culture as the beliefs employees have about what management believes and values; in my present terminology, organizational culture captures the attributions employees have about the gods management worships—the cost-cutting god, the risk-taking god, the customer god.

The focus groups I have conducted with employees reveal the reciprocal relationship between experiences and attributions: Climate causes culture, but the reverse is also true. This fundamental reciprocity is where the rapprochement between climate and culture exists for me—two complementary ideas that reveal overlapping yet distinguishable nuances in the psychological life of organizations.

Organizational climate and organizational culture permit avenues for understanding the ways work organizations are experienced by those who are part of them. There is rich material there for those of us interested in these experiences, but there is also the potential for furthering the understanding of organizational performance in related domains. A more strategic focus for organizational culture scholars might provide such leverage, and a more passionate focus for organizational climate researchers might make the climate construct as useful for management as it once appears to have been (McGregor, 1960).

Perhaps the most significant contribution that a rapprochement of the siblings might achieve is an increased understanding of how to achieve more durable organizational change. Values and beliefs are very difficult to change, even at the individual level. We know, however, that changes in behavior can yield changes in beliefs—and changes in the variables associated with climate might provide a useful entrée to achieving the changes in behavior that will result in changes in the more fundamental beliefs and values required for durable organizational change. It is time for the kids to come home, make up, and create a more complete understanding of the psychological life of organizations.

COMMENTARY

![heading rule]

# Sense and Nonsense About Culture and Climate

*-- Edgar H. Schein*

Writing some comments for a hand-book of this scope is a formidable task. But then, the climate/culture arena poses formidable challenges to us, both intellectually and empirically. Having struggled with both issues since the early 1980s, I want to make some general comments and try to clarify several issues.

## WHY IS IT IMPORTANT TO DIFFERENTIATE CULTURE FROM CLIMATE?

On the practical level, culture and climate as organizational descriptors are on the rise. More and more managers in organizations are talking about changing their cultures, creating new cultures, figuring out the impacts of their cultures, or preserving their cultures. When one examines what they are actually talking about, much of it has to do with what we would and should call climate.

*Culture,* in popular managerial parlance, usually refers to how people feel about the organization, the authority system, and the degree of employee involvement and commitment—the "soft" stuff, all of which refers more to climate than culture. Managers need to learn that where culture may matter most is in its impact on the "hard" stuff, such as strategy and structure. Most managers are quite blind to the fact that their strategies and structures are dominated by cultural assumptions and that histories of success and failure hardwire these cultural assumptions into their thinking.

Much of the confusion about the impact of culture could be reduced if we were clearer about (a) whether or not we are trying to change the climate and (b) how the underlying cultural assumptions would aid or inhibit that change process. Creating a climate of teamwork and openness is a common goal nowadays, but it is the rare company that figures out how cultural assumptions about individualism, about managerial prerogatives, and about respect for authority based on past success may make teamwork and openness virtually impossible. The structure of the reward system in most U.S. organizations is likely to be so completely individualistic that it should be no surprise that even a well-conceived and highly motivating program of team building has minimal and only temporary results. Recall how quality circles failed in the United States—not because workers don't care about quality, but because workers did not want to sit around in groups to talk about it.

The Singapore Economic Development Board has figured out how to deal with this issue by defining *individual* managerial potential in terms of the "ability to create a *team.*" So the board still rewards individuals, but it rewards those individuals who have track records of being able to attract others to work with them (Schein, 1996b). The point is that the board realizes that the culture is embedded in the reward system and it is at that level that things have to be examined and, if necessary, changed. The resulting "climate" of teamwork and the effectiveness of project teams is striking in that organization.

The second reason for bothering with this distinction is empirical. It seems obvious to me that organizations have climates that individuals feel immediately upon entering them. Climate is embedded in the physical look of the place, the emotionality exhibited by employees, the experiences of visitors or new employees upon entry, and myriad other artifacts that are seen, heard, and felt. It is equally obvious that climate does not explain itself. We need other variables to explain why different organizations feel different. My own resolution of this dilemma is to define climate as a cultural artifact resulting from espoused values and shared tacit assumptions. To understand climate fully, one must dig deeper and examine values and assumptions. In other words, to understand what goes on in organizations and *why it happens*

*in the way it does,* one needs *several* concepts. Climate and culture, if each is carefully defined, then become two crucial building blocks for organizational description and analysis.

## HOW SHOULD WE DEFINE AND THINK ABOUT "CULTURE"?

A chronic issue in conceptualizing "culture" seems to be whether we should think of culture as a "state" or static property of a given group/organization or as a human process of constructing shared meaning that goes on all the time. Culture creation from the latter perspective can, in fact, be viewed as one of the unique characteristics of humans, being based on our capacity for self- and other-consciousness. The answer, of course, is that both meanings have utility for theory construction.

I would propose that a useful way to think about this issue is to take a cue from the anthropologist Marshall Sahlins (1985), who argues that one cannot really understand certain social phenomena without understanding both the historical events and the cultural meanings attributed by the actors to those events. Although it is undeniably true that we produce culture through perpetual enactment and sensemaking, it is equally true that the actors in those same social events bring to them some prior meanings, stereotypes, and expectations that can be understood only in a historical context. Culture production in the enactment sense, then, is either the perpetuation or the change of some prior state, which can be thought of as the culture up to that point. And one can describe that culture as if it were a "state" of the existing system, even as one knows that the system is dynamic and perpetually evolving. The direction of that evolution will be a product of several forces: (a) technological and physical changes in the external environment, (b) changes in the internal dynamics of the social system, and

(c) historical circumstances that are fortuitous or serendipitous.

For example, let me offer my oversimplified summary of Sahlins's very sophisticated analysis of the death of Captain Cook at the hands of the Hawaiians. He notes several of these forces as they evolved historically. Because Captain Cook was viewed as a god (as predicted in the Hawaiian mythology), the sexual favors offered to his sailors by the Hawaiian women were viewed as gifts and as opportunities to relate to the divine. The sailors' cultural background defined this as a version of prostitution, however, for which they felt they should pay. When they offered to give the women something in exchange for the sex, the women asked for something that was scarce in Hawaiian society, namely, metal. Once the loose metal on board the sailors' ships had been used up, the sailors began to pull nails from the ships themselves, weakening the vessels structurally. Hence, when Captain Cook set sail, he discovered that the ships needed repair and ordered a return to harbor. In Hawaiian mythology, a god returning under these circumstances had to be ritually killed. At the same time, the Hawaiian social structure was undergoing change and became permanently transformed because the subordinate role of women in the society was altered by their ability to acquire metal, a scarce resource that gave them social power.

When one contemplates this wonderful analysis, it appear pointless to argue whether culture can be viewed as a state of the system (clearly there was a culture in Hawaii and a different culture on board the British ships) or as a process of enactment (clearly the interaction of these two cultures produced events that had profound impacts on both of these cultures). For me the major lesson is that *when we have access to historical data we should use it*. When we analyze organizational cultures, we should reconstruct their histories, find out about their founders and early leaders, look for the critical defining events in their evolution as organizations, and be confident that when we have done this

we can indeed describe sets of shared assumptions that derive from common experiences of success and shared traumas. And we can legitimately think of these sets of assumptions as "the culture" at a given time. That description will include subcultures that may be in conflict with each other, and there may be subunits that have not yet had enough shared experience to have formed shared common assumptions. In other words, culture as a state does not have to imply unanimity or absence of conflict. There can be some very strongly shared assumptions and large areas of conflict and/or ambiguity (Martin, 1992) within a given cultural state.

At the same time, we can study the day-to-day interactions of the members of an organization with each other and with members of other organizations to determine how given cultural assumptions are reinforced and confirmed or challenged and disconfirmed. We can analyze the impacts of these perceptual interactive events in order to understand how cultures evolve and change. This process could be especially productive in organizations undergoing mergers, acquisitions, and joint ventures of various sorts. For example, Faure (personal communication, May 1999) has analyzed the negotiation tactics that occur in the various joint ventures that the Chinese have launched with non-Chinese partners, and notes that for such a venture to succeed the partners-to-be must sometimes develop agreement on as many as 150 or more separate items.

It becomes a matter of choice whether one elects to focus one's cultural research on building typologies of cultural "states," categories that freeze a given organization at a given point in time, or on analyzing the moment-to-moment interactions in which members of a given social system attempt to make sense of their experience and, in that process, reinforce and evolve cultural elements. Both are valid methodologies, and in practice they should probably be combined, or researchers should choose research methods that suit the problems they are trying to solve.

## THE CLINICAL RESEARCH MODEL FOR STUDYING CULTURE

I have learned the most about culture when I have been involved as a consultant in trying to help an organization deal with specific issues on which it needed some help. The issue here is that in the normal flow of things cultural data are unintentionally concealed; the "natives" are not conscious of what it is they take for granted. The researcher then has the problem of how to observe phenomena that occur at that level without, at the same time, upsetting the natives by delving into areas that may be defined by them as private, or even unwittingly intervening in those cultures by raising questions that the natives may never have thought about. Anthropologists have solved this problem by living with the groups they are attempting to study, but this is very time-consuming and requires great care on the part of the researcher so as not to influence the culture unduly.

An alternative that has been given far too little attention academically is for researchers to draw observations and build theory from the data that are revealed when people ask for help (Schein, 1987, 1993b). This tradition has worked well in the study of personality, in that therapists, whether psychoanalysts, behavior modification specialists, or Gestalt psychologists, have inevitably been able to see into deeper layers of the personality just through their diagnostic and intervention efforts. For living systems, Lewin's dictum that "you cannot really understand a system until you try to change it" is an absolutely valid principle of research. To build variables from these deeper insights seems like a very appropriate way to study living systems, and that applies especially to complex systems such as groups and organizations.

There is a strong tradition of applied anthropology built around participant observation in the works of Mayo and Roethlisberger, Whyte, Dalton, Hughes, Becker, and Goffman. Recent examples include Van Maanen's (1973, 1988) studies of police departments and Disney theme parks, Zuboff's *In the Age of the Smart Machine* (1988), Kunda's *Engineering Culture* (1992), and Thomas's *What Machines Can't Do* (1994). What all of these studies have in common is the researchers' reliance on participant observation. What is insufficiently spelled out in these studies, however, is how the observers got into the systems in the first place and why they were tolerated and given data.

A researcher has basically three routes into an organization: (a) infiltration, in which the participant observer becomes a true insider; (b) a formal research role agreed to by the insiders; and (c) a formal clinical role, in which the insiders ask the outsider to come into the organization as a helper/consultant. I want to compare the pros and cons of these three roles for the study of culture. In the infiltration model, the cultural artifacts are very salient, and the newcomer feels them immediately. However, just feeling them does not enable the researcher to decipher them, and there is a danger of the researcher's projecting the meanings of his or her own culture onto another culture. The ethnographic solution is for the researcher to remain in the system long enough to figure out what things mean or to seek informants with whom he or she can forge a new kind of relationship. In building that relationship, the researcher must have something to offer, usually in the form of feedback of the results. However, this is rarely enough to motivate real collaboration on the part of informants. My hypothesis would be that only when the members of the culture see the ethnographer as helpful in the here and now do they really open up and tell him or her what things really mean.

I believe the same is true for the researcher who negotiates entry by promising feedback. He or she is allowed limited entry but is not really told what things mean and what is really going on until insiders feel comfortable that he or she will be helpful rather than harmful to them. "Gaining entry" then becomes functionally very similar to evolving a clinical relationship with the client where the goal is organizational improvement of some sort.

What distinguishes the clinician/consultant at the outset is that the problem or issue to be addressed is initially defined by the client, not the researcher. The client is willing to pay for a service, and this creates a different psychological contract—on the one hand, the area of inquiry is delimited initially by the client, but on the other, the consultant is licensed to ask deeper questions, to dig into dirty laundry, because that is necessary to doing the job. As I have argued elsewhere, the clinician still has to worry about establishing a relationship of trust in which the inquiry process becomes a shared intervention between the consultant and the client (Schein, 1999b).

The conclusion I draw from this analysis is that any form of inquiry into organizational culture, whether researcher or client initiated, will be successful in digging out the deeper layers of the culture only if the inquirer and the client system form a mutually trusting and rewarding relationship. Research and clinical work begin to merge, no matter how they were initiated. If the research is done without the direct involvement of the organization, it is doubtful that the researcher will be able to decipher the deeper layers of the culture (Schein, 1999a).

## CAN CULTURES BE CATEGORIZED OR PROFILED?

All culture and climate researchers start with some mental models of what they are looking for, based on their own education and empirical predilections. So we should not kid ourselves that we can go into an organization as a tabula rasa and just let the culture "speak" to us. Even how we experience the artifactual level, what we see and hear as we enter an organization, is biased by the perceptual and conceptual filters we bring to the situation.

The issue, then, is not whether the researcher will start with a priori dimensions in studying the organization, but how broadly he or she will cast the net and what kind of theoretical model the research will start with.

My prime objection to questionnaires as research tools for the study of culture is that they force researchers to cast their theoretical nets too narrowly. Even researchers using the 500-plus item personality scales, such as the MMPI, have to decide ahead of time what kinds of items to write and thereby limit the domain of inquiry. The advantage of the ethnographic or clinical research method is that we can consciously train ourselves to minimize the impacts of our own models and to maximize staying open to new experiences and concepts we may encounter. In the end, we may well sort those experiences into the existing categories we already hold, but at least we will have given ourselves the opportunity to discover new dimensions and, more important, will have a better sense of the relative salience and importance of certain dimensions within the culture. The issue of salience is very important because not all the elements of a culture are equally potent in the degree to which they determine behavior. The more open group-oriented inquiry not only reveals how the group views the elements of the culture, but, more important, tells us immediately which things are more salient and, therefore, more important as determinants.

As to the categories themselves, it seems to me that most of the questionnaires that have been developed draw their initial dimensions from narrow sociopsychological theories and ignore broader models developed by anthropologists and sociologists. Even functionalism narrows one's scope somewhat, but at least an effort to define all of the functions that cultural solutions must address forces us to cast the net widely. In this regard I have found it empirically useful to start with a broad list of "survival functions" (what any group must do to survive in its various environments and fulfill its primary task) and "internal integration functions" (what any group must do to maintain itself as a functioning system). This distinction is entirely consistent with a long tradition of empirical research in group dynamics that always turns up two critical factors in what groups do: (a) task functions and (b) group building and maintenance functions. Ancona (1988) and others have pointed out that we must add a third set to these two: boundary maintenance functions. Task and boundary maintenance functions are my external survival issues, and group building and maintenance functions are my internal integration issues. We may then construct different lists of what specific dimensions of behavior, attitude, and belief we will look for in each domain, but at least we have a model that forces us to cast the net widely and a reminder that culture is for the group the learned solution to all of its external and internal problems.

If we then look a little deeper, drawing again on anthropology and sociology, we find broad cultural variations around deeper, more abstract issues that link less with social psychology and more with cognitive psychology. How do we fundamentally view the world and our relationship to it? How does our language create perceptual and thinking patterns that differ fundamentally? One of the first lessons of Anthropology 1 is that the Eskimos have 30 words in their vocabulary for kinds of snow, and this reflects conceptual and perceptual skills that are different from those of peoples living in the tropics.

In this regard it is puzzling that the seminal work of Florence Kluckhohn and Fred Strodtbeck (1961) on comparative value systems has not led to more culture research. In their effort to compare the cultures of Native Americans, Anglos, and Hispanics in the American Southwest, they developed a number of very useful "deep" dimensions reflecting the nature of human nature, the relationship of humans to their surrounding environment, the nature of human activity, the nature of human relationships, and basic orientations toward time. Also underutilized is the work of England (1975) on managerial values that deals specifically with how in a given culture one arrives at "truth." If one combines these

dimensions with some of those identified by Edward Hall (1966, 1976, 1983) on concepts of space and spatial relationships, and with more recent concepts about the nature of the "self" in different cultures, one has a pretty good template of what culture covers at this deeper level. I do not see how any questionnaire, no matter how well designed, could even begin to get at some of these dimensions. However, in group interviews with representative samples of "natives" one can observe and ask about various of these dimensions if one has been given license to do so because one is perceived to be helping the natives solve some problem.

"Culture" questionnaire scores do correlate with various indexes of organizational performance, but these measures are more appropriately measures of climate than measures of culture. Because climate is an artifact of culture, such scores may measure some of the manifestations of underlying cultural assumptions, but because they do not empirically check what those deeper assumptions are, it is not clear what the correlations are based on. For example, certain aspects of climate can reflect coercive management, and the organization's effectiveness could be due to the potency of management rather than the particular norms being enforced.

To deal with this issue, researchers often ask on their questionnaires about employees' *desired* norms and test whether movement over time toward those norms correlates with organizational effectiveness. Some evidence exists along these lines, but there is a further problem. Unless the underlying assumptions are checked, it is not possible to determine ahead of time whether or not it will be possible for the organization to move in the direction of the new norms. It may be that the error variance in the correlation hides an important empirical fact—that movement toward certain desired norms is aided or constrained by the pattern of underlying assumptions. An ideal research design would measure the present and desired norms, and then check in the underlying assumption set (through group interviews that get at assumptions) why discrepancies exist between the present state and the desired state in the first place. It is the causes of those discrepancies that management needs to understand in order to determine what kind of culture change program to launch to achieve greater organizational effectiveness.

A further point is that management should seek not to change culture, but to change effectiveness. Only if it can be shown that the culture is actually a constraint should one launch a culture change program. Demonstrating that culture is a constraint requires, however, more than a questionnaire study. When one digs for underlying assumptions, one typically finds that some cultural assumptions actually will help achieve the kind of effectiveness desired, and that only some elements of the culture may be discovered to be constraints. Because culture change is intrinsically difficult, time-consuming, and anxiety provoking, it is far more desirable to work with supportive assumptions to achieve whatever new norms are desired.

grams fail because they do not take into consideration the underlying culture. In other words, surveying climate and specifying a desired climate are not enough. One must analyze the underlying cultural assumptions.

If culture and climate are to become practical, usable concepts, practitioners will have to learn how to do culture assessments as part of any change program. Articulating new visions and new values is a waste of time if these are not calibrated against existing assumptions and values. When such assessments are done, it is usually found that there are elements in the culture that can be used positively to create new ways of working that are more effective, and that is far preferable to "changing" the culture. In this regard, I agree completely with Cooperrider and others who have developed the concepts and methods of "appreciative inquiry" (see Cooperrider, 1990; Cooperrider & Srivastva, 1987). It is better to build on what is working than to obsess about what is not working. It is easier to evolve the culture than to change it.

## CAN THE CULTURE AND CLIMATE CONCEPTS BE USEFUL TO THE PRACTITIONER?

Climate can be changed only to the degree that the desired climate is congruent with the underlying assumptions. One cannot create, for example, a climate of teamwork and cooperation if the underlying assumptions in the culture are individual and competitive, because those assumptions will have created a reward and control system that encourages individual competitiveness. One cannot create a climate of participation and empowerment if the underlying assumptions in the culture are that subordinates should do what they are told and should expect their bosses to know what they are doing. One cannot create a climate of openness if the history of the company has been to punish the messenger for bad news. All too often, change pro-

## CROSS-CULTURAL COMMUNICATION: THE ROLE OF DIALOGUE

Cultures exist at regional and national levels, at the industry or institutional level, and at the organizational level. There are also occupational cultures and subcultures within organizations based on functions and tasks. Part of the reason organizations do not work well, part of the reason we have wars, and part of the reason we have difficulty reaching consensus on major global problems such as maintaining a healthy environment is that we cannot communicate very well across cultural boundaries. We have excellent data that show how differently various groups perceive their environments based on different shared tacit assumptions, but we have very few tools for helping people to improve communication across those boundaries.

The recent emphasis on "dialogue" (Isaacs, 1993, 1999; Schein, 1993c) may help, in that dialogue theory is focused on getting acquainted with one's own assumptions. We cannot appreciate another culture if we are not aware of our own cultural filters. Dialogue theory assumes that each human has his or her own set of assumptions from which he or she operates, and when such assumptions are shared across a group with shared experience we have not only the presence of the assumptions as filters but the motivation to hold on to those assumptions as a way of expressing our membership in the group. If we are to gain any understanding of another group's assumptions, we must get into a communication mode that legitimates self-examination and acknowledges that perception and thought are anything but objective.

It would therefore be highly instructive for both researchers and practitioners to form dialogue groups and begin to examine their own assumptions in a group context. Such an examination will reveal the subtle operation of cultural forces as well as make visible where different assumptions lead to different behaviors and often conflicts. Once assumptions are surfaced and stated, mutual understanding increases and a basis exists for finding common ground. I hope that this *Handbook* will stimulate more people to think about culture and to seek a deeper understanding of its operation in themselves and in others.

# Preface and Acknowledgments

*-- Neal M. Ashkanasy*

This volume is a joint project undertaken by three scholars from diverse backgrounds around the world. In the following, I trace the history of this project from a personal perspective and acknowledge the contributions of those who have been involved.

I am a former engineer, now an organizational psychologist and management scholar, based at the University of Queensland in Australia. Celeste Wilderom is an intraorganizational scholar, working currently at Tilburg University in the Netherlands, and Mark Peterson is a cross-cultural organizational scholar based at Florida Atlantic University in the United States. The team of contributors to the *Handbook* comprises 57 scholars and practitioners from an even wider variety of backgrounds and scattered across the globe. It is little wonder, therefore, that this volume is such a unique document. The following is a brief outline of its genesis.

The origin of the *Handbook* goes back to my dissertation in the 1980s, in which I needed to include measures of organizational culture in a model of leader-subordinate relationships. Although this was initially only a minor component of my work, it soon became a consuming interest. As I developed this interest, however, I became aware that there were many unanswered questions. In response to this, I began to organize local colloquia on the topic, culminating in 1994 with a "caucus" held during the annual meeting of the Academy of Management in Dallas, Texas. Some of the contributors to this volume were present at the caucus, including Allen Bluedorn, Ray Zammuto, and Celeste Wilderom. It became evident at the caucus that there were many others who harbored questions similar to mine, and we agreed that I should set up an e-mail discussion group to continue our debates. The e-mail list, set up in January 1995 and later named Orgcult, currently has 400 subscribers.

It was at the 1994 Academy of Management meeting, too, that the three editors of this handbook first got together. I recall a very pleasant evening, sitting on the veranda of the Outback restaurant in Dallas and discussing our various research interests. Following that meeting, Celeste Wilderom and I first raised the idea of a symposium at the 1996 Academy of Management meeting in Vancouver. Al Bluedorn and Ray Zammuto were participants, together with Jan Beyer. The symposium attracted a full house, and that interest encouraged Celeste and me to seek further horizons.

In 1995 I was also on sabbatical, and I spent the fall semester at Penn State University. The sabbatical gave me a further opportunity to network in the United States. In particular, I got to meet Ben Schneider and Bob House. Bob invited me to join the cross-cultural GLOBE (Global Leadership and Organizational Behavior Effectiveness) Research Project as the Australian country co-investigator. Through GLOBE I was able to extend my networks further, including meeting Marcus Dickson, who later agreed to contribute the GLOBE chapter to this *Handbook*.

It was Ben Schneider, however, who proved to be the key person in facilitating this volume. It was through Ben's advice and influence that Celeste and I were able to approach Sage Publications with our proposal. Although Ben was not in a position to join us as coeditor, he has assisted us greatly through every stage as a "consulting editor." During the early months of 1996, working largely through the Orgcult network, and with Ben's assistance, Celeste and I were able to put together the proposal for the *Handbook*. At the 1996 Academy of Management meeting in Cincinnati, Celeste and I presented our proposal to Sage and met for the first time with Sage acquisitions editor Marquita Flemming. Marquita was very enthusiastic about the project from the outset, and we soon had a contract.

Although we had a signed contract, we were still concerned about the lack of an American contact. Celeste and I valued Ben's advice and assistance, but we were keen to have an American associate working with us directly. Then we recalled that evening in Dallas when we had discussed working with Mark Peterson. In fact, I had already been corresponding with Mark on other aspects of my research, so it was natural that I should call him to offer him a chance to participate. Mark also has a wonderful network of colleagues working in cross-cultural research, and he has coordinated that section of the *Handbook*.

Once Mark was on board, we began work on the book in earnest, recruiting additional authors and cajoling everyone to get their manuscripts in on time. I am pleased to be able to say that we have lost only three of the original authorship teams—a remarkable achievement, given the diverse geographic locations of the authors and editors. Indeed, with the three editors evenly spaced around the world's time zones, one can say that work went on 24 hours a day.

In the end, we believe that, together with our authors, we have produced a wonderful compendium of current research, theory, and practice in the field of organizational culture and climate. I cannot emphasize too much how greatly we value the contributions of our authors.

Finally, on behalf of Celeste, Mark, and myself, I must thank Sage editors Marquita Flemming and Harry Briggs for their perseverance and help. Without their advice and support, this project would never have come to fruition. I would also like to express my appreciation to my assistant, Camille Jackson, whose help throughout the project has been invaluable. Last, but certainly not least, I thank my coeditors, Celeste Wilderom and Mark Peterson, for their contributions, collegiality, and scholarship.

# Introduction

*—— Neal M. Ashkanasy, Celeste P. M. Wilderom,
and Mark F. Peterson*

Why do we analyze organizational culture and climate? How do our analyses help us make organizations better? Where do these topics fit among the major issues facing not only organizational studies but social science as a whole as well as contemporary society? The contributors to this volume answer different parts of these basic questions and answer them in different ways.

In this introduction, we offer a guide to how the different parts of these questions fit together and where the different ways of answering them fit within organizational science and social science. We begin by considering the histories of organizational climate and organizational culture research in order to understand why these have been and continue to be topics of interest. We then turn to the ways that scholars working within various social science traditions and from the major lines of theory in these traditions understand the constructs of culture and climate. Our discussion then moves to the implica-

tions of historical and conceptual contexts for the study of an organization's culture, including the roles of nation and industry. Because we anticipate an audience of both readers interested in influencing organizations and others interested in clearly articulating how organizations operate, we conclude with a discussion of practical implications and directions for research.

## WHY ORGANIZATIONAL CLIMATE AND CULTURE?

People concerned about organizations sometimes want to look comprehensively at the ways whole organizations or major organizational subunits operate. How can they do that? The answers different people have given to this question have depended on when they were writing and what they have meant by *comprehensively.* Every area of social science could be drawn on to answer this sort of question, but not all have been equally used. Meyerson (1991), for example, has drawn our attention to the intrinsic ambiguities in organizational culture research. In the context of this *Handbook,* several chapters note insights about organizational culture from economics. Economic transactions, however, are used less often to represent fully what happens within organizations than in the study of more focused problems of agency relations and the origins of organizations within market systems (Barney & Hesterly, 1996). Similarly, behaviorist psychology that uses reinforcement models to represent what people do has not been dominant in organizational culture and climate research, although a number of helpful models of organizational learning draw insights from classical and operant learning theories. Systems theories and earlier structural-functional theories seeking to draw analogies between and to show relationships among all aspects of life were dominant for half a century. In organizational studies, these reached their most complete form in reviews by Katz and Kahn (1966, 1978), but seem now to be more a part of our intellectual heritage than an identifiable, active force (Ashmos & Huber, 1987). Clearly, the structural contingency theories reviewed and integrated by Mintzberg (1979) introduced significant new variables and continue to influence organization theory (Donaldson, 1996). Nonetheless, our sense is that these theories have occupied a niche in the field as middle-range theories of structure and of organization-environment relationships, and thus do not provide a holistic view of an organization. Although each of these kinds of theories is referenced on occasion in this volume's chapters, the authors place emphasis elsewhere.

Indeed, organizational studies scholars often want to do more than look at the slice of organizational life represented by a particular organization's current crisis, a particular set of variables, or a particular experimental paradigm. In this case, scholars often appeal to organizational culture and climate. In other words, when organization scholars want to view organizations comprehensively, we seem to find it more useful to draw from areas of social science that include constructs such as shared attitudes, values, and meanings that chunk the world into bigger bits than transactions and behaviors. Whether that preference is wise or not is open to debate, but the emphasis of the contributors to this volume on shared attitudes, values, and meanings reflects the current status of the field of organizational climate and culture more than it represents the editors' systematic selection. Even between the two closely related areas of culture and climate, the balance of attention has swayed toward organizational culture, with its emphasis on values, actions, and meanings, as the better way to talk about organizations and organizational subunits as wholes. The contributors draw most from the psychology and sociology of attitudes, values, and cognitions, and from the anthropology of societies. The labels *organizational climate* and *organizational culture* find their historical roots in these fields.

## LEWIN, LIKERT, AND THE HISTORY OF ORGANIZATIONAL CLIMATE

The study of organizational climate preceded that of organizational culture. Reichers and Schneider (1990) provide a historical overview of both in which they note the sequence of major studies in each area through the late 1980s. Climate research derives from a confluence of field theory and the quantitative study of attitudes within organizations. *Field theory* is the label Lewin (1948, 1951) and his colleagues gave to their attempts to represent any particular social process as part of a larger context or field. Their emphasis on context was closely linked to the Gestalt psychology of perception being contemporaneously developed by other German immigrants to the United States during the middle decades of the 20th century. Theirs was a context of neither a sociological grand theory seeking to generalize from basic patterns in the development of civilizations nor an anthropological ethnography seeking to understand a particular society comprehensively. Context in field theory was limited to aspects that one most needed to understand a particular individual or group phenomenon, such as a child's education. Climate as a way of characterizing context was also not overwhelmingly complex, nor did it display delicate nuances. Instead, as originally theorized, it fell into three major categories: autocratic, democratic, and laissez-faire.

Lewin, Lippitt, and White (1939) coined the term *climate* to describe the attitudes, feelings, and social processes that occurred among groups of boys at an American summer camp. They interpreted particular interventions in the boys' activities as having different effects depending on climate. In their view, a climate context could be created through leadership. Democratic, autocratic, and laissez-faire styles of leadership were important not as behaviors per se, but as dependable means of producing a social situation, a climate. Once a leader produced a climate context, particular interventions, such as the leader's absence from a room, had radically different effects depending on climate.

Did Lewin really believe that social context could be produced by leaders so easily? Without a doubt, he did. Leadership by individuals had created climates on a national scale within his personal experience. His analysis of groups was a microcosm of his analysis of the development of fascism in Germany. He sought to replicate on a smaller scale the transformation of the German education system and German society in general into the fascist society of the 1930s and 1940s (Lewin, 1948). Fascism was a societal climate that Lewin hoped to discredit scientifically, so that its ideology and political processes would not spread while it was being defeated militarily. The society that he was trying to encourage was the democratic society of the United States, to which he had emigrated. The society he worked to create was a democratic ideal state, the state of Israel.

Social climate in Lewinian theory represented context that could extend in comprehensiveness all the way from a national society down to a group of boys at summer camp. When it appeared in organizational studies, however, the meaning of climate changed. It is not certain how the idea would have developed had it not been for Lewin's premature death in 1947. Shortly thereafter, his successor as director of the Research Center for Group Dynamics, Dorwin Cartwright, moved the center to the University of Michigan to become part of the Survey Research Center within the Institute for Social Research (ISR). Cartwright followed interests at the group level rather than at the organizational or societal level. Eventually, that move brought Lewin's legacy into direct contact with another quite different line of work at ISR, that of Rensis Likert.

Likert is best known for two things that helped define organizational climate research. One is the Likert scale for measuring attitudes, a technology that greatly increased the influence of attitude research throughout the social sciences. The other is the "System 4" view of effective management (Likert, 1961). Lewin had written about social climates that he knew from both personal and documented experience, such as the German educational system, and other climates that he created experimentally. The problem Likert took on was different. He wanted to study climates that he could neither know quite so personally nor create. His problem was how best to capture the climate of an organization so that he could work with the organization's senior managers to monitor and promote its comprehensive improvement. The Likert scale that he had invented for sociological and psychological research provided a starting point to capture an organization's climate. Climate came to be represented by an aggregation of individual data from attitude scales, and a well-known set of controversies about the adequacy of these measures to the task Likert wanted to accomplish with them was set off. Reichers and Schneider (1990) note the sequence of key studies as these controversies evolved. Their current status is discussed in this *Handbook* by, among others, Payne (Chapter 10); Schneider, Bowen, Ehrhart, and Holcombe (Chapter 1); Ashkanasy, Broadfoot, and Falkus (Chapter 8); and Cooke and Szumal (Chapter 9).

The use of surveys to represent climate was the dominant way in which we in organizational studies through the 1960s and 1970s provided an overall sense of the social processes within organizations. Reichers and Schneider (1990) note that by the early 1980s, a combination of forces redirected the attention of scholars and organization change consultants to organizational *culture* as an alternative way of looking at overall organization functioning. Among these were the international forces discussed by Brannen and Kleinberg in Chapter 24 of this volume. Also, the role of psychology departments versus business schools changed, as did the priorities of funding agencies such as the Ford Foundation, the Rockefeller Foundation, the U.S. Office of Naval Research, and the National Science Foundation, on which the researchers at the ISR and other climate researchers had relied.

## ANTHROPOLOGY AND THE HISTORY OF ORGANIZATIONAL CULTURE

The analysis of organizational culture brought the field of management back to aspects of Lewin's concept of social climate that many felt the organizational climate literature had neglected. Many in the field felt that the organizational context within which managers take specific actions is at best only roughly approximated by what a survey can represent. Climate surveys were not ending with simple, comprehensive, powerful categorizations analogous to the climates of Lewin's boys' camps or the climates that distinguished fascist from democratic nations. And the field seemed to be getting weary of endless technical haggling about whether attitudes and perceptions of individuals could be aggregated to represent something at the organizational level, what metric should represent agreement, what criterion should be used to justify aggregation, which particulars are most important in the increasingly overwhelming morass of organizational behavior variables generating inconsistent, weak, contingent relationships, and on and on.

We learned that the masters of climate analysis were excellent scholars able to handle complex statistical problems of measurement, aggregation, and contingency. Many scholars who were interested in the kind of straightforward, powerful constructs that Lewin and Likert introduced, however, did not want to spend their careers bogged down by what they felt to be the technical minutiae of surveys. The idea of climate was not dead, and it still remains vigorous, as the climate chapters in the present volume indicate. In our view as editors of this *Handbook,* much of the critique and impatience with climate research is not helpful. For example, the fact that some people find statistics tedious does not mean that statistics are not useful. Similarly, if an approach to research reveals the world to be more complex than one would like, then simplifying the world may not always be the best choice. Our sense of the history of the field, however, is that many felt that climate was losing ground as the best way of representing the holism many wanted. What would be a better way to represent context, and where should the field look for this better way? Many scholars began to look to cultural anthropology, only vaguely realizing what they were doing.

The influence of the organizational culture articles and books, starting with Pettigrew's (1979) seminal article, through Hofstede's (1980a) and Schein's (1985) books, and including the contributions of other pioneers of organizational culture in the early to mid-1980s, is noted by Reichers and Schneider (1990) and described in many chapters of this *Handbook;* we will not duplicate comments about these. The history of the organizational culture field needs less comment because it is more recent, better known, and better represented by other authors in this volume than is the history of organizational climate. The history of organizational culture research is the history of how a field dominated by scholars steeped in psychology and sociology has learned from cultural anthropology. This learning has included adding bits of anthropological thinking—topics, variables, ways of doing research, ways of thinking—to organizational scholarship as well as welcoming newcomers with strong anthropological orientations to organizational studies. This process is ongoing and one in which we are now participating rather than just documenting. In order to participate effectively, we will consider something about the traditions in anthropology from which the study of organizational culture has drawn. We will then use these traditions as a basis when we move from our historical review to a discussion of major topics in current organizational culture and climate research.

Although organizational scholars are likely to be aware of the history of organizational culture research, the history of the anthropological traditions from which it might draw is likely to be less familiar. Culture has been the domain of anthropology, so the study of organizational culture has brought ways of thinking holistically about systems of meaning, values, and actions from anthropology into organization studies. The difference among schools of thought within anthropology that seems to us to have the most significance for current controversies in organizational culture analysis is a difference in focus on the culturally unique compared to the culturally general. A corollary is a difference in openness to highly structured analysis and quantification. Many anthropologists provide detailed, inductive accounts that were designed to bring out the unique qualities of particular societies. Mead (1928/1949) indicated a desire to question the values and practices of Western societies by comparing them to Eastern, ancient, small, or nonindustrial societies. Geertz (1973) has shown more interest in studying a broader range of cultures, including modern and modernized ones, and indicates a greater awareness than Mead of anthropology as basic science having implications other than critique of one's culture of origin. Others, like Malinowski (1923/1947, 1935/1965b), were equally interested in doing ethnographies, but did them from a functional motive—to identify systematically the generalizable problems that all societies face and to compare the ways different societies handle them.

Those forms of organizational culture scholarship that advocate working from direct experience with an organization and relying heavily on inductive intuition to describe an organization's culture (e.g., Schein, 1985) draw heavily on the ethnographic tradition in cultural anthropology. The intent is to represent all aspects of a society or an organization, including the more easily and less easily specified. Within this approach, there is particular interest in documenting characteristics of a particular society or organization. This tradition, however, is not monolithic.

Ethnographic analysis can follow from a functional, comparative motive, but need not do so. Malinowski (1923/1947) was a self-proclaimed functionalist who argued that all societies face the same universal problems. Anthropologists such as Kluckhohn and Strodtbeck (1961) and Kroeber and Kluckhohn (1951), from whom many of the contributors of the international chapters in the present volume draw, tend to take a similar position. Geertz (1973), however, is equally an ethnographer, but not a functional one. For Geertz, any potential for comparing cultures is not rooted in some inherent set of problems that societies or organizations face in common. Ethnographic studies of organizational culture often take this same position.

The relationship between the unique and the general has been debated in anthropology just as it is being debated in organizational culture analysis. Some scholars, such as Headland, Pike, and Harris (1990), see a constructive opportunity in moving back and forth between theoretical schemes designed for application in many cultures and those designed to represent the nuances of a particular culture. The ideal in this sort of interchange involves both producing an increasingly complete generic theory and doing full justice to each society's unique features. Particular parts of the generic theory will have meaning in some societies, but not in others. The value of general theory, in this view, is to compare where comparison is possible and also to help local informants penetrate beyond the fish-in-water problem of insiders' not being able to describe themselves for lack of a comparison other.

Other scholars see generic theory as working against rather than for understanding of particular societies. Geertz's (1973) interpretative theory of culture has been particularly influential, as reflected in the frequent citation of his work in many chapters in this volume. Geertz questions even the biological basis of human universals. Those who question functional arguments such as the systems theory position that all organizations inherently create certain problems (differentiation, coordination requirements, and such) are following a similar line of thought. As scholars in other fields have attended to interpretivist viewpoints from anthropology, this influential approach to anthropology has not only influenced organizational culture but has moved broadly into psychology through ethnopsychologies unique to particular parts of the world (Kim & Berry, 1993).

The history of anthropological work, however, should not be mistaken for a history of nonquantitative, inductive analysis. Even further in the direction of generality, anthropologists such as Murdock (1940) have produced extensive coordinated projects designed to structure research in a way that brings unity to work by large numbers of otherwise unconnected scholars, projects that continue to the present (Burton, Moore, Whiting, & Romney, 1996). Murdock's (1940) anthropology of the Human Resource Area Files is a comparative one based on not just a small number of universal functions, but a more detail enumeration of universal categories of variables. Were anthropologists able to construct surveys that would measure attitudes of Eastern, ancient, small, and nonindustrial societies, would they do so? Some no doubt would. We can think along with anthropology to look for ways to understand and to study organizational culture, but anthropology provides a set of debated concepts and methods rather than a monolithic alternative to the methods of climate research.

We consider below the implications for ontology, epistemology, and methods of these debates about the general and specific and other discussions in anthropology that reverberate in organizational culture analysis. A review of anthropology finds evidence of instances where it is modern and scientific as well as postmodern and political, where it is cognitive as well as behavioral, and where it is inductively empiricist as well as theoretically structured. Organizational culture scholarship has sometimes mistaken anthropology for a particular approach to anthropology, particularly the Geertzian approach that contrasts most with organizational climate, rooted as it has been in social sciences other than anthropology (Hunt, 1994). Trice and Beyer (1993), for example, strike a familiar chord when they argue that whatever difficulties there are in defining organizational culture, it most decidedly is not organizational climate.

## ANALYZING ORGANIZATIONAL CULTURE AND CLIMATE

Our reason for beginning with history is to understand the present problems with which we began this chapter, notably, why and how do we study wholes? A present question is, What do we now mean by *organizational culture* and *organizational climate*? A number of scholars, including Trice and Beyer (1993), have offered definitions that fit particular lines of theory they are seeking to develop. Such definitions are entirely appropriate. They provide particular lines of theory with consistent sorts of codes, like a Napoleonic code in law. Given, however, that this introduction sets the stage for chapters representing a variety of perspectives, it seems to us that a common-law approach to definition—working from common usage—will suit our purposes better. The common-law approach is especially appropriate given that Lewin's original use of the concept of climate seems to have been qualitatively altered as the climate literature became closely linked to configurations of attitudes. Similarly, as organizational culture has come to be represented by dimensions and theorized in terms of ideologies, some cultural anthropologists might find the term *organizational culture* to be an unintelligible oxymoron. We will avoid the issues about inconsistencies in definition and the difficulties these present for cumulative knowledge. Common usages of the terms *climate* and *culture* reflect different views of ontology, epistemology, and methods. Our preference is to note different views. The contributors to this volume use the ideas of culture and climate within their own chapters that are consistent with the heritages from which they draw. As such, our approach is consistent with Denison's (1996) view that climate and culture are not strongly differentiated. Instead, they represent different but overlapping interpretations of the same phenomenon.

Definitions of climate and culture reflect three different kinds of ontologies. The most common is a structural realist ontology. Organizations exist as structures that have a variety of properties, including climate and culture. From a structural realist perspective, an organization is a kind of structure that has a climate and a culture. A second ontology is a social construction ontology that places emphasis on the varying regularity in events that happen and gives observers room to select which sets of events to group together into a culture. From a social construction perspective, discernible regularities in events constitute a culture. Here, certain kinds of cultures, reflecting regularities in what we call *work-related events* (see Smith & Peterson, 1988), constitute an organization. An organization, in this view, is a kind of culture. A third ontological view treats organizations and cultures both as linguistic conveniences. Concepts such as organization and culture serve the heuristic purpose of helping us think. Structures, processes, and events are constructed or discarded as found helpful by a particular party, so that the correspondence to anything apart from the construction itself is secondary.

Definitions of climate and culture can also reflect three epistemological approaches. Deductive approaches emphasize broadly applicable cultural dimensions or analytic categories. Researchers gain knowledge by constructing these dimensions, looking to see where organizations fall on them, and then revising the dimensions when they notice previously overlooked phenomena. Inductive approaches emphasize investigators' capability to derive categories by directly observing particular organizations. Not only relationships among variables but the variables themselves may be unique to particular organizations. The second type of epistemology, the inductive approach, tends to recognize the presence of the tacit elements that always shape the experience of specified constructs and that can sometimes be made explicit (Polanyi, 1958/1962). Finally, radical approaches view observers as less dispassionately interested in accuracy than they are in producing constructions that reflect their own interests (Morgan, 1986, 1997).

The methods for studying organizational climate and culture include administering surveys designed to reflect generalized concepts, conducting interviews with key informants and focus groups, observing behavior patterns, collecting artifacts, and engaging in direct interactions with organization members to develop a personal intuition for the culture.

Some configurations among ontology, epistemology, and methods are more inherently compatible and are found together more often than are others. Adopting a realist ontology along with a radical epistemology, for example, seems more manipulative than most scholars would find comfortable. Still, ontology, epistemology, and methods can be found in a variety of combinations in the chapters in this volume.

Organizational climate fits easily within these categories of definition. The concept of organizational climate is currently being used to describe configurations of attitudes and perceptions by organization members that, in combination, reflect a substantial part of the context of which they are a part and within which they work. It is usually conceived of as being structurally realist, deductive, and based on survey methods. Following from the dimensions of climate surveys, climate can be broken down into various aspects corresponding to organizational behavior topics such as leadership, group dynamics, job characteristics, and satisfaction. The climate literature has evolved since the 1970s to add topics such as organization citizenship in recent years, and even to embrace elements of ethnographic research (e.g., Poole, 1985), but it traces back unambiguously to the legacy of Likert scales and the organizational psychology of the 1960s and 1970s. Denison (1996) has noted further that quantitative, survey-based methods are now often seen in the culture literature (e.g., Denison & Mishra, 1995; Hofstede, Neuijen, Ohayv, & Sanders, 1990; O'Reilly, Chatman, & Caldwell, 1991). In effect, the contributors to this volume whose work fits this mold, such as Ashkanasy et al. and Cooke and Szumal, use methods typical of psychology and sociology to deal with phenomena more traditionally emphasized in mainstream anthropology.

The common law of usage that we follow to define organizational culture is more diffuse. Culture can be defined using the same sort of structural realism, deduction, and survey use as found in climate research. Where do people following such a conception of culture see a difference from climate? Clearly, Ashkanasy et al. (Chapter 8) and Cooke and Szumal (Chapter 9) believe that a difference lies in the variables studied. Climate research draws from the organizational behavior variables studied through the 1970s, before organizational culture analysts brought vision, meaning, and similar topics to the fore. From the standpoint of its practitioners, quantitative organizational research uses clearly understood methods to remove an artificial veil of mysticism and, although not comprehensive, captures many of the important elements in culture. From the standpoint of scholars drawing from other culture traditions, on the other hand, this is not culture at all, but only climate research with new labels.

Indeed, many organizational culture scholars would argue that an ontology, epistemology, and method appropriate for studying whole cultures is better provided by the interpretative traditions within anthropology. After all, the problem taken on by anthropology always has been to understand the systems of meanings, values, and actions that characterize whole societies. In fact, the authors of a number of the chapters in this book, including Brannen and Kleinberg (Chapter 24) and Helms Mills and Mills (Chapter 3), are looking in that direction. Further, because anthropology is a no more homogeneous field than any other in the social sciences, the approaches anthropologists have taken to such topics vary considerably.

## CENTRAL TOPICS IN ORGANIZATIONAL CULTURE IDENTIFIED IN THIS BOOK

When we study the culture and climate of an organization or an organizational subunit, by definition we do so to take a holistic perspective on the organization or the subunit. The central topics in these fields reflect attempts to get a handle on the whole of an organizational unit (either the organization as a whole or a subunit). Organizational climate researchers have sought to get at the whole by representing a configuration of attitudes and perceptions. Some organizational culture researchers, like climate researchers, have used methods that require organizational members to articulate aspects of their cognitions and feelings using surveys, but have replaced climate questions about attitudes and perceptions with questions about values. Values have a broader scope of implications for meanings and actions than do attitudes and perceptions. Many scholars find values to be better suited for capturing the whole of an organizational unit than the attitudes and perceptions studied in climate research. Others in the field find analyses of values too incomplete, too focused on the relatively static and specifiable aspects of organizational units to fulfill the interest in holism. As an alternative, scholars of sensemaking and meaning have viewed the interest of holism to be served best by capturing systems of meanings and the ways in which meanings come to take shape in an organizational unit. A few organizational culture scholars avoid talking about meaning and sense, preferring instead to describe symbols, artifacts, and other visible expressions of culture as things in themselves. Regardless of how studied, an interest in analyzing organizational units as whole entities requires a view as well of the larger context of which organizations and their subunits are a part and of the smaller elements, the individuals, within them.

## Values

Values were quick to become part of the language of organizational culture. They are evident in the contributions to this volume by Ashkanasy and his associates (Chapter 8) and by Cooke and Szumal (Chapter 9) about quantifying culture. Zammuto, Gifford, and Goodman (Chapter 16) describe the Quinn competing values approach to culture, and Stackman, Pinder, and Connor (Chapter 2) describe the Rokeach values tradition.

The idea of values has meaning both in the realm of psychology that is familiar in organization studies and in some lines of anthropological theory. The idea of values has provided a way to talk about something that is at once social, cognitive, and behavioral. A construct that can link these three domains has the potential to be quite powerful. Because values are social, they reflect the history of experiences and understandings that characterize a group of people or society. Because they are cognitive, they reflect the history and experience of individuals with a group of people or a society. Because they are reflected in behavior, values typical of a group of people or held by one person affect actions and interactions. Because the idea of values allows the same label to be used for quite different kinds of purposes at different levels of analysis, the concepts can also be quite confusing.

The anthropological sense of values reminded psychologically oriented organizational scholars that what we had come to call individual differences among an organization's members are not entirely idiosyncratic. From the work of Hulin and Blood (1968), we were already familiar with the idea that individual differences do not occur simply at random, but are a function of socialization into communities. But people are socialized into something or some things prior to their membership in any particular organization. The values in a society precede the values of an individual. The idea of organizational culture expands the domain of socialization to a global scale and draws attention to insights from anthropology. These insights have implications for the ways organizations could engage in socialization themselves and fit readily into theories and applications of organizational psychology.

Values were not a major part of organizational climate research, but they provided organizational culture researchers with an easy transition from dimensions for studying attitudes and perceptions to dimensions for organizational culture. Values seem such a natural part of a society's cultural tradition that it is surprising that organizational culture research did not take value dimensions from some source in cultural anthropology. Kroeber and Kluckhohn (1951), in a review of culture concepts that helped define the concept of culture in anthropology, noted that values were a particularly significant part of the central core of culture definitions. Anthropologists, however, did not follow up by providing a set of value dimensions in the next 30 years that organizational scholars could readily apply. The tendency of cultural anthropology to deal with ancient and largely nonliterate societies militated against the development of standardized measures of values. Still, the basis for developing a generalized theory of values was present in anthropology. Malinowski (1939/1944) identified basic human problems about which societies needed to develop values. Kluckhohn and Strodtbeck (1961) began to document cultural differences in values. Inkeles and Levinson (1969) took on the task of specifying universal problems of society, but they did so out of a composite literature from psychology and sociology as much if not more than from anthropology. In Chapter 25 of this volume, Hofstede and Peterson note Hofstede's (1980a) reliance on the Inkeles and Levinson categories in his analysis of national culture. However, no one has yet systematically drawn from either these categories or any others that are more strictly anthropological to construct value dimensions for analyzing organizational culture. Instead of drawing from the work of anthropologists, researchers have used three main sources in attempting to understand values in organizational culture research. The most frequently used work is that of another American psychologist, Rokeach (1969, 1973), whose influence is much less evident in the climate tradition. Contributions to this volume by Stackman et al. (Chapter 2), Rose, Kahle, and Shoham (Chapter 27), and Sagiv and Schwartz (Chapter 26) represent the state of the art in values research based on

Rokeach's work. The second source is the competing values framework developed by Quinn and his colleagues, work that looked to the organizational behavior and climate literature for ideas about values that underlie organizational behavior and climate dimensions. Zammuto and his associates review this work in Chapter 16. The third source is the work of Geert Hofstede, a Dutch engineer who collaborated closely with Americans in an American multinational organization. The contributions here by Hofstede and Peterson (Chapter 25), Payne (Chapter 10), and again Rose et al. (Chapter 27) discuss some of the issues and applications.

For some organizational culture scholars, pointing to values was not meant to identify any particular set of specifiable values that could be used as variables to compare organizations. In fact, the purpose was quite the contrary. Martin and Frost (1996) remind us that part of the original stimulus and sustaining drive behind organizational culture scholarship has been dissatisfaction with structured, particularly quantitative, analysis. Much of the anthropology of the 1980s is not an anthropology that systematically enumerates functions, but is one of critical theory and postmodernism (Alvesson, 1995; Alvesson & Deetz, 1996). Organizational culture analysts appealed to values as a characteristic of people that had been neglected in organization studies, an element of humanity that was particularly resistant to being structured and quantified. Other scholars have been quite anxious to measure values and compare people, organizations, and nations based on them.

Scholars, including those who have contributed to this *Handbook*, generally agree that values are socially constructed. Nonetheless, views vary as to how much is "out there" that inheres in the nature of people or social situations and that gives structure to values. Kluckhohn and Strodtbeck (1961) argue that all societies face the same basic problems and that responses to these problems give structure to universals in the things upon which societies must place value. That is not to say that there are universals in everything societies must value, but there are universals in problems about which societies must reach some working value consensus. Rokeach (1969) argues that characteristics of human needs create "terminal values" that become taken-for-granted assumptions, which shape responses to the rest of life's experiences. Functionalism means that there are problems to which all societies or all people must respond. Several functional perspectives from anthropology are represented by chapters in this book, particular in Part V. Tyrrell (Chapter 5) draws from Malinowski's functionalism. Hofstede and Peterson (Chapter 25) as well as Sagiv and Schwartz (Chapter 26) draw from a functional tradition of values reflected in the work of Kluckhohn and Rokeach.

The analyses of values offered by authors in the present volume tend to be structured. The idea of values in social science precedes the idea of organizational culture, and scholars finding value in studying values systematically found a strong heritage from which to draw. Stackman and his associates (Chapter 2) draw from one of the more established lines of empirical research about values in social science, Rokeach's theory of values. This theme is developed further in other sections of the *Handbook*. In Chapter 26, Sagiv and Schwartz modify Rokeach's scheme to take it into international studies.

Rokeach's (1973) interest in values was the interest of a psychologist. His line of work links psychology back into philosophy, as in his distinction, developed by Stackman and colleagues, between instrumental and terminal values. Rokeach's work is also focused on distinguishing values from other psychological constructs, such as beliefs and attitudes.

All of us maintain some professional skepticism about the link between what we believe and what we say we believe. This skepticism certainly applies to statements about values. Skepticism about what people say in questionnaires is part of this. Rokeach (1969, p. 2) agreed, but he used question-

naires anyway. In their contributions to this volume, Stackman and his colleagues as well as Zammuto and his associates describe ways to use questionnaires and other structured research methods effectively as part of research into values.

## Symbols

Organizational culture research has helped us appreciate symbols in a way not developed in the climate literature. In Chapter 4, Rafaeli and Worline remind us of the significance symbols have, both for organization members and for outsiders encountering organizations. Soeters (Chapter 29) shows the distinctive position symbols have within certain communities of organizations.

Tyrrell (Chapter 5) takes our attention back to a transition point in social anthropology during the early part of the 20th century, when its practitioners stopped relying on intermediaries such as translators and key informants. At that point, anthropologists began to interact directly with members of preliterate societies by learning their languages and living for extended periods with them. Malinowski, the pioneer in the direct analysis of preliterate societies, took observables as the only firm ground for theory.

Language, in Malinowski's (1935/1965b) view, is a specific form of behavior and is more closely akin to nonlinguistic behaviors than to cognitions. Malinowski's work was developing during the period in psychology when introspection as a means to give cognitive meanings to events was competing with the physically oriented approaches of physiological psychology and behaviorism. As with behaviorism in psychology, anthropologists in Malinowski's tradition sought convergence among observables without trying to draw inferences back to cognition. After all, these scholars might argue, is it not obvious that people misrepresent their real values and meanings, sometimes because real values may not be socially acceptable and sometimes because the speakers themselves do not really understand their own motives?

The anthropologically oriented chapters dealing with symbols in the present volume follow other anthropologists who have used linguistic and nonlinguistic symbols as evidence for social and cognitive meanings and values. Still others, such as Harris (1979) and Pike (1954/1960), have focused mainly on language along with nonlinguistic symbols as a clue to meanings. Rafaeli and Worline take this view. Perhaps verbal and nonverbal behavior do not correspond all the time, but, they would argue, is not verbal behavior still a form of behavior? And is not the relationship between the two a part of a society's culture itself? In Chapter 24, Brannen and Kleinberg use the idea of "recontextualization" to describe the process by which symbols given a particular meaning in one society are given new meanings when the symbols are moved to other societies.

### Actions

Prior to the advent of organizational culture analysis, organization scholars were more familiar with the literatures of psychology and sociology than with other social sciences. The "culture" part of organizational culture scholarship has drawn us into anthropology's world of ancient and exotic civilizations. Studying ancient civilizations is quite a bit easier, to say the least, if one looks at artifacts reflecting symbols and behaviors. For example, the Aborigines, Aztecs, Incas, Polynesians, and Caribs who met Europeans for the first time several hundred years ago are no longer available to be interviewed, to complete surveys, or to permit unobtrusive observation.

Organizational scholarship has long been affected by the tension between modeling observables and modeling cognitions in the various traditions of psychology. The status of surveys and interviews compared with observation recurs in the organizational literature. A similar distinction appears in anthropology, and the distinction is reflected in the anthropologically oriented chapters in this volume. Tyrrell (Chapter 5) in particular draws on work that, although not wholly rejecting ideas of values and cognitive constructions of meaning, has certainly placed greater emphasis on actions. For Tyrrell, communication behavior over the Internet is the basis for a new kind of community or organization subject to its own unique forms of exchange, social contracts, function fulfillment, and game playing—in short, its own culture.

### Cognitions, Emotions, and Meanings

The question of meaning has brought anthropology, psychology, and linguistics into contact in the past. Ogden and Richards's (1923/1947) edited volume *The Meaning of Meaning* equates meaning with the correspondence of symbols with thought, reference, or idea and of these with a referent thing or event. Their formulation was brought into social anthropology through the support of Malinowski (1923/1947). The theoretical element that forged the union was context—Malinowski's social anthropology, like Ogden and Richards's theory of meaning, drove scholars' attention toward the problem of how, and how much, context affects meanings. Discourse about culture was about the context for any instance of meaning. Discourse about organizational culture has come to be about the way organizational context shapes the meanings and actions of organizational members. Many applications of organizational culture analysis suggest ways in which organization leaders can influence a broad range of specific behaviors of individuals by influencing the context of values within which they work.

While the "culture" in organizational culture theory was bringing anthropological insights into organizational studies, the fields from which organizational studies had traditionally drawn were undergoing other changes. A cognitive revolution that affected the way meaning was understood was occurring in psychology and spreading into sociology and management science. Constructs such as values, attitudes, beliefs, and personality structures were being used less as a way of explaining the meanings people give events. These traditional constructs were being reinterpreted, and at times supplanted, by ideas of scripts, schemas, knowledge structures, monitoring mechanisms, and prototypes. In recent years, the emotional side of life in organizations has also been analyzed (e.g., Ashforth & Humphrey, 1995; Weiss & Cropanzano, 1996). People were coming to be viewed as continuously engaged in creating meanings. Analyses of meaning have affected the way we look at such classic management topics as motivation (Bandura, 1997), group process (Argote & McGrath, 1993), leadership (Smircich & Morgan, 1982), and socialization (Isabella, 1988; Louis, 1980). We anticipate that there will be increasing interest in identifying and quantifying collective feelings operating in work settings. In particular, future research is likely to focus on the degree to which such feelings relate to and shape organizational climate and values.

### The Individual in the Culture

The sort of holism that defines organizational climate and culture leaves a great deal of ambivalence about whether mention should be made of the individual. One of the most intense controversies in organizational climate research is whether it is genuinely holistic organizational research or just the psychological study of groups of individuals.

Individuals sometimes find their way into organizational culture discussions. A visionary individual who can shape culture is sometimes evoked. This person tends to be treated abstractly as a source of vision rather than as a whole person with a variety of motives and a life before, after, and outside his or her role as visionary. In theories of meaning, individuals are sometimes evident as occupants of roles (as Peterson & Smith treat them in Chapter 6 of this volume) or as members of social networks (as discussed by Kilduff & Corley in Chapter 13). Most often, however, the organizational culture is the active subject and the individual is the object, the "thing" to be brought into the organization or, as Major describes it in Chapter 22, the object to be socialized. In effect, a form of cultural control of organizational members exists.

## THE CONTEXTS OF AN ORGANIZATION'S PRESENT CULTURE

People, history, and stakeholders' institutional frames—a theory to account for the sources, emergence, current status, and future development of an organizational culture must account for all of these. Key individuals include founders and subsequent change agents. History includes key events an organization has encountered while it developed and the practices established, stories told, and assumptions made as they were shaped by the organization's responses. Institutions include nations, industries, and otherwise circumscribed sets of actors and normal practices.

People and history are most in view in this book in discussions of organizational culture change (e.g., Hatch, Chapter 15; Michela & Burke, Chapter 14; Weber, Chapter 19; Wiley & Brooks, Chapter 11; Zammuto et al., Chapter 16) and socialization (e.g., Gunz, Chapter 23; Major, Chapter 22). Authors who deal with culture emergence, such as Major, describe the process of formation. Those who deal with changing existing cultures, such as Markus (Chapter 18) and Sathe and Davidson (Chapter 17), describe the kinds of interventions attempted and the struggles to see the changes accomplished.

Institutions are most in view in the chapters about national and occupational culture context. Hofstede and Peterson (Chapter

25), Rose and his colleagues (Chapter 27), and Sagiv and Schwartz (Chapter 26) describe the effects of national context. Soeters (Chapter 29) focuses on the effects of occupational culture and treats national culture as a secondary influence. Dickson, Aditya, and Chhokar (Chapter 28) do the reverse. Bluedorn (Chapter 7) goes one step further and addresses the dimension of time itself as a variable that affects perceptions of and responses to organizational culture.

## IMPLICATIONS FOR RESEARCH AND PRACTICE

We began this introduction with a question: Why analyze organizational climate and culture? For reasons reflected in the various topics covered in this *Handbook,* we believe that people study organizational climate and culture because of the insights such study can offer for practice, organizational research, and social science at large.

### *Implications for Practice*

The first issue for practitioners is whether organizational culture and climate make a difference. From a practitioner's point of view, there seems little point in worrying about these phenomena unless they have tangible outputs. This has, of course, been a central issue for researchers of organizational culture and climate from the very beginning, and it continues to be a thorny one. In Chapter 12, Wilderom, Glunk, and Maslowski address the nexus between culture and performance, and conclude that methodological shortcomings in most of the studies conducted to date leave this question open. They invite researchers to invent "fresh" (probably eclectic) theory.

Organizational culture has contributed toward the tradition of treating organizational change as comprehensive transforma-

tion. When trying to change something in an organization, we begin as individuals seeking to influence a whole and find that even that whole is what it is because of larger social institutions. The organizational culture literature reminds us that those hoping to initiate organizational change face a daunting task and provides insights about what to consider when facing it. Michela and Burke (Chapter 14) and Wiley and Brooks (Chapter 11) describe much of the current state of knowledge about what we can do to change whole organizations. The movement toward thinking about comprehensive rather than piecemeal change was already part of the heritage of organizational climate and systems theory, but culture added some topics and perspectives that were less evident before.

One element that organizational culture added was the visioning that senior leaders can provide (e.g., Schein, 1985). Leadership research was part of the climate tradition emerging from the Michigan group, but that was largely supervisory-level leadership research. Senior leaders created programs that influenced organizational climate. With the advent of organizational culture, these leaders promoted change by creating visions (e.g., Bass, 1985). If we did not get that message adequately through Peters and Waterman (1982) and Bennis and Nanus (1985) in the early years of culture analysis, we certainly got it through their many successors (see, in this volume, Dickson et al., Chapter 28; Granrose, Huang, & Reigadas, Chapter 30; Hatch, Chapter 15).

Another element added by organizational culture was the appeal to the substance of values and the place they have in organizational formation and change. Values were part of the national culture literature as reflected in all of the international chapters in this volume. As Beyer, Hannah, and Milton (Chapter 20) and Virtanen (Chapter 21) indicate, we already knew from the commitment literature of the late 1970s that shared values mattered. The organizational culture literature went on to identify types of values to which senior managers could appeal and tensions in other values that might occur by appealing to anyone (Zammuto et al., Chapter 16). Each of the chapters dealing with organizational change reflects a recognition of comprehensiveness, organizationwide leadership, and values as part of any change process.

## Implications for Organizational Research

Another reason for studying organizational culture and climate research is that it has directed our research about organizations and organizational subunits as entities. Each chapter in this volume notes research implications for its own specific topics. More broadly, however, organizational climate research helped keep us from overindividualizing organizations. When we study even attitudes toward job satisfaction or organizational citizenship, we are not studying only individuals, we are studying people in a social context. When we study individual perceptions, be they of group characteristics, leaders, or jobs, we are not studying the unique perceptions of each person uninformed by others. Multiple individuals are reacting to some of the same experiences and situations. People talk with one another about their groups, leaders, and jobs. The perceptions of one person shape the interpretations of others. A climate evolves. Survey questions being answered by individuals are simultaneously being answered by collectives. Much of the development in organizational research about the sense in which individuals are individuals compared to organizational members has occurred through climate research.

Organizational culture research has also contributed to organization studies at large. It has been the medium for importing a number of ideas, particularly from anthropology, that would otherwise receive less attention. It has contributed significance to the study of values and to understanding the way meanings develop. It has also directed scholars' at-

tention to the incompleteness of surveys and to possible ways of both improving them and using alternative methods. The concept of organizational culture has also been part of the position of some scholars drawing from interpretative theory in anthropology, who suggest that we should study each organization in its own right. Those who take this position warn us to be wary about transplanting ideas from setting to setting or developing general organizational theories. Even more than climate research, the study of organizational culture has given us ways to recognize that organizations are more than a collection of individuals.

Many of the controversies into which the *Handbook of Organization Studies* (Clegg, Hardy, & Nord, 1996) delved arose from the encounter between organization studies rooted in psychology and sociology and organizational culture ideas rooted in anthropology. The postmodern emphasis throughout that volume reflects the influence of a brand of anthropological research that challenges mainstream truths of industrialized societies by pointing out alternative ways of thinking and living, and by pointing to the varying interests and views of multiple parties. Donaldson's (1996) chapter in that volume reflects the struggle that one line of sociologically grounded organization studies, structural contingency theory, had in maintaining its influence. As Donaldson's work indicates, anthropology certainly did not have full sway to reshape organization studies even in the area of organizational culture. Psychology was well entrenched in organization behavior and, together with sociology, was also well established in organization theory. Political science long had a consistent presence whenever discussion in the field turned to power. Economics was taking hold in both organization theory and strategy just as the literature of organizational culture was developing (Barney & Hesterly, 1996). The relationship between anthropology and other fields is reflected in much of the discussion about the relationship between organizational climate and culture, and is a recurrent theme throughout this *Handbook* (e.g., see Hatch, Chapter 15).

This volume stays closer to the source of these controversies in organizational culture research and theory. The study of organizational culture is important not only because of the insights it offers about organizations, but also because of the position it has held as the primary point of contact among several fields of social science. The nature of anthropology remains less familiar to organization scholars than do psychology and sociology, especially for those whose research agendas and methodological orientations were shaped in the early 1980s or earlier. Anthropology somehow retains a mystical quality in organization studies. Chapters in the present volume about values and about interpretative approaches help demystify it. Issues in the field of organizational culture reflect dynamics both within cultural anthropology and in the relationship between it and other social science disciplines.

Controversies stimulated by the interaction among various social sciences in organizational culture research have been well represented by the organizational culture chapter in the *Handbook of Organization Studies*. In that chapter, Martin and Frost (1996) argue that alternative ways of analyzing meanings have become central to the struggle among four different perspectives on research and theory within the community of organizational culture scholars. The *integration perspective* on organizational culture focuses on commonalities within an organization in the values or criteria against which meanings are evaluated. Analyses in this vein document consistencies throughout an organization that distinguish it from others. Applied work within this perspective advocates various ways of promoting a common value base among organization members so that the processes they use to give meaning and take action can be readily coordinated. The *differentiation perspective* explores themes such as the combined effects that various kinds of programs in human resources and other areas have on meanings, the interplay of formal/informal cultures and enacted/espoused values, and the variability among an organization's subcultures. These themes all center on how meanings relate to value criteria. The *fragmentation perspective* highlights chaos in the process of making meanings. Meanings are neither predictably affected by programs nor particularly affected by unitary cultures or even subcultures. Attempts to influence meanings have random effects. The view that cultures provide a unifying base from which culture members look at the world is abandoned. *Postmodern perspectives* use meanings to analyze power. The emergence of meanings is interpreted as the emergence of power. Martin and Frost (1996) advocate the postmodern perspective as an addition to the first three, originally proposed by Martin (1992) and Meyerson and Martin (1981). They view dynamics among the four perspectives as power dynamics designed to promote the interests of various groups of analysts.

Our own view is that there is more substance in choices as to the most useful approach to organizational culture analysis than the achievement of power, especially if power is viewed as a way of shaping the prestige of particular sets of scholars. There is more at stake than this. The topic of organizational culture is at an intersection between fields, and the personal interests of particular scholars who happen to fall at that intersection may not determine where social science will go.

Our view of the perspectives that Martin and Frost (1996) describe is that there is a sense in which it is groups of analysts that come to be constructed and given identity by the meanings with which they become associated. Martin and Frost's framework of four organizational culture perspectives may even perform a sort of reification on people. It transforms categories of researchers into groups even though the group members may not identify with one another or interact in ways that are typical of a distinctive, self-aware community. Not just people and groups but also meanings and meaning frameworks like organizational cultures can in themselves have considerable power, substance, and reality. But in taking this view, we realize that we are placing emphasis on social forces over individual power in shaping the power dynamics underlying interpretation processes. The organizational culture literature brings out debates of just this sort.

## Implications for Social Science Research at Large

The study of the internal workings of organizations also contributes to research in the social sciences outside organization studies. Organizational culture has become a new meeting ground of anthropology with sociology and psychology. In entering organization studies through the lens of organizational culture, anthropology encountered the other social sciences in a new way. For most of the 20th-century history of social science, anthropology had found its niche in speaking about distant, ancient, or small societies, societies that were viewed by the mainstream of industrialized societies as pragmatically marginal. Anthropology was shaped by several kinds of values and motives, and developed methods and methodological controversies particularly associated with its niche. Anthropological discussions in the post-World War II years about meaning, grounded theory, and interpretation (Geertz, 1973) provided a potential point of contact with other social sciences, a point of contact that fed into the development of organizational culture research.

By moving into organizational analysis, anthropology has taken a step further as not only a basic social science discipline, but an applied one as well. In particular, organizational culture analysis, when done as a branch of anthropology, has been imbued with the pragmatic intensity that comes from the tremendous effect that businesses have on the lives and audiences of scholars working, as most do, in industrialized countries with market economies. It has provided anthropology with an opportunity to see if its tools and ways of thinking are adequate for the task of analyzing a kind of society traditionally de-emphasized: not just the primitive society, but the society of modern (and postmodern) organizations. In so doing, organizational culture research has raised questions about anthropology's conception of primary groups and of communities. It has also given anthropology settings for understanding how symbols and meanings interact, settings with which anthropology's audiences are likely to be familiar. Organizational culture research stands in contrast to the study of ancient societies or societies for which anthropology's audiences have less direct intuition than the ethnographic fieldworker reporting an experience.

Through the analysis of organizational culture, anthropology also has added to psychology and sociology new sets of topics and issues to address. From studying values in distinctive societies, anthropology has encouraged the sociological study of values as a basis for comparing societies and the psychological study of values as a basis for comparing people. This has prompted other disciplines to face the question of whether their presumed universality is actually a disguised ethnocentrism. In the psychological study of people as people, do we understand people properly as being fundamentally similar despite their contexts? Psychology had already debated idiographic research. Although some concluded that personality dimensions may not be particularly useful, or that the personality constructs needed to study any particular individual should be at least adapted to that individual, the field still emphasizes generalizable dimensions. It had also debated ethnopsychology. In particular, can we really use a small number of universal personality dimensions broadly to predict how people will behave in all parts of the world (Digman, 1990), or do we need to derive new personality dimensions for distinctive societies? Similar issues now can be raised for psychological research within organizations. Is seeking validity generalization an appropriate ideal for personality-based selection? On the other hand, should we consider not only revalidating the same instrument in different organizational cultures but reconstructing instruments for different cultures? Are surveys and laboratory manipulations the best way to do research? Or do we need to employ inductive methods to develop idiographic or culturally relative psychologies?

Finally, and from the broader perspective, does it make sense to have a general sociological theory of societies or of the nature of societal institutions? To what extent are we imposing an inappropriate set of categories when moving from the study of one society to another? And from one organization to another?

Our sense is that these kinds of questions are really about relationships among the social sciences, and that they are being debated in the forum of organizational culture research and theory. The chapters in this volume represent a diversity of views from scholars in different disciplines and illustrate the changes that research stimulated by organizational culture and climate are still making to organizational studies. The labels *organizational climate* and *organizational culture* continue to provide a focus for theory, research, and practice, and we expect them to continue to prove useful. Even if attention shifts to other labels, however, the contribution of work in these areas to organization studies and social science will remain. People will continue to be concerned at times with wholes rather than with parts, with both the more verifiably specifiable and the less specifiable, with the individual and the collective, and with the dynamic contributions of different social sciences competing and cooperating to influence and explain organizations and societies.

# PART I

# Culture and Climate

The contributors to this first section of the *Handbook* consider basic ideas in organizational culture, ideas of values and meanings and how they are represented and communicated in different kinds of communities. Value perspectives and meaning perspectives are potentially competing and potentially complementary. Value perspectives have tended to be rooted in functional theories of society. Research appealing to values tends to take the position that there are dimensions of values equally meaningful to large segments of the world and that different parts of the world, including different organizations, have positions on value dimensions. Meaning perspectives have tended to come from interpretative perspectives on society. The position is either that there are no functional dimensions at all or that attempts to identify dimensions should be set aside.

We begin with a chapter by Schneider, Bowen, Ehrhart, and Holcombe because of the historical precedence of climate research. Schneider and his colleagues deal specifically with the climate for service but argue that the principles they develop serve as a model for other applications of the organizational climate perspective. Their discussion, however, sets the theme of the *Handbook,* in that climate is presented as shared subjective experiences of organizational members that have important consequences for organizational functioning and effectiveness.

In Chapter 2, Stackman, Pinder, and Connor deal more specifically with organizational culture. These authors take a values perspective, noting the current status of values research in organization studies by comparing work values and personal values, the extent to which values can change, levels of analysis in organizational values research, and ethical issues in making personnel decisions based on employee values.

In Chapter 3, Helms Mills and Mills take an interpretative view and apply it particularly to gendering. They use culture as a heuristic to highlight holism, interconnectedness, and context for the focal issue of gendering. Their theoretical interest is in what generates shared meanings about issues such as gender. Through power dynamics within organizations, rules come to be established that shape meanings. Rules create a coherence in organizational practices regardless of variability in values or attitudes.

The authors of the next three chapters take the use of symbols and interpretation a step further. In Chapter 4, Rafaeli and Worline develop the theme of symbols that has been central to interpretative theories of culture. Symbols are directly experienced and give a concrete form to what would otherwise be abstract meanings. Symbols reflect organizational culture, trigger internalized values, provide a shared frame of reference, and integrate systems of meaning throughout an organization.

This is followed by Chapter 5, in which Tyrrell emphasizes interpretation perspectives in anthropology but draws as well from functional views that have been the source of cultural analyses of values. He reconsiders the concept of culture as a holistic way of understanding communities by using the example of how culture can be applied to cybercommunities. In so doing, he considers the nature of social institutions, how they are bounded, and how they change.

Peterson and Smith provide the final chapter on interpretation and symbols. These authors identify events as the objects of the interpretation processes that occur within cultures and identify a set of sources of meaning that can aid analysis of the ways events are interpreted. In principle, different sources of meaning can offer meanings associated with different values and, in the process of doing so, add a political element to creating meanings.

The last chapter in Part I provides an interesting alternative perspective on culture: time. Bluedorn introduces three temporal dimensions—polychronicity, temporal focus, and temporal depth—and shows how these dimensions are reflected in personal and social views of the world. This is an original perspective, and Bluedorn calls for scholars to "expand upon the nascent findings" he reports and to "explore other temporal variables and relationships."

# 1

## The Climate for Service

### Evolution of a Construct

—— *Benjamin Schneider, David E. Bowen,*
*Mark G. Ehrhart, and Karen M. Holcombe*

This chapter is about a special kind of organizational climate, the climate for service. *Climate for service* refers to the sense that people who work for and/or come into contact with an organization have with regard to the service quality emphasis of the organization. Both employees of organizations and customers of organizations experience service climate, employees with regard to the emphasis on service excellence they experience and customers with regard to the experiences they have when served, including the level of service quality they receive. In this chapter we deal with both what employees experience and what customers experience, while recognizing that other parties to the organization—such as suppliers—also experience its service climate (Schneider, White, & Paul, 1997).

In what follows, we first briefly explore the thinking and research about the generic concept of organizational climate. We then provide a relatively comprehensive treatment of thinking and research on service climate. The focus on service and service climate serves two purposes. First, the focus is meant to illustrate the strategic usefulness of the climate construct. That is, if management is interested in the degree to which employees are behaving consistent with a given formulated strategy, then it is useful to examine that strategy in terms of climate. Focusing on climate acknowledges the centrality of employees to success of the strategy and further acknowledges the importance of employees by going to them for information about organizational practices related to the strategy. Second, the focus on service acknowledges the centrality of services to the contemporary business scene. Because services have several characteristics that distinguish them from goods, the organizational attributes on which organizations must focus to be successful at providing services may also be different (Bowen & Schneider, 1988). To anticipate a bit, we will conclude that the climate construct is alive and well and useful as a heuristic for research and application on and in contemporary business organizations.

## A BRIEF HISTORY OF THE STUDY OF ORGANIZATIONAL CLIMATE

Climate research is grounded in the Gestalt psychology of Kurt Lewin. From Gestalt psychology comes the critical notion of the whole—the gestalt—meaning that individual elements of perception are formed into wholes that represent more than the simple sum of the specifics of the individual elements. A table, for example, is more than the sum of four small pieces of wood and one large piece of wood. Organizational climate is a gestalt that is based on perceived patterns in the specific experiences and behaviors of people in organizations. That is, when experiences and behaviors are perceived to be patterned in particular ways, the gestalt that the pattern connotes in the abstract constitutes the climate of the situation. In other words, the sense people make of the patterns of experiences and behaviors they have, or other parties to the situation have, constitutes the climate of the situation.

Lewin, Lippitt, and White (1939) introduced the concept of climate into the vocabulary of social psychology. They used the terms *social climate* and *social atmosphere* interchangeably to connote the psychological conditions created by leaders of boys' groups. They were interested in the consequences of leader behavior on the behavior displayed, in turn, by the boys in the groups.

After training different leaders to behave in democratic, authoritarian, and laissez-faire leadership styles, they then observed the effects of these leadership styles on the boys. The boys in the democratic condition displayed higher levels of cooperation, higher levels of participation in class work, and more openness toward the leader and each other than did boys in the other groups but were no more productive (in terms of raw productivity) than boys in the authoritarian condition. The boys in the democratic condition, however, liked being part of their groups more than did the boys who were in the other groups, and boys in the authoritarian condition least liked their groups. Lewin et al. concluded that the atmosphere that emerged in the democratic clubs was characterized by a broader range of positive experiences for the boys (including having fun) than was true in either of the other conditions.

But the democratic atmosphere was not only more positive; it was also much less negative. In the authoritarian condition, for example, the boys displayed many more dominating behaviors than were found in the democratic and laissez-faire conditions. In addition, the only boys to drop out of the groups were under the authoritarian condition, and it was under the authoritarian condition that the boys most displayed dependence upon the leader. In Marrow's (1969) biography of Lewin, he quotes Lewin's own reaction to the results observed for the autocratic leader: "There have been few experiences for me as impressive as seeing the expressions on children's faces during the first day under an autocratic leader. The group that had been formerly friendly, open, cooperative, and full of life, became within a short half-hour a rather apathetic-looking gathering without initiative" (p. 127).

There are several important points to note about this research. First, the role of the leader was paramount in this effort, perhaps having been stimulated by Lewin's experiences as a Jew in Germany prior to his emigration to the United States. Second, the climate or atmosphere of interest was not measured through the boys' perceptions but documented in the behavioral and attitudinal differences displayed by them under the three conditions. Third, more than immediately social or interpersonal issues emerged related to leadership style—fun, for example, was also a difference that was identified across the groups. Fourth, the research was a field experiment on an important social issue. Finally, the research was designed not to test a complete theory but to gather information as well as test some general hypotheses. In contrast to the myth that Lewin only believed in theory ("There is nothing so practical as a good theory"), Marrow (1969, p. 128) notes that Lewin was interested in both theory and data, the one building on the other in evolving spirals. Perhaps most crucial for the future of the climate construct is the second point above: Climate is an abstraction defined by a set of behaviors and attitudes but existing as an abstraction of those behaviors and attitudes.

World War II interrupted research like the Lewin et al. study, but shortly after the war several scholars followed in the social climate tradition, especially at the University of Michigan, where Lewin had helped to establish the Center for Group Dynamics. For example, Morse and Reimer (1956) published a study on the influence of participation in decision making on process and outcome variables for four clerical divisions of a large company. In a field experiment, they showed that under a nonparticipation condition productivity improved 25%, whereas in a participation condition productivity improved 20%. However, in the nonparticipation condition there were large drops in loyalty, attitudes, interest, and involvement in the work (specifically, feelings of responsibility for work). Following on work such as that of Morse and Reimer, first Likert (1961) and then Katz and Kahn (1966), also at the University of Michigan, produced scholarly works emphasizing the human context of work organizations for organizational per-

formance and organizational effectiveness, with an emphasis on both productivity outcomes and human outcomes. Thus, similar to Morse and Reimer, Likert as well as Katz and Kahn emphasized the idea that there is more to organizational performance than short-run productivity and that the conditions (atmosphere, climate) created in the workplace for employees can have important consequences.

There were other writings and research of a similar sort at about the same time—what might be called "the magical 1960s" so far as an emphasis on organizational climate is concerned. For example, Argyris (1957, 1960) wrote about the inclination for work organizations to infantilize workers through the nonparticipatory, nonchallenging work processes they imposed upon employees. In a similar vein, McGregor (1960) wrote of the "managerial climate" created in organizations as a function of their "managerial cosmology."

It is fair to say that research and thinking on climate since Lewin have focused on the role of the leader, as did McGregor. For example, in his famous writings on Theory X and Theory Y, McGregor (1960) emphasized the role of the manager in creating a "managerial climate," by which he meant the climate of the relationship between leader and subordinate—trusting, participative, supportive, and so forth for the Theory Y leader. In McGregor's words: "Many subtle behavioral manifestations of managerial attitude create what is often referred to as the psychological 'climate' of the relationship" (p. 134). McGregor went on to elaborate that managers implement their beliefs in people (Theory X or Theory Y) through their behavior, and it is this behavior that (a) reflects their attitudes toward people and (b) creates the climate of the relationship.

The explosion of research on organizational climate in the 1960s took many forms. For instance, the development of survey techniques for the assessment of organizational climate began right around 1960. In educational settings, for example, Pace and Stern (1958) developed a measure of college climate based on Murray's (1938) need-press theory. In business settings, early measures were those developed by Litwin and Stringer (1968) and Schneider and Bartlett (1968). Litwin and Stringer conducted several laboratory research projects directed at exploring the role of a leader's style in creating work conditions for the manifestation of the needs being simultaneously studied by McClelland. Frederiksen, Jensen, and Beaton (1972) also explored the effects of climate on performance in a laboratory setting. They examined performance on an in-basket as a function of different climates created for subjects in the directions for the in-basket. Schneider and Bartlett (1968, 1970; see also Schneider, 1972), on the other hand, developed a measure of life insurance agency climate in an attempt to show that individual-difference predictors of life insurance agent performance are moderated by the climate of the agency in which the agent works.

For Litwin and Stringer (1968), Frederiksen et al. (1972), and Schneider and Bartlett (1968, 1970), the inclusion of individual-difference variables with the organizational climate construct represented a somewhat futile early attempt to cross levels of analysis in the prediction and understanding of individual behavior. It is fair to say that this early work proceeded under the assumption that climate serves as a moderator of individual differences–individual performance relationships. Indeed, Campbell, Dunnette, Lawler, and Weick concluded in their 1970 review of organizational climate research relevant to the prediction and understanding of managerial behavior that what they called "environmental variation" is an important consideration for such prediction and understanding.

In England, on the other hand, the intensive and extensive Aston studies (see Payne & Pugh, 1976) attempted to establish the relationship between organizational structure and organizational climate. This research proceeded under the seemingly reasonable assumption that the structure of the organiza-

tion (hierarchy, size, span of control, and so forth) yields the gestalt that is climate. Here, too, however, the results were more modest than expected, even though the research effort was dramatic in terms of the number of organizations sampled and the number of employees involved. Precisely what the dimensions of organizational climate are and how to interpret data on those dimensions constituted perplexing issues, and individual researchers, going off in their own directions, were not resolving them.

At the same time researchers were dealing with the problem of understanding the dimensions and the cause of organizational climate, throughout the 1960s and into the 1970s three additional issues lurked in the background of research on organizational climate. The first was the discomforting feeling that the focus on individual levels of analysis for an "organizational" construct was conceptually inappropriate. The second, related to the first, was that climate conceptualized and measured as an individual variable was merely old (job satisfaction) wine in new (climate) bottles. The third was the equally uncomfortable feeling that when the construct was treated as an organizational-level variable, little was known about the reliability of the data being aggregated to produce the organizational variable. Hellriegel and Slocum (1974) resolved the first issue, proposing that when climate is conceptualized and measured at the individual level of analysis it constitutes "psychological climate," and when the construct is conceptualized and studied as an organizational (or at least beyond individual) variable it is "organizational climate." This convention received quick acceptance and is still operational today, with almost no research being accomplished any longer on psychological climate.

Guion (1973) addressed the relationship between climate and satisfaction most directly by making the argument that unless there is essentially 100% agreement among the respondents in an organization, all one has is another measure of individual job satisfaction. In fact, it is now obvious that he was simultaneously clarifying both the construct label and the aggregation issue. The immediate response to his claim that climate is satisfaction was a series of papers showing that climate data and satisfaction data are not at all necessarily correlated, even at the individual level of analysis (LaFollette & Sims, 1975; Schneider & Snyder, 1975). On the issue of aggregation and levels of analysis, Roberts, Hulin, and Rousseau (1978) presented a preliminary discussion of the issues in their excellent early book, elaborated on later by Rousseau (1985) and Schneider (1985), the latter with specific reference to not only organizational climate but organizational culture as well.

The data aggregation issue, as the king of Siam would have said, was a puzzlement. People trained basically as psychologists with a focus on individuals were delving into organizational realms without the tools they needed. The Roberts et al. (1978) book exploring levels of analysis problems and a detailed exploration of levels issues by Jones and James (1979) framed the issues well. Then James, Demaree, and Wolf (1984) suggested a procedure for indexing the reliability of aggregated data that seems to have made the measurement-oriented climate researchers happy. The James et al. procedure, combined with the later Dansereau (e.g., Dansereau & Alutto, 1990) WABA technique, brought the last of the three issues into the light for resolution.

Paradoxically, at about the same time that many of the issues with which climate researchers struggled were resolved, organizational culture (Pettigrew, 1979) as an alternative way to conceptualize the gestalt of organizations for their members emerged— and it has come to dominate the research literature. We will not concern ourselves here with the issues of differentiating climate and culture, for those are dealt with elsewhere in this volume. Suffice it to say here that ignoring the methodological issues that climate researchers resolved, especially those issues concerned with the reliability of aggregates, has not enhanced the scientific quality of cul-

ture research and thinking. For example, consider the definition of culture as shared values or shared beliefs or shared meanings. Use of the word *shared* in almost all definitions begs the question of how much is actually shared. Or consider the concept of culture strength, strong and weak; certainly an index of agreement or sharedness would facilitate study of this idea. We might speculate that some of the inconsistencies in the study of organizational culture (see Trice & Beyer, 1993) or some of the debate over whether organizational culture can be related to important organizational financial outcomes (see Siehl & Martin, 1990) may in part be attributable to a failure to grapple with these methodological issues.

Not that research in the more measurement-oriented climate tradition has lacked debate. Here, too, there was a dearth of research revealing strong relationships between climate and other important organizational outcomes. Reviews by Schneider (1975) and Payne and Pugh (1976) followed the Hellriegel and Slocum (1974) and Campbell et al. (1970) reviews, with none of them able to find convincing support for a relationship between organizational climate and other important indicators of organizational performance and effectiveness. For a while, the only work going on in climate seems to have been new reviews of the literature.

Schneider's (1975) review of the literature on organizational climate concluded with the thought that the generic concept of organizational climate is so amorphous and inclusive that the results from the measurement of climate are conceptually amorphous. What climate is measured in a 10-dimension measure of organizational climate? To Schneider it seemed that the measures had become so multifaceted that they no longer focused on Theory X or Theory Y managerial climate (McGregor, 1960), or on the inclination for banks to hire "right types" (Argyris, 1957), or on the fit of needs to campus characteristics (Stern, 1970), or on any specific kind of climate. He proposed the idea that climate has to have a focus, a target—that climate research has to be a climate *for* something. The *something* of interest might involve issues as diverse as the climate for safety (Zohar, 1980), the climate for sexual harassment (Fitzgerald, Drasgow, Hulin, Gelfand, & Magley, 1997), the climate for well-being (Burke, Borucki, & Hurley, 1992), and, as in the present case, the climate for service. Although our focus in this chapter is on the last of these, the principles that have evolved for conceptualizing and studying this specific focus of organizational climate apply to all manner of climates. The basic principle is that, in its generic form, the organizational climate construct has so many potential facets as to not have any focus whatsoever, with all of the attendant predictive problems associated with such measures. Thus from personality research (Tett, Jackson, & Rothstein, 1991) to attitude research (Fishbein & Ajzen, 1975) we know that, unless the predictor variable is conceptually and operationally linked to the criterion variable, the probability is low that even a modest relationship between the two will emerge. The same logic applies to the idea that, unless the climate that is conceptualized and measured is tied to the specific *something* of interest, the relationship between the climate measure and random available criteria of interest will be modest at best. In this spirit, we now introduce the reader to the research on the climate for service.

## THE CLIMATE FOR SERVICE

Schneider (1973) conducted the first research on the climate for service, arguing that the climate construct applies to customers, too. In his early research, Schneider focused on the degree to which branch banks create for their customers a "warm and friendly atmosphere." In the development of the customer surveys used in this project, Schneider interviewed a number of bank customers about their experiences. As the interviews progressed, he realized that the customers were speaking not only about the interpersonal nature of teller-customer relationships, but about other facets of the branch environment as well. For example, customers discussed the orderliness of the branch, the equipment and machinery in the branch, and the degree to which teller turnover was high or low. Schneider hypothesized, based on these interviews, that perhaps similar sets of experiences were being had by employees; if so, then employee experiences and customer experiences should be correlated. Specifically, he reasoned that the climate for service created for employees would be related to employees' behavior, which, in turn, should influence the climate for service experienced by customers.

In a series of papers, Schneider and his colleagues documented the relationship between employee experiences of service climate and customer experiences of service climate and service quality (Parkington & Schneider, 1979; Schneider, 1980; Schneider, Parkington, & Buxton, 1980), findings replicated in 1985 by Schneider and Bowen. Perhaps the most important finding emerging from what has come to be called *linkage research* was that the climate experiences reported by employees were validated by the experiences of the customers they served.

The early research by Schneider and his colleagues demonstrated a significant linkage between employee branch service climate data and customer experiences with branches. The unit of analysis in these studies was the bank branch, not the individual employee or individual customer. The surveys used to collect the employee data tapped multiple dimensions of organizational functioning that had emerged from interviews with employees about the kinds of practices and expectations they experienced at work that told them that service was or was not important. In this research, service climate itself was not measured directly; the multiple dimensions assessed defined service climate. That is, in keeping with the earliest history of research

---

**TABLE 1.1** Items Defining the Managerial Behavior Scale

My branch manager supports employees when they come up with new ideas on customer service.
My branch manager sets definite quality standards of good customer service.
My branch manager meets regularly with employees to discuss work performance goals.
My branch manager accepts the responsibilities of his/her job.
My branch manager gets the people in different jobs to work together in serving customers.
My branch manager works at keeping an orderly routine going in the branch.
My branch manager takes the time to help new employees learn about the branch and its customers.

---

on climate, the specific elements that connoted the gestalt were the data of interest. What Schneider and his colleagues really showed, then, was that specific facets of organizational functioning as described by employees that were directly or indirectly reflective of service were, in turn, related to customer experiences.

In the era of the early linkage research, employee surveys were considered to be assessments of employee morale or job satisfaction and, at best, indicators of such employee behaviors as absenteeism and turnover at the group and individual levels. In fact, in a particularly interesting study, Smith (1977) apologized for showing at the department level of analysis that more satisfied employees are less likely to be absent when it is difficult to get to work (as in a blizzard). That is, Smith apologized for not conducting individual-level analyses.

What Schneider and his colleagues showed was the criterion-related validity of employee reports for strategic organizational-level outcomes beyond outcomes associated with employees (i.e., employee turnover and employee absenteeism). To put this in context, one should remember that this research was being done prior to the days of employee empowerment, self-managed work teams, and so forth; this was still the era when the manager made all decisions, typically without consultation with or participation of lower-level employees. In addition, this was an era when all reviews of the literature reported es-

sentially no relationship between employee attitudes and employee performance (Brayfield & Crockett, 1955; Vroom, 1964). Finally, this was the era before organizational citizenship behavior (Smith, Organ, & Near, 1983) rescued research on job satisfaction by revealing that it (job satisfaction) actually correlates with an important behavior other than absenteeism and turnover.

It is useful at this point to present several of the scales contained in the early research as examples of the issues measured for both employees and customers. Table 1.1 shows the items used to assess managerial behavior from the employee's vantage point, and Table 1.2 shows the items used to assess branch administration from the customer's vantage point. In the studies done with these measures, the scale intercorrelations across 23 branches of one bank (Schneider et al., 1980) and 27 branches of another (Schneider & Bowen, 1985) were approximately .70 ($p < .01$).

Note that the items contained in both surveys were worded in terms of specific behaviors. For the Managerial Behavior Scale, almost every item refers to what managers do *with regard to service*—plan for service, reward ideas on service, and so forth. For the customers, the Branch Administration Scale items refer to specific actions on the part of branch employees or specific practices they experience—such as taking charge when the bank gets busy or messing up the opening of a new account (reverse scored). This inclination in climate items to focus on specific be-

---

**TABLE 1.2** Items Defining the Branch Administration Scale

An officer (or someone else) takes charge of things when the branch becomes overcrowded.
It sometimes seems to me that tellers have to walk all over the place to get things done. (Reverse)
When I've opened new accounts, or had to change old ones, something usually got messed up. (Reverse)
My branch has an adequate supply of deposit and withdrawal tickets.
I sometimes feel lost in the branch, not knowing where to go for certain transactions. (Reverse)
It is difficult to know who to call or where to write when I need specific bank-related information. (Reverse)

NOTE: Items followed by "Reverse" were reverse scored.

---

haviors and practices rests on the assumption that it is these very activities that, in the collective, determine the climate of a setting for those in contact with it. As noted earlier, climate is a gestalt, a whole that is constructed and can be identified based on specific activities, behaviors, and experiences. Climate is thus inferred from the presence of parts; service climate is inferred based on the presence of parts relevant for service, whether from the employee's or the customer's perspective.

Our focus here on the Managerial Behavior Scale should not lead to the conclusion that this was the only dimension of climate for service assessed through the employee survey. Three other dimensions (customer orientation, systems support, and logistics support) emerged from principal-components analysis of the originally conceptualized 10 dimensions, but we need not go into detail about them here. It is important, however, to note that following on Lewin et al. (1939) and McGregor (1960), leader and/or manager behavior continues to be an important facet of the identification of the causes of climate.

For the customer survey there were also more dimensions to service climate than branch administration. Additional scales measured courtesy/competence of staff, adequacy of staffing levels, and employee morale (perceptions of the job satisfaction of employees), and these were reduced through principal-components analysis from an original 10 a priori dimensions of customer experiences.

It may be interesting to note parenthetically that this early (1980) linkage research was very difficult to get published. Reviews of the articles focused on the small sample sizes (How can one trust an $N$ of 23?), the absence of analyses on the individual employees and/or the individual customers, and questions about the climate construct itself. The latter questions concerned issues having to do with levels of analysis, especially the following: How can data collected from individuals be aggregated to produce a unit (branch) score?

As noted earlier, this question is central to the conceptualization of climate in general and service climate in particular. The answer to the question has several components. First, bank branches are what customers experience in their visits to bank branches. Customers use more than one teller, more than one platform person (opening new accounts), more than one customer service representative, and so forth; they experience the *branch*. A corollary of this principle is the idea that if customers experience the branch, then it is what the typical customer experiences in the branch that is relevant both conceptually and practically. That is, (a) the climate of the branch is that which the typical customer experiences and (b) management is not usually concerned with individual customers—customers in the aggregate are management's legitimate concern. If the customers are to be studied in the aggregate, then employee data must also be aggregated. We will have more to say about this issue later. For now, we want to introduce the thinking from services marketing that also emerged in the 1970s and 1980s, at the same time the early service climate research was being accomplished. We do this because what has come to be called *services marketing* has had important consequences for theory and research on service climate.

## THE CONTRIBUTIONS FROM SERVICES MARKETING

Services marketing concerns the study of customers of service organizations as opposed to the study of customers of packaged goods. Early works in services marketing concentrated on defining service and the ways that the production and experiences of services differ from the production and experiences of goods. Indeed, services marketing scholars, more than researchers in organizational psychology or organizational behavior, have produced several important conceptual pieces on issues related to the management of service organizations (e.g., Davidow & Utall, 1989; Gronroos, 1990; Normann, 1984; Zeithaml, Parasuraman, & Berry, 1990) and there are now textbooks for students of services marketing that include implications for organization design (Zeithaml & Bitner, 1996).

### The Nature of Services

Writings and research in marketing have revealed, for example, that the relatively intangible nature of services makes the delivery of services difficult, because delivery can be coequivalent with services themselves. In other words, when something is intangible, the essence of it is contained in the delivery. For example, attendance at the symphony is an intangible experience, and it is the music that is the service. Due to intangibility, research on service quality has produced several dimensions that appear to capture many of the issues intangibility generates: reliability of delivery, assurance, empathy, and responsiveness during delivery (Zeithaml et al., 1990). It is important to note here that just as there is disagreement over the measurement and conceptualization of employee job satisfaction, there is similar controversy in the conceptualization and assessment of service quality and customer satisfaction with service quality (for a review, see Oliver, 1997). The concept of intangibility has furthered the understanding of the importance of the total situation for customer experiences of service quality. Here we cite just a few illustrative examples (interested readers should see Zeithaml & Bitner, 1996, for more details):

1. Research on the complexity of "servicescapes"—the physical nature of service settings—reveals the importance of the surroundings for setting/meeting customer expectations (Bitner, 1992).
2. Research on "recovery"—attending to customer problems after errors have been made—shows how the personal touch can literally recover customer satisfaction and in some cases enhance it (Heskett, Sasser, & Schlesinger, 1997).
3. Studies of attributes of the service itself (such as price) show that these attributes also influence customer expectations and perceptions (Guiltinan, 1987).

The theory is that intangibility makes these other aspects of the total situation more important for customers than is true when tangible goods are involved.

Services also tend to be produced and consumed simultaneously, placing heavy interpersonal demands on the employees who interact with customers—and those customers can vary considerably from one another, creating tension or stress in service workers that might not be present for workers on an assembly line. Good examples of this phenomenon are any services provided at sites where customers must line up and wait to receive service: banks, supermarkets, post offices, and so forth. Each customer in line is an unknown with regard to specific requirements and the way he or she will react and behave. Contrast this uncertainty with the certainty attached to the next piece coming down the manufacturing assembly line. Or consider the fact that many services require customers to be coproducers, such as in fast-food restaurants and department stores. This coproduction requirement places employees and customers in proximity to one another not only physically but psychologically, as they share a common space with a common goal.

Good research has been conducted on the tensions and stress associated with service work and customer contact. For example, Parkington and Schneider (1979) have shown that role stress is associated with employee perceptions that management wishes them to follow the rules rather than empathize with customers. In addition, they note that in branches where role stress is highest, customers report that they receive poor service quality. Weatherly and Tansik (1993) found that boundary workers in service roles differ in the ways they cope with the role stress of their work: some negotiate, some increase their effort, some avoid customer contact, and some attempt to preempt customers. Their research reveals that negotiators experience higher levels of role stress, those who put more effort into their work experience higher levels of job satisfaction, and those who preempt or avoid experience lower levels of job satisfaction. The important point to be made here is that the attributes of service create for both employees and customers sets of circumstances that can be very different from those associated with the production and delivery of goods—and both employees and customers behave and respond differently because of those differences.

## Technological Determinism of the Climate for Service

Intangibility, simultaneity, and coproduction are unique to the nature and production of services, and they have implications for the types of organizational designs that will emerge in service organizations. This idea follows from a credible, long-established "technological determinism" perspective in organizational theory (Perrow, 1970; Thompson, 1967; Woodward, 1958), which holds that the type of technology used by the firm to transform inputs to outputs is a critical contingency in determining what organizational design will be appropriate. In brief, the theory proposes that organizational structure must be designed to allow for the efficient and effective operation of the technology. In our context, this implies that the unique characteristics of service technologies require different organizational arrangements from those that would be appropriate for manufacturing or goods technologies. In turn, these service organization arrangements, and the ways employees behave under them, influence the climate for service.

Bowen and Schneider (1988) developed a set of generic implications of service technology for issues of organizational design in service organizations. They describe how the three defining attributes of service and service production (intangibility, simultaneous production and consumption, and customer coproduction) lead to a number of "organizing contingencies," which then imply certain "organizing principles." For example, intangibility leads to there being limited tangible reference points available to customers for assessing the quality of service received. Thus, as described earlier, the total situation becomes important for the customer. In turn, this suggests the organizing principle of enhancing the climate for service that is experienced by both employees and customers. That is, in the absence of tangible cues from the service itself, it is important that the "atmospherics" of the setting send a strong quality message.

A second organizing contingency is introduced into service organizations through the service attribute of simultaneous production and consumption. This characteristic of the production and delivery of service makes it difficult to decouple production and delivery of a service; this is the "high customer contact" notion introduced by Chase (1981). This is particularly true when customers are involved in producing the services they consume. These attributes make it impossible for quality control to be exercised through a supervisor's being present in the middle of every service encounter or through the pulling of a defective service encounter before it is delivered, as is possible in the manufacturing and distribution of products. This leads naturally to the idea that everything the organization can do to enhance a service climate—from selection and training to reward systems and leadership style and from managing the servicescape to managing recovery and relationships (Schneider & Bowen, 1995)—must be invoked to guide behavior and ensure quality. The rule is that the more elements of the situation connote service excellence, the stronger the service climate will be and the more customers will be likely to experience that service climate and service quality.

### Relationship Marketing

Another contribution from the field of services marketing to the development of research and theory on service climate involves what has come to be called *relationship marketing* (see Christopher, Payne, & Ballantyne, 1991). The concept of relationship marketing was introduced by Berry in 1983 (as cited in Berry, 1995), but has gained popularity and attention only since the early 1990s (Berry, 1995). Previous to the introduction of this concept, the goal of most marketing departments was to bring in new customers rather than to retain old ones. As Rust, Zahorik, and Kenningham (1996) describe it, "Until recently, then, marketing efforts have been focused on 'creating exchanges' rather than managing long-term relationships

with customers" (p. 374). In other words, in earlier times firms' interactions with customers were transactional in nature; the focus was on attracting customers through price and then being efficient in delivery. More recently, organizations have recognized the need for and importance of forming stronger, longer-term relationships with customers to ensure the organizations' future productivity and survival. The basic goal of relationship marketing, then, is "to develop reasons for the buyer to consider the seller more than the source of single transactions, but rather as a dependable source for solving many needs" (Rust et al., 1996, p. 377).

In the early linkage research conducted by Schneider and his colleagues, the issues involved were not as richly conceptualized as these ideas from marketing permit. In addition, from an organizational design and organizational change perspective, the increased emphasis on the subjective world of the customer has enhanced the practical usefulness of the linkage concept. Growing concern for customer satisfaction and for service quality has resulted in the establishment of a number of consulting firms specializing in linkage research (e.g., Gantz Wiley Research, Sirota Consulting), the development of new journals devoted to services research (*International Journal of Service Industry Management*, *Journal of Services Research*), and the implementation of courses in business schools on services management (see, e.g., Sasser, Hart, & Heskett, 1991). Service quality has become big business, both in business and in business schools.

## RECENT ISSUES RELEVANT TO SERVICE CLIMATE AND CUSTOMER SATISFACTION

### Refining the Linkage Between Employee and Customer Attitudes

Schneider et al. (1997) applied the concept of relationship marketing to the service climate literature by investigating the relationship between the focus of the organization's service initiative and customer perceptions of service quality. More specifically, they asked the following question: Is the relationship between internal organizational functioning and customer service quality perceptions stronger (a) when the organization's interactions with customers are transactional, emphasizing efficiency and price, or (b) when the organization's interactions with customers are used to form relationships with customers, where the emphasis is on expressing care and concern for the customer and his or her needs? By using archival data from two previous service climate studies, Schneider et al. show that employee reports on dimensions of service that emphasize customer relationships are more strongly related to customer perceptions than are employee reports on dimensions of service that emphasize the transaction and efficiency. Indeed, although both aspects of service are important as correlates of customer perceptions of quality, the data show that the relationship-oriented aspects of service delivery as described by employees have the most substantial relationship to customer perceptions.

Recall that issues of relationships have been central to the generic study of organizational climate. Many organizations use generic employee attitude surveys, sometimes called climate surveys or culture surveys, for the assessment of these relationship and attitudinal issues. Some researchers have shown that data from these more general attitude surveys are also related to customer satisfaction. Perhaps research by Organ (1988) showing that employee attitudes might be related to something after all emboldened other researchers to attempt to seek additional important correlates of these attitudes. Or perhaps the increased attention being accorded levels of analysis issues in employee survey data (Klein, Dansereau, & Hall, 1994; Ostroff, 1992) served to motivate aggregation of such data to the unit level of analysis. Whatever the cause, Wiley (1991) was one of the first people to begin thinking along these

lines. He and others have shown that employee job satisfaction and commitment surveys, when aggregated to the unit level of analysis, do in fact reveal significant relationships with customer satisfaction and customer commitment data (see, e.g., Tornow & Wiley, 1991; Ulrich, Halbrook, Meder, Stuchlik, & Thorpe, 1991). And these results are not just for branch banks; they cover industries as diverse as retailing, truck rental, and consulting as well.

One project in this regard that is of some interest is a study conducted by Schneider, Ashworth, Higgs, and Carr (1996) pertaining to an insurance company that had attempted to link employee survey data with customer satisfaction but found the relationships to be rather weak and unstable. Schneider and his colleagues designed a new measure for the company that focused on actual internal organizational functioning conceptually related to service and showed that over time, the measure (a) yielded stable data and (b) was related to customer satisfaction and customer intentions to renew their policies. That is, over an 18-month period, the relationship between employee climate data and customer satisfaction and intention data became stronger than did the reverse relationship, suggesting support for the implicit hypothesis that employee climate experiences yield employee behaviors that *cause* customer satisfaction. But there are several problems with this presumed causal stream. First, Ryan, Schmidt, and Johnson (1996) found that customer satisfaction over time was significantly related to employee perceptions but that the reverse was not true. Second, Schneider, White, and Paul (1998), in a study to be described in more detail below, found a clear reciprocal relationship over time (2 years) between employee perceptions and customer satisfaction.

Our present conclusion is that the issue of causality is, as usual, more complicated than our implicit linear causal thinking would suggest. The issue obviously requires additional conceptual work and data collection over meaningful periods of time, but we conclude for now that in service organizations where the relationship between employee and customer is both physically and psychologically close, a mutual influence process would seem to make sense. Thus customers *tell* employees what they are thinking about the service they receive and how (un)happy they are, and customers *experience* what employees are feeling (recall the Employee Morale Scale noted above in the discussion of early service climate studies). Indeed, Bowen (1983) hypothesized the strong relationship between customer and employee perceptions, arguing that in the "emotional labor" (Hochschild, 1983) world of service delivery employees are even more responsive to customers than they are to their own supervisors.

## Integrating Marketing and Organizational Perspectives

In addition to the relationship marketing integration reviewed earlier (Schneider et al., 1997), another concept central to marketing, market segmentation, has been integrated conceptually into thinking about organizational design and customer satisfaction. This work has underscored the idea that the very concept of service quality itself may be too generic. The logic is that what is seen as service excellence in one market segment may be seen as poor service quality in another. Consider service at a fast-food restaurant that is speedy, accurate, and delivered in a pleasant physical space: excellent service—for a fast-food restaurant. Chez Francois down the street cannot get away with this level of service if it charges Chez Francois prices and serves fine French food. *Segment* is critical.

*Market segment* refers to the service firm's strategic focus. For example, is it pursuing a cost-leadership or differentiation strategy (Porter, 1980)? Relatedly, what type of service delivery system will be needed to be consistent with this business strategy? Both of these strategic considerations are tied to the

market segment and the set of customer expectations the firm has targeted as its competitive arena. Market segmentation rests on the assumption that there is more than one way to serve customers effectively because customers have different needs and expectations at different points in time and/or for different reasons (e.g., income level). The implementation of the most effective service strategy depends upon the basis on which the firm is trying to compete. Customers in different market segments hold different expectations regarding what constitutes good service—as our example contrasting the fast-food restaurant and Chez Francois reveals.

Table 1.3 presents eight potential market segments based on three types of customer expectations: expectations for *speed* (responsive, reliable, and quick service that meets promised deadlines), expectations for *tender loving care* (TLC; courteous, understanding, empathic, friendly, and offering interpersonal service), and expectations for *customization* of service (encompassing various dimensions of the core service, including issues such as the dress and appearance of personnel, the physical facility in which the service is delivered, and the degree to which customers can choose the attributes of the core service itself).

Because firms must be at least adequate on each attribute in order to stay in business, there are no minus signs in the table. Organizations could aim to be average (0) or excellent (+) on any or all of these dimensions, depending on the market segments they are targeting. The type of service delivered is thus aligned with the expectations of the customers who are being served in a given market segment. Businesses must obviously create and maintain service climates that are appropriate for the market segments in which they wish to compete. Indeed, Chung (1996) has found support for the hypothesis that when a business implements human resources practices that fit the market segment, the customers the business serves are more satisfied.

**TABLE 1.3**    Market Segmentation Based on Three Facets of Service Delivery

| | Customer Expectations for | | |
| Market Segment | Speed | TLC | Customization |
| --- | --- | --- | --- |
| Adequate service | 0 | 0 | 0 |
| Speedy service | + | 0 | 0 |
| Friendly service | 0 | + | 0 |
| Fancy service | 0 | 0 | + |
| Good service | + | + | 0 |
| Cold service | + | 0 | + |
| Warm service | 0 | + | + |
| Terrific service | + | + | + |

SOURCE: Based on Schneider (1994).

It is clear that much is going on relating organizational issues to customer satisfaction, much of which would not fall under a traditional "climate" rubric. What has happened is that numerous organizational practices and employee attitudes vis-à-vis those practices have been shown to be reflected in customer satisfaction. That is the good news. The bad news is that much of the work is scattered, much of it has different (or no) conceptual clarity or links to prior work, and its relevance to the service climate construct itself is unclear.

### Merging the Generic and Strategic Climate Perspectives

In a recent article, Schneider, White, and Paul (1998) attempt to integrate the early climate research on generic facets of organizational functioning with the more specific strategic focus of more recent eras. To accomplish this integration, they propose that the existence of a climate *for* something (such as service) requires a generic climate for employee well-being to facilitate work accomplishment. They reason that specific strategic climates are unlikely to achieve the intended outcomes unless they are built on a strong foundation. They propose that issues such as training, equipment, leadership, and participation in decision making provide this strong foundation. In addition, they integrate research from marketing that has shown that "internal marketing" or "internal service" also provides a strong foundation on which a service climate may be built. *Internal marketing* refers to the degree to which employees inside an organization serve each other well. The model is actually quite simple: Generic work facilitation and internal marketing yield a foundation on which a climate for service can be built. The climate for service comprises a number of facets (such as those described earlier), which in turn are related to customer service climate perceptions and customer satisfaction. A test of the model using structural equation modeling over a 3-year period revealed an excellent fit to the data collected in 132 branches of a bank. As noted earlier, a reciprocal effect of customer perceptions on employee perceptions was also found.

This reciprocal effect, in which customers appear to have an effect on what employees experience as their firm's service climate, suggests some new ways of thinking about how management can enhance an organization's climate for service. Management can positively leverage customers' perceptions of service quality through service design choices, pricing, hours of operation, location—that is, through approaches other than focusing on internal service climate dimensions per se. This, in turn, can lead to positive customer behaviors that might favorably influence employee reports about the climate for service in which they work.

A second interesting feature of Schneider, White, and Paul's (1998) study is the researchers' attempt to measure directly the gestalt of climate. Schneider and his colleagues designed a single global measure of service climate comprising one summary item from each of the specific dimensions of climate assessed. For example, one of the global climate items was "How would you rate the leadership shown by management in your business in supporting the service quality effort?" This item summarized a four-item measure of managerial behavior and was one of seven items in the global service climate indicator.

## Managing Creation of a Climate for Service

Employees in organizations today have grown cynical about organizational change efforts, and their cynicism is not unwarranted. Many organizations focus their efforts on the latest fad, in search of a "quick fix." They charge the human resources department with increasing employee morale, for example, or with training employees on how to deliver superior service. Exhortations follow (smile more, look cheery, make eye contact, answer the phone within three rings)—along with coffee mugs proclaiming the importance of customers—and the organization is now a service quality powerhouse! The result is another failed attempt to make real change; the resultant appropriate employee cynicism is predictable.

The issues we have discussed so far in this chapter provide some insight into alternative tactics for bringing about a change to a

service climate that will yield improved service quality and customer satisfaction. These alternative tactics would emphasize the idea that the total pattern of important organizational activities emphasizing service quality must be in place for a service climate to exist—from the physical facility to managerial practices, from internal marketing to human resources practices, and from operations management to marketing management. In the absence of this patterning of activities with service as a frame of reference, a service climate cannot exist.

But what actual organizational activities require this form of patterning and this focus? The key, in our experience, is for management to consult with the people who work at the boundaries of the organization serving customers. One fact is clear from the research studies reviewed here: Employees have valid information about what requires attention, because what they report is related to what customers experience. The second key to establishing a climate for service is that the organization must pay attention to more than human resources issues—marketing and operations management, for example, play critical roles in creating a service climate, and all functions must be aligned to deliver quality service to customers (Schneider & Bowen, 1995).

## CONCLUSION

Lewin opened the door for an understanding of the psychology of organizations for the members of organizations. The issues are conceptually complex because climate is a variable that is both in the heads of organizational members and an attribute of the setting. Climate is the subjective world of the organization, but it is at least as real for those who come in contact with the organization as the physical setting itself. By saying that climate is the subjective world of members, we do not at all mean that there is no sharedness or commonality in what that subjective world is. *Subjective* merely means that individuals in settings actively perceive those settings and attach meanings to the patterning of activities they experience. Numerous studies have shown that people do agree in their perceptions of their situations and, further, that different parties to a setting—such as employees and customers—also converge in their perceptions.

The study of climate has evolved over the years from a molar, general perspective to a more strategic focus, linking climate perceptions to a specific criterion of interest, such as safety, innovation—or service. We have focused in this chapter on a climate for service and the myriad organizational arrangements necessary to create it. The many practices in departments of human resources, marketing, and operations all need to be in alignment with a strategic focus on service. If safety or innovation were the criteria of interest, the same principles of climate creation would apply—namely, the strategic focus needs to be clearly visible in organizational practices. It is the strategic focus of organizational practices that determines a setting's climate.

Climate for service is unique given its visibility to both employees *and* customers. This explicit recognition of the customer has shaped research and offered directions for practice in the area of climate for service. In research, it has yielded linkage research that shows the climate experiences of employees are validated by the experiences of the customers they serve. The shared perceptions of employees and customers have also forged points of integration between the two disciplines of organizational behavior and marketing. So-called linkage research (Wiley, 1996) has become an important business, providing organizations with information on the issues requiring attention if customer satisfaction is to be improved. In practice, insights have evolved concerning how to design human resources management practices to create a climate for service that fits the expectations of a targeted market segment of customers. Additionally, it appears that the climate for service is associated with customer retention and the profits that derive from it.

In sum, we have traced the evolution of climate for service from its roots in early climate research to its more recent treatment as a strategic focus. A summary lesson from these years of study is that when climate is more than an abstraction, its consequences for employees, customers, and overall organizational effectiveness are tangible and real.

# 2

## Values Lost

### Redirecting Research on Values in the Workplace

*—— Richard W. Stackman, Craig C. Pinder, and Patrick E. Connor*

The concept of values has been central to the organizational sciences and workplace relations for decades (e.g., Blood, 1969; Brown, 1976; Connor & Becker, 1975; Rosenberg, 1957; Selznick, 1957; Sikula, 1971). Moreover, the continuing interest in organizational culture (see Connor & Lake, 1994; Frost, Moore, Louis, Lundberg, & Martin, 1991; Trice & Beyer, 1993) has revitalized and sustained that interest in recent years. To consider values in the workplace is to probe the very reasons people work and why they behave in the ways they do in their jobs (Posner & Munson, 1979; Sikula, 1971). Values are key determinants of attitudes, which in turn affect work-related (and all other) behavior (Becker & Connor, 1986; Connor & Becker, 1975, 1994). For example, values lie at the core of individuals' conscious career decisions (Judge & Bretz, 1992) and the affective reactions people have to their jobs (Locke, 1969).

Values also play a role in the decision-making processes of managers (Connor &

AUTHORS' NOTE: Preparation of this chapter was made possible by the support of grants awarded to the second author by the Social Sciences and Humanities Research Council of Canada and by the Centre for Labour-Management Studies, and to the third author by the Kaneko Foundation and Willamette University. We thank Lois Fearon for her dedicated library research during the early stages of the project. We are also grateful to Tom Knight, David McPhillips, Bruce Meglino, Lilach Sagiv, Shalom Schwartz, Gordon Walter, and Ray Zammuto for their helpful comments.

Becker, 1994, 1995; Posner & Munson, 1979; Ravlin & Meglino, 1987a) as well as in the organizational dissension activities of workers (Graham, 1986). Alternatively, they have been found to be related to prosocial behaviors at work (see McNeely & Meglino, 1992). At a more sociological level, societal and corporate values have been cited as major parameters in issues related to corporate social responsibility, corporate ethics, and similar concerns (Balazs, 1990). Finally, values (and differences among values) have been studied at the global level: Investigators have examined and compared the typical value structures of managers and workers from different countries as a means of understanding the differential meanings of work and, in particular, the problems associated with cross-cultural trade and business (e.g., England & Lee, 1974; Hofstede, 1980a; Schwartz & Bilsky, 1987, 1990).

However, considering the extant research on values today, how much do we truly know about values and the roles values play in individual behavior? As Connor and Becker (1994) have noted, scholars' understanding of values—both in general and in the workplace—has been compromised. This has occurred, in part, through researchers' lax operationalization of the values construct itself and through the proliferation of new instruments and questionnaires that are rarely reconciled with earlier such instruments, making the accumulation of a coherent body of knowledge virtually impossible.

With the exception of studies such as those by Sagiv and Schwartz (1995) and Homer and Kahle (1988),[1] most past research has concentrated on the effects of single values, thereby neglecting the complex nature of value structures (Homer & Kahle, 1988; Schwartz, 1996b). Past research has also been plagued by the use of value lists that fail to cover the full range of values that are likely to influence behavior, and by the failure to view value systems as integrated wholes that entail trade-offs among competing value priorities (Schwartz, 1994, 1996b).

Finally, researchers have tended to focus their attention on the relationship between attitudes and behavior—especially behavior and behavior outcomes as influenced by the theory of reasoned action (see Ajzen & Fishbein, 1980; Feather, 1992; Fishbein & Ajzen, 1975). There has been some debate as to how successful these studies have been, because, in part, researchers have been studying behavior without a clear understanding of values and the roles values play in causing behavior (Feather, 1992; Homer & Kahle, 1988). Hence, even though values are both a powerful explanation of and an influence on human behavior, it remains a mystery how values cause preferences to be formed, and it is even more mysterious how values cause individuals to act upon their preferences (Connor & Becker, 1994; Homer & Kahle, 1988).

In this chapter, after first defining values, we examine six issues that are integral to these questions: value descriptiveness, the attainment of value specificity and generalization, the concept of a so-called central value system, value stability and change, levels of analysis and the anthropomorphism error, and ethics.

## VALUES DEFINED

Nearly two decades ago, Kilmann (1981) reviewed definitions of values published to that time. The general sense of these definitions is that values are objects, qualities, standards, or conditions that satisfy or are perceived to satisfy needs and/or that act as guides to human action. In much of the organizational literature dealing with values, the framework and definition advanced by Rokeach (1969) has been particularly popular: "an enduring belief that a specific mode of conduct or end-state of existence is personally and socially preferable to alternative modes of conduct or end-states" (p. 160). In Rokeach's conception, values entail attention to both *means* (such as acts) and *ends* (such as outcomes of various sorts): Values are "global beliefs (about desirable end states or modes of behavior) that underlie attitudinal processes. In particular, they serve as the basis for making choices" (Connor & Becker, 1994, p. 68).

Conceived as global beliefs, values are neither attitudes nor behaviors. Instead, they are the building blocks of the behavior of and the choices made by individuals. Attitudes, on the other hand, are cognitive and affective *orientations toward specific objects and situations.* Behavior is the manifestation of a person's fundamental values and corresponding attitudes. Schwartz (1996b) states that attitudes and behavior are guided not by the priority given to a single value but by trade-offs among competing values that are implicit simultaneously in a behavior or attitude (see Rokeach, 1973; Schwartz, 1992; Tetlock, 1986). Feather (1992, 1995) treats values not only as generalized beliefs about what is or is not desirable, but also as motives. Both needs and values can influence a person's cognitive-affective appraisal of a situation in relation to both means and ends. Feather's (1992) expectancy-value approach, in which values induce valences on events and potential outcomes, bridges the gap between knowing and doing.

Two key issues are important to any understanding of the values-attitudes-behaviors relationship: observability and applicability. Behavior is the most readily observable variable, with attitudes and values successively inferential (Connor & Becker, 1994; Feather, 1995). Values underlie and affect attitudes, which in turn underlie and affect behavior. In other words, attitudes result from the application of values to concrete objects or situations. As for applicability, values are conceived of as global, transcending all situations, whereas attitudes apply to specific objects, persons, institutions, and situations.

## Values Versus Work Values

One issue of major contention in the values literature has to do with a distinction be-

tween values (in the general sense) and work values—a concept that implies the existence of particular sets of values that govern employee work behavior, in all of its forms.

Most conceptions and definitions of *work values,* per se, are consistent with most general definitions of values in the broader sense, but they focus on work, work behavior, and work-related outcomes (e.g., Wollack, Goodale, Wijting & Smith, 1971). One typical definition is provided by Pine and Innis (1987), who conceive of work values as "an individual's needs and priorities and consequent personal dispositions and orientations to work roles that have the perceived capacity to satisfy those needs and priorities" (p. 280). A more recent definition is provided by Nord, Brief, Atieh, and Doherty (1988): "We define work values as the end states people desire and feel they ought to be able to realize through working" (p. 2).

The controversy has to do with whether there is any benefit added—such as conceptual clarity, applied insights, or scholarly utility of any sort—in distinguishing between values in general and values related to the workplace. Seligman and Katz (1996), who studied the reordering of values with respect to specific issues (such as abortion and the environment), argue that, on the one hand, the stability of a general value system is necessary to express the coherence of the self over time and situations. However, the multiple-value-system perspective (e.g., represented by work values and family values) would suggest that value systems are dynamic and that the value system a person constructs in any given situation is very much dependent on the context in which he or she is asked to do so. Consequently, value systems would be stable in a particular context because they would be flexibly attuned to context where these systems would be informed and influenced by the general value system (Seligman & Katz, 1996).

We return to this issue below and propose a means of reconciling the two opposing sides. For the sake of parsimony in the following sections, we refer only to *values* in our discussion.

## VALUE DESCRIPTIVENESS

An issue of fundamental importance to the study of values is that of descriptiveness and how it trades off against parsimony. Rokeach's (1973) early list of values comprised 18 "terminal" and 18 "instrumental" values that purported to apply to the multitude of roles and settings in which individuals may find themselves.[2] Since then, Schwartz (1992, 1994) and his colleagues (Prince-Gibson & Schwartz, 1998; Sagiv & Schwartz, 1995) have extended Rokeach's list by expanding the number of value types, sharpening some of the definitions of value types, and specifying the content of the values within categories. Schwartz's work was instigated by four questions germane to our present concerns:

1. Do values form some universal set of types?
2. Does the universal set include all types of values to which individuals are likely to attribute at least moderate importance as criteria for evaluation?
3. Do values have the same or similar meanings among the differing groups of persons under study?
4. Does a value structure exist such that there are consistent conflicts and compatibilities among values?

Schwartz (1992) derived and refined a list of 56 specific values and a set of 10 value types, specifying the dynamic structure of relations among these value types. His work has yielded a circular structure of wedges of value types, suggesting that the pursuit of different value types can be compatible—or incompatible—depending on how close together the types are on the circular map that represents his model. Any particular value type tends to be associated with value types that are adjacent to it on the map, whereas associations between types diminish as they are separated on the circumference of the wheel (Schwartz, 1992). Table 2.1 lists the value types, with each described in terms of its central goal (and followed, in parentheses, by specific values that primarily represent it). The circular model reflecting relationships among the various types is shown in Figure 2.1, and the entire list of 56 separate values is presented in Table 2.2. Table 2.3 presents the 36 instrumental and terminal values found in Rokeach's (1973) Value Survey, enabling a direct comparison of the two typologies as well as an assessment of the degree to which Schwartz's work has added descriptiveness to that of Rokeach. Notwithstanding the extra descriptiveness and precision added by Schwartz (1992) to Rokeach's (1973) typology, we believe neither list is sufficiently descriptive for an understanding of human behavior in any specific role or setting (such as an employee at work). That is, the values identified by Rokeach and Schwartz may, in many cases, be defined at levels that are simply too abstract to be of any descriptive, predictive, or even prescriptive use in work settings.[3] Indeed, both lists can be compared to that offered in the Organizational Culture Profile (OCP; O'Reilly, Chatman, & Caldwell, 1991), which is composed of statements that represent both terminal and instrumental values (see Table 2.4). Such a contrast highlights the trade-off between parsimony and descriptiveness. Although the OCP may offer more descriptiveness for specific purposes, such as organizational analysis, it lacks the parsimony offered by the other two typologies. Hence, for example, Rokeach's shorter list is missing values that capture such OCP dimensions as fairness, confronting conflict directly, and working in collaboration with others—specific values that may be useful in organizational work.

Schwartz (1994) argues that researchers need to consider more specific details of a situation when relating behaviors to general values that are transsituational in nature. Schwartz also acknowledges that the value

---

**TABLE 2.1**    Schwartz Motivational Values Types

| *Type* | *Description* |
| --- | --- |
| Power | Social status and prestige, control or dominance over people and resources (social power, authority, wealth) |
| Achievement | Personal success through demonstration of competence according to social standards (successful, capable, ambitious, influential) |
| Hedonism | Pleasure and sensuous gratification for oneself (pleasure, enjoying life) |
| Stimulation | Excitement, novelty, and challenge in life (daring, a varied life, an exciting life) |
| Self-direction | Independent thought and action—choosing, creating, exploring (creativity, freedom, independent, curious, choosing own goals) |
| Universalism | Understanding, appreciation, tolerance, and protection for the welfare of all people and for nature (broad-minded, wisdom, social justice, equality, a world at peace, a world of beauty, unity with nature, protecting the environment) |
| Benevolence | Preservation and enhancement of the welfare of people with whom one is in frequent personal contact (helpful, honest, forgiving, loyal, responsible) |
| Tradition | Respect, commitment, and acceptance of the customs and ideas that traditional culture or religion provide the self (humble, accepting my portion in life, devout, respect for tradition, moderate) |
| Conformity | Restraint of actions, inclinations, and impulses likely to upset or harm others and violate social expectations or norms (politeness, obedience, self-discipline, honoring parents and elders) |
| Security | Safety, harmony, and stability of society, of relationships, and of self (family security, national security, social order, clean, reciprocation of favors) |

SOURCE: Adapted from Schwartz (1996b, p. 3).

---

types may apply to all situations, although the specific values that constitute the value types could change. Because values are expressed in specific situations, much can be gained from alternative methods that embed values in concrete and varied everyday situations, such as school, work, or family contexts (Schwartz, 1992). Although such operations are less likely to reveal basic universals, they are important for clarifying the individual and cultural differences that arise when values are expressed in specific judgments and behaviors (Schwartz, 1992). We believe, therefore, that Schwartz's typology may serve as a useful starting point for the study of values in work organizations. In the meantime, we are left with this question: Is it possible somehow to reconcile the notion of general values with that of so-called work values?

## ATTAINING SPECIFICITY

We propose here a model that incorporates both value generality of the Rokeach or Schwartz variety and value specificity reflecting a high degree of work-related relevance. To do so, we adapt Schwab's (1980, 1999) model of the relationship between conceptual and operational levels in the conduct of social science research.

For Schwab (1980), it is critical that researchers' theoretical models and hypotheses relate independent and dependent variables at relatively abstract levels. At the same time, the models must be explicit about what is and is not to be included in the concepts involved. At issue is the correspondence between the concept, as it is defined, and the empirical (operational) indicator(s) chosen. It is critical to

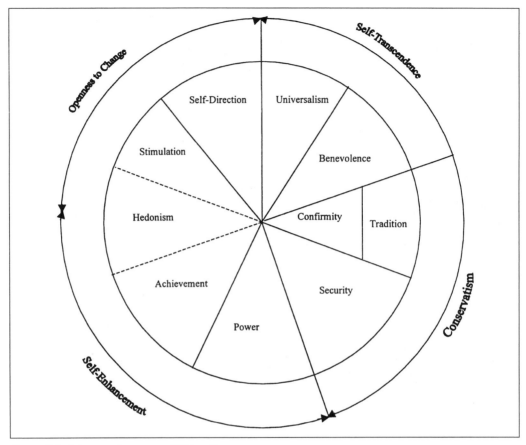

**Figure 2.1.** Schwartz Structure of Value Systems
SOURCE: Schwartz (1992, p. 45). Reprinted by permission of Academic Press.

differentiate between concepts, which by nature are relatively abstract, and the empirical indicators that are chosen to measure them.

How might Schwab's model be relevant to the issue of the descriptiveness of values for the workplace? We propose that this model might be adapted, or modified, through the addition of a third, intermediate level of definition. That is, one could conceive of values, per se, in the most abstract of terms, analogous to Schwab's conceptual level (see Figure 2.2). It is at this level that Schwartz's (1994) values list offers the most benefit. The values are carefully defined, but certainly not in operational terms; rather, they are defined in abstract terms, making them quite portable, universal, and more or less pan-situational.

Next, if one were to consider a level of abstraction that lies between Schwab's conceptual and operational levels, one would be able to translate Schwartz's generally defined values into terms that are relevant to particular settings, such as the workplace. In this second level, the values would still be defined nonoperationally, but in terms that make particular sense to work, working, and workplace issues. Finally, at the "lowest" of the three levels—the one that corresponds directly with Schwab's operational level—would be the values that are reflected in direct, empirical terms, such as those that are generated by questionnaires, interviews, or other empirical tools, such as the Survey of Work Values (Wollack et al., 1971). These operational measures would still have to be reconcilable upward to the second concep-

**TABLE 2.2** The Schwartz Value Survey

| | | |
|---|---|---|
| Equality | Self-discipline | Influential |
| Inner harmony | Detachment | Honoring of parents and elders |
| Social power | Family security | Choosing own goals |
| Pleasure | Social recognition | Health |
| Freedom | Unity with nature | Capable |
| A spiritual life | A varied life | Accepting my portion in life |
| Sense of belonging | Wisdom | Honest |
| Social order | Authority | Preserving my public image |
| An exciting life | True friendship | Obedient |
| Meaning in life | A world of beauty | Intelligent |
| Politeness | Social justice | Helpful |
| Wealth | Independent | Enjoying life |
| National security | Moderate | Devout |
| Self-respect | Loyal | Responsible |
| Reciprocation of favors | Ambitious | Curious |
| Creativity | Broad-minded | Forgiving |
| A world at peace | Humble | Successful |
| Respect for tradition | Daring | Clean |
| Mature love | Protecting the environment | |

SOURCE: Schwartz (1992, pp. 60-62).

**TABLE 2.3** The Rokeach Value Survey

| *Terminal* | *Instrumental* |
|---|---|
| Comfortable life | Ambitious |
| Exciting | Broad-minded |
| Sense of accomplishment | Capable |
| World at peace | Cheerful |
| World of beauty | Clean |
| Equality | Courageous |
| Family security | Forgiving |
| Freedom | Helpful |
| Happiness | Honest |
| Inner harmony | Imaginative |
| Mature love | Independent |
| National security | Intellectual |
| Pleasure | Logical |
| Salvation | Loving |
| Self-respect | Obedient |
| Social recognition | Polite |
| True friendship | Responsible |
| Wisdom | Self-controlled |

SOURCE: Rokeach (1973, pp. 26-32).

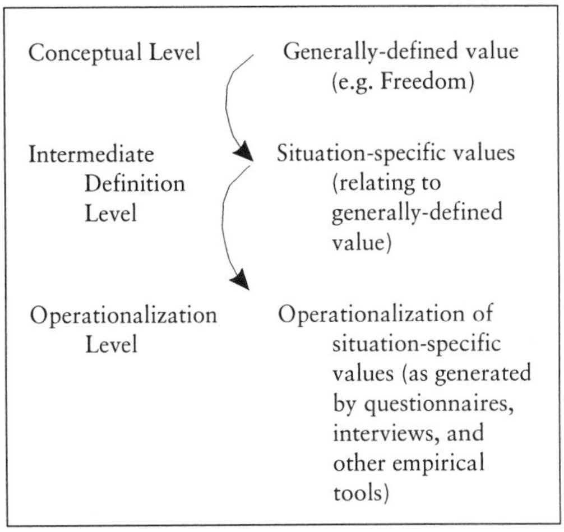

**Figure 2.2.** Modified Schwab Model
SOURCE: Based on Schwab (1980).

tual level (i.e., they would still have to pass the test of construct validity), which in turn must pass the test of relevance to the general values at the most abstract level.

By expanding Schwab's (1980, 1999) two-level model into a three-level one in this

**TABLE 2.4** The Organizational Culture Profile Item Set

| | | |
|---|---|---|
| Flexibility | Fairness | Security of employment |
| Adaptability | Respect for the individual's rights | Offers praise for good performance |
| Stability | Tolerance | Low level of conflict |
| Predictability | Informality | Confronting conflict directly |
| Being innovative | Being easygoing | Developing friends at work |
| Being quick to take advantage of opportunities | Being calm | Fitting in |
| A willingness to experiment | Being supportive | Working in collaboration with others |
| Risk taking | Being aggressive | Enthusiasm for the job |
| Being careful | Decisiveness | Working long hours |
| Autonomy | Action oriented | Not being constrained by many rules |
| Being rule oriented | Taking initiative | An emphasis on quality |
| Being analytical | Being reflective | Being distinctive—different from others |
| Paying attention to detail | Achievement orientation | |
| Being precise | Being demanding | Having a good reputation |
| Being team oriented | Taking individual responsibility | Being socially responsible |
| Sharing information freely | Having high expectations for performance | Being results oriented |
| Emphasizing a single culture throughout the organization | Opportunities for professional growth | Having a clear guiding philosophy |
| Being people oriented | High pay for good performance | Being competitive |
| | | Being highly organized |

SOURCE: O'Reilly et al. (1991, p. 516).

manner, we believe that we can reconcile the argument in favor of adopting parsimonious, general value sets (such as Schwartz's) with the alternative position that calls for assessing "work values." That is, so-called work values, as measured, could be directly reconciled with general values, as conceptualized.

### Generalizing the Approach

We can broaden this approach by operationalizing the general values of the Schwartz variety into terms that are specific in settings other than the workplace, such as a person's family or community relations. Again, the problems of construct adequacy and deficiency must be addressed. A general value such as "freedom" therefore may be operationalized in one set of measures when one is interested in people's work roles, but in entirely different terms when one's interest is in their activities in the general community. The measures would vary across settings, but they would all be ultimately reconcilable at the most abstract (Rokeach- or Schwartz-like) levels.

Such an approach also permits a look at the comparative relevance of values across situations. Again, consider the value "freedom," which Rokeach (1973) equates with "independence." Let us suppose that having freedom—independence, autonomy, discretion—in one's workplace is a matter of some significance to a person. The imposition (or relaxing) of directive rules and procedures by management therefore will likely speak directly to that value. Hence "freedom" is a highly salient value for that individual at work. On the other hand, this value may not be nearly as relevant in that person's life within the family setting. That is, independence, autonomy, and discretion simply may not be especially germane to the normal flow of activities and relationships he or she experiences at home. Thus summing a person's regard for freedom across all contexts loses the point; it offers little descriptive power in any particular setting. In other words, the benefit—descriptively, predictively, and prescriptively—of operating at the most abstract levels (such as via Rokeach's or Schwartz's typologies) may be more apparent than real. Moving "downward" into the operational levels provides more power for using the concepts of values in any and all particular contexts.

This approach is summarized graphically in the amoebalike model shown in Figure 2.3. The frames and squares composing the grid shown in the figure represent some of the various settings of importance in a person's life. The lengths of the various "tentacles" shown in Figure 2.3 correspond to the relative importance of particular values (or value sets) as measured at the "lowest" of the three levels from the adapted Schwab model. As Rokeach (1973) puts it, "Different subsets . . . are activated in different social situations" (p. 14). People adjust their value priorities to their circumstances. They downgrade values made unattainable by their role opportunities and constraints, and they upgrade those that are attainable (Kohn & Schooler, 1983; Schwartz & Bardi, 1997). Thus we can see that "freedom" is less important to the person portrayed when family relations are at issue than it is to his or her work attitudes and behavior. In this way, the amoeba portrays intraindividual differences in value importance because it conditions "importance" on the forum or setting involved. A different value (such as "ambitious") would, at a given time, be represented by an amoeba of a different shape on the same grid. In fact, one could simultaneously superimpose any number of "amoebae" (see Figure 2.4) onto a given grid at a given point in time to reflect how different values array themselves for a person in relative importance—depending on the context in question.

The amoeba model also permits an analysis of changes in values within a single person over time as well as the relative importance of particular values across persons at a given time. For example, one can imagine the lengths of the various tentacles representing a value such as "freedom" changing over time as an individual goes through various life experiences that affect how he or she thinks about work, family, and other roles and contexts in life.

In summary, we do not suggest that there is anything more to this representation than a visual parallel; we imply neither metaphoric nor literal similarity between amoebae and value structures (see Bourgeois & Pinder, 1983; Pinder & Bourgeois, 1982). Instead, we offer the amoeba model as one graphic way to examine the relative strengths of values within and among people, over time and/or in different settings of interest.

## THE CONCEPT OF A CENTRAL VALUE SYSTEM

Rokeach (1973) defines a personal value system as an "organization of principles and rules to help one choose between alternatives, resolve conflicts, and make decisions" (p. 14). The current management literature is dominated by his view that this organization is hierarchical, in which a personal value system is conceptualized as consisting of a rank ordering of individual values. As Rokeach notes in a work published shortly after his death, "A hierarchical conception directs our attention to the idea that although the number of values that individuals and societies possess is relatively limited, values are capable of being weighed and arranged against one another to lead to a very large number of permutations and combinations of value hierarchies" (Rokeach & Ball-Rokeach, 1989, p. 775).

We suggest that strict adherence to this view may have limited the advancement of

Work                    Hobbies

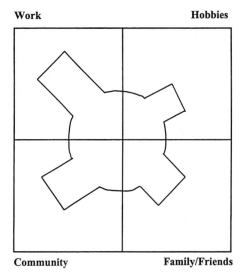

Community              Family/Friends

**Figure 2.3.** Amoeba Model: Freedom

scholars' understanding of values. Ravlin and Meglino's (1987b, 1989) work on the transitivity of values, for example, has led them to conclude that value hierarchies do "seem to exist"; however, these hierarchies are flexible when the values in question are of equal or nearly equal importance.[4] Thus a be-

Work                    Hobbies

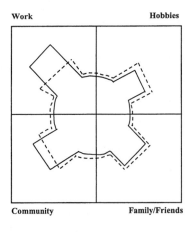

Community              Family/Friends

—— *Freedom*
------ *Ambitious*

**Figure 2.4.** Amoeba Model: Freedom and Ambitious

lief in the immutability of values with respect to a particular rank order may be misguided. In fact, Chusmir and Parker (1991) propose that individuals may have two different hierarchies of values, one for personal/family life and another for work life.[5] In his research, Schwartz (1992, 1994) has applied a rating, not a ranking, method when studying values. He argues that rating does not force respondents "to discriminate among equally important values or to compare directly values they may experience as incommensurable because one expresses personal, and the other social, goals" (Schwartz, 1994, p. 26).

If indeed different value hierarchies are salient for different situations, values would seemingly vary in rank order when compared across situations. We illustrated this possibility earlier when we introduced the amoeba model. Therefore, instead of comprising a rank ordering, a person's value system may be described as comprising a number of levels, ranging from the most explicit to the most basic. Borrowing from Hunt (1991, pp. 220-224; see also Connor & Lake, 1994, pp. 46-56), we liken a value system to a peeled onion; this conception is shown in Figure 2.5.

Values depicted near the center of the figure are hypothesized to be more important than those closer to the periphery; they are nearer the "core" of the individual's being. Instead of a rank ordering of one value relative to others, value systems may be conceptualized as an ordering of values sets in relation to other values sets. We believe that it is not meaningful that one value is more important than another in a rigid hierarchical sense; rather, it is probable that there is a set of core values for any individual that is more important—more deeply held—than another set of values. People feel strongly about their central values (Feather, 1995). It is these core values that allow us to speak of an individual's central value system, much as some managers and organizational scientists speak of an organization's core value system (Chatman, 1991). Such a system is said to exist within an organization when a number of particular values concerning behaviors and the way things are done in the organization are shared by key actors operating in powerful and important units and positions.[6]

One could also posit that those values composing the central value system are less changeable in relation to values residing at layers further from the core. If values do "change" in importance, then values would move from layer to layer, either outward or inward. The value itself would not change, but its importance in relation to other values would. The relative changeability of individual values and the conditions under which such "movement" might occur are two subjects that seem ripe for empirical examination. It is worth noting here that values are positive, and therefore individuals need not pay a penalty for reordering their value priorities (Seligman & Katz, 1996).

## *Recapitulation*

In summary, we offer the peeled-onion metaphor as a means of addressing and possibly reconciling previous views and debates in the values literature pertaining to the following critical questions:

1. Are values arranged hierarchically within persons?
2. Is the relative importance of a person's values changeable?
3. Are some values more changeable than others?
4. Is it useful to think of values-in-context (such as in the concept of "work values"), or is it more appropriate to consider people's values as general constructs that transcend settings to influence attitudes and behaviors?

We suggest that values ought to be considered in sets, such that certain sets of values become more or less important in guiding a person's attitudes and behavior depending on the context. It is reasonable to assume that different sets of values (as opposed to single values) will increase and decrease in relative

importance for an individual across time and differing contexts. To illustrate these arguments, we have offered two heuristic devices, one suggestive of an amoeba on a grid, the other reflective of the multilayered structure of an onion.

## THE CHANGEABILITY OF VALUES

Two issues are central to the matter of the changeability of values. The first pertains to the degree to which values in a society change at the aggregate level, over long periods of time. The second concerns the natural, developmental alterations that occur in individuals' values as they age, mature, become educated, and experience life. We examine only the latter issue here by asking the question, How stable or malleable are individuals' values?

According to Rokeach's (1973) theory, confronting an individual with information that is discordant with his or her values may influence those values or lead the person to alter them. As Rokeach and Grube (1979) put it:

> Long term changes in human values can be brought about as a result of a *self-confrontation* treatment in which individuals are given feedback and interpretations concerning their own and significant others' values. . . . the awareness of such inconsistencies arouses a state of self dissatisfaction and, moreover, as one means of reducing this negative affective state some individuals will change their values to become more consistent with self-conceptions. (p. 24)

To test this proposition, Rokeach and Grube asked university students to rank Rokeach's instrumental and terminal values in the manner he usually employed in his research. Then they asked students who possessed extremely high and extremely low rankings for various

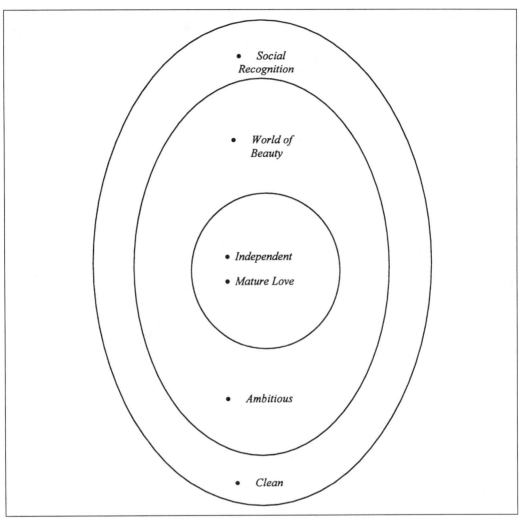

**Figure 2.5.** A Peeled-Onion Conception of a Personal Values System
SOURCE: Suggested by Hunt (1991, p. 227).

values to indicate whether they would increase the importance of those values in American society if they could do so, and whether they would resist attempts by others to reduce the importance of the same values in American society. In the second phase of the project, Rokeach and Grube actually confronted students with extremely high and low rankings for the value "equality" with experimental treatments designed to cause the sort of discomfort described in the quotation above.

The results of the project's two phases converged to suggest that self-confrontation may, in fact, be capable of causing people to alter their values, but only in directions those holding the values permit to occur. In other words, Rokeach and Grube conclude that the *arbitrary* manipulation of values (meaning manipulation by outsiders of a person's values in any direction) is not likely to be feasible. In short, they conclude that fears about the possibility of capricious, multidirectional changes of any person's values by outside agents are without basis. A person's values are robust and subject to change only to the degree that the individual permits them to be so.

In a rare longitudinal study, Armon (1993) adopted a theoretical perspective unlike any other discussed in this chapter or elsewhere in the traditional literature dealing with work and values. She employed a "structural developmental" approach to values—one that envisions how people's values are multi-dimensional, containing both moral and nonmoral qualities.[7] Armon's focus was on the question, "What is good work?" Her sample was small (N = 50, including 33 adults, ranging from 23 to 72 years), but she followed her participants and assessed their views on what constitutes "good work" four times over a 12-year period.

In brief, Armon found that many of the participants in her sample matured through a five-stage developmental sequence in which what they valued in work became less visceral, less instrumental, and more heavily directed toward the pursuit of such values as ethical conduct, assistance of other individuals, and having a positive net impact on the world at large. In addition, she found that these participants progressed through an identifiable developmental sequence (with no differences between the men and the women). Progression through the stages was related to education: Participants who advanced toward less selfish, more worldly values were more highly educated than those who did not. Further, those who were more developed tended to have more often witnessed critical life events—mostly work related—that featured ethical problems or dilemmas that had to be addressed or that required them to address issues of their own self-identity and integrity.

Armon's research is encouraging because it constitutes a rare longitudinal investigation of the natural development of values. However, it is also remarkable in that the literature has yet to address adequately the meaning and processes of "change" in a given value for a particular individual. For example, change may represent a reordering either within or among values. In other words, does the value actually change (such as a person's valuing honesty after having not cared about being honest or dishonest) or does the value change in relative importance to another value (an individual's now valuing economic goals more than comfort goals even though he or she may still value comfort goals quite highly)?

Ultimately, we need to know more about the malleability of values (for which we have offered two abstract models, the amoeba and the peeled onion) for two reasons: First, Rokeach (1969; Rokeach & Ball-Rokeach, 1989) has posited that one can best change an individual's behavior by focusing on and attempting to alter his or her value system rather than the behavior itself; second, one must have some knowledge of the malleability of values before one can locate them at any sort of value-hierarchical layer or importance stratum (á la the peeled-onion model of Figure 2.5).

## LEVELS OF ANALYSIS AND THE ANTHROPOMORPHISM ERROR

Many theorists believe that values (or shared values) are the sine qua non of cultures and of organizational cultures in particular (e.g., Meglino, Ravlin, & Adkins, 1989; O'Reilly et al., 1991); however, some infer incorrectly from this that it is useful to think of organizations, per se, as having values.

Years ago, Rokeach (1979) wrote:

The value concept is an especially powerful one for all the social sciences because it can be meaningfully employed at all levels of social analysis. . . . It is just as meaningful to speak of cultural, societal, institutional, organizational, and group values as it is to speak of individual values. If individual values are socially shared cognitive representations of personal needs and the means for satisfying them, then institutional values are socially shared representations of institutional goals and demands. (p. 50)

He then opined that it is the role of various societal institutions to instill particular values or value sets among the citizenry, and that the resultant value profile of a community reflects the comparative success of various institutions in inculcating their respective values among the people. There is a sort of value specialization within institutions (such as churches, schools, and police). There is also a degree of value sharing among them, such that the values espoused by various institutions—although they may compete for influence among the people—are, at the same time, somewhat compatible and in harmony with one another.

A logical error that many organizational participants make is in anthropomorphizing the organizations in which they work or with which they otherwise interact. Organizations are thereby thought of as having, in some sense, minds, memories, hearts, and other distinguishing properties of *Homo sapiens*. As a consequence, people speak of "loving" the Vancouver Canucks (of the National Hockey League), and employees of Harrod's say they hope that Harrod's will "remember" them when it is time for them to receive raises.

Although it is true that organizations are composed of people and can be defined as systems of interactions and events linking people (Katz & Kahn, 1978), it is a logical error—an error of composition—to attribute, other than metaphorically, human properties to aggregations of individuals such as groups, organizations, and institutions. In short, organizations do not have minds, memories, or hearts; they do not possess aspirations, loves, or fears (Pinder, 1998).

Likewise, organizations do not possess values or needs. Rather, key players in organizations, as individual human beings, possess values and needs, and sometimes the most powerful of these people can influence the goals and policies of their organizations in directions that are consistent with their own values and needs. In fact, in the work quoted immediately above, Rokeach (1979) describes five methods by which institutional values can be measured. Four of these methods require an assessment of the value structures of individual "gatekeepers" or "special clients" related to the institutions in question. In other words, although Rokeach claims that aggregations of people have values, he recognizes that, operationally, one must assess the values of key individual players to make sense of the concept.

We believe that there are several ontological and epistemological problems with this view and the research approach it requires. First is the matter of determining *whose* individual values are to be assessed and then aggregated to yield a composite definition of the "organization's values." Second is the issue of how, arithmetically, such values or value profiles (see Connor & Becker, 1975) are to be aggregated. Third are the possible ethical problems of (mis)leading lower participants and interested outside parties (such as customers, clients, and others) about the "values of the organization," as if these values have the same qualities as those possessed by individual persons (such as trustworthiness, loyalty, and honesty). Attributing kind or benevolent "values" to a more or less loosely coupled social system can be irresponsible.

Finally, there is a practical problem: In general, it is logical to assume a degree of coherence or agreement among the value structures of an organization's gatekeepers (or *elite groups*, as Hage & Dewar, 1973, refer to them). It is possible that the perceptions of values held by members of an organization may vary by hierarchical level, such that people nearer the top of the chart may believe in and/or espouse values that are very different from those held by people at the bottom. It is also apparent that an organization's "culture" is made up of multiple cultures, varying across functional, ethnic, age, and professional groups (Trice & Beyer, 1993). Hence to portray a single organization as having a "strong culture" is to imply that value congruence exists, in abundance, throughout the entire organization. To the extent that this is not so, it becomes meaningless to speak of an organization's (singular) culture and, therefore, of its values. The transporting of an individual-level trait or concept (in this case, values) to a level of analysis higher than that of single individuals is, at best, a metaphorical use of the terms involved. At worst, it is a logical error that can confound analysis and understanding of how organizations work (see Pinder & Bourgeois, 1982).[8]

A case study of the Levi-Strauss organization exemplifies the problem ("Managing by Values," 1994). Robert Haas possessed a strong desire to promote the values of empowerment, employee involvement, and equal opportunity. Despite his position as chairman and CEO, by which he presumably had substantial power and ability to influence, he ran into considerable difficulty in implementing his policies in accordance with those values. Apparently this was because those values were not shared by other powerful people in his company and, likely, because of the simple inertia that often surrounds significant organizational change (Connor & Lake, 1994).

The key point here is that it is critical to keep individual-level concepts (such as needs and values) focused on and devoted to an understanding of individual-level problems and phenomena. Other terms, representing other concepts for dealing with group, organizational, and institutional issues, should be created, invoked, or utilized as appropriate.

## ETHICAL ISSUES

We began our discussion by identifying a number of values issues (e.g., value descriptiveness and central value systems); not the least of these is a set of ethical concerns. Within broad limits, it seems that employers assume that they have a right, as part of the employment contract, to attempt to influence the values of employees. Likewise, it seems that employees often share that assumption, tacitly at least; they believe that their employers have the right to make them over in ways that will increase managerial control as well as employee uniformity and predictability.

In fact, some celebrated organizations have been cited as especially effective in their techniques of employee homogenization (consider companies known for their particularly strong cultures, such as IBM, Mary Kay, and Disney). Likewise, the "boot camps" of all military and quasi-military organizations are prime examples (the U.S. Marine Corps is especially proud of its effectiveness here). In a less pronounced way, many colleges and graduate schools employ Outward Bound experiences and other forms of bonding rituals early in the orientation of new students for the sake of generating strong cultures and uniformity in behavior and standards.

Meglino and his colleagues explicitly define organizational culture in terms of values and the concept of strong culture in terms of value congruence among organizational members (see, e.g., Meglino, Ravlin, & Adkins, 1989, 1991). An organization is said to have a strong culture to the extent that there is a high degree of consistency among its members in terms of their shared belief structures, values, and norms. "If there is no substantial agreement that a limited set of values is important in a social unit, a strong culture cannot be said to exist" (O'Reilly et al., 1991, p. 493).

Such aggregate homogeneity among the value structures of organizational actors has long been thought to be a source of job satisfaction, commitment, job proficiency, and long tenure for employees (see Brown, 1976; O'Reilly, Caldwell, & Mirable, 1992; O'Reilly et al., 1991). In addition, value homogeneity among members enables managers to make safe assumptions about the likely behaviors of their subordinates when first-order control mechanisms (such as rules) or second-order mechanisms (such as direct supervision) are not present (Adkins, Ravlin, & Meglino, 1992; McDonald & Gandz, 1992).

We believe that, at some point, a question arises concerning the ethical limits of the rights of employers (as well as of administrators in organizations such as graduate schools of business) to attempt to socialize, homogenize, deindividuate, and standardize the values and behaviors of lower participants and clients. What are the limits to the loss of individual rights and freedoms that can reasonably be expected or accepted in the greater context of a free society?

Heckscher (1988) notes that a central element of managerialism has been the development of a shared culture, or corporate value system.[9] This feature, he observes, is antithetical to some fundamental beliefs of North American society:

> This aspect is the source of some of the strongest emotions that have been aroused by managerialism. Our society retains a deep suspicion of social values from its historical struggles against religious oppression. The right to believe in whatever we please is one of our most cherished freedoms. We tend to emphasize impersonal and rational values because they protect us from arbitrary uses of personal power. *Thus any attempt to build shared values arouses suspicion.* On the other hand, there seems to be an equally deep social longing for the sense of community that has been shattered by bureaucracy, a longing that creates an unresolved tension in many of our institutions. (pp. 95-96; emphasis added)

Going a step further: It is currently understood that selecting employees on the basis of certain personal traits and characteristics (such as sex, race, and age) is unethical as well as unlawful. So this question remains: If it is fundamentally unethical for employers to attempt to achieve value homogeneity by *manipulating* employee values and belief structures, what makes it ethical for employ-

ers to presume to select job applicants on the basis of their apparent value structures?

Such questions are seldom raised, at least in the management and organizations literature, and such practices are rarely examined from the point of view of ethics, informed consent, freedom, and human dignity. Clearly, by their very nature organizations require control and predictability. There seems to be an irony here: An organization's interests lie in recruiting members who will behave ethically. Consequently, the organization engages individuals with particular values or tries to socialize and then standardize the values of those individuals to ensure ethical behavior. Thus the questions become: In attempting to effect values standardization, is the organization behaving ethically? And where are the limits? Who is to decide?

## Summary

We believe that research is needed that will give special emphasis to an examination of the ways in which values convergence is instigated and managed by work organizations. Although sociologists and cultural anthropologists have periodically paid attention to the issue of value change, their focus has been primarily at the aggregate, societal level (for early reviews, see Pine & Innis, 1987; Zytkowski, 1970). By contrast, the focus of the research we propose would be the changing of individual values, particularly as demanded by employing organizations. An important collateral stream of study should investigate the moral and ethical dimensions of deliberate attempts on the part of organizations to select employees on the basis of their values (when recruited) as well as employers' attempts to socialize people's values, once hired, to conform to the norms desired by power elites.

Such research would have to be different from previous studies in a number of ways. First, longitudinal designs will be needed to track the process of values convergence among samples of organizational members. (Most studies in this area conducted to date have merely examined degree of congruence at a point in time and correlated this with outcome variables.) The consequences of congruity or lack of congruity are not at issue here; rather, the emphasis would be on *how* congruity comes about, especially on those aspects of organizational socialization and reward systems that instigate and promote congruity.

## CONCLUSION

The role that values play in the study of work organizations and of the people in them is indisputable. However, if the study of values is to contribute further to the organizational sciences, future values research should be redirected to consider new modes of thinking about values and their role in the workplace. By way of summary, we offer the following principles, which best represent these new concepts and modes of thinking.

In the future, values research will be best served by the following:

1. A comprehensive yet parsimonious conceptualization of values that has theoretical generality and sufficient distinctiveness to workplace issues to foster theories of work motivation and other workplace issues.
2. The translation of these abstract, generally defined values into terms relevant to particular settings (e.g., work, working, the workplace) before operationalization. These operationalizations must ultimately be reconcilable at the most abstract level to foster the development of general theory.
3. Consideration of values in sets (and not in hierarchical arrays), such that certain sets of values become more or less important in guiding a person's attitudes and behavior, depending on the context.
4. Attention first to the meaning and processes of "change" in a given value for a particular individual before consideration of whether values actually change or change only in relative importance to each other—either individually or in sets.
5. Awareness that individuals have values—organizations do not.

## NOTES

1. Sagiv and Schwartz (1995) found that personal values accounted for a substantial proportion of individual variation in readiness for outgroup contact, whereas Homer and Kahle (1988) demonstrated that values were more strongly associated with nutrition attitudes than with shopping behaviors. Nutrition attitudes influenced natural food shopping, thus supporting the mediating role of attitudes.

2. Terminal values represent ultimate end goals of existence, such as wisdom, equality, and family security; instrumental values represent the behavioral means of achieving various end goals, such as living a life that is honest, ambitious, or logical (Rokeach & Ball-Rokeach, 1989). Research by Schwartz (1992) casts strong doubt, however, on the significance of the terminal/instrumental facet in organizing people's values, as the distinction does not affect the way people relate to values. Weishut (1989) notes that many instrumental values can be transformed into terminal phrasing (i.e., into nouns) and terminal values can be transformed into instrumental phrasing (i.e., into adjectives). Schwartz (1992) has concluded, on the basis of his and Weishut's work, that only one form is needed to measure values.

3. Rokeach's values may also be too abstract to be of precise utility in other particular settings, but our purpose here is to deal with values in the workplace, so we limit our attention to that setting.

4. Transitivity is the axiom that states, If $A$ is greater than $B$ and $B$ is greater than $C$, then $A$ is greater than $C$.

5. Chusmir and Parker (1991) found that male and female managers reported strikingly similar work values, whereas their personal value rankings showed substantial differences.

6. We take issue in a later section with the concept of "organizational values."

7. Because Armon's (1993) theoretical background is highly unusual and rooted in moral philosophy, we do not provide complete details on her theory base and methodology here. We refer interested readers to her original work.

8. The concept of "trust" is problematic at the time of this writing, for these reasons (see Zaheer, McEvily, & Perrone, 1998).

9. *Managerialism* is an umbrella term used to refer to a range of managerial techniques that go back decades, most of which have had as their goals increased employee satisfaction and productivity, usually through some form of work redesign or participation schemes. See Enteman (1993) for an extensive discussion of the ideology of managerialism.

# 3

# Rules, Sensemaking, Formative Contexts, and Discourse in the Gendering of Organizational Culture

## —— *Jean C. Helms Mills and Albert J. Mills*

In this chapter we use organizational culture as a heuristic for making sense of the gendering of organizations (Mills & Tancred, 1992). We argue, following the feminist notion of gender as a cultural phenomenon (Oakley, 1972), that the study of discriminatory practices at work can benefit from a holistic approach that takes into account the interconnections among the various processes and practices that characterize a particular entity. To this end, we offer an organizational culture perspective as a useful framework for capturing the all-embracing character of gender discrimination at work.

We propose a rules approach to the study of organizational culture (Mills, 1988a, 1988b; Mills & Murgatroyd, 1991) as a perspective suited to the task of uncovering gendered aspects of organizational realities. We develop a detailed account of the rules perspective to show how the approach can be used to make sense of various aspects of gender discrimination at work. We then discuss some of the limitations of the rules approach and review selected theoretical developments, specifically the work of Unger (1987), Blackler (1992, 1993), and Weick (1995), that may help to overcome those limitations. We close the chapter with an outline of the rules approach in practice and suggest ways the approach may be applied to the problem of gender discrimination.

AUTHORS' NOTE: Our sincere thanks to Mary Jo Hatch, Keith Marcus, and Mark Peterson for comments on an early draft of this chapter.

## CULTURE AS A METAPHOR FOR UNDERSTANDING THE GENDERING OF ORGANIZATIONS

For years, feminist scholars have contended that notions of womanhood and manhood are socially constructed, that although there are basic physiological differences between people, it is not those differences per se that determine our understandings of "men" and "women" but the way that cultural factors shape our understanding of the differences. Oakley's (1972) distinction between "sex" (as the basic physiological differences between men and women) and "gender" (as culturally specific patterns of behavior that may be attached to the sexes), although not uncontested (Acker, 1992; Calás & Smircich, 1992, 1996; Rakow, 1986), has served as a basic starting point for feminist studies of discrimination (Mackie, 1987). This simple distinction represents a holistic approach to gender by contending that notions of womanhood and manhood are outcomes of a multitude of factors that include language, attitudes, patterns of behavior, symbolism, dress, patterns of belief, value systems, stories, rites, rituals, ceremonies, and physical artifacts. This has generated numerous feminist studies of the relationship between cultural milieu and gendered outcomes (Ginsburg & Tsing, 1990).

Within this framework there have been various studies of gender and work (Armstrong & Armstrong, 1990), but feminist studies of organization are more recent (Mills & Tancred, 1992). Feminist organizational analysis has drawn attention to numerous discriminatory practices and processes at work, including in language and communication (Tannen, 1994), structure (Witz & Savage, 1992), dress (Rafaeli, Dutton, Harquail, & Mackie-Lewis, 1997), organizational discourse (Burrell, 1992), sexuality (Hearn, Sheppard, Tancred-Sheriff, & Burrell, 1989), and symbols, images, and forms of consciousness (Acker, 1992). These studies have been invaluable in addressing important aspects of the gendering of organizations.

In recent years, two major developments have encouraged the view that organizational problems in general and sexual discrimination in particular can be addressed through a focus on a particular organization as a culture or as a system. First, a change in the way that legislation in North America characterizes the nature of workplace discrimination has moved emphasis away from individual *intent* to a "systemic approach" focused on the *outcomes* of workplace practices. In the 1971 landmark case of *Griggs v. Duke Power Co.*, the U.S. Supreme Court held that "if an employment practice which operates to exclude [minorities] cannot be shown to be related to job performance, the practice is prohibited" (quoted in Abella, 1984, p. 201). This approach was taken up in Canada by the Royal Commission on Equality in Employment, which characterized the root cause of workplace inequities as "systemic discrimination." Reporting in 1984, the commission advocated that employment equity be addressed through an examination of workplace structures and practices, arguing that the problem lay in "the structure of systems designed for [white able-bodied males]" and in "practices based on white able-bodied males' perceptions of everyone else" (Abella, 1984, pp. 9-10).

The systemic approach paralleled a second development in the field of management education and practice that argued for an organizational culture perspective on the problems of organizational behavior and effectiveness. Advocates of this approach, moving away from the study of the purely "formal" and "rational" aspects of organization, argued that organizations are like "miniature societies," with unique configurations of heroes, myths, beliefs, and values (Brown, 1998; Ott, 1989). This focus is potentially invaluable to legislators and policy makers because it exposes the *processes* through which discriminatory practices are developed and maintained. Sadly, however, the culture debate has almost totally ignored the role of gender (Mills, 1988a).

The notions that gender is a cultural phenomenon and that organizations are best understood as miniature cultures provide compelling support for an organizational culture approach to the gendering of organizations, an approach that is capable of capturing the complexity of arrangements and relationships that come to constitute a particular set of discriminatory behaviors. This has generated debate among gender-focused organizational analysts (Alvesson & Berg, 1992; Alvesson & Billing, 1997; Mills, 1988a, 1988b; Mills & Murgatroyd, 1991; Ramsay & Parker, 1992; Smircich, 1985) and has led to, as yet, a limited number of studies of gender and organizational culture (Aaltio-Marjosola, 1994; Aaltio-Marjosola & Lehtinen, 1998; Aaltio-Marjosola & Sevøn, 1997; Gherardi, 1995; Korvajarvi, 1998; Morgan, 1988; Wilson, 1997), including a rules approach (Mills, 1994, 1995, 1996, 1997a, 1997b, 1998).

## ORGANIZATIONAL RULES AS CULTURAL FRAMEWORK

We begin our approach to organizational culture with the proposition that, as a concept, it is a useful device, or heuristic, for conceptualizing the problem of discrimination at work. As some scholars have argued, organizational culture can be seen as a "root metaphor" for making sense of organizational realities (Allaire & Firsirotu, 1984; Morgan, 1997; Smircich, 1983). That does not mean, however, that we entirely reject the notion of organizational culture as a "real" entity. We certainly believe that "real" (i.e., embodied) persons engage in "real" organizational activities (i.e., the perception of acting within a limited entity), and that the organizational lives of those persons are shaped by "real" (i.e., felt) experiences. Thus, from our perspective, organizational culture is a useful metaphor for attempting to capture a configuration of factors that influence lived experiences, in particular the ways in which people experience gendered realities. However, as Alvesson (1995) contends, metaphors are limited if they cannot provide important insights into organizations.

From our perspective, the notion of organizational culture must move beyond descriptions of factors that cohere to form a more or less consistent set of practices and experiences to explanation of what causes those factors to cohere in the first place. In contrast to symbolist approaches (e.g., Schein, 1992), which focus on "understanding the processes through which organizations are reproduced as shared systems of meaning" (Reed, 1992, p. 168), we seek to understand what is behind those processes, what it is that generates and maintains organizational processes, and what the implications are for the construction of "shared meanings." This search for an organizing principle mirrors the pioneering work of Eldridge and Crombie (1974) and the more recent work of Trice and Beyer (1993). Whereas Trice and Beyer (1993) center on responses to "uncertainties and chaos" (p. 2) and Eldridge and Crombie (1974) center on "strategic choice" as the dynamic that creates "the cultural distinctiveness of an organisation" (p. 89), we find a more compelling argument in Clegg's (1981) focus on organizational control, particularly the idea that control is achieved through "rules" that "formulate the structure underlying the apparent surface of organizational life" (p. 545). Eldridge and Crombie's (1974) argument that organizational cultures arise out of choices to "the problem of acquiring, combining, and making use of resources" (p. 89) underplays the role of ownership (i.e., the purposes and goals of the organization) and the exercise of power and control that precede the ability to make choices or, in the case of Trice and Beyer (1993), to deal with uncertainties.

It is our assumption that organizations are specific collectivities of people whose activities are coordinated and controlled in and for the achievement of defined goals. That is, organizations arise out of the desire of some individuals or groups (e.g., entrepreneurs, shareholders, policy makers, philanthropists, social activists) to achieve certain ends. In the process, they recruit or employ other people to help them to achieve their ends, and this creates pressure for the coordination and control of the various activities that people engage in. This, in turn, leads to the development of a series of rules, or "outline steps for the conduct of action [that], depending upon combinations of circumstances and actors, [will] be experienced as controlling, guiding and/or defining" (Mills & Murgatroyd, 1991, p. 30).

Our focus on control and the development of rules arises out of a concern "to formulate a more systematic understanding and explanation of the political and ideological practices through which 'organisations' are assembled and sustained as viable social collectives" (Reed, 1992, p. 133). It is an approach that Reed (1992) has termed "managerial realist," arguing that the "development of the rule concept is itself theoretically grounded in a model of the organisation as an interrelated network of social practices through which a wide multiplicity of activities are assembled to form institutionalised frameworks or patterns of collective action sustained over time and place by a matrix of rules" (p. 183).

The rules concept provides a framework that offers an explanation of common action without implying a unity, or pattern, "of beliefs, values and learned ways of coping with experience" (Brown, 1998, p. 9). Indeed, we contend that rules simultaneously serve to contain differences of opinion, beliefs, and values while resulting in practices that give the appearance of unity of purpose. In this regard, the rules approach has been categorized as a "differentiation perspective" in contrast

to an "integration" or a "fragmentation" perspective (Martin, 1992). The notion of tensions beneath the surface of organizational rules stands in contrast to the "integration perspective" that views organizational culture as "an internally consistent package of cultural manifestations that generates organization-wide consensus, usually around some set of shared values" (Martin & Frost, 1996, p. 602). The notion of unified practice as the outcome of rules, on the other hand, can be contrasted with the "fragmentation perspective," with its focus on "lack of consistency, lack of consensus, and ambiguity [as] the hallmarks . . . of culture" (Martin & Frost, 1996, p. 609). In this latter regard we would argue that the difference is one of emphasis. We do not disagree with the contention that organizations are marked by inconsistencies, divisions, and ambiguity, but we would argue that these things are often only part of an overall experience that feels coherent. Take, for example, an airline that expects its female flight attendants to smile at all times when performing their duties. There is considerable evidence that people differ sharply on the purpose of this type of performance; some flight attendants may see constant smiling as professionalism (Musbach & Davis, 1980), some may see it as degrading (Kane, 1974), and some may see it as sexual (Baker & Jones, 1967). Management and customers may also vary on the meaning of the flight attendant performance. Nonetheless, despite ambiguity and disagreement, constant smiling is a common practice in the performance of female flight attendants and imposes a common situation on a number of disparate actors. This and other rule-bound activities serve to give airlines a feel of coherence and order.

We agree, however, with the fragmentation perspective that the appearance of unity and meaningfulness is created by powerful organizational actors (Martin & Frost, 1996, p. 608), but would add that the "power" of those actors is rooted in their position relative to the construction and maintenance of organizational rules. The problem is that neither the activity of powerful actors nor the existence of rules fully explains why less powerful actors "buy into" aspects of the dominant meanings within an organization; we shall return to this problem later.

There are two elements to the rules approach: the rules themselves and the actors who engage in the process of establishing, enacting, enforcing, misunderstanding, and/or resisting rules. "Rules" ("phenomena whose basic characteristic is that of generally controlling, constraining, guiding and defining social action"; Mills & Murgatroyd, 1991, pp. 3-4) exist in written and unwritten, formal and informal, legalistic, normative, and moralistic forms. Rules do not "wholly rely for their efficacy on being known or understood by each and every member of a given situation into which they are applied" (Mills & Murgatroyd, 1991, p. 4), but they do arise out of the enactment of organizational actors who differ in their rule-making powers. This approach attempts to synthesize "both the enabling and constraining aspects of rule-governed conduct" by taking into account "the inescapable fact that rules are created by actors but that they simultaneously constrain the action alternatives to them over a series of decision-making situations" (Reed, 1992, p. 183).

## Formal Rules

The context for the establishment of an organizational culture, we would argue, is the establishment of a series of formal rules that come to dominate organizational activities, in particular the "manner in which groups and individuals combine to get things done" (Eldridge & Crombie, 1974, p. 89). By *formal rules,* we refer to those expectations and requirements, either written or unwritten, that are routinely associated with the pursuit of organizational purposes, activities, or goals that are perceived as legitimate or "normal." It is hard to avoid a rationalized view of organizations and hence of organizational culture because organizations are formally established, constituted by a series of formal, written rules, and often present themselves in a coherent light through such things as marketing and corporate image. Clearly, this overly rational image of the organization is not the whole reality, but it is an important element of the experience of organizations. Formal rules constitute an important aspect of the experience of organizational life through such things as recruitment and hiring practices, job descriptions, and a variety of "human resources" practices governing absences, leaves, health benefits, wage and salary rates, promotion steps and processes, disciplinary action, and even dress codes; these rules may exist in written form (e.g., as in a requirement to wear a uniform at specific times) or as unwritten expectations (e.g., an expectation that people will come to work in "appropriate" business attire).

Formal rules are established in response to a number of factors that start with the perceived purposes of the founding members (e.g., profitability, political power, charitable work) and the desire of those in charge to lay down a set of guidelines and limitations to those whom they recruit. This process continues and is modified by those who subsequently take over positions of power and authority within the organization. Beyond the specific needs for coordination and control by organizational managers, rules enter the life of an organization in various ways, including through legal requirements (e.g., laws governing commerce, labor, occupational health and safety, and employment equity), the introduction of technology (i.e., machinery, tools, skills, and/or work methods that require specific modes of operation), the employment of specific management practices (e.g., scientific management, reengineering, total quality management), the reproduction of dominant social values about the relative worth of men and women and/or of different ethnic/racial groups (e.g., the establishment of unequal pay rates or differentiated recruitment practices based on gender), the development of social practices designed to integrate employees (e.g., workplace social clubs, sports teams, dinner-dance events), and the establishment of job specializations and practices to deal with perceived environmental demands (e.g., a process of differentiation or divisionalization as a company moves into new markets or areas).

## Informal Rules

In the process of formal organizational development a series of informal rules develops alongside, and sometimes in contradiction to, formal rules. By *informal rules,* we refer to those norms of behavior that arise within the context of workplace associations but that do not develop to meet the defined goals or activities of the organization. People develop various forms of association at work (e.g., social groups, friendships, unofficial pressure groups) beyond those that are officially defined (e.g., specific units, divisions, and departments). In the process of developing informal groups or relationships, people typically develop norms that govern aspects of their behavior. Sometimes informal rules may complement formal rules, such as friendships that contribute to a sense of corporate belonging and identity (Wicks, 1998); sometimes informal rules may come into contradiction with formal rules, as in the classic Hawthorne studies, where informal groups of workers pressured each other to restrict output (Rose, 1978); and sometimes informal rules may have little or no effect on formal rules, as in a situation where the casual dress of students, in conformity to an informal dress code, does not affect the scheduled lecture that they are attending. Regardless, informal rules are an important influence on the life of an organization.

## Rules and Organizational Actors

In the words of Reed (1992), "The rule concept forms a linking function in that it connects forms of action to structural features by focusing on the diverse social practices through which actors construct rule matrices that shape their interaction and the institutionalized forms which it reproduces" (p. 183). Rules are primarily the creations of actors, but, once established, they appear as structures standing over and above people. People develop rules in several ways. Principally, rules develop and are changed by powerful actors such as founders and senior managers (Trice & Beyer, 1985); on occasion, a strong or "unbalanced" personality can have a disproportionate influence on a culture (Kets de Vries, 1989). Others (managers, supervisors) are then charged with enacting and enforcing rules, and, in the process, rules are negotiated, unintentionally misapplied, and/or resisted (Mills & Murgatroyd, 1991). Rules are also developed by actors as responses to unique situations, and rules are influenced by metarules as actors reproduce social values (e.g., discriminatory notions of women) that become embedded within organizational rules (e.g., pay inequities). In short, rules are established and changed through a series of interactions and yet are usually experienced as something beyond the control of people. Insights into the human basis of rule development and change can assist organizational actors in taking a more informed and confident approach to the problem of organizational change and in addressing workplace inequities in particular.

## Rules as Organizational Culture

It is the configurations of informal and formal rules that shape the culture of an organization as it deals with various legal requirements ("state rules"), adopts or adapts to extant management practices ("reproductive rules"), utilizes technology ("technical rules"), absorbs, reflects, or attempts to change the social attitudes that members bring to the organization ("extraorganizational rules"), develops human resources practices ("social regulative rules"), and attempts to control aspects of its external operating environment ("strategic rules") (Clegg, 1981; Mills & Murgatroyd, 1991). Specific configurations of rules provide the basis for patterns of behavior that appear as "the way things are done around here." In other words, rules form the experiential framework of organizational culture, but they develop and change through the actions of numerous actors as they establish, enact, enforce, misunderstand, resist, and/or break the rules. It is the configuration of rules and the actors involved that constitute a specific culture. Thus we can say that "organizational culture is viewed as being primarily composed of a particular configuration of 'rules,' enactment and resistance" (Mills, 1988a, p. 366).

## Studying Organizational Cultures Over Time

As Reed (1990) has observed, metaphors are problematic in that they do not provide insight into the historical development of specific organizations. We share the view that as cultures are, by definition, entities that have been established over time, they should be studied over time (Dellheim, 1986). We also share the view that organizational cultures should be viewed in social context (Kieser, 1989), that to understand a specific culture we need to know something about not only the internal dynamic of rule development but also the contribution of the broad social context to the process. In particular, we believe that a longitudinal study of the culture of an organization helps to identify how cultures become gendered and, importantly, how they change (or can be changed) over time (Mills, 1994). With that in mind, we now turn to an outline of the rules approach in practice, drawing largely on examples from a study of the gendering of British airline culture from 1919 to 1997.

## APPLYING THE RULES APPROACH TO THE GENDERING OF ORGANIZATIONAL CULTURE

A rules approach to the study of organizational culture sets out to address gender discrimination by uncovering the deep-rooted aspects of gender discrimination and, in the process, exposing their mundane nature; by revealing the role of actors in the construction of gendered practices; and by identifying how rules change.

In seeking to uncover the deep-rooted aspects of gender, we focus on practices that discriminate against women but also on the ways in which organizations contribute to notions of femininity and masculinity. It is a controversial approach both within feminist organizational analysis (Calás & Smircich, 1996) and within postmodernist accounts of organizational culture (Hatch, 1997). Certainly, we agree with the argument that concepts of "woman" and "man" are "unstable" and may ultimately contribute to discrimination through their reference to essentialist categories. That does not get past the problem that those very categories have real consequences for embodied persons who are discriminated against on the basis of assumed sets of gender characteristics. We attempt to manage the tension by addressing discriminatory practices in a way that encourages a questioning of the concept of gender itself. In other words, we are interested in the impact of discrimination both *on* women (and men) and on the construction *of* women (and men).

In studying an organization's culture over time, we use a focus on employment practices (i.e., the hiring and promotion of women) to track changes in the ways in which images of women (and of men) are constructed. In a study of British Airways, for example, at least eight different periods can be identified, including the absence of female employees in the period 1919-1924, the growth of female clerical work in the 1930s, and the rise of the woman manager in the 1990s (Mills, 1994). Each of these eras is associated with a different corporate image of women and men (Mills, 1995).

Rules contribute to the construction of discriminatory practices in different ways: Some have little or no obvious link to the process of gendering, some have direct and obvious links, and others are indirectly or subtly linked to the process. Organizations differ in the configuration of rules that compose their cultures. Thus it is important to identify (a) those rules that significantly contribute to the gendering of organizations, (b) those rules that *collectively* contribute to the gendering process, (c) those rules that arrest the process of discrimination, and (d) how rules change and become more or less gendered in the process.

## Formal Rules and the Gendering of Organizational Culture

The initial purposes and goals of an organization may or may not directly encourage the development of discriminatory practices. In some cases it is clear that the formal rules of an organization deliberately or effectively exclude women from all (e.g., men's clubs) or part (e.g., commercial airline piloting before 1965) of the organization (Mills, 1998; Rogers, 1988). In other cases it may not be the goals of the organization per se but the intervention of other rules that encourages gendered practices. The provision of an airline service, for example, is not obviously gendered, and when commercial aviation was established in Britain in 1919 it was a new industry without the baggage of old and existing practices, gendered or otherwise. Yet, from the beginning, despite the existence of women flyers and a number of former members of the Women's Royal Air Force, women were excluded from all but clerical positions; it took many years before British Airways (and its predecessors) employed

women in the positions of manager (1939), engineer (1942), flight attendant (1946), and pilot (1987) (Mills, 1997b). In such cases explanation must be sought in the intervention of other rule-generating activities.

Technology and its associated rules constitute a prime area for the generation of discriminatory practices (Cockburn, 1991). It is not the material aspect (machinery, tools, and the like) of technology that is gendered, but how the associated skills and modes of operation are understood and practiced. The skills of piloting and the organization of flight crews, for example, were practices that were strongly influenced by the wartime air forces, which restricted flying to men. The first commercial airlines reproduced those gendered associations and established formal technical rules that reinforced flying as a male occupation, and for a considerable time this affected the recruitment not only of pilots but of flight attendants (Mills, 1994, 1996). In a similar vein, the skills and organization of secretarial work have come to be associated with women and have led to formal rules whereby men are excluded from consideration for such positions (Pringle, 1989).

Formal rules that arise out of the practice of managing and organizing may appear gender neutral in intent, but, as feminist studies have revealed, they are often heavily gendered not only in their outcomes but in the assumptions underlying them. Schein (1994), for example, has documented how both male and female managers have tended to associate management with masculine characteristics. Other feminist researchers have revealed a link between bureaucratic practice and masculine values, discourse, and/or worldviews (Ferguson, 1984; Martin, 1990b; Morgan, 1988; Witz & Savage, 1992). More recently, it has been argued that some of the newer managerial practices, such as total quality management and business process reengineering, incorporate both feminine and masculine characteristics (Fondas, 1997), a view that is contested by others (Kerfoot & Knights, 1993).

In some organizations, gendered formal rules may arise out of a series of activities (e.g., sports and social clubs) designed to "incorporate" employees and give them a sense of belonging. Such activities can be gendered where they exclude and/or re-create narrow images of women and men. For example, Crompton and Jones (1984), who conducted a study that identified a relative lack of commitment among female as opposed to male employees, argue that the root cause lay in management's valuing of those who took an active part in the company's male-oriented sports and social club.

More pervasive, although not necessarily overt, are those extraorganizational rules that reflect dominant social beliefs about the relative nature of men and women. These beliefs become embedded in both formal and informal rules and contribute to the gendered nature of "the way things are done" in an organization, justifying failures to hire, promote, and pay equitable wages to women. For example, in an era that stresses an association between masculinity and danger, we would expect to find organizations restricting to men any jobs labeled as dangerous. This was the case with piloting, which for many years was seen as a dangerous and *therefore* masculine occupation. In more recent times, with airline companies emphasizing the skill rather than the danger of flying, a sociolegal stress on employment equity has weakened previous associations between masculinity and flying. Gendered understandings also contribute to the formal rules of an organization through a series of "external" influences that include legal, interorganizational, and institutional links.

Legal rules are far from gender neutral (Razack, 1991; Wolf, 1991) and may contribute to the construction of equitable practices or to a strengthening of discriminatory practices. The former situation can be clearly seen in regard to antidiscriminatory and employment equity legislation that has demonstrably contributed to the reduction of inequitable practices in major U.S. and Canadian corporations (Abella, 1984). On the other hand, as various court challenges have revealed, certain laws serve to support gendered practices on the grounds of "market need" (Wolf, 1991). It was legal intervention that established the exclusion of women from British Airways' flight crews for many decades; establishing Imperial Airways (British Airways' predecessor) in 1924, the British government effectively excluded women from a range of airline work by requiring that 75% of all airline pilots, ground personnel, and administrative staff be recruited from the Royal Air Force, the Reserve, or the Auxiliary Air Force (Penrose, 1980). This legal requirement contributed to the fact that more than 90% of all the airline's jobs were held by men until 1942 (Mills, 1997b). The rule changed when it fell into disuse in the face of wartime exigencies. More recently, changes in gendered airline practices have been achieved through legal challenges by women activists inside the industry (Hochschild, 1983; Nielsen, 1982).

Interorganizational linkages contribute to the development of formal rules that may or may not be gendered. Across the airline industry, for example, standardized recruitment practices have contributed to gendered outcomes, whereas the development of "code share" ticketing arrangements has not. Whereas legal rules *effectively* excluded women from British airline flight crews in the 1920s, international agreements of the 1924 International Commission for Air Navigation (ICAN) and the 1925 International Civil Aviation Organization (ICAO) deliberately banned them (Cadogan, 1992; Penrose, 1980). Cases of this type can be and have been dealt with through legal action: The ICAN and ICAO bans were rescinded in 1926. More difficult to deal with are those "isomorphic," or institutional, practices (DiMaggio & Powell, 1991) that influence organizations in subtle ways. In the development of an onboard airline service, for example, British airlines simply copied existing practices in comparable first-class transportation systems, employing the gendered title (steward), dress (white jacket), and physiological associations (men) of first-class rail and oceangoing liner service provision (Mills, 1997a). Interestingly, when United Airlines decided to hire female nurses as flight attendants in 1930, this established a practice that was copied until the late 1950s by almost all other airlines: United Airlines' employment of nurses was a compromise between using female employees to encourage more men to fly and avoiding charges of "impropriety" by marketing the women as "nurses" (Hochschild, 1983; Nielsen, 1982). Today, the long association of flight attending with women and of piloting with men has created a powerful set of rules that has proven difficult to erode: formal rules that may be supported in large part by the existence of a network of informal rules.

## Informal Rules and the Gendering of Organizational Culture

Informal rules, in contrast to formal rules, arise out of interpersonal relationships that are relatively free of mediating factors of organizational structure or goal orientation. A workplace friendship, for example, although facilitated and developed within a formal context, will owe more to personality and group dynamics than to the perceived demands of the organization. As such, informal rules are more directly influenced by gender dynamics than are many types of formal rules, because "doing gender" (Rakow, 1986) is a constant aspect of organizational life (Hearn & Parkin, 1987).

As Acker (1992) contends, gendered structures and practices develop through (a) interactions, (b) gender divisions of work, (c) symbolism, and (d) the mental work of individuals. People's interactions at work are more or less influenced by preexisting experiences of gender roles—husband/father, mother/daughter, and the like (Collinson, 1988; Pollert, 1981). This can result in "sex role

spillover," where, for example, female subordinates and coworkers are routinely treated as surrogate wives, daughters, or lovers, leading in some cases to office romances and in more invidious cases to a climate of sexual harassment (Gutek, 1985). It can also result in challenges and confrontations where people resist gender stereotyping. Interpersonal relationships are also influenced by the existence of gendered divisions of work roles in which some jobs and positions are mainly or exclusively occupied by men or women (Hearn & Parkin, 1987). In such cases the "opportunity structure" may contribute to narrow images of the respective capabilities of women and men, encouraging, for example, informal rules against fraternization with the "opposite sex" and people of either "sex" in higher positions (Kanter, 1977). Symbolism, ranging from the use of the term *girls* to pinup posters on the walls, can serve to strengthen narrow images of femininity and masculinity in the minds of those involved.

## Organizational Actors and Gendered Cultures

When one is analyzing the gendering of an organization's culture, it is important to look beyond the rules to their enactment and ask, Who are the key players involved in the maintenance or change process? In common with most theories of organizational culture, we look to the founders and senior managers of a company to analyze their roles in the process of culture development (Pettigrew, 1985), but we are also interested in the contributions of other organizational members to the process (Schultz, 1995).

Senior managers can influence the gendering of cultures in numerous ways. The commitment of top managers to a program of employment equity, for example, has been shown to have strong influence on outcomes (Agocs, Burr, & Somerset, 1992). In the more routine generation or countering of gendered rules, the role of the senior manager may be less overt. When Jan Carlzon took over as CEO of Scandinavian Airlines System in 1980, he completely revamped the organization and, in the process, profoundly influenced the airline's culture. This led to "improvements" in service provision that some claim degraded women, who were trained to "call all the men sir, look them between the eyes, keep your mouth half open" (quoted in Sampson, 1984, p. 216). The market success of the overall changes contributed to the maintenance of the new gendered practices. On the other hand, in the same time frame, the CEO of the Bendix company in the United States attempted to redress discrimination by promoting a woman, Mary Cunningham, to the position of corporate vice president—an action that was eventually derailed by a series of informal rules in the form of sexual innuendo that forced Cunningham out of the company (Cunningham & Schumer, 1984).

At other organizational levels, people are not mere recipients of rules; through enactment, interpretation, compliance, and resistance, people contribute to both the maintenance and the changing of rules (Bradshaw & Wicks, 1997). Thus every time someone turns down a female applicant for a job on the grounds that "this has always been men's work," that person is maintaining a gendered practice. Every time someone challenges the sex typing of jobs, he or she is undermining a gendered rule.

Together, analyses of the formal and informal rules and the key actors involved in a culture over time can help to identify those mundane practices that maintain and challenge discriminatory practices, and how practices change over time. However, the application of a rules approach raises questions about the microprocesses through which rules are generated and maintained, and this has led to exploration of recent social psychological theories of organizing, including the work of Foucault, Blackler, and Weick.

## RULES AND SOCIAL PSYCHOLOGICAL PROCESSES

### *Foucault and Discourse*

Although the notion of organizational rules is useful for capturing the various expectations that guide and constrain behavior, it does not explain how some of those expectations *cohere* into a way of thinking or behaving, or how coherence is contested and rule-bound behavior changed. Although clearly not a social psychological approach, the work of Foucault provides a useful way of understanding not only how organizational actors generate and act according to consistent behavior expectations, but how they come to resist dominant notions (Mills, 1993).

Focusing on "histories of experience," Foucault contends that human subjectivity is constructed within and as a result of given "discursive practices" constituted as discourse (see Gutting, 1996). In other words, discursive practices give rise to a multitude of experiences, some of which are translated into expectations or rules of action through the development of various discourses. Thus, for example, a number of experiences of doing gender are generated in an organization, but to take on the power of rules some of those experiences need to cohere in a way that "makes sense" to a significant number of people. As Sawicki (1996) expresses it, "Discursive practices that construct gender are rule-governed structures of intelligibility that both constrain and enable identity formations" (p. 300). The notion of discourse, the empowering of certain ideas through their appearance as "knowledge," helps to explain how certain rules become accepted by those involved. In the words of Walkerdine (1990), "Femininity and masculinity are fictions linked to fantasies deeply embedded in the social world that can take on the status of fact when inscribed with the powerful practices . . . through which we are regulated" (quoted in Ussher, 1991, p. 13).

Through the analysis of key discourses in the life of an organization, it is possible to track dominant sets of rules and explain their power and weaknesses over time. For example, in the early days of commercial aviation, discourses of piloting and flight attending had at their center particular images of masculinity—respectively, "the heroic flyer" and "the white-coated steward" (Mills, 1998). The association of danger, professionalism, and masculinity with flying existed as a powerful discourse within British Airways (and many other airlines) until recently. Not until the mid-1980s did these associations begin to unravel sufficiently to allow the recruitment of women pilots. It was a discourse that was continually supported by male-only recruitment practices in the industry itself and in the military air forces, by continual wartime images of the male pilot, and by the practice of recruiting retired air force pilots as commercial flyers. It took considerable challenges to the exclusion of women from military piloting and combat roles, alongside challenges to commercial airline practices, to weaken the discourse of male piloting. The discourse of flight attending as a male occupation, on the other hand, weakened relatively quickly. The role of airline steward developed in the middle of the 1920s as a strictly male occupation, yet by 1930 United Airlines hired the first female flight attendants and a number of airlines followed: British Overseas Airways Corporation (BOAC) and British European Airways (BEA) were, in 1946, among the last to employ females. Analysis of the discourse indicates that the power of the masculine associations was only as strong as its links to practices in other transportation industries, which, in any event, were not strongly associated with dominant notions of masculinity. Indeed, the main weakness of the masculinity focus was the characterization of the steward as, for example, someone who was "completely dedicated to the passengers and their comfort; experienced and consistent; part psychologist and part actor; methodical and meticulous; small, agile, quick-moving, deft and proud" (from *Imperial Airways Weekly News Bulletin*, September 8, 1936; quoted in Mills, 1998, p. 178). In the face of other market strategies, it was not difficult to adapt this image in support of the employment of female flight attendants, and the association of masculinity with stewarding eventually lost its power (Mills, 1996, 1998).

## Weick and Sensemaking

We are particularly drawn to Weick's (1995) theory of sensemaking because of its focus on meaning and identity (Helms Hatfield, 1997, 1998; Helms Hatfield & Mills, 1997). Indeed, as Weick (1985) puts it, the culture metaphor is significant insofar as it bestows meaning on an otherwise disparate set of events.

Weick's (1995, pp. 17-62) outline of the "properties of sensemaking" provides a useful way of conceptualizing the "genderation" of rules (i.e., the way gender rules are developed). Central to Weick's notion of sensemaking in organizations is "enactment," which refers to the construction of social reality through action that is then (retrospectively) made sense of by the actor or actors involved. People act in one way or another, and in so doing come to make sense of their actions in ways that constrain and provide opportunities for future actions. How people come to construct social realities through enactment is influenced by the "ongoing" nature of sensemaking, the "enacted cues" that people use to build sensible stories around, the situational and "social" contexts in which "retrospective" understandings occur, the need for "plausibility" in story construction, and the impact of sensemaking activity on "identity construction." More problematic is the theory's downplaying of power and politics and the assumption that sensemaking is a gender-neutral universal process.

The notion that sensemaking is "grounded in identity construction" meshes well with the idea of rules as experiences that influence a gendered sense of self. Nonetheless, although Weick (1995) contends that "people learn about their identities by projecting them into an environment and observing the consequences" (p. 23), he does so in a way that downplays the role of more powerful actors. Although focused on "action," Weick's theory centers on the imposition of ideas on situations that have consequences for those beyond the primary sensemakers. This is at its clearest where Weick references managers as sensemakers who "construct, rearrange, single out and demolish many 'objective' features of their surroundings" (cited in Hatch, 1997, p. 41). Thus, although it may be true that everyone can be said to engage in sensemaking, it is far from clear that everyone is equal in the process. It is also not clear that people are equally interested in enacting realities that come to dominate others' sensemaking, or in the creation of ordered understandings of reality. From a feminist perspective, there is some concern that sensemaking may, in itself, be a theory that is grounded in the construction of a white, Western male identity.

By emphasizing the role of power in Weick's theory of sensemaking while downplaying its (male-associated) universalizing assumptions, we can make use of important directions the theory provides for a rules approach. To begin with, through an examination of the role of founders and senior managers in the enactment of rules, we could usefully explore the particular ways that sense was made of specific events, especially challenges to the gendered order and the extent to which there was a felt need to impose "order, clarity and rationality" on events (Weick, 1995, p. 29). For example, perceived market pressures to introduce female flight attendants led managers at BEA and BOAC, in 1946, to develop a policy of "desexualization" that allowed them to employ women in a way that de-emphasized the feminine characteristics of female "stewards" (Mills, 1997a).

The notion of the "ongoing" character of sensemaking as a series of reference points for making sense of new events and dealing with interruptions to existing plans and actions is invaluable in directing us to explore how particular rule activities at any one time serve to maintain gendered order and how challenges to certain rules are dealt with through reference to those rule activities. Similarly, the notion of "enacted cues" suggests that it may be possible to identify significant elements in the development of rules that have served to define particular situations. The ICAN and ICAO banning of women from flight crews in the 1920s, for example, referenced women's menstrual cycles as a central reason. This acted as a cue for wider notions of the physiological and psychological unsuitability of women for flying (Cadogan, 1992). The "retrospective" character of sensemaking (i.e., that "people know what they are doing only after they have done it") can be traced through such things as corporate materials with a view to revealing how enacted rules (e.g., the recruitment of all-male flight crews) influenced gendered notions at a subsequent point in time.

The issue of "plausibility" (i.e., "socially acceptable and credible" accounts) is also an interesting idea that directs our attention to the peculiar ways in which gendered rules are maintained and resisted. Exploration of the success or failure of certain gendered accounts may help us to identify factors that make certain prejudices credible. Also, the notion of "resistance" as "confronting the activity of the environment" (Weick, 1995, p. 33) leads us to think that changes to certain gendered rules may be uncovered not only in evidence of confrontational action (e.g., union action, legal challenges) but in prominent examples of viewpoints that question existing ways of making sense of an activity. For example, *British Airways News,* the airline's in-house journal, contained a number of letters in the 1970s that questioned not so much the restriction of flight attending to women but the meanings (e.g., a focus on the bodily features of the job holders) and labels (e.g., "girls") attached to the practice.

Finally, the "social" character of sense-making (as a "social process" whereby "conduct is contingent on the conduct of others, whether . . . imagined or physically present"; Weick, 1995, p. 39) strengthens our view that not only does the enactment of rules have consequences for all involved—shaping the sensemaking contexts in which new rules are developed and in which identities become known—but it is not shared meanings or, as Weick (1995, p. 42) suggests, shared experiences that influence collective action, but the existence of rules of action that are understood (and experienced) in different ways by those involved.

## Blackler and Organizations as Activity Systems

The work of Blackler (1992, 1993) offers a way of understanding not only the micro and macro contexts within which rules are enacted but the possibilities of change (Helms Hatfield, 1994, 1996). For our purposes, Blackler's work on activity systems provides a more comprehensive explanation of the "social" element in Weick's notion of sensemaking while providing a way of conceptualizing links among sociocultural factors, discourse, and organizational rules. Curiously for a theory developed out of post-Marxist accounts, Blackler downplays the role of power, a fact that is particularly evident in his notion of "emancipation" as a process of making people aware of the social constructionist "dynamics of their situation" (Blackler, 1993, p. 872).

Central to Blackler's work are the related notions of activity and activity systems. Drawing on the work of Vygotsky, Blackler (1992) defines activity as "a sociocultural interpretation imposed on the context by the participants themselves" (p. 289); that is, activity is not merely "action" but the interrelationship between the processes of acting and making sense of the action. Thus, for exam-

ple, the activities of a male engineer should be seen not simply as engagement in the physical act of engineering (e.g., machine tooling), but as a process that is framed by a particular understanding of what engineering is (e.g., a masculine undertaking involving the exercise of certain skills). "Activity" alone does not tell us anything about the roots of the sense that people impose on an action, and this is where Blackler (this time drawing on the work of Engestrom) develops the notion of activity systems. *Activity system* refers to "the context of actions" that is constructed, by social actors, through a series of influences that "mediate the interactions between the individual and his or her context; by the appearance of traditions, rituals, and rules that mediate the relationship between the individual and her community; and by a simultaneous emergence of a division of labor that mediates the relationship between the community and the actions of its members" (Blackler, 1993, p. 868). Thus a social actor draws upon broad understandings to make sense of a particular activity. In our example above, the engineer does not simply make sense of *his* activity from a peculiar personal understanding of the situation (although this is always a possibility); rather, he draws on established notions of the masculine character of engineering tools, skills, and knowledge.

Through exploration of key aspects of social life that contribute to the construction of an activity system, Blackler reveals the potential for organizational change. Here, while consistently focusing on contradictions and ambiguities within and between activity systems, Blackler's understandings of the "essentials of such contexts" shift from an emphasis on Unger's notion of formative contexts to an emphasis on Engestrom's model that includes "culture, division of roles, and physical artifacts" (Blackler, 1993, pp. 868-869). In brief, Unger (1987) contends that "the origins of social arrangements lie in past social conflicts and the institutional and imaginative arrangements that followed their resolution," and that such "'formative contexts' are deep seated and pragmatic in their effects on everyday life [and] provide an implicit model of how social life should be led" (cited in Blackler, 1992, p. 283). Unger's notion of formative contexts links activity at the local level with dominant social assumptions about the character of social life, explaining how people come to reproduce existing practices. For example, it is not unreasonable to speculate that in Britain following World War I, a dominant social viewpoint that "a woman's place is in the home" (Pugh, 1992) influenced the hiring practices of those involved in airlines (Mills, 1994) and other types of organizations, with imaginative action leading eventually to institutional practices and the development of gendered rules.

Although Unger "recognizes . . . the privileged hold that certain groups and traditions have upon the mass culture [exerting] a unifying influence over expectations and ideals" (Blackler, 1992, p. 280), he nonetheless provides "a somewhat restricted account of human agency," having little to say about how "the distinctive characteristics of a formative context may be learned and internalized by those affected by them" (pp. 287-288). To this end, Blackler turns to Engestrom for answers; sadly, in the process, he loses sight of the role of dominant actors. Engestrom's focus on processes of mediation—"of *tools* between subject and object, of *rules* between community and subject, and of the *division of labor* between community and object" (Blackler, 1993, p. 869)—appear as no less vague in their specifics than Unger's concept of formative context but is important in focusing attention on the ideas that (a) different elements, or essentials, contribute to the construction of an activity system; (b) each essential may contain conflictual and ambiguous elements; (c) an activity system can be composed of actors who are more or less influenced by different essentials or reflect a different aspect of an essential; and (d) an activity system may contain conflicting and

ambiguous ideas. From this perspective, change can occur when actors confront or are confronted by conflict and ambiguities in their activities. For Blackler (1993), this can help managers and others to effect change by making participants aware of the social constructionist nature of their activities and "encourag[ing] people to stand back from their everyday routines and to perceive the overall pattern that such routines fall into" (p. 881).

From our perspective, the notion of organizations as activity systems encourages a focus on different areas of dominant social, institutional, and local practices in the maintenance of a particular set of gendered rules and the role of conflict and ambiguities in how those rules change or might be changed. Thus, for example, in order to explain how the hiring practices of BEA and BOAC shifted from a policy of "desexualization" in 1947 to the selling of eroticized images of women in 1960 (Mills, 1997a), we would need to examine the contribution of such things as local practices (e.g., female flight attendants actively seeking a more "feminine" look to the uniforms they wore), institutional practices (e.g., the hiring of women for an increasing number of different jobs and the further development of segregated work), broad social understandings and practices (e.g., the role of fashion and beauty contests in the social construction of images of women and men), and the potential for contradiction within and between levels (e.g., "positive" changes in the employment of women in a range of jobs versus the strengthening of segregated work; changing definitions of women as employees versus a changing emphasis on the bodily presentation of women).

Insights from the work of Foucault, Weick, and Blackler help to strengthen elements of the rules approach by providing a level of explanation for how rules are made sense of (Weick) and how rules develop a dimension of coherence (Foucault) and change (Blackler) over time.

## APPLICATION

At first sight, the rules approach may appear overly complex, asking the practitioner to consider not only key organizational rules, discourses, and formative contexts but the sensemaking frameworks of the actors involved. We would answer such concerns in two ways. First, we make no apology for focusing on the complexities of organizational life, because to untangle "the way things are done" in a given place it is important to unravel the various interconnections; too many "quick-fix" models falsely suggest that it is possible to overcome deep-rooted attitudes and behaviors in a short space of time.

Second, we would argue that the model is not that difficult to operationalize. To begin with, it is important that the practitioner work collaboratively with organizational clients to establish the desired element of change (e.g., the creation of a more equitable pay system). Then, through a series of interviews, observations, and content analysis, the practitioner can (a) document the extent and nature of the problem (e.g., comparable rates of pay between men and women at all levels of the organization; information gathered through company data and/or surveys of employees), (b) identify extant rules that contribute to the (discriminatory) practice (through analysis of dominant themes gathered through interviews, observation, and analysis of corporate documents), (c) identify key organizational discourses that appear to support the practice in hand (again drawing on analysis of dominant themes), (d) identify key sociocultural influences (formative context) on the practice (drawing on identifications of those influences by informants and undertaking selected content analysis of extant themes within the industry, profession, or occupation), (e) identify major sensemaking differences among salient actors involved in the construction of the selected practice (information through interviews and observations), (f) identify any significant ambiguities and conflicts in the different levels of influence (information through conflicting and unclear themes), and (g) confront those involved with the "findings" and help them to find ways not only to address the specific problem but to establish a process of reflection and negotiation that serves to question the purposes of particular sets of rules.

As a final word, we would say that we do not see the problem of addressing the gendering of organizational culture as an easy process. Power and politics will continue to play key roles. However, power is gained not only from structural position but within relationships to rules and to discourse. By questioning rules, sensemaking frameworks, discourse, and formative contexts, we are in some small but important way destabilizing existing frameworks of power.

# 4

# Symbols in Organizational Culture

## –– *Anat Rafaeli and Monica Worline*

If you will, imagine yourself walking through the front door of a glass office building on the corner of a bustling downtown city block. People are swinging leather bags full of documents and wearing Armani suits and Ferragamo shoes as they walk past flower stands where vendors sell loose roses and fresh-cut sunflowers. As you push open the heavy, darkened door, you see a reception desk across the wide marble floor. Inset in the marble is a replica of a compass surrounding the logo of the organization, and above it a set of clocks reports the time in different parts of the world. A woman wearing a suit, matching lipstick, and a cordless headset directs calls over a vast switchboard that becomes visible as you approach the uniformed security agent who gives you directions. You enter the elevator and ascend, and when the brass-trimmed elevator doors open, you find yourself in a glassed-in entryway that allows a sweeping view of a long conference table and the city 30 stories below.

Humor us with another imaginary voyage. It's been a long day at work, and you realize there's nothing in the house for dinner. You decide to go out for some quick food. You cross a wide parking lot leading into a small entryway with automatic doors that open into a waiting area where other people are standing. Resting your hand on the metal posts that direct you into your place in line, you look up to see a menu that is posted on the wall along with pictures of food. Looking around, you see a sticky linoleum floor and a colorful play area. When you finally get to the front of the line, the young person working at the cash register cannot seem to get your order correct. She calls a manager, who appears holding a heavy bundle of keys to correct her mistake.

So, where have we been? There are many ways to answer that question. We could name specific businesses, but we haven't been quite detailed enough to do that. We could give the most general answer: "two organizations." But we feel we know more than that. It would not be surprising to learn that the first is called Morgan Stanley or Barclay's. Nor would it be a shock to find the second called McDonald's or Happi House. How do we understand so much from very brief descriptions of imaginary travels? The answer is symbol, which is a powerful, physical indicator of organizational life. We know that these are different places by the things we find there. We know a lot about each place through our associations and inferences from objects such as switchboards, elevators, conference tables, cash registers, linoleum floors, and plastic trays.

The people in the two places are also symbolic. We are not surprised to find a young person in a polyester uniform working in the fast-food environment. Nor are we surprised to find that she makes mistakes. We match our expectations of behavior to the surroundings in which that behavior occurs. In a fast-food environment, the symbols tell us that the young worker has a limited set of responsibilities and that her job requires a limited amount of knowledge. We know this from the pictures on the buttons of her cash register and the manager's keys, which appear when the young cashier makes a mistake. The symbols in the reception area of a corporate office—including a person wearing a red suit—impress upon us a receptionist with more responsibilities and competence. The smooth technology symbolized in her cordless headset and the size and visibility of the switchboard she controls are symbols of the size and buzz of the corporation, and of the corporate attributions to this receptionist.

That a few symbols can convey such powerful meanings and what those symbols accomplish in and for organizations constitute the subject of this chapter. We first define *symbol*. We then detail four functions of symbol in organizational culture that add up to our assertion that physical cues in organizations integrate feeling, thought, and action into shared codes of meaning. The first function of symbol is to reflect basic and shared values or assumptions. Building on work in anthropology, we argue that symbols represent underlying values, assumptions, philosophies, and expectations of organizational life. The second function of symbol is to influence behavior by eliciting internalized values and norms. Extending work in social psychology, we argue that people act out the roles in which they are placed. Awareness of those roles is influenced by symbol. The third function of symbol is to facilitate member communication about organizational life. Sociological frame analysis shows that symbols act as frames of reference that facilitate conversation about abstract concepts. Symbol's final function is integration. Drawing on semiotic analysis, we argue that organizational symbols capture the systems of meaning that integrate emotion, cognition, and behavior into shared codes. It is these shared codes that undergird organizational culture and, indeed, organization.

## SYMBOL: A DEFINITION

Students of organizational culture seek to reveal the shared systems of meaning that construct organizational life and provide its structure and vitality. To understand the cultural system of an organization is to understand the reactions, interpretations, and actions of organizational members, as well as how those actions, thoughts, and feelings are shaped by the collectivity. In this chapter, we make the case that such understanding is impossible without careful attention to organizational symbols. Symbols are integral to organizational life. They are not simply by-products of organization; rather, they are elements that structure members' active construction of sense, knowledge, and behavior (Rafaeli & Kluger, 1998).

Symbol is important even for organizational "members" who may not be considered to be "insiders." Mills and Morris (1986) have argued that even as a visitor to or a customer of an organization, an individual is a partial employee. Rafaeli (1997) argues that the concept of membership is complex, with overlapping and competing dimensions. Rafaeli's analysis illustrates how membership may be characterized by physical or temporal relationships, contractual relationships, production relationships, or cultural relationships. For the purposes of this chapter, we maintain this broad definition of membership. We will argue that members who make meaning from organizational symbols are not simply employees, but also visitors, vendors, suppliers, managers, and customers.

What do we mean by the term *organizational symbol*? A dictionary definition of *symbol* refers to a thing that stands for an idea, as a dove stands for peace (Chevalier & Cheerbrant, 1994). However, this definition gives the impression that the pairing of symbols with contents is random or malleable. We disagree with this impression. We use *organizational symbol* to refer to things that stand for the ideas that compose the organization, but we move away from the assumption of randomness. Artificial intelligence research has focused on symbols but has regarded the relationship between symbol and meaning as essentially arbitrary. We do not share this view.

We consider organizational symbols to be visible, physical manifestations of organizations and indicators of organizational life. Symbols take on important meanings in organizations, meanings that are defined by cultural and social conventions and interactions. In our definition, symbols are things that can be experienced with the senses and used by organization members to make meaning. Symbols are noticed through sight, sound, touch, and smell. Symbols are experienced as real, and their impact has significant organizational consequences. Things such as organizational layout, organizational landscape, or organizational dress are examples. Although some research has implied that symbols are easily manipulated, we will show that symbols are powerful indicators of organizational dynamics that are not necessarily

easily changed. Thus symbol as discussed here comprises both the physical setting of an organization and the objects within that physical setting, and stands for the meanings, experiences, and ideas that people have in and about symbols in the context of the organization.

In general, people have a keen sense of the consistent connotations of symbols: where we find one symbol, we expect to find others that confirm or reinforce the connotations of that symbol (Kluckhohn, 1942; Pettigrew, 1979; Trice & Beyer, 1984). Simply switching between the description of a "wide marble floor" in the first paragraph of this chapter and the "sticky linoleum floor" in the second creates an incredible destabilization of the images found there. The same happens if we switch "brass-trimmed elevator" with "play area." Where one expects to find food or play areas, one does not expect a wide marble floor, and vice versa. To understand objects in a scene, people rely on both local and global contextual features and the consistency between them (deGraef, deTroy, & D'Ydewalle, 1992). The basic dynamics of the motivation to preserve consistency in situations, including consistency between internal and external cues, guide cognitive efforts to understand a scene (Festinger, 1957; Rogers, Lee, & Fisk, 1995; Siddiqi, Tressness, & Kinia, 1996). Making meaning in a scene is a product of both internal associations and the matching of internal and external cues (Kaplan & Kaplan, 1983). The ability to recognize objects and use them as guides to action has been central to human evolution and survival; this ability draws upon both affective and cognitive processes (Kaplan & Kaplan, 1983).

One of the potential flaws of studying organizational culture through symbol, however, is that the meanings given to a symbol by a researcher are not necessarily the meanings inferred by organization members (Schein, 1990). People encountering symbols read these symbols through their own individual eyes, and the symbols acquire meaning in the organization through recurring experiences. Importantly, only a connection between symbols and underlying organizational values provides a full understanding of both symbols and culture (Pondy, Frost, Morgan, & Dandridge, 1983; Schein, 1990). People's interpretations of symbols may differ, and, as with most communication, it is the interpretation rather than the intention that wins the day (Berger & Luckmann, 1967; Collins, 1994).

As we have demonstrated in the opening paragraphs of this chapter, however, even occasional visitors are sensitive to the connotations of symbol and engage in their meaning-making activities. Thus the connections between symbol and meaning are not random. To uncover consistency and connections between symbols and organizational values, the researcher's responsibility is threefold: to recognize the symbols in a specific context, to unravel members' interpretations in this context, and to verify the reliability of these interpretations across multiple members. Traditional tools of interjudge reliability and reliability over time need to be incorporated into the study of symbols (Epstein, 1986; Guion, 1976). We argue that a careful researcher can obtain a wealth of knowledge about organizations by exercising these responsibilities. We also note below some methodologies that can be useful in research on organizational symbols.

## SYMBOL: A REVIEW

Most available scholarly attention to the physical settings of organizations has focused on ergonomics. The Hawthorne studies, and others like them, examined the influence of physical factors (e.g., temperature, noise, space) on productivity and employee well-being. Some researchers examining the spatial configurations of organizations have found them to influence social interactions, arousal levels, affective reactions, morale, and perceived control as well as such work outcomes as performance and satisfaction (Baron, 1994; Davis, 1984; Goodrich, 1982; Marans & Spreckelmeyer, 1982; Oldham, Cummings, & Zhou, 1995). This line of research provides a foundation for our discussion in this chapter.

Specific findings support the assertion that physical layout is not only a practical influence but also a critical set of symbols. Office visitors, for example, have been found to form impressions of their own comfort and welcomeness in an organization, and about the personality of the person who works in the office, from physical items such as desk placement, tidiness, and decoration (Campbell, 1979; Morrow & McElroy, 1981). Some aspects of physical layout have been found to reflect similar meanings across a variety of contexts (Campbell, 1979; Morrow & McElroy, 1981; Ornstein, 1986). For example, Ornstein (1986) has shown that office space occupied by a large, polished desk placed in the back of a spacious office is seen as identifying a distant and powerful executive, no matter the industry. Ornstein further found that people viewing pictures of a reception area made attributions about the organizational climate based on different clusters of symbols.

Other physical qualities have symbolic power as well. In retail environments, store design has been shown to have the power to alter shoppers' emotions and buying behaviors (Babin & Darden, 1995; Donovan & Rossiter, 1982; Rafaeli & Kluger, 1998). Organizational dress has been argued to affect both individual- and organizational-level outcomes, such as compliance with occupational role requirements, communication of organizational values, and identification of organizational members by nonmembers (Rafaeli & Pratt, 1993). And it has been argued that organizational obstacles have impacts on both employees' interactions with customers and customers' perceptions of service, because employees who overcome obstacles in the organizational environment are seen as symbols of high-quality service (Brown & Mitchell, 1993).

Researchers from the architecture tradition have called the interaction of activity and setting "place" (Canter, 1997). In this view the idea of symbol is not merely a backdrop against which organizational action happens. Rather, place is a system of environmental experience that incorporates the personal, social, and cultural aspects of activity within an environment. Our analysis of symbol in organizations draws on the theory of place, because we hold that the location and objects that make up the environment are central to the personal, social, and cultural aspects of experience in that environment. We thus take an environmental approach to symbol and the information that it conveys. Objects and organizational landscapes are powerful indicators of social and cultural meaning rather than simply arbitrary signs.

An understanding of symbol can also draw from theory about aesthetics. Environmental psychology makes a case for the influence of aesthetic experiences on behavior and also posits a complex relationship between the actor and the environment (Kaplan, 1992). Gagliardi (1990a) proposes that the tangible, sensory aspects of the organization make up its aesthetic experience, which is the basis for all other types of experiences. In this view, the organization is experienced as the things, machines, products, and places that make it up. The things people create and use on a regular basis are concrete extensions of the self, and individuals invest psychological energy in these things (Csikszentmihalyi & Rochberg-Halton, 1981). In aggregate, this can be argued to be true of organizations: Physical objects are concrete manifestations of the psychological dynamics of organizational life.

Our analysis does *not* address all aspects that have been previously argued to be symbolic. We do not discuss the symbolism of managerial action (Peters, 1978; Pfeffer, 1981) or the ways in which actions are interpreted to have symbolic meanings within an organization. Also beyond our scope are symbolic messages or symbolic scripts within organizations (Gioia, 1986) and symbolic

events in the histories of organizations and their effects on organizational image and reputation (see Bromley, 1993; Fombrun, 1996; Sutton & Callahan, 1988). Such symbolic meanings within organizations encompass different dynamics. This distinction can be blurry, as in the case of organizational storytelling, which comprises both symbolic actions and sensual objects (Jones, 1993; Martin, Feldman, Hatch, & Sitkin, 1983). Yet the distinction serves the important purpose of separating the dynamics of symbolic action from the dynamics of symbolic representation. It is the latter with which we are concerned here.

## FUNCTION 1: SYMBOL AS REFLECTION OF ORGANIZATIONAL CULTURE

Organizational culture has been construed as a network of meanings or shared experiences and interpretations that provides members with a shared and accepted reality (Pettigrew, 1979; Schein, 1990; Trice & Beyer, 1993). In their first function, symbols provide a tangible expression of this shared reality (Dandridge, Mitroff, & Joyce, 1980).

At the level of the psyche, Freud (1989) identified the symbols in his patients' dreams as reflections of their underlying fears and psychoses, arguing that these are important cues for psychotherapy. The idea is that symbols reflect underlying values or realities. It is commonplace in disciplines such as anthropology to study cultures through their symbols (Geertz, 1973). This idea has also been applied to organizational culture (Schein, 1983; Trice & Beyer, 1984). Schein (1990) specifically identifies symbol as the first layer of culture, comprising the observable artifacts that make up the sensory experience of the organization. Gagliardi (1996) concludes that symbols "enable us to take aim directly at the heart of culture" (p. 568) because they represent and reveal what is tacitly known and yet unable to be communicated by an organization's members. Thus, in the first function of symbols, members make meaning from them. Looking at obvious physical manifestations of an organization can tell us more than we might suppose.

The intuitive yet powerful association between symbol and culture is evident in this news story about toys in the workplace:

A 3-foot toy blimp was enough to persuade Web site developer Eva Bunker, 26, to take a job at a start-up company in Dallas instead of at a more established business. The blimp arrived while she happened to be visiting, and employees started screaming with delight. (Aubrey, 1998, p. A8)

Eva Bunker, as a potential employee, read and interpreted the toy blimp as a symbol that reflected the start-up company's values. The symbol tipped the scale in that organization's favor as she made her employment decision.

Thus symbols can tell us much of what we know about organizations. As the tangible, sensory, felt experiences in organizational life, symbols are a way to understand the organizations they reflect. Through our sensing of symbols, we come to feel as if we know the organization. This process may suggest that symbols help bridge the gap between feeling and thought in organizations. Symbols spark feelings (Takahashi, 1995) and work to make feelings outwardly recognized and objectively real (Sandelands, 1998). Because of processes of aesthetic interpretation and sensemaking, the emotional experience sparked by symbols leads to a cognitive understanding of the organization (e.g., Dean, Ramirez, & Ottensmeyer, 1997; Gagliardi, 1990b; Weick, 1979). Thus we argue that symbols, in their first function, act as a bridge between members' emotional and cognitive reactions: Symbol sparks feelings and helps make those feelings comprehensible.

## FUNCTION 2: SYMBOL AS A TRIGGER OF INTERNALIZED VALUES AND NORMS

Research in social psychology has demonstrated that people often act out the roles in which they are placed (Katz & Kahn, 1978). Various types of symbols elicit this behavior. A common colloquialism reflects this dynamic: We speak of a person's putting on his or her "researcher hat" or "teaching hat," meaning, of course, not that the person changes attire, but that he or she dons behaviors appropriate to a particular role. In a vivid and tragic example of different behaviors being triggered by different "hats," the engineers who objected to the launching of the *Challenger* space shuttle were told: "Now put on your managerial hat and take off your engineering hat. We need to make a managerial decision" (quoted in Magnuson, 1986, p. 41; see also Timmons, 1991). These alternative "hats" involved making a decision that would be conservative and would respect engineering constraints versus a decision that would be risky but committed to the managerial goal of displaying the success of the project (Vaughn, 1996).

Carver and Scheier (1985) documented the impact of symbols in a powerful series of studies that explored various aspects that control human behavior. They placed people in a laboratory in front of either a mirror or a camera and predicted that these symbols would determine the attention to subjects' public aspects of self (e.g., Do I look good to others?) or private aspects of self (e.g., Do I feel good to myself?). Indeed, those placed in front of the mirror were made more aware of their own values and internal emotional states, whereas those in front of the camera were made aware of other people's values and opinions. The symbols in the environment presumably guided people toward behavior that was appropriate for the situation. Rafaeli (1989) posited the same hypotheses with respect to organizational smocks and name tags. She found that organizational norms were practiced more frequently when organizational attire was present. Thus our assertion of the second function of symbol in organizational culture: to elicit internalized values and norms that guide action in a given situation.

Social learning theory suggests that people learn through association (Bandura, 1977). Behavior therefore comes to be associated with symbols that act as cues in the environment. Berkowitz (1993) and his colleagues demonstrated that angry people exposed to a weapon were willing to administer more punishment than were those who did not see a weapon. When symbols are associated with internal states or feelings, their physical presence can evoke the associated states and feelings. In organizational contexts, a symbol that prompts internalized feelings provides a way to understand and act upon those feelings. Thus symbol serves to link feeling, interpretation, and action in organizations.

Some theorists, such as Gagliardi (1996), have proposed that our unconscious reading of symbols is a way of thinking and a form of communication that is more basic than conscious cognition. Lurie (1981) writes:

Long before I am near enough to talk to you on the street, in a meeting, or at a party, you announce your sex, age, and class to me . . . and possibly give me important information (or misinformation) as to your occupation, origin, personality, opinions, tastes, sexual desires, and current mood. I may not be able to put what I observe into words, but I register the information unconsciously. . . . By the time we meet and converse we have already spoken to each other in an older and more universal tongue. (p. 3)

Basic psychological research supports the idea of symbol as an unconscious form of communication. Work by Bargh and his colleagues suggests that a person's motivations and goals may be triggered directly by the environment (see, e.g., Bargh, 1990; Chen & Bargh, 1997; Wegenr & Bargh, 1988). In one intriguing study, people were unconsciously primed with a stimulus for rudeness, a neutral stimulus, or a stimulus for politeness. Subjects were asked to unscramble 30 sentences, half of which contained words related to rudeness (or politeness), and then ask the experimenter for the next task. The experimenter was talking to another person when the subject needed to ask for the next task. People who were unconsciously primed for rudeness interrupted the experimenter sooner than those who were neutrally primed, and people who were unconsciously primed for politeness waited longer to interrupt than those who were neutrally primed. In another study, people who were unconsciously primed with stereotypical descriptors of elderly people in a sentence-unscrambling task walked more slowly down the hall as they left the experiment than did other people (Bargh, Chen, & Burrows, 1996). This idea that unconscious affective and cognitive processes guide our behavior is also supported in environmental psychology (Kaplan, 1992). Thus the experience of symbols is a form of communication without verbal or conscious intervention.

Organizational examples of this function of symbol are ubiquitous. In the medical profession the symbol of the white coat is explicitly used to elicit appropriate and desired behavior. Becker, Geer, Hughes, and Strauss (1961) describe a ceremony in many medical schools that requires graduating medical students to put on white coats as part of their acceptance of a commitment to patients and to medicine. Feinberg (1986) found that students were willing to spend more on products when credit cards were left on a table in front of them. And McCall and Belmont (1996) demonstrated that the presence of a credit card company insignia on a restaurant bill tray resulted in significantly higher tips than when no insignia was present. Store layout and retail environments have been shown to affect buyers' actions through their emotions (Babin & Darden, 1995; Dawson, Bloch, & Ridgway, 1990; Donovan & Rossiter, 1982). In general, environments that are experienced as pleasant prompt spending beyond what the individual had intended, and store environments that are pleasant and also arousing increase the time customers spend there and their willingness to interact with employees (Donovan & Rossiter, 1982).

Symbol in service organizations is especially important because service is an intangible quality, leading customers in service environments to rely on tangible cues or physical evidence to evaluate both the service and their satisfaction with the service (Zeithaml & Bitner, 1996). Bitner (1992) describes the physical environment in which services are delivered as a "servicescape," as in "service landscape," to capture the dynamics by which symbols influence customer feelings, behaviors, and choices. As Rafaeli and Kluger (1998) argue, the facade of a restaurant evokes in customers a particular pattern of emotions and behaviors with respect to that restaurant.

Methodology from a line of study called *dramaturgy*—the study of human interaction as performance—can support an understanding of how symbols guide the actions of organizational life. Dramaturgy draws on Goffman's (1959) notion that everyday behavior is a form of self-presentation. The goal of dramaturgy is to uncover how humans accomplish meaning in their lives, with social interaction proposed as the key source of meaning (Brissett & Edgley, 1990). One idea largely unexplored by dramaturgy is that humans also interact with the physical environment. Just as with social interaction, interaction with symbols offers people meaning. One illustration of such interaction is provided by Scheiberg (1990), who found that employees use personal decoration of their work spaces to manage their own emotions on the job—for instance, through focusing on a poster of the ocean hanging over the desk to calm down. Similarly, Suchman (1983) found that employees in an accounting office interacted with office records in dramaturgical fashion; they used the symbol of orderly records and tidy record keeping as guides to their work routines, even though the organizational reality did not allow such routines.

Rafaeli and Pratt (1993) and Van Maanen (1978) have illustrated how a police uniform makes people outside of the police organization accept orders or instructions unquestioningly, even if they have never engaged in social interaction with the particular police officer. Using the notion of dramaturgical interaction with symbol, Rafaeli, Dutton, Harquail, and Mackie-Lewis (1997) examined the everyday decisions that administrative employees made about how to dress at work. Using individual decisions about what to wear to work as interactions with organizational symbol, they found that people in administrative positions navigated their way through the organization using dress. This navigation included placing themselves within and distinguishing between hierarchical levels, distinguishing functional areas, and interpreting relevant organizational events by learning about and complying with appropriate organizational dress codes.

In sum, the second function of symbol builds on the first. In reflecting an organizational culture, its first function, symbol acts as a bridge between feeling and thought. In its second function—as an influence—symbol is a bridge from feeling and thought to action. This bridge relies on the feelings and thoughts with which symbols are associated to elicit the behaviors appropriate for the situation.

## FUNCTION 3: SYMBOL AS A FRAME FOR CONVERSATIONS ABOUT EXPERIENCE

There is no looking without a frame through which to see. Studies of everyday experience suggest that simply perceiving the world involves the activity of forming conjectures about what came before and expectations about what will come next (Goffman, 1974; Weick, 1979). We construct what we see largely through expectations built upon what we have seen before (Kaplan & Kaplan, 1983). As observers of everyday events, we actively project our frames of reference onto the world and expect what we find to match what we are looking for. When our frames of reference match our circumstances, the frameworks of our experience are largely invisible to us. When the circumstances do not match our frameworks, we are jarred and feel that something is wrong or out of place. And we want to talk about it.

The third function of symbol is to make these frameworks outwardly visible and available for discussion by organizational members. Symbols help people communicate and share their frames of thought. The frameworks of a particular social group constitute a central element of its culture and require a mode of communication (Goffman, 1974).

Money is a classic example of symbol functioning as frame. Presumably the most important thing about a budgeting process is the allocation of money. However, the result of a budget may be less about the spending of money than it is about the expression of organizational values and the quest for legitimacy (Feldman & March, 1981). Olsen (1970) describes how in the budget-making process, community members in Norway use money to express their values and beliefs. The budget in this case provides a vehicle for conversation about priorities. Feldman (1997) describes a similar process among university housing administrators in the United States. In both cases, the budget has become a symbol that both frames members' experiences and facilitates conversations. Money functions as a symbol to allow conversation about such abstract notions as organizational identity, values, priorities, and beliefs.

Symbol as a means of communication can also occur at the organizational level, wherein, for example, an organizational identity in the minds of the public is established through symbolic or aesthetic means (Schmitt & Simonson, 1997). Consistency in symbolic aspects of product design and advertising considers these organizational-level actions to be organizational communication with potential customers (Aaker & Meyers, 1987; Ogilvy, 1985; Schmitt & Simonson, 1997). For example, the design of the Coca-Cola logo maintains an identical physical appearance in multiple nations around the world. This remains true even though the script used in different languages is different, as illustrated in Figure 4.1. The Coca-Cola symbol is a method of consistent organizational-level communication to customers around the world.

Organizational-level communication through symbols is also important to members employed by the organization (Dutton & Dukerich, 1991). Employment ads, annual reports, and other formal means of organizational communication rely on symbols to communicate to both insiders and outsiders. Instances of transition call up eloquent examples of the use of symbols. Schmitt and Simonson (1997) describe the splitting off of Lucent Technologies from AT&T. The new company wanted to establish an identity for itself and for the public through a new name, logo, and advertising campaign. All employees received a brochure that announced the new name, Lucent, and suggested that the name represented light and clarity. Along with the new name was a picture of the bright red, hand-drawn "Innovation Ring" logo, which was said to symbolize knowledge and "the creativity of our people" (quoted in Schmitt & Simonson, 1997, p. 28). Although symbols such as logos may seem arbitrary, they are not. Discussions of a new name, a new logo, and other organizational symbols provide a way for organizational members to understand the identities and values that come along with a major organizational change.

Many difficult and abstract issues in organizations are shrouded in discussions of dress codes, employment and product advertising, annual reports, logos, titles, and other orga-

Figure 4.1.

nizational symbols. This is not limited to what Dandridge et al. (1980) refer to as "verbal symbols," such as myth and legend. It is the case that members' stories themselves are symbols that can prove invaluable in organizational analysis (Jones, 1993; Martin et al., 1983), but we refer here to a simpler and more experiential function of symbol. Simply put, organizational symbols offer a language for organizational discussion. Schneider (1998) reports on the responses of an academic hiring committee to a job candidate who showed up for an interview in green polyester pants. After the interview, "for 10 minutes [the committee members] ranted about the cut, the color, the cloth. Then and only then did they move on to weightier matters. He did not get the job" (p. A12). This discussion was ostensibly about green pants. But the discussion of color, cloth, and style was also a discussion about important organizational questions, such as, Who is this person? Will we enjoy working with him? Will he fit here? In this vein, one scholar justified the importance of the discussion by saying, "If you don't know how to dress, then what else don't you know? Do you know how to advise students or grade papers?" (quoted in Schneider, 1998, p. A12). Even in the seemingly appearance-neutral academic world, Schneider (1998) argues, "clothes . . . help determine if someone will fit into a particular institution" (p. A12). The symbol of dress provided the hiring committee with an avenue for discussion of their goals, fit within

their environment, their identity, and the identity of the ideal candidate.

In a case study of nurses on a hospital rehabilitation unit who had requested a change in dress code, Pratt and Rafaeli (1997) discovered that the nurses' social identities were at the heart of the discussion. When nurses were talking about street clothes versus medical scrubs, they were actually talking about underlying philosophies related to their patients, their work, and their professional identities. The nurses used the symbol of organizational dress to represent and talk about the conflicting identities. The bulk of the issues represented by the two values of organizational dress in this case are summarized in Table 4.1. In essence, through their conversations about dress, the nurses were attempting to answer the question: Who are we as nurses on this unit? To resolve the question about the organizational dress code was also to resolve deeper conflicts about the purpose and identity of the organization and its members.

In short, the third function of symbol is to provide a vehicle for conversation and communication among organizational members. A careful cultural researcher can uncover meaning by exploring the uses of symbols in everyday conversation (Spradley, 1979). As a frame for organizational experiences, symbol provides a currency for discussion of otherwise abstract or ambiguous notions that are critical to the organization. Researchers can gain some understanding of an organiza-

| TABLE 4.1 | Conflicting Cultural Assumptions in a Rehabilitation Unit as Apparent in a Conversation About Organization Dress | |
|---|---|
| *Nurses should wear street clothes.* | *Nurses should wear scrubs.* |
| Rehabilitation Assumptions | Acute-Care Assumptions |
| Patients wear street clothes. | Patients wear pajamas. |
| Patients walk around. | Patients stay in bed. |
| Patients are disabled, but able to care for themselves. | Patients are sick, dependent on medical staff. |
| Patients stay in the unit 1-4 months. | Patients stay in the unit less than 1 month. |
| Patients learn to function in regular, nonhospital environments. | Patients' treatments require special equipment, such as Ivs and ventilators. |
| Nurses teach patients. | Nurses take care of patients. |
| A team of professionals develops a treatment plan for each patient. | Each individual professional applies his or her expertise individually to patients. |
| Families participate in the care of patients. | Families visit patients; medical treatment is left to professionals. |

SOURCE: Adapted from Pratt and Rafaeli (1997).

tional culture by listening carefully to conversations about symbols.

## FUNCTION 4: SYMBOL AS AN INTEGRATOR OF ORGANIZATIONAL SYSTEMS OF MEANING

Dandridge et al. (1980) propose that symbols have a consensual function that allows people to make sense of the organization and to find their place within it. Weick (1979) notes that managers work primarily with myth and symbol in the amorphous role of management. We extend this idea to argue that, in its fourth function, symbol integrates multiple, competing, and potentially even conflicting systems of meaning in an organization. A 1998 television commercial for a U.S. hotel chain provides an illustration of an elegant use of symbol to accomplish an acute sense of integration:

Mr. Richardson dashes into the hotel lobby and tells the desk clerk, who hands him a card key, that he must be at a multi-million-dollar business presentation in 10 minutes, but his shoes are soaked because he has just had to run through the rain. With a glance from the desk clerk, a bell-boy steps up, takes off his own shoes, and scoops up Mr. Richardson's dripping bags, leaving dry shoes at the guest's feet and getting him swiftly on his way.

Many of us would love to stay at this hotel, or are at least impressed by the quality of service it provides. How do we know? There are many symbols, but we would probably really like to stay at the hotel because of the shoes. Symbolically, the staff of the hotel will give you the clothes off of their backs (or feet, as the case may be). Metaphorically, the shoes are a small but important piece of the hotel's servicescape and dress patterns (Bitner, 1992; Rafaeli & Pratt, 1993). The shoes are drawn in the commercial to symbolize the total quality service one can expect to receive at this hotel. More subtly, the shoes are also a symbol of the prestige of the hotel. Note that the bellboy wears the same type of shoes as an important and high-powered corporate executive. A hotel where the people at the lowest levels share a dress code with highly prestigious clients must be an elegant hotel. Hence the shoes symbolize not just service, but also status. Together, they symbolize the organization.

What we have shown is how one symbol in an advertisement—a pair of shoes—suggests two themes or codes that are key to the operation of a hotel: service and status. We propose that additional symbols in this organization—the card keys, the luggage carts, the lobby, the elevators, the letterhead, receipts, annual reports to shareholders, and images in employment advertising—will also evoke the same two themes of service and status. In the imaginary conversation between the hotel and its audience, the important themes in the life of the hotel are communicated through its consistent use of symbol.

More broadly, symbols—as the physical manifestations of organizational life—help organizational members and observers integrate their experiences into coherent systems of meaning. The physical environment helps people encountering an organization make sense of it as a coherent idea. The fourth function of symbol ties together the first three functions. In the first two functions, the physical objects that are experienced by organizational members elicit emotional reactions and guide member interpretations and actions. In the third function, symbol allows communication about these reactions or actions. In the fourth function, as integrator, symbol reveals codes that undergird the organization. These codes are patterns of interpretation and understanding that are shared by organizational members. Thus the fourth function of symbol in organizational culture is to act as integrator.

The methods of semiotic analysis are useful for understanding how symbols provide an integration of an interpretative frame (Manning, 1987). Semiotics considers the world of organizations to be a system of signs. A sign is defined as the relationship between a symbol and the content conveyed by the symbol. The assumption in semiotics is that the link between expression and content is determined by the conventions of the individuals involved, which are called codes (Barley, 1983; Manning, 1987). A code consists of a set of symbols, a set of contents conveyed by the symbols, and rules for combining them (Barley, 1983; Eco, 1976). Codes thus specify meanings of a set of symbols within a culture. In using semiotic methods for studying organizational culture, the coders are the members of the organization and the codes are the systems of meanings that are shared in the organization. Semiotic analysis suggests that in order to study an organization's culture fully, one must uncover the relevant symbols, the content conveyed by the symbols, and the rules that bind them.

Multiple symbols in an organization can be easily coherent or well fitting. Fluid and coordinated relationships among organizational symbols are likely to lead to good aesthetic experience or "beauty," as in the hotel example above. Aaker's (1994) analysis of General Motors' experiment with Saturn reveals how organizational symbol can help in the construction of a successful and well-integrated organization. The Saturn Corporation began with a new name that did not tie it to its parent company, General Motors, and that company's associated image and reputation (Fombrun & Shanley, 1990). It also began with a clear mission statement, a new manufacturing site, new advertising, and new sales policies that set it apart from GM. The integrated message that Saturn sought to communicate is represented in the slogan "A different kind of company, a different kind of car" (Aaker, 1994, p. 115). As Aaker explains: "The slogan provides a core meaning while allowing a host of specific features and programs to be introduced without becoming lost or creating confusion" (p. 124). Core organizational symbols in this case integrated member experience, providing avenues for them to make sense of a host of organizational actions.

As is evident in the Saturn case, it is not one symbol that accomplishes integration. Understanding the Saturn organization involves looking at everything from the manufacturing plant to the product design to the showroom to the advertising. Yet, because change in the pattern of symbols is inevitable, given forces toward organizational change, integration of symbols may be lost over time. Aaker (1994) aptly notes that the early Saturn experience is marked by a synthesis of organizational symbol that gives the organization strong aesthetic relationships. However, later Saturn experience may not be so clear-cut. Uncovering the symbols and systems of meaning that have changed or developed in conflict with the original integration may be important to understanding the change in organizational culture.

Thus understanding organizational cultures involves the examination of complete systems of signification and meaning located in historical fields. Understanding organizational culture change involves tracing these meaning systems through time. The organization as a cultural system is created through the integration of socially shared interpretations of symbols, and its study precludes a simple focus on a specific symbol or a timeless individual.

At any point in time, multiple symbols may not be well integrated. This is likely to occur when there are cultural clashes within organizations and dissimilar codes are in operation. According to semiotics, an analysis of these symbols would reveal the internal conflicts (Meyerson, 1990) or the lack of cohesion of the organizational culture (Martin, 1992). The nurses described by Pratt and Rafaeli (1997) are a case in point. As summarized in Table 4.1, there were two cultures envisioned for the rehabilitation unit, and members were divided between them. The clash of cultures was manifest in arguments about organizational dress. The alternative values assigned by the nurses to the symbol of dress reveal the two systems of meaning or the two codes that operated in the organization. One code (street clothes) was the official interpretation of the organization as a rehabilitation unit. The other code (medical scrubs) was an unofficial view of the organization as a medical unit. As Pratt and Rafaeli illustrate, when cultural researchers turn their attention to understanding the codes that are generated by organizational symbols, an integrated perspective of the organization is revealed.

In short, a semiotic analysis of symbols is not independent of an analysis of the first three functions of symbol. Rather, it extends these functions and yields a more comprehensive analysis. The fourth function of symbol, that of integrator, unravels deeper codes of meaning that underlie organizational actions, reveals how members link symbol and content, locates the organization in specific historical fields, and brings us closer to an understanding of behavior within organizations.

## SOME CONCLUSIONS

Our broad message is that an important part of understanding organizational culture is the careful reading and analysis of organizational symbols. Such an analysis needs to examine the emotions, thoughts, and actions that symbols may engender and the integrated systems of meaning that they convey. This analysis continues previous assertions that when management wishes to create versatile and culturally rich organizations, it must attend to organizational symbols (Dandridge, 1983; Dandridge et al., 1980; Peters, 1978).

Our analysis suggests that symbols serve four functions in organizations. They reflect underlying aspects of culture, generating emotional responses from organizational members and representing organizational values and assumptions. They elicit internalized norms of behavior, linking members' emotional responses and interpretations to organizational action. They frame experience, allowing organizational members to communicate about vague, controversial, or uncomfortable organizational issues. And they integrate the entire organization in one system of signification.

Simple lip service to organizational culture through manipulation of a few symbols cannot suffice, however. We have only briefly noted how each of the four functions can be explored. A serious examination requires both depth and breadth of attention to the multiple symbols that abound in organizations. Our analysis supports the argument that organizational symbols have the power to facilitate or hinder smooth organizational functioning. Inattention to the multiple aspects of organizational symbols may lead to the possibility of a lack of shared interpretative codes among organizational members. This is perhaps easiest to see when a product does not match the quality symbolized by its advertising or brand name and therefore loses out in the market (Aaker, 1994; Schmitt & Simonson, 1997). We argue that this is also the case in relation to symbols such as organizational dress and office layout.

The process we propose is dynamic rather than static. A study of symbols in an organization is never completed, because symbols and the meanings people make of them change and adapt, both to one another and to the external environment. Organizational members, from customers to competitors to employees to managers, continuously read and respond to the organizational landscape. Without careful monitoring, the study of symbols can become misleading and antiproductive. However, with careful attention to symbol and the conversations, thoughts, emotions, and actions of organization members, the study of symbols can provide a deep, rich, and worthwhile understanding of organizational cultures.

# 5

# Hunting and Gathering in the Early Silicon Age

## Cyberspace, Jobs, and the Reformulation of Organizational Culture

-- *Marc W. D. Tyrrell*

The concept of corporate culture has a varied history in a number of disciplines. Most of these conceptions have treated "culture" as a variable arising out of structural conditions, rather than as an interactive, ongoing process operating between individuals and structures. In this chapter, I argue that a fundamental reconceptualization of culture is necessary at the level of basic theory. Drawing on current work in anthropology, I present one possible reformulation, using examples from job search communities and cyberspace to illustrate my argument. In particular, I concentrate on some of the effects of cyberspace on the bounded form of culture that makes up "organizational culture."

One of the greatest problems facing both academics and practitioners today concerns how to develop basic theoretical models for organizational cultures that will act as attractive communities and still be economically viable in the current environment. In order to reconceptualize culture, I draw on three traditions within anthropology: the social anthropology of Bronislaw Malinowski (1884-1942), the symbolic anthropology of Victor Turner (1920-1983), and current work in evolutionary psychology. In part, these choices stem from my desire to recast "culture" as a holistic concept, which is how it is conceived by most anthropologists (Jordan, 1994) and several organizational culture researchers (e.g., Trice & Beyer, 1993;

see also Beyer, Hannah, & Milton, Chapter 20, this volume).

## FOUR PROBLEMS IN REFORMULATING THE CONCEPT OF "CULTURE"

In the following subsections, I address four particular problems: the roles of institutions within a culture, how communities are defined, how we locate territories, and how we chart the changes in each of these through time. The necessity of examining each of these problems stems from one basic situation: Anthropologists use the term *culture* with two completely different connotations (see Jordan, 1994). The first concerns the ability of humans to generate symbolic and material "interfaces" (artifacts, organizations, belief systems, and the like) between themselves and their environments. The second meaning refers to the *specific,* historically situated interface structures of a particular group, a meaning often referred to as "the culture of . . . [a specific group]."

### Problem 1: The Concept of Culture

The term *culture* derives from the Latin *cultura,* "cultivation," and is allied to *cultus,* the past participle of *colere,* "to till" (Skeat, 1958). The term has connotations of cyclical time and reverence, where past patterns are repeated to produce the same results time and time again and, in the process, become "sacred." For some, "culture" is the norms, values, and beliefs of a group (e.g., Deal & Kennedy, 1982; Enz, 1988; Kroeber & Kluckhohn, 1952; Peters & Waterman, 1982). In this "integrationist" definition, culture is viewed as "an internally consistent package of cultural manifestations that generates organization-wide consensus" (Martin & Frost, 1996, p. 602).

To my mind, when applied in the term *organizational culture,* this definition presup-

poses that culture is generated at the level of an organization (e.g., the culture *of* IBM derives *from* IBM). Such an assumption has been undermined by Trice (1993), who notes the importance of organizational (Trice & Beyer, 1993) and occupational subcultures. Trice's (1993, p. xi) working definition of "culture" as ideologies and cultural forms (e.g., symbols, ceremonies, myths) goes some way toward redressing the problem. First, he de-emphasizes the equation of "culture" with "values" by pointing to specific cultural forms as components of "culture." Second, by developing the concept of occupational and organizational subcultures, he has made a de facto argument that organizations are composed of differing groups, each of which may be said to have its own community and culture.

Once we recognize that the term *culture* has two separate and distinct meanings, depending on which level of analysis is referenced, much of the confusion over the concept disappears (Jordan, 1994). Given these two distinct meanings, *all* historically situated "cultures," whether they are organizational, occupational, or national, are "cultures of . . ." and stand in sharp contrast to the *ability to produce* a culture. By drawing distinctions between different "cultures of . . ." and neglecting their interaction with the ability to produce culture, we have needlessly limited our understanding of how specific cultures are both changed and maintained. "Cultures of . . ." are constantly being negotiated and generated; they are an emergent property of human interaction with our natural and social environments and take the form of organizations, languages, belief systems, and other "structural" elements.

### Problem 2: The Conceptualization of Institutions

What is needed, then, is a model that explains the role of culture and the system of organizations within cultures. The type of model I am proposing draws its inspiration from the work of Bronislaw Malinowski. Although Malinowski is frequently assumed to be merely a precursor to Parsons in the functionalist paradigm (an assumption that was encouraged by Parsons himself; see Parsons, 1957), this assumption is false. Where Parsons (1957, p. 11) viewed culture as a shared symbolic system, Malinowski (1944/1960) saw culture as the interface (symbolic, material, and organizational) between individuals and their environment, and this was reflected in his major ethnographies (Malinowski, 1922/1961a, 1935/1965a).

A second major difference between Parsons and Malinowski lies in their conceptualizations of an "institution." For Parsons (1957) an institution is "a complex of institutionalized role integrates which is of strategic structural significance in the social system in question" (p. 39). Parsons went to great lengths to distinguish between his definition and Malinowski's, which Parsons characterized as "referring to a concrete social system or . . . a group" (p. 59). Although Malinowski (1945/1961b) argued that an institution is "a group of people united for the pursuit of a simple or complex activity" (p. 50), he made no requirement that the members of the institution be united in a single space or time. Furthermore, Malinowski's definition of an institution includes not only the "concrete social system" or bounded social group, but patterns of action and interaction, material artifacts, norms and perceptions, and purposive "values." In one instance, Malinowski (1945/1961b) asserted that an "institution" is equivalent to an "organized system of human activities" (p. 49).

Malinowski (1944/1960, chap. 11) argued that all cultural organizations (institutions) appear as specific ways to meet particular needs and/or desires. These, in turn, produce a series of secondary or derived needs that stem from the operation and maintenance of various institutions. On top of these, there are also a series of what he termed "integrative imperatives," symbol systems designed to maintain group cohesion (Firth, 1957; Malinowski, 1944/1960, chap. 12). For Malinowski, the institution is

the primary interface between individuals and their environments. Institutions embody the composite answers (material, perceptual, and organizational) of a culture to particular needs, problems, and desires.

Even as the analysis of the "culture of . . ." deals with a sliding scale of group size (e.g., national to regional to organizational), so too does Malinowski's analysis of institutions. This is clearly shown in his analysis of land tenure in the Trobriands (Malinowski, 1935/1965, especially chaps. 11-12). Malinowski analyzed land tenure, a concept that did not exist in the Trobriand society of 1914, through an extensive examination of the institutions that surround land use, access rights to land, the technology of gardening, the magic of gardening, kinship rights, the distribution of crops, and so on.

Although he never developed the observations further, Malinowski's work points toward two key relationships: First, institutions may operate only in specific perceptually defined territories; second, the relationship between institution and community is poorly developed. This relationship between institution and community is important, because the term *community* refers to the attachment of an individual to an institution (see the discussion in the subsections below on how community is defined and on the function and basis of communities; on attachment, see Beyer et al., Chapter 20, this volume). For organizational cultures, the overlaps among institution (organization), community, and territory become critical.

## Problem 3: How Is Community Defined?

The concept of "community" was somewhat problematic for Malinowski. In general, he viewed communities as the source of institutional "authority," a not unreasonable view for an individual examining small-scale societies. He also recognized other forms of communities, including what we would now refer to as communities of practice, although he based them around experience and iden-tity (e.g., kinship and parakinship structures; see Sahlins, 1972) in a manner similar to the concept of occupational subcultures dis-cussed by Trice (1993).

For Malinowski, the core of the concept of community is relationships between individ-uals: their mutual expectations, obligations, rights, and responsibilities. Communities au-thorize institutions, prescribe their deploy-ment, define their propriety, and act as test-ing grounds for their validity. Communities are not, in and of themselves, autonomous. Rather, they are parts of a larger web of social relations that define any particular society and the relationship of one society to another (i.e., the "world-system" in which that soci-ety operates). Communities are described as the living sites of culture(s), incorporating one or more institutions within their bound-aries and acting as a focus for social action and experience (i.e., the lived experience of the operation of one or more institutions). As such, they serve to create a sense of "us" grounded in a commonality of experience and understanding and, by extension, a sense of "them."

One way of viewing the range of needs, de-sires, and problems "solved" by a commu-nity is to consider the community as a topo-logical "domain" (see Tyrrell, 1998). Each community has its own domain, which may range from answering a specific need to an-swering many needs. Currently, most indi-viduals are members of multiple communi-ties and also have shifts in their needs over their lifetimes. As such, the relative impacts of any single community on an individual vary according to the breadth and relative importance of the need(s) covered by that community at particular points in time. A more concrete expression of this may be seen in the current mobility of employees in high-tech firms. Their current organizations/com-munities may not be able to meet their cur-rent or projected needs and, as a result, they are susceptible to being "headhunted" by other firms that are capable of meeting those needs.

Numerous authors have assumed that for a community to exist there must also be an associated settlement site (for an overview, see Wellman, 1998, pp. 10-11). This is the same as arguing that for any work to take place, there must be a factory or office build-ing—it is an assumption that is being rejected with increasing frequency, as current trends toward telework clearly show (I discuss cybercommunities further below in the sec-tion on communities as communicative net-works).

Wellman (1998, p. 10) notes that many definitions of community contain three com-mon criteria: interpersonal networks that provide sociability, social support, and social capital to their members; residence in a com-mon locality; and solidarity sentiments and activities. If we accept these criteria, espe-cially if we are examining communities that develop within particular organizations, then we must rework the concept of "site" in such a manner that we can account for, among other things, distributed work teams. These three criteria may be transformed into the following:

- Social networks that give access to institu-tions that provide active and potential affec-tive and material support and resources
- A common site in which and through which these affective and material resources may be provided
- A set of solidarity sentiments and activities (i.e., structures and rituals to promote at-tachment)

## Problem 4: Territories and Sites

The assumption of the necessity of a physi-cal site as a precondition to the existence of a community is, at first glance, a matter of common sense. It is, however, axiomatic in anthropology that numerous groups have no permanent physical locations (e.g., hunting-and-gathering societies and many pastoralist societies). Rather than single locations, such as villages or neighborhoods, these groups share in territories.

Territories contain the locations, or "sites," in which and through which institutions, organizations, and communities operate. In this formulation, "institutions" are prior to "organizations." This is an extension of Malinowski's thought, where a single "charter" may enable the existence of multiple organizations that draw on it. The term *location,* however, does not refer to a specific "place" in physical reality, but to a location in perceptual reality that may or may not be restricted to a particular place and will shift along with changes in the perceptual reality. Institutional "territory" may be equated with specific organizations or social roles, although any particular territorial claims will be in a state of constant redefinition (Abbott, 1988).

Within any specific territory, the sharing of resources takes place both in physical sites (e.g., factories, meeting rooms, Internet relay chat rooms) and in nonphysical "sites" (e.g., artifacts, asynchronous communicative media). Because many types of institutions may be "stored" in potential in artifacts, there is no requirement that the originator of the support be present or even alive at the time of transmission.

### Summation

In this section I have introduced four interlinking concepts: culture as environmental interface (the culture of . . .), institutions as organized systems of human activity, communities as the living sites of culture, and territories as the locations of communities. All four of these concepts are necessary for the construction of our general model of culture.

All of these concepts operate on a "sliding scale." In other words, each may be applied to any component of an organization (e.g., department, work group), to the organization as a whole, and to the general social environment(s) in which the organization operates. In the next section, I examine the concept of community in greater detail, in order to unravel the concept and show what communities are based on and how they may develop in cyberspace.

### COMMUNITIES AS COMMUNICATIVE NETWORKS

In the preceding section, I argued that the traditional interpretations of what a community must be do not hold up, particularly in the face of the Internet and its impacts. We must now ask what characteristics are necessary for "a common site in which and through which affective and material resources may be provided."

I would suggest that one characteristic is that of the medium of communication, both in its structuring and in its form. In other words, how do people within a community communicate? As Harold Innis (1964, p. 33) has noted, media have, by their physical nature, a bias toward the dissemination of knowledge over either space or time. A high bias toward spatial dissemination would normally indicate a low bias toward temporal distribution, and vice versa. The resulting communities have been broadly characterized along their communicative lines: oral cultures, literate cultures, and digital cultures (see DeKerckhove, 1995; Ong, 1982).

### Territory in Cyberspace?

This concept of a territory, rather than a single site, comes to the fore with the advent of cyberspace. Although many virtual communities are defined, at least for research purposes, as communities—a corporate intranet, a personal Web site, an Internet relay chat (IRC) channel, a listserv—this is frequently not the case. The community operates over a number of different sites, the sum totality of which defines the territory of that community. The individual sites are just that—sites. Each site, however, has its own peculiar bias of communication—a time-space trade-off dependent upon the technology.

In cyberspace, the bias of communication runs along two axes: (a) a bias in time from asynchronous (e.g., e-mail) to synchronous (e.g., chat rooms) communication and (b) a bias in event form from completely non-interactive to fully interactive (see Ferguson, 1998; Tyrrell, 1998; Tyrrell & Ferguson, 1998). The perceptual "geography" of cyberspace created by these biases ranges from the "stable" formations of asynchronous, totally noninteractive sites (e.g., data storage sites such as the SEC), through midrange "resource" sites (e.g., interactive database sites such as ZDNet), to highly interactive, interpersonal exchange-based sites (e.g., listservs, chat rooms).

The linking of various sites into coherent, subjective "wholes" produces territories in which communities evolve. These communities may be of *any* type, from a work team to a virtual corporation to a medical support group. Indeed, the integration of these communities into current organizational cultures has been of major concern, especially in the area of telework (see Davies, 1996).

## The Function and Basis of Communities

I use the term *function* in its biological, rather than sociological, sense to denote the current, rather than original, effect/use of a particular pattern of interaction. As such, the function of a community is to share specific affective and material resources. Given that this sharing is not, of necessity, dependent upon any particular point in space or time, is there some commonality upon which it is based? In order to answer this question, we have to move the basis of the discussion from Malinowski to the later work of Victor Turner, which centered on the symbolic/cognitive level of interaction. For our purposes,

the key concept we need to examine is Turner's concept of *communitas*.

In *From Ritual to Theatre*, Turner (1982) argues that there is a distinct relationship between the structures of a community and what he has called *communitas* (Turner, 1969, 1982). For Turner (1982, p. 50), communitas stands in a "figure-ground" relationship with social structure. Communitas erupts spontaneously and, if the experience is held to be useful and/or desirable, it is encapsulated within a structure (i.e., as an institution) and passed on to others.

Turner (1982, p. 58) sees a relationship between this institutionalized communitas and Csikszentmihalyi's concept of "flow." For Csikszentmihalyi, the flow state exists when

players shift into a common mode of experience when they become absorbed in their activity. This mode is characterized by a narrowing of the focus of awareness, so that irrelevant perceptions and thoughts are filtered out; by loss of self-consciousness; by a responsiveness to clear goals and unambiguous feedback; and by a sense of control over the environment. . . . it is this common flow experience that people adduce as the main reason for performing the activity. (quoted in Novak & Hoffman, 1997, p. 3)

Flow is the *subjective* experience of a particular type of event. It channels the participants into a set mode of perception that blocks out extraneous perceptions and, by doing so, achieves specific ends. When coupled with particular "structures" (e.g., game-specific rules and specific relations between the game and other structures), flow experiences, and the ends they produce, become one particular form of institutions— "games." I use the term *game* here specifically because of the "self-contained" nature of flow experiences, games, and events. It is an analogic convenience that has the advantage of being a collective concept that implies material resources, rules of action, and experiences generated through their usage. It also highlights the relationships among "play," "games," liminality, and communitas (see Turner, 1982).

Any given flow experience contains both material and affective outcomes, and is a component in a relational web composed of other flow experiences. Obviously, a flow experience is an "affective resource" in that it engenders a sense of control and accomplishment, but it also provides *material* resources, at least inasmuch as the game produces particular ends. Thus, by way of example, when salesmen speak about being "in the groove," they are referring to the subjective flow experience.

The flow experience serves to produce a sense of communitas between people who share the same, or similar, games: a sense of "commonality" that engenders an "us-ness" that provides a common ground for communication between otherwise disparate people. It must be noted that there is no requirement that the affective and material outcomes of a game must be "positive"; games will serve the same communicative and communitas building function even when they are negative.

The relevance for organizational cultures of this model is clear. Flow experiences act as the shared bases for occupational, departmental, and work team subcultures. They provide the subjective, experiential basis for individual attachment to particular (sub)organizations that allows for the continuing production of organizational cultures.

## Community Boundaries

What is distributed within a given community is not the actuality of a singular flow experience, although this *may* be available, as much as it is the *potentiality* for one or more particular flow experiences. In other words, communities supply their members with the rules to one or more games and the potential opportunity to engage in those games. As such, access to particular games, and the sense of "we-ness" produced by these games, serves as one boundary defining a community.

A second boundary is the utility of resources. Communities, by their very placement within larger environments, will inevitably adapt to whatever their "local" conditions are, and this adaptation will produce a variance between (a) the production of specific games and (b) the relative importance of different games. Given this situation, it is not surprising that some communities contain specific games that are completely absent in other communities, and others have adapted to produce games that are only occasionally required by the general societies in which they operate. This second type may be referred to as "contingent communities," because they center on specific culturally recognized contingencies.

## Summation

Culture is an integral composed of partly autonomous, partly coördinated institutions. It is integrated on a series of principles such as community of blood through procreation; the contiguity in space related to coöperation; the specialization in activities; and last but not least, the use of power in political organization. (Malinowski, 1944/1960, p. 40)

We can clearly see from the preceding argument that communities may be transient, contingent, and differentiated in their needs/answers domains. These domains include specific "games" and larger "metagames" (i.e., linked sequences of games for which the outcomes are both longer in time and greater in product than those of any component game). The exchange of information is critical for maintaining both the boundaries and the necessity of the community. As such, we can conceive of the intersection of communities and the territories in which they operate as the "playing field" within which these games and metagames operate.

In the preceding sections, I have attempted to draw out and expand upon the key components of Malinowski's model of "the culture of . . . ." These components are as follows:

1. Institutions, which are expanded from a community's means of satisfying fundamental human needs to include games and metagames
2. Territories, which are expanded from physical locales that circumscribe groups that interact frequently to systems creating opportunities for communication and participation in basic need fulfillment or constructed games
3. Communities, which are expanded from intersubjective networks of relationships that deploy and authorize a comprehensive set of institutions covering the full range of human needs to networks that are more specialized and focused in the institutions that they support

For Malinowski, each of these components must be considered in order to produce an adequate analysis of a particular "culture of . . . ." Indeed, these components are critical in order to allow us to place organizational cultures (and subcultures) in the broader social environment. This broader environment will, inevitably, have an impact on its component cultures, producing a situation of conflict, accommodation, and syncretism (see Malinowski, 1945/1961b, chap. 7). For Malinowski's "argonauts of the western Pacific" (the Trobrianders), the broader social environment was other, similar communities occupying the surrounding islands. For today's "argonauts of cyberspace," the broader social environment is composed of multiple communities, each of which satisfies particular needs.

In addition to constraints placed on a particular culture by the broader social environment, Malinowski (1944/1960, pp. 75-84) argued that any theory of culture must, ultimately, be based on biology. Unfortunately, Malinowski's work in the area is based solely on stimulus-response psychology. Although

Malinowski (1944/1960, p. 132) did attempt to link individual biology to symbolism, his model must now be considered hopelessly out of date in light of current knowledge of neurophysiology. Models that are more in tune with current neurophysiological knowledge include biogenetic structuralism (Laughlin & d'Aquili, 1974) and evolutionary psychology (Cosmides & Tooby, 1992; for less neurologically sophisticated models of symbolism, see Alvesson & Berg, 1992; Gagliardi, 1990b). In addition, Nicholson (1997) has discussed the application of biological systems components to organizations.

By arguing that any theory of culture must be based on biology, Malinowski meant not only the meeting of biological needs, but also the integration of biological systems components such as mental modules and the interface between biology and technology. In the next section, I consider two such constraints that, although unknown to Malinowski, fit his model perfectly.

## THE STONE AGE MIND IN THE MODERN COMMUNITY

Our modern skulls house Stone Age Minds. (Cosmides & Tooby, 1997, p. 11)

This phrase holds the conclusions of a number of evolutionary psychologists (e.g., Barkow, Cosmides, & Tooby, 1992; Cosmides & Tooby, 1997). The argument, following Cosmides and Tooby (1997), runs as follows. The brain is a physical system composed of numerous dedicated computational modules that have evolved over time to meet specific environmental problems. Because humans have spent the vast majority of our evolutionary history as hunter-gatherers, most of our neural circuitry has evolved to meet challenges faced by hunting-and-gathering societies.

## The Cheater Module as a Facet of Stone Age Minds

The most basic problems Stone Age humans had to solve involved dealing with the environment around them. Cosmides and Tooby (1992, 1997) argue that these environmental problems were not solely technical (food, shelter, clothing, and so on)—they were also social:

> Our ancestors have been members of social groups and engaging in social interactions for millions and probably tens of millions of years. To behave adaptively, they not only needed to construct a spatial map of the objects disclosed to them by their retinas, but a social map of the persons, relationships, motives, interactions, emotions, and intentions that made up their social world. (Cosmides & Tooby, 1992, p. 163)

Cosmides and Tooby (1992) show that reciprocal altruism cannot operate unless some mechanism for detecting "cheaters" is available. In this instance, "cheaters" are defined as people who accept benefits but do not pay the cost for those benefits as expressed in a social contract agreement. Cosmides and Tooby review a series of experiments that test a number of possible ways to detect cheaters and come to a number of conclusions, two of which are of direct relevance here. First, cheater detection does not occur unless the rule evoked has the cost-benefit representation of a social contract. Second, the module embodies the implicational procedures specified by computation theory (e.g., "If you take the benefit, then you are obligated to pay the cost" implies "If you paid the cost, then you are entitled to take the benefit"; Cosmides & Tooby, 1992, p. 206).

The implications of the existence of the cheater algorithm are directly relevant to a number of the current problems facing various organizational cultures (see Nicholson, 1997). Many of these problems arise from changes in the social environmental. Although the cheater algorithm does not detect cheaters unless there is a "social contract" (an accepted "ideology," in Trice & Beyer's [1993] language), it does detect attempts to alter or subvert the social contract. In effect, the cheater module operates as a form of social control for both the individual and the group.

But social contracts, ideologies, are adaptations to particular environmental situations. What happens when a "social contract" is maladapted to a new social situation? Probably the greatest changes in the social environment in recent centuries have stemmed from the adoption of new technologies. Each new wave of technological adoption has sparked massive responses to the changed social contract. And yet the adoption of new technologies has been a part of humanity for millennia.

## Homo Faber and Cyborg Technology

The augmentation and/or replacement of human labor with machines and tools is a characteristic of the human species. Even before the development of *Homo sapiens,* our remote ancestors were members of the genus *Homo faber*—a symbiotic genus with biological, cultural, and technological components (Barkow et al., 1992). For Malinowski (1944/1960), culture requires "artifacts, techniques, organization and symbolism" in order to exist (p. 136). The impact of technological change on particular adaptive instances cannot be underestimated.

Laughlin (1996) has developed a four-stage model of human-machine (cyborg) development. Although this model addresses the augmentation of humans with machine components, it also captures differences in human-machine interactions at a variety of levels, including that of production processes and cultural adaptation (see Tyrrell, 1996a).

The first stage, which is characteristic of preindustrial societies, is the extension of the skeleton and outer shell of the human. The second stage extends the human muscular system and, although present in preindustrial societies, it does not become dominant until the Early Industrial Age. In order to achieve its fullest expression, second-stage cyborg technology requires the development of "stand-alone" technology in two areas: (a) the harnessing of constant, efficient power sources, and (b) mechanical systems that replicate specific muscular tasks.

Third-stage cyborg technology involves the replacement and/or augmentation of the peripheral and autonomic nervous systems. In production, this is analogous to the development and deployment of digital and analog monitoring and control systems that operate in "real time" but separate the human from the immediate site of production (e.g., NPC systems, stock tickers, telephones, intercoms). Fourth-stage cyborg technology augments and replaces parts of the central nervous system. At present, it is characterized by the development and deployment of stand-alone decision-making technologies capable of interacting with their environment and exercising some control over it (e.g., expert systems). Fourth-stage technologies modify the very means by which humans both perceive and conceive their external environments. As such, they extend and modify both the ability of individuals to produce culture and the environment in which that culture will be produced.

Consider one simple example. The introduction of computerized monitoring has shifted some professions from work situations in which individuals exercised their own judgment to situations in which computer programs make decisions (Braverman's [1974] deskilling argument; for examples, see Garson, 1988, pp. 71-159). Clearly, such shifts affect both the attachment of individuals to organizations and the skill requirements of these positions.

Each stage of technological extension changes not only the technology employed but also the social relations in which that technology is placed. As such, it has an intimate effect on what games (as discussed above) an individual can be involved in, because technological change may render specific games obsolete and create new games. Changes in game availability cause changes in living communities, rendering some obsolete and opening up needs for new ones. Although changes in human-machine relations may be initiated in a fairly short period, there is a definite time lag in cultural adaptation to the new situation (see Brinkman & Brinkman, 1997). This lag is especially evident in the development and deployment of new social contracts. In the following section, I examine the shifts that have taken place in the last several centuries surrounding the concept of "job."

## CHANGES IN THE MEANING OF "JOBS"

I noted earlier that organizational cultures exist in a broader social environment. The time has now come to leave Malinowski and Turner behind and illustrate how this broader environment has had an impact in one particular area: jobs. I have chosen this example for two reasons. First, for the past two centuries, individuals have tended to define themselves by their employment situations. Individuals' jobs have provided not only much of their self-images, but also access to many of the games that allow them to define themselves as part of communities and, hence, part of distinct cultures (see Trice, 1993; Trice & Beyer, 1993).

My second reason for examining jobs is somewhat more complex. For the past century or so, organizations have acted as the main forum for integrating different occupational cultures into (relatively) coherent, purposive social units. In part, this has been managed through an increasingly bureaucratic approach to the definition of organizational social roles (see Weber, 1964). This integration has produced certain characteristic organizational cultures based around a specific social contract (see Whyte, 1956). However, changes in the very nature of organizational bonds, especially communicative bonds, have led to both accusations of betrayal (i.e., activation of the cheater modules in relation to organizational contract; see Bennett, 1990) and changes in the de facto social contract.

In the following subsections, I use the terms *Early Industrial Age* (circa 1760-1860), *Middle Industrial Age* (circa 1860-1914), *Late Industrial Age* (circa 1914-1980), and *Early Silicon Age* (circa 1968 to the present) to distinguish broad temporal and organizational categories. These designations derive from the convention of archaeology "stages" established by C. J. Thomsen in 1819, although precise dates are impossible to determine, because practices from one "age" continue into the next (for parallel arguments, see Barley & Kunda, 1992; Eastman & Bailey, 1998).

## Jobs in the Early and Middle Industrial Ages

Bridges (1994) notes that before the Industrial Revolution, the word *job* referred to "any task that was a single piece of work" (p. 31). By the 1830s in England, the term shifted to its modern connotations of, to use Bridges's words, "the way most people today get their money, their status, and many of their friends—in addition to their sense of belonging, their feeling of being productive, and their hopes for a better future" (p. 30).

Two key changes in the social and technological environments mark this shift. First, the organization of much human labor ("work") was broken down into a series of small "jobs" that were organized sequentially—Adam Smith's discussion of pin making is a good example (in *Wealth of Nations*, I:i). The second key change was the introduction of an efficient mechanical system of generating power—the Watts steam engine. Both of these changes stem from a combination of the institution of "scientific rationality" as developed during the Enlightenment with the institution of mercantile capitalism. These two developments combined to produce a situation in which machines not only could but should be used to replace humans at manufacturing tasks independent of the natural environment. The maladaptation of the older social contracts to the new social environment produced during this period are well-known and have been described by many authors (e.g., Braverman, 1974; Polanyi, 1944).

## Jobs in the Late Industrial Age

Whereas the Early Industrial Age concentrated on the mass production and distribution of raw commodities (such as coal, iron, and cotton), the Late Industrial Age concentrated on the mass production of consumer goods and services. The Late Industrial Age centered on the increased abstraction and codification of work-task-related knowledge, coupled with a shift from a social contract based on exchange to one based on redistribution (see Polanyi, 1944, 1977).

By the 1950s, this redistributive social contract had produced what Ruitenbeek (1963) termed the "organizational society," inhabited by the "organization man" (Whyte, 1956; see also Granick, 1960). The organization had become the primary environment in which individuals competed and provided the major arena for individual self-definition (Osterman, 1984; Tyrrell, 1996a, 1996b; Whyte, 1956). This period is characterized by a social contract wherein loyalty to and conformity with the expectations of the organization are exchanged in return for security (Bennett, 1990; Grossman, 1988; Kalleberg, Knoke, & Marsden, 1995; Morin, 1991; Tyrrell, 1994).

## *Jobs in the Early Silicon Age*

The Late Industrial Age has been characterized by a number of trends in three general areas. First, there has been a generalized replacement of human with machine labor. Second, the cognized and operational environments (Rappaport, 1968, pp. 237-242) of most large organizations have been extended to encompass the entire globe and low Earth orbit. Third, there has been a centralization and intensification of C3 functions (command, control, and communications) and, in many cases, a shifting of these functions from humans to digital technologies (e.g., expert systems).

The current culmination of these trends, the Early Silicon Age, is characterized by several key structures. First, the productive capacity of the Late Industrial Age sectors of the economy far exceeds the possible demand, whereas this situation is reversed in the service and information/knowledge-intensive sectors of the economy (see Rifkin, 1994). This can be seen in the rapid development and growth of the so-called high-technology sectors: computers, robotics, biotechnology, and precision instrumentation (Beck, 1992). It can also be seen in the chronic labor shortages currently reported in these sectors.

Second, the destruction of trust in the bureaucratic organizational forms and the social contracts of the Late Industrial Age has produced a situation of generalized uncertainty for both the employee (i.e., How long will I work here?) and the employer (i.e., How can I keep my good employees?). Rather than trusting organizations, the newly developing social contract places trust in the communities and personal networks over the organization and can be characterized as operating on reciprocity (see Mauss, 1950/1990; Sahlins, 1972; for a detailed discussion, see Tyrrell, 1995).

Third, the development and deployment of rapid, interactive communications technologies (especially communications technologies such as the Internet, intranets, EDI, and the World Wide Web) has produced new environments that give many people unprecedented access to specialized communities of interest. Although these electronic communication networks are by no means the only new forms of community, they are among the most readily observable and accessible, and they are having effects similar to those of the introduction of the printing press (see McLuhan, 1962; Niccoli, 1990; Ong, 1982).

## COMMUNITY AND LIVELIHOOD IN THE EARLY SILICON AGE

The intersection of a new social contract centered on reciprocity and the rapid deployment of new electronic networks has produced a situation that is unique in human history. Humans in the Early Silicon Age have access to more games and, hence, more communities than ever before. Furthermore, investments in time (e.g., for travel and research) have been significantly reduced while there has been a concomitant rise in the variety of games that are accessible.

In this section, I want to highlight some of these games and communities, with particular reference to those centering on job searching. I have chosen job-search games and communities for one main reason. Unlike the situation of the Trobriand Islanders studied by Malinowski, for members of present-day Western societies the action of acquiring a livelihood (a job) has been separated from kinship and local spatial community. And, unlike in organizations of the Late Industrial Age, acquiring a livelihood has now been separated from individual organizations and takes place in multiple organizations on a contingent basis (e.g., term and contract employment, job shifting, consulting).

Every major job-search book and organization embodies the idea that individuals, not organizations, are responsible for their futures (e.g., Bolles, 1993; Bridges, 1994; Swartz, 1997). This idea is in direct opposition to the loyalty-for-security social contract of the Late Industrial Age. As such, this has had a serious impact on how organizational cultures are conceived by employees and on employees' reactions to intraorganizational attempts to secure their loyalty.

## Job Seekers: A Contingent Community

Job-finding clubs, outplacement programs, and self-help groups for job seekers fall into the category of contingent communities. First, the contingency of being unemployed is well recognized and expected within our culture. Second, these clubs, groups, and programs contain a small number of professional counselors, a somewhat larger number of "alumni," and, usually, a very large number of unemployed participants. Third, clearly recognized affective and material resources are transmitted. Thus job-seeking groups are clearly communities as discussed earlier in this chapter.

Although cyberspace is still conceived of primarily as an adjunct to "real space" job-search communities (e.g., formal outplacement programs), there are indications that a job-search function has developed in many on-line communities. Specific job-search sites have operated on the Internet since the mid-1980s, primarily in the form of Usenet news groups and bulletin board systems. In recent years, however, the spread on the World Wide Web has generated a number of dedicated job-search sites such as Monster Board.

## Job-Seeking Games in Cyberspace

At this point in time there are a number of metagames available to a person who wants to generate an income. Although the most common metagame is still employment by an organization, there are other options, such as self-employment (as a consultant or entrepre-

neur), contract or temporary work, and franchise opportunities.

Each metagame contains its own specific component games, the most common of which are opportunity identification, opportunity research, and specific job-search skills (e.g., networking, interviewing, and researching; see Tyrrell, 1995), all of which are accessible via the World Wide Web. Opportunity identification (finding out about the existence of a job) has been augmented by the recent shift of many corporations toward electronic human resource management systems. Put simply, the cost of advertising a job on the Web is one-tenth that of using "normal" methods.

Opportunity research may be described as discovering the context of the opportunity and the company. Until (roughly) 1996, most of this information was gleaned from personal networks and from library research using annual reports, news articles, and publicly available private and government-mandated reports (e.g., SEC filings, Standard & Poor's ratings). By the end of 1996, most of the *Fortune* 500 corporations had established corporate presences in cyberspace that make available most of this information, as had many government agencies (e.g., the SEC filings).

The area of job-search skills training has also shifted into on-line settings, ranging from informal job discussion sites through articles on specific skills to full job-search manuals. Although the majority of this information is static or, at best, asynchronous FAQ (frequently asked question) sheets, several sites are experimenting with synchronous IRC-based training in networking and résumé preparation.

Training, at least in the form of information and advice, for research, networking, and interviewing is available via the Internet. General research and advice became available in 1993 via the Riley Guide, which is still the definitive resource for on-line job searching. The definitive guide to networking on the Internet was produced by Phil Agre in 1994 and is constantly being updated.

Finally, there are numerous guides to interviewing that have appeared on-line in the past few years, and several interactive simulations have also been made available.

## Interactivity and the Development of Settlements

The increase in interactivity stems from the deployment of new programming standards for the HTML language, coupled with the availability of highly interactive programming scripts (e.g., CGI scripting, Java, and UML) and simplified programming interfaces (e.g., HotDog, MS FrontPage). Not only has it increased the interactivity of Web sites and their ease of production, it has led to the development of Web pages that combine asynchronous and synchronous sites.

This combination of asynchronous and synchronous media into a single settlement is currently forming the basis for several communities of job seekers. Where the territory of a given cyberspace community used to be defined by a single site and that site's links to other sites, we now find the development of full-fledged, if specialized, settlements. Some of these settlements, such as Monster Board, might be termed "ports of trade," because they are functionally equivalent to those studied by Polanyi (1977).

This situation has advanced considerably since 1997 with the introduction and spread of e-mail and Web-accessible human resource information systems (HRIS). Of particular interest are the companies that are now using these systems exclusively (e.g., Canadian Tire). It is quite plausible to believe that by 2010, the vast majority of employment opportunities, at least in North America, will be available only via electronic interfaces—either job-listing boards or digital HRIS operations.

The deployment of digital HRIS operations coupled into the Internet and the development of major job-listing boards increase the importance of timely information for job seekers. This, in turn, stimulates the "need" for access to specialized communities for technical skills (e.g., How do I post my résumé?), for opportunity identification, and for increased participation in job-seeking communities where these resources are available.

All of these factors combine to produce a multiplicity of contingent communities that contain information about opportunities. Most of these contingent communities are outside of the control of any single organization; they exist in the spaces between organizations and, as such, are part of the social environment of organizations. At the same time, they both enhance organizations and serve as a way of detaching individuals from organizations, first by showing them other options and then by enhancing the newly emerging social contract.

## Some Effects of Contingent Nonemployment on Organizational Cultures

In several other papers, I have discussed the role of reciprocity in job-search strategies, both in the "real world" (Tyrrell, 1995) and in cyberspace (Tyrrell, 1996a). In these papers, I have argued that there are distinct parallels between the distribution systems of hunting-and-gathering cultures and those of modern job seekers. The problem for most organizational cultures is that almost everyone in the organization, from the CEO down to the mail clerk, is either engaged in an ongoing job search or subject to headhunting. Organizations have themselves become contingent communities, as can be seen in the development of a two-tier employment system in the United States, where most new jobs are outsourced to temporary agencies (see Rifkin, 1994, pp. 190-194).

One central point that many of us have forgotten is that all individuals are members of multiple communities. Even as the relative importance of our work communities is dropping, the importance of electronic and other networking communities is increasing.

This shift in relative importance may well be viewed as a "fragmentation" of our source of moral order, even as Durkheim (1893/1984) saw it. But, if I am correct in diagnosing the new social contract as based on reciprocity, this is not the case.

Every reciprocity system that has existed has relied on moral action by its participants (see Malinowski, 1935/1965; Mauss, 1950/1990; Sahlins, 1972). In these systems, "moral action" is located in three separate areas: the individual, the network, and the community(ies) involved. We can see indications of this tripartite system starting to come into place. Consider, by way of example, the development and, more important, the purchase of career-planning seminars for currently employed people. This is a form of moral action by a community (an organization) toward an individual (an employee). A second example comes from the growing discussions on the ethics of business. A third, and final, example comes from the dawn of our species history: We can detect cheaters in reciprocal obligation systems as easily as we can detect cheaters in other forms of social contracts.

## FROM OCCUPATIONAL CONTINGENCY AND ON-LINE COMMUNITY TO ORGANIZATIONAL CULTURE

I started this chapter by noting the need to develop basic theoretical models for organizational cultures that will act as attractive communities within the new social contract and still be economically viable. I have argued that, in order to solve this problem, we need to rework our basic concepts of organizational culture. The model I have proposed drew initially on the work of Malinowski, and I have extended it through the addition of elements from evolutionary psychology and symbolic anthropology. In this model, the concept of a social contract (ideology in Trice & Beyer's [1993] meaning of the term)

relies not on a philosophical basis but on an evolved psychological one.

The deployment of the Internet has only speeded up the process of a shift in social contracts from redistributive forms, where the organization was the major domain in individual life, to reciprocity. To paraphrase Durkheim (1893/1984), we are moving from mechanical solidarity, through organic solidarity, to electronic solidarity, where fragmented sets of communities replace aspects of both the communities Malinowski envisioned and Industrial Age organizations.

I have used shifts in the concept of "job" and the development of job-seeking communities as illustrations in this chapter for several reasons. First, the concept of employment within an organization has not, to my mind, been challenged enough. Recent trends in types of employment clearly indicate a shift away from organizational employment toward temporary and contingent work, and this is already having an effect on organizational cultures. Second, the very existence of viable alternatives to organizational employment creates a situation that undermines the validity of many organizational cultures. Why should I work for an organization that I "know" will fire me at the drop of a hat, when I could be working for myself?

What, then, can be said about the very concept of "organizational culture"? Clearly, organizational cultures are, from the position I have been advocating, contingent communities. Thanks to the deployment of the Internet and other forms of electronic communication, any given organization may well act only as a minor domain for an individual amid a sea of other, more attractive, communities and competing organizations. What we need to do now is develop specific ethical models that can generate proper moral codes for each new "age" based on both the lived realities of that age and "human nature" (see Nicholson, 1997). These moral codes can then be transformed into specific sets of needs/answers that may be grafted into particular organizational cultures and provide us with a normative theory. But that, as the saying goes, is for another article.

# 6

# Sources of Meaning, Organizations, and Culture

## Making Sense of Organizational Events

*-- Mark F. Peterson and Peter B. Smith*

Organization scholars use the term *event* to talk about elements that social actors abstract from social processes (Peterson, 1998). Anyone who participates in an organization does so by interpreting events and influencing the meanings that other parties give them. This chapter is about how an organization's culture reflects the way different sources combine to give events meaning.

Among the principal advances that organization theorists have made since the 1980s has been to appreciate how the distinctive situations or events that occur in organization life are given meaning. Weick's (1995) sensemaking perspective is the best-known exam-

ple. The study of meanings builds on earlier attempts to overcome excessive rationality in organization theory (e.g., March & Olsen, 1976, pp. 10-23). It rebalances attention away from making decisions and toward interpreting events. We sometimes make decisions, but we are always making sense of events. Talking about organizational culture has become a way of talking about making sense. Trice and Beyer (1993) center their analysis of organizational culture on ideologies comprising beliefs, values, and norms through which events are given meaning.

Scholars' time and energy shifted toward analyzing how events are given meaning as many began to question the potential held by

AUTHORS' NOTE: We would like to thank Greg Rose and the editors for helpful comments on an earlier draft of this chapter.

the contingency theories that dominated discussion during the 1960s and 1970s (Peterson, 1998). Organizational contingency researchers were having difficulty using generalized characterizations of situations. Plausible contingency theories in areas such as leadership (Smith & Peterson, 1988) and organization design (Doty, Glick, & Huber, 1993) were not receiving the empirical support that many anticipated. Donaldson (1996) indicates that contingency research has become more successful as theories and methods have improved. However, the difficulties contingency researchers faced through the 1970s coincided with a movement of other lines of thought into organization studies to direct scholars' attention elsewhere. Perrow (1970), Galbraith (1973), March and Olsen (1976), and Weick (1979) recommended that we study how organizations give meaning to particular, time-bound situations rather than study generalized contingencies. A few scholars doing both qualitative (Isabella, 1990) and quantitative (Rentsch, 1990) research have followed this advice. In so doing, constructs such as degree of uncertainty have been taken from contingency research and reshaped for constructing taxonomies of events (Peterson, 1998). The result has been the replacement of studies of, say, the implication that a generally uncertain environment has for an organization's typical management practice with studies of how particular uncertain events affect an organization at those specific times when the uncertain events occur.

During the same period in the late 1970s and early 1980s that organization scholars were becoming interested in sensemaking, the role that national culture was thought to play in international competition led scholars to attend to organizational culture (Trice & Beyer, 1993, chap. 1). The literatures on how meanings are made and on national culture, although following from different motives, converged. The convergence was fortuitous. Ideas about how organizations make meanings combined with theories of values

from international culture research to shape organizational culture theory (see, in this volume, Hofstede & Peterson, Chapter 25; Sagiv & Schwartz, Chapter 26; Stackman, Pinder, & Connor, Chapter 2).

## ORGANIZATIONAL CULTURE AND MEANING MAKING

Where do meanings come from? Trice and Beyer (1993) use the label *ideologies* for "shared, relatively coherently interrelated sets of emotionally charged beliefs, values, and norms that bind some people together and help them to make sense of their worlds" (p. 33). Weick (1995, pp. 111-113) incorporates Trice and Beyer's definition into his own view of sensemaking. Organization scholars struggle with the sense in which ideologies are things that have force in themselves rather than things that must be mediated by something more concrete. Weick's (1995, pp. 24ff.) emphasis that sensemaking is retrospective can be misconstrued as vitiating the power of ideological frameworks themselves. It would be a mistake to view meanings and meaning frameworks as having little consequence except as retrospective explanations. Still, even if we view meanings and ideologies as having power, we find it somehow disquieting to have them floating in the air like disembodied souls. We want to bring them to earth by attaching them to something we can touch. We like to associate them with social actors—people having substance we can see, nations having boundaries we can cross, organizations inhabiting buildings we can enter. But must meaning frameworks really be concretized?

Role theory gives power to meanings by giving meanings a teleology. Although rooted in the past, roles are charged with expectations and so shape the future. As developed by Merton (1957a) and brought into organizational analysis by Kahn, Wolfe, Quinn,

Snoek, and Rosenthal (1964), role theory connected meanings to the influence exerted between individuals. Different role senders could take different ideological perspectives or apply the same perspectives in different ways when seeking to influence powerfully the use a receiver makes of a perspective. The simple word *sender* covers a broad range of power relationships, from explicit to implicit, and influence approaches, from the coercive to the normative. In all cases, however, role senders politicize ideologies and bring them to earth by applying them to particular events experienced by particular people at particular times.

But is role theory inordinately structural? Can one ever talk about meaning frameworks themselves as having influence without attaching them to particular individuals, groups, organizations, or societies? We find that organization members sometimes treat emergent meanings as quasi-actors with life and power in themselves. For example, a shared vision can tie the interests of an organization to something that, if not eternal, is at least beyond the mundane. Although a vision may have an initiator, once established, it can have power apart from any identifiable actor. Such things are the "that's how things are around here" or "that's what they say" that point to established belief and practice with only the vaguest intimation of a specific actor. Neoinstitutional theory gives meanings a power that supersedes that of explicit structures (Powell & DiMaggio, 1991; Scott, 1995) and in so doing turns reification on its head. People and organizations do not always make meanings. Sometimes meanings make people and organizations what they are by defining their characteristics and roles.

We take the position that it is helpful to treat identifiable, structural entities such as people, groups, and organizations as sources of meaning, and that it is also helpful to treat things like ideologies in themselves with only loose links to structures as equally influential sources of meaning. From a grammatical standpoint, we have found that by endorsing the idea that meanings as well as people can be active subjects, we, like others who write about making meanings, may appear to view managers as merely passive and reactive. We need to be careful in our choices as to active and passive voices in this chapter. At most points, we will follow usual writing conventions by allowing physically identifiable social actors to be subjects. We will present ourselves as arguing this or that. Scholars will be said to contribute this or that. At other points, we will give meanings or meaning frameworks the status of actors. Meanings will do things. Meanings will sometimes happen with disturbingly little sign of who is making them happen.

In the remainder of this chapter, we shall first provide a model of meaning making stimulated by role theory. We will then discuss precedents for what we have been calling our event management variant on the sensemaking theme (Peterson, 1998; Smith & Peterson, 1988). Most of our discussion will be about the sources of meaning from which organizations and their members draw and the ways these interrelate in influencing how events are given meaning.

## THE PROCESS OF MEANING MAKING

In the ongoing experience of organization life, things happen, events occur. Figure 6.1 summarizes the process by which organizational events are given meaning. The social actors who give meaning include individuals, organizations, and larger systems. Although the kinds of structures each uses to interpret events are quite distinct (Argote & McGrath, 1993) and the scope of the meaning frameworks each uses increases in complexity with the complexity of the system, all share similarities as interpreting systems (Peterson, 1998; Van de Ven & Poole, 1990).

Through an interplay between what is actually occurring and characteristics of social

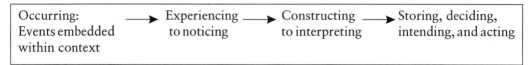

Figure 6.1. Phases in Sensemaking of Events

actors, attention is selectively given to some events. Events not noticed as discrete things can be experienced as part of the ground against which other things are noticed (Peterson, 1998; Polanyi, 1958/1962). Crystallizing and giving focus to an event by abstracting it from tacit context begins the process of constructing and interpreting it. Meaning making proceeds through the linking of events to existing interpretative structures. The process reaches closure as social actors modify or add to their interpretative structures and sometimes, but sometimes not, generate actions, choices, or intentions. Making a decision or taking an action is only one way to resolve an interpretative process. More often and more universally, interpretation is resolved by a more subtle change in interpretative structures. A person's thinking or an organization's culture may occasionally change radically, but it is always changing incrementally.

### Roles: A Starting Point for Theories About Sources of Meaning

How do we represent the more concrete sources of meaning, the structural parties, that become involved in meaning making? Merton (1957a) developed role theory to provide a way to distinguish among people and analyze their influence without equating a particular person with a particular function. The idea to separate a structural thing such as a role from any single function was part of the transition in organization studies from structural-functional theory to systems theory. Rather than equating roles with func-

tions, Kahn et al. (1964) based their role taxonomy on explicit authority relationships— superior, subordinate, or colleague. Although the role stress scholars (e.g., House, Schuler, & Levanoni, 1983) who mark the major application of Kahn et al.'s research occasionally refer to more generalized social norms closer to the cultural concept of ideology, their focus remains highly personalized. In role theory, meaning does not come from disembodied rules, cultural principles, norms, or ideologies, but comes from or is made salient by particular categories of people.

Role theory fits the rational ideal of modern organizations. The culture of an organization could be defined as modern from the point when people were assigned explicit status—superior, peer, or subordinate—in ways intended to affect how they relate to one another. Role analysis has been a useful starting point for understanding how meanings are given, but the more recent movement away from overrationality in organization theory recognizes that the implications of roles are not fixed or self-evident.

Hutchins's (1991) analysis of how crew members responded to events when a ship's engine failed illustrates both the utility and limits of categorizing sources of meaning according to formal role status. The crew adapted preexisting role relationships to produce new relationships more suitable to the handling of an emergency situation. During the emergency, the captain retained a pivotal role. However, behaviors toward the captain—what might otherwise be presumptuous interruptions, for example—reflected new role relationships. These may have been latent, emerging only in the crisis; they may have emerged ad hoc as needs arose and ended without a trace when nonemergency operations resumed; or they may have reshaped all role relationships. Hutchins's point is that pragmatically functional aspects of relationships within a role set based on each person's skills and the needs of an immediate situation will sometimes be more significant than will explicit roles. However, role relationships do not always spontaneously adjust to crises. Helmreich's (1994) detailed analysis of the crash of a Colombian airliner at Kennedy Airport indicates that the plane went down because crew members failed to challenge the captain's evident errors. Both analyses indicate that considering relationships according to superior, colleague, and subordinate status corresponds to aspects of role differentiation that are meaningful in many formal organizations. Both indicate as well that explicit assignment to formal roles is a social intervention that is likely to affect someone's thoughts and actions, but is not a conclusion that wholly determines actual role relationships.

## The Need to Augment Role Models

Other lines of work also suggest that personalized views of where meanings come from should be augmented. Kohlberg (1969), for example, argues that using the expected responses of other people as a basis for ethical choices characterizes only one stage of moral development. At other developmental stages, people address ethical dilemmas by referring to law, norms, or principles. We leave the particulars of when people use different sources of meaning to make moral judgments or interpret situations for other analyses (e.g., Peterson, 1998). The point for the present chapter is that such work indicates that we need to incorporate less personalized sources than roles into social-interpretation models.

## ORGANIZATIONAL SOURCES OF MEANING

We have argued that a taxonomy for sources of meaning needs to include both ideologies in themselves and a set of structural sources for which explicit roles provide only a beginning. Ideologies and structures have provided the two bases for categorizing sources of meaning in organizational culture theory. Trice and Beyer (1993, pp. 44-72) propose a typology of ideologies to capture the alternative frames that shape our understanding of the world. They evoke strain theory to indicate that societies continually strive with the disintegrating forces produced by conflicting frames. Competition among ideologies shapes an organization's culture. Ideologies fill the theoretical place of functions in earlier theory by specifying the contents of values that social actors can pursue. Trice and Beyer do not detail the links between ideologies and particular parties or structural devices that communicate, support, or assert these ideologies. How should we take the next step? To identify particular parties with particular ideologies would be to take a step backward. Doing so would take us into the nonproductive dialogue between classical Marxist attempts to identify specific ideologies of structural classes such as proletariat and bourgeoisie and the failed attempts to equate structures with singular functions.

Our alternative for identifying sources of meaning has been to follow the direction of role theory by specifying structural categories, but to do so in a way that allows for the influence of nonexplicit roles and less evident actors. Deal and Kennedy (1982) stimulated discussion of organizational culture with an account of roles unlike anything role theorists had previously envisioned. They populated organizational cultures with a delightful set of characters that included priests, whisperers, and gossips. These characters exert influence, along with occupants of traditional roles, by using such symbols as heroes, rites, and rituals. Deal and Kennedy give less attention to the ideological content of meanings offered by these characters, but such hidden structural sources of meaning show us how one might bring the kinds of ideologies of which Trice and Beyer speak to earth without portraying them overrationally.

We have followed a similar course by studying ways in which parts of an organization's social structure shape meanings. In our empirical projects (e.g., Peterson, Elliott, Bliese, & Radford, 1996; Peterson, Smith, Bond, & Misumi, 1990; Smith, Peterson, & Misumi, 1994), we leave room for the influence of ideologies per se as a set of norms that organization members experience as existing apart from any particular structural source. In so doing, we are leaving room for Deal and Kennedy's denizens of the implicit cultural world to have their sway. We leave the task of identifying types of ideologies for other chapters in the present volume, such as Zammuto, Gifford, and Goodman's (Chapter 16) discussion of competing values and the various formulations of national and organizational value types proposed in the chapters that make up Part V.

Table 6.1 shows the intraorganizational sources of meaning that we identified a decade ago (Smith & Peterson, 1988, p. 81). The explicitness of the institutional support that a larger system provides for particular sources of meaning is reflected in three levels of "formality." In this chapter, we first update our 1988 analysis by considering the more conventionally acknowledged sources of meaning that are located within the organization and the way these are being treated in the organizational culture literature. We then extend our earlier set by providing examples of extraorganizational sources that can also affect organizational culture.

## Rules as Sources of Meaning

Two lines of theory that appeared at the dawn of the organizational culture era treat explicit rules as givens that stand on their own to guide meaning and action. Stewart (1982) used "demands" and "constraints" to represent formal rules in a management model that treats leadership as the subsequent exercise of "choices." Katz and Kahn (1978) took a similar view by describing leadership as creatively "interpolating" within rules and procedures. The possibility that leadership can include bending or breaking rules or that explicit rules may really not be operative was left largely out of the discussion. Neither model provided a mechanism for an organization's sensemaking process as a whole to change, undermine, or avoid explicit demands, constraints, or rules.

As organizational culture theory has been drawn away from even these quasi-rational models, the question that the preparation of explicit rules and procedures answers has changed. For rational theory, the question was: What rules should be formulated to accomplish the purposes of organizational leaders? Rules were the epitome of rationality. The problem of bureaucratic management, scientific management, and, more recently, strategic management has been implementation. *Implementation* here means that rules must be properly formulated and followed. The question of rules in theories of organizational culture now changes into: How do rules on paper operate as interventions? The answer lies in the relationship between this cell of Table 6.1 and all the others. For explicit rules or known norms to be operative, they need to be supported by other sources. Martin, Feldman, Hatch, and Sitkin (1983) provide a rule-breaking story illustrating that to IBMers, mundane rules and procedures apply even to the CEO. This type of story indicates how the actions of one source of meaning, in this case superiors, spread through a storytelling network, can support an organizational culture for following rules.

Organizational culture viewed purely as a local ideology or "how we do things around here" disconnected from the parties holding the ideology fits squarely into the second category in the first column of Table 6.1. As for written rules and procedures, the force of un-

**TABLE 6.1** Intraorganizational Sources of Event Meanings

| Formality of Structures | Rules | *Intraorganizational Sources* | | | |
|---|---|---|---|---|---|
| | | Superiors | Colleagues | Subordinates | Self |
| Explicit structures | Formal rules | Formal downward influence | Formal lateral influence | Formal upward influence | Formal self-management |
| Implicit conventions | Established norms | Established downward influence | Established lateral influence | Established upward influence | Established self-management |
| Emergent aspects of culture | Emerging norms | Ad hoc downward influence | Ad hoc lateral influence | Ad hoc upward influence | Ad hoc self-management |

written rules is affected by their support from other sources. Organizational culture is often viewed as a set of unwritten, informal, or unspoken rules that affect meanings and behavior (e.g., Van Maanen & Barley, 1985).

Weick (1995) tells us that sensemaking is an emergent process. The potential that similar meanings can emerge from similar events under similar circumstances, or for sensemaking to begin to be institutionalized, is represented by the bottom cell in the first column of the table.

Organizational culture theory and sensemaking theory differ in their emphasis on this cell compared to the bottom cell in this column. Sensemaking analyses tend to emphasize dynamics and change in the process of making meaning. Organizational culture analyses tend to emphasize the influence that institutionalized understandings, like established unwritten rules and written rules, have on subsequent meaning making.

## Superiors as Sources of Meaning

The second column of Table 6.1 reflects leadership. Leadership can be exercised as an explicitly recognized role (first row of the table), as an established, implicit role (middle row), or as an emergent process (bottom row). The early literature on managing meanings was quickly accompanied by articles about how leaders influence meanings (Pondy, 1978; Smircich & Morgan, 1982). Similarly, as the organizational culture literature developed, the idea that leaders can influence organizational culture followed closely (Bass, 1985; Burns, 1978; House, 1977). Theorists have analyzed the cognitions and values of both leaders and followers to integrate leadership with sensemaking and organizational culture (Hunt, 1991; Lord & Maher, 1991; Smith & Foti, 1998; Smith & Peterson, 1988).

Organizational culture scholars who talk about leaders usually have in mind a manager appointed to a very senior position exerting influence over an entire organization. This vantage point differs from that of most post–World War II leadership studies about relationships that lower-level leaders have with subordinates. Upper-level transformational leaders are said to use a vision to shape the meanings that others place on events (Den Hartog & Verburg, 1998; House, Wright, & Aditya, 1997). In Trice and Beyer's (1993) language, transformational leaders select among an industry's or society's ideologies and articulate them in a way that is meaningful for a particular organization facing particular challenges. Scott (1995) reminds us that making senior leaders pivotal is consistent with the way early institutional theorists treated the chief executive as key to shaping meaning frameworks.

Leaders need not wait for events to occur. Leaders can shape meanings by drawing attention to particular events and evoking meanings to support their views. For example, countless CEOs have sought support for downsizing or austerity measures by directing their organizations' attention to actions by global competitors that could be read as signaling a threat to their own organizations' well-being or survival. In organizational culture theory, leaders make their visions concrete by projecting the implications that present events have for a desired future. In so doing, they influence which other sources of meaning are important. For example, an appeal to the value of tradition to meet competitive threat is an appeal to rules and current leadership. An appeal to the virtue of innovation could be an appeal to seek meanings from extraorganizational sources or innovative staff groups or task forces. An appeal to solidarity, to stand together, could be an appeal to seek meanings from other organization members.

Organizational culture theory opens up less fully explored directions for leadership research additional to the way that senior executives can tie organization success to members' personal values. The ethical and community contribution aspects of leadership are beginning to receive attention as well (Craig & Gustafson, 1998). Despite some limited efforts to reinterpret classic leadership research in sensemaking terms (e.g., Peterson & Sorenson, 1991), work remains to be done on how leaders at all levels shape meaning. For example, it may be natural for lower-level supervisors in some contexts to press subordinates to meet high performance demands and at the same time show personal concern for the subordinates. It fits an ideology that com-

petitive pressures make self-sacrifice necessary for long-term well-being (Peterson, Peng, & Smith, 1999).

## Colleagues as Sources of Meaning

Normative theories of organizational culture tend to minimize the significance of explicit rules apart from broad mission statements and to limit leadership to the shaping of organizational vision. They suggest instead that strong cultures promote reliance on colleagues (see, e.g., in this volume, Michela & Burke, Chapter 14; Zammuto et al., Chapter 16). Brannen and Kleinberg (Chapter 24, this volume) describe how culture change programs promoting team-based work system designs have been supported by the U.S. interpretation of and response to Japanese management systems. These programs followed earlier participation experiences such as quality of work life, sociotechnical systems, sensitivity training, and human relations programs in general (Barley & Kunda, 1992).

Despite occasional overzealousness of organizational culture authors in advocating that organizations should be centered on peer relations supported by strong organizational cultures, organization members certainly do much of their work with others who are neither clearly superiors nor clearly subordinates. Some researchers argue that lack of consensus about superior-subordinate relationships is much more the rule than the exception (Morley & Hosking, 1984). Multination studies suggest that superior-subordinate rankings tend to be less clear and fixed in some English-speaking nations and in northern European cultures than in many other parts of the world (Hofstede, 1980a). Joint interpretation of situations and the taking of coordinated action are likely to require more negotiation and less direct exercise of power in cultures that show this type of ambivalence about hierarchical differences. Colleagues may also play particularly important third-party roles in interpreting events when large status differences place strain on direct interaction between superiors and subordinates (Miller & Jablin, 1991).

A literature is rapidly developing about trust within organizations that suggests that trust affects the operation of collegial relations. Trust affects all relationships, but it plays a larger part in lateral than in hierarchical relationships. In any relationship, events occur that can make a party vulnerable (Bigley & Pearce, 1998). Trust affects whether occasions of vulnerability are experienced as opportunities to support or to harm the other party. Rousseau, Sitkin, Burt, and Camerer (1998) suggest that an organizational culture supporting trust can be based on the salience of trustworthy exchanges for individual benefit (calculative trust), an organization's history and mythology of trustworthy behavior (relational trust), or an established system of rewards and sanctions corresponding to trustworthy behavior (institutional trust). To the extent that trust exists among people of similar status and power, events can be interpreted from the standpoint of joint problem solving rather than self-interest. Research remains to be done as to how best an organizational culture can support various bases of trust, and about what implications each basis really has for lateral relationships.

## The Special Case of Staff Specialists

Specialists express belief systems and techniques originating in industries and professions. Support staff specialists (e.g., marketing research staff) provide information and expertise, and technostructure specialists (e.g., accountants) design rules and procedures (Mintzberg, 1979). Support staff specialists are the intraorganizational sources of meaning for understanding unusual events, particularly events related to such domains as law, economics, and technology outside the expertise of other organization members. Technostructure staff express industry-based techniques obtained from education and

knowledge of industry sectors to recommend ways of handling routine events. Barley (1990) describes the discussions that radiologists have with technologists to interpret such events as problems with machines and X-ray images. This is one of the few studies that describe the role staff play in sensemaking and organizational culture.

The organizational culture literature places the staff specialist in an equivocal position. Is the technostructure role reduced as direct coercion and control are replaced by visions and norms? Is the support staff role changed from providing information to executives to providing information to teams? Is the specialist role reduced as people take on broader responsibilities and have more direct access to knowledge bases previously requiring much greater specialized expertise? The thrust of the normative organizational culture literature is to de-emphasize staff in favor of individual expertise and peer collaboration. However, as an empirical question, the role of staff remains open for research.

## Subordinates as Sources of Meaning

The organizational culture literature has brought renewed interest in participation by increasing the attention that managers and scholars give to the effects that lower-level employees can have on the meanings that managers give to events. Western scholars quickly learned that Japanese management programs such as quality circles and "ringi" systems include substantial influence by lower-level parties, but it took much longer for them to appreciate that this influence occurred within a context of deference to authority (Lincoln & Kalleberg, 1990; Smith & Misumi, 1989). Several studies have documented upward influence through such mechanisms as persuading, manipulating, and providing information (e.g., Porter, Allen, & Angle, 1981; Schilit & Locke, 1982). Research into upward influence and impression management recognizes that subordinates are not passive; rather, they actively influence the ways superiors interpret their behavior and work situations. Subordinates who have good technical skills and who support their superiors are often drawn upon (Graen & Scandura, 1987) through formal participative mechanisms, informal understandings, or as part of the kind of emergent process that Hutchins (1991) describes, as noted above.

### The Self as a Source of Meaning

A good deal of what organization members do when making sense of surrounding events is to draw on what they experience as their own backgrounds, their "selves." Markus's (1977; Markus & Zajonc, 1985) theory of "self-schemas" has become central to the way self is currently understood in psychology. We expect that a great deal of what one experiences as self has roots in meanings drawn from other sources. At what point does one draw from a particular source so routinely that one loses any awareness that a viewpoint one adopts is not inherent, but was originally learned from this other source? A manager in a bureaucratic organization learns that rules are indeed frequently implemented. A manager in a participative organization learns that involvement in decision making is expected by relevant peers and subordinates. At an early stage in organizational socialization, these two managers may differentiate what they themselves view as appropriate from what is typical of their organization. At a later stage, organizational practice may come to be a more fully integral part of the self. Our own studies have shown that among managers in almost 40 nations, reliance on one's own experience and training is typically found to be the most endorsed source of event meaning (Smith & Peterson, 1995). This is probably best interpreted as showing that being an effective manager in any type of organizational culture requires not just the imposition of an individual's perspective derived from initial training but also an internalized and autonomous understand-

ing of what types of meaning are tenable and coherent within a given context.

Markus and Kitayama (1991) advance the theory of self by indicating that the distinction between the self and the collective is experienced quite differently in various parts of the world. They argue that in Western nations, where an "independent" construal of self prevails, the self is seen as an autonomous actor. In contrast, in other regions of the world an "interdependent" construal of self is found; selfhood involves an internalization of the demands and expectations of specific, social "others" within one's ingroup (Erez & Earley, 1993).

In the view we are presenting here, we follow the Western perspective by treating norms, laws, and other parties as major alternative sources of meaning to the self. This allows us to acknowledge that in certain well-studied parts of the world such a separation does occur. At the same time, we acknowledge that in some other contexts, the individual's "own experience and training" largely reflect internalized representation of the perspectives of other relevant sources of meaning.

The unique individual is not a focus of organizational culture analysis, but the operation of organizations that accommodate unique individuals is. Even more clearly than had climate research, organizational culture theory indicates that managing organizations is not the same as managing a set of discrete individuals or even departments. By moving attention away from the self to the collective, it has helped overcome the excessive self-focus in some lines of theory from which organization studies has drawn. For example, "self" in the social psychology of attribution tends to limit the sources of meaning that a focal person can call upon to his or her own prior experiences and training. In attribution theory, others are objects for comparison, not active meaning givers. Some approaches to social learning theory place the individual in a context of meaning sources. Sadri and Robertson (1993) have found that a sense of self-efficacy, the belief that one has the ability to carry out a course of action that will achieve the outcomes that one wishes (Bandura, 1997) is related to individual performance. Rather than being just an exercise in self-development, social learning theory recognizes that an individual's socialization into an organization includes the individual's changing and negotiating the sources of meaning that he or she uses to interpret events.

## Current Status of Intraorganizational Sources of Meaning in Organizational Culture Theory

In our earlier description of event management (Smith & Peterson, 1988), we distinguished among sources of meaning inside an organization. The specific responsibilities and functions associated with roles often explain more than does their formal status relative to one another. Taking Deal and Kennedy's (1982) labels, whether an organizational culture's priest is your colleague or your subordinate may not matter as much as whether the person's status is as designated worrier. For example, some theories of trust apply similar ideas to relationships regardless of role category. This work leaves room to consider whether the elements of trust that most affect a relationship are affected by relative status in the explicit hierarchy.

## EXTRAORGANIZATIONAL SOURCES OF MEANING

When Trice and Beyer (1993) describe sources of ideology, they look outside an organization. Their sources include transnational cultures, other organizations' cultures, regional and community cultures, industry ideologies, organization sets, and occupational ideologies. As for intraorganizational sources of meaning, we find it helpful to consider both structural and quasi-structural

extraorganizational sources, including the following:

- International, national, and local societal rules
- Primary groups
- Professional and occupational rules
- Professional peers
- Other rules and parties
- Societal self

Like intraorganizational sources, extraorganizational sources vary in their degrees of explicitness and precedence, and in the degree of consensus as to their endorsement. For example, explicit societal rules take the form of national or international laws, implicit conventions take the form of widespread norms about what is right, and emergent aspects of national culture reflect newer or less widespread norms that compete for influence with established explicit rules and implicit norms. These are certainly mediated by the meanings offered by intraorganizational sources. However, they also stand apart to directly affect meanings given to organizational events as members listen to the media, talk with friends and family, and consider personal views developed apart from their organizational experiences.

When we move outside an organization, the scope of potentially significant sources increases exponentially. We discuss below several external sources and ways of thinking about these sources, which we have selected because they are likely to be especially useful for an understanding of organizational culture.

## External Stakeholders as Sources of Meaning

Organizational scholars are using stakeholder analysis as a larger-scale analogue to role theory by specifying social structures as extraorganizational sources. Stakeholders are parties who have an interest in the actions of some focal party (Mitchell, Agle, & Wood, 1997). The specific ideologies or cultural priorities that stakeholders draw from tend to be downplayed. Instead, analysts have been interested in issues such as how unequal resource dependencies between a focal party and a stakeholder affect the relative power that accrues to the parties. In effect, when an ideology finds a stakeholder with the resources to support it, the ideology becomes influential.

The varied purposes to which stakeholder analysis has been put illustrate the varied kinds of meanings that a social actor can give to events. One issue in giving meanings is to ascertain whether or not a state of affairs is effective. Stakeholder theories treat a social actor's effectiveness as depending on the interests of a particular party (Pennings & Goodman, 1977). Mason and Mitroff (1981) suggest how senior organization leaders should use stakeholders to give meaning to such events as strategy proposals. They argue that leaders should evaluate such proposals by anticipating the reactions of an organization's numerous stakeholders. Quite a bit remains undetermined and open to research about the influence that stakeholders have on organizational culture, both directly and as mediated by internal parties.

## Family and Friends as Sources of Meaning

Families affect meanings both as socializing agents expressing societal norms and as continuing influences on meanings in the workplace. Interest in the family as an issue in work-nonwork relationships continues with renewed spirit as knowledge workers fulfill role responsibilities away from traditional work sites and as dual-career couples (see, e.g., Perlow, 1998) seek to reconcile conflicting schedules. The influence of family on how one goes about doing business comes into the organizational literature through studies of cultures where such influence is more typical than that described in the U.S. and European literatures (e.g., Tsui, 1998; see also Granrose, Huang, & Reigadas, Chapter 30, this volume). It also appears as networks built on bonds of family and friendship ties become economically significant, as in immigrant entrepreneur communities (Waldinger, Aldrich, Ward, & Associates, 1990). Family has a tremendous effect on expatriate adjustment (Adler, 1997, pp. 263-294), but the particulars of how family affects the meaning expatriates give to their situation remain for further research.

The pervasive Weberian tradition of separating work from nonwork is still reflected in the limited discussion of family in organizational culture research. This separation leaves much to research about the influence of the family in, say, the visions offered by a chief executive, the different meanings organization members give to self-sacrifice compared to family sacrifice on behalf of an employer, and the effect of organizational socialization on people having different family socialization.

## Owner-Agent Interactions: A Special Case of External Sources

Agency theory is seldom discussed in organizational culture analysis, but it has the potential to offer insights into the dynamics of distinctive parties within a single organizational culture. The classic agency problem can be viewed as one where owners and managers put different meanings on events that provide cues to organizational performance (Eisenhardt, 1989). The economic self-interests of owners encourage them to interpret events such as changes in market conditions as presenting opportunities for profits and share values. Managers, on the other hand, share these interests to some extent, but also pursue other ends. If owners reward managers according to the size of the organization, the managers may place organizational growth, which increases their personal wealth, above share value, which increases owners' wealth. If managers are not rewarded for either growth or profitability, they may place emphasis on stable, secure markets, which would reduce the effort required of them.

Agency theory is ripe for rethinking based on theories of culture and meaning. It began by identifying the many conditions under which managers will interpret market conditions using criteria other than those applied by owners. It has been extended to analyze conditions under which any given set of parties will interpret events in incompatible ways due to differing economic interests. Agency theory is moving from its origin in the owner-manager problem framed by neoclassical economics and developing into a theory of the way in which any parties in a relationship influence one another's actions by influencing the meanings each gives to events (Peterson, Rodriguez, & Smith, 2000).

### *Interorganizational Systems: Environmental Scanning, Imitation, and Institutional Processes*

Institutional theory explains how organizations use information from one another and about one another to make strategic, structural, and managerial choices (Scott, 1987, 1995). Levitt and Nass (1989), for example, describe the processes of mimetic, coercive, and normative isomorphism in the way textbook editors react to the event of receiving a manuscript submission. Editors can follow mimetic processes to evaluate the submission by comparing that event with competing products from other publishers. Editors can be coerced to accept pressure from governmental bodies legislating textbook content. Editors can also follow normative processes in publishing based on established industry practices and associated academic disciplines. Managers have come to recognize that effectively functioning organizational cultures have competitive value that is

difficult to imitate because of their social complexity (Barney, 1991). Because difficult does not mean impossible, organizations actively look to one another to compare the meanings being given to events having market, technology, or other significant implications.

## RECONCILING SOURCES OF MEANING WITHIN AN ORGANIZATION'S CULTURE

We have now updated and extended our earlier taxonomy of the sources of meaning that organization members, groups, subcultures, and whole organizations use. All of these actors can supplement their own frameworks for interpreting events by drawing from frameworks within and outside particular organizations' cultures. Each must handle the alternative meanings offered by different sources. Different sources can certainly be most closely aligned with different ideologies. Even the same source can express different ideologies under different circumstances. Cognitive consistency and strategic management notwithstanding, neither people nor social systems are bound to be completely consistent. The taxonomy of sources of meaning we propose helps to structure a number of issues for organizational culture scholarship.

### *Reconciling Sources of Meaning: Beyond Roles and Rules*

The idea that divergent role expectations can cause strain opens a door to the study of strain attributable to all kinds of sources. Ambiguity is uncertainty about what to do, what to think, and what meaning to give to events due to the meanings offered not just by role senders, but by all sources. Conflict is not just role conflict, but incompatibility among alternative meanings from internal and external, role and nonrole sources. Researchers, including ourselves, have been satisfied to measure role stresses and assess their relationship to a limited set of criteria (Jackson & Schuler, 1985; Peterson et al., 1995). We need to extend the idea of role stress to include stress that is attributable to all potential sources of meaning.

Perhaps reaction against the heritage of rational models of rules has dissuaded organizational culture scholars from concertedly analyzing the way rules combine with other sources. In our view, the more important insight from organizational culture theory is not that rules do not matter, but that they, like all other sources, do not stand alone.

### Reconciling Sources of Meaning: Social Interpretation or Power Struggles?

Perhaps most important for organizational culture research and theory, carefully working through the nature of sources of meaning has the potential to promote discussion between the two most distinctly different approaches to understanding organizational culture: the social-interpretation and power-based approaches. Are organizational cultures forums for interactions among ideologies, or are they forums for interactions among ideologues? New events provide the stimulus to social process in either case, but how should the process of giving them meaning best be modeled?

Our taxonomy of sources refers to some entities, such as superiors and family, that seem closer to competing power holders, and other entities, such as unwritten rules and widespread societal beliefs, that are closer to social interpretation. In our empirical projects (Smith & Peterson, 1995; Smith, Peterson, & Wang, 1996) and in the examples of sources we have discussed, we have used labels for things that organization members are likely to concretize. We have not explicitly included informal roles such as priest and whisperer in our taxonomy, not because they are unimportant, but because organization members are less likely to identify them readily. Despite some organizations' attempts to tame them by appointing "corporate ombudsmen" or "chief knowledge officers," Deal and Kennedy's (1982) creatures still lurk in the shadows. We fear they may even become transformed into entirely different corporate beings when brought into the light.

As denizens of the culture world, they and the less visible processes that go on to give events meaning help us encompass both power and social interpretation. They are part of what we implicitly represent without naming when we ask people about the influence of "unwritten but accepted ways of doing things around here" and "widespread beliefs in your country about what is right." How do practices become accepted if not written? Partly through observation and imitation by people in their explicit roles as managers, accountants, or engineers, but partly also through the stories told and actions taken by people in informal roles as culture preservers and transmitters.

Social-interpretation views emphasize the content of what Trice and Beyer (1993) and Weick (1995) would call ideologies, but we prefer to soften into meaning frameworks. Power views emphasize the interactions among parties designated according to both their explicit organizational roles and their implicit ones. Our view is that there is a world out there that is not sufficiently unequivocal and singular to determine social constructions fully, but that certainly constrains them. It is within such constraints that alternative meaning frameworks and powerful social actors interact to give events meaning. Organizational culture researchers would do well to analyze simultaneously the events that occur and are noticed, the meaning frameworks through which these events can be viewed, and the powerful social actors who seek to influence which meanings prevail.

Our view implies some particular directions for research, among which are the following:

- Continue to use qualitative methods in sense-making analysis, but also use established insights from sensemaking to construct quantitative measures, particularly of the sources organization members use to create meanings.
- Create measures of stress that cover sources of meaning in addition to roles.

- Increase research attention to sources of meaning traditionally overlooked in the United States, such as family and national norms.
- Use the success and continuing stresses of other lines of organizational research, such as contingency theory and agency theory, to identify topics and concepts for study in sensemaking research.

# 7

# Time and Organizational Culture

### —— *Allen C. Bluedorn*

What is as fundamental as time? Yet time has been almost totally ignored as a research topic in the organization sciences. Indeed, prior to the 1980s, the organization science studies that had gone beyond the physicist's $t$ in the consideration of time could almost be counted on the fingers of one hand (e.g., Clark, 1978; Ditton, 1979; Jaques, 1976; Roy, 1960; Webber, 1972; Zerubavel, 1979). Unfortunately, this work received less attention than it deserved. In the early 1980s, Jaques's (1982), McGrath and Rotchford's (1983), and Zerubavel's (1981) work generated more attention, functioning as a harbinger of things to come, such as the work of Bluedorn and Denhardt (1988), Clark (1985), Das (1986), Dubinskas (1988), Gersick (1988, 1989), and Schriber and Gutek (1987). But if time is so fundamental, why has it taken so long to emerge as an important issue in organizational research and, especially, as a major topic in organizational culture research?

Two explanations seem plausible. First, time has been considered a constant rather than a variable, and who studies constants? In experimental research the independent variable must take on at least two values, and in regression analysis, how often does anyone attend substantively to the equation's constant? By the 20th century, the physicist's $t$ had become institutionalized as *time*—even in the social sciences—without the realization that much of the belief complex surrounding this view was actually a social construction. And when something becomes deeply institutionalized, it goes unnoticed—the second explanation for time's neglect.

Edward T. Hall has observed that time is fundamental to human existence because "everything in life occurs in a time frame—

AUTHOR'S NOTE: The preparation of this chapter was supported by summer research fellowships from the College of Business and Public Administration at the University of Missouri–Columbia. I would like to thank the three editors for their thoughtful suggestions and guidance throughout the development of this chapter.

most of which is taken for granted" (quoted in Bluedorn, 1998a, p. 110). The key is that most of the time frame is "taken for granted," existing at the level of culture that Schein (1992) calls basic underlying assumptions, the most fundamental level of culture in which perceptions, thoughts, and feelings are "unconscious" and "taken for granted." Time as the physicist's *t* became a taken-for-granted constant over the past millennium in the Western world. For evidence, consider the disconcerting response people experience when they first encounter Einstein's time dilation concept (Davies, 1995). Time dilation is disconcerting because it means time is not a constant, but constant status is a basic underlying assumption in the social construction of clock time, the physicist's *t*. As Schein (1992, p. 23) notes, because of the human mind's need for cognitive stability, any challenge to a basic assumption—and few assumptions are more basic than those about time—will produce anxiety and defensiveness (e.g., people's response to the concept of time dilation). Thus time has come to be unconsciously seen as a constant, a firmly and deeply embedded assumption in Western cultures.

My argument in this chapter is based on a different assumption. I believe that time varies and varies tremendously along many dimensions, several of which I will consider later in the chapter. More specifically, I will address the nature of time and reveal several temporal forms. Following a discussion of temporal ontology, I will present polychronicity, temporal focus, and temporal depth as dimensions not just of time, but of organizational culture. I will consider the relationships these dimension have with other dimensions of organizational culture, including their implications for organizational change.

Please note that despite my focus on time and *organizational* culture, temporal studies from other levels of analysis (e.g., individuals, societies) will often enter the discussion, because so few studies have been conducted about time as an organizational culture phenomenon.

## TIME IS A COLLECTIVE NOUN

St. Augustine spoke for his era when he wrote: "What is time then? If nobody asks me, I know: but if I were desirous to explain it to one that should ask me, plainly I know not" (1912, p. 239). And his statement is as cogent today as it was 1,600 years ago. Yet an equally cogent answer can be given to this most fundamental of questions: What is time, then? It is a collective noun. Less cryptically, just as contemporary financial theory describes the organization as a nexus of contracts (Jensen & Meckling, 1976), time is a nexus of temporalities, a concept that Fraser (1975) developed into a model of temporal ontology.

Fraser (1975, p. 436) proposed an explanation of time in which time's meaning varies as a function of the level of existence. In his original formulation, he identified six "semiautonomous levels of nature": electromagnetic radiation (e.g., the universe at the time of the "big bang"), indistinguishable particles (the elementary particles of quantum mechanics), ponderable mass (planets and stars), cyclic and aging orders of life (living organisms), individuals' mental functions (the mature human mind), and society's communal functions, which were characterized by the following temporalities, respectively: atemporality, prototemporality, eotemporality, biotemporality, nootemporality, and sociotemporality (for descriptions of these temporalities, see Fraser, 1975, 1978a, 1978b, 1987). Although he identified six levels, his original formulation specified only the characteristics of the temporalities associated with the first five. In his later work, Fraser (e.g., 1978a, 1978b, 1987) developed the sixth temporality, the sociotemporal, but then apparently abandoned it, because a subsequent discussion of the model included only the first five temporalities (Fraser, 1994).

Fraser may have deleted the sociotemporal level from his hierarchy of six nested temporalities because of conceptual difficulties. References to people living and working in societies and "the timing of collective action through synchronization and schedules" and "the creation and maintenance of value systems that guide the conduct of members of a society" (Fraser, 1987, p. 188) are on solid social science ground. Societies, organizations, and other social groups do these things. But postulating the conceptual need for "an integrative level that would correspond to the total family of man" (Fraser, 1978a, p. 423) and a "time compact globe . . . in the process of being created" (Fraser, 1987, p. 368) may have added unnecessary restrictions to the definition of sociotemporality. The sociotemporality of a hunting-and-gathering society composed of 100 people is just as real and complete as that of a possible worldwide society. Thus the specification of a humanity-encompassing, time-compact-globe construct seems overly constraining, and this difficulty may have led Fraser to abandon sociotemporality.

Fraser may have abandoned it, but we need not. The discussions of the temporal dimensions of organizational culture that follow are all firmly embedded in such a level, a level that includes the domain of organizational culture.

## DIMENSIONS OF SOCIOTEMPORAL TIME

In this section I will present some of the dimensions along which sociotemporal times may differ. Because so little empirical research has been conducted on time and organizational culture, not every dimension along which times might differ can be covered in depth, and many such dimensions exist. For example, Schriber and Gutek (1987) developed scales to measure 13 temporal dimensions of organizational culture, including punctuality, schedules and deadlines, and work pace. Instead of trying to cover all possible dimensions, I will discuss the cultural dimension, polychronicity, about which a considerable amount of empirical organizational culture research has and is being conducted. This discussion is followed by examinations of temporal focus and temporal depth, cultural dimensions with promise for future organizational culture research.

### Polychronicity

Polychronicity is the set of values and beliefs people hold about organizing and sequencing activities. Hall (1959) introduced the polychronicity concept in his seminal work *The Silent Language*, albeit in a discussion of "monochronism" (pp. 153-155). He presented the polychronicity concept as a continuum anchored by two temporal archetypes: monochronic time, in which people prefer to attend to and do only one thing at a time (Hall, 1983, pp. 45-46); and polychronic time, in which people prefer to be involved in many things at once (Hall, 1983, pp. 45-46). Ambiguities occur in Hall's work about whether polychronicity per se is limited to the how-many-things-at-a-time dimension, or if it is part of a larger construct involving such matters as leadership style, punctuality, and commitment to schedules (Hall, 1976, p. 17; 1983, p. 53; Hall & Hall, 1990, pp. 13-15). His most recent treatment of the matter indicates the more focused meaning: "In the strictest sense, a polychronic culture is a culture in which people value, and hence practice, engaging in several activities and events at the same time. Monochronic cultures are more linear in that people prefer to be engaged in one thing at a time" (Hall, quoted in Bluedorn, 1998a). Most polychronicity researchers (e.g., Bluedorn, Kaufman, & Lane, 1992; Kaufman, Lane, & Lindquist, 1991; Schein, 1992; Slocombe & Bluedorn, 1999; Tinsley, 1998) have followed the more tightly focused conceptualization, as will I in this discussion. Thus polychronicity is the extent to which people (a) prefer to engage in two or more tasks or events simultaneously and (b) believe their preference is the correct way to do things (Bluedorn, Kalliath, Strube, & Martin, 1999). It is a template for behavior that is held largely out of conscious awareness and is often so well institutionalized that it is taken for granted as the only way to do things.

## The Measurement of Polychronicity

Hall used qualitative observation procedures to determine the level of polychronicity displayed by an individual or group. This approach to measurement helped him to develop the concept as well as to characterize several parts of the world (e.g., Northwestern Europe and the United States displayed lower levels of polychronicity than societies in either Latin America or the Mediterranean world; see Hall, 1983). More recently, a psychometric alternative to observational techniques has been developed.

Marketing researchers Kaufman et al. (1991) developed a four-item individual-difference measure of polychronicity, the Polychronic Attitude Index. Using it, they found individual polychronicity negatively correlated with role overload and positively correlated with working more than 40 hours per week, as well as with social group and club membership.

Although Kaufman et al.'s (1991) efforts had been aimed at developing a polychronicity scale as an individual-difference measure, Hall's work dealt with polychronicity primarily as a cultural variable; but Hall, too, has discussed it as a possible individual-difference variable (Bluedorn, 1998a). To argue that polychronicity is either a cultural or an individual-difference variable, but not both, forces one into the absurd situation of having to ignore either the obvious systematic polychronicity differences among cultures or those among individuals. Values and beliefs about the same thing can be parts of both culture and personality, so fatuous arguments about polychronicity being only one or the

other serve no good end: It is both an individual and a cultural variable.

Building on Kaufman et al.'s (1991) work, Bluedorn et al. (1999) conducted a scale-development project in which our goal was to produce a psychometrically sound measure of polychronicity as an organizational culture variable. We gathered data from 13 samples ($N = 2,190$ respondents) and conducted a wide range of reliability and validity tests, all of which strongly supported the scale we were developing (e.g., a median alpha coefficient of .84 over 11 samples). This effort produced the 10-item Inventory of Polychronic Values (IPV), which has facilitated research on polychronicity's relationships with other organizational variables, including other dimensions of organizational culture. (For presentation of the complete IPV and a full account of its development and psychometric properties, see Bluedorn et al., 1999.)

One can modify the IPV to measure an individual's polychronicity values largely by changing the "we's" in its items to "I's," which changes the referent from the respondent's group (e.g., department, organization) to the respondent him- or herself. Recent research on the individual polychronicity values version of the IPV has revealed psychometric properties comparable to those reviewed in this chapter for the culture version (Bluedorn, 1998b).

## Polychronicity and Other Dimensions of Organizational Culture

Earlier, I raised the issue of whether the broader or more focused polychronicity concept should be used to define polychronicity. Although I have adopted the more focused definition, Hall's (e.g., 1983; Hall & Hall, 1990) description of a broader complex is still useful because it specifies other variables to which polychronicity should be related and how it should be related to them. In particular, polychronicity should be negatively correlated with an emphasis on holding to schedules and deadlines and to being on time (punctuality).

Bluedorn et al. (1999) tested these relationships with data from two large hospitals ($N$ = 1,204 respondents). The respondents completed the IPV *and* Schriber and Gutek's (1987) punctuality and schedules-and-deadlines scales about their departments. We created departmental scores for these three variables by calculating the means from each scale for each department, after which the scores were correlated. Consistent with Hall's conclusions, polychronicity was significantly and negatively correlated with both punctuality values ($r = -.22, p < .001, N = 198$ departments) and schedules-and-deadlines values ($r = -.22, p < .001, N = 198$ departments), identical correlations to two decimal places. Hall (1983; Hall & Hall, 1990) also indicated that punctuality and schedules-and-deadlines values should be positively correlated, which they were ($r = .39, p < .001, N = 199$ departments—the slightly different $N$ for the polychronicity correlations is due to missing values). Thus these findings support a nomological net (Cronbach & Meehl, 1955) proposed by Hall. They also support the focused polychronicity concept described earlier and used by most polychronicity researchers (e.g., Kaufman et al., 1991; Onken, 1999; Slocombe & Bluedorn, 1999; Tinsley, 1998), because the correlations' magnitudes (i.e., $r$s of −.22) are not large enough to support combining the three constructs and their measures into a single construct and scale. To do so would create problems of information loss and ambiguity (Carver, 1989). (For a general discussion of the issues involved with developing questionnaire measures of organizational culture, see Ashkanasy, Broadfoot, & Falkus, Chapter 8, this volume.)

In our aforementioned work, Bluedorn et al. (1999) took the approach of measuring dimensions of organizational culture by aggregating individual perceptions of cultural dimensions to calculate group scores on those dimensions. Current methodological thinking supports this approach to measuring group-level phenomena if sufficient agreement about the group property is demonstrated among the group's respondents. Such agreement can be demonstrated statistically by a sufficiently high $r_{wg}$ (James, Demaree, & Wolf, 1984, 1993) or by acceptable results from a within-and-between analysis (George, 1990; George & James, 1993). Other approaches to measuring cultural phenomena, such as direct observation and identifying tangible manifestations of polychronicity or any other organizational culture dimension, would not only be viable measurement alternatives, they could play an important part in a triangulation measurement strategy. And should such a triangulation approach be successful, it would make a powerful case for the assessment of the dimension being measured. Dubinskas's (1988) collection of four ethnographic studies of the temporal aspects of organizational cultures illustrates the utility of qualitative methods for the study of organizational culture's temporal dimensions, as does work by Cotte and Ratneshwar (1999) and Perlow (1997, 1998, 1999), and Conte, Rizzuto, and Steiner's (1999) investigation of polychronicity as an individual-difference variable has approximated the triangulation approach suggested here.

## Polychronicity and Other Organizational Variables

Onken (1999) collected data from 20 telecommunications and publishing companies and used the IPV to measure polychronicity. She administered a questionnaire to multiple respondents in each company, and, after aggregating the responses by company, she found several relationships that extended Bluedorn et al.'s findings. First, polychronicity values correlated significantly and positively ($r = .44, p < .05$) with the extent to which the organizations valued speed as measured by Schriber and Gutek's (1987) pace-of-work scale augmented with two items from their future-orientation-and-quality-versus-speed scale. Second, she found significant positive correlations between polychronicity and two traditional organizational performance indicators—return on assets ($r = .17$, $p < .10$) and return on sales ($r = .20$, $p < .10$)—which indicate a modest direct effect of polychronicity on performance. Thus Onken's research revealed statistically significant relationships between polychronicity and organizational performance as well as between two temporal dimensions of organizational culture: polychronicity and speed values.

### Polychronicity and Individual-Organizational Value Congruence

So far, I have discussed polychronicity primarily as a group-level phenomenon (e.g., department, organization), but polychronicity is also an important individual-difference variable. Because individuals vary in polychronicity, as do cultures, an important issue is the relationship between the two, to wit: What results from congruence between individual and group polychronicity values?

This question is a specific case of a more general question: What consequences obtain from individual-organization value congruence? Research on this more general question indicates that congruence affects a variety of outcomes, including job satisfaction, organizational commitment, and turnover (see, e.g., Chatman, 1991; Meglino, Ravlin, & Adkins, 1989; O'Reilly, Chatman, & Caldwell, 1991). Theoretical support for these findings can be found in a variety of perspectives, but attraction-selection-attrition (ASA) theory (Schneider, 1987; Schneider, Goldstein, & Smith, 1995) seems most direct. According to this theory, individuals search for and are attracted to organizations whose cultures contain values and beliefs similar to their own. In a complementary fashion, organizations are more likely to make job offers to individuals who share the organizations' values. Then,

after a job is accepted, the more congruent the individual's and the organization's values, the more readily the individual will be socialized by the organization and the more likely he or she will be to stay.

Following ASA theory, one would expect more fundamental values and beliefs to have especially important impacts on the attraction-selection-attrition process—even if the individual is not conscious of holding a specific value or belief. Consequently, given my previous argument that polychronicity is a fundamental cultural and individual value, and hence is held below the level of conscious awareness, the effects of congruence between individual and organizational polychronicity values should manifest themselves when this form of congruence is examined by itself rather than having to be part of congruence between larger sets of values.

To investigate the value-congruence question as it applies to polychronicity values, Slocombe and Bluedorn (1999) sent questionnaires to 5% of all living graduates of the College of Business and Public Administration at the University of Missouri–Columbia. We asked respondents to reply to one set of items about their personal polychronicity preferences and values and to a second set of items about the polychronicity behaviors and values they experienced in their work units. These responses allowed us to assess individual–work group polychronicity value congruence in terms of its impacts on several individual outcome variables.

Slocombe and Bluedorn (1999) found statistically significant positive relationships between individual–work unit polychronicity value congruence and (a) perceived fairness of performance evaluations, (b) perceived level of performance evaluation by supervisor and coworkers (how highly respondents believed their supervisors and coworkers evaluated the respondents' work), (c) willingness to exert effort on behalf of the organization, (d) desire to remain a member of the organization, and (e) belief in and acceptance of the organization's goals. The last three of these outcomes are components of organizational commitment (Porter, Steers, Mowday, & Boulian, 1974), a variable with an important and enduring status in organization science. As such, these congruence effects indicate polychronicity has an important impact on individual behavior and outcomes in organizations. Because these results were produced through the use of the analytic procedures specified by Edwards (1994; Edwards & Parry, 1993), greater confidence can be attached to the validity of the findings than if we had employed the analytic methods more commonly used in congruence research.

### A Parallel Process Suggested by the Polychronicity-Similarity Findings

Similar to the findings reported above about the congruence of individual and organizational polychronicity values, Jaques's (1976, 1982) work on the time span of discretion suggests comparable outcomes might occur concerning this time-horizon-like variable because of its fundamental importance. *Time span of discretion* refers to the longest time targeted for the completion of assignments in organizational work roles (Jaques, 1982, p. 130), and Jaques (1976) has observed that levels in organizational hierarchies consistently differentiate themselves by the average time spans of discretion associated with their respective positions. Moreover, individuals of the same age vary in how far into the future they can plan and accomplish activities (Jaques, 1982). Therefore, as with polychronicity value congruence and following ASA theory logic, individuals should be differentially attracted to the level in an organization's hierarchy in direct proportion to the similarity between how far into the future the individuals can plan and accomplish projects and the time span of discretion associated with the hierarchical level's positions. Such differential attraction and retention would likely create and reinforce unique subcultures by hierarchical level within an organization, or at least promote different cultural values and beliefs focused

on matters such as time horizons, one of the key variables associated with the main topics presented in the following section: temporal focus and depth.

## Temporal Focus and Depth

Temporal focus and depth have customarily been so intertwined conceptually that some authors have treated them as a single construct. To emphasize the point that two constructs are involved here, I have chosen labels for them that emphasize both their origins and the differences between them. Moreover, only one aspect of the depth dimension has usually been considered (depth of the future), thereby reinforcing the necessity to draw much-needed attention to its other aspect (depth of the past). Thus I will introduce and discuss each construct separately and with new labels before proposing an integrative model for them.

### Temporal Focus

Kluckhohn and Strodtbeck (1961, pp. 13-15) proposed time orientation as one of five value orientations addressed by all cultures. To them, time orientation refers to the way all societies deal with the "three time problems": conceptions of past, present, and future. They describe these three orientations as a "timeless, traditionless, future-ignoring present" flanked by a realizable future and a past whose traditions are to be either maintained or restored. Following Kluckhohn and Strodtbeck, Maznevski and Peterson (1997) note that past-oriented societies look to tradition and precedent for meaning and use the past to anticipate the future, whereas present-oriented societies try to resolve problems quickly, with little regard for long-term implications, such implications being the primary concern of future-oriented societies.

Hofstede and Bond (1988) identified a similar dimension in their cross-cultural research. They describe "Confucian dynamism" (later labeled *long-term versus short-term orientation;* see Hofstede, 1993, 1997a) as a dimension varying from a future orientation to a past-and-present orientation. An advantage of this dichotomy (future versus past-and-present orientation) over the Kluckhohn and Strodtbeck trichotomy is that it avoids the knotty problem involved in determining the boundaries between the past and the present and between the present and the future. How long is now? is a daunting question, both epistemologically and ontologically.

Even if Confucian dynamism avoids a tricky conceptual difficulty in Kluckhohn and Strodtbeck's (1961) framework, both approaches share two problems. First, many other temporal dimensions exist in addition to a concern with the past, present, or future (e.g., polychronicity, time span of discretion). Second, the past- and future-orientation constructs do not distinguish between the short-term past and future or between the long-term past and future. Yet a culture that emphasizes a 3-month future or past would be different from one that emphasizes a 10-year past or future. For these reasons, I label the degree of emphasis on the past, present, and future as *temporal focus* rather than time or temporal orientation. Calling this construct time or temporal orientation implies that the concern with past, present, and future is all there is to time, which is clearly false, and using the word *focus* more directly indicates that this construct is about the emphasis placed on past, present, and future.

As just described, a past orientation could refer to a cultural orientation that varies according to the amount of the past the culture emphasizes. Similarly, a future orientation can vary regarding the portion of the future a culture emphasizes. And these points are not just hypothetical possibilities. To investigate them, I administered a questionnaire to students at the University of Missouri–Columbia that included several items about how far into different regions of the past ("recently," "a middling time ago," and "a long time ago") and future ("near future," "midterm future," and "long-term future") they

thought about when they considered these temporal realms. After summing the three items in each of these scales as measures of past and future temporal depth, respectively (alpha coefficients .75 and .83, respectively), I correlated each scale with the respondents' scores on Usunier and Valette-Florence's (1994) Orientation Towards the Future and Orientation Towards the Past scales. The correlation between my future temporal depth scale and the Orientation Towards the Future scale was $r = .18$ ($p < .001, N = 480$); it was $r = .07$ ($ns; N = 471$) between my past temporal depth scale and the Orientation Towards the Past scale. This statistically nonsignificant correlation and the other small correlation both indicate that temporal focus and temporal depth are different constructs. Although collected at the individual level of analysis, these data provide empirical support for treating temporal focus and temporal depth as distinct constructs. Consequently, I now turn to a consideration of temporal depth as a construct in its own right.

### Temporal Depth

Most of the literature dealing with temporal depth discusses it under the time-horizon label and focuses almost exclusively on future temporal depth. Using Ebert and Piehl's (1973, p. 35) time-horizon definition as a base, I define temporal depth as the temporal distances into the past and future that an individual typically considers when contemplating events that have happened, may have happened, or may happen. That organizational cultures differ in temporal depth is a point made by Ouchi (1981) in his description of modal Japanese organizational cultures (Theory J) as having longer time horizons than modal American organizational cultures (Theory A).

Unfortunately, Ouchi (1981) is almost alone in his treatment of temporal depth as an important element of organizational culture. One other discussion of temporal depth as an attribute of organizational culture is found in Quinn and McGrath's (1985) work linking future time horizon to the competing values model of organizational culture (Quinn & Rohrbaugh, 1983; Quinn & Spreitzer, 1991). Quinn and McGrath describe rational (rational goal) and developmental (open systems) cultures as being characterized by shorter time horizons than consensual (human relations) and hierarchical (internal process) cultures.

Most of the remaining research on temporal depth has been focused on other properties of the organization and its environment, such as environmental uncertainty, organizational size, and organizational life cycle (Judge & Spitzfaden, 1995). Thus temporal depth, at least future temporal depth, appears to be related to several mainstream organization science variables, but the relationships do not seem to be either consistent or stable (Judge & Spitzfaden, 1995).

*Integrating the Temporal Focus and Depth Constructs*

As already noted, originally the time-orientation construct included what I have called temporal focus and temporal depth. Although I have distinguished these two constructs, it may prove useful to combine them in a new way. Combining the dichotomy from the Confucian dynamism version of temporal focus (past versus present-and-future orientation) with a dichotomization of the temporal depth construct produces the two-by-two diagram in Figure 7.1.

Although it is not my purpose here to develop a new theory based on the temporal typology presented in Figure 7.1, organizations in different cells of this diagram should act differently regarding a wide range of matters, including organizational decision making, strategy formulation, personnel practices, and orientations toward innovation and change. An organization with a shallow past orientation would likely be different from one that tends to look to the deep future. Indeed, Judge and Spitzfaden's (1995)

finding that strategic managers employ portfolios of time horizons suggests that this typology may oversimplify things. Nevertheless, I present it here to emphasize the point that two constructs—temporal focus and temporal depth—are involved, not one.

In the next section, I discuss additional temporal depth studies because of their implications for organizational change, especially changes in organizational culture.

## TEMPORAL DIFFERENTIATION, ENTRAINMENT, AND CHANGE

An axiom of mainstream organization theory is that organizations must use increasing numbers of integrating mechanisms as they differentiate to maintain or enhance their effectiveness (Lawrence & Lorsch, 1967). Lawrence and Lorsch (1967) have described temporal differences as some of the most profound ways in which organizations culturally differentiate themselves internally. This differentiation's source is the organizational

*(continued)*

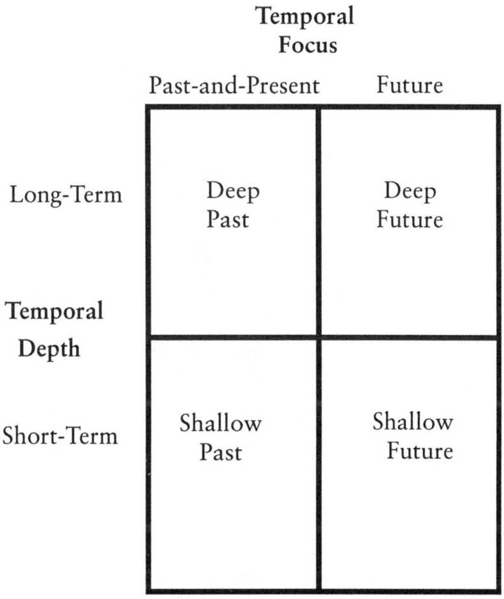

|  | Temporal Focus | |
|---|---|---|
|  | Past-and-Present | Future |
| **Long-Term** | Deep Past | Deep Future |
| **Temporal Depth** | | |
| **Short-Term** | Shallow Past | Shallow Future |

**Figure 7.1.** The Cross-Classification of Temporal Focus With Temporal Depth

units' efforts to align their time horizons with the time span of feedback from their respective environments, the time span of feedback being the time required to learn the results of actions taken by the units. Bluedorn and Denhardt (1988) have interpreted this alignment between time horizons and time spans of feedback as a form of the basic integration process known as entrainment.

Entrainment is the adjustment of the pace or cycle of an activity to match or synchronize with that of another activity (Ancona & Chong, 1996, p. 253); it is a fundamental organizing process across all realms of existence (e.g., Fraser's levels described earlier). Descriptions of how entrainment organizes and coordinates human affairs have been presented by several authors (e.g., Ancona & Chong, 1996; Bluedorn, 1997; Bluedorn & Denhardt, 1988; Gersick, 1994; Hall, 1983; McGrath & Kelly, 1986). Given that entrainment is a temporal phenomenon itself, it is not surprising that it is a fundamental mechanism for achieving the integration required by temporal differentiation (i.e., different temporal foci and depths, varying degrees of polychronicity, and so on).

### Entrainment and Polychronicity

Entrainment may explain Slocombe and Bluedorn's (1999) findings about the correlates of individual–work group polychronicity value congruence. Polychronicity concerns preferences for ways of sequencing activities. As described earlier, Slocombe and Bluedorn found that as individual and work-unit similarity regarding these preferences increased, several positive outcomes seemed to follow (e.g., greater levels of organizational commitment). When increasing similarity involves preferences for activity patterns, it is only a small step to suggest that these patterns are aligned, or at least more aligned than when preferences are less similar. The importance of such alignment, and of activity patterns, is revealed in research showing that even when work results are of objectively equal quality, the activity schedules followed

to produce them affect the evaluation of the work's quality (Persing, 1991). Similarly, an entrainment interpretation of Slocombe and Bluedorn's results indicates that people may respond more favorably to work situations in which the sequence of activities more closely approximates their own preferred modes of sequencing tasks and activities. This may be why Hall (1983) has said of the two archetypes that anchor the polychronicity continuum, "Like oil and water, they don't mix" (pp. 45-46). They don't mix because as polychronicity values diverge, they become harder and harder to align, harder and harder to entrain.

### Entrainment and Temporal Depth

As described earlier, Lawrence and Lorsch (1967) discovered that organizational subunits aligned their future temporal depths with the time span of feedback provided by their environments, meaning the cycles of subunits' activities became linked to the cycles of information produced by their environments, which suggests the environment is a determinant of differentiation by temporal depth across an organization's units. But an organization's or department's environment may not be the sole entraining force—history seems to matter as well.

Most research conducted on organizational temporal depth has focused on *future* temporal depth—with three notable exceptions. The first is Larwood, Falbe, Kriger, and Meising's (1995) research on managerial vision, in which they found a statistically significant positive correlation between future and past temporal depth: The longer the past depth, the longer the future depth. The second study, conducted by O'Connor (1998), focused on the role of narrative in strategic management and revealed a link between perceptions of an organization's past and anticipations of its future. In one case study, the organization attempted to cope with the unknown future by searching for guidance in the company's origins, especially the origins of the qualities and attributes that made the firm unique. Thus a function served by memories of an organization's past may be to help it cope with the uncertainties inherent with movement into the temporal frontier represented by its future. And the longer the organization's past, the larger the database from which its members can extrapolate and project into the future. In the third study to consider both past and future depths, El Sawy's (1983) provocative results are not only consistent with this interpretation and Larwood et al.'s and O'Connor's findings, but, as I will discuss in the next subsection, they suggest a method for changing the temporal depths in an organization's culture, albeit perhaps only temporarily.

## Change

The attempt to move an organization's culture, even a department's culture, to a new value or belief is one of the greatest challenges facing any manager, and the temporal dimensions of culture may be the hardest to change of all, because they are some of any culture's most fundamental values and beliefs. Their intractability is revealed by the abject failure of attempts by both Republican France and Soviet Russia to radically change the definition of the week (Zerubavel, 1985). The failure of two such regimes that applied hideous force to promote their ends demonstrates well the self-maintenance power of culture's temporal dimensions.

Even so, the findings from two studies suggest ways to facilitate such culture change efforts. The first of these studies is El Sawy's (1983) aforementioned research. El Sawy conducted an experiment with bank CEOs and found that the CEOs who were first asked to think about the past before considering the future in a planning scenario thought farther into the future, about 4 years farther, than the CEOs who did not first think about the past. On a geological or cosmic time scale, 4 years is not long, but in contemporary North American human affairs, it is long enough to shift from the boundary of the short term to the threshold of the long term.

Indeed, an intriguing extension of this research would be experimental manipulations of the length of time into the past the participants were asked to think about before working on the planning scenario, to see if longer times into the past would generate concomitantly longer future depths in the planning scenario, as both Larwood et al.'s (1995) positive correlation and El Sawy's initial findings suggest. If these positive correlations between past and future time horizons can be replicated in other research, a reasonable interpretation can be made in terms of entrainment: Organizations entrain their future temporal depths with their past temporal depths. They may not entrain their temporal depths with the exact precision of a clock or calendar metric, but they may do so in at least the ordinal sense that the longer the past depth, the longer the depth of the future. Thus entrainment may serve as a mechanism that not only integrates individuals to organizations, but likely helps integrate the temporal dimensions of organizational culture, too.

The relationship between past and future temporal depths suggests ways to alter the latter. Research on polychronicity also reveals a relationship with change. In my own work, I administered an individual-difference version of the IPV and Trumbo's (1961) Orientation Toward Change at Work scale to two large samples of undergraduate students at the University of Missouri–Columbia (Bluedorn, 1998c). In both samples, I found statistically significant positive correlations ($rs$ between .30 and .40) between polychronicity and change orientation: The more polychronic respondents were more positively oriented toward change. Although these data were from the individual level of analysis, they suggest that as organizations become more polychronic, they become more susceptible to change. These findings suggest this relationship for at least two reasons. First, Das's (1986) work reveals that individuals will tend to use their own temporal depths on behalf of their employing organizations (i.e., the longer the individual's temporal depth, the longer the temporal depth he or she will employ on behalf of the organization). If this holds true for other values, polychronic individuals will try to behave more polychronically in organizations, and, given the positive correlation between polychronicity and change orientation, they will also be more receptive to organizational change in many areas, including culture change.

A second reason is more theoretically based, coming from Schneider's (1987) previously discussed ASA theory. If, as the theory argues, individuals and organizations with similar values will attract each other and over the long run organizations will reflect the values held by their members, polychronic organizations will attract and hire more polychronic members, members who are also more positively inclined toward change. Hence the organizations will become more receptive to change as well.

## CONCLUSION

As I have discussed, the nature of time varies by the level of existence (Fraser's hierarchy of temporalities). In this chapter, I have presented several temporal dimensions of organizational culture within the sociotemporal level, three of which—polychronicity, temporal focus, and temporal depth—I have discussed at length because they have been investigated as attributes of organizational culture or show the potential for being used to address meaningful questions in future organizational culture research.

The selection of the topics covered in this chapter should not be taken to imply that these are the only potentially important temporal topics for the study of organizational culture (see, e.g., the 13 dimensions identified by Schriber and Gutek, 1987; see also the work by Levine, such as Levine & Bartlett, 1984; Levine, Lynch, Miyake, & Lucia, 1989, which suggests that the pace-of-work dimension may have important implications for employee health). However, in the contemporary study of organizational culture, time has seldom even been mentioned as a potential topic of investigation (major exceptions being the work of Bluedorn & Denhardt, 1988; Bluedorn et al., 1999; Dubinskas, 1988; Ouchi, 1981; Schein, 1992; Schriber & Gutek, 1987), so it is important to explain what time is and why it has been ignored. And if time has not even been mentioned in much of the organizational culture literature, obviously it has rarely been studied as an organizational culture phenomenon. So it is important to discuss the three temporal dimensions—polychronicity, temporal focus, and temporal depth—that have been the topic of most time-focused organizational culture research.

It is my hope that this chapter has revealed the potential of time and temporal variables for expanding our understanding of organizations, their cultures, and behavior within them. The task of future research is to expand upon the nascent findings reported here and to explore other temporal variables and relationships. Without such developments, our knowledge of organizational culture will be incomplete; there will be an important lacuna in our understanding. We are thus provided with an imperative to study the temporal aspects of organizations. And if not now, when?

# Measurement and Outcomes of Organizational Culture and Climate

A recurrent theme of this *Handbook* is that organizational culture and climate are conceptually and empirically closer than had previously been assumed. In particular, in order for the culture and climate constructs to represent real phenomena, it is axiomatic that there must be both a means to measure them and discernible outcomes. The chapters in Part II deal with these issues from a variety of perspectives, but nonetheless can be characterized as lying at the quantitative end of the methodological spectrum.

The part opens with three contributions on measurement of organizational culture and climate. In Chapter 8, Ashkanasy, Broadfoot, and Falkus review the development of questionnaire-based measures of culture, based on Schein's levels of culture. They then describe how they assembled a multidimensional measure that they call the Organizational Culture Profile and discuss the difficulties they encountered in validating the new instrument. They conclude by noting that questionnaires have a role to play in culture research, especially when complemented by other qualitative date. In Chapter 9, Cooke and Szumal review the well-known Organizational Culture Inventory and demonstrate how the use of a questionnaire measure can lead to useful insights into key facets of organizational functioning. In the third chapter in this group, Payne addresses directly the overlap between measures of organizational culture and climate. He shows how a questionnaire measure of "cultural intensity" can be used with the collaboration of organizational members to reflect cultural integration and fragmentation. As such, he concludes that "climate is . . . not as different from [culture] as I once thought."

The next two chapters in Part II relate to the outcomes of organizational culture and climate. In Chapter 11, Wiley and Brooks detail how measures of organizational climate can be employed to gain important insights into high-performing organizations. They describe the linkage research model and, based on this model, extensively review published accounts linking culture measures to indicators of organizational effectiveness and performance. In Chapter 12, Wilderom, Glunk, and Maslowski examine more directly the issue of the nexus between culture and organizational performance. They provide an extensive and critical review of the extant literature and conclude that problems of inconsistent and often unreliable measurement continue to cloud the picture in this important area of research.

In this part's final chapter, Kilduff and Corley provide a fresh alternative view of culture measurement and performance by drawing upon the developing literature based on social network theory. The social network approach is a quantitative procedure, but it is different from the other quantitative approaches described in Part II, focusing on the network of relationships that exist between organizational members. Kilduff and Corley review the social network literature and identify a range of central dimensions that are likely to impinge on cultural issues. Although untested to date, their approach suggests a new and potentially valuable approach to measuring organizational culture.

In summary, the six chapters in Part II provide a fairly comprehensive overview of quantitative approaches to the measurement and assessment of organizational culture and climate. As we have noted in our introduction to this volume, the distinction between climate and culture, once seen as conceptually and empirically clear, is no longer clear-cut. Although we still have a long way to go before we really understand how culture and climate are reflected in organizational outcomes, the chapters in this section provide background and ideas that we hope will encourage and facilitate further research in this important area of organization science.

# 8

# Questionnaire Measures of Organizational Culture

–– *Neal M. Ashkanasy, Lyndelle E. Broadfoot, and Sarah Falkus*

Although the concept of organizational culture has been prominent in organizational and management literature since the 1970s (Barley, Meyer, & Gash, 1988), scholars still disagree on the best way to measure it (see O'Reilly, Chatman, & Caldwell, 1991; Rousseau, 1990a). Some writers have suggested the use of multiple methods (e.g., Martin, 1992; Rousseau, 1990a), but these methods are often complex, expensive, and time-consuming. What is borne out by the literature, nonetheless, is that questionnaires can play an important role in the quantitative analysis of organizational culture (Reichers & Schneider, 1990; Rousseau, 1990a).

In this chapter, therefore, we address questionnaire measures used in the assessment of organizational culture. We present our discussion in two major sections. In the first, we explore the role of quantitative measurement in cultural research and the level of cultural understanding that may be allowed by such measures. We also present a typology for the classification of culture questionnaires that draws on Schein's (1985) three-level model of culture. We use this typology to facilitate a review of the literature in the area, including an examination of specific questionnaire measures. In the second main section of the chapter, we discuss issues concerning the validation of multidimensional descriptive measures of organizational culture. This discussion is based on our own research experiences in the early stages of development of the Organizational Culture Profile (OCP). Our intention is not to present a technical case for the validity of the OCP; rather, we utilize the development process we experienced as a vehicle to illustrate the difficulties researchers face in developing and validating organizational culture questionnaires. Finally, and based on this discussion, we suggest key issues to be addressed in future research.

## A REVIEW OF ORGANIZATIONAL CULTURE SURVEYS

As Meek (1988) argues, organizational culture is an all-encompassing concept that needs to be broken into manageable proportions for study. To facilitate this, we have adopted Schein's (1985) three-level typology as a framework for categorizing the different perspectives of organizational culture. In Schein's view, culture derives from an underlying pattern of assumptions that members of an organization come to share as a result of common experiences in their working life. These assumptions, in turn, are reflected in and give meaning to expressed values and observable artifacts and patterns of behavior (see also Sathe, 1985a).

Grundy and Rousseau (1994) make the point, however, that Schein's (1985) model of culture implies a complex, multilevel phenomenon that can be construed in many different ways. In light of this complexity, we agree with Marcoulides and Heck's (1993) view that delineation of culture's parameters must start with a realistic admission of its limitations. Given the focus of this chapter on quantitative measurement of culture, we are necessarily limited to observable and measurable manifestations of culture as represented by the shallower levels of Schein's typology. Another way of explaining the limits of a quantitative study of organizational culture is provided by Smircich's (1983) distinction between two facets of organizational culture: as something an organization *has* and as something an organization *is*. The limit of our definition is therefore to view culture as something that an organization has.

A further implication of this line of reasoning is that each of Schein's (1985) levels of culture is amenable to a different research method. Thus, according to Rousseau (1990a), the appropriate means of assessment depends on the cultural level to be examined. The shallower layers of culture are more explicit and can be appropriately studied using a structured and quantitative approach (Ott, 1989; Rousseau, 1990a).

## The Role of Quantitative Measurement

Because quantitative assessment of organizational culture is limited to the more observable and accessible levels of culture, it is important that we state at the outset of this chapter why a measurement perspective is worthwhile. In the first instance, scholars such as Martin (1992) have noted that quantitative assessment of organizational culture has been criticized in the past because of a strong monomethod bias in the field. The emphasis on higher abstractions of organizational culture, coupled with researchers' perceiving "either/or" choices among methods, has led to the use of qualitative methods nearly to the exclusion of quantitative techniques. In Martin's view, such monomethod approaches are too naive. Although Martin argues for a need to include qualitative data in culture studies, the essence of her case is that there is a need for a multilevel and multimethod conceptualization. In this respect, Schein's (1985) three-level typology provides a distinctive role for both quantitative and qualitative measurement. Further, as the elements of culture become more conscious and observable to participants in a study, they become more accessible to standardized assessment (Rousseau, 1990a). For example, it is generally agreed that surveys represent an efficient and standardized means of tapping the shallower levels of Schein's typology. The deepest level of culture, on the other hand, can be investigated only through more intensive observation, focused interviews, and the involvement of organizational members in self-analysis (Ott, 1989; Rousseau, 1990a; Schein, 1990). The thrust of this argument is that there is a clear and continuing role for quantitative measures as a means of assessing the less abstract levels of organizational culture.

An alternative view, however, is that the usefulness of quantitative measurement may not be definitively restricted to the shallower levels of organizational culture. Instead, as Deal and Kennedy (1982) have argued, there may be grounds for maintaining that the three levels of culture are unified, especially when a culture is strong. In this case, quantitative measurement of organizational culture may have the potential to tap deeper levels of culture (see also Ott, 1989; Rentsch, 1990). It has even been posited that organizational culture may be rooted in perceived practices rather than values (Hofstede, Neuijen, Ohayv, & Sanders, 1990), and therefore offer a window into the operating environments of organizations. Although this conclusion may be caused by the relatedness of practices and the values they reflect (Neuijen, 1992), such questions serve to emphasize further the potential of quantitative measures to increase our understanding of organizational culture.

Finally, we note that survey methods have characteristics that render them especially useful for organizational culture research. As we have noted above, self-report surveys allow respondents to record their own perceptions of reality. Because behavior and attitudes are determined not by objective reality but by actors' perceptions of reality (Rentsch, 1990), it is clearly appropriate to focus on perceptions rather than on reality. Further, from an organizational development point of view, self-report measures offer internal credibility to organizational members, which is likely to increase the likelihood that members will accept the results of the survey. Researchers have cited numerous other advantages of survey assessment and of quantitative techniques generally. These include allowing replication and cross-sectional comparative studies, providing an accepted frame of reference for interpreting data, helping the evaluation and initiation of culture change efforts in organizations, and provid-

ing data that can be analyzed through multivariate statistical techniques (see Cooke & Rousseau, 1988; Xenikou & Furnham, 1996).

## Classification of Survey Measures of Organizational Culture

Having considered the role of quantitative culture measurement and construct issues, we now turn our consideration to the nature of published questionnaire measures of culture. The interest in organizational culture noted by Barley et al. (1988) has given rise to a variety of questionnaires designed to assess the phenomenon, and even the most cursory of comparisons reveals that there are significant differences among them. What a number of authors have found to be particularly unfortunate is the lack of consensus concerning questionnaire format or style (see Frost, Moore, Louis, Lundberg, & Martin, 1991; Furnham, 1997; Ott, 1989; Rousseau, 1990a). We find also that the lack of a theoretical basis for many of these instruments is further cause for concern on the part of cultural researchers and practitioners. Wilderom, Glunk, and Maslowski (Chapter 12, this volume) comment on the difficulties this problem has created for assessment of the impacts of culture on organizational effectiveness and performance.

In this chapter, therefore, we seek to compare a diverse range of questionnaires by presenting a new typology for the classification of culture measures. In conducting the research described in the second major section of this chapter (Broadfoot & Ashkanasy, 1994), we reviewed a wide range of organizational culture surveys and sought to present them in a consistent framework that would allow for comparison. In doing so, we determined that surveys can be classified as either *typing* or *profile* scales, with three subcategories of profile scales (see Figure 8.1). Typing surveys are those that classify organizations into particular taxonomies. Profile surveys

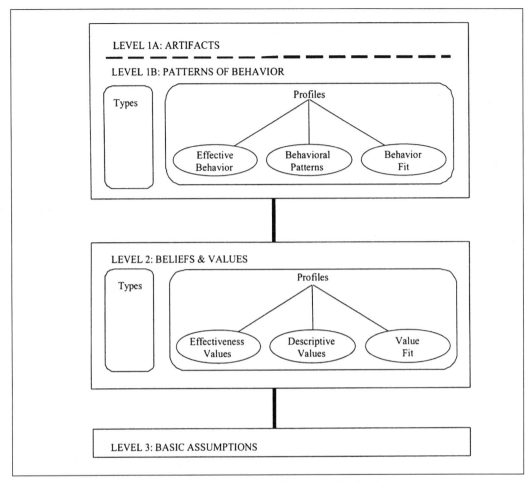

**Figure 8.1.** Quantitative Instruments Operating at Different Levels of Culture

are concerned primarily with the description of an organization's culture. A brief overview of each type follows.

*Typing surveys.* Typing surveys are those that use standardized instruments to yield discrete sets of organizational culture "types." Usually, the types are accompanied by detailed descriptions of behaviors and values associated with them (e.g., Margerison, 1979; Myers-Briggs, 1980). Thus typing allows respondents to understand the consequences of their type-category membership and also to compare their types with others (see Myers-Briggs). The work of Cooke and Rousseau (1988), for example, suggests that

typing can help managers to articulate their visions of change, expressing them in terms of behaviors needed from organization members. The use of typing also is beneficial for tracking the process of cultural change in organizations (see Ashkanasy & Holmes, 1995).

In summary, then, typing surveys identify organizations as belonging to one of several possible mutually exclusive categories. The typing approach is subject to three limitations, however. The first of these is an implication that all organizations of a particular type are similar, or should be similar, neglecting the unique nature of cultures (Schein, 1985). The second limitation is that typing implies discontinuous categories, something that is difficult to sustain on theoretical grounds (Rousseau, 1990a). The third limitation is that not all organizations necessarily conform to particular types, whereas others appear to be mixtures of types (Deal & Kennedy, 1982).

*Profiling surveys.* Profiling surveys are concerned with giving descriptions of organizations by measuring the strengths or weaknesses of a variety of organizational members' beliefs and values. The different scores on several culture dimensions, generated by the varying outcomes for different beliefs and values, provide a profile of an organization's culture. Profiling surveys differ from typing surveys in that they categorize organizations in terms of multiple categories of norms, behaviors, and values or beliefs that are not necessarily mutually exclusive.

Profiling surveys can be further divided into three subcategories: effectiveness surveys, descriptive surveys, and fit profiles. Effectiveness surveying is the most prevalent approach, assessing the values that are thought to produce cultures associated with high levels of organizational effectiveness and performance. Descriptive instruments measure values, but no evaluation of an organization's effectiveness is made on this basis. Fit profiles look at the congruence between individuals and the organization. The three approaches are based on a common notion that important characteristics of organizational culture can be viewed as properties comprising distinct variables that reflect measurable dimensions (Likert, 1967; Schein, 1990).

## Literature Review and Comparison of Survey Measures

Two of our primary purposes in this chapter are to provide a summary of the literature in the area of survey measurement and to discuss a representative sample of culture measures. The typology that we suggest constitutes one approach to classification. In Table 8.1, we classify 18 instruments published over the period 1975 through 1992. The sample of measures listed in Table 8.1 is by no means exhaustive. Our intention is only to illustrate the different approaches that can be taken. Surprisingly, a search of the literature revealed that little significant development of new survey measures has taken place since 1992. A notable exception is the GLOBE instrument developed for a major cross-national study of organizational culture and leadership (see Dickson, Aditya, & Chhokar, Chapter 28, this volume). At the time of this writing, however, the GLOBE survey was still in a developmental stage. We believe that the 18 measures we have selected constitute a representative sample of the population of organizational culture instruments. In addition to categorization, Table 8.1 shows for each scale the level of culture addressed and the number of dimensions measured, as well as format, validity, and reliability. This selection of parameters is similar to those examined by Rousseau (1990a).

The instruments included in Table 8.1 represent the work of both academic researchers and consultants. They were published over an 18-year period and were reported in academic journals and popular books. The levels of culture at which they are targeted vary from behaviors to beliefs and values. The instruments vary in format, although most use Likert-style response scales. In terms of validity and reliability, however, only the instruments offered by Cooke and Lafferty (1986) and O'Reilly et al. (1991) have been reported as reliable and possessing consensual, construct, and criterion validity. Finally, although we can describe the nature of the instruments, our pivotal interest is in the level of culture that each measure taps. This requires that we look briefly at the theoretical basis of each to differentiate among them according to the level of culture each aims to assess. Instruments operating at each level measure culture in different ways, leading to differing understandings of organizational cultures.

**TABLE 8.1** Summary of the Organizational Culture Instruments in the Derivation of the OCP

| Author | Year | Level[a] | Dimensions | Type | Format | Reliability | Consensual Validity | Construct Validity | Criterion Validity |
|---|---|---|---|---|---|---|---|---|---|
| Allen & Dyer | 1980 | 1 | 7 | behavior[b] | Likert | | | X | X |
| Kilmann & Saxton | 1983 | 1 | 4 | behavior[b] | paired | X | | X | X |
| Cooke & Lafferty | 1986 | 1 | 12 | behavior[b] | Likert | X | X | X | X |
| Harrison | 1975 | 1/2 | 15 | typing | rank | | | | |
| Handy | 1979 | 2 | 9 | typing | rank | | | | |
| Margerison | 1979 | 2 | 24 | typing | Likert | | | | |
| Organization Technology International | 1979 | 2 | 5 | descriptive | Likert | | | | |
| Glaser | 1983 | 2 | 4 | typing | Likert | | | | |
| Harris & Moran | 1984 | 2 | 7 | effectiveness | Likert | | | | |
| Sashkin & Fulmer | 1985 | 2 | 10 | effectiveness | Likert | | X | | |
| Enz | 1986 | 2 | 22 | fit | Likert | X | | X | X |
| Reynolds | 1986 | 2 | 14 | descriptive | Likert | X | | | X |
| O'Reilly et al. | 1991 | 2 | 24 | fit | Q-sort | X | X | X | X |
| Woodcock | 1989 | 2 | 12 | effectiveness | Likert | | | | |
| Hofstede et al. | 1990 | 2 | NA | descriptive | Likert | | | | |
| Lessem | 1990 | 2 | 7 | typing | rank | | | | |
| PA Consulting Group | 1991 | 2 | NA | descriptive | Likert | | | | |
| Migliore et al. | 1992 | 2 | 20 | descriptive | Likert | | X | | |

SOURCE: Based on Broadfoot and Ashkanasy (1994).

## Instruments Measuring Patterns of Behavior

Of the 18 instruments in Table 8.1, 3 focus on the first level of Schein's (1985) typology, patterns of behavior, although it may be more accurate to say that they focus on either patterns of behavior or the *norms* for these patterns. Allen and Dyer's (1980) Norm Diagnostic Index (NDI) is the earliest instrument in the set. The NDI consists of a collection of dimensions along which an organization can be described in terms of the behaviors of its members (Rousseau, 1990a). The NDI is a profile and therefore does not have an integrative framework to link its elements together. The other instruments in this set, developed by Kilmann and Saxton (1983) and Cooke and Lafferty (1986), are based on two bipolar dimensions. The first dimension, common to both instruments, is a focus on people versus task. The second dimension is also common, but it has been given two different labels. It represents the degree to which people are encouraged to avoid conflict and to protect themselves versus being innovative and risk taking (Rousseau, 1990a). Kilmann and Saxton refer to this as a short-term versus long-term focus, whereas Cooke and Lafferty describe a similar dimension as security versus satisfaction. The two instruments also vary in their application. The Cooke and Lafferty measure, for example, can be applied as a typing or as a profiling instrument (Cooke & Rousseau, 1988; see also Schein, 1990).

## Instruments Measuring Values and Beliefs

The remaining 15 of the organizational culture instruments listed in Table 8.1 address Schein's (1985) second level of organizational culture: beliefs and values. These instruments capture the espoused beliefs and values of an organization's members (Ott,

1989). We discuss the typing and profiling categories separately below.

### Typing Instruments

The earliest of the typing instruments in the set is that developed by Harrison (1975), who describes his instrument as a measure of "organizational ideology" (see also Harrison, 1979; Saunders, 1984), defined as systems of thought that are the central determinants of the character of the organization. Harrison describes four types of organizational ideology: power, role, task, and self. Harrison's work was developed further by Handy (1979), who conceptualized the four ideologies as elements of organizational culture in line with Schein's (1985) definition. Handy uses metaphors based on the Greek gods to symbolize organizational culture, an idea he attributes to Harrison. Although popularly successful, Handy's version differs little from Harrison's original.

Margerison (1979) introduced a different typology instrument to aid in the assessment of organizations based on three types: bureaucratic, innovative, and supportive. Margerison conceptualized these three key areas as operating on two dimensions: bureaucratic versus innovative and low versus high supportiveness. According to Margerison, a culture is effective if it reinforces an organization's purposes and strategies.

The third typing instrument, developed by Glaser (1983), is based on the work of Deal and Kennedy (1982), who conducted a review of hundreds of corporations and found that they fell into four general categories or types of cultures. These categories are determined by two factors: the level of risk and the time taken to receive feedback on success. They include a "process" culture type and a "bet your company" culture type. It is worth noting here that Deal and Kennedy point out that organizations in reality may conform to a mixture of types, although they still advocate typing as a means to aid managers' understanding of the nature of their organizations.

Lessem's (1990) is the most recent of the typing instruments in the set. Lessem conceptualized four culture types as being defined by four dimensions for both performance and aspirations: primal, rational, developmental, and metaphysical. According to Lessem, organizations either strongly or weakly fit within each type. Aspirations and performance are designed to measure the extent to which the organization aspires to and actually carries out its goals.

It is difficult to compare the instruments in the typing group because they are based on distinct theoretical frameworks that may have only a tenuous basis in mainstream organizational culture research (e.g., Handy, 1979). A further problem is that the typing can be ambiguous. Harrison (1979), for example, notes that although organizations have a dominant type, they can also manifest characteristics of more than one type. Also, because there is a lack of independence among the scales being measured in typing surveys, such measures violate the assumptions of most statistical tests and therefore present problems for the establishment of reliability and validity. Nonetheless, typing is advocated primarily because it provides a global description for organizational members of what the culture of the organization is like. Typing is also beneficial for tracking the process of cultural change in the organization (Ashkanasy & Holmes, 1995; Deal & Kennedy, 1982).

### Profiling Instruments

The second type of survey at the level of values comprises profiling instruments. These measure a variety of beliefs and values, resulting in separate scores on a number of dimensions. The instruments also vary in the extent to which the items are explicitly tested. As noted earlier, profiling surveys can be further divided into subgroups: descriptive values, effectiveness values, and value fit.

We define and discuss each of these categories below.

*Descriptive profiling instruments.* The descriptive profiling group comprises those instruments that measure values but do not attempt to attach any significance to those results. Instruments in this group are differentiated from those in the effectiveness profiling group in that they do not imply any evaluation of the organization's effectiveness. The descriptive value profile provides a picture of the intensity with which each value is held by organizational members. According to Margerison (1979), in most consulting applications the scores are fed back to the members, who are invited to discuss the results and to attribute meaning to the scores. Margerison notes further that a primary benefit of the survey-feedback approach is obtained through the organizational members' discussion and interpretation of the results.

The earliest instrument in the set is the Management Value Inventory (Organization Technology International, 1979). In essence, the focus of this survey is on dichotomous dimensions described as task versus social and security versus risk (similar to the Level 1 instruments described earlier). The profiling instrument developed by Reynolds (1986) has similarities to the Management Value Inventory, but it describes culture in terms of affective and expressive dimensions.

The descriptive values instrument developed by PA Consulting Group (1991), which designed it for use in an Australian organization, is an example of a typical consulting organizational culture survey. The emphasis in this instrument is on the environment and the extent to which the organization is client focused. The instrument developed by Migliore, Conway, Martin, and Stevens (1991) is interesting in that it explicitly incorporates a strategic planning dimension. Migliore et al. justify the inclusion of this dimension by describing it as reflecting underlying assumptions and therefore indicative of the key force behind decision-making processes in the organization.

Geert Hofstede's (1980a; Hofstede et al., 1990) continuing research in the area of cross-cultural manifestations also uses a descriptive values instrument. Cross-cultural research aims to examine the relative strengths of organizational and national culture (Triandis, 1994). For the purposes of Hofstede's research, however, the objective was not to determine which of the cultures is the most effective, because this assumes that the culture of one country can be more effective than that of another. Finally, it should be noted that this measure is distinct from the well-known scale employed by Hofstede (1980a) in his cross-national study of values in the IBM Corporation (see Hofstede & Peterson, Chapter 25, this volume).

*Effectiveness profiling instruments.* The focus of the second group of profiling instruments is on the values that the organization needs to be effective. According to Gordon and DiTomaso (1992), most empirical research has attempted to relate culture to organizational outcomes through an effectiveness trait approach, described by Saffold (1988) as a focus on values that are thought to produce a "strong" culture. Others, such as Kotter and Heskett (1992), Schein (1985), and Weick (1985), however, have disputed the idea that more or stronger culture is necessarily better; they argue that the relationship is contingent on environmental factors. Nonetheless, the effectiveness profiles still constitute a major category of organizational culture measures.

Harris and Moran's (1984) survey is our first example of an effectiveness profiling approach. The instrument focuses on the effectiveness of managers and the organization, including leadership and communication. These dimensions are proposed to influence the extent to which the leaders are effective and the organization is successful. Sashkin and Fulmer's (1985) instrument is another example of the effectiveness approach. Sashkin and Fulmer describe the values they measure as those that must be present for the work to get done. These values include attending to people, managing "hands-on," and believing in common organizational philosophy. The final effectiveness profiling scale was developed by Woodcock (1989) and focuses on actions required by management to achieve organizational success. In this instance, strongly held values are seen to be essential to organizational effectiveness.

*Fit profiling instruments.* The third subset of value profiles are those that look at "fit." The theory underlying this approach is that the extent of congruence between values held by the organizational members and management determines organizational effectiveness (O'Reilly et al., 1991; Weber, 1996; see also Weber, Chapter 19, this volume).

The instrument developed by Enz (1986) was the first to focus on this congruence between the organization and the individual. Enz claims in particular that the perceived congruence between the individual and the organization affects both employee and management behavior. This notion has been developed further by O'Reilly and his associates (1991), who found support for the usage of a fit approach in organizational culture research. Rousseau (1990a) describes the O'Reilly et al. instrument as the most popular at the time he was writing, although this is debatable. Nevertheless, the instrument has been demonstrated to have both reliability and validity, and it has also proved useful as a descriptive profile (see, e.g., Windsor & Ashkanasy, 1996).

## Summary

Our purpose in this discussion has not been to provide an in-depth theoretical analysis of each of the measures. Clearly, such an exercise is beyond the scope of this chapter. Instead, we have focused on some of the key dimensions and concepts that are purported to underlie each scale. In particular, we have illustrated the diversity of conceptual approaches that have been employed. We have also provided a useful taxonomy of the instruments based on the levels of their application and the purposes for which they are intended (see Figure 8.1). We have divided the instruments into those that focus on patterns of behavior and those that measure values and beliefs, and have further categorized them into typing and profiling instruments. Typing instruments provide global descriptions of organizations in terms of ostensibly mutually exclusive categories, whereas profiling instruments focus on specific organizational variables that are not mutually exclusive. We have further subdivided the profiling instruments into three subcategories: descriptive, effectiveness, and fit profiles. Descriptive value profiles do not prescribe the type of culture an organization should possess, whereas effectiveness and fit profiles do.

In the next section, we discuss the problems we encountered in the early stages of trying to validate a multidimensional descriptive profile instrument. This case serves to illustrate the issues that need to be addressed in the development of a valid and reliable instrument.

## VALIDATING A NEW MEASURE
## OF ORGANIZATIONAL CULTURE

In the following discussion, we draw primarily on our own experiences during the development of the Organizational Culture Profile. The OCP is a quantitative, descriptive profiling questionnaire that was designed to measure 10 dimensions of organizational culture in terms of patters of behavior and behavioral norms. It was specifically intended to answer the call for greater focus on empirical and theoretical validation of quantitative measures of organizational culture (Broadfoot & Ashkanasy, 1994; Kopelman, Brief, & Guzzo, 1990). Given the issues raised by the measures reviewed above, it should be instructive now to consider the difficulties that we encountered in the early stages of development and validation of the OCP. In particular, we focus on the concep-

tual issues that arose in this process and suggest lessons for future research in this field.

### The Organizational
### Culture Profile

The development of the OCP was motivated by the literature review discussed above, which revealed a variety of often conflicting theoretical positions and a lack of empirical support for many of the measures of organizational culture. In the original development of the OCP, we sought to create a valid tool that would be reflective of the emerging research perspectives on culture. Our aim was to overcome the problem of which dimensions to include in a measure of organizational culture by deriving the dimensions directly from those being used in the organizational culture literature. In particular, by surveying the literature to identify the main theoretical dimensions that have emerged across many studies, we hoped to tap into the collective knowledge base of scholars working in this field. We saw this as a novel and comprehensive way of addressing the problem of defining which dimensions to include in a questionnaire, and one that would avoid researcher bias or theoretical preference. This approach also ensured that the maximum item pool was generated for the derivation of the dimensions.

The 18 surveys reviewed in the first section of this chapter formed the basis of the OCP. Our selection built upon the summary of 7 surveys undertaken by Rousseau (1990a), although we elected also to include some practitioner surveys. Rousseau had excluded practitioner instruments on the grounds that they lack supporting validity research. This argument, however, falls down because so many of the academic instruments were equally bereft of research. Indeed, instruments preferred by practitioners may be better able to convey meaning to management than to academics. Support for this approach comes from Barley and his colleagues (1988), who found that academics often lag behind practitioners in their use and conceptualization of organizational culture (see also Xenikou & Furnham, 1996).

To determine the dimensions for this new measure, we listed all the dimensions used in the 18 surveys and derived 15 underlying themes. We calculated the total number of items in each and then reclassified those with low numbers. This process led to the 10 summary dimensions, representative of the major dimensional categories we identified in organizational culture literature. We then chose 41 items from this list to represent the 10 dimensions, with selection based on generality, discriminability, readability, and nonredundancy (O'Reilly et al., 1991). Where appropriate, we modified the items to ensure consistency of expression within the scale. We adapted a further 9 items specifi-

cally for the OCP to deal with concepts addressed in past surveys but not covered by a single item. To keep the survey a manageable length, we limited the number of items to 5 per dimension. The 10 dimensions are described in Table 8.2.

## Preliminary Reliability and Validity Evidence

We have established the rationale for the development of the OCP in the discussion above. To validate the measure, we initially administered the survey to 151 respondents from an Australian regional health care authority. Results, however, provided only mixed support for the reliability and validity of the OCP. We found that the reliabil-

**TABLE 8.2** The 10 Dimensions of the Organizational Culture Profile

| Dimension | Description |
| --- | --- |
| Leadership | The role of leaders in directing an organization, maintaining its culture, and serving as role models |
| Structure | The degree to which the organizational structure limits the actions of members, looking at the influence of policies and procedures on member behaviors and the concentration of power in the organization |
| Innovation | The organization's risk preference: the willingness of the organization to take risks and the encouragement it shows for innovation and creativity |
| Job Performance | The degree to which the organization emphasizes task performance—the extent of task orientation and whether performance is rewarded |
| Planning | The extent to which the organization has clear goals, has plans to meet those goals, and strives to follow those plans |
| Communication | The free sharing of information among all levels within the organization where possible, the direction it takes (bottom-up, top-down), and the importance of rumor in communication |
| Environment | The extent to which the organization is responsive to the needs of its clients and the extent to which it is influenced by and influences the actions of other similar organizations |
| Humanistic Workplace | The extent to which the organization respects and cares for individuals; represents the people end of the task-versus-people dichotomy |
| Development of the Individual | The extent to which the organization expends sufficient effort in providing opportunities for members to develop their skills and rewards development with career advancement and challenging work |
| Socialization on Entry | The time new members take to settle in, the degree to which employees feel they understand the organization, the extent of formalization, and the effectiveness of the socialization process |

ity of the culture dimensions was variable, suggesting that some may have been in need of reworking. Reliable dimensions (Cronbach alpha > .80) were Leadership, Planning, Communication, and Humanistic Workplace. Three other dimensions approached acceptable reliability (Cronbach alpha > .70): Environment, Job Performance, and Development of the Individual. Broadfoot and Ashkanasy (1994) suggested that the remaining three dimensions (Structure, Innovation, Socialization on Entry) should be used with care and were perhaps in need of revision if higher reliabilities were not achieved in subsequent studies.

Support for the OCP's validity was partially obtained in significant correlations between organizational commitment and the four reliable dimensions: Leadership, Planning, Communication, and Humanistic Workplace ($rs$ from .67 to .79). Broadfoot and Ashkanasy (1994) concluded that these four scales had potential in the further development of a valid measure of organizational culture. Finally, principal-axis factor analysis with Varimax rotation showed that, although all items loaded on at least one dimension, only three factors underpinned the OCP, two of which had acceptable psychometric properties. These two factors were labeled, respectively, Innovative Leadership (alpha = .91) and Rules Orientation (alpha = .69).

### Follow-Up Validation Study

Our initial research was aimed primarily at the derivation of OCP items, with testing limited to a single organization. The second stage of validation and testing was carried out using a larger sample by Falkus (1998), who collected data from 297 respondents in 14 Australian organizations in the telecommunications, finance, and retail food industries. Exploratory and confirmatory factor analyses were utilized in the study to ascertain support both for the original 10-factor structure of the OCP and for the 2-factor solution that emerged in the initial validation

study. The exploratory factor analysis (principal axis with Varimax rotation) supported a 20-item 2-factor solution. We have labeled these factors Instrumental (alpha = .82) and Expressive (alpha = .87). Confirmatory factor analysis indicated that an 18-item version of the 2-factor solution produced a good fit. The final 2-factor structure also bore similarity to the corresponding factors identified in the initial validation study (although the Expressive factor is a reversed version of the Rule Orientation factor found in the initial study). Further, and as we found in the initial study, the 10-dimensional structure was not supported in the exploratory factor analysis. Nevertheless, results based on confirmatory factor analysis were more positive; although the overall fit statistics were somewhat disappointing, residual indices and factor loadings were encouraging. (Details can be obtained directly from the first author.)

Irrespective of the mixed results from the factor and reliability analyses, the OCP performed well in terms of the validity indices. Within-group agreement ($r_{wg}$) and significant between-group differences were found for both the 2-factor and the 10-factor models. For the 10-factor model, predictive and concurrent validity was strongly supported for 9 of the 10 dimensions, with correlation coefficients supporting all but 1 of the hypothesized relationships with satisfaction, commitment, and performance (the exception was Structure). Multiple regression analysis, however, showed that there was considerable overlap among the 10 dimensions. Regression results for the 2-factor model, on the other hand, showed that the Instrumental and Expressive factors were significant and independent predictors of organizational effectiveness, job satisfaction, and organizational commitment.

At this point, therefore, it would seem to be appropriate for us to conclude that there was strong support for the validity and reliability of a 2-factor solution. The Instrumental and Expressive factors were found to be reliable, had good validity, and had similarities with the emergent dimensions from our initial validation study. The 2 dimensions are also similar in content to the major facets of culture measured in other organizational culture surveys.

The question now, however, is whether it is worthwhile persevering with the original 10-dimensional representation or whether the 2-dimensional model is sufficient to describe organizational culture. We feel in particular that there are important lessons for the field in this discussion and suggest that future research will need to resolve the important issues that we raise here.

## How Many Factors?

From our discussion so far, it appears that the 2-factor model that has emerged from the validation studies is psychometrically the more correct. However, from a point of view of contribution, it is doubtful whether such a conclusion is really useful. A 2-factor measure of organizational culture would join the ranks of similarly narrowly delineated measures, without addressing the need for a more comprehensive measure of organizational culture. Indeed, we argue that, in organizational culture studies, the more parsimonious solution is not necessarily the most useful one, from both theoretical and practical perspectives.

Throughout this discussion, it is important to remember that the rationale for the development of the OCP was the absence of an existing comprehensive measure of culture summarizing the relevant dimensions of culture. Results of factor-analytic studies, although instructive, do not necessarily invalidate this aim (DeShon & Landis, 1997). Although the tendency for quantitative measures to take a reductive view of organizational culture has in the past prompted calls for qualitative assessment of organizational culture research, such a view is clearly simplistic (Denison, 1996; Marcoulides & Heck, 1993; Martin, 1990a). In this respect, some quantitative researchers have begun to question the tenet of parsimony that is generally pursued by their colleagues. DeShon and Landis (1997), for example, have argued that

the statistical summarizing evidenced in previous factor analysis of a goal commitment measure may mask the true dimensions of the construct. In the specific domain of organizational culture, it is also coming to be more recognized that reductive approaches may be counterproductive. Hawkins (1997) has noted that researchers should take care not to "reductively simplify the depth and richness of the culture perspective of organizations" (p. 420). In this light, we advance four reasons for the retention of the more complex, nonreductive, 10-dimensional structure of the OCP.

First, it is important to note that the 10-dimensional structure of the OCP was not necessarily empirically rejected in the present survey. Hurley et al. (1997), for example, argue that satisfactory goodness-of-fit indices can be difficult to achieve in a model with so many constraints. As a consequence, more emphasis needs to be placed on interpretation of residual statistics and parameter estimates. In the validation study, these latter statistics indicated that there was support for 9 of the 10 dimensions of the OCP as discrete constructs. Further, the one that was not supported in this test (Communication) performed satisfactorily in other tests (e.g., Cronbach alpha).

Our second point is that interpretation of factor analysis needs to be made in the context of the aim for data reduction. Factor analysis explains the covariances and intercorrelations between many observed items by grouping highly correlated items with relatively few underlying latent variables (Hurley et al., 1997; Thompson & Daniel, 1996). It is often overlooked, however, that even though factors have overlapping variance, they can still have discriminating effects and measure meaningfully different constructs. Well-known constructs such as job satisfaction and commitment, for example, are highly correlated, but are recognized as residing in distinct theoretical domains. Overly parsimonious factor solutions may lose this discriminability.

Third, researchers such as Cooke and Rousseau (1988) and Harris and Mossholder

(1996) maintain that multidimensional measures serve a useful purpose in the detection of subcultures (Sackmann, 1992; Trice, 1993) and in discriminating effects of particular dimensions on outcome variables. What has not been established, however, is how many dimensions a measure needs to be classified as a multidimensional instrument in this way. In Falkus's (1998) study, the validation results suggested that more than two factors were necessary for the OCP to realize its measurement potential. For instance, between-group differences were found for hierarchical level only on the original Development of the Individual dimension, and not on either of the emergent factors.

Our fourth point concerns the interpretability of cultural studies based on multidimensional profiling surveys. Jick (1979), for example, has proposed "triangulation" as a method of combining quantitative and qualitative data. This approach allows the researcher to capitalize on the advantages of quantitative methods and at the same time to capture a richer picture of the organization that is often not amenable to quantification (see also Hawkins, 1997). In this respect, multidimensional profiling surveys such as the OCP hold a major advantage over more restrictive measures. This is because the comprehensive coverage of the multiple dimensions facilitates more specific description and interpretation and is therefore closer to the richness of the qualitative descriptions. In the particular instance of the OCP, the dimensions were developed from a review of a wide range of literature and are therefore interpretable in language that should be familiar to qualitative researchers.

Together, these reasons provide justification for continuing to persevere with multidimensional questionnaires in future development of organizational culture measures. We argue that organizational culture researchers need to take care not to use oversimplified measures. Although such measures often can have good psychometric properties, there are dangers that such oversimplification can result in key aspects of organizational culture being missed. In particular, multidimensional surveys such as the OCP provide important benefits in terms of interpretation and organizational diagnosis.

## Suggestions for Future Research and Development of Multidimensional Questionnaires

So far, we have presented a case for use and development of a multidimensional measure of organizational culture. Our experiences with the OCP, however, suggest that there are six aspects of the development process that will need careful attention in future research.

First, it is important that the dimensions being measured are clearly distinguishable. Overlapping dimensions may make subsequent interpretations difficult. DeShon and Landis (1997) make the point that the different aspects covered by distinct factors should be optimized as far as possible, without merging the dimensions. They note that this can be achieved through the addition of new items, deletion of low-reliability items, and revision of existing items to reduce ambiguity. In the OCP validation study, for example, items varied in their contributions to factors, with some deletions leading to more reliable and valid factors (Falkus, 1998).

The second point is a corollary of the first. There is a need for further research to establish a more theoretical basis for questionnaire measures. The OCP was developed following a review of the literature that identified 10 consistent themes. Although this procedure offered several advantages, as we have outlined above, it could well be that the difficulty we experienced in differentiating the factors in the OCP resulted from a lack of a unified theoretical foundation.

The third issue is that a wide spectrum of respondents needs to be used in validation studies (see Hawkins, 1997). In the case of the OCP, both of the studies we have described were based on limited samples. Respondents in the initial study were health care professionals, and those in the follow-up validation study were middle-level managers. More and larger samples are needed to address this deficit; such samples would simultaneously allow greater scope for application of confirmatory factor analysis techniques.

Fourth, it is clear that longitudinal studies are necessary to establish causal relationships between culture dimensions and outcome variables (Brown & Greenberg, 1990; Saffold, 1988). Many of the issues we have addressed in development and testing of the OCP remain unresolved because of the lack of data to establish causal relationships.

Our fifth point is that controls for environmental stability and cross-cultural issues are needed to establish the psychometric properties and validity of culture measures (see Dickson et al., Chapter 28, this volume). This information could also be used in studies examining the complex integrated relationships among the organization's environment, its structure and purpose, its culture, and resulting outcomes (Marcoulides & Heck, 1993; Saffold, 1988).

Finally, we recognize that future research requires qualitative information regarding the nature of the organizational sample, its industry, its subcultural makeup, and how these groups interact.

## CONCLUSIONS

Our purpose in this chapter has been to provide a review of questionnaire measures of organizational culture, focusing in particular on some of the challenges that we encountered in attempting to validate a new multidimensional profiling measure of culture, the Organizational Culture Profile. We have presented our discussion in two main sections. In the first, we introduced a new typology of questionnaire measures, which we used to facilitate a review of the literature and a discussion of 18 published questionnaire measures. In the second section, we discussed the issues that we encountered in developing the OCP. Although the OCP has already been used with some success by some researchers (e.g., Kekele, 1998), we do not suggest that this instrument is necessarily the best one to use. Our intention has been to utilize the OCP to illustrate the difficulties faced by researchers in developing and validating organizational culture questionnaires.

We began the chapter with the statement that questionnaire measures of organizational culture are based on a restricted conception of organizational culture as something an organization has, rather than something an organization is (Smircich, 1983). In this respect, we acknowledge that quantitative questionnaire measures of culture are bounded in their range of application. Schein (1996a), in particular, has stressed that an understanding of the deeper levels of culture must be the fundamental aim of organizational culture research. Consequently, the exclusive use of quantitative methods is bound to prove inadequate in many situations. We therefore advocate the adjunctive use of qualitative methods as a means to extend the boundaries of application of quantitative measurement of organizational culture. Combined with the qualitative data, questionnaire measures provide a standardized means to assess organizational culture.

Finally, we argue that research is needed to develop further multidimensional measures of organizational culture such as the OCP. In particular, multidimensional measures offer greater interpretative power than simpler questionnaires, especially when used in conjunction with qualitative methods. In this light, we feel sure that measures such as the OCP will have a continuing role in advancing our knowledge and understanding of organizations.

# 9

## Using the Organizational Culture Inventory to Understand the Operating Cultures of Organizations

-- *Robert A. Cooke and Janet L. Szumal*

The Organizational Culture Inventory (OCI; Cooke & Lafferty, 1987) is a quantitative instrument that measures 12 sets of behavioral norms associated with three general types of organizational cultures: Constructive, Passive/Defensive, and Aggressive/Defensive. Since its introduction, the OCI has been used by thousands of organizations and completed by over 2 million respondents throughout the world. It has been used for a variety of purposes, including to direct, evaluate, and monitor organizational change (e.g., Gaucher & Kratochwill, 1993); identify and transfer the cultures of high-performing units (Human Synergistics, 1986); study and enhance system reliability and safety (Haber, O'Brien, Metlay, & Crouch, 1991); facilitate strategic alliances and mergers (Slowinski, 1992); promote collaborative relations within and across units (Leeds, 1999); and test hypotheses on the relationships among culture, outcomes, and antecedent variables (Klein, Masi, & Weidner, 1995). This wide range of applications has produced an extensive information base regarding the ways in which culture operates in different types of organizations.

In this chapter, we briefly describe the OCI, its underlying conceptual framework, and the behavioral norms it measures. We then propose a theoretical model of "how culture works" based on findings reported in previous studies, along with the results of new analyses of OCI data. These findings and results illustrate how the behavioral norms measured by the inventory are related to individual-, group-, and system-level criteria of effectiveness, as well as to antecedent variables (which can serve as levers for cultural change). The theoretical model also explains why the operating cultures of organizations are often inconsistent with their missions and the espoused values of members, and why culture is not always related to effectiveness in the manner expected.

## THE ORGANIZATIONAL CULTURE INVENTORY

The OCI assesses 12 sets of norms that describe the thinking and behavioral styles that might be implicitly or explicitly required for people to "fit in" and "meet expectations" in an organization or organizational subunit. These behavioral norms specify the ways in which all members of an organization—or at least those in similar positions or organizational locations—are expected to approach their work and interact with one another.

### Conceptual Framework

The behavioral norms measured by the OCI are defined by two underlying dimensions, the first of which distinguishes between a *concern for people* and a *concern for task*. The second dimension distinguishes between expectations for behaviors directed toward fulfilling higher-order *satisfaction* needs and those directed toward protecting and maintaining lower-order *security* needs. Based on these dimensions, the 12 sets of norms measured by the OCI are categorized into three general "clusters" or types of organizational cultures, which are labeled Constructive, Passive/Defensive, and Aggressive/ Defensive. Empirical support for these clusters, and therefore the construct validity of the inventory, has been provided by the results of principal-components analyses presented elsewhere (e.g., Cooke & Rousseau, 1988; Cooke & Szumal, 1993; Xenikou & Furnham, 1996).

The 12 behavioral norms measured by the OCI are described in Figure 9.1. Constructive cultures, which are characterized by norms for Achievement, Self-Actualizing, Humanistic-Encouraging, and Affiliative behaviors, encourage members to interact with *people* and approach *tasks* in ways that will help them to meet their higher-order *satisfaction* needs. Passive/Defensive cultures, characterized by Approval, Conventional, Dependent, and Avoidance norms, encourage or implicitly require members to interact with *people* in ways that will not threaten their own personal *security*. Aggressive/Defensive cultures, encompassing Oppositional, Power, Competitive, and Perfectionistic norms, encourage or drive members to approach *tasks* in forceful ways to protect their status and *security*.

### The OCI Circumplex

Respondents' OCI scale scores are plotted on a circumplex (see Figure 9.2), a circular diagram on which the distances between the behavioral norms reflect their degree of similarity and correlation (Guttman, 1954). Behavioral norms on the right-hand side of the OCI circumplex reflect expectations for behaviors that are people oriented; those on the left-hand side reflect expectations for behavior that are relatively task oriented. Norms toward the top of the circumplex promote behaviors that are directed toward the fulfillment of higher-order satisfaction needs; those near the bottom promote behaviors directed toward the fulfillment of lower-order security needs.

The statistically normed OCI circumplex allows members of an organization to compare their results to those of others who have completed the inventory. The bold center ring in the circumplex reflects the median score for each of the 12 styles. More specifically, the concentric circles (from the center of the circumplex outward) represent the 10th, 25th, 50th, 75th, 90th, and 99th percentiles, or progressively stronger norms along each of the 12 styles.

| | |
|---|---|
| **Constructive Cultures**<br> | **Achievement norms** (11): Members are expected to set challenging but realistic goals, establish plans to reach those goals, and pursue them with enthusiasm.<br><br>**Self-Actualizing norms** (12): Members are expected to enjoy their work, develop themselves, and take on new and interesting tasks.<br><br>**Humanistic-Encouraging norms** (1): Members are expected to be supportive, constructive, and open to influence in their dealings with one another.<br><br>**Affiliative norms** (2): Members are expected to be friendly, cooperative, and sensitive to the satisfaction of their work group. |
| **Passive/Defensive Cultures**<br> | **Approval norms** (3): Members are expected to agree with, gain the approval of, and be liked by others.<br><br>**Conventional norms** (4): Members are expected to conform, follow the rules, and make a good impression.<br><br>**Dependent norms** (5): Members are expected to do what they're told and clear all decisions with superiors.<br><br>**Avoidance norms** (6): Members are expected to shift responsibilities to others and avoid any possibility of being blamed for a problem. |
| **Aggressive/ Defensive Cultures**<br>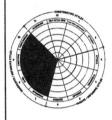 | **Oppositional norms** (7): Members are expected to be critical, oppose the ideas of others, and make safe (but ineffectual) decisions.<br><br>**Power norms** (8): Members are expected to take charge, control subordinates, and yield to the demands of superiors.<br><br>**Competitive norms** (9): Members are expected to operate in a "win-lose" framework, outperform others, and work against (rather than with) their peers.<br><br>**Perfectionistic norms** (10): Members are expected to appear competent, keep track of everything, and work long hours to attain narrowly-defined objectives. |

**Figure 9.1.** Descriptions of the Behavioral Norms Measured by the Organizational Culture Inventory
SOURCE: Reprinted by permission. Copyright © 1987, 1989 held by Human Synergistics, Inc.

### Ideal Versus Current Cultures

Beyond assessing the current operating cultures of organizations, the OCI is used also to identify the ideal cultures for organizations and subunits. A parallel form of the inventory, the OCI-Ideal, asks respondents to consider the extent to which members *ideally* should be expected to exhibit the 12 behav-ioral styles to maximize individual motivation and organizational performance (Cooke & Lafferty, 1994).

The ideal profiles generated by members of organizations usually emphasize a preference for Constructive behaviors. For example, the ideal profiles for organizations in the United States, Australia, Canada, New Zealand, and the United Kingdom typically show strong expectations for Constructive behaviors, moderate to weak expectations for Ag-

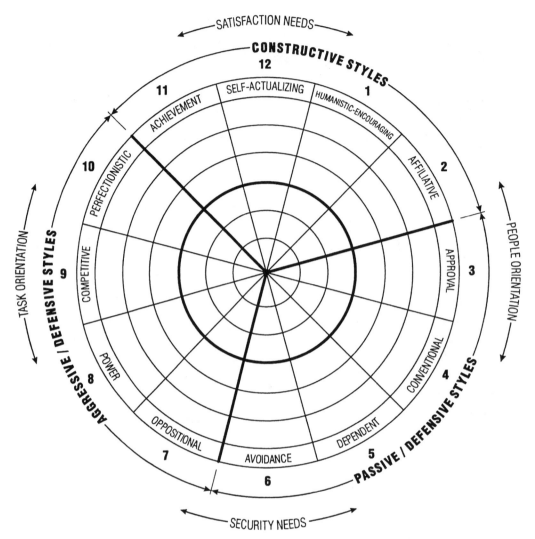

**Figure 9.2.** The OCI Circumplex
SOURCE: Reprinted by permission. Copyright © 1987, 1989 held by Human Synergistics, Inc.

gressive/Defensive behaviors, and weak expectations for Passive/Defensive behaviors. Ideal profiles for organizations in countries outside the Anglo cluster (e.g., Latin Europe, Latin America, and the Far East) also tend to be characterized by strong expectations for Constructive behaviors; however, expectations for some of the Defensive styles tend to be pronounced as well.

Similarly, differences across industries—and across organizations with different environments and technologies—can be observed, but such differences are much smaller than those who embrace "contingency" the-

ories of culture might predict. For example, researchers studying "reliability-oriented" systems, such as nuclear aircraft carriers, have questioned whether those organizations "would function as well under cultural features found in other [performance-oriented] organizations" (Roberts, Rousseau, & La Porte, 1994, p. 158). However, OCI-Ideal surveys administered in nuclear power plants, chemical and oil refineries, and reliability-oriented military units consistently produce ideal culture profiles that are predominantly Constructive. Similarly, research findings indicate that reliability-oriented sys-

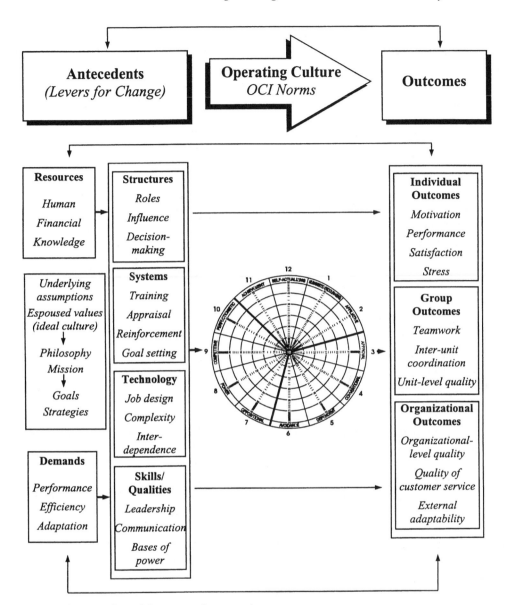

**Figure 9.3.** Theoretical Model: How Culture Works
SOURCE: Reprinted by permission. Copyright © 1987 held by R. A. Cooke (model) and Human Synergistics, Inc. (circumplex).

tems (e.g., nuclear power plants) with Constructive norms perform better under emergency conditions than do those with more Defensive norms (Shurberg & Haber, 1992).

More generally, responses to the OCI-Ideal are based in part on societal values and beliefs regarding how things work and the types of behaviors likely to lead to individual and organizational effectiveness. Given the relatively strong individualistic, weak uncer-

tainty avoidance, and moderate power distance societal values (Hofstede, 1980a), respondents in the United States strongly endorse Constructive norms as those most likely to promote performance—regardless of the types of organizations they are describing. Similarly, the emphasis on certain Defensive norms found in the ideal profiles generated for organizations in Latin European, Latin American, and Far East Asian countries likely reflect their stronger collectivistic, power distance, and/or uncertainty avoidance values (Hofstede, 1980a).

## THEORETICAL MODEL: HOW CULTURE WORKS

Although the operating cultures of organizations have been viewed as a direct function of the assumptions and values shared by members and, in turn, as important determinants of individual and organizational performance, research with the OCI suggests a more complex picture of how culture really works (see Figure 9.3). First, the model proposes a disconnect between underlying assumptions and espoused values on the one hand and operating cultures in terms of behavioral norms and expectations on the other. This disconnect is due to the direct influence of structures, systems, technology, and skills/qualities—which do not necessarily reflect underlying assumptions and values—on the operating cultures of organizations.

Second, the model proposes a relation between culture and outcomes consistent with, for example, the work of Kotter and Heskett (1992). Their description of the effects of adaptive versus nonadaptive cultures on organizational performance, problem solving, enthusiasm, and innovation suggests that Constructive (as opposed to Defensive) norms should lead to effectiveness. Our model, however, shows that a number of other factors are causally related to outcomes—and these factors can suppress or counteract the effects of cultural norms.

Finally, the model displayed in Figure 9.3 proposes that organizational resources and environmental demands play an important role in explaining inconsistencies among values and philosophies, operating cultures, and organizational effectiveness. Resources and demands account for the misattributions often made when organizations with dysfunc-

tional cultures appear to be successful. They also explain why attempts to overcome or bypass the negative effects of a Defensive culture (through the use of structures, systems, and technology to control members' behaviors directly) may appear to be effective—at least temporarily along certain criteria of effectiveness.

## THE CULTURE DISCONNECT

Conceptual models of organizational culture (e.g., Schein, 1981; Trompenaars & Hampden-Turner, 1998) suggest that the more salient aspects of culture (as measured by the OCI) should reflect, and be shaped by, the more fundamental aspects of culture, such as the underlying assumptions and values shared by members (reflected in responses to the OCI-Ideal). Consistent with these models, our perspective on "how culture works" shows that the assumptions held by members (internalized or unrecognized beliefs and values) and their espoused values (what they say is important) influence the mission and philosophy of their organization and its strategies and goals. However, in contrast to other models, our perspective is that values, missions, goals, and strategies have only marginal impacts on the operating cultures of many organizations.

This disconnect between values and mission on the one hand and norms and expectations on the other is illustrated by data collected from approximately 90 organizational units. The managers of these units were asked about the clarity and strength of their organizations' values, philosophies, and missions; their subordinates were asked to complete the OCI. Although the results of correlation analyses suggest that Constructive norms are related to strong philosophies and Defensive norms are related to weak missions, none of the coefficients were significant, and a few were close to zero. Similarly, the same managers were asked about the importance (or value) their organizations place on specific sets of behaviors corresponding to the Constructive, Passive/Defensive, and Aggressive/Defensive behavioral norms. The correlations between values and norms were in the expected direction, but, again, were not significant.

It is not unusual to see strong Defensive cultural norms operating in organizations with mission statements emphasizing high-quality service, innovation, teamwork, and the growth and development of members and correspondingly Constructive OCI-Ideal profiles. As Lawler (1996) notes, the mission and values statements drafted by top managers are often disregarded by organizational members, as well as by those who wrote the statements. How can the operating cultures of these organizations be so diametrically opposed to the cultures that members deem to be ideal? The reason is that the norms that emerge in many organizations are not a direct function of the values and assumptions of leaders and founders, but rather are determined by the organizational conditions and realities that members face on a day-to-day basis.

## THE IMPACTS OF STRUCTURES, SYSTEMS, TECHNOLOGY, AND SKILLS/QUALITIES ON OPERATING CULTURES

The behavioral norms that emerge in organizations are products of members' collective learning regarding what it takes to get things done and succeed—or to stay out of trouble and survive—in the system. In discerning what behaviors are appropriate, members may react cautiously or even skeptically to mission statements, change programs, and what managers "say" they want. Instead, they infer what is expected on the basis of cues or signals from the forces they face on a daily basis. These forces—which include structures, systems, technologies, and skills/

qualities—may or may not be consistent with the more fundamental aspects of the organization's culture. Nevertheless, they determine whether members come to believe that they should behave in Constructive versus Defensive ways and shape the true operating culture of the organization (as shown in Figure 9.3). We describe below the ways in which these factors shape and reinforce behavioral norms, basing our discussion on analyses of data from the OCI, manager interviews, and other sources. These other sources include the Organizational Effectiveness Inventory (Cooke, 1997), a survey that measures outcomes of culture as well as potential levers for change.

### Structures and the OCI Norms

*Structure* refers to the manner in which components are ordered and coupled to create an organization (Georgopoulos, 1986). Within organizations, structure manifests itself along multiple dimensions, including centralization of authority, hierarchy of influence, and degree of role specification. These dimensions shape the operating culture by making possible or requiring certain types of behaviors and ruling out or making difficult other types of behaviors. Possibly for these reasons, structures have been proposed to constitute a necessary (but not sufficient) lever for culture change (Cummings & Worley, 1998; Miles, 1997b; Nadler, 1998; Nevis, Lancourt, & Vassallo, 1996).

The correlations reported in Table 9.1 illustrate some of the ways in which dimensions of structure are related to behavioral norms. For example, the positive correlation between role specification and Constructive norms suggests that the specification of clear (although not necessarily narrow) roles promotes Constructive behaviors by defining incumbents' responsibilities, reducing uncertainty, and enabling members to take initiative and be proactive. Similarly, the correlation between the amount of influence exercised by members across organizational

**TABLE 9.1**   Correlations: Structures, Systems, Technology, and Skills/Qualities as Related to Culture

| Antecedents (levers for change) | OCI Norms[a] | | |
| --- | --- | --- | --- |
| | Constructive | Passive/ Defensive | Aggressive/ Defensive |
| *Structure* | | | |
| Role specification[a] (*n* = 358) | .28*** | –.00 | .06 |
| Total influence[a] (*n* = 610 to 611) | .39*** | –.10* | .01 |
| Hierarchy of influence[a] (*n* = 610 to 611) | –.24*** | .27*** | .15*** |
| Centralization of decision making[b] (*n* = 327) | –.18** | .17** | .03 |
| | | | |
| *Systems* | | | |
| Fairness of appraisals[a] (*n* = 107) | .61*** | –.14 | .06 |
| Rewards—use of praise[a] (*n* = 466) | .48*** | –.23*** | –.04 |
| Punishment—use of criticism[a] (*n* = 466) | –.24*** | .29*** | .31*** |
| Goal clarity[a] (*n* = 515 to 516) | .28*** | –.14** | –.06 |
| Goal difficulty[a] (*n* = 515 to 516) | .13** | –.13** | –.04 |
| Participation in goal setting[a] (*n* = 515 to 516) | .21*** | –.25*** | –.19*** |
| | | | |
| *Technology* | | | |
| Job design—autonomy[a] (*n* = 466) | .30*** | –.29*** | –.15** |
| Job design—skill variety[a] (*n* = 466) | .37*** | –.18*** | –.09* |
| Job design—task identity[a] (*n* = 466) | .22*** | .00 | .01 |
| Job design—task significance[a] (*n* = 466) | .21*** | –.10* | –.03 |
| Job design—feedback[a] (*n* = 466) | .15** | –.04 | –.02 |
| Job complexity—data[c] (*n* = 312) | .16** | –.21*** | –.05 |
| Job complexity—people[c] (*n* = 312) | .22*** | –.21*** | –.12* |
| Job complexity—things[c] (*n* = 312) | .02 | –.07 | –.11 |
| Interdependence[a] (*n* = 156 to 157) | .27** | –.09 | .00 |
| | | | |
| *Skills/qualities* | | | |
| Leadership—interaction facilitation[a] (*n* = 265) | .51*** | –.17** | .07 |
| Leadership—task facilitation[a] (*n* = 265) | .43*** | –.11 | .10 |
| Leadership—goal emphasis[a] (*n* = 265) | .48*** | –.21*** | .00 |
| Leadership—consideration[a] (*n* = 155) | .47*** | –.13 | –.06 |
| Bases of power—organizational[a] (*n* = 156 to 157) | .10 | .24** | .36*** |
| Bases of power—personal[a] (*n* = 156 to 157) | .53*** | –.22** | –.13 |

a. Based on employees' reports (aggregated to the unit level).
b. Based on managers' reports.
c. Based on data from the U.S. Department of Labor (1991).
*$p < .05$; **$p < .01$; ***$p < .001$.

levels (i.e., total influence as defined by Tannenbaum, 1968) and Constructive norms suggest that expectations for proactive and positive behaviors are strong when members at all levels of the organizational hierarchy exercise influence.

On the other hand, hierarchy of influence (estimated by computing the difference between the influence of members at the bottom of the organization and the influence of those at the top) is negatively related to Constructive norms and positively related to both sets of Defensive norms. Centralized decision-making structures are also negatively correlated with Constructive norms and positively correlated with Passive/Defensive norms. Such structures serve as a constant reminder to members of the need to follow rules and directives while suppressing opportunities to approach their work and interact with others in self-fulfilling ways. More generally, organizational structures (which may or may not reflect shared values) shape the operating culture by influencing the behaviors that members come to believe are necessary and appropriate.

with Constructive norms (see Table 9.1). Similarly, the use of praise for good work is positively correlated with Constructive norms and negatively correlated with Passive/Defensive norms. In contrast, the use of criticism when mistakes are made is negatively related to Constructive norms and promotes self-protective (both Passive/Defensive and Aggressive/Defensive) norms.

The degree of member participation in the setting of job-level goals is also positively associated with Constructive norms and negatively associated with both Passive/Defensive and Aggressive/Defensive norms. Systems that produce clear goals are positively associated with Constructive norms and negatively associated with Passive/Defensive norms. Finally, reasonably challenging goals are related to the strength of Constructive norms; goals that are too easy or too difficult to achieve are related to Passive/Defensive norms. Thus, although the foci of organizational systems can direct members' attention and behavior, such systems implicitly shape organizational culture simply as a function of their design and implementation.

## Systems and the OCI Norms

*Systems* refer to the interrelated sets of procedures—such as human resource, information, accounting, environmental scanning, and quality-control systems—an organization uses to support its core activities and to solve problems. Organizational systems, particularly those for human resource management, have been proposed by others to be a potentially powerful lever for shaping and changing the culture of an organization (Allen, 1985; Schein, 1983; Sethia & Von Glinow, 1985; Ulrich, 1997). More generally, research with the OCI indicates that human resource systems, simply by virtue of their design and implementation, have impacts on norms and expectations that go beyond the specific behaviors these systems are designed to reinforce.

For example, the perceived fairness of performance appraisals is positively correlated with

## Technology and the OCI Norms

The methods by which an organization transforms inputs into outputs also shape behavioral norms and expectations. The impact of technology on culture was first suggested by Trist and Bamforth's (1951) classic study of coal miners, which describes how a change in technology led to a new set of norms. Later, Hackman and Oldham (1980) diagnosed technology at the job level and identified a set of core job characteristics causally related to outcomes such as work motivation and performance. These same core characteristics, as well as other dimensions of job design, shape individual normative beliefs and shared behavioral expectations, particularly when members of an organizational unit are performing similar jobs.

Jobs that provide high levels of autonomy, skill variety, task identity, task significance, and feedback are positively associated with

Constructive norms (see Table 9.1, which presents results for those units in which members held the same or similar jobs). Conversely, jobs that lack autonomy and skill variety are associated with both sets of Defensive norms, and those that have little significance in terms of their impact on people are associated with Passive/Defensive norms.

Similarly, job complexity with respect to working with data is positively associated with Constructive norms and negatively associated with Passive/Defensive norms. The complexity of jobs with respect to working with people is related positively to Constructive norms and negatively to both sets of Defensive norms. More generally, jobs that are simple and routine implicitly establish norms for compliant and "detached" behaviors and suppress expectations for achievement, growth, and collaboration.

Finally, the degree of interdependence among members is positively associated with Constructive norms. When interdependencies are sequential or reciprocal, the job performance of incumbents is contingent not only on the performance of others but also on their ability to coordinate their activities. Thus technologies based on teams, self-regulating work groups, and sociotechnical approaches appear to require, and are likely to promulgate and reinforce, Constructive operating cultures.

### Skills/Qualities and the OCI Norms

The skills and qualities of organizational members, particularly those who hold leadership roles, can shape, reinforce, and change the culture of an organization or subunit (Allen, 1985; Human Synergistics, 1986; Kotter & Heskett, 1992; Nevis et al., 1996; Schein, 1983). Because of their position in the organizational hierarchy, managers tend to be viewed by other members as role models—whether or not they exemplify their espoused values or the philosophy of the organization. Additionally, the leadership behaviors of managers—which reflect their interpersonal and organizational skills—can shape the culture by constraining or facilitating members' work activities and interactions with others.

For example, leadership styles that emphasize interaction and open communication among employees (interaction facilitation) and the achievement of goals (goal emphasis) are positively associated with Constructive norms and negatively associated with Passive/Defensive norms (see the bottom of Table 9.1). Leaders who demonstrate concern for employees (supportiveness) and help them identify ways to solve problems and complete their assignments (task facilitation) are also more likely to promote Constructive cultures than are leaders who do not demonstrate these styles. Similarly, reliance on organizational bases of power (legitimate, reward, and coercive power) is positively associated with Defensive norms. Conversely, reliance on personal bases of power (expert and referent power) is positively associated with Constructive norms and negatively associated with Passive/Defensive norms.

More generally, the skills and qualities of members at all levels can influence an organization's operating culture and the subcultures of its units. Constructive norms are likely to emerge when members' interpersonal and communication skills are well developed and when their behaviors exemplify these skills. Conversely, when members lack the skills and qualities needed to perform their jobs, they tend to approach others in Defensive ways (Szumal, 1998), increase the security needs of those around them, and inadvertently establish norms for, and patterns of, Defensive behavior.

### THE IMPACT OF OPERATING CULTURE ON OUTCOMES

Although organizational outcomes are influenced by myriad factors, the OCI norms are expected to have effects that are discernible and significant. Specifically, strong norms for Constructive behaviors should lead to desirable outcomes (e.g., individual motivation, performance, job satisfaction, teamwork, quality of work relations, and quality of customer service) and should minimize undesirable outcomes (e.g., social loafing and stress). Conversely, expectations for Defensive behaviors, particularly those that are Passive, should have the opposite impact, according to our model of how culture works. The findings reported by others, along with analyses carried out on the previously mentioned OCI data set (which also contains manager interview and Organizational Effectiveness Inventory data), illustrate the relationships between norms and various effectiveness criteria.

## The OCI Norms and Individual Outcomes

As shown in Table 9.2, Constructive norms are positively associated with members' reports regarding motivation and job satisfaction and managers' reports of the percentage of their employees demonstrating high levels of performance. Constructive norms are also negatively related to members' reports of stress and managers' reports of the percentage of employees who engage in social loafing. Conversely, expectations for Passive/Defensive behaviors are negatively associated with employee motivation and job satisfaction and are positively associated with employee stress and the percentage of employees who engage in social loafing and put forth little effort. Finally, Aggressive/Defensive norms are negatively correlated with employee job satisfaction and positively correlated with stress.

The results reported in Table 9.2 are based on correlations conducted on unit-level data; that is, the responses of individual members were aggregated to the unit level prior to analysis. Similar findings, however, have been reported at the individual level with respect to the relationship between culture and stress (van der Velde & Class, 1995) and that between culture and member satisfaction (Haley, 1998; Klein, Bigley, & Roberts, 1995; McDaniel & Stumpf, 1995; Rousseau, 1990c).

Additional insight into the impact of operating cultures on employees is provided by other studies incorporating the OCI. For example, Haley (1998) found that Constructive norms were positively associated with *affective* commitment (that is, commitment based on emotional attachment to the organization). On the other hand, Lahiry (1994) found that Defensive norms (particularly Passive/Defensive) were positively related to *continuance* commitment (that is, when people stay with their organizations because they feel that the costs of leaving are relatively great). Finally, Weidner (1997) has shown a positive relationship between Constructive norms and the trust of hospital personnel in their supervisors and the organization.

## The OCI Norms and Group Outcomes

Our analyses (Table 9.2) show that Constructive norms are positively associated with employees' reports regarding teamwork and unit-level quality and with managers' reports of the quality of work relations among employees. In contrast, Defensive norms have a detrimental effect on employees' ability to work together, as reflected in both their own perceptions of teamwork and their managers' reports regarding the quality of work relations.

The link between the OCI norms and these group outcomes is probably neither direct nor simple; instead, it is likely that other factors are involved and operate as intervening or causally prior variables. For example, other variables that have been found to be associated with the OCI norms—including communication self-efficacy (Leeds, 1999), conflict resolution styles (Keenan, Cooke, & Hillis, 1998), and group cohesion (Hsieh, 1998)—potentially are causally related to

TABLE 9.2   Correlations Between Culture and Outcomes

| | OCI Norms[a] | | |
| Outcomes | Constructive | Passive/ Defensive | Aggressive/ Defensive |
|---|---|---|---|
| *Individual outcomes* | | | |
| Motivation[a] (*n* = 409 to 410) | .56*** | −.33*** | −.08 |
| Social loafing[b] (*n* = 446) | −.23*** | .18*** | .04 |
| High performance[b] (*n* = 352) | .17** | −.08 | .02 |
| Job satisfaction[a] (*n* = 606 to 607) | .60*** | −.32*** | −.13** |
| Stress[a] (*n* = 314 to 315) | −.25*** | .21*** | .21*** |
| *Group outcomes* | | | |
| Teamwork[a] (*n* = 598 to 599) | .44*** | −.25*** | −.17*** |
| Quality of work relations[b] (*n* = 447) | .20*** | −.16*** | −.08* |
| Unit-level quality[a] (*n* = 107) | .59*** | −.13 | .11 |
| *Organizational outcomes* | | | |
| Quality of customer service[a] (*n* = 369) | .58*** | −.19*** | .07 |

a. Based on employees' reports (aggregated to the unit level).
b. Based on managers' reports.
*$p < .05$; **$p < .01$; ***$p < .001$.

outcomes such as teamwork and quality of work performed.

## The OCI Norms and Organizational Outcomes

Quality of customer service is one of the most important and most commonly measured outcomes in studies of organizational culture. As shown at the bottom of Table 9.2, quality of service (measured on the basis of members' perceptions) is positively related to the strength of Constructive norms and inversely related to Passive/Defensive norms. These findings are consistent with those of A. S. Klein et al. (1995), whose analyses suggest that this relationship is further explained by employees' perceptions of control.

Quality of customer service has been considered in a number of cultural analyses of health care organizations (e.g., Haley, 1998; Kosmoski-Goepfert, 1994; Shortell et al., 1991). Haley's (1998) study is particularly interesting in that it included patient satisfaction data and other quality indicators (e.g., "untoward events" such as medication error rates and patient falls). Consistent with Haley's hypotheses, patient satisfaction was positively related to Humanistic (Constructive) norms and negatively related to Dependent (Passive/Defensive) norms. In contrast, rates of medication errors and patient falls appeared to be higher in units with Constructive cultures and lower in units with Defensive cultures. Based on qualitative data collected on the units and previous research on the discrepancies between the number of untoward events that *actually occur* in hospitals and the number that are *reported,* Haley proposes that Constructive norms encourage and permit nurses to report problems; in contrast, Defensive norms may impede the reporting of errors by forcing members to look good and to please those in positions of authority.

Beyond quality of service, cross-sectional studies on culture have considered a number of other organizational-level outcomes. A reanalysis of OCI data on supermarkets (Human Synergistics, 1986) found that Achievement (Constructive) norms were positively related to sales per square foot of selling space as well as to subjective measures of store effectiveness. Klein (1992) found a significant relationship between the Constructive norms and sales growth in a study of apparel stores. Thornbury's (1994) study of 17 units of four European companies showed that effectiveness in dealing with change was positively related to Constructive norms and negatively related to Passive/Defensive norms. Rousseau's (1990c) study of multiple units of a large fund-raising organization demonstrated that Passive/Defensive norms were negatively related to the generation of revenues.

Evidence that the norms measured by the OCI are causally related to performance is provided by cultural change programs that have been evaluated longitudinally (Dale, 1997; Human Synergistics/New Zealand, 1998; "IBM Division Reborn," 1998; Sarkis, Sanders, & Pattillo, 1992; United Auto Workers, 1990). Such programs were designed to bring about cultural change and performance improvements by means of interventions directed at systems, structures, technologies, and/or skills. These case studies, although not based on controlled experimental designs, lend support to the notion that culture has an impact on effectiveness.

## THE EFFECTS OF RESOURCES AND DEMANDS ON HOW CULTURE REALLY WORKS

Although culture likely has an impact on effectiveness, our experiences with using the OCI, along with the observations of others (e.g., Kotter & Heskett, 1992; Nadler, 1998), suggest that the success of an organization can also affect all the other variables in our model and create inconsistencies between the different levels of culture and between culture and outcomes. Specifically, our model of how culture works is reinforced by two critical sets of variables: *resources* and *demands*. The variables in the first set, which are partly based on the organization's historical performance or effectiveness, include financial reserves, members' technical expertise, and patents and copyrights, as well as more tangible resources. The variables in the second set include demands for performance, efficiency, adaptation, and change. These demands emanate from various sectors of the environment (including customers, suppliers, competitors, and shareholders, as well as the local community and larger society) and, like resources, partly result from the organization's prior effectiveness and impact on its environment.

As shown in Figure 9.3, resources and demands influence outcomes at the individual, group, and organizational levels both directly and indirectly. Holding other factors constant, the magnitude of an organization's resources has a direct and positive impact on such outcomes, whereas the magnitude of the demands placed on it has a negative impact. Organizations with vast resources and little or no competition are simply in an advantageous position to grow and prosper relative to those that have limited resources and are operating in highly competitive and demanding environments. At the same time, resources and demands can influence structures, systems, technologies, and skills/qualities and, in turn, shape the organization's operating culture. Culture disconnects (discussed earlier) occur when these factors are more influential in shaping systems and related antecedents than are the espoused values of members or the organization's mission or philosophy.

More generally, the direct and indirect effects of resources and demands on outcomes explain why a subset of organizations with Defensive cultures nevertheless appear to be relatively effective. We discuss these dynamics below in terms of the defensive misattribution of success and the culture bypass.

## The Defensive Misattribution of Success

Resources and demands, particularly when the former are substantial and the latter are minimal, can have a greater bearing than cultural norms on the short-term performance of an organization. Organizations that enjoy strong franchises, munificent environments, extensive patents and copyrights, and/or massive financial resources are likely to perform quite adequately, at least in the short term and possibly even over the long term, if environmental pressures for innovation, adaptation, or flexibility remain minimal.

However, the indirect effects of resources and demands on outcomes are not always consistent with the direct effects, particularly when managers lose sight of important core values and/or the factors that led to the organization's success in the first place. Although an abundance of assets and a nonthreatening environment can make it "easy" for an organization to perform effectively, these same factors provide members with slack resources and obliterate accountability and feedback on the true impacts they are having on the organization (Zoltners, Sinha, & Murphy, 1997). Managers can "get away" with implementing ineffective systems, designing organizational silos and unwieldy hierarchical structures, introducing technologies that destroy motivation, and providing leadership based on questionable skills (Nadler, 1998)—and, in the process, creating an Aggressive and/or Passive organizational culture.

This dynamic is further complicated by managers' tendencies to assume that the organization is functioning well, that resources and environment conditions will not change, and that current successes will continue. In such situations, it is particularly difficult to gain managers' acceptance of, or support for, the need for cultural change. Although they accept their Defensive OCI cultural profiles, attribution theory and self-serving biases (Levy, 1993) almost assure that they will attribute successes to themselves and failures to external factors. Because they created the dysfunctional culture (or inadvertently allowed it to emerge), they credit it as being the source of the organization's effectiveness. Systems thinking, however, would reveal that their effectiveness is a function of a complex array of factors. Although the impact of culture may be overshadowed by the impacts of resources and demands, Constructive norms would nevertheless enhance the performance of these organizations, increase their adaptability, and protect them from being blindsided by forceful and unanticipated environmental changes.

## The Culture Bypass

The culture bypass is another dynamic that accounts for inconsistencies among values and philosophy, operating culture, and organizational effectiveness. Certain organizations adopt strategies for their operating units that produce negative cultures but are nevertheless successful—at least in terms of specific criteria of performance. These strategies typically revolve around special resources, proprietary technologies, or standardized products that provide the organization with some type of competitive advantage—often in terms of cost. The technologies implemented, and the structures and systems put into place to support them, are implicitly designed to "bypass" culture or its impact by directly controlling members' behaviors. Unfortunately, many of these substitutes for culture promote norms for Defensive behavior and, ultimately, have negative effects on members and, sometimes, the organization.

The culture bypass can be observed most frequently in organizations that have substantial resources, operate in environments with considerable competitive and other pressures, and have many geographically dispersed units (e.g., branches or stores) that carry out the same or similar activities. Examples of such organizations can be found in the fast-food, banking, and other service (e.g., hotel) industries, where highly efficient technologies for operations at the store or branch level have been developed to maintain control, promote consistency, and reduce the need for a highly skilled or expensive workforce. In terms of our model of culture, the strategy is to emphasize systems, structures, and technologies and to downplay the importance of members' skills and culture with respect to task accomplishment.

For example, to control members' behavior and performance, jobs within culture-bypass organizations are carefully specified and designed to be simple. However, because such jobs inherently lack the core characteristics associated with motivation and satisfaction, centralized structures and systems are needed to reinforce the technology to assure that employees do what is necessary and maintain standards. Although initially intended to bypass culture or to overcome its effects, these systems and structures inevitably lead to the emergence of fairly strong Defensive cultural norms. Beyond affecting employees' behavior and performance, Defensive norms lead to marginal levels of commitment and increased turnover (Cooke & Szumal, 1993). In response, jobs are further simplified to make it easier to replace and train people, which, in a recursive manner, results in even stronger Defensive norms. Although questions might be raised about customer satisfaction and employee growth, culture-bypass organizations often appear to be successful, at least temporarily, from financial and internal business-process perspectives.

Nevertheless, there is reason to believe that the culture-bypass strategy is suboptimal and that Constructive cultural norms could enhance the effectiveness of the operating units of these organizations. For example, when stores or outlets within the same firm are considered, research indicates that Constructive norms have a positive impact on outcomes such as job satisfaction, perceived quality of service, and sales growth (Klein, 1992). Further, unpublished case studies based on the OCI have identified markedly strong Constructive cultures in some units of companies that seem to operate on the bypass strategy. Without exception, these units performed above average if not exceptionally in terms of sales, employee satisfaction and retention, and perceptions regarding customer service.

## CONCLUSIONS

Our model of how culture works, in consideration of organizational resources and demands, requires further testing and possible elaboration. Particularly useful would be multivariate studies across industries permitting analyses of the potentially contradictory direct and indirect effects of resources and demands on effectiveness. Additional studies within industries (and across multiple units within single organizations) would also be useful in that they control, to an extent, for factors such as resources and demands. There is also a need for this type of research across countries. We have noted that the societal norms prevailing in certain countries lead to more Defensive OCI ideal profiles. This finding raises questions regarding the impact of Constructive and Defensive norms on the effectiveness of organizations in Southeast Asian, South American, and Latin American countries. Finally, action research studies based on quasi-experimental designs with control groups (subunits, stores, departments) would provide important information on the effects of cultural change programs on behavioral norms and outcome variables.

The culture disconnect, the defensive misattribution of success, and the culture bypass highlight the importance of alignment, systems thinking, and organizational learning to cultural change. The frequency with which we have observed cultural disconnects suggests that many organizations need to bring their missions and goals into alignment with shared values and assumptions, and then make appropriate changes or improvements in systems, structures, technologies, and skills of members. Operating cultures are molded on a day-to-day basis, thus strategically directing a culture requires not only the clarification of visions and values but also the identification of indirect (and otherwise unanticipated) consequences of changes in technologies, structures, and systems. In turn, organizational learning and similar interventions designed to enhance systems and critical thinking (Argyris, 1982; Senge, 1990) may be prerequisite to cultural change in many organizations. Ironically, organizational learning and systems analysis are inconsistent with the Passive/Defensive and Aggressive/Defensive norms prevailing in those organizations most in need of cultural change. Thus quantitative data that clearly portray the direction of an organization's culture and its impact on effectiveness are needed to reveal the inadequacies of current strategies and to motivate learning at the individual, group, and organizational levels.

# 10

## Climate and Culture

*How Close Can They Get?*

—— *Roy L. Payne*

The idea of using climate-like ideas to measure culture was first proposed, as far as I know, by Siehl and Martin (1988), although the idea of using a variety of data to "triangulate" on a subject/ situation was proposed by Denzin (1978). Siehl and Martin describe a study of a *Fortune* 500 company in which they used observation, open-ended in-depth interviewing, and archival materials to "focus on espoused values and on cultural forms and practices that supported or refuted those values" (p. 85). They then used these data to design a questionnaire that had five sections: espoused values, company jargon, organizational stories, tacit knowledge, and beliefs about practices. The espoused values section contained five core values, and respondents were asked to rate the importance of those values to the company and to themselves personally. The section on company jargon listed 20 company words that respondents were asked to define. Of these, 12 were technical and 8 were related to company values, such as the importance of "working the issue" to achieve consensus. The stories section described four stories that were well-known throughout the company. Each story indicated three moral outcomes, only one of which was consistent with the views of long-term employees. Respondents were tested to see how many they got correct. Siehl and Martin tested respondents' grasp of "tacit knowledge" by presenting two paragraphs from the company report in which every fifth word was left blank. Respondents had to provide the missing words, and answers were coded as totally correct, partially correct, or incorrect. The measurement of beliefs about company practices really assessed ideological commitment to the company rather than knowledge of company practices. Five items of information about the company were described, but the numerical information was left out. Respondents had to choose one of two answers for each item, not knowing that both were actually wrong. The true answer lay between the two, and the logic of the measure was that a respondent's biasing of answers to the more favorable response would indicate greater ideological commitment. The results showed that even new recruits were aware of important company values, but the longer they were in the organization, the more they picked up about the jargon and the stories, and the stronger they became in their ideological commitment. The importance of Siehl and Martin's study is that it demonstrates that quantitative approaches can be used to assess cultural concepts and to make comparisons across cultures and subcultures.

Duncan (1989) was inspired by Siehl and Martin's work and carried out a study in a public health care setting. He also used a combination of observation, interview, and questionnaire data and discovered interesting differences across some cultural values between the data generated by the questionnaire and the interview data. Furthermore, because of the observations of eight observers and personal interviews with the staff, he was able to explain the discrepancies between the questionnaire and interview data, and why the culture had produced them.

Having derived the idea from those described above, my aim in this chapter is to explore the concepts of culture and climate to see how closely the methods of studying organizational climate can assist in the study of organizational culture. Before I present the details of the arguments, I define both concepts and their relationship to each other.

## THE CONCEPT OF CULTURE

In her entry for the concept of organizational culture in the *The Blackwell Encyclopedic Dictionary of Organizational Behavior,* Joanne Martin (1995) distinguishes three traditions in cultural research and concludes that, to define culture and to study it empirically, researchers require all three. The first she calls the *integration perspective.* Under this set of assumptions, people in the culture share a common set of values, a common set of norms that are clearly expressed to and understood by the vast majority of people identifying themselves with the culture. Usually, a charismatic leader has generated the set of beliefs and values, and his or her role in propagating them is often cultivated through stories and myths that are well-known to members of the culture. In modern organizations these cultural assumptions are sometimes expressed in "mission statements." Company logos, uniforms, and ceremonies are used to educate and indoctrinate newcomers to the organization. Because of the wide and strong consensus that exists in such cultures, they tend not to change gradually but through revolution, where a new set of values and beliefs replaces the old one. Martin notes that this is one of the most widely held views of organizational culture and the one most widely propounded by managers and consultants, as the belief is held that such "strong cultures" lead to better organizational performance and effectiveness.

Researchers who have studied organizations from this perspective have largely relied on the reports and claims of senior managers/professional employees who are held to understand the culture and are involved in selling it to the rest of the people in the organization. The degree to which the rest of the organization has actually bought into the culture is frequently problematic and often not questioned. Certainly, the evidence that such strong cultures are common is unsound, as is the claim that a strong culture necessarily leads to greater effectiveness. Martin (1995) concludes that "integration studies offer managers and researchers a seductive promise of harmony and value homogeneity that is empirically unmerited and unlikely to be fulfilled" (p. 378).

The unlikelihood of all members of a large, complex organization agreeing about its aims and methods lies at the heart of Martin's second tradition, which she calls the *differentiation perspective*. Organizations contain people who come from different social and ethnic backgrounds and who perform different roles; these roles vary in the power and authority they carry and the rewards and obligations that derive from them. Thus the people fulfilling these different roles have different interests and different motives. At the same time, they have to cooperate to some extent, or the organization will fail and none of them will get their interests met. Hence there are degrees of differentiation, and the subgroups or subcultures need to learn to cooperate with each other and to resolve the conflicts that inevitably flow from their differences in ownership and involvement. Mintzberg's (1983) division of organizations into five parts (the strategic apex, the middle line, the operating core, the technostructure, and the support structure) exemplifies the structural aspect of differentiation, although he is less concerned with indicating how the divisions are often associated with subcultural differences in race, age, gender, social class, and mixtures of all these. Differentiation in an organization often results from pressures in the wider environment in which it is embedded—social, political, economic, and physical/environmental. In this perspective the thing that distinguishes an organization's culture is the way it manages this nexus of forces and the environment it is in. Change tends to result from environmental pressures and occurs incrementally rather than dramatically. As Martin points out, the assumption that there is consensus within the subcultures remains powerful and therefore suffers the weakness of the integration perspective.

The third tradition for understanding culture takes differentiation to an extreme. Martin (1995) calls this the *fragmentation perspective*. Contemporary cultures, she argues, are so riddled with ambiguity in terms of aims, values, norms, and beliefs that they inevitably fragment into ever-changing subgroups. Ideas, needs, and motives are continually shifting: "To the extent that consensus exists, it is issue-specific and transient" (Martin, 1995, p. 380). Understanding culture, then, is about understanding the ambiguities of life as it is at the present. This perspective rejects the idea that relationships among people can achieve any lasting consensus or consistency. Power relationships alter to respond to current changes in the environment, which trigger the need for people to respond in order to protect their own self-interests. The idea of planned change is anathema to people holding this view of the nature of social reality. Martin criticizes researchers holding this tradition for perpetuating a methodological tautology: Fragmentation and ambiguity are what they look for, and fragmentation and ambiguity are what they find—unambiguously.

Having exposed this conceptual differentiation, Martin (1995) offers a form of integration by proposing that those who study organizational culture need to take all three perspectives into account, because using all of them will provide a greater understanding of the whole. This concurs with Gareth Morgan's (1986) argument for studying the "images" of organizations and reading the scripts each image creates. This is not to argue that using the three approaches to collecting data and interpreting them will achieve triangulation (Denzin, 1978) and provide a coherent view with which other researchers and/or cultural members would agree. Rather, it is to say that by taking all three perspectives into account, a researcher can better understand the dynamics of the whole culture. Each perspective involves the subjective interpretation of the culture, whether the methods used to collect information about it are quantitative or qualitative. Some measure of integration, differentiation, and fragmentation will be present in all organizations at any one point in time. It is a matter of how much of each there is, where in the organization it is occurring, and why.

So, culture is complex in reality, and as a construct. What about climate?

## THE CONCEPT OF ORGANIZATIONAL CLIMATE

In 1990, Schneider edited a book that attempted to distinguish culture from climate, and none of the contributors came to any clear conclusion. Denison (1996) has attempted to end the "paradigm wars" that he perceives to have existed between culture and climate researchers. He concludes as follows: "A comparison of this recent culture research with the 'organizational climate' literature of the 1960s and 1970s shows a curious similarity and suggests that it is becoming increasingly difficult to distinguish some of the cultural research from the earlier climate paradigm on the basis of either the substantive phenomenon or the methods and epistemology" (p. 644). In terms of definitions of culture and climate, I certainly agree with Denison that many are easily substitutable for each other. Denison, however, presents a helpful comparison of the two concepts, which appears here in Table 10.1 (my own minor alterations to Denison's lists appear in the table in italics).

Denison's comparisons illustrate well that culture is very different from climate but they also share the common ground of trying to describe and explain the relationships that exist among groups of people who share some sort of common situation/experience. What Table 10.1 illustrates is that they use very different methods to do it. Culture researchers derive their methods from anthropology, and climate researchers derive theirs from the nomothetic traditions in psychology. Weick (1969) describes the GAS framework for comparing different approaches to social/psychological research: $G$ stands for

**TABLE 10.1.** A Comparison of Culture and Climate, After Denison (1996)

| Focus | Culture | Climate |
|---|---|---|
| Epistemology | contextualist | nomothetic/ comparative |
| Point of view | natives' *(via researcher)* | researcher's *(via natives')* |
| Methodology | qualitative | quantitative |
| Concern | values and assumptions | consensus of perceptions |
| Theoretical foundations | social construction/ critical theory | $B = f(P \times E)$ |
| Discipline | anthropology/ sociology | psychology |

NOTE: Additions to Denison's comparison appear in italics.

generalizable, $A$ for accurate, and $S$ for specific. It is proposed that no single piece of research can simultaneously satisfy these three requirements. Culture research is more accurate and more specific than climate research, but it is much harder to generalize from, other than in the application of the concept itself. Climate research is (possibly) more generalizable, but it is less accurate and less specific, although it may still provide a useful description of a single organization and an even more useful comparison with other organizations. Thus, although it is difficult to distinguish definitions of culture from those of climate, it is possible to claim that climate is a way of measuring culture. The question I am asking is, How close can it get to doing that, given the meaning of culture as defined by Martin? To explore this question, I describe below a three-dimensional model of culture that is an elaboration of a framework I first published in Warr's ed-

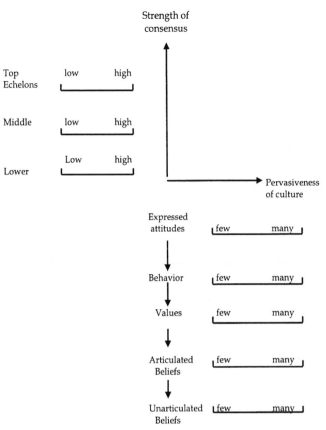

**Figure 10.1.** Cultural Coordinates

ited volume *Psychology at Work* (Payne, 1996).

## A THREE-DIMENSIONAL MODEL OF CULTURE

Figure 10.1 presents the two main dimensions of the original framework. There is a problem with the figure in that the horizontal dimension of pervasiveness contains two different concepts: pervasiveness and psychological intensity. *Pervasiveness* refers to the range of beliefs and behaviors that the culture attempts to define and control. In a religious order this is very wide. The culture determines what you should think, what you should do, when you should do it, how you should do it, how you dress, how you address others, what is right, what is wrong, and what punishments and rewards are associated with obeying or betraying. Traditional Japanese manufacturing organizations influenced a much greater range of behaviors and beliefs than did similar large Western organizations. Much of their success has been attributed to the greater commitment and control this generated in the workforce (Ouchi, 1981). IBM expected its employees to behave as "IBM people" and, in the 1970s at least, attempted to influence how people dressed and behaved at work, but not in their own homes. Apple Computer encouraged more casual dress and a greater range of acceptable social behavior at work (but not in the home). Organizations that employ many part-time (casual) workers attempt to influence only a very narrow range of behaviors and expressed attitudes (i.e., only those relevant to the performance of the job at work).

Attempts to influence beliefs and behaviors vary in their psychological intensity. Organizations can attempt to influence what people do and think by manipulating their attitudes—that is, by making people think positively about the organization and about how to treat customers, colleagues, and bosses. If they are successful, then the behavior associated with the attitude frequently follows too—they achieve attitudinal commitment (Meyer & Allen, 1991). In some cultures, the emphasis is on the control of behavior. In organizations where control is important (e.g., prisons, the military, some schools, some assembly-line workplaces), managers are more concerned with making sure employees do what is required than with whether or not they like it. Positive attitudes often flow from behaviors that are rewarded (Stajkovic & Luthans, 1997), and the psychological intensity increases when the attitudes and behaviors become central values or core beliefs for the person. For many people who work in prisons, the military, and manufacturing organizations, the goals and values they serve become very important and highly valued. At this level of intensity, behavior is controlled from within the person. When operating at the level of attitudes and behavior directly, the control is largely external to the person through the control of rewards and punishments. Powerful though they are, beliefs of this sort are still open to rational evaluation. They can be reconsidered, changed in the light of experience. When they reach the point where they are not open to rational thought, and are so fundamental to the person's view of reality and of his or her own identity that they are undiscussable, then they are almost beyond change, although the "road to Damascus" (or Microsoft) remains open. At this point they are "taken for granted." They are the "way things are." As suggested in Figure 10.1, they represent a scale of psychological intensity.

The vertical dimension in Figure 10.1 takes us back to Martin's integrated perspective. The dimension is called *strength of consensus* to emphasize the point that cultures vary in strength. In the organizational culture literature in particular, it is almost taken for granted that the word *culture* means a strong culture. That strong cultures necessarily lead to effective organizations is a major managerial myth (Martin, 1995). As Figure 10.1 indicates, however, it is quite possible to get strong consensus about cultural issues, but the content may differ at different levels in the hierarchy. This is, of course, an example of a differentiated culture. If the consensus were to occur both horizontally (across divisions and departments) and vertically, then it would become a fragmented culture. The three dimensions are brought together into the "culture cube" illustrated in Figure 10.2.

In terms of this model, a highly integrated culture would be one in which there is consensus throughout, about a pervasive range of issues, which are accepted by the members as deeply held values, with many operating at the level of the "taken for granted." As Figure 10.1 illustrates, this is the province of religious orders, cults, and clans rather than work organizations, although some work organizations are more like this than others (e.g., traditional large Japanese organizations). As the model suggests, a culture could achieve high consensus over a narrow range of beliefs and behaviors and work at a deep level of intensity too.

A most important point needs to be added to this framework. That is: What specific things are the focus of any particular culture? What are the specific values promoted by leaders? What are the specific behaviors members are expected to act out? How are these promulgated? What myths are told and retold? What symbols and artifacts are used, and when and where are they displayed? Which members of the culture are allowed to display them? What sorts of ceremonies take place and who attends them? What sorts of language will be used? Although I have suggested that the dimensions in Figure 10.2 are the main dimensions, it should not be forgot-

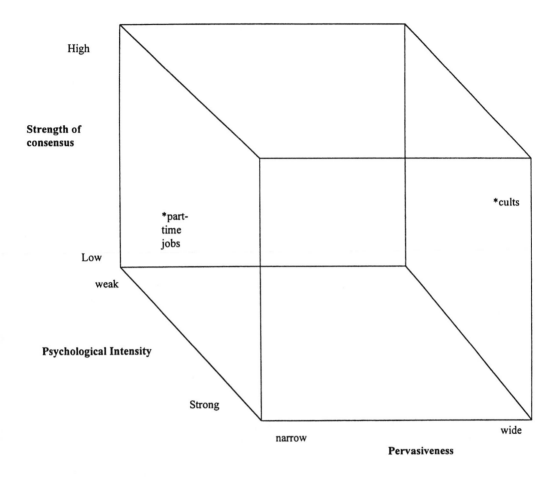

**Figure 10.2.** A Three-Dimensional Model of Culture

ten that it is the content of cultures' values/beliefs that truly distinguishes one culture from another. Indian temples, Indian gods, Indian ceremonies, Indian social systems are quite different from Anglican ones in their content, even though they both occur in large religious buildings, worship a god, and specify which kinds of people can do what, when, where, how, and why.

Strictly speaking, content is a category rather than a dimension, but content can be treated as a set of variables. The best-known organizational example of this is the work of Hofstede (1980a). Using a data set from a survey of values carried out in IBM organizations around the globe, Hofstede identified

four dimensions and was able to show how the dimensions differentiated across national cultures even within the relatively strong organizational culture of IBM. Hoppe used the same measure in China, and a fifth dimension has been added to the list (Hofstede, 1991). Descriptions of these five dimensions follow, along with examples of the national cultures that have been found to be high and low on each of them:

- *Power distance:* Values about the degree to which power should be concentrated or dispersed throughout different levels of the organization. For example, at IBM, power was concentrated at the top in Indonesian offices and was much more dispersed in Austria and Israel. (the question of "Who?")

- *Uncertainty avoidance:* The degree to which deviance from established norms and values can be tolerated. Low tolerance was found for uncertainty avoidance in Greece and Portugal compared to Sweden. (the question of "How?")

- *Individualism/collectivism:* The degree to which culture/climate encourages social cohesion versus individual independence and self-reliance. Australia and the United States were found to be more individualist and Pakistan more collectivist in the IBM data set. (the questions of "Who?" and "How?")

- *Masculinity/femininity:* The degree to which assertiveness, or dominance of others, is approved versus caring and nurturance of others. Within IBM, Japan was more masculine and Sweden more feminine. (the questions of "Who?" and "When?")

- *Confucian dynamism:* The degree to which there is concern for the maintenance of traditional social orders (e.g., the family, the dynasty) versus more individualist, liberal social orders based on negotiation rather than on obligation. Countries in the Far East tend to be more traditional than those in Western democracies. (the question of "Why?")

Although it is easier to see that these dimensions differ across national cultures, it is obvious that they also raise some fundamental issues for cultures of any kind. Who has power and why? Should we encourage risk taking? Do we value change? How should the individual be treated? Should the group be more important than the individual? Is tradition more important than innovation? How do we manage relationships between the sexes? These dimensions represent a reasonable starting place for consideration of how cultures differ in content, and even more so in the ways they shape the management of that content—that is, through the management of symbols, ceremonies, rites, and the artifacts that accompany them, as well as through traditional and evolving legal systems. The content of some cultures might not be relevant at all to other cultures: witchcraft or animism,

for example, or the accumulation of material objects and wealth.

## GETTING CLIMATE CLOSER TO CULTURE

My purpose in describing the three-dimensional model of culture was to elaborate it so as to make it easier to operationalize. The consensus aspect of the model has been a key problem since measures of climate were first developed. In developing climate measures for schools, Pace and Stern (1958) developed a series of true/false statements and used them to describe an aspect of climate only if more than two-thirds of the people in the school endorsed them. Guion (1973) has argued that the proportion should be nearer to 90%, but most researchers have used Likert-type scales rather than binary scales and have taken the mean score as an indicator of the climate. The problem with this approach is that it ignores the variance around the mean, which can be considerable. Efforts to cope with this led to the use of the intraclass correlation and later the $r_{wg}$ (James, Demaree, & Wolf, 1984) as means of assessing whether there is sufficient agreement to justify the use of the mean as an indicator of the climate. Having developed these statistical tools, researchers were faced with the question of the size of the coefficients. I will return to this later; for now, suffice it to say that there are ways of measuring the degree of consensus and thus the strength of the climate.

The content has also been developed in the sense that there are many organizational climate questionnaires that cover a range of content (Furnham & Gunter, 1993) as well as questionnaires aimed at specific sorts of organizations, such as schools and colleges (Stern, 1970). Some have been developed to measure specific kinds of climates, such as the safety climate (Zohar, 1980) or the service climate (Schneider, Wheeler, & Cox, 1992). Some are also broad in the things they cover and thus indirectly tap the concept of

**TABLE 10.2**   The Cultural Intensity Questionnaire

This questionnaire is designed to describe your organization's culture, with an emphasis on measuring how strong it is. This is achieved by getting you to describe how many people hold certain views, for example, and by assessing how intensely the culture is felt by considering whether it is primarily held as an attitude, largely expressed as behavior, or rooted in deeply held values/beliefs. Your initial reactions to the questions may well be your most accurate, so if in doubt, be guided by those thoughts.

The questions all have the same format. For each aspect of culture you are asked to indicate how many people would (a) publicly express a positive attitude toward it, (b) behave that way (whatever their attitude), (c) have it as a deeply held value (whether they behave that way or not), (d) have it as such a fundamental belief that it is "taken for granted" without them necessarily expressing their awareness of it.

*Example*

With respect to "Giving a fair day's work for a fair day's pay":

| | *all/most people* | *many* | *some* | *few/none* |
|---|---|---|---|---|
| (a) People would express a positive attitude toward it | 4 | 3 | 2 | 1 |
| (b) People behave in line with it | 4 | 3 | 2 | 1 |
| (c) People value it deeply | 4 | 3 | 2 | 1 |
| (d) It is so fundamental here, it's just taken for granted by | 4 | 3 | 2 | 1 |

Sometimes all the answers will be the same, but often there will be inconsistencies among attitudes, behaviors, and values or beliefs. A culture is strong when most people adopt it and there is consistency of values, beliefs, and behaviors.

Please complete the scoring sheet by answering sections a-d for each of the items on the following page(s).

*Example Climate Items*
With respect to:

1. Putting the customers' needs first
2. Disciplining people for failing to follow rules and procedures
3. Supporting members of the organization who need help
4. Promoting an identity through the use of ceremonies
5. Promoting and supporting green issues
6. Recruiting good people and rewarding them accordingly
7. Empowering people at all levels of the organization

**ANSWER SHEET**

Enter a number from 4 to 1 in columns a to d.

| (a) attitude | (b) behavior | (c) value | (d) taken for granted |
|---|---|---|---|

Question Number:

1. Customers
2. Disciplining
3. Creating identity
etc.

pervasiveness. No researchers, to my knowledge, have systematically concerned themselves with the concept of pervasiveness per se. Stern's (1970) measures contained 300 items designed to tap the degree to which the climate creates a "press" for each of 30 needs. The Business Organization Climate Index had 20 scales (Payne & Pheysey, 1971). The Organizational Culture Inventory (Cooke & Lafferty, 1989) has 12 scales with 10 items in each, and the Organizational Culture Profile (O'Reilly, Chatman, & Caldwell, 1988) measures 9 scales with 54 items. Factor analysis of these longer measures tends to reduce them to 3 or 4 dimensions. Second-order factor analysis of Stern's 30 scales reduced them to only 2 dimensions.

Where climate measures have been least satisfactory is in the measurement of what I have called intensity/depth. Most climate questionnaires ask people to agree or disagree with descriptions about the organizational environment. The descriptions might be about leaders' behavior, whether decisions are shared, how people treat each other, and so on, but they don't systematically examine whether the target description is about attitudes, behaviors, values, or taken-for-granted beliefs. The three-dimensional model can help to do that.

Table 10.2 presents an example of how the instructions and response format for a climate instrument could be designed to achieve this; I call it the Cultural Intensity Questionnaire. The items are used merely to indicate the range of issues that can be investigated in this way. Item 1 is about concern for customers, 4 about managing culture itself, 5 about environmental values, and 6 about who gets into the organization. None of these really fall within the categories defined by Hofstede; item 3 is about social support and could be seen as an aspect of feminism, item 7 concerns empowerment and can be seen as power distance, as could item 2, which is about discipline. More important for the question of concern—How close can climate get to culture?—the framework can be used to encourage members of the culture to define their own content. The items presented in Table 10.2 are just examples that can be used or rejected if they are not relevant to the culture under examination. This process is most economically done either in small groups that are representative of different parts of the organization or in groups that are drawn from different parts of the organization to sample systematically potential differences in culture. A more costly, but more thorough, method would be to employ the multimethod approaches described at the start of this chapter (Duncan, 1989; Siehl & Martin, 1988). It is worth noting that it may also be worth recording what the culture is not. The advantage of creating content in this way is that the items can be constructed in ways that make use of the company's own history, language, myths, ceremonies, and systems. I have used this in workshops, and people soon get the hang of designing items. Furthermore, they can answer in the format described in the table and can distinguish between behaviors and values that are (or are not) consistent with those behaviors. It is also worth noting that this response format is directly consistent with the concept of climate itself. The respondents are required to act as reporters about the collectivity qua collectivity, not as respondents who report their own experiences of the culture that are then aggregated (i.e., psychological climate), which is the case for some climate measures (Lawton, Patterson, Maitlis, Payne, & West, 1997). The format is a good one for assessing consensus. If everybody is agreeing that most people believe or value something, and that this value is deeply held, perhaps taken for granted, then one can reasonably assume that it is a strong component of the culture. In Martin's (1995) terms, it will identify an integrated climate.

However, the climate literature is replete with examples of the failure to find high levels of consensus. This has led to the use of cluster analysis to identify clusters of individuals who do see the climate in similar ways. Jackofsky and Slocum (1988) carried out a two-phase study in a hotel and showed that at the first phase one of the clusters was consistent with membership of a department, although this was not replicated in the second phase. They were able to show that clusters differed on other variables, such as job satisfaction, and attributed this to respondents' sharing the common experience of the climate. I have criticized this approach, arguing that such clusters should be treated as meaningful only if they have some other psychosocial identity (e.g., are members of a department, a clique, the same profession/trade, or the like; Payne, 1990). Patterson, Payne, and West (1996) sought to find a situation where a common task and physical proximity could be expected to create climate clusters/collectives, but failed to do so. Sparrow and Gaston (1996) made more positive progress, and I have recently been a journal reviewer of at least one paper that has used some creative ways of pursuing this form of analysis.

On reflection, however, this thinking is rooted in the integrated perspective. Perhaps it would be just as useful to use climate data to explore systematically where there are reasonable levels of consensus in different parts of the organization (i.e., teams, levels, subgroups, working parties, and the like) but differences across them: the differentiated perspective. It would also enable the researcher/consultant/CEO to explore the nature of the differences in terms of pervasiveness of the content, degree of intensity related to different areas of content, and degree of consensus about each of these. If there is no consensus, then one has a good empirical indicator of the degree of fragmentation, again for different aspects of content. A statistic such as $r_{wg}$ could be used to measure the *degree* of consensus by level of segment and by the content area. High consensus at different levels and over different content areas would indicate a differentiated culture and identify the nature of the differentiation. Longitudinal studies of fragmented organizations would reveal just how fast the content of the issues that lead to temporary integration change, and over which sorts of issues they change. These kinds of data would inevitably lead to a search for the ambiguities, conflicts, and "causes" that provide the energy for such activity. In other words, data that are seen as "noise" by those holding the integrationist view of climate can be seen as information by those taking the differentiation or the fragmentation perspective.

## MEASURING THE DEGREE OF CONSENSUS

This use of measuring the degree of consensus does raise issues of how consensus is measured and what constitutes a practical degree of consensus. As indicated earlier, there is a debate about which index is most suitable and what size of index indicates a degree of consensus high enough to be acceptable to somebody with the integrated perspective. I have drawn attention to this issue in an essay in honor of Derek Pugh (Payne, 1997), but with the sole aim of testing the integrationist perspective. Accepting that information about disagreement is of just as much use as information about agreement casts things in a different light, but the importance of knowing the level of consensus becomes even more important if climate measures are to be used to reflect all three cultural perspectives.

As I have noted, there has been a debate about which index is the best for measuring the degree of consensus/agreement about the climate. The main protagonists have been James, Demaree, and Wolf (1984, 1993), Yammarino and Markham (1992), and Kozlowski and Hattrup (1992). Despite this well-known problem, studies of climate still use the mean score and fail to test for degree of agreement, or test for it using coefficients of agreement, but ignore them if the levels fall below those recommended (0.7) on the grounds that this is what others have done in the past. Zammuto and Krakower (1991), for example, published the coefficients of

**TABLE 10.3** Summary Statistics of Bootstrap Results ($n = 40$)

| Scale | Minimum | Maximum | Mean | Standard Deviation | Skewness | Kurtosis |
|---|---|---|---|---|---|---|
| 1 | 0.00 | 0.87 | 0.696 | 0.116 | −1.908 | 5.680 |
| 2 | 0.33 | 0.90 | 0.795 | 0.106 | −1.556 | 4.987 |
| 3 | 0.00 | 0.87 | 0.686 | 0.069 | −2.148 | 7.291 |
| 4 | 0.38 | 0.90 | 0.795 | 0.128 | −1.701 | 5.161 |
| 5 | 0.00 | 0.89 | 0.729 | 0.062 | −2.501 | 11.056 |
| 6 | 0.00 | 0.87 | 0.694 | 0.116 | −1.978 | 6.430 |
| 7 | 0.00 | 0.87 | 0.685 | 0.113 | −1.529 | 3.620 |
| 8 | 0.00 | 0.78 | 0.369 | 0.241 | −0.340 | −1.202 |
| 9 | 0.00 | 0.89 | 0.720 | 0.102 | −1.811 | 5.643 |
| 10 | 0.00 | 0.86 | 0.656 | 0.140 | −1.850 | 4.715 |
| 11 | 0.00 | 0.90 | 0.737 | 0.102 | −1.948 | 6.761 |
| 12 | 0.00 | 0.87 | 0.521 | 0.211 | −1.045 | 0.374 |
| 13 | 0.00 | 0.89 | 0.649 | 0.158 | −1.793 | 4.169 |
| 14 | 0.36 | 0.90 | 0.756 | 0.073 | −1.209 | 2.363 |
| 15 | 0.00 | 0.90 | 0.741 | 0.095 | −2.253 | 10.091 |
| 16 | 0.00 | 0.88 | 0.680 | 0.135 | −2.085 | 6.405 |
| 17 | 0.00 | 0.82 | 0.585 | 0.171 | −1.603 | 2.613 |

agreement for the different quartiles of their sample of 332 colleges. For the top 25% the average coefficient was 0.66, and for the lowest quartile it was only 0.2, but all organizations were used in other analyses.

The most widely used coefficient is the one recommended by James et al. (1984) and further justified by these authors in 1993: $r_{wg(j)}$. My colleagues and I have investigated the properties and parameters of this index. Our analyses are based on a revised version of the Business Organization Climate Index (Payne, Brown, & Gaston, 1992; Payne & Pheysey, 1971). The revised version has 17 scales, each of which has 8 items that are answered on a 4-point scale ranging from *definitely true* to *definitely false*. The revisions from the original 20 scales involved cutting some scales out and creating new ones to deal with things like the management of culture, information technology, quality, and customer service.

The measures were completed by 2,150 people from 56 U.K. organizations, which ranged in size from 70 to 7,100 employees. Of these organizations, 9 were in retailing and distribution, 24 in manufacturing, and 23 in the service sector. There were 163 senior managers, 803 supervisors, and 1,155 operator-level employees. The results of our analyses appear in Padmore, Gaston, and Payne (1993) and Padmore and Payne (1995).

In the 1993 Padmore et al. study, the within-groups coefficient, $r_{wg(j)}$, was calculated for each of the 17 scales in each of the 56 organizations. The purpose was to see how the size of coefficients varied under different assumptions. Initially, it was assumed that the responses would show no systematic sources of variation other than true response variance. Thus responses to each item would follow a uniform distribution, leading to an expected variance of 1.25. Indices estimating this value may be regarded as upper-bound estimates of the true level of consensus (Kozlowski & Hattrup, 1992). Other forms of response bias were studied having variances of 1.00 and 0.89, which are moderately skewed distributions. These three distributions were felt to represent possible real distributions, and the indices for each of them were displayed as box and whisker plots (Tukey, 1977).

There were large variations in the indices of consensus by scale, but even more important for the integrationist perspective, there were many organizations with low consensus across many of the scales. Each organization was examined separately using the lower estimate of variance (0.89). Accepting the guideline of 0.7 as a standard, Padmore et al. declared organizational consensus to exist if (a) this was achieved for 75% or more of the scales and (b) no other scale was lower than 0.5. Applying this rather liberal standard, we found that 35 out of 56 organizations met the criteria. On this evidence, the findings of many studies that relate climate to anything else must be considered highly suspect.

This is a pretty crude way of proceeding, however, and in the 1995 Padmore and Payne study we sought a more refined set of guidelines by using bootstrapping techniques (Efron, 1979). These techniques involve repeatedly resampling from the sample to produce an empirical description of the sampling distribution of the statistic. The statistic used here was again $r_{wg(j)}$, used as an indicator of degree of consensus within a group. The degree of consensus actually observed was compared to a bootstrap estimate of what might be obtained under the assumption of no differences between organizations. All individuals are treated as representatives of the population, so samples of any given size can be created from the population by resampling with continuous replacement from the entire sample. The values of $r_{wg(j)}$ can be calculated for the facsimile samples and an empirical description of its distribution calculated, assuming no consensus within organizations. A

comparison of these with the statistics actually obtained from real organizations provides a way of estimating the degree of consensus in the organizations themselves.

Assuming no interorganizational differences, 1,000 samples were constructed using different sample sizes (from 10 to 60) that are similar to the sample sizes in the data set itself. Table 10.3 shows the statistics for the sample size of 40 for each of the 17 scales (the complete set of results appears in Padmore & Payne, 1995). It is obvious from Table 10.3 that even in randomly drawn groups the mean size of the statistic is close to the 0.7 recommended to show adequate levels of consensus. Many past studies have clearly not demonstrated adequate levels of agreement to claim the mean represents the organization's climate on any particular dimension.

The box and whisker plots for the "real" data are presented in Figure 10.3. They assume a variance of 0.89. It is obvious that some scales show much less consensus than others. Scale 8, which measures Scientific and Technical Orientation, and Scale 13, which measures Interpersonal Aggression, produce wide distributions within the 56 organizations studied here. Given that the organizations span distribution, manufacturing, and service, the wide distribution on Scientific and Technical Orientation is perhaps understandable. Interpersonal Aggression may be more subject to individual-difference effects than other variables.

Scales 2, 4, 9, and 14 have coefficients above 0.8 and relatively small variances. They measure Questioning Authority, Orientation to Quality, Intellectual Orientation, and Rules Orientation, respectively. These all show higher levels of consensus than would be expected by chance. When the actual values were compared to the upper 10% cutoff point of the bootstrapped critical values for the sample size of 40, three organizations were found in which all 17 scales were significant, 18 organizations had 12 scales or more, and 24 had more than half the scales significant.

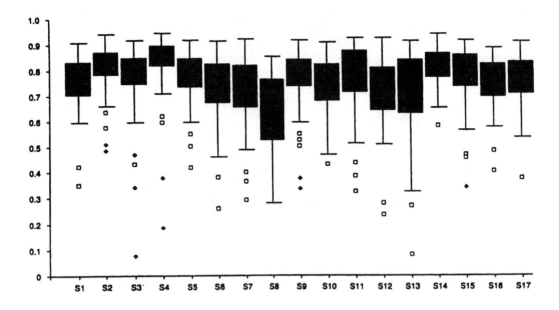

**Figure 10.3.** Box Plot of $r_{wg(j),0.89}$ by Scale

From the point of view of the present discussion, it can be argued that the three organizations are clear examples of cultures that conform to the integrationist perspective. The 32 that failed to have half the scales showing consensus can be seen as fragmented. What is perhaps more important is that through the use of this approach it is possible to compare levels of staff, or departments/divisions, to explore where consensus lies or where fragmentation is greatest. This approach is consistent with the search for the differentiated perspective. It is also obvious that one could look for agreement or disagreement across particular scales or factors of climate to see whether consensus or fragmentation differs by content. No doubt the high concern we show for comparison and generalization will involve the use of some scales that are standard, and it would be interesting to compare degrees of consensus on these with scales that have been generated by the organizations themselves. One would hypothesize that the latter should show higher consensus.

## CONCLUSION

With the use of climate scales that are designed in collaboration with members of the organization, and with acceptance that measures of agreement can be used to reflect integration and fragmentation, the climate approach can be seen to be a useful indicator of culture. Climate is not culture, but it is not as different from it as I once thought, and redesigned along the lines described above it can play a useful role as a research tool, and perhaps an even more useful role as a diagnostic approach to understanding individual organizations and monitoring change within them. Climate can get us closer to culture.

# 11

## The High-Performance Organizational Climate

### How Workers Describe Top-Performing Units

*—— Jack W. Wiley and Scott M. Brooks*

A significant body of research has emerged over the past 20 years that examines the relationship between how employees describe their work environments and the relative performance success of those work environments. Wiley (1996) has termed this body of research *linkage research* and has provided the following definition and purpose: "Linkage research involves integrating and correlating data collected from employees with data in other key organizational databases. The purpose of linkage research is to identify those elements of the work environment—as described by employees—that correlate, or link, to critically important organizational outcomes such as customer satisfaction and business performance" (p. 330).

Wiley (1996) summarized the approximately 20 studies then published, which included both qualitative case studies and quantitative empirical studies. From this summary, he developed the linkage research model, which is depicted in Figure 11.1. The linkage research model provides a comprehensive framework for integrating all previously published work in this field. It suggests that the more present certain organizational or leadership practices are in a given work environment, the more energized and productive the workforce. In turn, the more energized and productive the workforce, the greater the satisfaction of customers and the stronger the long-term business performance of the organization. The model gives special consideration to the moderating effects of work characteristics (such as closeness of

**Figure 11.1.** The Linkage Research Model
SOURCE: Copyright 1996 Gantz Wiley Research. Reprinted by permission.

customer contact or the transaction volume of the performed work) as well as to the mediating effects of time—that is, it is over the long (versus short) time perspective that a focus on customer results is beneficial to business performance.

We have several purposes in this chapter. First, we summarize recent linkage research studies and evaluate their consistency with conclusions reached in Wiley's (1996) previous review. Second, we introduce and briefly describe three new linkage research studies as further illustration of the linkage research model. Third, we summarize the results of the three new studies, blending them with those of previous research, to describe in greater clarity and detail how higher-performing units differ from lower-performing

units within their respective organizations. And finally, we discuss the implications of our conclusions for both the measurement of work environments through the use of employee surveys and the creation and maintenance of higher-performing organizational units.[1]

## REVIEW OF RECENT RESEARCH

In this section we focus primarily on linkage research published since the previous review by Wiley (1996). We summarize studies conducted in a variety of settings, including banking, insurance, retail, utilities, fast food, and business services. Wiley (1996) discussed earlier and in some detail the most common design for conducting empirical linkage research as well as the challenges associated with that design. We present here the findings produced by such studies. We discuss two major types of studies: concurrent and longitudinal.

## Concurrent Studies

In a very common setting for linkage research, branch banking, Johnson (1996) conducted a study evaluating various climate-for-service components against a criterion of customer satisfaction. Participants in the study consisted of 538 employees and 7,944 customers across 57 branches of a large bank. Employees completed a survey assessing their perceptions about the performance of their organization in managing the delivery of quality service. Customers completed surveys assessing their satisfaction with specific service issues. Results showed that all climate-for-service components were significantly related to at least one facet of customer satisfaction. Seeking and sharing information about customers' needs and expectations, training in delivering quality service, and rewarding and recognizing excellent service were the practices most highly related to customers' overall satisfaction with service quality.

In the utility industry, Thompson (1996) examined the hypothesis that those work units perceived by employees as being more progressive in their human resource practices have superior performance. The units of analysis in this study were 71 districts of a large utility having primary responsibility for customer service and sales. Districts ranged in size between 50 and 200 employees each. Progressive human resource practices were measured using the Vision Progress Index, which consists of employee survey items measuring the following topics: Core Values, Customer Commitment, Business Dimensions, Communication, Safety, Business Results, Empowerment, Innovation and Risk Taking, Rewards and Recognition, Community Involvement, Environmental Responsibility, and Team Work. The research findings supported the hypothesis; that is, the units with the most progressive human resource practices were also the units with higher customer commitment (an employee measure), customer satisfaction (an external customer measure), and profit contribution margin. In addition, those same units also achieved significantly lower grievance, absenteeism, and safety incident rates. Subsequent qualitative analysis determined that the presence of a caring, involved leader was the critical ingredient in unit success.

In a unique study conducted among franchisees in four industries (restaurant, business aids and services, automotive products and services, and retailing nonfood), Morrison (1997) examined the influence of franchisee job satisfaction on four organizational outcomes: franchisee performance, organizational commitment, congeniality of franchisor relations, and intention to remain. Using a mail questionnaire, Morrison collected data from 307 franchisees in four different industries. Although the study uncovered many useful findings, most relevant to this chapter are the findings that franchisee satisfaction had a significant and positive correlation with each of the four included measures of organizational outcomes. Although satisfaction is different from climate, there are often overlaps in how the two are measured. In this study, for example, satisfaction was measured not only by a single global measure of satisfaction taken from the Job Diagnostic Survey (Hackman & Oldham, 1974), but also by the much broader 20-item form of the Minnesota Job Satisfaction Questionnaire (Weiss, Dawis, England, & Lofquist, 1967), which addresses a number of dimensions of the work environment.

In a business services industry setting—namely, within a large security systems company with 160 offices throughout the United States—Schmit and Allscheid (1995) explored the relationship between employee attitudes and intentions and customer satisfaction. They examined the results from a total of 3,464 employees who completed a survey containing 36 items reliably measuring Supervisor Support, Management Support, Service Support, Monetary Support, and Perceived Service-Product Quality. Customer satisfaction data were collected from a total of 31,362 customers who completed an 8-item survey. All of the employee measures except Supervisor Support were significantly and positively related to customer satisfaction. Schmit and Allscheid subjected the data to a series of rigorous analytic techniques and concluded that the "findings suggest that top management must take an active role in establishing a service climate by showing direct support for service imperatives and concern for employees' welfare" (p. 532).

## Longitudinal Studies

Perhaps the most significant change in linkage research studies conducted in recent years is the emergence of longitudinal studies. As Wiley (1996) noted in calling for such research in his earlier summary of this topic, longitudinal studies have the advantage of providing information concerning the causality or directionality of relationships. In fact, the linkage research model implies that leadership practices precede employee results, which precede customer results, which precede business performance. The model also implies that, as the leadership value system continues to be regarded as the foundation for achieving higher customer satisfaction and stronger business performance, it becomes self-reinforcing.

The first such study to address this question of directionality was conducted by Schneider, Ashworth, Higgs, and Carr (1996). Working in a major U.S. insurance company, these researchers designed an employee survey that focused on strategic objectives of the firm and measured the degree to which frontline employees perceived that certain strategic initiatives were being carried out. They collected data from approximately 7,000 employees, working in 27 different regions of the company, over four successive quarters. Simultaneously, they collected customer data (including data on both satisfaction and likelihood of policy renewal) from approximately 50,000 customers during each of these same four quarters. To analyze the relationship between the employee and customer data, they used cross-lagged panel analysis, a statistical technique that explores sets of correlations collected over multiple points in time to reveal the most likely causal sequence. The pattern of relationships that emerged suggested "that the causal arrow runs from employee to customer data, rather than the reverse, over time" (p. 702). This implies that changes in managerial practices, as observed by employees, preceded changes in customer perceptions and intentions.

In a study conducted by Ryan, Schmit, and Johnson (1996), relationships among employee attitudes and turnover, customer satisfaction, and organizational unit performance were examined at the branch level of a large automotive finance company. Using data from 142 branches in 2 consecutive years, the researchers revealed several significant relationships between attitude factors and employee turnover, customer satisfaction, and performance indicators. Given that they had data over two time periods, Ryan et al. used structural equation modeling techniques to suggest the causal relationships among these sets of variables. Before doing so, they collapsed three employee attitudinal factors (Job/Company Satisfaction, Supervision, and Work Group/Teamwork) into a general factor labeled Morale and found little to indicate the causal nature of a morale-productivity relationship but some evidence suggestive of customer satisfaction as a cause of morale. Ryan et al. provide some potential explanations for this finding and strongly caution against generalizing about causal direction from this research.

A chain of fast-food restaurants was the setting for research reported by Donthu, Bernhardt, and Kennet (in press). Across 382 restaurants, they collected data from 3,009 employees and 342,308 customers, incorporating those data with 12 months of restaurant performance measures. Although they found a positive and significant relationship between employee and customer satisfaction in any one given time period, when analyzing the data collected concurrently, they found neither employee satisfaction nor customer satisfaction to be significantly predictive of business performance. However, the analysis of time-series data revealed that a positive and significant relationship existed between changes in customer satisfaction and changes in the business performance of the firm. The authors conclude that the impact of an increase in customer satisfaction on profits, although obscured in the short run by many factors, is significantly positive in the long run.

Finally, Schneider, White, and Paul (1998) tested, among other things, the premise that climate for service causes customer perceptions. Data were collected at multiple points in time from employees and customers of 134 branches of a bank. Support for one of the major contentions was found, namely, that individual climate-for-service scales—customer feedback and interdepartment service—as well as the measure of global service climate were positively and significantly related to overall customer perceptions. However, they also found, using structural equation modeling, a relationship of reciprocal causality between service climate and customer perceptions of service quality. Even so, the authors suggest the commonsense notion that the key to positive customer perceptions of service quality is found in organizational and leadership practices that emphasize listening to customers and creating conditions that will meet those customers' expectations and needs.

## Conclusions From the Literature Review

In general, recent linkage research studies appear highly consistent with previous research and with the linkage research model in particular. All of the concurrent studies found positive relationships between the components of the model they examined. Johnson (1996), Morrison (1997), and Schmit and Allscheid (1995) all found significant and positive relationships between how favorably members of an organization described their work environment and how satisfied customers were with product and/or service obtained from that organizational unit. In addition, Thompson (1996) demonstrated that significant relationships also exist between how favorably employees describe their work units and various outcome measures, such as higher profit contribution margin and lower grievance, absenteeism, and safety incident rates.

As noted previously, longitudinal studies attempt to provide insight into the causality or directionality of these relationships. All of the reported longitudinal studies indicate (as do the concurrent studies) that positive relationships exist. Schneider, Ashworth, et al. (1996) demonstrated that changes in employee opinions about their work environment preceded changes in customer satisfaction and intention. In a similar fashion, Donthu et al. (in press) found that increases in customer satisfaction predicted increases in unit profitability. Both of these studies support the directionality implied by the linkage research model—that is, from leadership practices and employee results to customer and business results.

On the other hand, the study by Ryan et al. (1996) offers no insights regarding the morale-productivity relationship, but it does provide some evidence suggesting that increases in customer satisfaction precede increases in morale. Notice, however, that this study focuses on the employee measure of morale. Morale is a very different concept from measures of climate in general and climate for service in particular. It has been our experience that as members of an organization align around key objectives (e.g., increasing customer satisfaction), and when measurements indicate that they are successful in achieving those objectives, employee morale increases. Although the resulting increase in morale may appear to stem from increases in customer satisfaction (or some other key initiative around which the organizational units are aligned and measured), in actuality it is the leadership or organizational emphasis being placed on a certain value (e.g., customer satisfaction) or outcome (e.g., operating efficiency) that precipitates the resulting improvements in both satisfaction and performance. In effect, this seems to support the conclusion of the longitudinal study by Schneider, White, and Paul (1998), which found reciprocal causality between employee measures of service climate and customer perceptions of service quality.

Table 11.1 organizes what the literature suggests are the most common work climate dimensions that are related to customer satisfaction and business performance. We have included the studies reviewed here as well as one other recent study conducted since the previous literature review (Wiley, 1996). The most frequently supported climate dimensions are those represented by the linkage research model.

From a review of the research it is clear that the patterns of relationships vary depending upon the criterion examined. Customer opinions regarding products versus services, for example, relate slightly differently to employee-perceived work climate dimensions. More important, different measures of business performance can sometimes yield substantially different relationships with work climate dimensions. Nevertheless, the few studies that have included business performance measures have all found significant relationships with at least some climate dimensions—in patterns consistent with the customer and climate dimension relationships. We acknowledge our oversimplification of the business performance criterion and leave its clarification to future research.

Taking the above into consideration, it would appear that strong support has emerged for the linkage research model, based on both concurrent and longitudinal studies. One natural next step is that of further and more exactly clarifying the dimensions—as observed and reported by employees—that separate top- and bottom-performing units of organizations. Given the variety of ways in which the work environment is measured, the question is this: What are the factors or themes, when more present in a work environment, that are associated with higher levels of organizational success? Important answers are provided in what follows: three case studies—built around the linkage research model—that allow us to provide a taxonomy of climate dimensions and descriptions reflective of successful organizations.

## CASE STUDIES

In this section we present three case studies, conducted by our colleagues and ourselves, representing distinct industries: banking, women's specialty retail, and business services. For all three cases, we briefly describe the settings and the databases analyzed, including employee and customer perspectives, as well as business results. Using the linkage research model as a guide, we present the climate dimensions significantly related to customer and business performance criteria. We further elaborate on these broad dimensions by focusing on the specific employee measures, at the item level, that achieve the most empirical support. Following these individual studies, we integrate the results into a summary that depicts how employees in successful organizations describe their work environments.

### Branch Banking

The setting of this case study is a large midwestern retail branch banking system. In brief, employee survey, customer survey, and productivity measures were integrated, using the bank's 133 branches as the unit of analysis. The employee survey contained 79 items

**TABLE 11.1**  Summary of Recent Literature on Employee Work Climate Dimensions Related to Customer Satisfaction and Business Performance

| Work Climate Dimensions | Overall Customer Satisfaction | Business Performance (various measures) |
| --- | --- | --- |
| **Customer orientation** | | |
| Customer focus (management support, systems, strategy) | Johnson (1996); Ryan et al. (1996); Schmit & Allscheid (1995); Schneider, White, & Paul (1998); Thompson (1996) | Ryan et al. (1996); Thompson (1996) |
| Employee estimate of customer satisfaction | Johnson (1996) | |
| Problem resolution | Schneider, Ashworth, et al. (1996) | |
| Recognition for service | Johnson (1996) | |
| **Quality emphasis** | | |
| Quality | Ryan et al. (1996) | Ryan et al. (1996) |
| Perceived service/product quality | Schmit & Allscheid (1995) | |
| Quality physicians | Kam & Brooks (1998) | |
| Recommend products | Schneider, Ashworth, et al. (1996) | |
| **Involvement/empowerment** | | |
| Flexibility | Kam & Brooks (1998) | Kam & Brooks (1998) |
| Empowerment | | Ryan et al. (1996) |
| **Employee training** | | |
| General training | Ryan et al. (1996) | Ryan et al. (1996) |
| Service training | Johnson (1996); Kam & Brooks (1998) | |
| **Information/knowledge** | | |
| Customer information | Johnson (1996); Schneider, Ashworth, et al. (1996); Schneider, White, & Paul (1998) | |
| Business information (goals, strategy, etc.) | Kam & Brooks (1998); Schneider, Ashworth, et al. (1996) | |
| **Teamwork/cooperation** | | |
| General teamwork | Ryan et al. (1996) | Ryan et al. (1996) |
| Cross-functional— between specific groups | Johnson (1996); Kam & Brooks (1998) | |
| Cross-functional—general | Schneider, White, & Paul (1998) | |
| **Overall satisfaction** | | |
| Job satisfaction | Donthu et al. (in press); Rucci et al. (1998); Ryan et al. (1996) | Morrison (1997); Ryan et al. (1996) |
| Company satisfaction | Rucci et al. (1998); Ryan et al. (1996) | Ryan et al. (1996) |
| **Employee retention** | | |
| Turnover | Ryan et al. (1996) | |

that, based on factor and internal reliability analysis, were categorized into 15 themes. Across the system of 133 branches, 2,422 employees completed the survey, yielding a response rate of 80%.

The customer survey contained 70 scaled items that, based on factor and internal reliability analysis, were categorized into 8 themes. For the purposes of this chapter, we present only Overall Satisfaction here (due to its universal, summary nature). The paper-and-pencil survey was mailed to customers' homes. In total, 15,455 customers responded to the survey, for a response rate of 34%.

Two key measures of business or operational performance were included in this research: Productivity Ratio, computed as the amount of branch bank revenue generated for every dollar of personnel expense, and Number of Teller Transaction/Full-Time Equivalent (FTE), a measure of the volume of transactions handled by tellers in relation to the number of full-time-equivalent teller staff. The business performance measures used were based on year-end data. We believed this would provide the most reliable assessment of business performance.

Table 11.2 presents the significant relationships ($p < .05$, two-tail tests) between the employee survey measures, as organized according to the leadership practices and employee results components of the linkage research model, and the customer and business performance criteria. Along with this branch banking study, Table 11.2 summarizes the empirical findings of the remaining two case studies as well. Not all employee survey items were identical across these three case studies. As a result, we combined similar concepts to facilitate the distillation of common findings.

## Specialty Retail

The setting of this case study is a large chain of 575 women's specialty retail shops. Employee survey, "secret shopper" evalua-tions (i.e., trained raters posing as shoppers), and sales growth performance were integrated using 69 shop districts as the unit of analysis. The employee survey contained 128 items, 100 of which were categorized into 19 themes based on factor and internal reliability analyses. Across the chain of 575 shops, 5,945 employees completed the survey, for a response rate of 54%.

As previously indicated, the client service evaluation was completed by mystery shoppers who were trained to visit each shop within the chain and observe and evaluate the shop's overall client service orientation. Individual ratings were given to each shop on such features of client service as greeting and approach, store image, service provided by employees, availability of merchandise, comfort of fitting rooms, and general impressions of the shop. Because many of the 56 items in the survey used yes/no or other checklist response options, traditional scale creation was not possible.

Two of the client service evaluation items were chosen as the criteria on which to focus: "Did the associate ask questions to determine your needs?" and "Did the associate suggest items in addition to those you inquired about?" These items were selected based upon their relationships to the key measure of financial performance: season-to-date same-store sales (shop-level percentage of sales improvement in comparison to the same period of the preceding year). Both client service evaluation items yielded significant partial correlations, .38 for asking questions to determine customer needs and .36 for suggesting additional items. Because employee survey confidentiality concerns necessitated aggregation to the district level (rather than the store level), it was judged appropriate to control for district size (measured by number of shops and number of respondents per district) and average company tenure of associates by district.

Table 11.2 also summarizes the findings for this specialty retail case study. The significant relationships presented all represent partial correlations.

## Business Services

The setting for the final case study is a major division of a multinational computer corporation that provides computer-based processing services to businesses, including payroll, tax filing, accounting, and human resource management functions. Employee opinion survey, customer satisfaction survey, and business performance data were aggregated using 31 districts as the unit of analysis.

The employee survey was administered to 2,287 employees, with 1,476 returns yielding a 64% response rate. The 66 scaled items were categorized, based on factor and internal reliability analyses, into 11 themes.

The customer survey was mailed to 6,425 customers, with 52% or 3,341 returning completed surveys. The 68 items were a priori grouped into 8 themes and confirmed as having acceptable Cronbach's alphas. For the purpose of this study, the theme selected upon which to focus our analyses was Overall Satisfaction. We chose this theme because of its summary nature. The business performance measures presented here include Profit as a Percent of Revenue (representing a bottom-line financial measure) and Responsiveness (representing an internal process quality measure).

Again, Table 11.2 indicates the relationships between the employee survey measures and the selected customer and business performance criteria. Due to a smaller sample size, fewer significant relationships were found for this study. The magnitudes, however, are roughly comparable to those of the first two cases.

## Case Study Integration

Although these case studies can be illuminating individually, and certainly are important to the client organizations, there are clearly some common conclusions we can draw. Using the results from these three case studies, along with previously published research regarding established linkages, we have developed a taxonomy, presented in Table 11.3, of how employees describe successful work environments. Based upon a now solid foundation of quantitative research, this taxonomy provides a more narrative description of the features of successful work environments. It illustrates in greater detail the values managers should emphasize and the practices on which they should focus in order to create high-performance organizations.

Viewed holistically, there is a very clear sense overall of the importance of leadership and the responsibilities of communication, vision, and demonstration of priorities. This suggests that a foundation to organizational success is the ability of a senior management team to create a credible and potent sense of confidence that the organization is well led.

## IMPLICATIONS

From the linkage research conducted to date, there are two rather clear implications for employee-based organizational measurements. The first is that properly designed employee-based measures of the work environment and organizational climate are key tools for the diagnosis of bottom-line organizational success. Such tools can be, as Schneider, White, and Paul (1998) note, measures of more than just opinions. The results of such diagnoses can identify a clear road map for organizational development and needed improvements.

The second implication is that when the objectives for climate and employee opinion measurement tools include understanding and having impacts on customer satisfaction and business performance, these tools should emphasize the leadership and organizational practices, as identified in the linkage research model, that have a demonstrated ability to predict these important outcomes. As a result, these measurement tools will focus on

*(text continued on page 189)*

**TABLE 11.2** Summary of Significant Relationships Among Work Climate Dimensions Implicit in the Linkage Research Model and Customer Satisfaction and Business Performance for Three Organizations

| Work Climate Dimensions | Retail Branch Banking Organization | | | Specialty Retail Organization | | | Business Services Organization | | |
|---|---|---|---|---|---|---|---|---|---|
| Leadership Practices | Customer Satisfaction | Teller Transaction | Productivity Ratio | Determining Customer Needs | Suggesting Items | Same-Store Sales | Customer Satisfaction | Responsiveness | Profit as % of Revenue |
| **Customer service** | | | | | | | | | |
| Strong emphasis on customer service | ** | — | | * | ** | | | * | |
| Company provides quality service | ** | | * | ** | ** | | | | — |
| Customer problems corrected quickly | ** | | ** | ** | ** | | * | * | |
| Delivers products/services in a timely fashion | — | — | — | ** | ** | — | — | — | — |
| Other departments help serve customers | * | | | — | — | — | — | | — |
| **Quality** | | | | | | | | | |
| Senior management committed to quality service | * | | * | | | | | * | — |
| Senior management demonstrates quality top priority | ** | | * | | | | | | |
| Manager provides service guidance | * | * | | | | — | — | — | — |
| Manager sets good example re quality | | * | | ** | — | — | — | ** | — |
| Rate work group quality | — | — | — | ** | ** | * | | ** | |
| Continuous improvement | * | * | | — | — | — | | — | |
| Set clear service quality standards | * | * | | * | — | | — | — | |
| Quality is priority vs. meeting deadlines | — | — | — | — | * | | — | — | |
| Quality is priority vs. cost containment | — | — | — | ** | | | — | | |
| **Involvement** | | | | | | | | | |
| Authority necessary to serve customers | * | ** | * | | | | | | — |
| Encouragement to be innovative | | ** | | — | — | — | — | — | — |
| Encouragement to participate in decisions | | ** | | | | | | | |
| Sufficient effort to get opinions | | ** | | * | | | | * | |
| Management uses good ideas employees have | | | | | | | | | |
| **Training** | | | | | | | | | |
| Have plan for training and development | — | — | | — | — | | — | | — |
| Opportunity to attend training | * | | | | | | | * | * |
| Given opportunity to improve skills | | ** | | * | — | — | | — | |
| Satisfied with training/development opportunities | — | — | | ** | | | * | * | |

186

| Work climate description | | | | | | | |
|---|---|---|---|---|---|---|---|
| Right training to help me improve | — | — | — | — | — |  | * | * |
| Product and services training | — | — | — | — | — |  | ** | ** |
| Training to do current job | — | — | — | — | — |  | * | * |
| Satisfied with on-the-job training | — | — |  | ** | ** |  | — | — |
| New employees get necessary training | — |  |  | * |  |  | — | — |
| **Information/knowledge** |  |  |  |  |  |  |  |  |
| Management gives clear vision/direction | — | — | — |  | * |  | ** | ** |
| Clear understanding of goals | — | — | — | — | * |  | ** | ** |
| Employees informed about issues | — | — | — | — | — |  | ** | ** |
| Other departments keep us informed | — |  |  |  |  |  | ** | ** |
| Enough warning about changes | — |  |  | — |  | * |  |  |
| Satisfaction with company information | — | — | — | — | — |  | * | * |
| **Teamwork/cooperation** |  |  |  |  |  |  |  |  |
| Cooperation to get job done | * |  |  |  | * |  | ** | * |
| Employees work hard to meet customer needs | — |  |  | — |  |  | — | — |
| Management encourages teamwork | — | * |  | — |  | * | * | * |
| Workload divided fairly | — | — | — | — | — | ** | — | — |
| Enough people to get work done | — | — |  | — | — | ** | — | — |
| Problems in group corrected quickly | — | — |  | — |  |  |  |  |
| **Overall satisfaction** |  |  |  |  |  |  |  |  |
| Rate job satisfaction | * |  | * | ** | * | ** | * | * |
| Like the work I do | * | * | ** | ** |  | * | * | * |
| Job uses skills and abilities | — | — | — | — |  |  | * | * |
| Work gives feeling of accomplishment | — | * |  | * | * | ** | ** | ** |
| **Company satisfaction** |  |  |  |  |  |  |  |  |
| Rate company as place to work | * | * |  | ** | ** | ** | * | ** |
| Would recommend working at company | * | ** |  | ** | ** | — | — | ** |
| Proud to work for company | — | * | ** | ** | ** |  | ** | ** |
| Confidence in future of company | — | ** | * | ** | * |  | * | * |
| Rate job security | — | ** |  | — | ** |  | — | ** |
| **Employee retention** |  |  |  |  |  |  |  |  |
| Not seriously considering leaving company | — | ** | * |  | ** |  | — | — |

NOTE: The work climate descriptions listed in the left column are abstracted across the three organizations and thus represent survey item content in summary form. A dash in a column indicates the item was not included in the survey for the referenced organization.
* $p < .05$; ** $p < .01$.

187

**TABLE 11.3**  Characteristics of High-Performance Organizations: The Employee Perspective

**LEADERSHIP PRACTICES**

*Customer orientation*

Employees see a strong emphasis on customer service, and in fact believe their organization does a good job of satisfying customers.

Customer needs are attended to quickly, whether in initial delivery of products and services or in the resolution of problems.

*Quality emphasis*

Senior management is committed to quality and demonstrates this priority in day-to-day decisions. These values are effectively translated and implemented by lower-level managers.

Employees can see that quality is a priority versus cost containment, and especially versus meeting deadlines.

Employees believe their work groups do quality work, as judged by clear quality standards, and are able to improve continuously.

*Involvement/empowerment*

Employees have the authority and support they need to serve their customers.

Employees are encouraged to participate in decisions affecting their work and, perhaps more important, to innovate.

Management solicits and uses opinions of employees in such a way that employees can see the connection.

*Employee training*

Employees have written development plans to take advantage of the formal and informal skill-improvement opportunities that exist within the company.

Whether on-the-job or formal, employees see they have the training to perform their current jobs well. This can include specific training on products and services or explicitly on customer service.

New employees are oriented and able to come up to speed quickly, without undue burden on existing staff.

**EMPLOYEE RESULTS**

*Information/knowledge*

Management creates and communicates a compelling vision and direction for the company.

Employees understand their role in the organization—how their goals fit into overall company objectives.

Employees report having enough information to do their jobs, including company information, advance warning of changes, and information from other departments.

*Teamwork/cooperation*

Employees both within and across departments cooperate to serve customers and to get the work done. This teamwork is actively supported by management.

Workload is managed effectively within a given work group—the load is divided fairly, and short staffing is not a significant barrier.

*Overall satisfaction*

Employees derive intrinsic satisfaction from their work, see a good match among their jobs, their interests, and their skills and abilities.

Employees are satisfied with and proud of their organization.

There is confidence in the company's ability to succeed, leading to long-term stability for the employee.

*Employee retention*

Employees value their relationship with the organization and have no short-term interest in leaving.

Longer-tenured employees are more efficient and create more value for the organization and its customers.

the values, practices, and resources that most separate organizational leaders and laggards.

From a measurement perspective, the starting point is the idea of employees as observers and reporters of the values and practices that define their work environments. When measurement tools are properly designed to capture "observations" and "reports" about what matters most in predicting organizational success, such tools produce information that represents a significant organizational asset. Moreover, as Kraut and Saari (1999) note, designing survey instruments and interpreting their results in light of models such as the linkage research model can dramatically enhance the value of employee survey efforts.

From the linkage research conducted to date, we can also identify five practical implications for organizational leadership in the quest to develop work climates and environments most productive of customer satisfaction and long-term business success. These implications focus on strengthening and improving leadership practices.

First, organizations should create and nurture a strong orientation toward serving the customer well and a strong emphasis on creating and delivering a high-quality product and service. Clear messages regarding these values must be communicated and driven throughout the organization through the establishment of clear standards and guidelines. Day-to-day decisions and choices made by management (e.g., the priority of quality versus cost containment or deadlines) must demonstrate the relative importance of these values.

Second, a high value should be placed on the input and involvement of frontline supervision and employees. This can be demonstrated through a variety of techniques aimed at engaging executive management and employees in dialogue and soliciting and using employee ideas. For example, and in relation to the first point above, leaders should attend to customer service shortcomings observed and reported by employees. In addition, executives and managers should encourage individual employees and teams to innovate,

recognize them for doing so, and ensure that employees have the authority to do what is necessary to serve their customers well, whether those customers be internal or external to the organization.

Third, organizations should ensure that employees are properly trained to perform the requirements of their jobs and should place special emphasis on the training of new employees. In addition, an organization's leadership must strongly encourage, through both formal and informal means, the continual development of employees' skills and their knowledge of products and services.

Fourth, leadership must create and communicate a compelling vision for the future of the organization such that employees know not only the direction the organization is heading but also how their individual roles fit into organizational success. The focus on communication must also include an emphasis on interdepartmental alignment and sharing of information. An ongoing, proactive communication style will build confidence in the leadership of the organization.

Fifth and finally, organizations are most effective when they operate in a cooperative fashion and with a spirit of teamwork. Teamwork will flow from a common sense of purpose and interdependence, along with equitable inputs and outcomes for all team members. Where barriers to teamwork exist, management must identify them and work to reduce or eliminate them. Care must be taken to ensure that workload is fairly divided and that adequate human resources are available to achieve the organization's goals.

The more the leadership of an organization adheres to the above practices, the greater the success the organization will achieve. In addition, under these conditions, the more intrinsically satisfied employees will be with their work and the more pride they will have in their organization. Employees will also have greater confidence in the organization's future and will be less likely to resign voluntarily and to seek employment elsewhere. This, in turn, contributes further to the organization's success, in that more highly tenured and experienced employees, all other things being equal, add more economic and marketplace value.

## FURTHER RESEARCH DIRECTIONS

Our primary objective in this chapter has been to elaborate on the specifics of how employees describe successful organizations. Future studies should build upon the practical relevance and the scientific foundation of linkage research. We list below a number of key additional areas that we suggest for future investigations:

- *Employees as informants:* We know that some employees are better informants about the work environment than others (e.g., Brooks & Kam, 1998; Lundby, Dobbins, & Kidder, 1995). Future investigations that take this reality into consideration will enrich our understanding of how opinions of different categories of employees relate differentially to customer and business results.

- *Causality/directionality:* Causality will always be an important and yet difficult issue to address. With the complexity of organizations and the measures involved, there may be multiple causality paths among many different kinds of measures. Researchers should work on finding causal support for paths between particular categories of constructs that are stable across organizations.

- *Criterion development:* With linkage research, as with much organizational research, most of the effort has been devoted to understanding the predictors (i.e., employee opinions) as opposed to the criteria (i.e., customer and business outcomes). Brooks and Kam (1998) found that employees can relate dramatically differently to different types of customers. Wiley (1998) has suggested that focusing on the most important and nonconflicting business performance measures will help an organization decide how to define and track its own success.

- *Setting:* There is evidence that industry and other characteristics of an organization can make a difference in how employees understand the value they create and how that value translates into customer reactions and subsequent business performance. For example, different types of units (e.g., mall versus freestanding retail stores; Brooks & Guth, 1999) and different markets (e.g., metro versus nonmetro bank branches; Wiley, 1996) attract and evoke different types of customer behavior and expectations. Additional research can help to determine what unit-level characteristics are important to include in the conduct of linkage research.

- *Economic impact calculations:* Recent work published about Sears (Rucci, Kirn, & Quinn, 1998) presents very compelling evidence about how unit improvements in employee opinions drive specific levels of customer satisfaction increases, which in turn generate specific levels of revenue growth. Although there are very sound methods for creating such models, they make certain assumptions about causality and variability in the measures that need to be firmly supported. Future research can clarify which approaches are the most valid.

## CONCLUSION

Within the domain of organizational climate, linkage research represents one of the most organizationally relevant and scientifically compelling avenues of study. Practically speaking, the combined weight of prior findings has led to exciting and useful frameworks such as the linkage research model and, as presented in this chapter, the characteristics of successful environments. Scientifically speaking, our increasing understanding of how employees come to understand and view organizational performance touches upon the very center of what it means to be effective and how employees are directed and motivated to participate. As researchers within the rapidly growing field of linkage research, we are directed forward by the questions yet to be answered, and the implications of what we already know provide unique motivation.

# NOTE

1. The employee opinion constructs discussed here seem to fall clearly under the category of "climate" rather than "culture" measures (for a review, see Denison, 1996). We acknowledge that there is some debate as to the appropriateness of linking organizational effectiveness to culture (Denison, 1996). There is significant support, however, for the appropriateness and value of establishing how specific climate measures are connected to a company's performance (e.g., Schneider, White, & Paul, 1998).

# 12

## Organizational Culture as a Predictor of Organizational Performance

*—— Celeste P. M. Wilderom, Ursula Glunk, and Ralf Maslowski*

Research on the link between organizational culture and performance/effectiveness has increased substantially during the past decade (Lim, 1995). Large-scale quantitative studies have been undertaken mainly in the United States (Denison, 1990; Denison & Mishra, 1995; Gordon & DiTomaso, 1992; Kotter & Heskett, 1992; Marcoulides & Heck, 1993; Petty, Beadles, Lowery, Chapman, & Connell, 1995; Rousseau, 1990c) and in Europe (Calori & Sarnin, 1991; Koene, 1996; Wilderom & Van den Berg, 1998). A wide variety of culture as well as performance indicators have been utilized, and they have been employed in various kinds of organizations and industries. What connects these studies is a strong belief among the researchers that the performance of organizations is attributable, in part, to organizational culture. Between a mere belief and hard scientific evidence, however, there is a world of difference. Central to this chapter is the question of evidence: Does organizational culture have, indeed, a positive effect on organizational performance?

Before we examine the available evidence for this proposition, we first provide a historical sketch of the relevant literature. We then address pertinent research challenges regarding the linking of organizational culture to performance. We thereby offer a framework for future testing of this link. We think that the field of organizational studies will not flourish without more solid evidence on the culture-performance (C-P) link (Smircich, 1983), but so far only a handful of scholars have been engaged in this admittedly daunting task. Yet much more sophisticated C-P research is needed. Such work is likely to provide convincing evidence for the idea that deeply rooted positive sentiments on the part of employees regarding their organizations

**TABLE 12.1**    Phases in the Organizational Literature on the Culture-Performance Link

| Phase | Time Span | Characteristics | Main Representatives |
|---|---|---|---|
| Emergence | World War II-1978 | mere suggestion of a link between culture and performance; no standardized measures of culture | Jaques (1951); Silverzweig & Allen (1976) |
| Promulgation | 1978-1982 | promulgation of the C-P link; mostly semiscientific literature | Ouchi & Jaeger (1978); Ouchi & Johnson (1978); Pascale & Athos (1981); Peters & Waterman (1982); Deal & Kennedy (1982) |
| Defiance | 1982-1990 | emphasis on literature review papers; ad hoc criticism on the C-P link | Carroll (1983); Reynolds (1986); Saffold (1988); Siehl & Martin (1990) |
| Testing | 1990-present | empirical testing of the C-P link; use of relatively sophisticated statistical analyses | See Table 12.2 |

are highly conducive to positive organizational results.

## HISTORIC OVERVIEW

The link between organizational culture and performance has a relatively long tradition in the field of organizational studies (see Table 12.1). Its roots can be traced back to the Hawthorne studies (Roethlisberger & Dickson, 1939/1975) and, more important, to the study of the Galcier Metal Works. In *The Changing Culture of a Factory,* Jaques (1951) focused on the customary and traditional ways of "thinking and of doing things, which is shared to a greater or lesser degree by all its members" (p. 251) and related these to the working behavior of the employees. Jaques was primarily interested in the social interactions among employees and the regularities that resulted from these interactions.

He did not explicitly study the effects of these social processes on the performance of the firm. His findings, however, point to culture as a serious barrier to productivity—that is, if the culture is not congruent with organizational structure or environment.

During the 1960s and early 1970s, organizational culture and its link to performance gained little attention. Most of the studies that addressed the culture of organizations were not concerned with the issue of performance or addressed it only in an indirect manner. Pfiffner and Sherwood (1960), for instance, noted in their popular handbook at the time: "Around each organization, then, there grow certain patterns of conduct and beliefs. These are considered 'right' for the organization. . . . They become the value system of the organizational members, and it is within this context that all members are expected to operate" (p. 250). Like Jaques, Pfiffner and Sherwood suggested that there might be a relationship between the culture and effectiveness of a firm, but they did not look into the nature of this link.

Silverzweig and Allen (1976) were the first to investigate explicitly the effect of a company's culture on its performance. On the basis of eight case studies, they suggested a close link between the culture and the performance of a company. Their cases involved firms from various branches that suffered losses or that intended to raise their effectiveness. They found that the performance of six of these eight organizations increased substantially after changes in their cultures, and that these improvements lasted for longer periods. Silverzweig and Allen's focus, however, was primarily on the culture change process, and the performance variables they used depended on the firm under study. Hence they gathered no comparative data, except concerning prior performance by the same firm. Their study thus had more value for research on the effects of cultural interventions than for an exploration of the relationship between culture and performance. Nevertheless, it must have given others some input for further research on the C-P linkage.

This indirect or implicit attention for the C-P evidence changed at the end of the 1970s, at which time explanations for the worldwide success of Japanese firms were being sought. At the forefront of this movement, Ouchi drew attention to the importance of workers' commitment and a unitary vision for a company's performance (Ouchi & Jaeger, 1978; Ouchi & Johnson, 1978). Ouchi argued that financial success of firms is attributable to their strong emphasis on certain humanistic values, such as concern for the well-being of employees and an emphasis on consensual decision making, which he found to be characteristic of most Japanese companies. In a similar vein, Pascale and Athos (1981) suggested, based on their experiences within 34 Japanese and American companies, that Japan's higher productivity was largely due to its focus on human relations. More specifically, they argued that a strong emphasis on the aspects of skills, style, staff, and superordinate goals would make the dif-

ference between high- and low-performance companies. What distinguished this period, it turned out, was a focus on the specific, more human-oriented content of supposedly successful corporate cultures.

A year later, Peters and Waterman (1982) fed that trend by claiming that what distinguishes highly successful from less successful companies is their so-called strong culture. In their widely cited book *In Search of Excellence,* they argued that superior firm performance is only to be achieved if companies move away from a pure technical, rationalistic approach toward a more adaptive and humanistic approach. Similarly, Deal and Kennedy (1982) suggested that organizational performance is enhanced by shared values, because such values act as an informal system that shows employees what is expected of them. In their view, an organization with a strong culture is not only able to respond well to its environment but able to adapt to diverse and changing circumstances.

This relatively popular and uncritical belief in the culture-performance link was criticized in the years that followed. Carroll (1983) questioned the approach taken by Peters and Waterman for its lack of comparison groups as evidence that the values of their excellent companies actually differed from those of other companies. Carroll indicated that some of the 36 firms that Peters and Waterman studied encountered serious financial problems only a few years after completion of their study. A subsequent journalistic follow-up of the companies in Peters and Waterman's sample, published in *Business Week,* gave rise to further doubts. Based on measures of financial performance, 14 of the original 62 "superior performers" apparently no longer passed the financial tests described in the book or had suffered significant declines in earnings ("Changing a Corporate Culture," 1984). A few years later, Reynolds (1986) presented a study in which he found that employee responses to a culture questionnaire in a company identified as "excellent" by Peters and Waterman did not differ from those in two other companies with less impressive performance. Finally, Hitt and Ireland (1987) studied 185 *Fortune* 1,000-type industrial firms, including 14 of Peters and Waterman's excellent companies. The results showed that, in terms of market return, Peters and Waterman's so-called excellent companies did not perform better than the other companies. Furthermore, the scores of excellent companies on some traits of excellence, such as closeness to customers and innovation, were not significantly higher than those of the other companies.

Owing to such results, the causal link between strong culture and corporate performance was seriously questioned by the end of the 1980s. Saffold (1988), for instance, acknowledged that a pervasive phenomenon such as organizational culture is likely to affect corporate performance, but he concluded that a "simple model for relating culture to performance no longer fits with the knowledge scholars have developed about the role culture plays in organizational analysis: a more sophisticated understanding of the tie between culture and organizational outcomes must be developed" (p. 546). Siehl and Martin (1990), following this argument, asserted that it might be possible that a link between culture and financial performance exists, but that the approach taken concerning content as well as methodology is on the wrong track. Even more critically, they argued that "the promise of a link between organizational culture and financial performance is empirically unsubstantiated, perhaps impossible to substantiate" (p. 241).

Despite this skepticism, the 1990s gave rise to a relatively large number of survey studies that empirically tested the assumed culture-performance link. This fourth phase (see Table 12.1) can be characterized by a renewed belief in a relationship between culture and performance. Researchers made great strides in developing and testing ideas that may explain this relationship, and some of them used relatively sophisticated statistical analyses (Koene, 1996; Marcoulides & Heck, 1993; Wilderom & Van den Berg, 1998). Yet most of the empirical studies reported in the 1990s had important conceptual and methodological weaknesses, many of which will be addressed shortly. A few of the major ones include the following:

1. Unknown or questionable construct validity of operationalizations of the two central variables (C and P)
2. Ambiguity about the direction of the C-P relationship
3. A relatively small number of participating organizations per study
4. Intraorganizational respondents that are not representative of entire organizational cultures

In the remainder of this chapter we will discuss the available culture-performance evidence and issues pertinent to obtaining more convincing evidence. What is the relevance of gathering further evidence on the prospective C-P linkage? In essence, such evidence would force us to provide a better understanding of the complex notion of organizational culture, plus it would, eventually, settle the degree of importance of an organization's cultural constellation vis-à-vis other important organizational variables, such as structure, strategy, and technology (Newman & Chaharbaghi, 1998).

## TEN EMPIRICAL C-P STUDIES

The widespread idea generated by the extensive writings on organizational culture is that the culture of an organization is an important key to the success of the organization. One might ask to what extent this idea is true or a mere management (guru) illusion (see also Kopelman, Brief, & Guzzo, 1990; Lim, 1995). In order to answer this question, we identified the published empirical research that explicitly studied organizational culture and its relationship to organizational performance/effectiveness. We did not take into consideration studies with "perceived organizational performance/effectiveness" as the main outcome variable. This measure is generally considered not "hard enough" when combined with independent variables consisting of perceptions, which standardized measures of culture invariably are (available solutions to this common method problem are hardly ever used in this area). We did not consider either the many case studies that speak to this issue, because their results are not comparable or conclusive. The first column of Table 12.2 provides references to 10 quantitative studies that we feel constitute the major empirical culture-performance studies to date.

The evidence summarized in the last column of Table 12.2 shows that each of these studies claims to show such a link. Taking these studies together, one could point to a body of evidence showing the existence of a significant C-P linkage. However, when interpreting the specific findings, we see little room for generalization. This is not only because of the studies' weaknesses but also because hardly any of them seem to have built on one another. They seem to be a set of studies that have very little relation to each other, despite their explicit claims to have tested the C-P link. Why is this so? First, all 10 operationalizations of the independent variable, organizational culture, as well as the outcome variable, organizational performance, differ greatly. Before we provide more general criticism on this line of organizational research, we will first take a closer look at the 10 extant studies listed in Table 12.2.

According to the guiding theory of Denison's empirical studies (see also Quinn's [1988] competing values model), a highly adaptable, high-involvement organization with a clear mission and widely shared organizational values ("consistency") will be most effective (Denison, 1990; Denison & Mishra, 1995). Both studies, even though varying in their operationalizations of the culture and performance variables, found this to be true, at least to some degree. Denison and Mishra (1995) found, for instance, that it holds only for large firms, whereas Denison (1990) noted earlier that

"the evidence for adaptability is less direct" (p. 178). The major problem with both studies is the operationalization of culture. In his 1990 study, Denison relied on data from the Survey of Organizations, a research project designed for other purposes. The scales utilized can at best loosely be labeled culture. In Denison and Mishra's study, the operationalization of each of the four cultural traits consisted of only two items, which is a narrow basis for the study of culture, particularly given that the validation information provided is not very convincing. The 1990 study, on the other hand, suffered from too many scales (21).

Rousseau's (1990c) operationalization of culture also consists of many scales, 12, the so-called normative beliefs, summarized into two dimensions (satisfaction versus security; see the second column in Table 12.2). Even though many intraorganizational issues are touched upon in the corresponding 120 items, this operationalization also fails as a best measure of organizational culture. Why? Even though it is a behaviorally descriptive measure of culture (quite fit for behavioral feedback in organizational change practices), its use is limited for the correlation of C to P. Culture was narrowed down to the two content dimensions, and the question still exists to what extent both dimensions (including their 12 constituent beliefs) are representative of an organization's culture. In other words, one is left to wonder if the resulting four types of culture cover the entire gamut of organizational cultural constellations. To our knowledge, other C-P research since 1990 has also failed to address this concern satisfactorily.

Calori and Sarnin's (1991) exploratory assessment of organizational culture also entailed a great number and variety of intraorganizational characteristics, worded and labeled differently. We have not seen a second use of this questionnaire in the literature (and this applies to all of the other standardized questionnaires utilized in this set of 10 C-P studies). In comparison with Denison's 1990 assessment, Calori and

**TABLE 12.2**   Empirical Studies on the Organizational Culture-Performance Link

| Reference | Organizational Culture Dimensions | Performance Measure | Organizations Involved | Respondents Involved | Evidence for the Culture-Performance Link |
|---|---|---|---|---|---|
| Denison (1990) | (a) involvement, (b) consistency, (c) adaptability, (d) mission | average over 6 years of (a) return on sales, (b) return on investment, (c) income/sales ratio, (d) income/investment ratio | 34 large U.S. firms from 25 different industries | 43,747 employees within 6,671 work groups | 1. Involvement is positively related to short- and long-term performance. 2. Consistency is positively related to short-term performance, but negatively related to long-term performance. |
| Rousseau (1990c) | (a) team- or satisfaction-oriented norms, (b) security-oriented norms | amount of money raised for community | 32 large units of a U.S. nationwide voluntary service organization | 263 paid staff members | Little emphasis on security-oriented norms is significantly related to high performance. |
| Calori & Sarnin (1991) | work-related values (12 dimensions) and management practices (17 dimensions)/culture strength | average over 3 years of (a) return on investment, (b) return on sales, (c) growth | 5 French firms with a single business, in mature industries pursuing a differentiation strategy | 280 managers and employees, excluding frontline workers | 1. Many values and their corresponding management practices were related to company growth. 2. Strength of culture is positively related to high growth. 3. Only a few values and practices were related to profitability. |
| Gordon & DiTomaso (1992) | (a) strength of culture, (b) adaptability, (c) stability | 6 years: (a) growth of assets, (b) growth of premiums | 11 U.S. insurance companies | 850 managers | Culture strength and adaptability are both predictive of short-term performance. |
| Kotter & Heskett (1992) | (a) strength of culture, (b) strategy-culture fit, (c) adaptability | average over 11 years of (a) yearly increase in net income, (b) yearly return on investment, (c) yearly increase in stock price | 207 U.S. firms from 22 different industries | 600 top managers | There is a positive but moderate relationship between culture strength and long-term economic performance. |

| Study | Culture/Climate Dimensions | Performance Measures | Sample | N | Findings |
|---|---|---|---|---|---|
| Marcoulides & Heck (1993) | (a) organizational structure, (b) organizational values, (c) task organization, (d) organizational climate, (e) employee attitudes | (a) gross revenue/product value ratio, (b) market share, (c) profit, (d) return on investment | 26 greatly varying U.S. firms | 392 employees | All culture dimensions have some direct or indirect effect on performance. |
| Denison & Mishra (1995) | (a) involvement, (b) consistency, (c) adaptability, (d) mission | (a) perceived performance, (b) objective performance as average over 3 years of return on assets and sales growth | 764 firms in five different U.S. industries | 764 top managers | 1. For large firms profitability is best predicted by stability traits such as mission and consistency. 2. Sales growth is best predicted by flexibility traits such as involvement and adaptability. 3. All cultural traits were positively related to return on assets, with mission as the strongest predictor. |
| Petty et al. (1995) | (a) teamwork, (b) trust and credibility, (c) performance improvement and common goals, (d) organizational functioning | (a) operations, (b) customer accounting, (c) support services, (d) employee safety and health, (e) marketing | 12 service units within a U.S. firm in the electric utility industry | 832 employees | Much teamwork is associated with high performance. |
| Koene (1996) | (a) process vs. results orientation, (b) employee vs. job orientation, (c) professional vs. parochial orientation, (d) open vs. closed culture, (e) tight vs. loose control, (f) normative vs. pragmatic | (a) store performance, (b) cost performance, (c) personnel performance | 50 company-owned Dutch supermarket stores of a large retail chain | 1,228 employees | Employee orientation and openness influence performance both directly and indirectly through their impact on the climate variables general communication and task communication. |

Sarnin's questionnaire also included items pertaining to the organization's "relation to its environment" (p. 53; see also Denison, 1990, p. 178)—an important aspect of any organization's culture for most of us.

One of the intriguing findings of the Calori and Sarnin study is a significant relation between a firm's growth (over a 3-year period) and "cultural intensity" and "cultural homogeneity." The latter two variables denote "cultural strength" and are considered similar to Denison's "consistency" notion. Denison (1990) found that "highly consistent management systems and little variability in the survey data appear to be better performers" in the short run (p. 178). Based on both studies, it would seem that having a strong culture is good for an organization only for a few years.

Let's see if the results of the two other studies that speak to this issue (Gordon & DiTomaso, 1992; Kotter & Heskett, 1992) confirm this inference. Clearly, Gordon and DiTomaso (1992) also found that "a strong culture, as measured by the consistency of perceptions of company values, is predictive of short-term future company performance" (p. 794). Yet Kotter and Heskett (1992) report a positive link between strength of culture and *long-term* economic performance. However, they also state that "the problem with the strong-culture theory, as we see it, is simply that . . . , it overlooks too much. Much too much" (p. 27). The fact that Denison and Mishra (1995) are silent about this issue (even though they measured "consistency") can be taken as some support for the latter ("there is more to it"-type) view.

Marcoulides and Heck (1993) used a structural equation model. They found that all their various intraorganizational factors influence organizational performance. Just as Denison had done in 1990, they labeled these factors together *organizational culture*—in our view, again too loosely. They nevertheless obtained results that are "congruent with the human resource management perspective, which has long advocated the development of effective methods of recruit-ing, evaluating, and compensating employees to enhance organizational performance" (p. 222).

Petty et al. (1995) found teamwork to be predictive of organizational performance. Their study is unique in the sense that both culture and performance were measured at two different points in time. Their culture measurement was quite particularistic—that is, it was created for the one firm within which the data were collected. Unfortunately, as is usual in the 10 studies under review, they provide very limited validation data.

Koene's (1996) dissertation study, as well as the study carried out by Wilderom and Van den Berg (1998), focused not only on the C-P linkage but on the leadership factor, often said to be different from culture yet often included in operationalizations of the organizational culture variable. Koene used the frequently cited Hofstede, Neuijen, Ohayv, and Sanders (1990) operationalization of organizational culture—perceptions of intraorganizational practices—but failed to extract all five dimensions.

Wilderom and Van den Berg (1998) found, with LISREL, an intriguing significant suppressor effect. They used a summary score for the variable of organizational culture, labeled *organizational culture gap*. Organizational culture gap is defined by the difference between perceived and preferred organizational practices; five new organizational practices or culture dimensions were employed. We will return to this potentially promising culture gap measure shortly.

Note, finally, that 9 of the 10 studies reviewed here (Petty et al., 1995, is the exception) report correlations in the context of cross-sectional designs. And only 3 of the 10 studies report objective performance data that were obtained after culture was assessed (Denison, 1990; Gordon & DiTomaso, 1992; Koene, 1996). Thus few of the studies summarized in Table 12.2 established causality. Hence most results could equally be "consistent with the hypothesis that effectiveness determines the cultural traits"

(Denison & Mishra, 1995, p. 220). The hypothesized predictive effect of C on P remains largely inferential.

In conclusion, the research evidence regarding the claimed predictive effect of organizational culture on organizational performance/effectiveness appears to be there, but not very convincingly so. Due to the utilized operationalizations of the culture variable and especially due to their uncertain validity, we are now not much further than we were in 1984, when Denison rightly stated that "there is little solid evidence about the impact of an organization's culture on performance" (p. 6). The fact that C-P studies where no such a link was found are not likely to be published and are thus underrepresented in the literature underscores this conclusion. Nevertheless, the great intuitive appeal of the C-P linkage, the preliminary evidence found so far, and the many research challenges involved in obtaining the evidence give some reason to still believe in this link. The great complexities involved in solid examinations of the C-P linkage point to the need for more sophisticated C-P studies. Hence in the remainder of this chapter we will address a number of challenges that this line of research entails.

## MAJOR C-P RESEARCH CHALLENGES

Researchers aiming to study the culture-performance link in a comparative way face at least three major questions. First, how do we best assess organizational culture? Second, how do we best assess organizational performance? And third, how do we best approach the relation between organizational culture and performance? In this section we discuss all three challenges, and we conclude that only if these three major questions are answered by the next phase of quantitative C-P studies can we more confidently answer the overriding question of the possible predictive effect of organizational culture on the performance of organizations.

## *How to Assess Organizational Culture*

The first research challenge in the context of quantitative C-P studies relates to the definition and measurement of the construct of organizational culture. As can be gleaned from the second column of Table 12.2, there are a multitude of underlying definitions of organizational culture, and no generally endorsed or applicable framework exists that allows us to measure and compare organizational cultures comprehensively. This variety of cultural characterizations found in the available studies is striking and reflects the equivocal nature of the construct of organizational culture. Some critics may even argue that in the 10 studies reviewed, "culture" has not been measured at all. Instead, they would say, assessments have been made of structural aspects of the organization and work-related values (Calori & Sarnin, 1991; Marcoulides & Heck, 1993), of normative beliefs (Rousseau, 1990c), of organizational climate (Denison, 1990; Denison & Mishra, 1995; Gordon & DiTomaso, 1992), or more generally of the practical functioning of the organization (Koene, 1996; Kotter & Heskett, 1992; Petty et al., 1995). This variety in organizational culture views is also reflected in the questionnaire items used, which refer to the attitudes of employees, to personal and organizational norms, to descriptions and evaluations of procedures, and to processes and structures in the organization, among other things. If assessments of organizational culture vary so widely, one may ask how we can ever accumulate (i.e., also compare) organizational culture knowledge. Let's see if we can, nevertheless, find some patterns in the results.

In the majority of the reviewed studies, analyses were focused on sets of intraorganizational content variables or dimensions labeled as organizational culture (e.g., involvement, consistency, adaptability, and mission). The only content dimension used repeatedly (i.e., in 4 of the 10 studies) was "adaptability." However, the great variation in its operationalization and especially the lack of validating information prevent clear comparisons and final conclusions. In other words, whether a highly adaptive intraorganizational culture (or, for that matter, any other cultural type) contributes to an organization's health or success is not firmly established. Although intuitively appealing and often claimed in organizational change practices, based on the evidence thus far, we are not sure if an adaptive organizational culture is always truly advantageous. Therefore, the validity of the C-P claim is undermined by the large variety of organizational culture operationalizations, especially their questionable construct validity.

A number of the empirical C-P studies reported "culture strength" on the basis of a summary or process score of organizational culture. This summary score, however, has not been widely accepted among scholars in the field (Kopelman et al., 1990; Schein, 1985; Weeks, 1994). Note also that the culture strength measure was used only three times in our set of studies, and each time operationalized differently. Hence, despite its popularity, particularly in managerial practice, we think of the evidence obtained with this score as insufficient to warrant any well-founded C-P claim. In other words, it is unclear if it will pay off for a firm always to strive toward a so-called strong culture, especially given that we have no consensus on what this really means or whether it truly matters, not to mention the tools to manage it.

Some have argued that an interaction effect between cultural content and cultural summary scores may be most powerful (Gordon & DiTomaso, 1992). The breadth or complexity of the culture construct makes this idea worth testing in future studies. Before one could test such an interaction proposition, one would need to have available a valid summary-type notion of organizational

culture. Moreover, one would require the availability of relatively large samples as well as a convincing, standardized questionnaire measure of organizational culture that is well connected to (organizational) culture theory—the latter requirement being the most prominent yet difficult to fulfill (see also, in this volume, Ashkanasy, Broadfoot, & Falkus, Chapter 8; Cooke & Szumal, Chapter 9).

A promising basis for further measurement development along those lines is offered through the summary notion of "culture gap," advocated originally by Kilmann and Saxton (1983). Based on two content dimensions, Kilmann and Saxton identified the pressures exerted by work groups on their members (actual norms) and, separately, the norms that should be operating to promote high performance and morale (desired norms). Unfortunately, little follow-up has been done on this work. Yet the notion of culture as a difference between an actual (perceived) and desired (preferred) state of affairs is tempting (see also Dickson, Aditya, & Chhokar, Chapter 28, this volume, on the GLOBE organizational culture view). It mimics typical depictions of culture as a layer cake, an onion, or, even better, a water lily (Hawkins, 1997)—metaphors that show that culture assessments cannot be based merely on the straight perceptions or attitudes of participants of given social settings, as climate often is. One can see organizational climate, then, as attitudes toward the organization at a given point in time and organizational culture as an explicit description and evaluation of typical organizational practices (Jones, 1983b). The organizational culture gap thus focuses on typical organizational practices and on employee registration and evaluation of those practices. Such a score thus explicitly incorporates two levels of culture, mainly description or registration and evaluation or appreciation. The latter assessment taps the deeper layers, where normative or subjective judgments regarding the organization's functioning reside. In the gap score the more superficial part of the culture is included through its focus on organizational practices—that is, on how organizations operate within (see also Pfeffer, 1997, who argues that the field of organization theory in its entirety should focus on organization practices). Use of an organizational culture gap score could thus potentially enlighten other parts of the field as well.

O'Reilly, Chatman, and Caldwell (1991) used a similar summary-type score of culture in their study on person-organization fit. Their research indicates that organizations with larger gaps between actual organizational norms and desired individual norms experience higher turnover. Wilderom and Van den Berg (1998) looked into the relationship between the average culture gap within organizations and their performances. This study suggests that, instead of striving for strong cultures, firms should attempt to reduce the gap between employees' preferred organizational practices and their perceptions of their organizations' practices. In brief, the empirical evidence for the impact of the organizational culture gap on organizational performance/effectiveness is still limited, but it forms, in our view, a fruitful basis for more refined future C-P research.

## How to Assess Organizational Performance

A second major point of considerable debate in the study of the organizational culture-performance link relates to the choice of a performance/effectiveness approach. We will first analyze the choices made thus far in this respect and argue for multidimensional (e.g., stakeholder) assessments of organizational performance within the context of longitudinal research designs.

For organizational performance researchers focusing on profit-seeking firms, the rational goal approach has traditionally been the dominant performance approach. It assumes that the pursuit of financial or economic goals (e.g., profit maximization) is the primary organizational objective (Venkatraman & Ramanujam, 1986). Rational goal performance is usually assessed using accounting-based indicators (e.g., profitability measures such as return on assets, return on investment, return on sales, return on equity). These measures provide aggregated performance information and have the advantage of being rather easily accessible and comparable across various types of industries. Yet they have also come under considerable criticism. Proneness to manipulation, lack of consistency in accounting methods, backward orientation, and short-termism have been the major points of criticism (see, e.g., Brown & Laverick, 1994; Kaplan & Norton, 1992; McGuire, Schneeweis, & Hill, 1986). Discontent with these popular financial and economic performance measures and the growing awareness that multiple and partly conflicting goals exist within profit organizations (e.g., short-term profit and quality) have challenged the dominance of the rational goal approach to organizational performance.

Multidimensional performance approaches, including nonfinancial and perceptual performance indicators, have recently met with wide approval in the conceptual performance literature (see Donaldson & Preston, 1995; Doyle, 1994; Preston & Sapienza, 1990). The multiple-stakeholder approach to organizational performance is one of the most promising alternatives to the rational goal approach (see, e.g., Connolly, Conlon, & Deutsch, 1980; Freeman, 1984; Tsui, 1990). It explicitly takes into account that organizations have multiple goals. Following this approach, an organization is considered effective if it balances the competing claims of various relevant organizational stakeholders (e.g., owners, employees, customers, suppliers, the community) and thus ensures their continuing cooperation. This approach corresponds with modern perspectives on business organizations as complex webs of relationships among interest groups or political arenas (e.g., Atkinson, Waterhouse, & Wells, 1997; Clarckson, 1995; Keeley, 1980).

Changes in business environments (increasing turbulence, globalization, and growing competition) as well as lively discussions about the social responsibility of business firms that started in the early 1970s have fostered the popularity of the stakeholder approach in the management literature. Moreover, the quality movement has also prepared the field for other than purely financial and economic performance approaches. As stated by Brown and Laverick (1994), the more a firm depends on the cooperation, loyalty, and goodwill of others (e.g., workforce, suppliers, customers), the stronger the argument becomes for including multiple stakeholders in performance assessments. In this view, the pursuit of purely profit-maximization goals is self-defeating. Financial and economic superiority is only one part of organizational performance, and it is the part that is mainly in the interest of top management and/or shareholders. Performance in terms of satisfaction of other relevant stakeholders is seen as the other complementing factor. Whereas financial and economic evaluation criteria are assumed to be indicators for short-term performance, stakeholder satisfaction criteria are seen as indicators of longer-term performance.

None of the 10 empirical studies on the culture-performance link summarized in Table 12.2, however, applied a stakeholder performance approach. Five of the studies applied pure financial and economic performance approaches based on accounting or stock market figures (Calori & Sarnin, 1991; Denison, 1990; Gordon & DiTomaso, 1992; Kotter & Heskett, 1992; Marcoulides & Heck, 1993). Rousseau (1990c), who focused on nonprofit organizations, applied a unidimensional input-oriented performance approach. The four remaining studies used multidimensional approaches to organizational performance, usually without referring to any specific theoretical basis for their choices of performance dimensions (Denison & Mishra, 1995; Koene, 1996; Petty et al., 1995; Wilderom & Van den Berg, 1998). Whereas Petty et al. (1995), Koene (1996),

and Wilderom and Van den Berg (1998) at least explicate the practical relevance of their chosen performance indicators, Denison and Mishra (1995) do not even provide such a rationale. This shows a general difficulty in multidimensional performance approaches. Although they have the potential to provide more meaningful results than narrow financial and economic approaches, the definition of relevant performance dimensions is less straightforward and clearly requires more consideration.

An important methodological point in C-P studies using multidimensional and perceptual performance approaches concerns the threat of common method bias. Whenever the measurement of both performance and culture is based on perceptual data stemming from a single information source, common method bias can become an issue. This is the case in two of the C-P studies reviewed: Whereas Denison and Mishra (1995) ignore this issue, Wilderom and Van den Berg (1998) do a better job by employing a procedure that corrects for common method variance.

It is difficult to draw any final conclusions concerning the performance approaches used in the 10 studies reviewed. In our view, researchers should no longer choose the rather straightforward and easily accessible financial/economic performance indicators. They should apply less convenient and more complex multidimensional performance approaches that include financial and economic performance indicators. From the 10 C-P studies reviewed in this chapter that apply a multidimensional performance approach, those of Petty et al. (1995) and Koene (1996) are most promising. They give at least some rationale for the performance indicators chosen and do a rather good job of objectively measuring the various dimensions. The application of a multidimensional performance approach is certainly more demanding in terms of conceptualization and measurement than a mere financial/economic approach. However, it has the advantage of fully acknowledging the reality or multidimensionality of an organization's functioning. We believe this is the only way to move forward in this area of organization studies.

## Substantiating the Assumed C-P Link

The third important challenge in research on the culture-performance link relates to the establishment of a theoretical basis for explaining the assumed relation and a useful and valid methodological approach for testing it. The resource-based approach provides a general framework for explaining why an organization's culture can be assumed to lead to increased performance. According to this approach, intraorganizational resources that are valuable, rare, and imperfectly imitable are assumed to provide a competitive advantage leading to a sustained record of superior performance (Barney, 1991, 1997). The organizational culture construct combines elements of tacit knowledge, social interconnections, and specificity that make a culture-based competitive advantage unique and extremely difficult for competitors to fathom and to imitate (Barney, 1986). A culture-based advantage can, therefore, be assumed to lead to a sustained record of superior performance. The most crucial question, however, is not addressed by the resource-based approach: What type of culture is so valuable that it leads to a culture-based advantage?

Our literature review reveals that different approaches to this question exist. Some writers argue that the advantage of organizational culture is based on value consensus or pervasiveness (culture strength), which serves as an informal coordination or control system and thus enhances smooth organizational functioning. Others focus more on the content of organizational culture for explaining a culture-based advantage. For instance, some assume that humanistic organization culture values are generally advantageous. Others argue that the value of specific cultural dimensions is contingent on contextual

factors such as industry type, technology, size, and national culture (see, e.g., Calori & Sarnin, 1991; Denison & Mishra, 1995). We would argue that all these approaches have their merit, and they all need more rigorous testing.

In all of the 10 studies presented in Table 12.2, the culture of the organization is believed to affect its effectiveness. However, relying solely on correlational techniques, most of the studies were not able to establish firmly the direction of this relationship (see Calori & Sarnin, 1991; Denison, 1990; Gordon & DiTomaso, 1992; Kotter & Heskett, 1992; Petty et al., 1995). This does not imply that correlational research is never helpful. On the contrary, a significant correlation might indicate that a causal relationship exists between the culture and the performance of a firm that should be investigated further. Unfortunately, this valuable function of correlational analyses is weakened due to the large number of culture and performance variables that are typically put to the test. Any significant relationship found may therefore be due to "fishing" rather than to any actual link between a cultural trait and a performance variable. Those objections are surmountable if the same prespecified relationships are tested in subsequent studies. After all, similar findings over a number of studies reduce the threat of fishing and strengthen the probability that an actual link exists between the culture and effectiveness of a firm. As noted before, however, the studies reviewed here differ widely in their operationalizations of both the culture and performance construct and should therefore not be considered repeat analyses of the same culture-performance relationship.

For empirically testing the hypothesis that organizational culture has a positive impact on performance, a longitudinal research design (measuring culture at an earlier point in time than performance) is preferable to a cross-sectional assessment. This holds especially for financial and economic performance approaches using backward-oriented performance indicators (e.g., accounting-based figures from previous book years). Of the 10 C-P studies reviewed, only 4 used a time lag (from half a year up to 6 years) between the measurement of culture and performance (Denison, 1990; Gordon & DiTomaso, 1992; Koene, 1996; Petty et al., 1995). Kotter and Heskett (1992) assessed culture retrospectively and in that way generated something like a longitudinal research design that is not very convincing. Denison (1990) combined long-term and short-term performance indicators showing a significant difference on the "consistency" dimension. The remainder of the studies measured organizational culture and performance at the same points in time (Marcoulides & Heck, 1993; Rousseau, 1990c; Wilderom & Van den Berg, 1998) or even used performance data that preceded the measurement of culture (Calori & Sarnin, 1991; Denison & Mishra, 1995). Although results obtained by these cross-sectional studies may provide some indication of a relationship between culture and performance, statements about the precise direction or nature of this relationship cannot be made.

In this context, it should be noted that the assumed direction of the relationship between culture and performance is not unquestioned. Schein (1985), for instance, has argued that certain values and norms develop from or are strengthened through successes of work groups within the firm. He points out, referring to the literature on group formation, that the effectiveness of actions taken by employees shapes the employees' values and norms, which become elements of the corporate culture. This implies that the performance of a firm influences its culture, or, in fact, that the relationship between culture and performance is recursive instead of linear. For that reason, Siehl and Martin (1990) have argued that we are in need of more longitudinal studies in which both culture and effectiveness are measured over a period of years. Denison and Mishra (1995) and many others second this, adding that this longitudinal research should be accompanied by in-depth measures of culture in order to

contribute to our understanding of the relationship between culture and performance.

Because most studies lack a clear theoretical conception of the nature of the culture-performance link, they may not, despite its presence, find a relationship between these two variables. Siehl and Martin (1990) elaborate this view and also suggest that culture may serve as a filter for factors that influence the effectiveness of an organization. Because these factors may differ between organizations, a more thorough understanding of the mechanisms at play is essential for research on the culture-performance link. The importance of including intermediate variables can be further illustrated by the work of Wilderom and Van den Berg (1998), who found no direct significant zero-order relationship between culture and performance. However, taking also the perceived performance and style of leadership into account, these researchers did discover that a significant relationship existed between culture and performance. This finding illustrates the importance of the development of more elaborate theories on the direction and contingencies in the relation between culture and performance (see Denison & Mishra, 1995; Kotter & Heskett, 1992; Quinn, 1988). Without such theories, we may draw overly simple or even misleading conclusions.

## OTHER CRITICAL ISSUES IN THE DESIGN OF C-P STUDIES

The remaining critical issues for the design of empirical C-P studies relate to the sampling of organizations, the types of respondents, and the levels of analysis used. Studies on the culture-performance link regularly use, although sometimes implicitly, a two-stage sampling procedure. The first stage involves the sampling of organizations to be included in the study. Subsequently, in the second stage, respondents within these organizations are selected. With the exception of the studies performed by Koene (1996), Marcoulides and Heck (1993), and Wilderom and Van den Berg (1998), in the 10 studies reviewed here at least one of these two sampling procedures was done insufficiently. For example, Calori and Sarnin (1991) handpicked five organizations, one firm per industry, but the firms chosen were not representative of their industries. Similarly, Rousseau (1990c) and Kotter and Heskett (1992) used convenience samples of employees and managers in their studies. Such shortcomings in sampling procedures seriously undermine the quality of the data obtained as well as the generalizability of results.

A related issue concerns the types of respondents involved in studies. Given that *organizational culture* refers to attributes of the entire organization, it seems crucial that researchers investigate organizational members who are representative of all the various hierarchical or other (potential subcultural) levels of the organization. It is even more astonishing that some studies purporting to assess organizational culture have included only managers or executives (Denison & Mishra, 1995; Gordon & DiTomaso, 1992; Kotter & Heskett, 1992). In the Denison and Mishra (1995) study, for example, all respondents were CEOs, resulting in the collection of data too narrow to be used as a basis for assessing the cultures of entire organizations. It is imperative that researchers investigate all sorts of organizational members, representative of all the various hierarchical, departmental, divisional, and/or professional organizational entities.

An even more important issue in C-P studies concerns the level of analysis and the aggregation of data. Given that culture is a construct at the level of the organization, individual responses need to be aggregated to this level before the relationship between culture and performance can legitimately be examined. Aggregating the data, however, has some theoretical and methodological implications. From a theoretical point of view, culture is often conceived of as a synergetic or holistic concept. This implies that we cannot

always equate the statistical mean or median of the data obtained with the culture of the organization. Moreover, even if we explicitly ask employees to characterize the cultures of their organization, it is unclear whether the variance in the answers of employees within the same organization should be interpreted as measurement error or as an indication of the amount of cultural strength.

The use of individual responses as input for the data analysis also contains a serious methodological flaw. It violates the rule of independent measures that is a precondition for many inferential techniques and will result in an overestimation of the actual relationship between the culture and the levels of performance of organizations. Researchers may avoid this pitfall by using elaborate techniques for analyzing the data, such as multilevel analyses (Bryk & Raudenbush, 1992; Goldstein, 1995). In multilevel analyses, the variance is attributed to the various levels (for instance, to the individual and the organizational level); such analyses therefore represent a more powerful means of investigating the relationship between culture and performance than a straightforward aggregation. For this reason, future multilevel C-P analyses are essential, particularly for relatively small samples of organizations.

## SUMMARY AND CONCLUSIONS

In this chapter we have reviewed large-scale empirical studies assessing organizational culture and organizational performance/effectiveness. We have shown that both variables have been operationalized in many various and, at times, ambiguous ways. This shortcoming, combined with the limited reported evidence, does not provide much backup for the idea that organizational culture predicts organizational performance. We have enumerated critical conditions under which new research on the C-P linkage is needed. The central issue is the development of additional theory on the assumed relationship. A preliminary conclusion of the foregoing is therefore that circumstances under which the culture of an organization's culture predicts high performance still have to be spelled out, primarily, by fresh (probably eclectic) theory development.

A second conclusion pertains to the use of the appropriate methodology for a given research question. The dominant underlying question of past C-P research and auxiliary writings has been: To what extent does a culture have to be shared among its individual members and/or units in order for it to be highly productive? We conclude that, due to the methodological shortcomings of the studies reviewed in this chapter, we have not been able to answer this question—the utilized culture strength measures seem too crude. In our view, investigating the degree of cohesion and/or intensity with which members of work groups pursue goals would be better done with experimental methods first (see, e.g., Podsakoff, MacKenzie, & Ahearne, 1997), so that the underlying psychological and economic makeup of members involved in strong cultures can be determined. That should help provide insights into the dynamic interplay of controllable work situations, employee cohesion, and various outcomes, at both the organizational/work group level and the individual level. A second question that has received a lot of attention in the literature on organizational culture concerns the degree to which these cultures have to be highly dynamic or adaptable in order for them to yield the best outcomes. Addressing that question would require, at the very least, standardized assessments of both culture and performance over time. Remarkably, only 1 out of the 10 representative studies discussed here met this condition (Petty et al., 1995)—however, without being able to extract generalizable results.

A third conclusion pertains to prospective approaches to operationalizing organizational culture. Given the dynamic nature of most organizations' environments and cultures, we postulate that the more organizational members place high value on and are actively engaged in the continuous improvement of the external as well as the internal side of their organization, the better the organization will fare in the long run. Testing this basic idea would require, among other things, a valid, standardized questionnaire of organizational culture that is explicitly and well connected to a widely acceptable operational definition of organizational culture (whereas most of the reviewed questionnaires are not). Wilderom and Van den Berg's (1998) organizational culture gap score may provide some promise in this respect. It taps members' perceptions or registrations of organizational practices (i.e., of how things are typically done; see Pfeffer, 1997) plus an assessment of how these same organizational practices ought to be, in the eyes of the same members. Hence an important superficial level of organizational culture (organizational practices) is connected in this assessment to deeper, motivational layers of the culture (or to deeply rooted sentiments). Thus, even though a complete new theoretically sound approach to quantitatively measuring organizational culture is not worked out yet, new leads are emerging.

Finally, although the quality of a new C-P study also stands or falls by a sophisticated performance approach, most extant C-P studies, we conclude, have spent far too little effort on this. Consequently, they tend to use convenient or easily accessible measures of organizational performance. We have argued in this chapter that it is crucial, also for the purpose of cumulative knowledge buildup on the C-P link, that researchers better face the challenges involved in valid and more comprehensive assessments of organizational performance. Thus, due to the complex nature of both the culture construct and the performance construct, the design of empirical studies to test the assumed culture-performance link has become a highly demanding task. Researchers studying this C-P link rarely approach these two constructs and their probably complex relationship with equal sophistication and depth. For example, the distinction made in the culture literature between short- and long-term performance is not well integrated with this distinction made in the recent organizational perfor-mance literature. We advocate making the-ory a priority in future empirical C-P stud-ies, so that the next (fifth) phase of the C-P literature (see Table 12.1) can be called the *theory-testing phase.*

# 13

## Organizational Culture From a Network Perspective

*-- Martin Kilduff and Kevin G. Corley*

In the study of human culture, an ethnographic approach tends to dominate. This approach focuses on the meanings and significance of the details found within each particular culture. The emphasis is on the rich textures of significance that surround ritual events and familiar interactions. Researchers engage in the direct study of the members of a particular cultural group. For example, Turnbull (1962) described his life among the Pygmies of the Congo, detailing the routines and activities that enabled them to thrive in the dense tropical forest shunned as uninhabitable by other peoples. The ethnographic approach emphasizes the multitude of ways in which human societies differ with respect to the ceremonies and rituals that endow interactions with meaning. The ethnographic perspective has achieved wide influence across disciplines, including work on organizational culture (e.g., Kilduff, Funk, & Mehra, 1997; Kunda, 1992). Our assumption here is that most organizational scholars are familiar with the ethnographic approach and traditionally associate this perspective with work on organizational culture.

The social network approach (also known as structural analysis) is less well-known in the organizational culture field. Social network analysts (particularly those who, like Mayhew, 1980, identify themselves as structuralists) tend to assume that the details of any particular culture are determined by an underlying system of relations. It is this underlying system that the researcher seeks to understand. Once the underlying system is captured, it can be compared with the underlying systems of other cultures, much in the same way that the deep grammar of a particular language can be compared with the deep grammar of another language (see Leach, 1976). In this approach, the details of the culture, or the language, are of interest only insofar as they allow us to access the structure behind the details.

The network approach draws inspiration from Marx, Durkheim, and Simmel. As Mizruchi (1994) points out, for these theorists (particularly Simmel), "the forms and patterns of social relations were more important than the content" (pp. 329-330). For example, Simmel suggested that many social situations could be analyzed in terms of one actor (a person or a group) exploiting a conflict between two other actors. Working within this structural tradition, network researchers have drawn attention to such structural properties as (a) the extent to which relations in a network tend to be organized around a central actor (Freeman, 1979), (b) the proportion of isolates in a social network (Blau, 1982), and (c) the extent to which actors can be grouped together on the basis of similarity of ties to others (White, Boorman, & Breiger, 1976). Network analyses help answer such questions as the following: How do people structure their social lives? How are the contradictions inherent in any social group represented? What are the underlying patterns of interaction, and what are the consequences of such patterns? The network approach has found numerous applications in anthropology (for reviews, see Johnson, 1994; Mitchell, 1974) and has widely influenced research across the social sciences, including, in the organizational studies literature, work that examines the effects of social networks on organizational outcomes (e.g., Barley, 1990; Krackhardt & Kilduff, 1990).

We try to accomplish two things in this chapter. First, we outline the traditional social network approach and show how it can be used in the study of organizational culture. Our aim is not to argue for the dominance of structural analysis but to raise awareness of an overlooked approach to organizational culture. Second, we focus on how poststructuralist approaches overcome some of the problems inherent in social network epistemology and how these approaches may help reconcile the structural analysis and ethnographic traditions. We conclude with some suggestions for future research on organizational culture from both structuralist and poststructuralist perspectives.

## A SOCIAL NETWORK APPROACH TO ORGANIZATIONAL CULTURE

With its origins in gestalt and field approaches to social phenomena (for a brief history, see Scott, 1990, pp. 7-38), social network analysis has become a set of powerful quantitative approaches to the analysis of relational data. The focus here is on the word *relational*: Structural approaches in general, and social network analysis in particular, take as the unit of analysis the relation between two entities rather than the entities themselves. For example, if we are interested in the culture of a small entrepreneurial company, one of the cultural aspects we could investigate might be the structure of relationships within the company. A social network approach would involve collecting data concerning relationships, such as friendship, advice, and communication. Specifically, we might ask each person in the company to look down a list of names of all other people in the company and check off the names of his or her personal friends, then to look down a similar list and check the names of those he or she goes to for help and advice at work, and so on for other relevant networks.

The collection of such data is premised on the importance of two concepts: embeddedness and social capital. These concepts are fundamental to the social network analysis of relations in organizations and integral to the emergence of social network theory. These concepts orient the researcher toward specific aspects of organizational phenomena.

### Orienting Concepts

*Embeddedness.* According to the embeddedness argument, work-related transactions tend to overlap with patterns of social relations (Granovetter, 1985). Thus business is embedded in social networks. This insight is used to explain how patterns of transactions between firms depart from what might be expected from a pure economic perspective. Entrepreneurs prefer to do business with contractors and others with whom they have ties of friendship or kinship rather than find exchange partners in the open market (Uzzi, 1996).

From this perspective, an organization's culture is directly influenced by its ties to other organizational actors. Organizations may suffer from a "liability of unconnectedness" (Powell, Koput, & Smith-Doerr, 1996), focusing internally and even punishing those who create links with competitors and other industry players. Thus some organizations may develop fortresslike cultures whereas others may create cultures that interact fluidly with the environments of other organizations. In some cases (e.g., Silicon Valley), the social network may span an entire geographic area, with each organization reflecting some aspect of a shared industry culture (for an illuminating discussion, see Saxenian, 1994).

Further, from an embeddedness perspective, resource flows within the organization are likely to depart from what a purely rational model might predict. People are likely to favor their friends with timely information, recommendations, interesting projects, and other career-building opportunities. The culture of the organization is created and re-created by individuals swapping stories, participating in rituals, applauding heroes, and trading in symbols. These patterns of interaction are likely to be embedded in social networks.

*Social capital.* Some organizations are characterized by a general altruistic regard for the well-being of the collectivity. Others are characterized by an opportunistic regard for individual advantage. From a social network perspective, these two very different kinds of cultures demonstrate the importance of social capital. The altruistic organization is

likely to be one in which social relationships are consistently maintained and repaired, where top management is active in promoting social links between and across hierarchical levels. In other words, the altruistic organization is one in which social capital (defined as the quality and extent of relationships existing in the organization) is high. The opportunistic organization is likely to be one in which social capital has become diseased (to use Burt & Ronchi's, 1990, graphic term), in the sense of being allowed to deteriorate into conflict between and within groups and hierarchical levels. According to the social network perspective, social capital is as important to organizational success as financial and human capital (Burt, 1992). Our contention in this chapter is that the extent of the organization's social capital can determine important aspects of organizational culture, such as levels of altruism, openness, and cooperation.

## Network Characteristics

Orienting concepts such as embeddedness and social capital direct attention to social networks in organizational settings. There are also specific characteristics of networks that are useful in the evaluation of culture in organizations. We present brief discussions here of density, centralization, reachability, and balance.

*Density.* A general measure of the degree of social interaction in an organization is density, defined as the number of connections in the organization as a proportion of the total number of connections possible (Scott, 1990). Thus organizations with higher density are those in which there are relatively more connections between people. Organizations of the same size can be compared to see how much social interaction is occurring within them. Thus the density of a friendship network or other positive-affect network represents a rough measure of cohesiveness, which is an important concept within the organizational culture literature. The denser the network, the faster rumors are likely to penetrate to all network members (Niemeijer, 1973, p. 47).

*Centralization.* Another measure important to the organizational culture literature is the extent to which organizations are focused on leaders. For any organization, a centralization score can be calculated that shows whether, for any social relationship, such as advice, people tend to be organized around the most central people (Scott, 1990). Further, we can investigate whether these people are themselves clustered together in a structural center or whether there are multiple centers spread throughout the organization. Thus we can assess the degree to which the organization is organized around one or more nuclei, and this may help provide one explicit indicator of how organic or mechanistic the organization is (Schrader, Lincoln, & Hoffman, 1989).

*Reachability.* Some networks are more efficient than others in the sense that larger proportions of the people in these networks can be contacted through the same number of steps. In network A, for example, all network members may be contacted if every person in the network contacts personal friends (one step) and friends of friends (two steps). In network B, by contrast, a two-step outreach effort may reach only 50% of the members. This is the idea behind reachability. Friendship networks with high reachability are those in which (a) there are relatively few isolates (e.g., people with no friends) and (b) relatively many contacts at each step. One measure of reachability is the average number of people reached per person over all possible steps (Mitchell, 1969, pp. 16-17). In high-reachability networks, cultural norms and values tend to diffuse rapidly to many people without distortion, putting conformist pressures on individuals within the network.

*Balance.* The two components of balance are reciprocity and transitivity. *Reciprocity* re-

fers to whether a link from ego to alter is returned from alter to ego: If John sees Glenn as a friend, does Glenn also see John as a friend? *Transitivity* refers to whether a link between two alters (each of whom is linked to ego) exists or not: If John is friends with Glenn and Scott, are those two others themselves friends? According to Heider (1958), there is a pressure toward balance in friendship networks. Recent work has confirmed that people tend to perceive friendship relations as reciprocated (Kenny, Bond, Mohr, & Horn, 1996; Kenny & DePaulo, 1993). Transitivity has been described as the "key structural concept in the analysis of sociometric data" (Holland & Leinhardt, 1977, pp. 49-50). Individuals who perceive their friendship relations as unbalanced may react with strong emotion rather than with cool analytic reasoning. Balance, from this perspective, functions as a deep-seated goal of human interaction (see discussions in D'Andrade, 1992; Fiske, 1992). Unbalanced networks may result in nervousness (Sampson & Insko, 1964) and dissonance (Festinger & Hutte, 1954).

The degree of balance in organizational networks indicates the extent to which informal relations are structured. Ego's perception of an unstructured region in the environment functions as a barrier that "makes action and therefore control difficult if not impossible" (Heider, 1958, p. 71). Highly balanced networks tend to resemble junior high school social systems, where members are locked into cliques that are themselves allied into mutually antagonistic camps (Davis, 1979). Networks characterized by relatively low balance may be hierarchical, with some network stars receiving many nominations that are not reciprocated. Low balance may also indicate that relationships in the system are undergoing change and that individuals are unaware of friendship opportunities. Balance, as a structural property of social networks, indicates the extent to which patterns of daily interaction tend toward stability.

How might data on such network characteristics (density, centralization, reachability, and balance) provide insight into a specific organization's culture? The answer depends, in part, on which organizational culture perspective the researcher takes. Martin (1992), in an influential text, identifies three perspectives (integration, differentiation, fragmentation) that make different assumptions and demand different analytic procedures. Different social network interpretations may be appropriate for each perspective.

## The Integration Perspective

The integration approach to organizational culture emphasizes harmony and homogeneity, and focuses on shared values and assumptions. Leaders tend to be portrayed as possessing extraordinary powers to create cultures that inspire loyalty, commitment, and increased productivity. People throughout the organization are viewed as agreeing about potentially divisive issues (see Martin, 1992, pp. 45-70).

*Consensus.* The first issue that social network analysis can address, from an integration perspective, is the issue of consensus itself. If culture is defined as knowledge stored in the minds of members concerning "how things are done around here," then it is possible to determine how much consensus exists in the organization concerning different cultural elements. Romney, Weller, and Batchelder (1986) provide a social network approach to this issue, an approach that also solves the problem of how to determine the cultural competence of each member of a culture—that is, how much knowledge each member possesses concerning the culture.

The analogy that Romney et al. (1986, p. 316) provide is to the game of tennis. Imagine that we wish to unravel the rules of tennis, and we conduct interviews with people who belong to a tennis club and with others who neither belong to the club nor play tennis. We would expect that tennis players would demonstrate more agreement among themselves concerning the game of tennis than would the

non-tennis players. Further, we would expect that some tennis players would be more knowledgeable than other tennis players. Thus the cultural consensus method allows the researcher to reconstruct the underlying rules from in-group members' responses and permits the identification of each person's knowledge concerning the underlying culture.

A similar approach to organizational culture focuses on people's interpretations of such cultural artifacts as goals, slogans, myths, and stories (Monge & Eisenberg, 1987). By content analyzing such interpretations, it is possible to identify which people share similar semantic frameworks. From these data, the researcher can build a network picture of where in the organization there exist groups of people with common understandings, where those with idiosyncratic understandings are, and who serves to link groups together.

These methods may help define what is unique to an organizational culture and what is merely shared among organizational members and nonmembers alike. Further, these methods may help answer one question that has dogged organizational culture research from an integration perspective: How much consensus does it take before one can say, yes, there is a distinctive organizational culture here? By calculating the average correlations or semantic overlaps among informants concerning aspects of organizational culture, researchers can estimate how much consensus exists in that organization for any particular cultural domain, and how the consensus is distributed among different parts of the organization. Researchers can also compare cultural domains across organizations to identify weak and strong cultures on specific domains.

*Schemas.* A second question that the social network approach can help answer is: Where does the shared knowledge underlying cultural consensus come from? The answer, according to social network research, is: through social interaction. An intriguing study of respondent recall has demonstrated that those who engage in regular social interaction over time as members of a formal organization tend to develop shared interpretative systems (or schemas) to organize relevant knowledge (Freeman, Romney, & Freeman, 1987). These schemas allow organizational members to see the world in closely similar ways. The schemas fill in the blanks in knowledge of the social world (Freeman, 1992) and bias perceptions in predictable ways (Kumbasar, Romney, & Batchelder, 1994).

*Cultural stability.* Organizational simulations (Carley, 1991) have taken this interaction model of organizational culture further by looking at how groups maintain cultural distinctiveness and stability in the face of turnover and new ideas. In particular, this work has examined what happens when information is exchanged between the members of two organizational subgroups: Inevitably the subgroups tend to merge. The assumption here is that subgroups are kept apart by differences in knowledge concerning such important cultural facts as code words specific to the social context, dress codes, and appropriate meeting places for cultural activities. Subgroups within the same organization have a large base of facts in common, but "behavior is controlled by small differences in who knows what" (Carley, 1991, p. 346). Social interaction produces shared knowledge, which tends to eliminate the cultural distinctiveness of subgroups. This work suggests that in the absence of communication barriers, group boundaries in organizations will tend to dissolve (Carley, 1991, p. 351), thus resulting in a tighter integration of the culture.

Carley's (1991) method also allows for estimation of the degree of cultural homogeneity of any social group at any one point in time. Her measure involves calculation of the percentage of facts shared between pairs of people concerning some cultural domain (p. 336). One of the main predictions of Carley's work is that, "regardless of its popu-

lation, knowledge, initial social structure, or initial culture, a one-group, fully-connected society will become increasingly homogeneous, both culturally and structurally" (p. 341). Eventually, in very stable organizations, behavior becomes completely ritualized because everyone knows everything, consensus is complete, and organizational members have no need of interaction to reach decisions. Hiring new people or bringing new cultural facts into the organization (e.g., new technology) can, of course, disrupt this harmony. Carley shows that organizational stability is less threatened by new facts than by new people, and that certain types of organizations (smaller, simpler cultures, more distinctive cultures) tend to reconstruct their cultures more successfully. (For a discussion of how socialization processes maintain cultural harmony, see Major, Chapter 22, this volume.)

## The Differentiation Perspective

The differentiation perspective weakens the assumption of homogeneity and harmony characteristic of the integration view. The differentiation perspective presumes the existence of subcultures that, as Martin (1992) writes, "co-exist, sometimes in harmony, sometimes in conflict, and sometimes in indifference to each other" (p. 83). This perspective does not dispute the existence of organizationwide norms and values, but it does emphasize that different groups within the organization can strategically promote their adherence to such values when it is useful to do so (Martin, 1992, p. 90). For example, everyone associated with the Chicago Board of Trade pays fervent lip service to an important organizationwide value: the ideal of free enterprise. But there are several different subgroups whose activities affect the workings of the Board of Trade. Social interactions tend to be within groups, and, thus, different interpretations of organizationwide values tend to develop. This was dramatically illustrated in 1979 when inside traders were threatened with massive losses by a coalition of new traders (led by the Hunt brothers of Dallas, Texas). The insiders arranged for the rules of trade to be changed to bankrupt the outsiders and save the insiders money: "Ideologically, the Hunts and their opponents on the exchange were fully agreed about the virtues of free enterprise, but this ideology of freedom was more a self-justifying belief than a description of the degree of discretion allowed by the rules of transaction on the exchange" (Abolafia & Kilduff, 1988, p. 187). In this case, all the subcultures (inside traders, outside traders, government regulators) involved in the running of the Chicago Board of Trade agreed concerning the importance of free enterprise. But whereas one group decried rule changes as interfering with free enterprise, the other group imposed rule changes to preserve free enterprise.

*Subcultures.* Social network analysis from a differentiation perspective helps identify important subcultures within any organizational context, such as the Chicago Board of Trade. To take a more general example, researchers can investigate the degree to which the social structure of friendship in an organization is patterned on occupational specialties. An ideal matrix (that is, a matrix created by the researcher to represent some ideal state of affairs) can be created based on the hypothesis, let us say, that certain occupational specialties (such as research and development) tend to encourage within-group ties, whereas other occupational specialties (such as sales) tend to encourage out-group ties. To test this hypothesis, researchers could correlate the ideal matrix (representative of the hypothesis) with the actual matrix (representing the data) and subject this perceived correlation to a significance test designed specifically for these kinds of data (e.g., Barley, 1990). Such an analysis can help confirm the existence of different patterns of interaction characteristic of different subcultures.

*Who controls communication?* A second, more detailed example of how structural analysis from a differentiation perspective might provide valuable insights concerning organizational culture is taken from research on one department of a large Japanese high-technology company (Kilduff & Funk, 1998). The network studied in this case was the communication network, and the data were collected not by questionnaire but through intensive observation by a participant observer. The department included 12 engineers who were building a new generation of machinery designed to manufacture computer chips. The network data were arranged in four 12-by-12 matrices to show (a) how many times each pair talked during 1 week at the beginning of the summer (observations made every 30 minutes), (b) how many times each pair talked during 1 week at the end of the summer (observations made every 30 minutes), (c) the total number of conversations involving each pair during 1 day at the beginning of the summer, and (d) the total number of conversations involving each pair during 1 day at the end of the summer.

These data were analyzed as a set rather than individually, given that engineers were frequently absent from the office. Thus the different data collection efforts helped capture enduring communication routines. The four matrices were submitted to an analysis that partitioned actors into cliques, that is, groups of individuals who tended to interact within group (Breiger, Boorman, & Arabie, 1975). Note that this type of analysis, as well as many other social network techniques, is available in user-friendly form as part of the UCINET software package for personal computers (Borgatti, Everett, & Freeman, 1992).

Two questions were asked of the communication data. First, were patterns of communication restricted by membership in functional subgroups? And second, was communication controlled by the hierarchy of authority in this organization? The analysis revealed that engineers tended to talk with members of other functional subgroups. Informal communication, therefore, crosscut formal departmental lines, knitting the department together rather than fracturing it into functional specialties. Thus the analysis revealed the existence of subgroups, but showed that the subgroups in this case were cooperative rather than antagonistic.

In answer to the second question, Kilduff and Funk found that the most central actors in the communication network were the top two administrators. In this particular case, centrality was measured as betweenness centrality—that is, the extent to which each actor controlled the flow of information from one part of the network to another (Freeman, 1979). There was, in fact, a significant correspondence between formal position in the organization and how much an individual controlled the information flow. The price for subgroup coordination, it appeared, was centralization of authority.

Network analysis, therefore, helped reveal the structure of communication within this work community. In particular, the researchers learned how the formal organizational structure of subgroups and hierarchy related to the informal structure of apparently spontaneous conversations. Social network analysis of this kind may prove valuable in uncovering the underlying structures of communication through which organizational culture is transmitted and reproduced. This kind of structural analysis can enrich a purely ethnographic approach to the same cultural site. (For an ethnographic treatment of this particular organization, see Kilduff et al., 1997.)

*Structural holes.* Because the differentiation approach to organizational culture emphasizes the importance of subcultures, relationships between subcultures are also highlighted from this perspective. To the extent that two subcultures have no social interaction links between them, we can say that a structural hole exists between those two subcultures (Burt, 1992). An organization that has many structural holes may tend to develop several distinct, and possibly incompatible, cultures as subgroups develop norms and values in isolation from each other. Thus

the organization may be rife with secrets, misinformation, and conflict. Further, the existence of such structural holes may encourage social network entrepreneurs within the organization to link two subcultures and in this way control communication and resource flow between noncommunicating groups. Thus a relatively invisible cadre of boundary spanners may spring up in the organization, promoting their own interests, possibly at the expense of the organization as a whole. For example, the workers at one manufacturing plant were divided according to their geographic origins within the industrial valleys surrounding the plant. One worker had systematically, over a 30-year period, and unknown to the management, supplied would-be employees with information on vacancies. As a result, he had links to all of the major subgroups within the plant. The firing of this man during a downsizing exercise precipitated strikes, resistance, and death threats that the individuals in top management were at a loss to comprehend (Burt & Ronchi, 1990).

## The Fragmentation Perspective

The fragmentation perspective weakens the assumption of homogeneity even further than the differentiation perspective by taking into account shifting identities and multiple interpretations (Martin, 1992, pp. 130-167). The emphasis in this perspective is on a web of individuals, with coalitions shifting and re-forming around specific issues (Murnighan & Brass, 1991). Two examples of studies from a fragmentation perspective may help illuminate this way of thinking about culture and social networks.

*Dyadic ties.* In a study of how the friendship network in an organization shaped the pattern of cultural attributions of organizational members, participants were asked not only to provide information concerning their personal friendships, but to rate every other person in the sample on seven constructs that prior exploratory research in this company had revealed as expressing vital aspects of the organization's culture (Krackhardt & Kilduff, 1990). These seven bipolar constructs included the dimensions "Inflexible, critical versus Flexible, tolerant" and "Goes by the book versus Prepared to cut corners." Two structural hypotheses were tested and supported. First, the researchers found that relative to pairs of individuals who were not friends, pairs who were friends tended to have similar patterns of cultural attributions. Second, they found that the more people tended to agree with their friends (concerning how they construed others in the organization on the seven cultural dimensions), the more they were satisfied with their jobs.

This research, therefore, showed a significant link between how pairs of individuals interpreted the culture of the organization and friendship formation. This study helps explain how, within the fragmented universe of a complex organization, friends can establish mutually reinforcing interpretative systems that may be resistant to management attempts at control. The friendship bond is one of the most powerful in human society. People are likely to resist management efforts to change values and opinions that are reinforced through daily interaction with friends. It is important to note that this fragmented view of organizational culture does not deny the possibility of a level of integration within the very same culture. Everyone in an organization, for example, may endorse the importance of values such as honesty and initiative, but people may differ as to how a specific behavior, such as insider trading, should be interpreted. Those accused of that behavior may claim that they are demonstrating initiative within the understood constraints of honesty. Others may conclude that such initiative falls outside the norms of what is considered acceptable. Within any organizational culture, the same set of values can lead to discrepant attributions about the same people.

*Malleability of social identity.* A second example of how structural analysis might provide valuable insights concerning organizational culture from a fragmentation perspective is taken from research on the malleability of social identity (Mehra, Kilduff, & Brass, 1998). In this research, an individual's social identity was found to depend not on some intrinsic attribute of the self, but on the specific social context within which the individual was currently enmeshed. Thus white women in an organization that was predominantly white and male tended to identify themselves more as women than as whites. But this identity could change instantly if the demographic context changed. This research supports the idea that the relative rarity of a group in an organization tends to promote that group as a basis for members' social identification. Therefore, an organization in which there are many groups of people and in which some groups are relatively underrepresented in terms of the overall demography of the organization may find the fragmentation approach to organizational culture helpful for its understanding of such phenomena as the tendency of underrepresented group members to show more homophily (i.e., solidarity within group) than majority group members.

As can be seen from the examples above, regardless of the perspective one takes in studying organizational culture, a social network approach to organizational culture can lead to insights. This approach highlights patterns of homogeneity, inconsistency, and fragmentation in the underlying structures of culture and provides the basis for awareness and understanding of the relational features inherent in every culture.

## POSTSTRUCTURALIST EXTENSIONS

### Structural Methods/ Ethnographic Humility

Structural analysis has come under critique for a variety of reasons that can be summarized under the rubric of intellectual hubris. Structuralists have been attacked for ignoring the judgment calls underlying their analyses and for pretending to reveal the truth of structure when more than one interpretation of structure may be possible. The structural approach also has been attacked for tending to reify existing structures rather than challenge them, thereby tending to endorse the status quo. Further, structuralism has been accused of neglecting the margins in favor of the center, thereby contributing to the continuing marginalization of underrepresented groups. Structuralists have also been criticized for dismissing individuals and individual action as epiphenomena, thereby removing human action from their accounts (Kilduff & Krackhardt, 1994), and for neglecting the importance of human agency in the creation and re-creation of society (Emirbayer & Goodwin, 1994). Finally, social network analysis has been criticized for an overemphasis on relatively esoteric methodology at the expense of substantive contributions to knowledge (for more details of these criticisms, see Agger, 1991; Giddens, 1987; Kilduff & Mehra, 1997; Rosenau, 1992).

One possible way to overcome these criticisms is, we suggest, for structuralist researchers to learn from their more qualitative colleagues an ethnographic humility. In other words, we suggest that researchers can borrow from recent developments in the ethnographic tradition to overcome many of the perceived problems of the structural analysis approach to studying phenomena such as organizational culture.

*Local knowledge.* In anthropology, there has been a distinct turn away from grand theorizing and toward recognizing the importance of detailed ethnographic understandings of specific contexts (Clifford & Marcus, 1986; Geertz, 1983). In principle, there is no reason structural methods, such as social network analysis, cannot be applied to such local contexts, thus offering a multimethod approach to the understanding of organizational culture (see, e.g., Barley, 1990).

*The margins.* Social network research has typically devoted tremendous attention to studies of the center, reflecting, perhaps, a general fascination in the organizational studies community with powerful elites. For example, there is a large literature devoted to examination of interlocking directorates in the U.S. economy (for a review, see Mizruchi, 1982). This intense focus on the center of social interaction often ignores the importance of the margins. Social network studies tend to focus on organizational elites, explicitly ignoring production workers and others who are of nonmanagerial status (for one example of this bias, see Krackhardt & Kilduff, 1990). Recent work has focused attention on those at the margins rather than at the center of social networks in organizations, with explicit attention, for example, to the social networks of ethnic minorities (Mehra et al., 1998). The same methods that are used to identify the most central actors in an organization can also be used to locate those at the margins and to study their distinctive patterns of interaction. A renewed emphasis on marginalization will help move organizational culture research away from its almost exclusive focus on the concerns of top management. (For evidence of how much organizational culture research tends to follow trends established in journals targeted at top management, see Barley, Meyer, & Gash, 1988.)

*Bringing the individual back in.* Similarly, structuralists have typically dismissed the importance of individuals, preferring to assume that individual attitudes and cognitions are epiphenomena produced by structural characteristics concerning which individuals are largely ignorant. For example, Mayhew (1980) derides the study of individuals as "a dead end" (p. 335). In a recent structuralist analysis, McPherson, Popielarz, and Drobnic (1992) assert, "The homophily [similarity] principle can be derived from social structure rather than be attributed to human agency" (p. 168). One of the most influential of structuralists has declared the person construct to be "polluting" (White, 1992, p. 3). These comments appear to represent an intellectual hubris that refuses to acknowledge any role for individual cognition or action. A recent study directly compared conventional structuralist predictions and predictions inspired by a poststructuralist emphasis on the importance of individual perceptions of social structure. To quote from the abstract: "Being perceived to have a prominent friend in an organization boosted an individual's reputation as a good performer, but . . . actually having such a friend (as assessed by conventional structural methods) had no effect" (Kilduff & Krackhardt, 1994, p. 87).

In applying social network analysis to the assessment of aspects of organizational culture, researchers can push beyond the limitations of structuralism and bring a more nuanced application of structural methods to the exploration of social interaction patterns in organizations.

## CONCLUSION

As we have demonstrated, social network and poststructuralist approaches can provide additional insight for researchers examining the cultures of organizations. Structural analysis can increase our understanding of the systems underlying an organization's subcultures and affords researchers access to more complex analyses of relational patterns. Poststructuralist approaches help integrate the perspectives found in structuralism and ethnography by applying the methodological techniques of structuralism while maintaining ethnography's consideration of individuals, attention to the margins, and acknowledgment of subjective interpretation.

The approach to organizational culture outlined in this chapter suggests new research questions, many of which are unlikely to emerge from conventional perspectives. The following are representative of unanswered questions that this review has prompted us to consider:

- How much consensus does it take before there is a distinctive organizational culture?
- Where does the shared knowledge underlying cultural consensus come from?
- To what extent is communication controlled by the hierarchy of authority in an organization? How does this influence the creation/maintenance of the culture?
- Are there differences between cultures in the role structural holes play and how they are filled by "network entrepreneurs"?
- How is the interpretation of cultural values negotiated among interacting individuals within the organization?
- How do social networks affect the transmission of culture to new hires?
- How important are isolates and marginalized individuals in cultural creation, maintenance, and change?
- How do subcultures emerge in organizations?

Progress in organizational research can be measured in many ways. Our preference is to measure progress by the extent to which new and exciting questions are being generated (see Kilduff & Mehra, 1997). Our network perspective represents not just a research agenda that promises to renew an area that some have declared moribund (e.g., Calás & Smircich, 1987). More than this, it helps begin to decode the systems of relations that underlie the apparent mutability of everyday life. Even as we celebrate the diversity that characterizes life in organizations, we can begin to understand the structures that sustain and renew stable patterns of norms, values, and behavior.

# PART III

# The Dynamics of Culture
# and Climate Change

The chapters in this part of the *Handbook* are concerned with organizational culture and the dynamics of organizational change. Common sense tells us that organizational culture change is a slow affair, because there is so often resistance to change at the different levels in an organization. On the other hand, one could also find many cases of organizational dissolution and other dramatic organizational changes (e.g., through crises, downsizing, restarts, or mergers and acquisitions) occurring at a fast rate. Common sense seems therefore to be an overgeneralization. Indeed, it seems to be far more appropriate to specify types of organizational change and the cultural dynamics associated with it. The chapters in Part III deal with these issues from a variety of perspectives.

In Chapter 14, Michela and Burke analyze the concepts of culture and climate with specific reference to organizational change for Total Quality or to implement strategy that calls for ongoing innovation in processes or products. These authors make the case that culture change depends in part on the degree of sophistication that top management displays in managing change. It is argued that leaders need to understand the nature and management of culture and climate if they are to accomplish the sorts of organizational changes most often associated with quality and innovation.

In Chapter 15, Hatch takes a different view. She acknowledges that leaders play a role in initiating change, but de-emphasizes the role of leadership in the change process itself. Hatch makes the point that organizational members throughout the organization continually remake culture on a daily basis. Thus overdependence on leadership as the crucial factor in culture change represents a serious oversimplification.

Zammuto, Gifford, and Goodman, in Chapter 16, make yet a different case. They argue that organizations with managerial ideologies that are control oriented tend to fail at culture change. They propose four content types of managerial ideologies, which are embedded within a larger social system, as the key elements in determining if change is to be successful.

In Chapter 17, Sathe and Davidson differentiate the literature on organizational culture change as either an ongoing process of incremental change or a single major transformation. The latter process is most commonly referred to in the change literature. They also buy into the leadership model of effective organizational culture change and discuss the types of motivators that are needed for change to succeed.

In Chapter 18, Markus refers to a different process altogether—he discusses a less spontaneous culture change (or "reproduction of organizational culture"), where the role of leaders is less pronounced than in transformational culture change. He concludes in particular that more knowledge on the dynamics of organizational culture will provide a key to the tricky issue of culture's persistence.

In the final chapter in Part III, Weber deals with the issues of culture change in the context of mergers and acquisitions. He also addresses the interaction between politics and culture change, a major avenue for future study of the increasingly important topic of culture change. In particular, Weber reports on the finding that turnover of managers of acquired firms is significantly greater when there are large cultural differences between the management team of the acquired and that of the acquirer.

# 14

# Organizational Culture and Climate in Transformations for Quality and Innovation

-- *John L. Michela and W. Warner Burke*

Twenty years ago, few managers outside of Japan knew very much about how to produce goods and services at the levels of quality that customers demand today, and some managers seemed not to care. Ten years ago, nearly everyone sought quality in some way, but the specific practices of quality (such as statistical process control [SPC] and broadcasting the voice of the customer [VOC] throughout the organization) were not sufficiently pervasive. Today these practices are fairly well understood and fairly widely implemented in their settings of greatest applicability (e.g., SPC in manufacturing). There is even talk that total quality management (TQM) is becoming absorbed into mainstream management practice and is, in this sense, fading in prominence (Schroeder, 1998). The future is said to belong to companies that satisfy customers not only through traditional quality but also through innovation, which promises products having new or enhanced value to customers (e.g., Woodruff, 1997).

However, as managers and scholars know well, understanding and even implementing worthwhile practices do not necessarily result in their intended benefits. Newspapers and other mass-media outlets have described various large-scale studies of TQM practice, usually with the conclusion that X (huge) percentage of firms have implemented at least some TQM practices, and Y (tiny) percentage of firms have expressed satisfaction with the results of these efforts. An explanation given frequently in the TQM literature for this state of affairs draws on the construct of organizational culture. Woods (1997) puts it succinctly: "Increasingly, organizations are discovering that quality management is more about cultural change than it is about any specific practices" (p. 49).

Indeed, awareness of organizational culture's importance, as reflected in the TQM literature, is impressive. For example, in a discussion of continuous improvement (or CI, which is one of the aspects of TQM most connected with organizational culture and climate), Jha, Michela, and Noori (1996) include organizational culture management in a short list of success factors for CI—a list that also includes leadership, planning, and training. This emphasis on culture has been supported by a tabulation of key words used in a commercial database of reference citations to articles on CI detailed by Michela, Jha, Noori, Weitzman, and Eickmeier (1997). In this tabulation, *corporate culture* (the specific term used in this database) was found to be more prevalent in articles on CI than key words such as *leadership, training, customer satisfaction,* and *organizational change*. The concept of organizational culture shows similar prominence in the expanding literature on innovation. For example, 25% of the pages in a recent book on innovation by Tushman and O'Reilly (1997) fall within chapters concerning culture and culture management.

Nevertheless, it is one thing to say that organizational culture is often invoked as an explanation for success and failures in quality or innovation, and it is something else to say that this explanation is sound. Our reservations about this explanation, at least as typically presented, are one impetus to our writing this chapter. Explanations that invoke a related concept, organizational climate, also have their shortcomings, as we will describe.

Despite these shortcomings, the concepts of organizational culture and climate have a great deal to offer to leaders and researchers. Leaders who understand the nature and management of culture and climate are well positioned to accomplish the major organizational changes often required for quality and innovation, because the culture and climate literatures point to many levers for change.

Researchers aware of the links of culture and climate to quality are, we believe, more likely to look in productive directions for explanations of quality or innovation program successes and failures.

In this chapter we will examine various connections between quality and innovation on the one hand and culture and climate on the other. In the most basic terms, the essence of this connection is that appropriate culture and climate promote successful organizational change for quality, and inappropriate culture and climate stifle it. Consequently, we will also give some attention to organizational change models and methods as they relate to concepts and models of culture, climate, quality, and innovation.

## HOW DOES A QUALITY ORIENTATION AFFECT EMPLOYEES' WORK?

One starting point for analyzing culture and quality is to look at the work that people do under traditional versus quality-oriented management. Traditionally, an employee has a job description that specifies tasks. When these tasks are accomplished along with those of employees with different job descriptions, the work of the organization gets done. For example, a purchasing clerk makes purchases and a receiving clerk makes records of raw materials received for use in manufacturing operations.

A quality orientation starts with analysis of the larger processes within which work activities of this kind are embedded. Is there a better way to organize jobs and departments so that the underlying process (obtaining raw materials) may be accomplished more efficiently and reliably? *Efficiency* is important for keeping final cost to the customer to a minimum. Minimizing this cost is important because the ultimate aim of quality management is to maximize *value* provided to customers, and value, in turn, can be understood as a ratio of benefit to cost. *Reliability* is important partly because it bears on cost, but also because it bears on the value ratio's numerator—benefit to customers. For example, it may be important to a customer to receive manufactured goods on a specific delivery date. An unreliable process for obtaining raw materials thus will reduce the manufacturer's capacity to perform in the manner desired by the customer.

The concept of reliability in quality is perhaps more familiar in terms of the characteristics of objects made from raw materials (e.g., Is every piston of the same length, diameter, and weight?) and of the raw material itself (Is the metal flawed in some way?). The reason your North American car is in the shop more often than your neighbor's Toyota is that Toyota has mastered the areas of quality management practice that correspond to the two aspects of this example—respectively, statistical process control and supplier management.

This chapter is not the place to delve into details of these or other topics in the field of quality management, such as analyses of the dimensions of value (durability, delivery time, and so on) as perceived by customers (e.g., Garvin, 1988). Instead, the point of the preceding is to begin to suggest the many changes to traditional work organization that a quality orientation requires, so that we can go on to consider effects of culture and climate on these changes.

When process improvement becomes everyone's job on a continuing basis, employees' scope of work is enlarged to include analyzing processes (e.g., flowcharting), measuring the performance of processes (e.g., percentage of pistons manufactured outside of tolerances), and using teamwork skills (e.g., coordinating team members' efforts, resolving conflicts). In effect, everyone has a role in process innovation. *Teamwork* actually has several meanings for quality. One meaning involves use of temporary teams for process analysis and improvement in settings such as manufacturing. Another meaning involves fostering cooperation of various departments or divisions when they all make contributions to an overarching process such as "order fulfillment." Still another involves ongoing production teams whose members may be multiskilled and whose work may involve a larger portion of total production as had been the case traditionally. Yet another involves groupings of service providers into units that may be encouraged to know their customers and be empowered to serve them well, in settings such as financial services, computer software, and telecommunications.

Of course, it makes no sense for frontline employees to do process analysis unless real process changes may result, or to reorganize workers into production or service teams unless real increases in responsibility and authority coincide. Thus these changes in work activities and team organization imply potentially sweeping changes in roles of managers, technical experts such as manufacturing or information systems engineers, and nonmanagement workers (Olian & Rynes, 1991). It is this depth and breadth of change that leads to the view of change for quality as culture change.

## WHAT IS A CULTURE FOR QUALITY AND INNOVATION?

### Values

Viewed through the lens of an organizational culture perspective, the concept of values takes on a strikingly prominent place in discussions of quality management. For example, a keynote speaker at a recent conference on quality began her remarks by listing the values that characterize quality-oriented firms (Flynn, 1998). Very similar lists, such as that in Table 14.1, are used frequently in management training and consulting on quality (e.g., Beecroft, 1995). In a recent review of 21 published works on quality management that mention culture explicitly, De Lima (1999) presents a comparable list of cultural values held to be important for qual-

**TABLE 14.1   Values of Total Quality Management-Oriented Organizations**

Customer-Driven Quality
Continuous Improvement
Fulfilling Work and Respect for Employees
Communication, Cooperation, and Teamwork
Management by Fact
Prevention of Quality Problems
Long-Range Strategic Focus
Public Responsibility

ity. As a final example, Camisón (1998) describes values as providing "the base of" TQM (p. 488).

Values, of course, are central to many definitions of organizational culture (e.g., Cameron & Quinn, 1999; Schein, 1985). Values are understood to influence a wide variety of specific behaviors, so if employees have the right values for quality, the behaviors should follow. One frequently used example is that of the Nordstrom department store employee whose value on satisfying the customer motivates a long drive to deliver goods needed right away by a customer. To the extent that this high level of service to the customer is consistent with company strategy, the value has promoted the behavior needed from the employee.

When writers describe culture as critical to success in achieving quality, they evidently have in mind this kind of motivational force. Assuming behavioral congruity with strategy, it is clearly a good thing if a retailer's employees are motivated to satisfy customers, which is to say, if they value customer satisfaction. Similarly, following Table 14.1, generally a manufacturer's employees should be motivated to improve production processes on a continuing basis (otherwise, competitors will get ahead through their process improvements).

An emphasis on values for managing employee behavior for quality has a special unity or coherence. This coherence follows from the premise that superior individual performance and organizational performance are possible only when the whole employee is engaged at work. The contrast again is with traditional management, which, in the extreme case of Taylorism, literally held that the employee could leave his or her "brains at home" because tasks and incentive structures had been, in theory, specified so precisely and optimally. Under values-based management, employees are given direction not in literal terms but in terms of objectives, goals, or desired end states. Employees then apply discretion in seeking these ends. That Nordstrom employee turns out to be a pretty good example of this notion. Presumably, no one said, "Drive a long way to deliver goods to customers"; instead, it was, "Do what is necessary to satisfy the customer" (see Tushman & O'Reilly, 1997).

Values-based management makes sense when Tayloristic task specification is either impossible or incongruent with the rest of the context, and this is certainly the case for organizations seeking the highest quality in goods or services. In the case of manufacturing, part of the task of frontline employees is to generate improvements in production processes on a continuous basis. This is an inherently creative and collaborative process. It cannot be fully specified, and if it could, the mind-numbing nature of highly specified work would drive out the creativity. Management by values applies at least as well to management-level employees as to those not on that level. For example, strong values on fulfilling work and respect for employees have many implications for how managers should treat subordinates and peers. In fact, all of the values listed in Table 14.1 can be imagined to inform managers' decisions and actions. Attempts to influence these actions instead by more specific directives would be impractical (e.g., overwhelming in number) and motivationally incongruent (e.g., demeaning by minimizing managerial discretion).

Management by values also can have payoffs with other professionals, such as software developers. For example, in a study of approximately 100 developers organized into 12 interdependent groups, values that had been instilled for satisfying customers, taking responsibility for self-management, and getting the job done ("can-do attitude") appeared to provide the opportunity and drive to overcome structural roadblocks to success in serving clients (Webster et al., 1998).

A "values" emphasis on culture has this immediate implication: For successful organizational transformation to quality, employees must acquire and follow values like those listed in Table 14.1. This requirement may lie behind the widespread belief that leaders must communicate, reward adherence to, and, perhaps, exemplify these values for quality (Daft, 1992; Waldman et al., 1998). Trice and Beyer (1993, p. 412) give the example of a new leader of a manufacturing plant who announced his (values-based) managerial philosophy and then "roamed" the organization like an evangelist converting people. To the extent that values are tied to identity (corporate or individual), pertinent actions for culture management also include management of artifacts that signal who we are (e.g., architecture and other aspects of style in the organization that say we are traditional, nontraditional, dynamic, warm, and so on) and repetition of stories that bear on values such as equality (as in the story of the IBM CEO who, like any other employee, was turned away at a security post when he lacked a required badge).

## Norms

The simplest definition of organizational culture—"the way we do things around here"—connects most closely with the concept of norms within the definition of organizational culture. In common and formal use of the term, *norm* has two aspects: what people typically do and shared understandings about what people are supposed to do. People tend to think that typical behavior is the right thing to do (a conversion from "is" to

"ought") because that has been their experience in many domains of life (D'Andrade, 1984; see also various sources in Shweder & LeVine, 1984). A good example from the domain of culture-based diets is the norm to avoid eating the shells of nuts. Most of us in Western societies probably think that is the right thing to do. But why? Are the shells poisonous? Indigestible? Unpalatable? Many of us may not know. The norm can be so strong that we never ask, and it may not even occur to us to try eating nutshells. Further, we may assume that we ought not eat nutshells. The same can occur with normative behaviors in organizations. In other instances, norms exert their effects through individuals' expectations that others will apply sanctions for violations of norms. By the fact that a behavior is normative, one can expect that others will also perceive it as normative and right, and insist upon it.

Like other concepts and corresponding processes of culture, norms and values are intertwined. Norms often imply identifiable values (e.g., cooperation as a value behind information sharing), so either or both may explain corresponding behavior. Nevertheless, these two concepts may imply somewhat different sequences of transformations for quality. With values, the desired behavior is expected to follow if the predisposing values are instilled. With norms, getting the desired behaviors, by whatever means, creates conditions in which people infer they are the right ones or, at least, the socially approved ones (including when people are explicitly socialized to conform to the norms).

The immediate implication is that appropriate norms are required for quality. However, this raises a problem to which we alluded in the opening of this chapter, that of circular definitions of the role of a culture for quality in attaining a quality orientation such as total quality management. That is, it is obviously circular to say that if we just had the right norms we would be a TQM organization—if TQM is defined as a set of shared practices equivalent to norms ("the way we do things"). Each reader of the quality literature must judge whether circularity is pervasive and whether the construct of culture has a useful purpose (see Newman & Chaharbaghi, 1998). One reason for concern is that the meaning of *culture* is often left unspecified in writings on quality management, and it does seem quite possible that, at least in part, a definition along the lines of "the way we do things around here" is often implied. However, it seems likely as well that some writers have in mind a basis for these norms in values, and others intend to emphasize how norms instigate processes of social control, as organization members implore others to conform to norms. Still other writers avoid the logical problems here by stating explicitly that instilling particular cultural values is important in the early stages of a quality transformation (Camisón, 1998; Scholtes & Hacquebord, 1988).

A further problem concerns how to instill norms for quality—such as sharing information across departments or making a habit of asking external and internal customers (other departments) for feedback on performance. This is, in essence, a problem of changing employee behavior on a broad scale. It seems likely that *if* behavior can be changed on a broad scale, and if that behavior turns out to be experienced by employees as *beneficial* in various ways (e.g., promotes company survival in a competitive industry; provides intrinsic satisfactions relating to growth, achievement, aesthetics, and the like; is appreciated and recognized in the organization), then values will follow and it will be meaningful to speak of having a culture for quality.

### Steps and Tools for Behavioral Change Toward Cultural Change

Burke (1994) describes his experience at British Airways, where a process of culture change for enhanced responsiveness to customers (including internal customers such as other departments) began by identifying behaviors that would be manifestations of the new culture. Then managers were trained through feedback and role or skill practice in these behaviors (e.g., communicating in an open manner, involving subordinates in decisions that affect them directly). Next, these behaviors were incorporated into performance appraisals. Finally, incentive pay for performing the behaviors was tied to these appraisals.

This example captures three areas of action commonly discussed in the quality management literature: training, measurement, and rewards. Training is one of the most widely cited "success factors" for quality (see, e.g., Jha et al., 1996). When quality involves new concepts, such as statistical process control, training is obviously necessary—a point to which we will return later. The main, further point from this example is that training in interpersonal behavior can also be necessary (see also Rubin & Inguagiato, 1991).

An emphasis on measurement is likewise ubiquitous in quality management (Kober & Knowles, 1996; Olian & Rynes, 1991). Measures may be taken component by component in manufacturing or transaction by transaction in service, but measures are also taken for quality performance by groups, plants, branches, and whole organizations (e.g., defect rate or dissatisfied customer rate).

There is much more controversy about the proper use of rewards to induce change in specific behaviors and, ultimately, culture for quality. Hackman and Wageman (1995) review writings of major figures, such as Deming and Juran, and arrive at a summary of advice on whether quality programs should include pay-for-performance schemes: "Do not do it." Although this view is based on a wealth of experience in trying to move organizations toward quality practices, it contradicts the notion of contingency in organizational behavior (i.e., the notion that blanket advice, pro or con, is unlikely to be useful "always and everywhere"), it is inconsistent with models of culture change that include rewards among the prominent levers

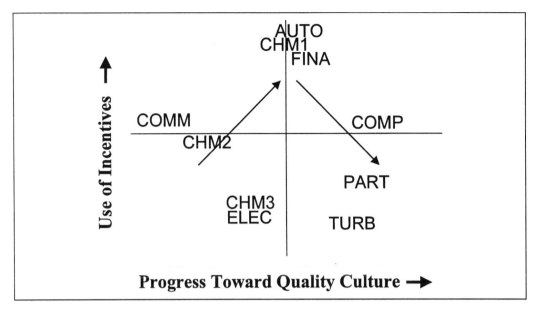

**Figure 14.1.** Interrelations of 10 Firms Seeking Quality, Based on Interview Data From Human Resources

for change (e.g., Kerr & Slocum, 1987; Sathe, 1985b), and it is inconsistent with research showing that it is possible to promote both intrinsic and extrinsic motivation simultaneously (see Hackman & Wageman, 1995).

Michela, Clark, Jha, and Noori (1998) studied this matter by asking managers in 10 firms to describe their approaches to quality, their organizational cultures, and any programs or systems of rewards or recognition for quality-related behaviors and outcomes. Their findings are depicted in Figure 14.1, which summarizes the interview comments quantitatively, as characterizations of each firm in terms of two dimensions: extent of progress toward a quality culture and use of tangible rewards (money, merchandise, and so on) as incentives for doing the work of quality. These dimensions were generated by a statistical procedure called multidimensional scaling. Data for this procedure concerned ratings of the 10 firms on attribute dimensions that emerged during the content coding of the interview notes.

By looking at specific comments from firms at various points along the horizontal continuum to total quality, Michela et al. inferred

that use of tangible rewards can help a firm to "get moving" toward quality if it is otherwise complacent or mired. One source of evidence consisted of comments by the manager of the firm labeled CHM1 (near the middle-top of the figure), who said, "We're about halfway along the continuum" from what her firm termed a "reward" culture to the "appreciative" culture the organization had set as its goal. This concept of the "reward" culture involved use of rewards to induce individuals and groups within functional areas to achieve high performance and make process improvements. In the "appreciative" culture, teamwork, performance, and improvement would be more intrinsically valued, and the primary reward would be recognition and appreciation by stakeholders—generally internal customers. Managers in firms at the far right of the figure described this "appreciative" kind of teamwork and recognition as characteristic of their firms. For example, the manager at a turbine manufacturer (TURB in the figure) said: "The continuous improvement culture has become ingrained in the way we do business. [We feel no] push to go back to some sort of incentive plan. What we're trying to do is create a team environment."

These observations do not mean that Deming and others were wrong in warning against use of extrinsic incentives for quality. Research on intrinsic motivation (for a brief introduction, see Michela, 1996) is convincing on the point that people tend to attribute their behavior to extrinsic rewards when these rewards are large or otherwise salient. Having made this attribution, people are less likely to acquire values that support the behavior, as they might if the intrinsic satisfactions or other benefits of the behavior were relatively more salient. Thus it appears that extrinsic rewards should be relatively small and should be used only when necessary (perhaps in a climate of low trust between labor and management). Real intrinsic reward should be available in quality-related behavior (e.g., opportunities to make sizable contributions to organization effectiveness and other attributes listed in Burke, 1982) and emphasis should be given to the recognition aspect of any reward given (consistent with the favorable effect on intrinsic motivation tied to the "informational" function of rewards, described in Deci & Ryan's [1980] cognitive evaluation theory).

Problems involving employees' feelings of fairness are another key reason to avoid use of extrinsic rewards for inducing behavioral change for quality. In particular, any proportion of cost savings returned to the innovator may not be seen as large enough, and the singling out of an individual or a group for a sizable payment may seem unfair to others who contributed—and thus may undermine a climate for cooperation.

These problems may be less acute for occupational groups such as the managers at British Airways (see also Hackman & Wageman, 1995). Managers generally have more autonomy than frontline employees, so accountability, measurement, and reward of the kinds described in that example may be experienced as more fair and motivating. In

any case, there seems to be a growing trend in labor-intensive industries (such as financial services) toward linking a portion of managerial pay to measures of behaviors thought to promote quality and service cultures. Concerns are often voiced about measurement per se, but otherwise the fairness and motivational benefits of this linkage seem to gain at least some acceptance.

## Schemas

In contrast to the emphasis that the concept of "values" gives to affective aspects of culture and the concept of "norms" gives to social and behavioral aspects, the concept of "schemas" emphasizes cognitive aspects, such as beliefs about the right way to go about doing things. As a general definition, a schema is a mental framework or structure for identifying or understanding things, actors, events, and situations. The simplest schemas provide the basis for seeing objects such as tables or faces, either in everyday visual perception or in representations (e.g., abstract art). For example, a table is defined by a parallelogram with three or four lines below it. More complex schemas allow us to recognize incipient interpersonal conflict or to formulate plans for heading off conflict.

Schemas are important in motivation generally and in understanding culture specifically, partly because they "bind" elements such as values and needs to action (see Pratkanis & Greenwald, 1989). This notion is reflected in writings of cultural anthropologists who have argued that a culture's hold over behavior derives not only from values and norms but also from the convincing rationales that often accompany values and norms (Shweder & LeVine, 1984). For example, a parent may tell a 5-year-old about the germ theory of disease as a rationale for hand washing.

Kilmann (1998) points to schemas as an important construct in corporate transformation generally, and Spencer (1994) indicates that an aspect of cultural transformation to quality is the acquisition of concepts that are schematic in scope. Quality-related schemas may be local or global in scope. Relatively local schemas include those that represent knowledge about specific quality practices, such as "root cause" analysis. More global schemas represent the meanings of encompassing terms such as *kaizen*. Schemas also vary in whether they are attribute oriented (e.g., one's schema for TQM might incorporate the attributes one thinks are characteristic of companies that follow this management philosophy) or event oriented (e.g., one could have a schema for the sequence of events necessary for large-scale organizational change, beginning, say, with formulating a vision).

Two devices used to discuss and analyze organizations may help to make the concept of schemas more concrete. One such device is a generic organization model, which may provide either a categorization of important variables (e.g., people, tasks, structure) or a more dynamic characterization of the organization (e.g., as an open system that relates to its environment in a manner analogous to an organism). Such a model functions schematically by helping to frame and reduce chaotic reality into more manageable and interconnected bits and pieces. Another device is a story, which may help explain the direction, meaning of, and rationale for organization change. Howard Gardner's (1995) work regarding the importance of the leader's story about a given change effort is particularly relevant here.

In the opening of this chapter we referred to reports of high failure rates in transformations for quality. Reger, Gustafson, DeMarie, and Mullane (1994) offer the bold suggestion that these failures are not to be explained by operational failures, as suggested in the reports, but by failures of management to create conditions for employees to acquire the encompassing understanding of quality and its rationale that our analysis of schemas entails. Reger et al. call this "reframing" but

cite the same theoretical sources (e.g., Fiske & Taylor, 1991) on which we have drawn in defining and distinguishing schemas. This reframing model further holds that change must be calibrated to organization members' likely acceptance of change. The zone of acceptance lies between a region where change is perceived as unnecessary and one where change is perceived as unattainable. One might address the necessity of change (emphasized also by Kotter, 1996, among others) in part by giving information about the firm's competitive position; one might address the attainability of change by showing what other organizations have done (as through employees' visits to other firms in benchmarking).

The general implication of schematic aspects of culture is that people must acquire many new concepts, which must fit together into a comprehensible whole. The existence of "quality colleges" (maintained by vendors of training for quality) attests to wide recognition of the learning requirements of quality. One can hardly "overcommunicate" about major organizational changes such as adoption of quality management practices (see Exterbille, 1996). Top managers, immediate supervisors, newsletters, and any other communication sources and media should provide rationales and concepts repeatedly.

However, training can and should be about more than skills, knowledge, and stated rationales. The training setting, away from day-to-day tasks, provides opportunities for employees to question rationales (and receive answers), check reality, express fears or frustrations, and obtain support from peers. On this matter, Bolman and Deal (1991, p. 376) comment that resistance to change can stem from fears of being unable to perform under new work arrangements. Training can address these fears directly by providing necessary skills and indirectly by providing opportunities for employees to receive peer support.

Through communications from management and among peers in a period of organizational change, employees may undergo change in two of the most fundamental schemas, those concerning individual and organizational identities. Indeed, lack of change in these schemas can be a major barrier to change when employees react to proposed change with the thought: That's just not who we are. We don't "give away the store" to our customers. We do the work but we don't design it. We aren't the revolutionaries in our industry.

Reger et al. (1994) discuss several approaches to and examples of the use of identity to gain leverage for behavioral and cultural change for quality. Often the basic idea is to make an aspect of existing identity salient (such as "We have a can-do attitude") and then provide contrary data in order to motivate action to close this identity gap. Direct customer interaction and benchmarking are two sources of such data.

### Evaluating the Contribution of the Concept of Culture to Quality Management

Inducing people to work in new ways for quality and innovation may involve overcoming past habits, values, beliefs, and identity. We have tried to show in the preceding discussion that concepts from the organizational culture literature provide many avenues for approaching necessary changes. Our main reservation is that this literature is quite interpretative in approach. That is, the actual evidence generally consists of writers' interpretations of what they have observed in organizations, in the absence of validated or other calibrated measures, and lacking research designs that allow strong inference. Kilmann (1998) notes this problem for a great deal of literature on organizational change; it is not unique to transformations for quality and innovation. If continued work on these topics encompasses a wide range of theoretical and disciplinary orientations (anthropology, social psychology, and so on) and design features (intensive single

case, content-analyzed multiple case), this should help to compensate for the uncertainties inherent in any particular study.

## WHAT IS A CLIMATE FOR QUALITY AND INNOVATION?

### Distinguishing Climate From Culture

Traditionally defined, organizational climate involves people's perceptions and experiences of the workplace in terms of warmth, trust, dynamism, ambiguity, and other affect-laden dimensions (James, 1982). A parallel, one-sentence definition of culture might emphasize how cultures influence the meanings of events at work (Burke, 1994), as when a competitive threat is assessed or a new way of working is attempted. (The concept of meaning integrates values and schemas from the preceding section and the concept of norms bears on one of the most basic meanings, how one should act.) Thus, although climate and culture are related (e.g., because warmth, trust, and so forth *are* meanings), they are also distinguishable. Culture influences people's orientations to one another, to work, and to the environment. Climate unfolds as people experience warmth, ambiguity, and so forth through actions and interactions (see also Denison, 1996; Schneider, 1975; Schneider, Brief, & Guzzo, 1996).

In contrast to the scores of articles easily uncovered on the topic of culture in quality management, our search on climate and quality yielded relatively few articles. Of course, this result could be an artifact of language; to some degree, writers use the term *culture* to include what we have defined as climate. However, use of the term *climate* is not randomly distributed in the quality literature with respect to the problems addressed, such as overcoming resistance to change or promoting cooperation and communication. The problem for which favorable climate is most often offered as the solution is innovation. For example, Fishman and Kavanaugh (1989) suggest that the "missing link" in quality is for supervisors to promote a group climate where people feel secure in offering improvement suggestions. They suggest further that climate is shaped substantially by behaviors of the supervisor, such as listening fully and giving recognition or otherwise being positive about employees' attempts at contributions.

Aside from the relatively focused climate dimensions featured in discussions of innovation, the broad dimensions of trust and its opposite, fear, recur in the quality and innovation literatures (e.g., Alexander, 1985; Kipnis, 1996; Sitkin & Stickel, 1996; Suarez, 1994). Deming (1986) includes among his principles that managers should "drive out fear" from the workplace because it is debilitating to the kinds of work required for quality (e.g., by making it dangerous to share information). Trust is an important topic not only in quality management but in organizational development generally today (Burke, 1997). Partly this importance stems from the increased need for trust in a period when hierarchical structures are being dismantled and employees' interactions are increasingly self-managed. The era of downsizing, huge CEO salaries, and corporate greed that coincided with the rise of quality management may also be a factor in the rise of concern with trust. Finally, there is hypocrisy in various forms, as when executives call for openness but hide impending changes from employees until they have all their facts together and all their ducks in a row.

We suspect that climate lurks in the background for quality management in other ways that have not been fully articulated in the literature. One indication comes from an observation made by Jha et al. (1996): Announcements by management of many quality programs, dating back to one of the earliest in 1894 (see Schroeder & Robinson, 1991), have been accompanied by announcements of actions to improve working conditions. This observation suggests that a climate of positive feeling toward the employer is necessary if employees are to change their ways of working as required for quality.

## Climate for Innovation

An analysis of organizational conditions for innovation offered by West (1990) and his colleagues (Anderson, Hardy, & West, 1990) makes reference to values and norms but ultimately hinges on climate. The empirical research in this line has concerned teams in an oil factory (Burningham & West, 1995) and other settings. The research model posits that the determinants of group innovativeness are participative safety, support for innovation, climate for excellence, and vision. Participative safety is a climate factor involving an expectation that one will be appreciated rather than vilified for offering suggestions in the innovation process. Support for innovation is basically a shared value that innovation is good. As indicated earlier in this chapter, these expectations and values may be instilled explicitly in socialization or implicitly in cultural messages. In addition, although it does not directly influence innovation, a climate for excellence often is helpful because people striving for excellence will naturally seek innovation when appropriate. Similarly, a clear, attainable, and consensually shared vision or mission is helpful because people become motivated to reach the goal by appropriate means.

In a discussion that addresses connections between innovation and many variables from organizational behavior and organizational theory, Anderson and King's (1993) coverage of organizational climate keys on a study by Nystrom (1990). In this study of a chemical manufacturer, climate was conceptualized as playing a role along with strategy, structure, and culture. Moreover, specific configurations of culture and climate factors were observed to coincide with particular levels of innovative or creative output. For example, the firm's most innovative division displayed relatively high conflict and low trust and harmony, although risk taking and debate were encouraged, as was playfulness.

Amabile's (1998) work on creativity offers additional insight into pertinent aspects of climate for quality and innovation. In one of her studies, she asked research and development scientists about characteristics of the organizational environment that facilitate or inhibit creativity (Amabile, 1988). The inhibitors most frequently mentioned by the scientists included an organizational climate marked by lack of cooperation across divisions and levels and lack of value placed on creativity by the organizational culture. Inhibitory organizational structures and policies, such as inappropriate reward systems, also were mentioned frequently. The opposites of these factors, such as a creativity-promotive culture, were mentioned frequently by the scientists as facilitators. Also noteworthy among the facilitators was a sense of freedom over one's work, particularly in the day-to-day conduct of one's work. Nystrom's study mentioned previously and other research cited by Amabile have pointed to freedom as a favorable factor as well.

Amabile (1988) characterizes managers' tasks in support of creativity as a balancing act. In the area of feedback about performance, the wrong amount or wrong kind of performance evaluation is detrimental. Too much or overly specified criteria for evaluation may inhibit risk taking. Too little evaluation leads employees to feel forgotten and thus unmotivated. Thus Amabile recommends "a constant, constructive, less formal exchange of information about a project's progress on the part of all team members and management" (p. 149). Arriving at a recommendation about another balancing act, applying the right amount of pressure, is more difficult. On the one hand, some amount of time pressure and possibly competition appears to be facilitative; on the other, too much pressure appears to lead to unimaginative solutions.

Amabile has offered an encompassing model of creativity and innovation that incorporates factors ranging from those at the highest level of organization (e.g., the mission statement for the organization as a whole) to the individual level (e.g., skills). Many aspects of Amabile's recommendations and model are consistent with one of the models of dynamics in organizational performance and change (particularly, transactional dynamics) that we describe in the next major section of this chapter. Before describing those models, we will complete the present section by examining one further connection of climate to quality and innovation.

## Climate for Technology Implementation

Comprehensive analyses of quality recognize that even when people are highly motivated as a result of culture, climate, and other factors, they can provide world-class goods and services only if they make use of the best available technology for the task. Klein and Sorra (1996) argue that organizational climate is a key factor in technology implementation and other innovation implementation. These writers adapted Schneider's (1990a) conceptualization of climate, involving employees' shared perceptions concerning whether specific behaviors (as related to innovation, for example) are "rewarded, supported and expected in a setting" (p. 384). Findings from employees with access to computer-assisted design and drafting systems in an engineering and construction firm provide an illustration. Although the technology had been adopted and installed, and employees had received sufficient training and rationales to use it, use for some time was sporadic at best. The problem appeared to stem from a combination of unfavorable conditions that Klein and Sorra term a climate—lack of rewards for using the new technology and failure to remove barriers such as sluggishness in the operation of the computer itself. In other instances, indicators of a poor climate for innovation implementation could include lack of training or coaching, failure to address concerns about change, scheduling or other time incompatibilities, and other shortcomings of organizational support for change.

A further aspect of Klein and Sorra's (1996) analysis suggests that when values (as discussed earlier in this chapter, in connection with culture) are incongruent with available innovation, implementation will suffer. One example involves an operational technology (as opposed to a mechanical or electronic one), statistical process control. Klein and Sorra cite Bushe's (1988) case study, in which manufacturing employees' high value on performance or production was seen as interfering with the change and learning required for SPC. They also provide other examples relating to teamwork, design for software development, and flexible production innovations.

In an article that is mostly about organization design and culture in relation to success in implementing advanced manufacturing technology, Zammuto and O'Connor (1992) discuss climate and individuals' motivation to maximize their skills with advanced technology. Various aspects of the employer-employee relationship that bear on climate features, such as security and warmth, appear to be key. For example, Zammuto and O'Connor cite Hildebrandt (1988) on the point that high-level learning about technology is more prevalent in "high-trust organizations." Walton's (1989) work on "high-commitment organizations" points in the same direction. High commitment is a two-way proposition: The employer promotes the employee's welfare in various ways, and the employee is fully engaged in learning and performance.

## Evaluating the Contribution of the Concept of Climate to Innovation

Some of the research reviewed in this section may be questioned concerning either the subjectivity in case-based, qualitative studies or the design limitations of correlational studies (such as a potential reverse causal se-

quence in which innovating groups might have given high ratings to participative safety *because* their ideas were well received). Nevertheless, some reassurance comes from the frequent harmony of the findings of various researchers using somewhat different approaches (Amabile, Anderson, Nystrom, West, and others). Indeed, there may be more empirical basis for saying climate is associated with outcomes (such as more output of innovative ideas) than for saying the same about culture.

However, this empirical superiority is somewhat offset by the greater conceptual ambiguity surrounding climate. One issue is whether many so-called climate effects are better termed culture effects, as they are based in motivation stemming from either values or social pressure. Another is whether the "summary" nature of the "climate for" construct (i.e., climate as the social and psychological encapsulation or upshot of a wide variety of possible objective conditions) is a strength or weakness. Klein and Sorra (1996) note astutely that comparison of innovation across organizations, despite tremendous variation in specifics of policies and practices, could be greatly fostered by a focus of research on the cumulative influences of training, rewards, user-friendliness, and so on, which is to say, on climate for innovation implementation. However, a hazard in this approach is that, depending on how it is measured, the "climate for" conception may not add anything beyond its components (training, rewards, and so on). Alternatively, it may collapse into outcome variables such as motivations thought to govern work behavior (e.g., if conceptions of both "climate for" and "motivation" include expectations about rewards for behaviors). Moreover, if a researcher finds the middle ground between these alternatives, this may undermine his or her making connections back to the specific factors that need action by management or forward to explain how associated consequences are generated.

The issues here are reminiscent of those in the field of work stress, where stress is seen as the cumulative result of a wide variety of environmental and personal factors. Kasl (1984) concludes that the statement "Stress can cause illness" is both tenable and virtually meaningless without further specification; the same seems to apply to "Organizational climate can promote quality and innovation." At the same time, just as the concept of "stress" may have real heuristic value, "climate" may point in productive directions for research and practice.

In order for the climate construct to contribute to true explanation of employee behavior—either as the "climate for" version of the construct or as discrete dimensions of climate—more complete theoretical accounts must be developed. These accounts may need to draw on the interplay of perceptions of the environment (e.g., what is permitted, or encouraged, or expected), personal preferences, motivations, and social processes (see Klein & Sorra, 1996; Michela, Lukaszewski, & Allegrante, 1995). For example, if a climate of freedom is associated with innovation, a proper account of this association might require a description of the motivational and behavioral processes and events that occur when freedom is perceived or experienced.

For the moment, the empirical findings provide ample basis for management attention to organizational conditions likely to influence perceptions and experiences encompassed by "climate." Some approaches to intervention, to achieve favorable organizational conditions, are the topic of the next section.

## COMPREHENSIVE PERSPECTIVES ON ORGANIZATIONAL TRANSFORMATION

The array of concepts, variables, and processes discussed so far in this chapter is potentially overwhelming. If all these factors must be considered in organizational change for quality and innovation, is there hope for the leader who seeks change? The answer is yes, because this huge task has been broken down into more manageable components in writings available in the quality literature and in the literatures on organization development and organizational change or transformation.

We favor writings in the latter literatures as points of departure for planning and initiating large-scale change for quality and innovation, because the models presented are comprehensive, systematic, and explicitly based on motivational and other psychological theory and research of the kind we reviewed in the earlier sections of this chapter. We will discuss three models in order to draw out three distinctions: transformational versus transactional dynamics, fixed-order versus contingent interventions, and orchestration versus improvisation.

## The Burke-Litwin Model of Transformational and Transactional Dynamics

Burke and Litwin's (1992) model, presented in Figure 14.2, is a useful framework for understanding organizations in at least two ways. It addresses (a) what drives individual and organizational *performance*, and in what priorities, and (b) how to conceptualize and implement *change*. For our purposes in the context of this chapter, we will concentrate on the change dimension.

It is pragmatic to think of organization change in terms of two levels: transformational and transactional. *Transformational* refers to fundamental, significant, and comprehensive change in an organization and is represented in the model by the top boxes: external environment (the forces from outside the organization that drive change, e.g., competition, changing technology, and/or market dynamics or globalization,

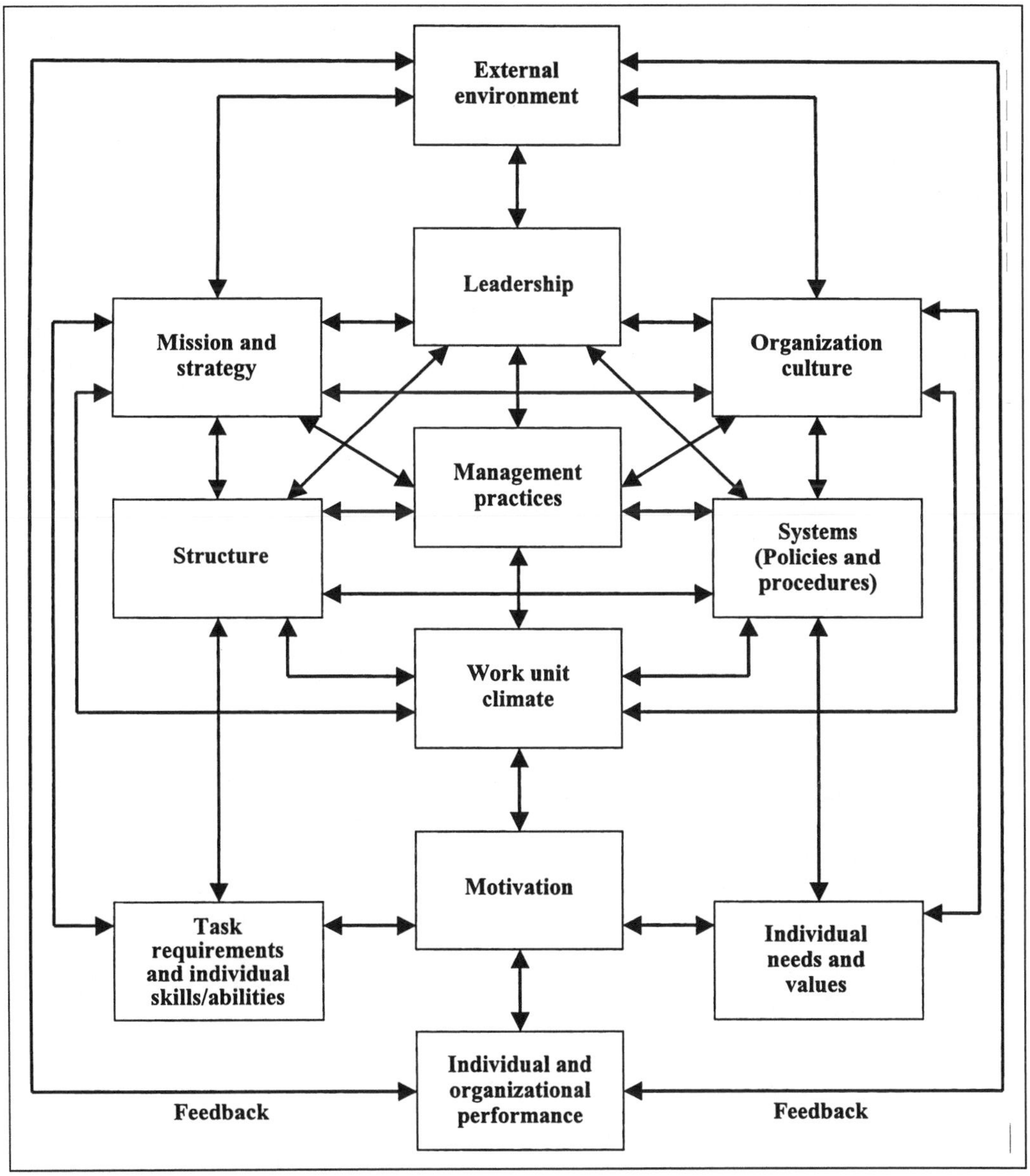

**Figure 14.2.** The Burke-Litwin Model of Transformational and Transactional Dynamics in Organizational Performance

new or reduced government regulations), mission and strategy (the purpose of and direction for the organization, including *how* to get there), leadership (executives who are responsible for coordinating all the boxes in the model), and culture (the way we do things, the overt and covert rules, or norms and values). Typically, transformational change occurs when organizational members and primary stakeholders (e.g., the board) respond to environmental forces with entirely new behavioral sets. New ways of working for quality (think "culture") are paradigmatic here. Organization transformation, then, requires (a) new organizational directions in response to environmental changes, (b) new behaviors that will implement the different directions *and* are linked to new values and norms that support the new directions, and (c) leadership that promotes these new behaviors, understandings, and values.

The *transactional* level refers to organization changes that are more operational, day to day, and in many cases associated with continuous improvement. This level is represented in the model by the boxes in the lower half: structure (organizational design, accountability, decision making, and how units relate to one another, including hierarchy), management practices (the daily behaviors of managers as they relate to their bosses, peers, direct reports, and other relevant constituents, e.g., customers), systems (policies and mechanisms designed to facilitate work, e.g., rewards, communication, measures), work unit climate (the collective perceptions by members of a local work unit about what is expected of them, their feelings about their manager and one another, work standards, recognition, and other dimensions), motivation and other factors that have direct effects on motivation congruence, task requirements and individual skills/abilities, and individual needs and values. Climate results from the transactions of a number of boxes in the model, but particularly management practices (e.g., Litwin & Stringer, 1968). Earlier, when we referred to the supervisor's role in group climate (Fishman & Kavanaugh, 1989) and to the balancing acts required of managers seeking innovation (Amabile, 1988), we were addressing transactions of this kind.

Diagnosing and monitoring employees' beliefs, perceptions, and motivations, especially those related to culture and climate, are critical to any change effort. A model of this kind can point to the types of questions to ask in this diagnostic process and how to interpret identified shortcomings (see Trahant & Burke, 1996). The value of culture or climate

diagnosis in the process of transformation to quality, specifically, is reflected in the work of Collard (1989). And, finally, it should be pointed out that

> executives and managers typically concern themselves with the left side of the [model]: mission and strategy, structure, task requirements and individual skills or abilities. In contrast, behavioral scientists are more likely to be concerned with the right side and middle of [the model]: leadership, culture, systems (especially rewards), management practices, climate, individual needs and values, and motivation. For a fundamental, large system change effort one should be concerned with the entire model and with a more effective integration of purpose and practice. (Burke, 1994, p. 138)

## Kilmann's Integrated Sequence of Eight Tracks for Transformation

A good example of a sequenced model of corporate transformation is the one offered by Kilmann (1998), which describes eight interconnected "tracks" or thrusts of organizational and personal development. These tracks are culture, skills, team, strategy, reward, gradual process, radical process, and learning process. Although we cannot fully describe the model here (see Kilmann, 1995), the following points are noteworthy.

Kilmann's model is distinguished by its proposal of a preferred ordering of the kinds of actions for transformation that we have been discussing throughout this chapter. Some of this ordering appears to be loose, and overlap in time is recommended (e.g., skills training begins while culture is still being addressed). Nevertheless, there is a definite starting point, culture, and some tracks are not to be followed until others have run their course (e.g., strategy and reward after culture and skills).

It should be noted that prescriptions for the ordering of actions for organizational change are fairly common in the literature focused more specifically on quality management (e.g., Camisón, 1998; Schmidt & Finnigan, 1992). However, some more general approaches, such as the Burke-Litwin model, imply a more contingent approach in choosing when to address the various components of the model.

*Culture* in Kilmann's model refers to norms about how people behave toward one another. In Kilmann's words, these are "dos and don'ts," not values. People can be specific in discussions of the corresponding behaviors, and they can call one another on norm violations. Within the culture track it is necessary to engender open communication and other behaviors that will enhance trust and other attributes of a positive social and task climate in the organization. Without these attributes, the difficult choices in reengineering or other sweeping transformations would be extremely difficult to discuss, let alone resolve. Support for innovation as adaptation to environmental requirements should also be fostered in this phase.

Finally, personal development and self-knowledge are as important as organizational development in Kilmann's approach. In part this is because radical organizational transformation bears on individuals' identities and attachments. Kilmann (1998) believes that people with strong egos—who know themselves and value their strengths —are better able to cope with radical change.

## Bartunek's Model of Schema Conflict and Resolution

In contrast to the two "orchestrated" approaches to organizational change just described, Bartunek's (1993) approach could be described as "improvisational." Bartunek's analysis of organizational change hinges on her version of the concept of schemas. Illustrating the approach, Bartunek examined the schemas of five categories of employees or other stakeholders (i.e., consultants) during an initiative for greater productivity in a food-processing firm. Bartunek distinguishes among these schemas in terms of (a) what each group wanted to arise from the initiative, (b) means to achieve desired ends, (c) expressed concerns, and (d) a summary label. For example, Bartunek labels the schema for local management "paternalism" because it sought productivity and quality-of-life enhancements through a system that would maintain management dominance in decision making. Machinists' "competition" schema sought to maintain pay differentials with other, less skilled groups by refusing to participate in the intervention.

The improvisational nature of this approach lies in how the particular content of different groups' schemas will differ across organizations. (This contrasts with the more universal nature of the boxes of the Burke-Litwin model or the tracks of Kilmann's model, for example.) Nevertheless, most organizations may be expected to contain groups with different goals, different ideal paths to goals, and so forth. In some instances the sources of these differences will be "occupational cultures," defined by von Meier (1999) as different mental models or cognitive representations of technology and work effectiveness that are adaptive for the occupational groups but may lead to conflicting evaluations of innovation.

Misunderstandings or different understandings of the most effective ways of working are not the only basis of logjams that occur in attempts at organizational change. Conflicting interests are also key. For example, local management might insist that its paternalistic orientation is necessary for everyone's ultimate benefit; line employees are unlikely to agree with this orientation if it means that their wishes will receive little weight in the decision process. In consulting practice, Bartunek induces the various groups to address each other's perspectives (schemas) explicitly. One of the functions of this direct engagement is to discover legitimate interests of the other, thus providing a basis for negotiation. Another function is to stimulate a dialectical process in which the status quo thesis and an alternative antithesis may become seen as reconcilable in a synthesis. Bartunek (1993) describes such an outcome for a religious order that arrived at a synthesis of two seemingly incompatible roles for itself in its community (somewhat as Reger et al., 1994, discuss in connection with identity-based change, described earlier). Finally, in direct engagement it may be discovered that notions about the legitimacy of conflict itself and acceptable ways of handling conflict are intrinsic to one or more groups' schemas, and that these notions must be addressed.

Conflict should be expected to lie under (if not above) the surface of many instances of change for quality or innovation. Over time, as ways of doing things become entrenched in organizations, many organization members acquire a stake in keeping things that way (e.g., in their job titles/authority, value of their skills). Change threatens these vested interests. A good starting point for further reading on this matter is Kanter (1988).

### Evaluating Systematic Approaches to Organizational Change for Quality and Innovation

It seems unlikely there is one best way to approach change in culture or climate for quality and innovation—which is why we have tried to present several different kinds of models for organizational change. Other relevant models may be found in Burke (1994). Even within each model, a contingent approach (informed by diagnostic data) is generally necessary, and elements may need to be combined from multiple models. For example, Kilmann (1998) does not recommend just jumping in with the first track in his model. He advises strategy analysis and diagnosis of barriers to strategy implementa-

tion before the tracks are scheduled and implemented.

## INTERPRETIVE AND CRITICAL PERSPECTIVES

Earlier in this chapter, we pointed to ideal values, norms, and understandings for quality. However, actual approaches to quality vary considerably. In a rich discussion that covers more ground than we can summarize here, Spencer (1994) conceptualizes this variation in terms of three models of organization: mechanistic, organismic, and cultural. She argues that in some respects or some implementations, TQM is basically an extension of the old, mechanistic model of organizations and maintains a whiff of Taylorism. Other writers have pointed to the *increased* stress felt by workers in manufacturing plants where TQM has yielded processes so well controlled and measured that production standards are extremely demanding and deviations are immediately detected and attributable to individuals or groups. The organismic model as presented by Spencer questions the "always and everywhere" TQM prescriptions, such as Deming's (1986) 14 principles, and reflects a focus that is relatively more external (toward satisfying customers) than internal (toward optimizing processes—consistent with its systems view of the organization). Organizations that operate according to this organismic model may provide opportunities for intrinsic satisfactions as discussed earlier, but they have not fully embraced the value on "fulfilling work and respect for employees" (see Table 14.1) that is central to Spencer's cultural model. For example, in the mechanistic and organismic models, managers are cast as designers and coordinators of the organizational systems; in the cultural model, they are seen as inspiring and exemplifying leaders, coaches, and mediators.

Spencer's "interpretative" orientation reminds us that writings like this chapter may themselves be value-laden rather than value-free. The organizational analyst's or change consultant's choice is to act either normatively, articulating and acting in accord with his or her own stated values, or contingently, as by focusing on obtaining valid data that a client may use to pursue whatever his or her goals may be (Burke, 1982, 1994, 1997). In an era when transformations to quality are sometimes accompanied by downsizing and other exercises of corporate power over individuals and societies (e.g., see Estes, 1996; Korten, 1995), we are comfortable in supporting the employee-oriented and society-oriented values that can be well aligned with total quality management. However, as Spencer's analysis of quality approaches and organizational models makes clear, this alignment is not automatic. Like any management approach, quality management principles may end up either helping or hurting people. It is our hope that this chapter can aid those who want to promote workplaces that are more rewarding and effective in all senses.

## SUMMARY AND CONCLUSIONS

The quote from Woods (1997) near the beginning of this chapter helped to set the tone and perspective for our approach, namely, that quality and innovation in organizations are inextricably intertwined with organizational culture. The question immediately raised is how to ensure an appropriate intertwining. The answer usually entails, at least at the outset of a quality emphasis, organization change, especially in the dimension of culture. To change culture, one must first understand it. We have therefore examined some of the fundamentals of culture—values and norms—highlighting examples that relate to quality and innovation.

Our discussion of these fundamentals has departed from most other analyses of organizational culture in its coverage of the concept of schemas, which we have defined as cognitive structures that help people to understand and explain complex matters such as the critically important dimensions of organizational change. We have noted that pertinent schemas can take at least two forms—models and stories—and that the concept of schemas appears in various forms in the literatures on culture, climate, quality, and innovation (e.g., as reframing).

We have also discussed the importance of key processes in cultural change, particularly training, measurement, and rewards. Training helps to orient organizational members toward the kinds of behaviors that will lead to a culture that stresses the importance of quality and innovation in their daily work. With respect to measurement and rewards, it is interesting to note that managers often say, "What you measure is what you get," and behavioral scientists just as often say, "What you reward is what you get." Both are correct. Yet great care must be taken with both to make certain that one is measuring the right behaviors to ensure individual and organizational performance for high quality and to ensure that the relevant behavior and performance are rewarded (Kerr, 1995).

Finally, in considering organization change, we have argued that it is important to make a distinction (yet understand the overlap) between culture and climate—organizational background and foreground, respectively. Culture may be the ultimate goal, but to get there, climate must be affected. The latter requires change in people's everyday experiences of the ways in which they are managed and their relations with one another.

With all of the complexities of culture change that we have considered, one can easily feel overwhelmed. Choices have to be made, priorities determined, and time and energy devoted to the effort. These complexities explain, in part, the reason so many culture change efforts are never realized. In addition, getting a change under way is one thing—keeping it going is quite another and more difficult matter.

Whether in the direction of higher quality and greater innovation or in the direction of customer focus and market orientation, organizational culture change is possible (see, e.g., Burke, 1994; Goodstein & Burke, 1991). To make it possible, those who want to make such change must pay attention to the dimensions of relevant organizational models that emphasize change, be clear about the direction and priorities of change ingredients and activities, and provide persistent and consistent leadership to make it all happen in the first place and then to sustain and renew the process.

# 15

# The Cultural Dynamics of Organizing and Change

## — Mary Jo Hatch

Max Weber (1864-1920) was one of the first to emphasize the dynamic aspects of cultural change, which he did in his theory of the routinization of charisma (see Weber, 1978; see also Schroeder, 1992). However, like so many sociologists and organization theorists after him, he used his dynamic theory to explain the stable and structured aspects of culture rather than to explain change itself (which he attributed to charismatic interventions of a unique and idiosyncratic sort). My own model of cultural dynamics, which is focused on organizations and based in anthropological as well as social constructionist and interpretivist traditions, makes observations similar to those of Weber but concludes that cultural processes (i.e., manifestation, realization, symbolization, and interpretation) account for both cultural change and stabil-

ity (Hatch, 1993). In this chapter I compare and contrast Weber's theory with my model in relation to the dual question: How do cultures change and who (or what) changes culture?

I undertake this comparison of the two theories of cultural dynamics not only out of historical interest, but because their contrasts permit these theories to make contributions to each other. Because collaborative achievements are based in differences, it is important to acknowledge what the differences between these two theories are. Perhaps most important, as a sociologist Weber operated at a higher level of abstraction and with a longer time horizon than I do as an organization theorist. Furthermore, where Weber emphasized leadership and its power bases and interests, my model is concerned with the symbolism and interpretation of leaders by other mem-

AUTHOR'S NOTE: My thanks to Celeste Wilderom and Keith Markus, who made helpful comments on an earlier version of this chapter.

bers of the organization. In considering leaders to be cultural artifacts, I continue the work of decentering leadership begun by Weber when he noted that the charisma of a leader must be validated by the recognition of his or her followers. Although Weber indicated that charisma involves subjectivity, he managed to avoid delving very deeply into this territory. My cultural dynamics perspective bears no such hesitations. In shifting between the objectivist and subjectivist understandings that have worried much of the debate surrounding organizational culture (Martin & Frost, 1996, give a good account of this debate), I explicate the role of subjectivity in the dynamics of organizational culture.

First I will present the essentials of Weber's theory of the routinization of charisma and then those of my own model of the dynamics of organizational culture (Hatch, 1993). In the latter section, I will discuss how and where Weber's insights about power relations might be incorporated into my model. Next, I will address the question of cultural change in relation to leadership and subjectivity, showing how and where my model extends Weber's theory and offering some ideas for future research. I conclude the chapter with some summary reflections on how cultures change.

## WEBER ON CULTURAL DYNAMICS

According to Weber (1978), all change in culture originates in the introduction of new ideas by a charismatic figure, but change at the level of everyday life follows the path of routinization of this charismatic influence. Thus it is in his theory of the routinization of charisma that Weber acknowledges the intermixing of his ideal types of authority, for in routinization, charismatic authority is complemented, extended, and engaged with everyday life through the offices of tradition, rationalization, or both.

Weber's theory of cultural change, according to Schroeder's (1992) insightful study of Weber's work, rests on three pillars: the routinization of charisma, the differentiation of the spheres of life (especially the religious, economic, political, and intellectual spheres), and the inner logic of worldviews (e.g., the meaning and coherence of a belief system). In Weber's (1978) words:

> The term "charisma" will be applied to a certain quality of an individual personality by virtue of which he is considered extraordinary and treated as endowed with supernatural, superhuman, or at least specifically exceptional powers or qualities. These as such are not accessible to the ordinary person, but are regarded as of divine origin or as exemplary, and on the basis of them the individual concerned is treated as a "leader." (p. 241)

Schroeder (1992) explains:

> The routinization of this authority occurs when this special endowment is either directly transmitted to others through heredity or devolves upon a group of followers. . . . the struggle between charisma and routinization describes the flux between the initially revolutionizing impact of beliefs and their eventual accommodation to everyday life. Not the origin of world-views, but their subsequent force in shaping conduct and social relations is important. (p. 17)

He continues:

> Once beliefs have come into existence through the assertion of charisma, their reception among certain strata depends on the predispositions of these strata. . . . These predispositions, in turn, depend on the social circumstances of the various strata, on their position in relation to other strata and on their common way of life. (p. 20)

Weber was particularly concerned with authority and the different forms of domination typical within premodern and modern societies. His focus on charismatic authority represents his explanation of how, under extraordinary circumstances including "suffering, conflicts or enthusiasm," revolutionary changes in worldviews and their consequent influence on social action occur within society (Weber, 1978, pp. 241-249). But Weber was cryptic about how the charismatic revolution occurs, saying only that

> the genuine prophet, like the genuine military leader and every true leader in this sense, preaches, creates, or demands *new* obligations—most typically, by virtue of revelation, oracle, inspiration, or of his own will, which are recognized by the members of the religious, military, or party group because they come from such a source. (pp. 243-244)

However, and perhaps most important, Weber (1978) positioned charismatic influence (and thus cultural change) in the subjective realm when he compared charisma with reason:

> The . . . revolutionary force of "reason" works from *without:* by altering the situations of life and hence its problems, finally in this way changing men's attitudes toward them; or it intellectualizes the individual. Charisma, on the other hand, *may* effect a subjective or *internal* reorientation born out of suffering, conflicts, or enthusiasm. It may then result in a radical alteration of the central attitudes and directions of action with a completely new orientation of all attitudes toward the different problems of the "world." (p. 245)

Rather than explain how the revolutionizing and reorienting occurs, however, Weber described what happens after the introduction of the revolutionary influence of a charismatic leader into a culture. In doing so, Weber seems to have mostly avoided the subjective element he identified in his theory of cultural change. Furthermore, instead of explaining how charismatic leadership is so influential, Weber explained why it is not more influential than it is (i.e., because it is routinized), and thereby opened the door to decentering leadership.

In Weber's theory, charisma is routinized to serve the needs and interests of everyday life within the culture. Weber proposed the processes of systematization and accommodation to explain how charisma is routinized. In the instance of systematization, carriers of the charismatic influence (Weber refers to these as "disciples" of the charismatic leader) link and extend it to everyday life, dissipating some of the revolutionary appeal of the initial influence through its association with the mundane. As Schroeder (1992) explains it: "A stratum of interpreters elaborates the belief-system so that it constitutes a coherent whole and its tenets are extended to apply to various aspects of everyday life" (p. 10).

Accommodation involves the politics of everyday life by which negotiations around the interpretations and implementations of the new beliefs and obligations shape and alter the charismatic influence in ways that bring it further into line with the familiar and that cause it to conform, more or less, to existing power relations. Schroeder (1992) explains:

> There is an accommodation of the belief-system to the interests of various strata of believers. As a result, its content corresponds more and more closely with what these strata, on the basis of their social position, had already been predisposed to believe or with their everyday conduct. (p. 10)

It is through routinization, Weber argued, that new ideas introduced by charismatic individuals constitute cultural change but are also transformed (routinized) by that very process (i.e., via systematization and accommodation).

According to Weber (1978, p. 146), charismatic authority cannot remain stable but must become either traditionalized or rationalized (or both). This is because of the demands of everyday life on the followers of a charismatic leader who not only wish to participate in the worldview of the charismatic leader, but also wish to maintain the stability of their social position and their material well-being (e.g., serve their family obligations and their political and economic interests). But the question is, what happened to change? In switching from the claim that charisma is the source of all cultural change to the theory of how this influence is diluted by routinization, Weber's theory of cultural change became a theory of cultural stability that explains not how leaders influence culture, but why leaders are not more influential than they are.

Weber (1978) made another, subtler contribution to cultural change theory in relation to the symbolic-interpretative aspects of this phenomenon. First, he relegated enormous power to leadership by labeling it charismatic (and mystifying charisma via associations with the divine, the supernatural, and the superhuman), and then he handed charismatic power over to the followers of the leader, noting in several places how, without a following, charisma disappears (e.g., pp. 242, 1116, 1123, 1148). Thus Weber maintained that charisma depends on the responses and interpretations of others. As he put it: "It is recognition on the part of those subject to authority which is decisive for the validity of charisma. This recognition is freely given and . . . is a matter of complete personal devotion to the possessor of the quality, arising out of enthusiasm, or of despair and hope" (p. 242).

Although Weber acknowledged that leaders would probably not regard their charisma as dependent on the attitudes of the masses toward them, he claimed that their authority nonetheless rests on how others regard them. He made this point when he said that "in general it should be kept clearly in mind that the basis of every authority, and correspondingly of every kind of willingness to obey, is a *belief*, a belief by virtue of which persons exercising authority are lent prestige" (p. 263). In this regard, Weber invited us to decenter leadership by giving at least the power to change, if not the idea for change, over to "those subject to authority."

Oddly, Weber seems to have been caught up in the leadercentric view from which he frees us. That is, Weber pointed to recognition as the source and sustenance of authority, but in labeling those who recognize authority "subjects" and "disciples," he indicated and reinforced belief in the dominance of leadership (whether this belief was his own is difficult to tell). Nonetheless, when Weber introduced the source of the belief that sustains authority as an "inner logic of world-views" (as quoted in Schroeder, 1992, p. 11), he placed leadership within the domain of culture (worldviews) and culture within the realm of subjectivity (*inner* logic). Thus the beliefs of cultural members determine not only how a leader will be regarded, but who will be regarded as a leader.

Another contribution Weber made to the theory of cultural dynamics was to anticipate the development of charisma in the direction of democracy. Weber (1978) claimed that "when the charismatic organization undergoes progressive rationalization, it is readily possible that, instead of recognition being treated as a consequence of legitimacy, it is treated as the basis of legitimacy" (pp. 266-267). Weber called this development "democratic legitimacy," but it is essentially a reinterpretation of the routinization of charisma. That is, Weber saw charismatic authority as the primary source of cultural change, but allowed that its routinization gave cultural members some influence within the change process. In his view, the "subjects of charismatic authority" alter the ideas leaders introduce to suit their everyday lives and political, religious, intellectual, and economic interests. In such a "democratic" view, these modifications to charismatic influence are themselves a source of cultural change. The change they introduce is to "validate" a leader's authority, and thus create a leader.

But why stop there? If "subjects of charisma" are able to alter or even create charismatic influence, would they not likewise be able to introduce some of their own? Such an extension to Weber's ideas about democratic legitimacy suggests that culture can be influenced by ideas that occur anywhere in its domain, regardless of their links to leadership or authority (although these links may moderate the degree of the influence in many cases). If this is possible, why stop with ideas generated within the culture? Ideas from beyond the culture could also be influential by being engaged by the same processes that serve charismatic authority or any other cultural change. It is this extension to Weber's theory that my model of the dynamics of organizational culture offers.

## HATCH'S DYNAMICS OF ORGANIZATIONAL CULTURE

The direct lineage of my cultural dynamics model (Hatch, 1993) lies in the work of Schein (1981, 1991a, 1992) and in the philosophies of Berger and Luckmann (1967) and Ricoeur (1976), who influenced the development of the symbolic-interpretative perspective within organizational culture theory. I intended the cultural dynamics model to address both the objectivizing (artifact-producing) and subjective (meaning-making) aspects of cultural processes. However, in retrospect, and especially via Schroeder's (1992) recent interpretation of Weber as a culture theorist, I have come to see equally strong links between Weber's enterprise and my own. Thus, although I did not originally formulate the cultural dynamics model in relation to Weber, it seems appropriate to make amends for this oversight now. The rewards for doing so are to link Weber's views on power relations and leadership to the cultural dynamics model and to give credit to Weber for his insights about the role of the subjective in cultural change. I will address leadership and subjectivity in the next section of the chapter. In this section I will briefly describe my cultural dynamics model and discuss how Weber's theory contributes to it by indicating how the role of power might be incorporated.

The cultural dynamics model integrates Schein's three-level conceptual model of artifacts, values, and assumptions with the concept of symbols and identifies four processes linking these phenomena: manifestation, realization, symbolization, and interpretation (see Figure 15.1). Building on the work of Schein (1992), I have described assumptions, values, and artifacts as follows:

> Assumptions represent taken-for-granted beliefs about reality and human nature. Values are social principles, philosophies, goals, and standards considered to have intrinsic worth. Artifacts are the visible, tangible, and audible results of activity grounded in values and assumptions. (Hatch, 1993, p. 659)

Symbols are defined as "anything that represents a conscious or an unconscious association with some wider, usually more abstract, concept or meaning" (see, e.g., Gagliardi, 1990a; Gioia, 1986; Morgan, Frost, & Pondy, 1983; Turner, 1990). In distinguishing between artifacts and symbols, I have raised the question of how artifacts (e.g., objects, behaviors, ways of speaking) are used to make and communicate meaning, thus linking the objectively observable to its symbolic interpretations.

### Manifestation and Realization Processes

Schein (1991a) refers to values and behaviors as "observed manifestations of the cultural essence" that he calls basic assumptions. This core of assumptions is linked to

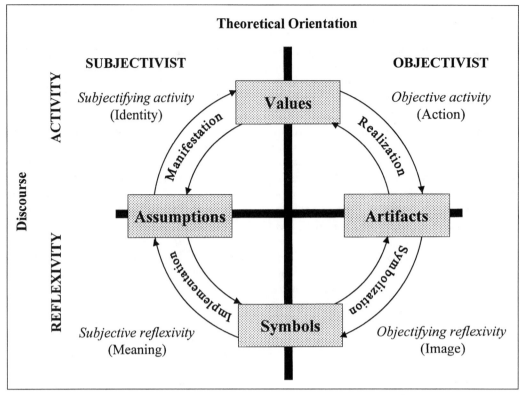

**Figure 15.1.** The Domain of Cultural Dynamics, Showing Objectivist and Subjectivist Theoretical Orientations Subdivided by the Discourses of Activity and Reflexivity

SOURCE: Hatch (1993, p. 685). Used by permission from the *Academy of Management Review.*

values and behavioral norms that, in turn, influence members' actions within the cultural domain. Manifestation occurs whenever specific values or behavioral norms are evoked perceptually, cognitively, or emotionally. Realization follows manifestation only when such evocations find their expression in outcomes or acts. Cultural values and norms then become realized in the products of culturally influenced action. These products are called artifacts. That is, artifacts realize underlying values and assumptions in the sense that they are made real (tangible, explicit, material) via actions that are culturally shaped and directed. The processes of realization refer to making something real, not in the sense of knowing causal laws that will guarantee its occurrence, but rather in the sense of translating it from the domain of

imagination or expectation into the sphere of social or material reality (Czarniawska-Joerges & Joerges, 1990).

I do not mean to suggest that images and expectations are unreal, but rather that what in everyday language we term *reality* differs from them in important ways. For example, we insist that our children distinguish between what they have imagined (e.g., monsters under the bed) and what is "real." It is to this commonsense distinction that I refer when I contrast manifestation and realization. However, realization is also closely linked to manifestation by a different logic: What cannot be imagined cannot be considered real. Thus, to some extent, manifestation carries the seeds of realization within it.

Nonetheless, there is ample reason to distinguish between manifestation and realization processes. First, manifestation can be distinguished from realization as action readiness is distinguished from action itself. Many things that are imagined are never acted upon. When manifestations are acted upon, they appear as artifacts (e.g., new objects, behaviors, or ways of speaking). Of course, they may never appear as artifacts, simply being replaced at some point by other manifestations. Because of the possibility that a given manifestation will never be realized, it is useful to maintain the distinction between these processes. A second reason for the distinction is that when artifacts from other cultures are encountered and absorbed into the focal culture, they appear in a realized state prior to being connected to cultural assumptions and values. As this connection takes place primarily through symbolization and interpretation, we turn now to consideration of these cultural processes.

## Symbolization and Interpretation Processes

A symbol always has meaning that points beyond its physical existence or form, as when a work of art transcends the medium of its expression (e.g., paint and canvas) to communicate with its audience. In addition to representing and conveying meaning, symbols have the power to "evoke emotions and impel men to action" (Cohen, 1976, p. 23). This power is to be found in the provocative, meaning-creating role of symbols. An artifact becomes a cultural symbol when it is used by members of the culture to make meaning (Ortner, 1973). For example, a national flag becomes a symbol whenever someone salutes it, waves it, or burns it. A symbol is an artifact in (meaning-creating) use.

Symbolization is the cultural process that links artifacts and meanings through the recognition of personal and social significance that is reflected in objects, acts, feelings, cognitions, or aesthetic responses. It is a self-involving process that is known by its

emotional, cognitive, aesthetic, and behavioral traces. In the flag example, the transformation of "flag as artifact" to "flag as symbol" occurs each time individuals interact with their flag. The symbolization of the flag may be accompanied by a lump in the throat (emotional trace), thoughts about patriotism (cognitive and moral trace), standing and saluting (behavioral traces), and/or an experience of beauty or truth (aesthetic trace). These traces give evidence of the processes of symbolization and can be described in terms of the experience of meaning.

For the individual, the particular pattern of behavioral, aesthetic, cognitive, and emotional traces (of the experience of meaning at a given moment in time) provides the basis for an interpretation of a symbol, but it is not itself the interpretation. Whereas symbolization transforms artifacts into symbols through the experience of meanings, interpretation specifies those meanings. Interpretation specifies meanings by locating the immediate experience associated with a symbol within the broader context of a history of cultural meanings and a geography of cultural artifacts (as will be explained more thoroughly below). Like symbolization, interpretation also involves emotion, cognition, aesthetics, and behavior, but it is a further set of emotions, cognitions, aesthetic responses, and behaviors that goes beyond the experience of meaning to articulate the meaning of a particular (symbolic) experience.

So far, I have described symbolization and interpretation as though they are phenomena that occur solely at the individual level of analysis. Whereas acts of symbol production and manipulation are located within individuals, symbolization affects and is largely affected by its social context (Morgan et al., 1983). Symbols appear at the surface of culture as artifacts and thus are publicly available to interpretation by persons other than those who produced them. As Salancik and Pfeffer (1978) point out in their social information processing theory, people observe the interpretative activities of others and make comparisons with their own interpretations in doing so. These comparisons constitute a social process through which cultural meaning comes to be constructed intersubjectively (Berger & Luckmann, 1967). Interpretation creates and is created within a domain located among and between the experiences of cultural members and their symbols and assumptions (another issue to which I will return below).

## The Dynamics of Manifestation, Realization, Symbolization, and Interpretation

In Schein's theory, artifacts located at the surface of a culture are realizations of underlying values that are manifestations of deeper assumptions. Meanwhile, as described within the interpretative view, meanings associated with cultural assumptions and values imbue artifacts transforming them via symbolization into symbols. When interpreted, these symbols (re)constitute and thereby have the capacity to alter the starting assumptions. Taken together, these four processes describe a continuous dynamic state within which members forge their cultural influences and respond to them (see Figure 15.1).

It should be clear from the discussion that none of the processes is causal, although all of them are logical. For example, values and assumptions do not force their way to the cultural surface in predictable forms. On the contrary, the same assumptions can, and do, support (through association rather than causality) a wide variety of values and artifacts that may be interpreted as compatible, contradictory, or ambiguous. (Empirical evidence of the occurrence of a variety of values, including conflicting ones, all traced to the same set of assumptions is provided by Schultz, 1995.) A better way to think about these relationships is to regard artifacts and symbols as expressions of assumptions and values rather than as their outcomes.

Of course, there is a backward spin to these processes, a retrospective or retroactive aspect (the counterclockwise arrows in Figure 15.1) that dampens the forces for change provided by the proactive or prospective aspects of the processes (the clockwise arrows in the figure). That is, existing assumptions predispose certain interpretations. These predispositions constrain the ranges of meanings that attach to artifacts in the making of symbols. This leads to a distribution of artifactual material that tends to normalize cultural meaning by making sure that material favoring the existing assumptions and values outnumbers that favoring any other worldview. This feeds into retroactive manifestation and realization processes that tend to confirm, through direct sensory experience, existing assumptions and values by the sheer volume of artifacts supporting the status quo at any moment in time. That is, retroactive manifestation and realization processes tend to confirm existing assumptions unless there is a revolutionary change in the retrospective interpretation and symbolization processes by which a vast number of existing artifacts are given new meanings all at once (e.g., via the influence of a charismatic leader, a paradigm shift).

The retrospective/retroactive aspects of the cultural dynamics processes are tantamount to what Weber described as routinization within which accommodation to existing political, religious, intellectual, and/or economic (power-based) interests occurs. It is here that Weber's theory makes a significant contribution to my model. Politics is out in the open in proactive manifestation and realization processes where the struggle to define what matters and how cultural members behave goes on in well-theorized ways put forward in theories of domination such as Weber's. In this view, those in power have more opportunity to realize their values and assumptions than do those not in power. These power-based theories, however, obliterate much of the interpretative perspective by suggesting that all meaning is created by those with power who externally impose it on others. My interpretative view, following along the lines of Weber's decentering of leadership, emphasizes that culture lies behind the determination of who gets power—only those who can be used to symbolize values and assumptions (what Weber called "the inner logic") will be able to sustain their power or their interpretation *as* leaders. Thus leaders are merely artifactual grist for the symbolic-interpretative mill of culture. This is not to argue that power does not matter, but rather to say that how power matters is up to cultural dynamics.

To see how cultural change occurs, one must follow the path of new meaning (e.g., from artifact to assumption versus the path of the reassertion of old meaning that travels in the opposite direction). This Weber attempted to do by suggesting that a charismatic leader introduces new meaning into a culture. But he failed to consider the processes by which someone is constructed as a charismatic leader, and he ignored the introduction of new meaning via routes independent of the charismatic individual. In particular, he ignored the influence of artifacts that come from outside the culture in question, and he downplayed human curiosity and creativity, by which novelty seeking constantly generates potential for change in cultural meanings.

My cultural dynamics model accounts for both the influence of artifacts from beyond the culture and the creative influence of cultural members other than leaders. Change can come from anywhere, but it comes in the form of artifacts and of the symbols created with them. In a nutshell, my cultural dynamics model presents culture as two counteracting forces, one oriented around the production of artifacts (sometimes called material culture) and the other oriented around the production of meaning. Both forces have active and reflexive modes and also accommodate both objective and subjective views (see Figure 15.1).

If we think of these counteracting forces as spinning wheels, one set inside the other as depicted in Figure 15.1, then the outer wheel continuously spins out artifact-strewn landscapes or cultural geography while the inner wheel spins a web of symbol-rich heritage or history within which future artifacts and symbols will be shaped and interpreted. These artifacts and symbols intertwine in human experience, providing the thread from which Geertz's (1973) famous web of culture is spun (a spiral or double helix may provide a better image of this thread than does the temporally flat model in Figure 15.1). It is important to note that the distribution of artifacts and symbols extant at a given point in time represents only the culture as it is *momentarily* configured by its dynamic processes. To give such a static description of culture would be to cut the thread that constantly spins culture. Therefore, it is only with reference to a living history (e.g., via narratives and storytelling) and a continuously traversed geography (i.e., moving between different views of the constantly changing landscape of material culture) that culture in its dynamic state can be appreciated, and this is essentially a subjective (or at least a highly personal) position.

## WEBER AND HATCH: CULTURAL CHANGE AND ITS IMPLICATIONS FOR LEADERSHIP AND SUBJECTIVITY

My cultural dynamics model is rooted in interpretative and social constructionist perspectives. However, it does not negate traditional realist views that can also be seen within the model; rather, it builds upon or overlays them. Specifically, realization and symbolization processes can be regarded as realist in the sense that they have objective aspects that are amenable to observation by others. Artifacts in particular, which are cultural realizations as well as the material upon which symbolization depends, are imminently observable by anyone who happens into their proximity. It is difficult to glean from mere observation, however, the cultural stories of their heritage and value in the eyes of organizational members or the roles they play when they are used to make meaning.

To understand and communicate with cultural symbols as an insider does, to act without violating basic cultural assumptions, norms, and values, or at least to know that one is violating them when one acts in particular ways, are subjective capabilities acquired through intimacy with a culture, a state that transforms the individual who acquires this deep knowledge. Thus once an individual has achieved cultural acceptance and understanding, his or her external-objective reasons for desiring such acceptance and understanding will have been altered by the experience obtained, which is why the question of cultural change has such a strong subjective element. People constantly act in ways that lead to cultural change because those acts are part of the dynamics of culture. However, when they perform these acts, their engagement alters the departure point such that the question of "What change?" becomes relativized as its original meaning is transformed. There can be no such thing as changing a culture from the outside—one must engage the culture to change it, and engagement changes what one sees, thinks, and feels by embedding one in the context of perceiving, thinking, and feeling that forms the culture.

That said, it is important to recognize that not all change originates inside the culture. There can also be influences from outside the culture in question. This happens, for instance, when cultures are merged or have other forms of contact (e.g., member sharing through joint ventures, partnering, alliances). The point is that cultures, especially in the globalizing world in which we live, are not closed; they are continuously bombarded by potentially influential new cultural material. Here the dynamic processes of symbolization and interpretation (Hatch, 1993) and systematization and accommodation (Weber, 1978) become especially important. Because artifacts are submitted to these processes, the beliefs and values they indicate in one context (e.g., the originating culture) may be modified or wholly transformed as they are drawn into the cultural dynamics of an organization or other social group that comes into contact with them (e.g., Brannen's 1992 "Bwana Mickey" example; see also Brannen, Liker, & Fruin, 1999).

Alternatively, there can be idiosyncratic actions within a culture. Whereas Weber focused on the portion of this dynamic in which a charismatic individual inserts or carries new ideas or other artifactual material into cultural processes, my model suggests that charismatic leaders are, in important respects, artifactual material themselves. Their importance lies in their potency relative to the artifacts that they deliberately introduce in order to alter the culture they represent and enact with their person. This is more than the familiar role modeling effect. People do not simply mimic leader behavior, they scrutinize it, test it, judge it, and use their interpretations to challenge, criticize, legitimate, and construct new behaviors of their own. That is, organizational members do not take leadership influence at face value, they process it as they would any other new cultural material (i.e., artifact). In this way, cultural members alter their own cultures by creating and using their leaders and other artifacts to make meaning and respond to it, something they do more or less continuously every day.

In the remainder of this section I will consider Weber's theory of cultural dynamics as a complement to my own in regard to the theories' mutual implications for leadership and subjectivity. I begin by examining the relationship between cultural change and leadership.

## Cultural Change and Leadership

My cultural dynamics model is similar to Weber's theory in that new artifacts (including charismatic individuals and their ideas) are symbolized and interpreted within the context of existing artifacts, symbols, assumptions, and values (Weber called them beliefs and obligations) whose meanings are formed and transformed within these processes. With respect to interventions designed to alter cultural beliefs, my model suggests that what leaders do (no matter what their intervention strategy) is to introduce new artifacts into the symbolic-interpretative field of organizational meaning making. Depending upon the relationship of the new artifacts to all the others that constitute the culture, which is a matter for cultural members to determine in the course of their everyday interpretative activities, the artifact either will or will not be used by other members of the culture to make meaning in ways different from the usual ways. Leaders can encourage this symbolizing activity through their own example (thus introducing more artifacts to be interpreted), but little or no change occurs unless other members of the culture make meaningful use of the artifacts introduced and thus transform them into symbols. From this point, what Weber referred to as systematization and accommodation to preexisting beliefs and obligations may take place—but so does change in beliefs and obligations.

To the extent that existing beliefs and obligations (or assumptions and values) overwhelm any new meaning created in the symbolization process, cultural dynamics consists of absorption of the new material within old frames of meaning, which are thereby reconstituted, giving the appearance of no change. However, even the slightest amount of new material represents some change and, as the process is ongoing, culture changes continuously, albeit in mostly imperceptible ways. Thus what Weber called routinization is really about dampening the revolutionizing impact of new meaning to a level of change tolerated by the culture. From the perspective taken in the cultural dynamics model, routinization does not prevent change, it makes change possible in part by blending it with stability (i.e., giving it conti-

nuity and coherence). Ironically, continuity and coherence facilitate change by making people comfortable enough to take new meaning on board.

This view comes very close to what Gagliardi (1986) terms incremental cultural change. In incremental cultural change, when new values are juxtaposed to old they do not subvert the cultural embrace of meaning or significance, but merely extend its reach. Gagliardi contrasts incremental to both revolutionary and apparent change. In apparent change, only artifacts are altered, with no consequence for meaning-making activities or for core values, assumptions, or beliefs. Revolutionary change, however, affects all these things through an alteration so profound that it destabilizes or destroys the entire meaning-making process and replaces it with another one (e.g., through severe downsizing or sudden additions of new members through acquisition or merger). In the case of revolutionary change, continuity is lost and a new culture having a completely new identity is created. According to my model, Gagliardi's three types of change (apparent, incremental, and revolutionary) are different moments in the ongoing processes of cultural dynamics.

Weber's notion of accommodation is important here because the interests of managers themselves may be the biggest impediment to cultural change that any organization faces. This is because some (most?) of the interests protected by the accommodation of new ideas to old meanings are managers' own. Although change agents might be attracted to the revolutionary model in their frustration over the pace of change within their organizations, it is generally believed that revolutions depose those in power. The problem is that few managers are willing to sacrifice themselves to achieve revolutionary change. Yet effectively altering a culture in a deep sense may require that management profoundly change or realign its interests. It is here that Weber's ideas about power relations contribute to the cultural dynamics model. That is, interpretations offered by those who are symbolically significant within a culture are artifacts whose symbolic potential is magnified by power relations. Social power is thus interpretatively associated with certain artifacts by virtue of their having been produced by those to whom the culture has assigned a certain level of significance. In other words, all artifacts are not created equal. For at least some period of time following an artifact's realization, the symbolic weight given to the "maker" is transferred to the artifact. This preassigned significance gives the artifact heightened attention within the symbolic field, at least for as long as the association lasts. This aspect of the dynamics of organizational culture gives managers a sizable capacity to resist cultural change as well as to lead it.

This brings us to the role of leader/manager in the dynamics of organizational culture. To grasp the implications of my cultural dynamics model, one must see leaders/managers as artifacts. That is, leaders/managers are cultural material with the potential to be used by others to make meaning. When used in this way, leaders/managers have influence that can contribute to cultural change. But it should be recognized that cultural change does not depend upon leaders/managers' intentions. The symbolic use of leaders/managers (along with other artifacts) by organizational members constructs the meaningful reality of the organization and thereby influences the course of cultural change.

My model of cultural dynamics suggests both retrospective and proactive approaches to the study of leaders as artifacts. One approach would be to do a historical study of a leader's rise to power (or at least of the events leading up to selection of the leader). Interviews of those who were directly involved in the selection process as well as those who observed it or just heard stories about it could be used to collect retrospective accounts. Analysis of these accounts in terms of the symbols, values, and assumptions they reveal

could be used to examine more closely how culture manifests and realizes the artifact of a leader. A second possibility would be to study how a leader/artifact is symbolized within a culture. An ethnographically trained observer could spend time documenting the ways that cultural members use their leaders to make meaning in everyday life, as well as the ways in which leaders attempt to influence (or control) interpretation processes. Interviews could then be conducted to collect and perhaps to coanalyze with organizational members their interpretations of the leader and their uses of him or her to make meaning.

In terms of managerial implications, cultural dynamics theory suggests that leaders/managers' intentions are interpreted rather than directly enacted (i.e., interpretation moderates the effects of leader intent). The more controlling of interpretative processes managers try to be, the more likely the managers will be interpreted with cynicism or skepticism, which can undermine their influence and eventually challenge their hold on power. This raises a key issue for managers: How should knowing about cultural dynamics inform managerial action? The answer is a tricky one, for as Weber (1978) pointed out, the basis of the charismatic claim to legitimacy lies in "the duty of those subject to charismatic authority to recognize its *genuineness* and to act accordingly" (p. 242; emphasis added). The issue of genuineness introduces the matter of aesthetic and emotional judgment, and thus the role of subjectivity in cultural change.

### Cultural Change and Subjectivity

Not giving adequate (or any) attention to subjectivity in cultural change has confused many managers and a considerable number of academics, whose lack of acceptance of subjectively based knowledge has led them to pursue cultural change programs in organizations on the principle of trying to change artifacts and symbols in the hope of affecting the subjective consciousness that is implicated in interpretation and manifestation processes. In short, limiting yourself to what can be objectively appreciated cuts you off from subjective engagement with others.

Let me explain my position in another way. Although humans, especially modern Western ones, have developed the capacity to ignore and even deny their subjectivity in favor of a belief that progress is good, science is progress, and science requires strict adherence to objectivity, those who embrace and explore subjectivity find that it is intertwined with objective experience (i.e., the experience that there is a world apart from our subjective sense of self). Some postmodernists (e.g., S. Hall, 1996) take this intertwining an additional step and argue that this means that selves are constructed entirely by cultural and social contexts that invent them (e.g., language gives them existence via allotment of the subject or object position in a sentence, a role within a narrative, or a voice in a discourse). I will not go quite this far; however, notice that my view of subjectivity does not deny the objectivist position but embraces it, giving the cultural dynamics model both an inside and an outside point of view (which are sometimes impossible to distinguish). I would argue that we simultaneously enjoy (or not) both an inner and an outer existence, the outer being perhaps best described as physical and studied via the physical sciences, whereas the inner-outer dual consciousness is more easily accommodated by shifting to the symbolic-interpretative perspective (see Hatch, 1997, for a basic discussion of symbolic-interpretivism in relation to both modernism and postmodernism in organization theory).

In the symbolic-interpretative perspective, culture is a collective expression of the continuity between the inner and the outer world. As such, we are able, through the study of culture, to engage the dynamic interplay between the subjective and the objective and experience the ways in which who we are interpenetrates the identities of other beings around us. In the act of interplay between self and others, the inner world finds its way into the outer. What can be coimagined and communicated finds its way into what is realized, culturally speaking. Of course, the opening occurs from both sides, and what has been realized has a tendency to infiltrate (and in many cases to shut down or close off) further imagination ("be realistic" or "get real" are typical expressions of this effect). Nonetheless, the possibility for change remains.

On the subjective side, change occurs (radically or incrementally) when imagination overtakes objective reality. But it is not as simple as dreaming, due to the collective properties of culture. Imagination must take hold, the image must be replicated in the inner worlds of other members of a culture (i.e., resonance occurs) such that via the collective (not necessarily consistent) weight of their changed perceptions, thoughts, and feelings, new possibilities are brought forth in artifactual form. This takes place as artifacts are responded to (symbolized), sparking further images, until a discernible transformation occurs (i.e., on a large enough scale to merit comment and perhaps a story, which is the point at which change is acknowledged as such).

Astute leader/managers desiring credit for change can be alert to these processes and at the critical point just prior to collective awareness can position themselves for notoriety by associating themselves with the change that is already taking place (e.g., via labeling or storytelling). Consider, for example, the myriad high-profile changes reported in the press, such as Iacocca's turnaround of Chrysler, or Gorbachev's of Russia. From the perspective offered by cultural dynamics theory, these were changes well under way when these men came to power; their brilliance was to understand what was going on well enough to represent it and thereby give the change a face—their own. But let us not constrain ourselves to consideration of whopping big change or even merely to those to whom we give credit for change. Let us consider the more crucial question of how change occurs, what actually happens, and what the limits and opportunities are that we face in regard to influencing these processes.

According to cultural dynamics theory (e.g., Hatch, 1993; Weber 1978), subjective human experience and its intersubjective communication are central to our understanding of cultural change. Cultural processes transpire through multiple channels of human awareness, including the five senses, mental ideas, emotional responses, and, as I will argue further below, aesthetic, moral, and intuitive capacities. Although senses, ideas, and emotions are commonly associated with individuals, it is the interrelationship of individual experiences of these across organizational space and time (or geography and history) that defines what we label culture. In other words, when we speak of culture we refer not only to one individual's experience of one artifact at one point in time, but to all members' experiences of all of their artifacts as these occur and interact over space and time. What is more, the capacity for intersubjective experience defines the domain of culture and, activated over space and time, creates a symbol-rich field of communicative activity and cultural expression.

In order for an artifact to symbolize meaning within a culture, it must be able to strike a chord that resonates within members of that culture. This capacity is synonymous with the term *symbol* as Jung (1923, 1959) defined it. In Jung's view, symbols involve appreciations that go beyond cognitive and emotional experience into domains we label aesthetic, moral, and intuitive. He suggested that within every culture will be found the same set of core symbols, called archetypes (e.g., the circle). Archetypes resonate within *all* humans and create the direct links between them that define humanity. Following Jung's reasoning, cultural symbols resonate with(in) cultural members and thereby implicate the entire range of individually situated

experiential capacities whenever individuals relate to their culture. This occurs in much the same way that archetypes relate humans to their humanity, although the effect of cultural symbols is more circumscribed and localized.

In this view, symbolism (the use of artifacts to make meaning) allows individuals to communicate with one another in ways that extend beyond the sensory channels through which information flows. When individuals stand in recognition of their flag, their participation activates aesthetic, intuitive, and emotional as well as cognitive and moral capacities. Thus, through personal engagement in cultural symbolism, each individual directly contacts his or her own culturally situated being in a context that enables emotional, intuitive, and aesthetic resonance with other members of the same culture. It is for this reason that individuals and their cultural contexts are difficult to distinguish—they are enmeshed, mutually embedded, and interpenetrating.

Groups of people living (or working) together develop intertwined consciousness and this intertwining manifests in patterns of action, expectation, and belief that become familiar parts of their everyday life. For example, rituals (e.g., forms of greeting or address) are common aspects of everyday life used repeatedly to communicate and to strengthen relationships and thus the community itself. The ritualized components of everyday life give a sense of stability, certainty, and belonging to what we have come to regard as culture. But culture itself is not solely about stability; its myriad changes are the ways by which culture maintains its vibrancy and relevance. For instance, a ritual could be reenacted with some members experiencing totally new meaning and, so long as the ritual form still did its connecting work, life would go on as an extension of the past while simultaneously incorporating change.

One might say that culture is based on a kind of intimacy; through emotional, intuitive, and aesthetic resonance, culture contacts its members in an intimate way (although not in the same way in each case). As is true for sexual intimacy, cultural intimacy requires an "other" who is taken to be the same or similar (i.e., someone with whom to share the experience). Culture derives from the resonance that occurs among members as they appreciate their own symbolic experience within a shared cultural context. Thus the members of culture are implicated in a mutually constructed (but not identically experienced) social context in which it is not necessary for them to share the meanings that they invest in particular symbols, but only that they regard at least some of the same symbols as meaningful and thus respond in emotionally, intuitively, and aesthetically resonant and mutually coherent ways.

Studying emotional, intuitive, and aesthetic resonance will no doubt require ingenuity. A starting point might be to locate such experiences using participant observation techniques. Researchers using their own subjective sensibilities to "feel out" such moments could identify coparticipants and witnesses to these moments and then invite the participants and witnesses to recount their experiences. A range of modes of expression might be used, from personal narrative to poetry or painting; these activities could be carried out individually and/or in groups. If researchers use groups, they might employ specifically group-based techniques, such as group narrative or group drawing (e.g., Barry, 1996). It might similarly be possible for researchers to conduct group analysis of the data collected or to conduct entire studies as cooperative inquiry (see Reason, in press; Reason & Rowan, 1981).

## CONCLUSION

Where Weber (1978) saw change occurring only via the rare appearance of the charismatic individual, my cultural dynamics model locates change in the trenches of every-day life in organizations (Hatch, 1993). My model does not present the stimulus to change strictly in terms of leadership, although this is clearly one important influence. Instead, it presents organizations as symbolic fields strewn with artifacts that interpreters (cultural members) use to make and communicate meaning. Leaders and the new ideas that they carry enter the dynamics of organizational culture in the form of artifacts. When leaders are caught up by the symbolic-interpretative processes of culture, however, they become symbols to which the influence of leadership is ascribed. Their symbolization depends on this use, and thus their meaning is made by the interpretative acts of cultural members, as Weber noted. Because it is cultural members who symbolize leader/artifacts, I put less store in change via leadership than did Weber.

How, then, does change occur in cultures? My cultural dynamics model suggests that culture never stops changing; rather, it is in continuous dynamic flux. What we think of as change is really a symbolic construction, a collective move to regard ourselves differently and declare that a transformation has occurred (e.g., via sensemaking techniques such as historicizing or storytelling). But new artifacts are continuously generated or found, presenting an unending parade of possibilities to remake meaning. Everyone involved in a culture remakes meaning daily, thus opportunities for change are ever present, as is change itself.

Our creative aspects, the imaginative dimensions celebrated in artists but possessed in some degree by all humans, constantly alter in more or less imperceptible ways the ground on which cultural meaning walks (e.g., the language in which we communicate, for instance, or the visual or aural images we choose to represent ourselves). It is at this microscopic level of everyday being (and becoming) that cultural change as we know it (or as we commonly conceptualize it) is engaged—not on the grand scale of Christ giving his sermon on the Mount, but at the level of small, imperceptible changes that occurred prior to this (and continued afterward), changes that brought people out to hear Him and predisposed them to listen. In this view, without seekers, the figure of Christ would have been inconsequential. The ground for change must be prepared well in advance of the appearance of the charismatic leader. My cultural dynamics model looks at the ground for change, and it is here that I feel it extends the theory of cultural dynamics initially proposed by Weber.

# 16

## Managerial Ideologies, Organization Culture, and the Outcomes of Innovation

### A Competing Values Perspective

—— *Raymond F. Zammuto, Blair Gifford,*
*and Eric A. Goodman*

anaging in a turbulent world is not easy, and managers are constantly looking for new concepts, tools, and techniques to help them cope with the demands of accelerating change. A multiyear research project by consulting firm Bain and Co. has shown that the overall corporate use of 25 leading management tools and techniques is on the rise. This annual survey found that the average company used 11.8 of these tools in 1993, 12.7 in 1994, and 13 in 1997 (Micklethwait & Wooldridge, 1996; Rigby, 1998). In 1997, Bain and Co.'s survey showed that the hottest management tools being used by organizations in its study

were strategic planning (90%), mission and value statements (87%), benchmarking (86%), customer satisfaction measurement (79%), pay for performance (78%), strategic alliances (68%), core competencies (67%), reengineering (64%), growth strategies (61%), and total quality management (TQM; 60%). The study also showed that the use of growth strategies, pay for performance, and benchmarking were on the rise; earlier favorites TQM, reengineering, and core competencies were on the decline (Rigby, 1998).

Unfortunately, managers often find that the management tools they adopt are not magic bullets. For instance, Bain and Co.'s

AUTHOR'S NOTE: This research was supported by a grant from the Center for Health Management Research. We appreciate the comments of Jane Davidson, Andrew Griffiths, Mark Peterson, and Robert Quinn on an earlier version of this chapter.

study found that 77% of executives reported that these tools promise more than they deliver (Rigby, 1998). This finding is consistent with other accounts of implementation failure across a range of managerial innovations (e.g., reengineering, TQM) and technological innovations (e.g., flexible manufacturing technologies, enterprise resource planning systems), where failure rates run above 50%. The result is that managerial innovations become management fads, things that are tried and then abandoned. Even when implemented successfully, critics charge, many tools often deliver "benefits" other than those their proponents intended. Reengineering, for example, which promises fast, flexible, highly efficient operations delivered through empowered teams, often delivers organizational chaos and sweatshop working conditions.

Frequently cited culprits in these failures are the implementing organization's culture and its underlying ideology of management. Ideologies that focus on managerial control, "have always 'dominated' the managerial community, in the sense that they are more prevalent and more tightly linked to managerial practice" (Barley & Kunda, 1992, p. 393). However, managerial innovations that are designed to empower line employees and create fast, flexible organizations require a different ideological mind-set. Champy (1995), for instance, notes that successful reengineering requires that managers "discard the fantasy of a corporate culture of *reflexive obedience* and undertake the hard work of creating a culture of *learned willingness* and *individual accountability*" (p. 29). However, it is difficult to change beliefs about how the world works, and managers often find themselves "living in a dual world: the real world and the world of officially sanctioned ideology. Thus, they talk about 'empowerment' but habitually hoard power, or they proclaim that they are 'reengineering' their organizations when they are really just firing a few of the more lackluster workers" (Micklethwait & Wooldridge, 1996, p. 18).

For many organizations, it seems that creating empowered, flexible, learning organizations that are efficient *and* fleet of foot is not something that comes easily.

In this chapter, we focus on the relationship between organizational culture and the outcomes of innovations. Our general argument is that the ideological underpinnings of an organization's culture affect how innovations are implemented and the types of outcomes that are observed. We use the competing values framework as a tool for understanding and studying differences in ideologies across organizations and illustrate our argument using data from case studies of two hospitals' TQM programs. In the final section of the chapter, we present a general model of how organizational ideologies affect the outcomes of innovations.

## MANAGERIAL IDEOLOGIES AND ORGANIZATIONAL CULTURE

Beyer (1981) defines ideologies as "relatively coherent sets of beliefs that bind some people together and that explain their worlds in terms of cause-and-effect relations. . . . ideologies explain the hows and whys of events, and affect predictions of the likelihood of outcomes. Ideologies may specify that some courses of action are far more likely to bring about desired outcomes than others" (pp. 166-167). In essence, ideologies are systems of belief about what works and what doesn't as individuals attempt to attain valued outcomes. As we will show in the following sections, two "types" of ideologies, organizational ideologies and managerial ideologies, play important roles in our analysis. Organizational ideologies are the belief systems shared by the members of a specific organization, whereas managerial ideologies comprise the broader conceptions of management that are institutionalized within the larger society.

The concepts of culture and ideology are closely intertwined at the organizational level of analysis (Louis & Sutton, 1991), as is evident from a comparison of Beyer's definition of ideology with Schein's (1992) definition of organizational culture: "a pattern of shared basic assumptions that the group learned as it solved its problems of external adaptation and internal integration" (p. 12). Both definitions emphasize shared beliefs about what works and what doesn't. Much of the theory and research on organizational culture, however, defines the concept more broadly to include idiosyncratic organizational manifestations of these beliefs in the form of myths, stories, rituals, structures, strategies, reward systems, and so on. The essential point is that "the actual content or substance of a culture resides in its ideologies" (Trice & Beyer, 1993, p. 33).

As a system of shared beliefs, an organization's ideology shapes action within the organization. Beyer's (1981) review, for example, shows how ideologies shape decision-making processes within organizations. Miles and Creed (1995) indicate that ideologies rationalize and legitimate the patterns of authority within organizations and argue that different ideologies emerge over time with new organizational forms. For instance, ideologies supporting hierarchical authority relationships in functional organizations do not fit the horizontal patterns of coordination characteristic of networked organizations. Thus we now see the emergence of new ideologies that rationalize and legitimate the networked organizational form. Meyer (1982b) has also found a relationship between organizational ideology and structure in that internal consensus about an organization's ideology can affect the need for formal coordination and control mechanisms. The greater the ideological consensus, the less the need for formalized structures.

Meyer and Starbuck (1993) argue that organizations' ideologies shape strategies and the power structures within them, which can make different types of organizational changes more or less difficult. For example,

they note that incremental strategic changes are relatively easy to accomplish because they reinforce an organization's ideology and power structure. Conversely, major strategic reorientations often generate resistance because they run counter to an organization's existing ideology and upset its prevailing power structure. Ideologies also influence organizations' reactions to environmental change. Meyer (1982a), for instance, has shown how the organizational ideologies of 19 hospitals influenced their responses to a major environmental jolt—a doctors' strike—and how differences in ideologies can affect the extent to which organizations learn from their experiences. Flexible, adaptive organizational ideologies enhance learning.

Managerial ideologies, broad philosophies of management embedded in society, become relevant to the analysis when we ask the question, Where do organizational ideologies come from? Beyer (1981) notes that "since all resources in organizations, including members, were obtained at some point from the environment, many of the ideologies and values held by members must be viewed as originating in the environment" (p. 168). Bendix's (1956) comparison of managerial ideologies in the United States and Russia, for instance, shows that they are products of those societies' broader cultures and that they evolved over time as those societies changed. The evolution of managerial ideologies has received attention from several scholars, such as Bendix (1956), Barley and Kunda (1992), Trice and Beyer (1993), Miles and Creed (1995), and Calori, Lubatkin, Very, and Veiga (1997). Although analyses of the processes of ideological change have differed, "scholars have converged on a common vision of how American managerial thought has evolved" (Barley & Kunda, 1992, p. 363), and different ideologies have emerged over time (we will discuss the content of these ideologies later). As important, as new managerial ideologies evolved, the older ones "never disappeared. Instead, images and practices central to each were gradually institutionalized" (Barley &

Kunda, 1992, p. 365), which leads to two of our key points.

First, institutionalized managerial ideologies form a common foundation for the ideologies of individual organizations. Managerial ideologies are imported into organizations from the institutional environment through many different mechanisms, such as business and professional education, occupational training, popular management books and magazines, and consultants. Thus managers in American society draw from a common, limited set of managerial ideologies that are the foundations for the assumptions, values, and beliefs on which individual organizations' cultures are based. Differences in what parts of these broad managerial ideologies are imported into organizations' ideologies lead to differences in organizational cultures.

Second, given their shared social basis, we can examine the common ideological elements within organizations' cultures and gain an understanding of how ideological similarities and differences affect individual and organizational behavior. We propose in the following sections that one theoretical model, the competing values framework, provides a conceptual tool for understanding the ideological underpinnings of organization's cultures as well as a method for studying ideological differences across organizations.

## THE COMPETING VALUES FRAMEWORK AND MANAGERIAL IDEOLOGIES

The competing values framework (CVF) was developed by Robert Quinn and his colleagues in a series of conceptual papers and empirical studies during the late 1970s and early 1980s (Quinn & McGrath, 1985). The best-known and most frequently cited of these is an empirical analysis of organiza-

tional effectiveness criteria presented by Quinn and Rohrbaugh in a 1983 *Management Science* article. This study showed that differences among the many effectiveness criteria in the literature can be better understood when they are organized along two axes. One axis reflects whether an organization focuses its attention inward, toward its internal dynamics, or outward, toward its external environment. The other axis reflects preferences for flexibility versus control in organizational structuring.

The flexibility/control dimension is particularly relevant to our analysis because it directs attention to coordination and control within organizations, which is an important basis for distinguishing among managerial ideologies. Barley and Kunda (1992) note that the progression most authors detect in the evolution of managerial ideologies over the past century parallels Etzioni's (1961) typology of control, with a shift from coercive to normative forms of coordination and control in organizations. There is a direct parallel in the CVF in that the control end of this dimension is associated with externalized (coercive) mechanisms of coordination and control, such as rules, policies, procedures, and direct supervision, and the flexible end is associated with internalized (normative), commitment-based mechanisms of coordination and control, such as training and socialization.

The CVF's four quadrants describe different valued outcomes that define effective organizational performance and means through which they are likely to be attained (see Figure 16.1). Essentially, each quadrant represents a set of valued outcomes and coherent managerial ideology about how to attain them. Taken together, the quadrants map out the major shifts that have occurred in both managerial ideologies and organizational theorizing over time. We review the model below to show how each quadrant represents a different managerial ideology present in the current institutional environment. We also use Scott's (1992) analysis to

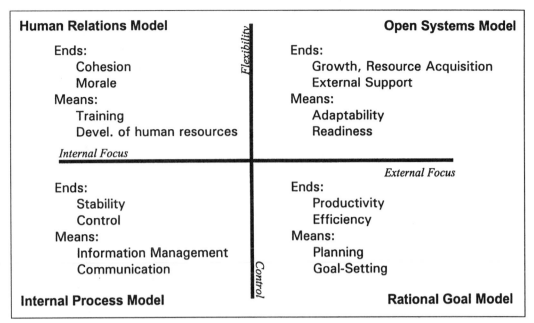

**Figure 16.1.** The Competing Values Model of Organizational Effectiveness
SOURCE: Adapted from Quinn and Rohrbaugh (1983).

show how each reflects a major theoretical orientation to the analysis of organizations. We employ findings from CVF-based research to develop a stereotypical snapshot of an organization within each ideological perspective.

### Internal Process Model

The CVF's control/internal focus quadrant is labeled the *internal process model* and represents Barley and Kunda's (1992) ideology of scientific management. Valued outcomes of stability and control are attained through means such as information management and communication. This quadrant is equivalent to Scott's (1992) classification of closed rational systems models, which were the earliest manifestations of organizational analysis. This philosophy of management was dominant in the early 1900s and reflected Weber's (1964) theory of bureaucracy, classical management theory (Fayol, 1949), and scientific management (Taylor, 1911). All these theories "portray organizations as tools designed to achieve preset ends, and all of them ignore or minimize the perturbations and opportunities posed by connections to the wider environment" (Scott, 1992, p. 101).

Table 16.1 displays several organizational characteristics that CVF-based empirical research has associated with the internal process model. Primary leadership roles associated with the internal process model are monitoring and coordinating. Structurally, this type of organization relies on vertical communication and formal rules, policies, and procedures for coordination and control. Interpersonal relations are marked by relatively low levels of trust, morale, and leader credibility and relatively high levels of conflict and resistance to change. Other characteristics shown in Table 16.1, such as management information system orienta-

**TABLE 16.1  Organizational Characteristics by CVF Quadrant**

| CVF Quadrant | Human Relations | Open Systems | Internal Process | Rational Goal |
|---|---|---|---|---|
| CVF dimensions | Flexible/internal | Flexible/external | Control/internal | Control/external |
| Ideological emphasis | People | Innovation and change | Stability and control | Task accomplishment |
| Leadership roles (Denison, Hooijberg, & Quinn, 1995; Quinn, 1988) | Mentor (caring, empathic—shows consideration) | Innovator (creative, clever—envisions change) | Monitor (technically expert, well prepared—collects information) | Producer (task oriented, work focused—initiates action) |
| | Facilitator (facilitates interaction—process-oriented) | Broker (resource oriented, politically astute—acquires resources) | Coordinator (dependable, reliable—maintains structure) | Director (decisive, directive—provides structure) |
| Structure (Buenger et al., 1995; Zammuto & Krakower, 1991) | Complex training demands; decentralized; less use of rules, policies, and procedures; less use of formal planning | Nonroutine task technology; interdependent work flow; less use of rules, policies, and procedures; less use of formal planing | Vertical coordination; routine task technology; formal rules, policies, and procedures; formal planning | Centralization, complex training demands |
| Interpersonal relations (Zammuto & Krakower, 1991) | Higher levels of trust Higher morale Higher levels of leader credibility Lower levels of conflict Less resistance to change | Higher levels of trust Higher morale Higher levels of leader credibility Lower levels of conflict Less resistance to change | Lower levels of trust Lower morale Lower levels of leader credibility Higher levels of conflict More resistance to change | Lower levels of conflict Lower morale Lower levels of leader credibility Higher levels of conflict More resistance to change |

| | Reactive | Proactive | Reactive | Neither reactive or proactive |
|---|---|---|---|---|
| Strategic orientation (Zammuto & Krakower, 1991) | | | | |
| Managerial communications (Quinn, Hildebrandt, Rogers, & Thompson, 1991: Rogers & Hildebrandt, 1993) | Relational/builds trust — Expressive, open, candid, honest, credible, believable, plausible, conceivable | Transformational/stimulates change — Strongly worded, emphatic, forceful, powerful, insightful, expansive, mind-stretching, visionary | Informational/provides facts — Rigorous, precise, disciplined, controlled, focused, clear, logical, organized | Instructional/directs action — Interesting, stimulating, engaging, absorbing, conclusive, consequential, decisive, action oriented |
| Management information systems (Cooper, 1994; Cooper & Quinn, 1993) | *MIS capabilities* — Computer-aided instructing; Interpersonal communicating and conferencing; Group decision supporting | *MIS capabilities* — Environmental scanning and filtering; Interorganizational linking; Doubt and argument promoting | *MIS capabilities* — Internal monitoring; Internal controlling; Record keeping | *MIS capabilities* — Modeling; Forecasting; Sensitivity analyzing |
| | *System characteristics* — User controllability, personalization, convenience, user feedback | *System characteristics* — Ad hoc usage, provision of multiple cues, wide and frequent access | *System characteristics* — Standardized, reliable, stable, precise and detailed information | *System characteristics* — Integrated systems, quantitative, time and accurate information |
| Group decision processes (McCarrt & Rohrbaugh, 1995) | Participatory process; Supportability of decision | Adaptable process; Legitimacy of decision | Data-based process; Accountability of decision | Goal-centered process; Efficiency of decision |

tion, decision making, and managerial communications, paint a consistent picture of the classic bureaucracy. This ideology focuses on the control of internal processes as the means to achieve valued ends. Some common terms used to characterize organizations emphasizing this managerial ideology are *bureaucratic, rule-bound, by-the-book,* and *top-down.*

### Human Relations Model

The CVF's flexibility/internal focus quadrant is labeled the *human relations model* and reflects Barley and Kunda's (1992) human relations ideology. This model emphasizes valued outcomes of cohesion and morale through means such as training and human resources development, and it is analogous to Scott's (1992) classification of closed natural systems models. These models include the work of human relations theorists, a tradition that began with the Hawthorne studies in the 1930s (Roethlisberger & Dickson, 1939/1975) and was further developed by others such as Mayo (1945), Whyte (1948), and Dalton (1959). As Scott (1992) notes, "Although this work caused our view of organizational structure to become more complex and flexible, as diffuse and conflicting goals were recognized and participants were endowed with multiple interests and motives, most of the work within this tradition restricted attention to the inside of organization" (p. 103).

As Table 16.1 shows, the primary leadership roles associated with this quadrant are mentoring and facilitating. Coordination and control are achieved through decentralized decision making and teamwork. Interpersonal relations tend toward higher levels of trust, morale, and leader credibility and relatively lower levels of conflict and resistance to change. This managerial ideology focuses on people as the means to achieve desired ends, and words such as *family, trusting, loyal, empowered,* and *collegial* are

typically used to characterize organizations with human relations orientations.

### Rational Goal Model

The CVF's control/external focus quadrant is labeled the *rational goal model* and parallels Barley and Kunda's (1992) systems rationalism ideology. Valued outcomes in this quadrant are productivity and efficiency gained through means such as goal setting and planning. This quadrant is analogous to Scott's (1992) classification of open rational systems models. Scott notes that "beginning in the late 1950s and continuing to the present, a new generation of theories have again focused on the organization as a rational system, but with a difference: now the organization is also viewed as an open system. The major challenge addressed by these theories was how to organize systems rationally in the face of environmental demands" (p. 104). Scott includes contingency theory (e.g., Burns & Stalker, 1961; Lawrence & Lorsch, 1967; Thompson, 1967), agency theory (e.g., Alchian & Demsetz, 1972), and transaction cost analysis (e.g., Ouchi, 1980; Williamson, 1975) in this classification.

Table 16.1 shows that the leadership roles in this quadrant emphasize providing direction and initiating action. Structurally, the rational goal model is associated with centralized decision making. Interpersonal relations are marked by lower levels of trust, morale, and leader credibility and relatively higher levels of conflict and resistance to change. This managerial ideology focuses on task accomplishment to achieve desired ends, and terms often used to characterize organizations with a rational-goal emphasis include *driven, goal oriented, achievers,* and *focused.*

### Open Systems Model

The CVF's flexibility/external focus quadrant is labeled the *open systems model,* and valued outcomes in this model are growth, resource acquisition, and external support through means such as adaptability and readiness. This quadrant is similar to Barley and Kunda's (1992) "organizational culture and quality ideology." This quadrant also is analogous to Scott's (1992) classification of open natural systems models, which arose to challenge the assumptions of the open rational systems models in the 1970s. As Scott notes: "These new models place great emphasis on the importance of the environment in determining the structure, behavior, and life chances of organizations: they are clearly open system models. However, the assumption that organizations behave as rational systems is strongly challenged in this work" (pp. 107-108). Organizational learning (March & Olsen, 1976), organizing (Weick, 1969), sociotechnical systems theory (Miller & Rice, 1967), and organizational culture (Martin, 1992; Schein, 1992; Trice & Beyer, 1993) are among the approaches that can be included in this classification.

The leadership roles associated with this quadrant focus on innovation, change, and the acquisition or resources (Table 16.1). Structurally, the open systems model is associated with an emphasis on informal coordination and control systems and horizontal communications. Interpersonal relations can be characterized as having higher levels of trust, morale, and leader credibility and low levels of conflict and resistance to change. This managerial ideology focuses on achieving desired ends through innovation and change. Terms such as *innovative, aggressive, adaptable,* and *entrepreneurial* are typically used to characterize organizations with ideologies emphasizing the open systems model.

## MIXED VALUES, MIXED IDEOLOGIES

As stereotypes, the quadrants paint internally consistent pictures of four sets of valued outcomes and the means by which to attain them. By juxtaposing the four quadrants along its two dimensions, the CVF makes it clear that each quadrant emphasizes different aspects of the organizing process—people, adaptation, stability, and task accomplishment—issues that are important for every organization. The opposing quadrants highlight inherent dilemmas in the organizing process that every organization needs to address—stability versus adaptation and people versus task accomplishment.

As Buenger, Daft, Conlon, and Austin (1996) note, the idea that organizations face competing demands along these lines had "been present, but unarticulated in the literature for some time. For instance, Parsons (1956) argued that system survival hinged on successful performance of four basic functions, and Perrow (1961) contended that all organizations must accomplish four critical tasks" (p. 559). The difference between the CVF and earlier work is that the CVF concisely captures the tensions among the different models, highlighting the paradoxes managers face. As Quinn (1988) notes, an overemphasis on any one of the quadrants can result in a dysfunctional organization. Overemphasis on the human relations model, for example, can lead to an "irresponsible country club"; on the internal process model, a "frozen bureaucracy"; on the rational goal model, an "oppressive sweat shop"; and on the open system model, a "tumultuous anarchy." Hence the CVF makes it explicit that organizations need to embrace elements of each of the four managerial ideologies. However, actions within an organization and its cultural manifestations are likely to reflect the most strongly held ideological components within it.

We argue that the relative balance of the four managerial ideologies within a particular organization's ideology has a major impact on how its members view an innovation, its intended outcomes, and how it is implemented. We also think that an organization's response to innovations that run counter to its ideology goes beyond the resistance that Meyer and Starbuck (1993) see being generated. Rather, the response is more likely to resemble Schön's (1971) dynamic conservatism, where social systems "fight to stay the same" (p. 32) and, when they can't defeat an innovation, co-opt it to protect the existing social order.

In other words, innovations with the potential to increase both operational efficiency and organizational flexibility are likely be implemented in a manner consistent with the organization's most strongly held ideological beliefs. Even though innovations such as TQM, reengineering, and high-performance work practices are often seen as vehicles of cultural change, they are likely to implemented in a manner that maintains and reinforces the organization's existing ideology. Control-oriented ideologies will beget more control; flexibility-oriented ideologies will beget more flexibility. The essential point is that managerial tools are just that, tools. Their ideational content is likely to be shaped during implementation by the prevailing organizational ideology.

## WHY MANAGERIAL INNOVATIONS HAVE UNINTENDED CONSEQUENCES

Consider the case of total quality management programs. According to its proponents, TQM is explicitly about changing organizations' cultures. Tuckman (1994), for instance, notes that "what differentiates TQM [from earlier quality approaches] is the emphasis placed on cultural change. . . . [It is] a cultural revolution that sets out to supplant hierarchy with informality" (p. 741), literally meaning a move from external to commitment-based mechanisms of coordination and control. Anderson, Rungtusanatham, and Schroeder's (1994) analysis of the conceptual underpinnings of Deming's principles shows the types of changes that TQM programs are supposed to engender. Five of the seven underlying dimensions that Anderson et al. identify—visionary leadership, internal-ex-

ternal cooperation, learning, employee fulfillment, and customer satisfaction—are characteristic of the human relations and open systems models of the CVF. The other two dimensions—process management and continuous improvement—fall within the realm of the internal process and rational goal models. Thus, within the context of the CVF, the expectation is that the ideological profile of an idealized TQM organization would be biased toward the upper two quadrants of the framework.

Chang and Wiebe (1996) employed a panel of TQM experts to determine the relative balance of the CVF's four value systems that would be found in an "ideal" TQM organization. Their results confirm the above-stated expectations. The "ideal" TQM profile is biased toward the human relations and open systems values, with less emphasis on internal process and rational goal models. In a study that supports Chang and Wiebe's findings, Shortell et al. (1995) examined TQM implementation in 61 U.S. hospitals and found that the greater the emphasis on human relations and open system models, the more likely the success of TQM implementation.

However, critics charge that successfully implemented TQM programs often have the opposite of their intended cultural effects and result in greater levels of managerial control instead of empowered employees. For instance, Eccles (1993) notes that one interpretation of TQM is that it

is meant to "empower" workers to police their own performance, but not to set their own goals or target levels, and that this really means a management goal of "total management control" because of "increased surveillance and monitoring of workers activities . . . heightened responsibility and accountability, the harnessing of peer pressure within "teams" . . . pushing back the frontiers of control . . . such that any gains made by workers are noticed and appropriated [by the firm]. (p. 17)

Spencer (1994) explains why this can occur. In discussing the underlying theme of process control inherent in continuous improvement efforts, he notes that TQM

> evokes comparison to Taylor's scientific management. . . . It controls activities to increase consistency, reduce waste, and speed the flow of work. . . . However, the extent to which process control is entirely mechanistic seems to depend on who conducts the audits, who designs and carries out the procedures, and who checks to make sure the procedures are done correctly. (p. 452)

In other words, TQM can empower line employees or increase managerial control, depending on how it is implemented, and the direction implementation takes depends on the organization's ideology. If, for example, an organization's ideology emphasizes managerial control, TQM implementation is likely to follow the path of least resistance and create a TQM system that maintains or increases control.

## A Case Example

We can illustrate this effect with some unintended findings from a study in seven of the hospitals included in the Shortell et al. (1995) study. Our study, conducted 4 years later, was concerned with the delivery of prenatal care services and focused on the obstetrics units within these hospitals. Shortell et al.'s study was organizationally broader in scope, assessing quality implementation in 10 different departments, including obstetrics. Although our study was not directly concerned with TQM, we used the CVF instrument employed by Shortell et al. to develop CVF profiles for each of these obstetric units. It became apparent early in our interviews that TQM implementation took different directions in these organizations and there had been noticeable shifts in their CVF profiles over time. Of the seven hospitals, six appeared to have made progress in implementing their TQM programs according to survey data collected from managers.

In order to illustrate the dynamics we observed, we focus on two of the hospitals that represent different patterns of TQM implementation. Both are large hospitals (more than 500 beds) located in major metropolitan areas. Both had experienced increasing competition with managed care organizations, and both had undergone major restructurings accompanied by layoffs. Obstetric unit staff nurses in both hospitals reported similar increases in workload and similar organizational changes, such as the combination of antepartum and postpartum units into mother/baby units, cross-training, a shift toward increased use of less skilled nursing personnel (certified nursing assistants and licensed practical nurses), and the implementation of performance-based compensation systems.

Figure 16.2 shows the competing values profiles for the obstetric units in Hospitals A and B based on the Shortell et al. data. Figure 16.2 also contains Chang and Wiebe's (1996) "ideal" TQM profile.[1] The profile for Hospital A emphasizes the internal process and rational goal models, indicating a control-oriented organizational ideology. The site visit report on Hospital A from Shortell et al.'s study describes an organization consistent with this type of profile. It notes that a lack of leadership stability, coupled with a hierarchical culture, had bred cynicism and mistrust throughout the organization:

> Employees look to top management (and particularly to their budget allocations) for signs of true priorities. Even so, some say the road to survival is to learn to give lip service to management initiatives until they blow over. One interviewee said that it is the department heads who really get things done because higher levels of management turn over so fast. . . . There is also a significant element of distrust of management. Among many employees, management is perceived as being interested only

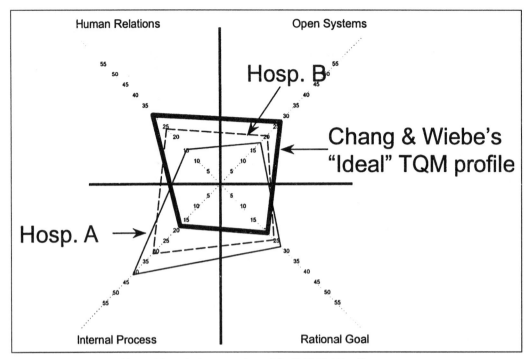

**Figure 16.2.** CVF Profiles at Time A Compared to "Ideal" TQM Profile

in money. A series of layoffs in recent years has contributed to this view. Among physicians, there is complaining that the hospital has played favorites in handing out economic benefits. Altogether, the medical staff was distrustful of management, and there has been a long history of generally hostile relations between administration and clinicians.[2]

A comparison of Hospital A's CVF profile with Chang and Wiebe's (1996) "ideal" TQM organization profile shows that Hospital A had a culture very different from what the experts indicate an ideal TQM organization looks like. Yet Hospital A demonstrated success in implementing its TQM program. For instance, one manager reported that "in terms of a productivity standpoint, we benchmark both internally within [our hospital system] and externally with 350 other hospitals and we get grouped by patient satisfaction. We also get grouped in terms of pro-

ductivity. [Our obstetrics unit] is right at 100 percent, we are probably the benchmark to work with."

Hospital B had a greater emphasis on the human relations model compared with Hospital A, and its profile more closely fit Chang and Wiebe's "ideal" TQM profile. Shortell et al.'s site report on Hospital B characterizes its culture as one

that emphasizes "perfectionism" and has traditionally been very financially driven. . . . Many aspects of this culture are very supportive of continuous quality improvement efforts. At the same time, some of these "perfectionist" tendencies may stifle risk taking, experimentation, and learning. Also, a number of people interviewed indicated that the past dominance of the financial paradigm can still be a negative influence on their quality improvement efforts. Nonetheless, the general consensus was the [Hospital B's] culture is changing.

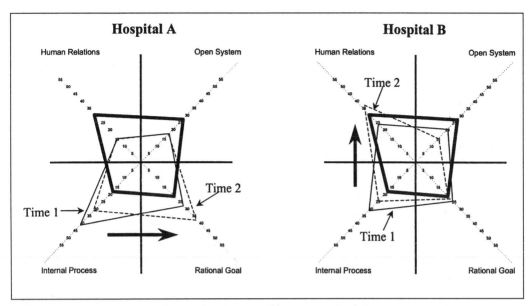

Figure 16.3. Hospital A's and Hospital B's CVF Profiles, Times 1 and 2

In the past two years greater emphasis has been given to the values and tenets of quality improvement, and they are beginning to see financial objectives within the quality improvement paradigm rather than the reverse.

The site report also notes that a "positive force has been nursing's shared governance model. It has served as an example of empowerment and has been an extremely supportive facilitator of quality improvement efforts." Hospital B has also demonstrated success in its quality programs. It is the largest hospital in a system that has received several national awards in recognition of its leadership in quality improvement.

If TQM is a vehicle for cultural change, as its proponents argue, one would expect that there would be changes in the organizations' CVF profiles over time. As Figure 16.3 shows, the CVF profiles for the obstetrics units at Hospitals A and B shifted over the 4-year period, but in opposite directions. At Hospital A there is movement along the internal/external focus axis from the internal process model to the rational goal model. This shift indicates that the organization became more externally focused and efficiency oriented. But there is no indication of the empowerment that is a hallmark of TQM. Conversely, the profile for Hospital B shifts upward along the flexibility/control axis further into the human relations model, which is consistent with increasing empowerment. We observed similar shifts in the profiles of four of the other hospitals in our sample that were having success implementing TQM. The profiles of two hospitals that were members of Hospital B's system and had profiles emphasizing the human relations model in Shortell et al.'s study also shifted further in that direction, as did Hospital B's profile. The other two hospitals had control-oriented profiles and exhibited the same shift experienced by Hospital A, toward the rational goal quadrant.

Spencer's (1994) observation that how the quality process is designed and carried out influences whether it is empowering or controlling helps explain the shifts in these profiles. For instance, managers in both hospitals reported that line staff were involved in the development of clinical protocols. Our interview data indicate that Hospital B uses existing groups within work units whenever possible to develop protocols and emphasizes communication during the development process between quality team members and individuals who will be affected but are not involved in the development. This type of horizontal communication is consistent with the communication patterns observed in organizations with an emphasis on the human relations model.

In contrast, staff nurses in Hospital A reported that standardized protocols, like other changes, come down from the administration, and the nurses have little, if any, input. This pattern is consistent with the top-down communications characteristic of control-oriented organizations. It also is consistent with the nurses' reactions to the other changes taking place in the hospital, which one nurse captured concisely, saying that management's perspective is "you have to do this, this is what is expected of you." Managers at Hospital A did not mention line employee participation when talking about changes in the hospital. They did, however, talk about communication and say that they felt the rationale for changes had been communicated effectively to line staff. One commented: "Our strategic mission couldn't be any more public. It's on the walls, in the bathrooms." The problem, as a couple of managers explained using the same analogy, is that "you can lead a horse to water, but you can't make him drink." Again, this is consistent with expectations from the CVF framework. Control-oriented organizations rely on top-down communication and experience higher levels of resistance to change than organizations with ideologies emphasizing the human relations and open systems models.

Clinical protocols also are used differently in these two organizations. In Hospital A, the protocols are rules to be followed. For instance, one nurse said, "If you don't follow them, you are talked to and told what to do in the future." In contrast, Hospital B's protocols are framed as guidelines for practice. Hospital B's quality program "statement of philosophy" notes that "all statements, protocols, recommendations, etc., are viewed and stated as tentative, transitory and iterative. . . . Each patient and physician is unique and it is understood that the [protocols] do not supplant professional judgment." Staff nurses reported that they could call patients' physicians and have orders changed when they thought the protocols were inappropriate.

We found through our interviews that the perceived empowerment at Hospital B has much to do with the shared governance system that was launched as part of the quality improvement effort. Many of the nurses at Hospital B, and at the two other hospitals in the same system, mentioned shared governance as having had a positive effect on their organizations. One nurse, for example, said that shared governance meant that "nurses decide on our own practice, we make the decisions." Another noted that her unit's manager "lets us make the decisions that we want to make. She'll sit in and listen, and if it's something we want to do, it's majority rule as long as it fits within the budget."

Several nurses offered the example of the development and implementation of a new peer evaluation system to explain how shared governance works. Many nurses did not like an earlier peer evaluation system because the goals were not task oriented and feedback from the annual peer reviews was anonymous. A task force of nurses at one of the system's hospitals designed a new peer evaluation system. In this new system, nurses select their goals from a list of patient-focused objectives and then are evaluated on an ongoing basis by two specific peer evaluators. This system makes feedback continuous throughout the year, rather than just at appraisal time, and makes evaluators accountable for their observations. Once developed, the plan moved through the hospital's and system's governance councils and was being implemented systemwide.

The effects of these differences in organizational ideologies are evident in the nurses' reactions to their organizations. As part of our study, nurses completed a short questionnaire that included items about job involve-

| TABLE 16.2 | Employee Attitudes by Organization | |
| --- | --- | --- |
| | *Hospital A* | *Hospital B* |
| Commitment | 3.03 | 3.72* |
| Empowerment | 2.76 | 3.32* |
| Job involvement | 3.33 | 3.47 |
| Job satisfaction | 2.98 | 4.02* |
| Intent to leave | 2.66 | 1.75* |
| *n* | 85 | 53 |

*Mean difference significant at $p < .05$ (5 = high, 1 = low).

ment, organizational commitment, empowerment, job satisfaction, and intent to leave the organization. Table 16.2 displays the mean scores for the two hospitals. Nurses at the two hospitals reported no difference with respect to their involvement with their job, the provision of nursing care to mothers and babies. However, their feelings about their employers were considerably different. Nurses at Hospital A reported significantly lower commitment to the organization, job satisfaction, and empowerment, and significantly higher levels of intent to leave the organization than did the nurses at Hospital B, findings that are consistent with those from earlier CVF research.

## IDEOLOGIES AND THE OUTCOMES OF INNOVATION

We think that the dynamics of implementation we observed in Hospitals A and B are generally applicable to the broad class of managerial and technological innovations that have the potential for increasing both operational efficiency and organizational flexibility. This type of innovation typically increases operational efficiency by streamlining and/or automating operations and increases organizational flexibility by making

organizational changes that enhance the horizontal flow of information and by empowering employees to make decisions. Examples include TQM, reengineering, high-performance work practices, flexible manufacturing technologies, and integrative information technologies such as enterprise resource planning systems. These kinds of innovations can be differentiated from those with other objectives. For example, benchmarking and dedicated automation focus on increasing efficiency, and customer satisfaction measurement and strategic planning tools aim to increase an organization's external focus, but neither of these types of innovations has an explicit agenda of increasing organizational flexibility.

Innovations with the potential to increase both efficiency and flexibility are dual-edged swords, because they are open to different interpretations depending on an organization's ideological perspective, which determines the focus of the implementation process. For instance, if an organization's ideology emphasizes managerial control, as was the case for Hospital A, attention is likely to focus on task-related efficiency benefits. Implementation will be directed toward streamlining and/or automating operations to gain such benefits. However, organizational changes that increase the horizontal flow of information and empower employees are likely to receive less, if any, attention because they run counter to control-oriented ideologies. Conversely, if an organization's ideology emphasizes commitment-based control, as was the case for Hospital B, attention is likely to focus on gaining an innovation's efficiency *and* flexibility benefits. Implementation is more likely to be directed toward streamlining and/or automating operations *and* toward making organizational changes that increase flexibility because they are ideologically consistent.

Organizational changes that enhance the horizontal flow of information and empower employees to make decisions are critical to gaining the flexibility benefits of this type of innovation. For instance, Zammuto and

O'Connor's (1992) study of advanced manufacturing technology implementation indicates that the flexibility benefits of advanced manufacturing technologies are more a function of an organization's structural flexibility than of the technologies themselves. Similarly, research on organizations that have successfully implemented other types of high-performance innovations (e.g., work teams, employee involvement or problem-solving groups, decentralized quality programs) shows that these innovations make organizational and human resource changes conducive to organizational flexibility (Osterman, 1994; Pil & MacDuffie, 1996). The implication, as Zammuto and O'Connor (1992) argue, is that different sets of outcomes are available to organizations, depending on the extent to which their cultures are, in terms of the CVF, control oriented or flexibility oriented. Organizations with control-oriented cultures are likely to fail at implementation or, when they implement changes successfully, to gain only the new technology's efficiency benefits. As the control orientation of an organization's culture decreases, implementation failure becomes less likely and the likelihood of the organization's gaining both the efficiency and flexibility benefits of a technology increases.

The rationale for this observation is contained in Schön's (1971) concept of dynamic conservatism. Schön notes that "social systems resist change with an energy roughly proportional to the radicalness of the change that is threatened" (p. 38). The radicalness of any given managerial innovation that has the potential for both efficiency and flexibility gains will vary according to the extent to which an organization's ideology is control oriented. The more control oriented the organization's ideology, the more radical the innovation's threat to the system and the greater the resistance that will be activated. Higher levels of resistance make implementation more likely to fail. As a result, the range of outcomes (i.e., failure, efficiency gains, efficiency *and* flexibility gains) available to an organization from such an innovation will vary depending on the organization's underlying ideology.

The relationship between outcomes and ideology is shown graphically in Figure 16.4. Consider the case of Organization 1, with an ideology that emphasizes control (e.g., emphasizes the internal process and/or rational goal models). An innovation that contains the seeds of both flexibility and control would be perceived as a radical threat to the interests of Organization 1's powerful members and subunits, whose roles and perquisites are sanctioned by the prevailing organizational ideology. Odds are that strenuous resistance to implementation would be encountered and implementation would fail. If resistance is unsuccessful at defeating implementation outright, Schön (1971) notes, "social systems tend to respond by changing—but by the *least change* capable of neutralizing or meeting the intrusive process" (pp. 49-50). Hence the innovation is co-opted and minimal organizational change occurs. As a result, the organization can attain the efficiency benefits of the innovation while preserving managerial control. But the organization cannot gain the flexibility benefits because it remains structurally inflexible. The organization cannot attain the innovation's flexibility benefits without further changes in the organization's structure, which would require changes in the organization's underlying ideology.

Organization 2's ideology is less control oriented than that of Organization 1, and the innovation is likely to be perceived as less of a threat and activate less resistance. As a result, the range of outcomes available to Organization 2 is broader, making implementation failure less likely and attainment of the efficiency benefits of the innovation more likely, and putting the flexibility benefits within the realm of the possible. This is the situation where an innovation with the potential for both efficiency and flexibility benefits may act as a vehicle for culture change, depending on how it is implemented.

Organization 3 has an ideology that is biased toward commitment-based coordina-

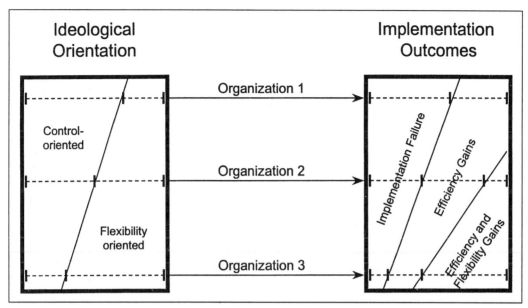

**Figure 16.4.** Managerial Ideologies and the Outcomes of Managerial Innovations
SOURCE: Adapted from Zammuto and O'Connor (1992).

tion and control (e.g., human relations and open systems models). The same innovation that would be perceived as a significant threat in Organization 1 would likely be perceived as an enabler in Organization 3, because it reinforces the organization's existing ideology. The introduction of the innovation would trigger less resistance, making implementation failure less likely and attainment of the innovation's efficiency *and* flexibility benefits more likely. Organization 3 is an example of the kind of organization to which such innovations come naturally. Unfortunately, the historical record of implementation failures suggests that such organizations are a clear minority.

## CONCLUSION

In concluding this chapter, we would like to draw attention to three points. First, both managers and researchers need to under-

stand that the benefits of managerial and technological innovations that have the potential to increase operational efficiency and organizational flexibility are asymmetric in that they cannot be classified simply as success or failure. Part of the reason for high failure rates and executive dissatisfaction with innovations that deliver less than their proponents promise may be related to the fact that the executives' organizations cannot achieve promised empowerment and flexibility outcomes because of their control-oriented ideologies. The implication is that managers in control-oriented organizations should think twice before adopting the "latest" management tools. Failed implementation efforts are expensive in terms of time and financial costs as well as the personal toll they take on the individuals involved. They also breed cynicism and distrust, which make later attempts at change more difficult. Resources available for buying the latest tools might be better spent on changes needed to make organizations' ideologies less controlling, which, in turn, will make them more hospitable venues for innovations with both efficiency and flexibility benefits.

Second, managerial and technological innovations promising cultural transformation should be viewed skeptically. Such innovations can change organizations' cultures, but, as often as not, changes may be in the opposite of the hoped-for direction. Markus and Benjamin's (1997) "magic bullet theory" of information technology-enabled transformation provides some insight into why this occurs. They note that too often, senior and implementing managers view innovations as "magic bullets" because they believe that an innovation, in and of itself, has the power to create organizational change. Senior and implementing managers

> play the role of designing and building guns. Builders of guns that fire magic bullets do not have to worry very much about who is going to aim and fire the gun. After all, magic bullets always hit the right target. So the gun builders can focus on the performance characteristics and aesthetics of their craft, without worrying about the shooter's aim or the targets' ability to dodge. (p. 57)

The subsequent hands-off approach to change management enables the forces of dynamic conservatism, not those of cultural transformation. The resulting co-optation of the innovation reinforces the organization's existing control-oriented ideology, instead of creating empowered employees and a flexible organization. The point is that these types of innovations can be used as vehicles for cultural change, but they will be effective only if senior and implementing managers commit the time, resources, and energy necessary to change the ideological underpinnings of the organization's culture.

Third, even though organizations' cultures contain many idiosyncratic elements, their underlying ideologies share a common basis in the managerial ideologies embedded in the larger social system. For this reason, we think comparative studies of the ideological aspects of organizations' cultures can be productively pursued. Such studies can yield deeper insight into the types of ideologies that lead to successful performance in different contexts and the mechanisms of change that are successful in organizations with different ideologies. The competing values framework provides one tool for doing this.

## NOTES

1. Chang and Wiebe (1996) used a Likert-type version of the CVF profiling instrument, whereas Shortell et al. (1995) and Gifford, Gallagher, and Zammuto (1997) used an ipsative version of the instrument. We converted Chang and Wiebe's profile to the 100-point ipsative format to allow comparison of the profiles.

2. The site visit reports from the Shortell et al. (1995) study quoted here and below are unpublished. Because the organizations involved were promised anonymity and the names of those organizations appear in the site report titles, we refrain from referencing these materials any further.

# 17

## Toward a New Conceptualization of Culture Change

*-- Vijay Sathe and E. Jane Davidson*

The surge of interest in the concept of organizational culture change over the past two decades has been no accident. Management theorists have worked to develop conceptualizations of culture change, and the importance of their work has been amplified by some fundamental changes in market conditions and the nature of work itself.

The "machine bureaucracy" (Perrow, 1986) of yesteryear, in which decision making was driven by rules, regulations, and precedent, is virtually obsolete, at least in business organizations (Nadler, Gerstein, & Shaw, 1992)—for example, rule-based customer service can be too slow and inflexible; customer expectations are now so high, and the pace of change in the organizational environment so rapid and so radical, that decisions must often be made quickly by individuals at the front line. To achieve this level of responsiveness, employees right down the chain of command must have a solid instinct for the organization's beliefs and values about what constitutes appropriate behavior. This is especially true for the new breed of knowledge workers (Drucker, 1985), whose managers lack the know-how to micromanage subordinates' knowledge-based decisions. Culture provides a sense of understanding of an organization's beliefs and values that is necessary when rules, regulations, and micromanagement cannot be used to control behavior or work procedures (Slater & Narver, 1995).

The other important change driving the increased importance of culture change is the dramatic increase in competition worldwide. This has largely been fueled by government deregulation, especially the weakening of protectionist trade policies, and increases in international trade. In a market characterized by improved innovation and swift imitation, a strong and productive organizational culture can be an important source of sustainable competitive advantage, because it is difficult to imitate (Barney, 1986; Prahalad & Hamel, 1990). An attractive corporate culture can also be a valuable lure for and retainer of top personnel.

These changes are forcing academics and practitioners to strive for a better understanding of organizational culture and how it can be changed. Unfortunately, their efforts are hampered by inconsistencies and contradictions in the literature on culture change. We begin this chapter by explaining these anomalies, and then we attempt to reconcile them. We then reconsider traditional ways of thinking about culture change and propose a new conceptualization.

## ORGANIZATIONAL CULTURE

The most commonly accepted definition of culture is that laid out by Edgar Schein (1985):

> A pattern of basic assumptions—invented, discovered, or developed by a group as it learns to cope with its problems of external adaptation and internal integration—that has worked well enough to be considered valid and, therefore, to be taught to new members as the correct way to perceive, think, and feel in relation to those processes. (p. 9)

According to Schein, culture may be studied at its most visible level through the examination of its *artifacts and creations,* which include physical space, technology, art, symbols, language, mottoes, and overt behavior. At the next level are the *values* espoused by individuals as the organization faces and deals with new situations. These represent "what 'ought' to be, as distinct from what is" (p. 15). Finally, at the deepest level of culture are the *basic, underlying assumptions.* When actions that are taken in response to problems of external adaptation or internal integration are seen to be effective, the values on which they were based become accepted as "truth," sink below the conscious level of culture, and become taken-for-granted assumptions that organizational members use to guide their behaviors and attitudes.

Sathe (1985a) has proposed a similar, but subtly different, conceptualization of culture. Sathe's model of culture also includes three levels: shared behavior patterns, shared rationalizations and justifications, and shared beliefs and values. Shared beliefs and values are expressed when people rationalize and justify (i.e., make sense of) shared behavior patterns or norms. One key difference between Sathe's (1985a) and Schein's (1985) models is that the former refers to the *actual* values shared by organizational members, rather than the *espoused* ones. According to Sathe (1985a), beliefs and values, although subconscious, can be altered once they are raised into consciousness. Because they are expressed through rationalizations and justifications, they can be uncovered through insight, challenged, and consciously changed. In this chapter we refer to the deepest level of culture as the actual, rather than the espoused, *beliefs and values* that underlie rationalizations and behavior patterns.

Lewin (1951) proposed one of the first theories of culture change. Although he does not use the term *culture change,* much of what Lewin refers to implies he was looking at what is defined here as culture. For example, he describes influencing a population to change in terms of breaking "social habits"—a strong indication that he is referring to norms, which are one manifestation of culture (behavior patterns). Lewin proposes three phases for changing group standards: "unfreezing," "moving," and "freezing" (p. 228). Much of the subsequent work on culture change can be organized into these three well-known phases, and Table 17.1 provides a summary of this work.

### Unfreezing

Lewin (1951) defines unfreezing as reducing the forces that maintain the status quo, or

# TABLE 17.1 Selection of Culture Change Literature Presented Using Lewin's (1951) Framework

## Unfreezing ("mindshift" focus)

Emotional stir-up required (Lewin, 1951).

Highlight inconsistencies between actual and espoused values (Argyris, 1993).

Need *both* disconfirming information and psychological safety (Schein, 1993a).

It is important to have a face-saving way of admitting mistakes (Martin, 1993).

Threats come from problems with internal coordination *or* external adaptation (Schein, 1985).

It is important to persuade people that external threats are serious (Deal & Kennedy, 1982; Kroeck, 1994; Sathe, 1985a; Wegbreit, 1992; Wind & Main, 1998).

Unfreeze by confronting reality through benchmarking and continuous, tough evaluation (Miles, 1997a).

Senior managers may need to create a perceived crisis *deliberately* (Hurst, 1995; Kotter & Heskett, 1992).

Engage in multiple scenario planning, so threats are recognized (de Geus, 1997).

Challenge the internal change agents with the problem, then put them in important positions and have them infiltrate the ranks of the resisters (Strebel, 1999).

## Unfreezing ("behaviorshift" focus)

Use negative shock (Van de Ven, 1993).

Change the *context*—strategy, structures, procedures and so on (Beer, Eisenstat, & Spector, 1990; Kanter, Stein, & Jick, 1992; Schein, 1985; Vollman, 1996).

## Moving

Attitude and belief change best achieved through *group* decision making, consensus building, and/or cognitive redefinition as a group (Deal & Kennedy, 1982; Lewin, 1951; Schein, 1985).

Best method is skillful, directed challenging and critical analysis of beliefs, values, justifications (Kotter & Heskett, 1992; Sathe, 1985a).

Keep "visioning" to a minimum; that is, don't force people into a predetermined mold (Miles, 1997a).

## Moving without unfreezing

Use "positive shock"—unexpectedly reward people for the new behavior. This allows the old behavior to be replaced without its being directly challenged (R. Gable, personal communication, April 17, 1998).

Focus on creating what isn't, not on destroying what is (Goss, Pascale, & Athos, 1993).

## Freezing

It is important to have visible success of new methods (Kotter & Heskett, 1992; Schein, 1985; Strebel, 1999).

Symbols and/or structural changes help institutionalize the new culture (Deal & Kennedy, 1982; Hurst, 1995).

Rather than punishing mistakes, rewards should be centered on the detection of errors as well as the achievement of new behaviors (Schein, 1993a).

## Alternatives to refreezing

Refreezing is neither possible nor appropriate (Argyris, 1993).

It is important to maintain a dynamic imbalance/disequilibrium (Ghoshal & Bartlett, 1996).

Only the deepest level of culture—beliefs and values —should be refrozen (Wegbreit, 1992).

The organization needs the adoption of adaptive values for change to persist (Miles, 1997a).

breaking "a well-established 'custom' or 'social habit'" (p. 224). Table 17.1 shows that writers on culture change have a number of different views on how unfreezing is achieved. These range from confronting individuals with the contrast between their beliefs and reality, or between their actual and espoused values, through deliberately creating perceived crises or threats, to manipulating the organizational context. The consensus on unfreezing appears to be that some sort of encounter with a surprising reality is necessary, although views differ about the most effective strategy for achieving this.

With regard to the differences among the writers' views, we can see two themes running through discussion of the unfreezing phase. These concern (a) whether behaviors or minds are the best targets for change and (b) whether the old behaviors and attitudes need to be confronted or substituted without confrontation (see Table 17.1). The latter of these two represents a largely untested idea in the area of culture change, and we will not specifically address it here. However, we will revisit the question of whether to target minds or behaviors in the next section, when we attempt to reconcile these contradictions.

### Moving

Lewin (1951) describes moving as increasing forces in favor of change—that is, pushing attitudes, values, and behaviors to a new level. An interesting contrast here is between (a) those who advocate emergent redefinition by the group and (b) those who support a more deliberate attempt to redefine beliefs and values in a certain way (see Table 17.1). Writers with a stronger orientation toward organization development—with its traditionally humanistic emphasis on facilitation and consensus building—tend to support allowing people to create their own versions of what should be. In contrast, those with stronger leanings toward organizational transformation—which has a more macro-level, strategic view of change—prefer to leave less to

chance, emphasizing a more deliberate push toward the creation of more specific beliefs and values deemed essential for the success of the new strategy.

The issue of whether minds or behaviors are best targeted also emerges in this section. The majority of writers suggest interventions with a heavy cognitive focus, aimed at forging a redefinition of beliefs and values, and most also suggest this is best achieved in a group setting. Thus the consensus here strongly favors an emphasis on changing people's minds (rather than behavior), at least initially. In contrast, one theorist suggests a purely behavioral intervention: "positive shock" (R. Gable, personal communication, April 17, 1998). Unlike negative shock, this is a force in favor of change (moving), rather than one against the status quo (unfreezing). Positive shock may be described as deliberate, norm-breaking positive reinforcement, designed to shock individuals into changing their behavior and to demonstrate that the organization's old beliefs and values no longer apply. For example, an organization trying to create a more innovative culture could use a surprise reward, such as a prestigious new award for "Mistake of the Month," delivered along with a description of why the mistake rewarded was an excellent one. The rationale behind positive shock is that extrinsic motivators will force behavior change, which will lead to a reconsideration of the beliefs and values on which the previous behavior was based.

### Freezing

Lewin (1951) defines freezing as the institutionalization of the new equilibrium, or "reconstructurization of the social field" (p. 233). There are two distinct approaches to the issue of freezing the new culture—one emphasizes the natural process by which new beliefs and values become "second nature," whereas the other focuses on the structural and procedural levers that can be used to institutionalize the new culture (see Table

17.1). Again, we see the question emerge as to whether the focus is more fruitfully placed on "mindshift" or "behaviorshift," and therefore whether intrinsic or extrinsic motivators should be employed in the freezing process. We address this question in the following section.

A more fundamental area of disagreement regarding the freezing phase is what, if anything, can or should be refrozen. Some writers argue that even the deepest underlying beliefs and values of the culture can be institutionalized, whereas others insist that this is possible only with more surface manifestations of culture. Further, several writers argue that the end state should be fluid, and not frozen at all. We also address each of these issues in the following sections.

## ISSUES IN CULTURE CHANGE

With Lewin's (1951) three-phase model as a starting framework, we now turn our attention to some of the main controversies in the literature on culture change. In the preceding section we have highlighted at least three unresolved issues: (a) whether and how basic underlying beliefs and assumptions can be changed, (b) whether emphasis is more fruitfully placed on intrinsic or extrinsic motivators, and (c) the timing and sequence in which these motivators are best employed. We will address the broader issue that has also emerged—whether or not the new cultural elements should be frozen—later in this chapter, when we reconsider the appropriateness of Lewin's change model for new organizational forms. The main issues, and the positions of various writers on them, are summarized in Table 17.2.

### Can the Deepest Level of Culture Be Changed?

Perhaps the most fundamental of the three controversies noted above is the extent to which culture can be changed. Can the deepest values and beliefs be altered? Schein (1985) argues that, although some of the more superficial ones may be changed, the deepest of the organization's underlying assumptions cannot be confronted or debated. Similarly, Argyris (1993) states that the organization's defensive routines are undiscussable, as is the undiscussability itself.

However, Argyris (1993) also argues in favor of comparing espoused values with those that are implicit in actions and words, suggesting that taken-for-granted defenses (i.e., beliefs and values) may be brought to the surface and addressed openly. This is what Sathe (1985a) describes as a key mechanism for culture change. He argues that the deepest level of culture (beliefs and values) *can* be brought into consciousness, challenged, and changed. Empirical research showing that basic belief structures may be consciously changed if they are made explicit supports this view (Bernstein & Burke, 1989).

### Conclusion

Here we find agreement that at least some beliefs and values can be changed; the disagreement is a matter of degree—Can the very deepest of beliefs and values be changed, or only those relatively close to the surface? In our view, the evidence clearly supports the possibility of altering beliefs and values at a deep enough level to refer to as culture change.

### Intrinsic Versus Extrinsic Motivators

Extrinsic motivators effect behavior change, whereas intrinsic motivators effect attitude, belief, and value change (Sathe, 1985a). There is general consensus that culture change consists of changing people's minds as well as their behavior. This raises two important issues: First, if both intrinsic and extrinsic motivators are necessary for sustained culture change, is emphasis more

TABLE 17.2   Summary of Issues in Culture Change

| | Yes, definitely | No, probably not |
|---|---|---|
| Can the deepest level of culture be changed? | Sathe (1985a): Can bring beliefs and values into consciousness and change them. Bernstein & Burke (1989): Basic belief structures may be consciously changed if they are made explicit. Argyris (1993): Defensive routines are generally undiscussable, but comparing espoused with actual values is possible in order to address discrepancies. | Schein (1985): Only some superficial beliefs and assumptions can be changed. Wegbreit (1992): Only surface levels of culture can be changed; not the deepest levels. |
| Intrinsic and extrinsic motivators | *Intrinsic* | *Extrinsic* |
| Primary emphasis | Lewin (1951): Persuasion only. Schein (1985): For young organizations. Bernstein & Burke (1989): Need belief change for behavior change. Harrison (1995): Extrinsic surface compliance and covert rebellion. Vollman (1996): Comparison of two large organizations; the one that mandated change down to the last detail generated fear, resignation, and sham compliance. Sathe (1985a): Intrinsic motivation essential if change is to be self-sustaining. | Skinner (1971) Schein (1985): For mature organizations Nadler et al. (1994): Rewards and punishments like promotion and sidelining are key signals of what really matters. Hurst (1995): Recognition better for innovation than compensation. Cotter (1995): Material and psychological recognition. Hope & Hope (1996): Important to measure and reward desired results. Sathe (1985a), Strebel (1999): For people who need a "push" to try something that will produce quick success, then intrinsic takes over. |
| | | *Mix* |
| | | Zaltman & Duncan (1977): Mix of facilitative, persuasive, and power strategies. Sathe (1985a): Mix, but don't overemphasize extrinsic. Strebel (1999): Use intrinsic for all but the resisters; use extrinsic then intrinsic for them. Quinn & Cameron (1988): Balance polarities; don't buy into false dichotomies. Schein (1993a): Mix of persuasion, guilt, and rewards. Litwin et al. (1996): Extrinsic → reactive behavior; intrinsic → purposive. Hambrick, Nadler, & Tushman (1998): Manage the and/also, not the either/or. |
| Timing and sequence of motivators used (if a mix is recommended) | *Intrinsic first* | *Extrinsic first* |
| | Give people a chance to buy in (Sathe, 1985a). Persuade the change agents first, then the bystanders and traditionalists; save extrinsic motivation for the resisters (Strebel, 1999). | Use extrinsic motivators to force a behavior shift in resisters, then use intrinsic motivators to achieve buy-in after they have seen the success stories (Binder, 1998; Sathe, 1985a; Strebel, 1999). |
| | | *Unspecified/depends on situation* |
| | | Zaltman & Duncan (1977) Quinn & Cameron (1988) Schein (1993a) Litwin et al. (1996) Hambrick et al. (1998) |

fruitfully placed on intrinsic or extrinsic motivators? Second, which is more effective, changing people's minds so that their behavior will change, or the reverse? In other words, in which order are intrinsic and extrinsic motivators best employed?

### Intrinsic Versus Extrinsic Motivator Emphasis

The majority of writers on culture change favor intrinsic over extrinsic motivators. For example, the emphasis in Lewin's (1951) work is on noncoercive persuasion and intrinsic motivation; rewards and punishments are not mentioned. Bernstein and Burke (1989) have also argued that a change in belief systems is necessary in order to produce behavior change. Harrison (1995) asserts that intrinsic motivators are superior to extrinsic ones, because the latter tend to produce "surface compliance and covert rebellion" (p. 159).

Intrinsic motivation may also be superior when the organization needs frontline staff to be able to cope with novel situations. Litwin, Bray, and Brooke (1996) assert that the use of extrinsic motivation produces "reactive" behavior, which will be possible only in learned situations. To achieve appropriate behavior in novel situations, "purposive" (goal-directed) behavior—which would require intrinsic motivation with respect to the goals—is necessary. According to Beer (1987), intrinsic motivation for change is generated through cultivation of *dissatisfaction* with the status quo.

Empirical evidence in favor of intrinsic motivators is provided by Vollman (1996), who describes two large organizations that implemented a top-down organizational change strategy. One mandated the implementation of a large number of detailed change initiatives. The other communicated potential problems the organization was facing and mandated a general approach, but left it up to the business units to decide what changes to implement. The latter resulted in the successful development of a culture of urgency, whereas the former gave rise to "fear, resignation, [and] sham compliance" (p. 237).

In contrast, Binder (1998) describes a large retail organization that implemented a detailed organizational change effort successfully by closely monitoring implementation at the behavioral level. Intrinsic motivation developed when the measurement system sparked a healthy sense of competition among the retail stores on their "behavioral scorecard" measures.

Rewards and punishments are not merely tools for shaping the behavior of the individuals receiving them; they are also symbolic. Nadler, Shaw, Walton, and associates (1994) report that rewards are "what employees most frequently mention as the real indicator of commitment to cultural values" (p. 162). Carefully watched signals include who gets promoted, sidelined, dismissed, and selected. Hope and Hope (1996) also stress the importance of measuring and rewarding desired results.

Litwin et al. (1996) argue that the *nature* of the rewards is a key determinant of how effective they are. They cite evidence from a number of their own studies showing that managers who relied heavily on financial incentives were ineffective—that is, their units failed to achieve performance targets. In contrast, managers who emphasized recognition and encouragement were much more effective in achieving targeted results. These findings are consistent with the arguments made by Hurst (1995), who describes how organizations that rely solely on compensation for recognition lose their power to innovate.

Few writers promote a strong emphasis on extrinsic motivators simply to induce behavior change. Some stress the use of intangible rewards and punishments aimed at increasing intrinsic motivation, whereas the majority frame extrinsic motivators as *symbols* that reinforce and help institutionalize desired beliefs and values (see also Hatch, Chapter 15, this volume).

Another view of extrinsic motivation is as a tool to "shock" the organization into unfreezing by presenting it with negative information about its own performance. For example, Miles (1997a) argues that an organization can generate the energy needed for transformation by *confronting reality* through ongoing benchmarking against customer expectations and competitor best practice, industry trend analysis, and diagnosis of internal strengths and weaknesses. Wind and Main (1998) propose benchmarking as a way to shock bureaucrats with the knowledge that other organizations have figured out better approaches than they have. This is framed as an important part of the learning process, as it allows the organization to "get rid of knowledge that is no longer or never was true" (p. 280).

An interesting variation on the theme of shocking the organization into unfreezing is positive shock (R. Gable, personal communication, April 17, 1998). A positive shock could initiate serious rethinking about what is really valued in the organization, replacing previous beliefs and values with seeds for new ones—without using any negative shocks to act directly on the forces of resistance. The above-described CEO award for "Mistake of the Month" is an example of a positive shock strategy.

In sum, most writers appear to agree that both intrinsic and extrinsic motivators are necessary to some extent and at some point in the change process. In our view, the balance of opinion appears in general to favor the superiority of intrinsic motivators.

### Timing and Sequence of Motivators

There is some disagreement in the literature concerning the use of intrinsic and extrinsic motivators, including the question of which should be used first. For example, Sathe (1985a) advocates a balanced approach and warns against the overuse of extrinsic motivators because they tend to produce only temporary behavior change that is not sustained in the long term. He suggests using a combination of intrinsic and extrinsic motivators to force an initial change in behavior, which can be sustained later through intrinsic motivation, provided the new behavior is seen to work. This is in contrast with Schein's (1961) assertion that coercive persuasion is an effective strategy for achieving belief and value change.

Strebel (1999) suggests that intrinsic motivators should be employed *before* extrinsic ones to convince first "change agents," then "bystanders," and finally "traditionalists" of the need to change, but they should be applied in the reverse order for employees who actively resist the change. Once the new methods are seen to work, resisters are more likely to buy into the change, provided they are offered a face-saving way of shifting position (i.e., a meaningful role) and a guarantee that there will be no recriminations for their having resisted initially. Those who still refuse to commit to the change will have to leave the organization.

In line with the previously noted consensus on the superiority of intrinsic motivators, there is general agreement that intrinsic motivators should be the first ones employed in the culture change process. Extrinsic motivators may then be used to (a) institutionalize the change for those who have already bought into it and (b) force behavior change in active resisters, in the hope that they too will become intrinsically motivated once they see that the new methods work. Finally, the option to leave, voluntarily or involuntarily, may be utilized as a last-resort extrinsic motivator for those who are still unable or unwilling to come on board. (For a detailed example of successful culture change using a mix of intrinsic and extrinsic motivators, see Sathe, 1985b.)

### Conclusion

We believe that change agents should seek a balance in the use of intrinsic and extrinsic motivators, taking care not to overemphasize the latter. In particular, extrinsic motivators other than positive shock should be used only after people have been given a chance to change. Given that the most effective combination is usually a mix of intrinsic and extrinsic motivators, the question of what kind of mix works best under what conditions is an important one for further research.

## TOWARD A NEW CONCEPTUALIZATION OF CULTURE CHANGE

In the previous sections, we have explored the range of views in the culture change literature using Lewin's (1951) three-stage model and have outlined three controversies that emerge within that framework. As we have noted, there are also some issues arising from the literature that call into question the unfreeze-move-refreeze framework itself.

In this section we turn our attention to these broader issues and to some other important considerations that will lay the groundwork for a new conceptualization of culture change. These include (a) whether there is such a thing as one best (e.g., "strong" or "flexible") culture and (b) whether there are identifiable phases or stages for achieving culture change (see Table 17.3). Having explored these, we will build on them by introducing the notion of cultural evolution and showing its connection to organizational learning. This will set the stage for a proposed new framework for conceptualizing culture change.

### Culture Strength Versus Flexibility

Peters and Waterman (1982) were widely influential in introducing the notion that strong cultures are superior to weak ones. In support of this idea, Kotter and Heskett (1992) found empirical evidence that strong cultures perform better financially. Kotter

and Heskett also discovered that certain themes in cultures—such as equal emphasis on *all* key constituencies (customers, stockholders, and employees) and emphasis on leadership (rather than management) at all levels—are associated with better performance. De Geus (1997) argues that large, long-lived companies tend to be very cohesive and to have definite "personas" (i.e., strong cultures), so that the employees feel part of one entity despite their organization's size.

Schein (1985) asserts that a strong culture is *not* better, and further that there is no preferred type of culture. Both Sathe (1985a) and Strebel (1994) have argued that organizations with weak cultures are flexible and adapt easily to external change. Sathe (1985a) explains that a stronger culture has (a) a greater number of important shared assumptions, which are (b) more widely shared throughout the organization and (c) more clearly prioritized in terms of relative importance. The greater the strength of the culture and the larger the magnitude of the proposed change, the greater the resistance to change. Radical change involves replacing a large number of central shared assumptions with less intrinsically appealing (i.e., more alien) assumptions (Sathe, 1985a). This suggests that a culture may be relatively easy to change if the most central and widely held beliefs and values are not targets of the culture change. Also, a culture with beliefs and values that are supportive of flexibility itself may be strong without inhibiting the organization's ability to adapt to its environment.

In support of the notion that strong cultural elements can be conducive to flexibility, Cooke and Szumal (1993) found greater organizational effectiveness to be associated with "constructive" cultures. Such cultures are characterized by humanistic and encouraging norms, which tend to support innovative work practices. Clearly, there is a strong linkage between culture and innovation, a topic discussed at some length by Sathe and Nemiro (1999).

**TABLE 17.3** Issues Relating to a New Conceptualization of Culture Change

| | *Yes—strong is better.*<br>*Phases within a change effort* | *Strong is not necessarily better.*<br>*Stages of cultural evolution* | *Yes—flexible/adaptive/constructive.*<br>*Continuous evolution* |
|---|---|---|---|
| *Is there such a thing as one best (e.g., "strong" or "flexible") culture?* | Peters & Waterman (1982): Anecdotal evidence of success. Kotter & Heskett (1992): Stronger → better financial performance. de Geus (1997): Large, long-lived companies have definite "personas" → sense of identity. | Sathe (1985a): Strong is difficult to change ⇒ can be problematic. Schein (1985): Ditto, and there is no particular culture that is better. Strebel (1994): Weak resistance to change ⇒ greater flexibility and adaptability. | Kotter & Heskett (1992): Certain characteristics of cultures are associated with strong financial performance. Cooke & Szumal (1993): Constructive → greater organizational effectiveness. See also organizational evolution. |
| *Are there identifiable phases or stages for achieving culture change?* | Unfreezing → moving → freezing (Lewin, 1951). Taking hold → immersion → reshaping → consolidation → refinement (Gabarro, 1987). Crisis → transformation → transition → stabilization → development (Levy & Merry, 1986). Efficiency orientation versus adaptation orientation (Pawar & Eastman, 1997)—organization open to transformational leadership in adaptation orientation. Balanced scorecard (Kaplan & Norton, 1996) 4-phase cycle: vision and strategy → communicating and linking → planning and target setting → feedback and learning → vision and strategy . . . | Model I → Model II theories-in-use; single-loop → double-loop learning (Argyris, 1993). Transactional → transformational cultures (Bass, 1998). Survival → defense → security → self-expression → transcendence (Harrison, 1995). Political → directive → values-driven leadership (Badaracco & Ellsworth, 1989). | Speed of learning increases as culture evolves to higher levels (Levy & Merry, 1986). "Climate of continuous change" allows organization to evolve (Lawler, 1996). Learning organization → [success] → performance organization → [crisis] → learning organization → [success] → . . . continuous cycle (Hurst, 1995). More highly evolved organizations are those that evaluate more effectively (products, personnel, policies, and change programs)—idea adapted from Scriven (1991). |

a. *Phases* are parts of the change process that generally follow one after the other, but may overlap. *Stages* are sequential steps that cannot be skipped. One stage must come to an end before the next one can begin.

## Conclusion

There is still considerable disagreement around the issue of whether strong cultures are intrinsically superior or resistant to change and therefore inferior. However, thinking over the past 15 years has evolved to some extent, with most writers now conceding that some elements of a culture can be strong as well as conducive to organizational flexibility. A potentially interesting avenue for future research would be to determine which aspects of culture fall under this category and how they can be developed in both new and existing organizations.

## Are There Identifiable Phases or Stages for Achieving Culture Change?

In a report on his observations of more than 100 attempts at organizational change, Kotter (1995) concludes that most failures are due to organizations' skipping or making mistakes at one of the eight necessary steps in the process:

1. Establishing a sense of urgency
2. Forming a powerful guiding coalition
3. Creating a vision
4. Communicating the vision
5. Empowering others to act on the vision
6. Planning for and creating short-term wins
7. Consolidating improvements and producing still more change
8. Institutionalizing new approaches

Levy and Merry (1986) list crisis, transformation, transition, and stabilization and development as the four stages of organizational change. Sathe (1994) proposes a seven-phase model:

1. Shock the organization.
2. Break the old mind-set.
3. Make the tough decisions.
4. Demand performance.
5. Track progress and begin vision creation.

6. Weed out those unwilling or unable to change; recognize and reward those willing and able to change.
7. Begin to build a culture of high competence and performance.

Sathe emphasizes the importance of avoiding the "vision trap" (Langeler, 1992), whereby the vision evolves into an excessively ambitious goal that can distract the organization from its important task of building things people will buy.

Whereas most change models take a linear form, Kaplan and Norton's (1996) "balanced scorecard" approach outlines a four-phase *cycle* for organizational change:

1. Clarifying and translating vision and strategy
2. Communicating and linking objectives and measures
3. Planning and target setting
4. Strategic feedback and learning (and back to the beginning)

## Conclusion

The linear models described relate to the process of managing a single, major organizational transformation effort resulting in an organizational form qualitatively different from that existing previously. In contrast, the "cycle" model appears to relate to an ongoing process of incremental change not involving major upheaval. We would argue that both types of models are valid and useful, but under different conditions—that is, depending on the type of change. The organizational transformation models seem most appropriate for guiding top-down change efforts, whereas the cyclical model might also lend itself to use for bottom-up change or organization development. Research comparing the relative success of organizations using these and other models would provide a valuable contribution to the literature.

## Stages of Cultural Evolution

In addition to describing phases of organizational change, it is also possible to view culture change as a long-term, evolutionary process. For example, Harrison (1995) has drawn on Maslow's (1954) hierarchy of needs to posit that there is a *hierarchy* of organizational cultures, and that organizations gradually evolve up the levels: survival → [defense] → security → self-expression → transcendence.[1] Harrison's self-expression and transcendence cultures are similar to constructive (Cooke & Szumal, 1993) and transformational cultures (Bass, 1998).

Harrison (1995) argues that organizations at the survival and defense levels are not amenable to having their cultures changed at all—they first need to solve their operational problems. In contrast, higher-level cultures can be transformed. This is consistent with Pawar and Eastman's (1997) assertion that organizations are "more receptive to transformational leadership during adaptation orientation than during efficiency orientation" (p. 92).

There are some parallels between the hierarchy of cultures posited by Harrison (1995) and Badaracco and Ellsworth's (1989) hierarchy of leadership philosophies: political, directive, and values-driven leadership. Political leaders concentrate on the political reality of decision making—coalitions, sources of influence, persuasion tactics, trade-offs, and compromises. In contrast, directive leaders strive to create a "marketplace for ideas," focusing on objective assessment of the company's situation and capabilities and on the strategic substance of decisions. Their goal is to lead the organization toward clear, specific, and compelling goals. The "self-expression" culture (Harrison, 1995) has strong parallels not only with the "marketplace for ideas" in the directively led organization of Badaracco and Ellsworth, but also with "Model II" learning (Argyris, 1993) and commitment-based management systems (see Zammuto, Gifford, & Goodman, Chapter 16, this volume). Finally, Badaracco and

Ellsworth's (1989) "values-driven" leaders are concerned with "shaping an organization so that its values, norms, and ideals appeal strongly to its individual members while at the same time making the company a stronger competitor" (p. 65).

De Geus (1997) describes how values are the key to diversity and innovation. They are different from vision and mission, which tend to focus on the line of business the company is in. In contrast, values define what it is that will still bind the work community together when the current line of business no longer exists in the world. Hurst (1995) also sees values as central to the task of revitalizing mature organizations. Action is taken because it is intrinsically valuable, rather than as a means to some clearly defined end goal. This allows outcomes to be novel or creative rather than predetermined.

In contrast with the hierarchical models of evolution, Hurst (1995) presents a circular model of organizational evolution; he suggests that success gives rise to increased rigidity as the resulting "performance organization" formalizes its procedures and structures in order to maximize efficiency. A crisis is needed to allow the rules to be broken so that the organization can revitalize and become free to choose how it operates again.

## Conclusion

Drawing on the various accounts of organizational evolution described here, it appears that *incremental* change, rather than culture change, efforts are predominantly used to improve organizational *functioning*. In contrast, most descriptions of (and prescriptions for) larger-scale organizational *transformation* or metamorphosis involve converting organizational cultures from the security culture to the next level, self-expression. We believe that this distinction goes some way toward reconciling these two rather different conceptualizations of organizational change. Weick and Quinn (1999) point out that episodic transformation becomes unnecessary for higher organizational forms—that is, once organizations acquire the capability to change continuously.

A difficult issue confronting the development of the "higher" forms of culture is the challenge of being an early adopter of the new culture. An individual who freely expresses new ideas and criticizes old ones, or challenges the very decision-making process itself, will become an easy target for those operating in the more political Model I mode. Future research might probe the kinds of strategies that would protect early adopters, thereby increasing the likelihood of successful culture change.

## Organizational Learning and Evaluation

A key feature of more advanced organizational forms appears to be their ability to learn. For example, Argyris's (1993) Model II learning promotes continual change through double-loop learning. Another key feature of learning cultures is their tolerance for mistakes. As Vollman (1996) puts it, "If change proceeds with no failures, the speed of change is probably too slow" (p. 243). This is consistent with Jack Welch's advocacy of "fast failure" at General Electric—those who get to failure first have the chance to be the first to learn about a new product, market, or technology.

Lawler (1996) has written of creating a "climate of continuous change" through organizational experimentation and an openness to "learning about the positive and negative effects of particular practices" (p. 254). Lippitt, Langseth, and Mossop (1985) and Mink, Esterhuysen, Mink, and Owen (1993) stress the importance of a strong evaluation function as part of the learning loop. For example, action research is a technique whereby the organization can experiment with a number of different approaches, then feed performance information back to the decision makers before they determine which option to implement on a larger scale.

Cotter (1995) advocates piloting innovations and being tolerant of mistakes early on.

Empirical support for both is provided by a large study sponsored by Shell in 1983, which found that long-lived companies were both sensitive to changes in the environment and tolerant of "outliers, experiments and eccentricities . . . which kept stretching their understanding of possibilities" (de Geus, 1997, p. 7).

Scriven (1991) posits the existence of an evaluation "gene," a characteristic that has driven the evolutionary survival of groups that critically evaluate and improve their own performance in a systematic way. The earliest examples are of tribes that evaluated and refined weapons and tools more effectively than did their enemies, but this is also true of organizations that experiment, evaluate, and learn more effectively than their competitors, including learning how to change more effectively. This idea is supported by Wind and Main (1998), who describe how the very successful Microsoft learns through "brutal critiques"—postmortems of finished projects that focus on the process to figure out not just *what* went wrong, but *why.*

Miles (1997a) also insists that organizational change efforts themselves must be rigorously assessed early in the corporate transformation process—values must be translated into concrete behavioral expectations, and people must be held accountable for modeling them.[2] However, in the change effort Miles describes at National Semiconductor, the emphasis in evaluation was clearly on financial indicators. Although goals were set for culture change, Miles provides little hard evidence that underlying beliefs or values actually changed.

Kaplan and Norton (1996) have warned organizations against focusing exclusively on financial indicators, advocating instead the balanced scorecard, which incorporates the valuation of the drivers of future performance (a company's intangible and intellectual assets) into the traditional financial accounting model. This shift away from demanding short-term measurable results reflects a realization of the importance of developing a culture that can be leveraged as a competitive advantage into the future.

Several other writers have also touched on the problems inherent in a narrow focus on financial data as indicators of success. Hurst (1995) points out that financial indicators make people look backward, rather than at indicators of future success, such as employee attitudes and customer satisfaction. De Geus (1997) provides some evidence from a large, Shell-sponsored study that multiple indicators may constitute a tool for survival. The study found that long-lived companies tended to recognize that "figures, even when accurate, describe the past. They do not indicate the underlying conditions that will lead to deteriorating health in the future. . . . Once the problems cropped up on the balance sheet, it was too late to prevent the trouble" (p. 7).

Proponents of the balanced scorecard advocate checking links between "softer" intermediate variables—such as culture, competence, and process capability—and financial outcomes. This allows the company to check the validity of the cause-and-effect theory underlying its strategy—a form of double-loop learning. This idea has very strong similarities to "theory-driven evaluation" (Chen, 1991), which allows one to distinguish between theory failure and implementation failure. Changes in intermediate and outcome variables are assessed separately from the links among those variables. If the variables are statistically linked but positive change has not occurred, the diagnosis is implementation failure; the reverse situation indicates theory failure. Even if both cultural and financial indicators have improved, theory failure would suggest that this was due to environmental causes rather than to the organization's strategy.

## A PROPOSED FRAMEWORK
## FOR CULTURE CHANGE

Lewin's (1951) three-stage model of organizational change has stood the test of time for almost five decades. However, its usefulness has recently been challenged with the emergence of more organic organizational forms. As the existence of these forms centers on a continuous process of adaptation and organizational renewal rather than a stable state, the "freezing" metaphor seems inappropriate for describing any part of the change process for such organizations. In addition, we need to incorporate the notion that an organization can be strong and adaptive at the same time.

By broadening the discussion of culture change to consider the possibility of cultural evolution, we have been able to gain a better understanding of where organizational learning fits into the advancement of organizations into higher forms. The task that remains is to place this alongside Lewin's (1951) model to arrive at a more comprehensive description of culture change that is useful to academics and practitioners alike.

Drawing on Harrison's (1995) hierarchy of organizational cultures and Argyris's (1993) distinction between Model I and Model II learning, we would like to propose a new framework for thinking about culture change. Figure 17.1 shows that change occurs in one of two "zones": Model I or Model II. In the Model I zone, we can see the familiar notion of a change effort that starts with one state and ends with another. It is to this type of organizational change—such as the implementation of total quality management (see Michela & Burke, Chapter 14, this volume)—that Lewin's (1951) unfreezing-moving-freezing model still applies.

As illustrated in Figure 17.1, we equate the Model I zone with Harrison's (1995) notion of "gratification-driven" cultures and the Model II zone with his "value-driven" cultures. Although this is slightly different from Harrison's original conception of this distinction, we would argue that a culture becomes value driven when there is open, Model II-like debate concerning what is right and wrong, good and bad. The main difference between the self-expression and transcendence levels is the extent of agreement on the

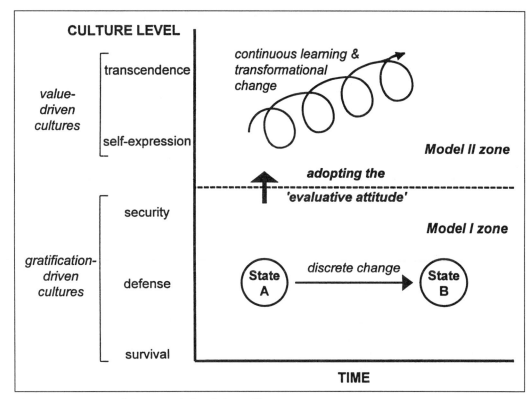

**Figure 17.1.** Proposed Framework for Culture Change

values against which results and actions are evaluated.

Figure 17.1 also illustrates our key assertion—that an organization must make this fundamental switch to the values of a learning organization in order to make the transition from the Model I to the Model II zone. We believe that an organization can do this most effectively by embedding the "evaluative attitude"—the relentless pursuit of the truth about quality and performance—firmly into its deepest cultural assumptions. This can be achieved through a powerful combination of leadership and implementation of high-quality evaluation systems.

Many people assume that evaluation is primarily an accountability-focused function that centers on control, measurement, and monitoring. Our intention here is to distinguish this management information system (MIS) activity, with its emphasis on goal achievement, from true evaluation. The latter consists of determining merit, worth, or significance—briefly, the extent to which the evaluand made the best possible use of available resources to achieve outcomes of maximum possible value (Scriven, 1991). Because competent evaluation necessarily involves the consideration of alternative uses of resources, its emphasis is much more heavily on expanding the organization's possibility horizons. In contrast, the "on time, on target, and on budget" emphasis of the MIS/monitoring model keeps the focus firmly within the existing frame. The "outside the box" thinking that characterizes true evaluation is what forms the basis of the evaluative attitude.

Once the evaluative attitude has become part of the culture, the organization will learn, evolve, and constantly renew itself with an agility that will surpass its competitors who are still immersed in attempts at discrete change. Fruitful avenues for research here would include comparisons of the financial performances of organizations that evaluate competently and those that do not, as well as the types of evaluation that yield the most valuable kinds of organizational learning.

## IMPLICATIONS FOR PRACTITIONERS

### Initiating Change

In order to reduce the forces in favor of the status quo (Lewin, 1951), it is first necessary to persuade people of the need for change. If a sense of urgency is not yet present, compelling evidence will be needed to convince them that the current way of doing things is not working.[3] Such evidence may be readily available; if not, it should be collected or created. People need the opportunity to work through their problems, understand how their own beliefs and values may be part of their problems, and find a face-saving way of admitting that previously valid beliefs no longer hold (Martin, 1993). It is especially important that people critically examine their *actual* beliefs and values, particularly in contrast with *espoused* ones.

The difficult task facing change agents is how to unfreeze the culture of the organization. In some cases, it may be possible to skip this step and go straight to the "moving" phase by mandating behavior change and backing it up with a measurement system that cannot be manipulated. However, this will be feasible only if (a) performance monitoring is logistically possible and relatively inexpensive, (b) the change agents can gather enough expertise in the planning phase to determine what should be done, and (c) the new behavior is likely to result in quick success, which will then fuel the development of intrinsic motivation for changing the beliefs

and values (i.e., create a culture consistent with the desired behavior, to sustain it in the longer term).

### Implementation Strategies

Organizationwide participation in the development of a solution can be extremely beneficial for achieving buy-in for the culture change, and for rapid adoption of desired behaviors once the new way of doing things is agreed upon. The emphasis at this stage too should be on the use of intrinsic motivators, as they are consistent with evolution toward a more advanced, value-driven culture. In contrast, the excessive use of extrinsic motivators would reinforce the beliefs implicit in a gratification-driven culture, thereby inhibiting evolution to the higher, more adaptive form.

If possible, methods consistent with the new culture should be piloted in a part of the organization where they are (a) most urgently needed and (b) most likely to produce visible results quickly. In order to maximize organizationwide belief in the feasibility of the new ways of doing things—and to ensure they *are* the best of all possible options before the organization invests heavily in their implementation—the organization should arrange for rigorous evaluation of the new methods in comparison with their most viable alternatives, including the status quo.[4]

During the piloting and implementation phases, it is important that the organization create an atmosphere of psychological safety for engaging in the new behaviors and testing the waters of the new culture. This encourages employees to verify for themselves the validity of the new beliefs and values, and to explore how they *personally* can contribute to the change effort. Managers and change agents can make an important contribution to the atmosphere of psychological safety by modeling the new culture, rather than merely generating rhetoric about it. The use of extrinsic motivators as symbols is also important at this stage. Reward systems should be designed to demonstrate the organization's commitment to the change—supporters of the effort should be promoted and rewarded in public, and punishment for mistakes during the learning phase should be scrupulously avoided.

Some individuals will not have bought into the new culture even after they have seen its methods succeed. Change agents need to give these resisters a "push" using extrinsic motivators, so that they at least try the new behaviors. People who still block the change even after being given every opportunity to voice dissent, learn new skills, and come on board should be sidelined or given the chance to leave the organization—the costs to morale and credibility of keeping them in their positions of power are simply too high.

## Building an Adaptive Culture

It seems clear that it is possible to create a culture that is strong, yet flexible. The most important consideration in institutionalizing the new culture is to embed only those beliefs, values, and practices that support organizational adaptation. The goal is to eliminate the necessity of unfreezing the organization in the future by retaining enough fluidity in most aspects of the organization's culture that "moving" will be simply a matter of changing speed or course (see Weick & Quinn, 1999).

We believe that three elements should be built into the organization in order to ensure its ability to perceive changes in the environment, learn from them, and change itself proactively. At the top of the menu is the refinement of organizational antennae so they can detect a very broad range of signals from the external environment. This is best achieved through a combination of scenario planning and the use of external resources to provide independent, critical, and objective views of the organization's position with respect to its competitors, customers, and other constituents.

The second priority is a system that mirrors these antennae *within* the organization, in order to eliminate surprises and ensure that erroneous knowledge is not embedded in the organization's memory. To support a culture that actively and continuously confronts reality, an organization needs to engage in thorough, ongoing critique of personnel, practices, policies, products, and change programs. This will prevent the development of conventional wisdom, which can hinder the organization's ability to innovate. In order to ensure that the system stays rigorous and honest, to provide for the injection of novel viewpoints, and to allow benchmarking against competitors, the organization should have outside evaluators conduct a "health check" periodically.

Finally, leaders need mirrors. To develop the kind of culture in which there are no "sacred cows," where everything is vigorously critiqued for the value it adds, commitment has to start at the top (Sathe, 1999). All true professionals actively seek feedback from their toughest critics (Scriven, 1991), and leaders should lead the way in this crucial task. This can be very difficult personally, but it is what everyone must do to develop and sustain a learning organization. Useful ways of getting such feedback include asking a trusted external adviser to collect 360-degree appraisals and critically evaluating and challenging top team members on their performance as change leaders (Sathe, 1999).

Although the details of what works will vary across organizations, we believe the approach outlined here provides a solid foundation for practitioners, based on a synthesis of some of the most up-to-date knowledge in the field. Given that the concept of continual change is a relatively new one, considerable scope is available for researchers and practitioners to inform the field, and for theorists and academicians to build on the current knowledge reviewed here.

There is a clear need to further our understanding of how culture change works under different conditions, as well as the processes involved in building and maintaining an adaptive culture. We would urge a strong research emphasis on rigorous evaluation of various organizational change strategies in terms of both effectiveness and cost-effectiveness, rather than the maintenance of a traditional, descriptive research focus.

## NOTES

1. Harrison (1995) argues that organizations do not normally pass through the "defense" level during evolution to higher levels. However, under pressure to evolve, they may inadvertently develop "defense" instead of "self-expression" cultures. Harrison characterizes the defense culture as a kind of "holding-on reaction . . . to prevent a descent to the level of survival" (p. 222).

2. However, Miles's (1997a) recommendation that external content consultants run the pilots and evaluate their own efforts to determine if organizationwide implementation is feasible is flawed by the substantial conflict of interest involved.

3. Note that, under Schein's (1985) definition, new cultural assumptions may be created in response not only to threats external to the organization, but also to problems with "internal integration." Therefore, it should still be possible (although harder) to initiate change in an organization in a relatively noncompetitive environment.

4. Executives often consider evaluation to be an unnecessary expense. However, even a very quick and inexpensive effort can have substantial payoffs, as some monumental failures in organizational change have demonstrated. A classic example is the productivity paradox, the finding by at least three independent studies (each conducted because the researchers could not believe the findings of the previous studies) that the officewide installation of personal computers in the United States, at least up to the early 1990s, did *not* result in increases in productivity that justified the cost (Harris, 1994). A major culture change effort requires the commitment of considerable organizational resources. Given that, allocation of, say, 5% of the budget to ensure that it works and that all alternatives are considered would be by no means excessive.

# 18

## Twelve Testable Assertions About Cultural Dynamics and the Reproduction of Organizational Culture

_-- Keith A. Markus_

I n these few pages, I want to engage you in a different conversation about organizational culture (OC). For the purposes of this chapter, I will assume that the definition offered by Schein (1991b) provides a workable approximation of what we mean by OC. Rather than approaching OC as a naturally inert structure in which change requires explanation, however, I approach OC as a dynamic system in a natural state of flux such that stability requires explanation. This provides a richer and more useful understanding of cultural dynamics and OC. Along the way, I offer 12 testable assertions that highlight some of the implications of this way of speaking about OC. To avoid empty ab-

stractions, I would like to begin with an example.

Perhaps the most memorable image from the _In Search of Excellence_ documentary (based on Peters & Waterman, 1982) is that of a Disneyland employee dressed as Goofy snapping into character as soon as the camera comes into his line of sight in a passageway closed to the public. We are told that this reaction reflects the strong culture of the Disney organization. We take this culture to be an enduring quality of the organization and assume that the same would hold were we to return to the same passageway tomorrow. Why should that be? Why should cultures persist? The venerable answer to this ques-

AUTHOR'S NOTE: I would like to thank Celeste Wilderom, John L. Michela, Daniel Yalisove, and Gwendolyn L. Gerber for helpful comments on earlier versions of this chapter.

tion is that cultures are relatively stable structures that will remain as they are until something changes them. It is the event of culture change that requires careful explanation in terms of cultural dynamics (Hatch, 1993; see also Chapter 15, this volume). In the absence of change agents, cultures remain as they are.

In this chapter, I will render plausible a different and seemingly paradoxical answer. Nothing could be more natural than to attribute culture's persistence to stability. Nothing would seem to threaten culture's persistence more than instability and flux. Despite these first appearances, a dynamic view of culture provides a more theoretically sound answer to the question of culture's persistence. Cultural dynamics are at least as important to our understanding of stability as to our understanding of change.

This assertion does not deny the value of the more familiar conversation in which culture is spoken of as a stable entity. The familiar conversation about OC has been invaluable to the establishment of OC as a unique and viable area of study in the face of fundamental criticisms of the culture concept (Guion, 1973; Hellriegel & Slocum, 1974; James & Jones, 1974; Johannesson, 1973; Johnston, 1976; Schneider, 1975; Woodman & King, 1978). While recognizing the knowledge that the familiar conversation has made possible, we can nevertheless seek further understanding of OC through alternative conversations. In the next section, I provide a transition from a static to a dynamic approach to OC. I then develop the notion of culture as actively reproduced in the face of flux, and in the remaining sections I explore various approaches to cultural dynamics.

## WHY DO CULTURES NOT FADE?

One way of speaking about OC describes culture as something that is attached to an organization, as a coat of paint is attached to a fence. Once a fence is white, we expect it to remain white until something acts to change

its color. Of course, things do act to change its color. Wind and rain will fade the painted fence just as we might expect turnover, a changing workforce, and daily interactions with those outside the organization to gradually fade an organization's culture.

We would expect culture fade, that is, if we viewed cultures as static and passive, like the paint on a fence. Familiar approaches to understanding OC, however, do not turn a blind eye to the reproduction of OC. Attention has been paid to the role of selection and socialization of new members (Sackmann, 1991; Schein, 1991a). In fact, transmission is an essential quality of an organizational culture, by Schein's definition. Socialization offers an explanation of how cultures reproduce themselves over the long term.

If cultures are thought of as stable in the short term but in need of dynamic processes to reproduce in the long term, then we need to determine where the short term ends and the long term begins. We can get away with a fuzzy line between the two so long as we are dealing with relatively stable organizations. As our world economy moves toward greater and greater dynamism, however, the awkwardness of this arrangement begins to assert itself. Fortunately, as rapid economic change leads us to examine the dynamic processes that reproduce OC in the very short term of day-to-day events, we gain a better understanding of how cultures resist fading over the long term.

An example may help to make the issue more concrete. In developing the example introduced above, I do not wish to imply that the Disney culture is limited to the role of the Goofy character. Rather, I wish to explore various aspects of the interaction as it is organized by layers of cultural practices, values, and assumptions. Granting that a given culture has been produced within Disneyland and that it has been duly transmitted to the employee who portrays Goofy, we may still ask what it is that maintains the culture. When the employee goes home, why is the culture still there when he or she returns the next morning? Granted that the culture is maintained, where is it maintained? We recognize that memories, practices, stories, and meanings all have a propensity to be lost over time. As the founding events that produced the culture recede into the past, we would expect their salience to diminish. People get distracted. They forget. They move on. All of this would suggest that the culture should fade. Nonetheless, cultures do not seem to fade.

Where are the cultures and what could be acting to maintain them? The venerable answer to the first part of the question is that cultures are in the head. Cultures are aggregates of individual beliefs, values, and assumptions that are held in common. Individual beliefs, values, and assumptions become culture by being shared. What, then, could be acting on the contents of organization members' heads to maintain the culture? The image of employees going home to practice culture memorization exercises is somewhat implausible. A more believable answer is that culture is reinforced through the practice of the culture itself: day-to-day interactions among organization members sharing in the culture (Bourdieu, 1972/1977; Hardy, Lawrence, & Phillips, 1998; Markus, 1997).

On the basis of the above reasoning, I offer my first testable assertions:

- *Assertion 1:* A cross-sectional analysis of cultural practices will not find a strong negative association between their strength (salience in the organization) and their age (time since introduction into the culture).
- *Assertion 2:* A longitudinal study of an emerging culture will not find that the culture is strongest at its inception and gradually weakens over time.

## THE REPRODUCTION OF ORGANIZATIONAL CULTURE

Moving toward a dynamic view of OC involves a shift of emphasis rather than a shift of paradigm. Theories and findings readily straddle static and dynamic approaches. What changes is the operative metaphor. Do we approach the periods between transitional states (Lundberg, 1985) as stable states, like the frames of a film? Or do we approach them as simply a different kind of flux, like the blinking pixels of a television screen actively maintaining a stable image? I will argue for the latter dynamic approach, seeking to explain the absence of change through dynamic processes. Metaphors (Lakoff & Johnson, 1980) and other rhetorical figures (de Man, 1983) blind us to some things as part of the process of facilitating insight into others. Nonetheless, this does not imply that all metaphors are created equal. Some offer more insight than others. In the remainder of this chapter, I will recommend a dynamic approach to OC on the grounds that, by and large, it offers greater insight into OC than does the static view without giving up the insights that the static view has lent us.

Taking a dynamic approach, we can envision telling a familiar sort of story about how Disneyland developed the culture attributed to it. The difference is that the development is seen as ongoing rather than something that has come to completion. The difference between the transition state and the comparatively stable state is a matter of degree. What Sathe and Davidson (Chapter 17, this volume) describe as freezing is only a relative slowing of the processes that does not reach absolute zero. Better put, the appearance of freezing is actively maintained by dynamic processes boiling within the culture, in much the same way that objects maintain their solidity through dynamic molecular processes.

The difference between the dynamic processes that maintain the culture in the individual and the socializing processes that transmit the culture to the new hire is likewise a matter of degree. Even the eldest of the old guard are daily subject to countercultural influences. They interact with others outside the organization's culture in each of the various other organizations to which they belong. If they are married, if they belong to social organizations, volunteer organizations, religious organizations—all of these involve acting in cultures other than that of the work organization. Similarly, incremental changes in the problems faced by the organization and by its members invite corresponding adjustments in how things are accomplished in the organization. These influences work against the maintenance of the culture of the work organization by imposing centrifugal forces on the members who practice the culture. The centripetal forces that maintain the culture must therefore be at work in the old hand as well as in the new hire. (For an elaboration of the relevant senses of centrifugal and centripetal forces, see Bakhtin, 1981.)

The image we are left with, then, is of a culture taking its basic features from a formative event, but day in and day out being shaped and reshaped through dynamic processes. At the level of individual day-to-day interactions, the culture is constantly being remade with minor variations, modifications, and adaptations. These small but incessant forces have long been recognized in the OC literature, but have not been given sufficiently serious consideration as cultural dynamics. The next section takes up the specific nature of these processes.

Before moving on, I offer two further assertions:

- *Assertion 3:* A longitudinal study of specific cultural practices will find that at least some practices become more salient in the organization over time.
- *Assertion 4:* A longitudinal study of specific cultural practices will find variability among the practices in the direction and degree of change in salience over time.

## THREE TYPES OF CULTURAL PROCESSES

We can now ask how the dynamic cultural processes that reproduce OC are to be understood. I will consider three alternatives: intentional processes, unconscious processes, and discursive processes. Intentional processes occur within individual conscious minds. Unconscious processes occur within individual minds but outside of consciousness. Discursive processes occur between individuals within sets of symbolic or communicative practices. In the process of articulating these three alternatives as distinct from one another, I also mean to suggest that each addresses limitations of the former.

### Intentional Processes

One alternative is to view the processes that maintain a culture as intentional processes. Cultures can be thought of as being composed of symbols with meanings projected by individuals into their environments. In the present discussion, intentional processes involve conscious projections, be they deliberate or not. In this view, the processes that maintain an organization's culture are conscious, willful acts aimed at maintaining a shared set of meanings.

So, when you come in to work the next morning, why snap into character at first sight of the camera? You snap into character because Disneyland is about something. It is about creating an illusion, lending reality to a certain unreality, and keeping that illusion in place. You value that illusion. It is important to you. It gives meaning to the small part that you perform. Snapping into character at first sight of a camera is your way of actively reaffirming those values and actively projecting those meanings onto the situation. So long as others see you as Goofy, the performance is successful and the illusion is intact. Of course, if there is a supervisor accompanying that camera crew, the act may also be a spontaneous expression of "Hey, look, I am following the employee manual and I do not want to get fired" (Van Maanen, 1991). Either way, it is an intentional act.

There is something very compelling about this account. It tugs at our heartstrings. It affirms our importance by putting us at the center of the action. It makes us feel good. In fact, there is quite a lot in this picture that is of value. Nonetheless, viewing OC as reproduced by intentional processes has inescapable limitations.

Consider the various levels of organizational culture outlined by Schein (1991a, 1991b): artifacts, values, and assumptions. As a cultural artifact, the snap into character is well enough explained as an intentional act. There is nothing inherently implausible about understanding this act as the projection of meaning into the environment. The employee is socialized into the meaning by being trained to perform Goofy. Snapping into character is a way to project the meaning onto the Goofy symbol. The camera crew is out to film backstage Disney employees. By this one employee's intentional act, they are now filming Goofy.

Underlying the act is a value. In this case, perhaps it is the value of the performance, maintaining the illusion for the visitors. The intentional explanation is less immediate at this level of culture. The employee need not be intending the value at the time of performing the artifact that reflects that value. The collective culture may maintain the link between the artifact and the value in the absence of the specific intention by the actor. We have all experienced the automatic performance of an oft-repeated act. It is at least as likely that the employee's mind was occupied at that moment by the novel stimulus of a backstage camera crew as it is that the employee was upholding the familiar cultural value.

At this point, it is only fair to recognize objections that the intentional explanation is capable of meeting. For example, it is no objection at all to argue that all of the values constituting the culture cannot remain in the employee's conscious awareness simultaneously. The employee need only be conscious of the particular value he or she is projecting at the moment. For the same reason, there is no serious objection in the fact that the employee cannot remain conscious of the values at all times. Again, he or she need only be conscious of the particular value at the moment of the intentional act. Furthermore,

as indicated above, it may not even be necessary that the employee consciously intend the value so long as the value is linked to another consciously intended meaning.

It is more difficult to reconcile the intentional explanation with shared assumptions, the deepest level of OC. Assumptions are understood as underlying organization members' conscious understanding, but not being a conscious part of those understandings. Conscious beliefs become assumptions as they drop out of conscious awareness. Assumptions are taken for granted to the point of dropping out of awareness. At first glance, it is difficult to understand how intentional acts could be the mechanisms that maintain cultural assumptions. Like most explanations, however, this one deserves a second glance. So long as assumptions are understood to be outside of conscious awareness, it is clear enough that they cannot be maintained through a direct intentional projection of their meaning on the symbols that represent them. Nevertheless, it is possible that they are maintained indirectly. That is, the intentional acts that directly project meaning on artifacts, and possibly values, may indirectly reproduce and maintain unconscious assumptions. The assumptions can be understood as implied by the conscious acts. Anything not completely implied by the conscious acts, however, cannot be explained by them. The immediate difficulty with this explanation, then, is that in order for assumptions to be completely implied by the higher-level components of the culture, they would have to be redundant with them. Like the conclusion of a deductive argument, they can contain no new content. As such, this explanation renders assumptions superfluous to OC.

One might conclude that the notion of subconscious assumptions is therefore superfluous to OC (J. L. Michela, personal communication, October 2, 1998). It is nonetheless difficult to reconcile such a conclusion with Schein's (1991a) persuasive arguments that just such a substratum is required to explain OC's stabilizing influence on organizational behavior. A purely intentional approach is hard-pressed to explain such a substratum within OC. Tests of the next two assertions may aid in clarifying this issue.

- *Assertion 5:* In their own sensemaking, organization members will construct narratives that make reference to individuals' being unaware of the meanings of things they say or do.
- *Assertion 6:* Ethnography will uncover meanings within an organization that will not occur naturally in the narratives of organization members, but organization members will recognize and consent to descriptions of these meanings as part of their culture once they are brought into awareness by a relative outsider.

The difficulty that the intentional explanation finds with unconscious levels of OC suggests a turn to unconscious processes as mechanisms to maintain OC. If unconscious elements of OC cannot be accounted for in terms of conscious processes, it is natural to turn to unconscious processes, because the above criticisms will not apply to such processes.

## Unconscious Processes

We have two distinct bodies of research in which unconscious processes have been developed in some detail: cognitive science and psychodynamic theory. There is a great deal of evidence that individual cognitive processing involves a great deal of unconscious processing (for a particularly colorful discussion, see Hofstadter & Dennett, 1981). Although this has found little application to issues of OC, it is worth pausing to formulate why this is the case. Although unconscious aspects of OC are not conscious, as culture they are shared. We are looking for an explanation of how they might be reproduced, outside of conscious intentional acts. There is no reason to believe that the same conscious meanings need correspond to the same sorts of unconscious cognitive processing. Differ-

ent brains can share the same symbols (Hofstadter, 1979). As a result, the conscious symbols would seem to be the only link between the individual unconscious processing and the shared culture. As that link has been brought into question in the previous subsection, it is not at all clear how individual-level cognitive processing could provide the sort of explanation we seek.

Psychodynamic processes, on the other hand, may come closer to offering a link between unconscious processes and the reproduction of OC.[1] Psychodynamic processes involve overt behavior, which provides a link to interaction between organization members and therefore to what is shared between them. My concern here will be limited to the application of psychodynamic theory to OC, something that is not representative of psychodynamic theory in general. For example, Schein (1991b) discusses the role of anxiety in the production of OC. The idea is that organization members are faced with similar sources of anxiety, and that shared cultural assumptions may arise as means of controlling that anxiety. A psychodynamic approach, then, would allow us to explain the maintenance of cultural assumptions outside of conscious awareness in terms of psychodynamic processes directed unconsciously at reducing shared sources of anxiety.

Establishing the particular anxieties and assumptions involved in the case of Goofy snapping into character would involve intensive ethnographic study and is most likely impossible after the fact. In the present context, however, we are concerned only with seeing that an explanation is possible, and not that it is necessarily true. In this spirit, some general conclusions can be drawn from some admittedly arbitrary speculation about Goofy.

For all we know, the employee portraying Goofy may have been a young college student with no economic anxieties who was simply working a summer job to earn a little extra spending money. Let us, regardless, suppose that the maintenance of personal income is a common source of anxiety, that the success of the theme park is seen as the means of avoiding financial difficulty, and that the success of the performance provides an object on which these anxieties are unconsciously condensed. The employee snaps into character at first sight of the camera because the presence of the camera crew threatens the success of the performance by undoing the illusion. This in turn threatens the control on the economic anxiety. Goofy wakes up with yesterday's culture because he also wakes up with yesterday's anxieties. The culture is reproduced through the artifact of the performance maintained through the psychodynamic process of collective anxiety management. The shared assumption is maintained because it serves to reduce the shared anxiety.

Without putting too fine a point on the matter, I see no grounds to deny the possibility of such an explanation. In fact, there would seem to be much to recommend Schein's general approach. It accomplishes everything that the intentional explanation accomplishes while also meeting the difficulties that the intentional explanation cannot. Local skepticism regarding the specific example may be well-founded, but it does not question the global possibility of some such explanation. The reader is free to substitute another set of specifics. A fully developed analysis would be considerably more complex and detailed.

The more interesting criticisms stem not from questioning the explanations that the psychodynamic approach offers, but from looking for the explanations that it does not offer. For example, Schein (1991a) assumes that all unconscious aspects of organizational culture were at one time conscious. Unconscious meanings are the same sort of thing as are conscious meanings. This leads us to ask if there might be meanings in a culture that were never conscious or that become conscious after originating as unconscious meanings.

The criticism that I want to develop here is that the psychodynamic approach adopts from the intentional approach a conception of meaning derived from conscious meanings and then constructs its conception of unconscious meaning in kind. Unconscious meanings are understood as meanings like conscious meanings that have fallen beneath conscious awareness. Because of this link between meaning and intention, the psychodynamic approach cannot account for meanings that are not intentional. At this point our familiar theoretical lexicon begins to fail us, so clarity favors a pause to distinguish the phenomenon under discussion from others that may be described with misleadingly similar language. Psychodynamic theory should have no difficulty in dealing with subconscious neural processing, the sorts of unintended meanings popularly referred to as Freudian slips, or even the notion that conscious meanings may have unexpected consequences that surprise us due to our limited processing capacity. Rather, the phenomenon that raises difficulties for the psychodynamic approach is a meaning that can be identified in an OC but that cannot be understood as projected into the environment by either a conscious or an unconscious mind.

Intentional meanings require a presence to mind, be it conscious or unconscious, but cultures are full of meanings that constitute an absence from mind. The reason for this is that we form meanings by distinguishing one from another—in exactly the way that I am now distinguishing intentional meanings from nonintentional meanings. Things thus assimilated will always have some differences, and things thus distinguished will always share some similarities. These differences and similarities are hidden in order that other similarities and differences may be revealed. These hidden qualities, or rather the very hiding of them, constitute nonintentional meanings—meanings that cannot be consciously or unconsciously projected by a mind because they constitute a necessary absence from mind.

A plausible hypothetical example will suffice to establish that this is a sensible criticism to make of the psychodynamic approach to dynamic cultural processes. On that cue, let us return to the task of explaining what it is that keeps Goofy ready to snap into character. The intentional approach allows us to understand the performance of the Goofy character as an intentional projection of the meaning of the Goofy symbol. The psychodynamic approach allows us to understand the continued projection of this meaning as satisfying a need, such as anxiety reduction, that may not be the consciously espoused reason for using the symbol. An exploration of the limits of the psychodynamic approach begins with an inspection of the pattern of distinctions in which this symbol is embedded.

Goofy snapping into character at the sight of a backstage camera crew is situated within several symbolic distinctions. The portrayal of Goofy requires that the actor be in character as opposed to out of character. The snapping into character occurs at the point at which the previously invisible camera crew becomes visible. The event occurs offstage as opposed to onstage. The members of the camera crew are characterized as guests, as opposed to Disney employees, or hosts. These and many other distinctions combine to form a symbolic matrix within which the Disney culture can be either performed or flouted. The material of this example is rich in potential, but it is enough to notice only a small portion of the hidden content of this matrix.

After snapping into character, the actor offers only a wave and continues down the corridor rather than stopping to greet the guests or pose with them for a picture. That is, Goofy continues to pursue the actor's objective of traversing the corridor, something that seems out of character for Goofy, but can be out of character only so long as we regard the actor as in character as Goofy. The sight of the guests transforms the heretofore backstage corridor into an offstage stage. It is simultaneously both onstage and offstage. The camera crew's guide is a Disney host, but the actor portraying Goofy must act toward the guide as Goofy, thereby treating the guide as a guest. A host to a guest becomes a hosting guest. To the guide, the actor remains an actor, the actor in character rather than out, but

still an employee to be evaluated as in or out of character. So to the guide the actor remains out of character—that is, the actor remains the actor—by stepping into the Goofy character. Furthermore, in the eyes of the guide, to be in the Goofy character is within the actor's character. Each of these knots in the symbolic fabric must remain unthought in order for us to think the seemingly simple thought that Goofy snaps into character at the sight of the camera crew in the backstage corridor. To address such phenomena, we need an approach that separates meaning from intention. Explanations in terms of discursive processes provide such an approach. Where both intentional and psychodynamic approaches fall short, a discursive approach allows us to press forward.

- *Assertion 7:* For any distinction between categories practiced within a culture, it is possible to identify similarities between the things thus distinguished and differences between the things thus assimilated into a common category (although not necessarily by means that would be accepted within the culture). Otherwise put, any distinction between Xs and Ys suppresses similarities between Xs and Ys as well as differences among Xs and among Ys.
- *Assertion 8:* Organization members will judge a person who makes an utterance consistent with the distinctions between categories practiced within the culture to present a better fit to the organization than an otherwise identical person who makes an utterance inconsistent with these distinctions.

## Discursive Processes

In the previous sections, I described intentional processes as involving the conscious projection of meanings and unconscious processes as projecting meanings without accompanying conscious awareness. Discursive processes differ from these in that the individual person or individual mind is not taken as the source of meaning. Instead, people are understood as agents produced by the discursive practices within which they interact. As such, discursive processes are processes that take place within a set of practices available to exchangeable participants.

A discursive explanation of the processes that reproduce OC begins with the separation of meaning from intention. It is not enough to separate meaning from the conscious projection of meaning, for as much is accomplished by the turn to unconscious processes. Rather, the discursive view wrests meaning free of its long-standing association with any individual's mental contents—be they conscious or otherwise. The hackneyed example, made all the more valuable through its familiarity, is to ask how it is that you might know that others mean the same as you by the term *red* (Locke, 1690/1997). You cannot get inside someone else's head to see what that person sees when looking at an object that you see as red. Likewise, you cannot invite that person into your head to show him or her what you see. All that you have to work with is a certain level of correspondence between what you call red and what the other person calls red, and perhaps a certain correspondence between your agreement that something is red and certain physical characteristics of the object in question. This typically leads one to conclude that (a) the meaning of *red* cannot be fixed to a particular conscious experience, and (b) the meaning of *red* lies in the regularities of its use (Wittgenstein, 1958).

In separating the meaning of *red* from the conscious experience of redness, it is important that we not go too far in the other direction. If we simply define *red* as what people call red, then we find ourselves in the embarrassing position of being unable to explain how it is that someone could mistakenly call something red (Dummett, 1978). Rather, we have to remain cognizant of the full complexity of the context of utterances about redness, including their capacity for error, duplicity, and playfulness (Derrida, 1988).

All of this sounds well and fine in the abstract, but once again it is time to reel in the abstractions by applying them to our example. To make this application, we have to take one more step into the discursive perspective. This perspective does not entail that people do not intend meanings when they use symbols (Hatfield & Mills, this volume). Instead, it recognizes that people do have intentions but seeks to explain these as dependent upon the systems of symbol use in which they are embedded. Our internal and external use of symbols rests upon the broader history of symbol use in the contexts in which we use them and among those with whom we share those contexts. Symbol use is symbol repetition wherein the very act of repetition refers back to previous repetitions and thereby confers new meaning (Derrida, 1988). Repeated symbol use never simply repeats because it always adds a repetition.

Explained in terms of conscious or unconscious processes, culture is something that the employee takes home in his or her head and brings back to work the next morning. In the discursive view, the culture resides in the workplace. Specifically, it resides in the context of symbol use and the concrete history of specific uses of specific symbols in that context. This is not to say that all share equally in the organization's symbolic resources (Bourdieu, 1991). It is only to say that in interpreting others' use of symbols, and in formulating our own, we refer back to the concrete history of use that surrounds us—what Foucault (1969 & 1971/1972) terms an archive and Bourdieu (1972/1977) a habitus. To the extent that we bring culture home with us, it is only in the form of our knowledge of that culture. It is only our internal cognitive map of the organization's patterns of symbol use (Sackmann, 1991), a map that will become dated if kept apart from the culture it maps.

In snapping into character, the employee repeats a familiar gesture. The context of use structures the meaning of the gesture and helps guide both the employee's understanding of it and others' understanding as well. To see this, transport the scene out of the backstage passage at Disneyland and into, say, a London subway tube. The lumbering Goofy gait adopted by the employee would not carry the same significance in that context. The contrast between being in character and out of character would be greatly diminished. Likewise, alternative reactions to the camera crew ("Hi, Mom!") would be interpreted with reference to the context of their prior use.

In the discursive view, then, the processes that reproduce an OC are the very processes that sustain symbol use. They are the references to the history of symbol use within the organization that are involved in every new use of a symbol. The artifacts, values, and unconscious assumptions are meanings that exist in the collective history of symbol use and are only reflected in conscious intentions or unconscious mental processes.

- *Assertion 9:* Organization members will construct narratives that make reference to symbols changing meaning in light of new information or changes in context.
- *Assertion 10:* Participants in an experiment given radically different interpretations of the same formal symbols and formal rules for manipulating the symbols can nonetheless engage in shared symbol manipulation activities.
- *Assertion 11:* Participants in such an experiment (Assertion 10) will rate their interlocutor's understanding of the symbols that they use in proportion with the degree to which their formal rules coincide if communication is limited to symbol manipulation.
- *Assertion 12:* Participants (Assertion 11) will not rate their interlocutor's understanding of the symbols in proportion to the degree to which their interpretations of those rules coincide.

*Reproduction of OC*

The order in which I have presented the three perspectives should be enough to indicate the importance that I place on the discursive view. Nonetheless, I would not want to leave the impression that the intentional view or the psychodynamic view is simply to be cast aside. To the contrary, all three perspectives have valuable roles to play in our understanding of the reproduction of organizational culture. Explanations of the ongoing reproduction of a culture within an organization can draw on intentional, psychodynamic, and discursive processes. Some combination of all three is most likely required to produce a complete explanation of the processes that maintain organizational cultures. Before concluding, I turn to a forceful criticism of the discursive approach to organization.

## A STRUCTURALIST CRITIQUE OF DISCOURSE ANALYSIS

Reed (1998) provides an articulate critique of a discursive approach to organization. The reader should consult Reed's chapter to appreciate his argument fully, because I cannot do it justice with these few comments. Reed argues that organization is an interplay between agency and structure. He then asserts that a discursive approach to organization cannot account for this interplay because it (a) replaces agency with discursively organized action, (b) replaces macro-level structure with micro-level discourse, (c) posits discourse as inherently ambiguous and undecidable, and therefore (d) cannot account for enduring organization or patterns of control.

Reed gives no attention to the well-known criticisms of the traditional structuralist approach that he advocates (e.g., Derrida, 1978; Hardy et al., 1998). Long ago, Plato (1974/375 BC) warned us against collecting conflicting arguments for and against a proposition under consideration. By ignoring Plato's advice, Reed is able to conclude his criticism with a triumphant flourish, but the reader cannot help feeling dissatisfied with having been left the task of weighing and balancing the competing arguments.

Reed's (1998) criticism is well-founded if narrowly applied to one prevalent but uninteresting interpretation of Foucauldian analysis. The effectiveness of the criticism, however, depends upon one crucial "assumption that the production and reproduction of discursive formations, as systems of thought which inform material practices, has a logic of its own *independent* of the social action through which it is made possible" (p. 209). There are two fundamental problems with this assumption that we will do well to avoid.

The first problem involves the pivotal notion of independence. It is not asking much merely to distinguish between the discursive practices within which individual action occurs and the individual action itself. It is going a few steps further to argue that there is some wiggle room between these two things. It is going a great deal further to suggest that individual action has no impact whatsoever on discursive practices. Nonetheless, it is this last notion of independence upon which the criticism depends. We readily avoid the criticism in recognizing that individual actions within a set of discursive practices also reproduce and modify those practices (Bourdieu, 1972/1977).

The second problem with the assumption is the claim that discourses are "systems of thought" that "inform material practices" (p. 209). Any dualism that opposes thought to material practices has no place in a serious attempt to understand either Foucault or discourse analysis (Foucault, 1963/1975; Hardy et al., 1998; Markus, 1998a; see also Helms Mills & Mills, Chapter 3, this volume). Reed himself is careful to develop this point earlier in his chapter, but lapses back into Cartesian dualism in formulating the crucial premise of his critique. Discourse is as material as the ink on this page and is as much a part of our world as are brick walls and marble staircases. Language cannot provide a neutral position from which to observe the world from without (Derrida, 1978; Markus, 1998b). As soon as an organization's discourse begins to seep into our talk about the organization, we begin to enter the organization. Organizational research is part

of the flux, and we should not allow ourselves to be seduced by structuralism's false promises of a fixed structure outside of the flux.

There is no difficulty in discussing the interplay between "agency" and "structure" from a discursive perspective. The problem lies in attempting to discuss agency and structure without recognizing the manner in which they are constituted through discursive practices. Treating our talk about agency and structure as if it were an ideal medium of thought that does not contribute to the manner in which "agency" and "structure" are socially constructed opens the way to all the traditional criticisms of structuralism.

## CONCLUSION

Our field has traditionally assumed stability and sought to explain culture change. Nonetheless, there is something to be gained by assuming change and seeking to explain stability. This advantage does not invalidate the knowledge provided by the former strategy, it simply seeks to press it further. Cultural dynamics emerge in a new light when we put them to use in explaining the persistence of cultures. In retrospect, explaining stability was a primary task for which OC was introduced into organization theory. Simply giving stability the name of culture does not suffice to explain it. Exploring the dynamic cultural processes behind the day-to-day reproduction of OC offers an explanation of stability in organizations.

The testable assertions that I have offered in the course of this chapter suggest means by which my argument can be tested. These are not merely rhetorical. By reversing stability and change as figure and ground, I hope to stimulate further research in the directions indicated by the assertions. Ultimately, however, I would like to see the field go beyond simply reversing the roles of stability and change. The reversal can serve as an intermediary step toward the collapse of the distinction altogether. If we come to think of stability as being achieved through dynamic processes of change, then we come to think of stability as a type of change. At that point the distinction between stability and change ceases to be useful as an analytic tool, allowing cultural dynamics to reach their full potential in organization theory.

In the space of these few pages I cannot pretend to have offered a comprehensive analysis. As readers, you will have already begun critically evaluating my arguments. Some of you may find the arguments persuasive, and others may not. Either way, if you have been engaged in the conversation, then I have achieved my goal.

## NOTE

1. I owe a debt of gratitude to Koji Takahashi for helping this dyed-in-the-wool discursive psychologist come to appreciate the value of a psychodynamic approach to understanding organizational behavior.

# 19

# Measuring Cultural Fit in Mergers and Acquisitions

— *Yaakov Weber*

Clashes between the cultures of the combining organizations in mergers and acquisitions (M&As) have received growing attention from both practitioners and academics in recent years (e.g., Ashkanasy & Holmes, 1995; Cartwright & Cooper, 1993a, 1993b; Davis, 1968; Lubatkin, Schweiger, & Weber, 1999; Marks, 1994; Nahavandi & Malekzadeh, 1988; Porter, 1985; Shrivastava, 1986; Weber, Ganzah, & Ben-Yemini, 1995; Weber & Pliskin, 1996; Weber, Shenkar, & Raveh, 1996). It has been suggested that such culture clashes have major implications for stress, attitudes, behavior, and turnover, especially for the managers and employees of acquired companies in both domestic and international M&As. Furthermore, culture clashes influence the effectiveness of the postmerger integration process, the integration of infor-

mation systems, and the financial performance and shareholder value of acquiring companies.

Although cultural fit has been acknowledged to be a potentially important factor in M&As failures, empirical studies that investigate the role of cultural fit in M&As remain a rarity. Moreover, relatively little has been done in terms of specification and operationalization of culture fit measures. As Cartwright and Cooper (1993b) suggest, "Culture fit and culture compatibility are well-used but ill-defined expressions" (p. 60).

The literature on culture clashes in M&As to date has three major limitations. First, most of it is based on observations by practitioners and consultants, with little theoretical or empirical support (e.g., Barrett, 1973; Davis, 1968; Gill & Foulder, 1978; Levinson, 1970; Pritchett, 1985; Searby, 1969; Sinetar,

1981). Second, the few empirical studies that have been conducted have each investigated the cultural clash in only one merger or acquisition (e.g., Blumberg & Wiener, 1971; Buono, Bowditch, & Lewis, 1985; Graves, 1981; Greenwood, Hinings, & Brown, 1994; Sales & Mirvis, 1984; Schweiger & DeNisi, 1991; Shirley, 1973, 1977; Weber et al., 1995). Third, although M&As differ with respect to such factors as relatedness and type of industry (e.g., Lubatkin, 1983; Nahavandi & Malekzadeh, 1988; Shrivastava, 1986; Weber, Lubatkin, & Schweiger, 1994), most studies have been conducted under the assumption that M&As are homogeneous and so have failed to consider the possibility that the impacts of culture clash on organizational effectiveness might vary from one situation to another.

The extant literature does not provide systematic empirical evidence on (a) why and how cultural differences may cause integration problems in M&As, (b) what factors are important for the integration of top management teams (TMTs) in M&As that may be affected by cultural differences, or (c) how any possible relationships between cultural differences and other factors, such as cultural tolerance, affect the behavior of the acquired TMT. Such evidence might be lacking because of the difficulty of gaining access to study M&As (e.g., Greenwood et al., 1994) and the unavailability of an instrument for measuring culture and cultural differences in M&As.

My goal in this chapter is to fill some of these gaps. Specifically, my aim is to describe an instrument for measuring culture in general and cultural differences in M&As in particular. In the next section, I review the literature on the role of culture and cultural differences in M&As. I then identify the important cultural dimensions and describe a study in which a culture scale tailored for top management teams in M&As was developed. Finally, I present the results of the study and discuss future research opportunities.

## CONTACT BETWEEN TWO CULTURES IN M&As

A merger or acquisition involves the combination of two or more organizations. This results in contact between two distinct top management cultures (e.g., Perry, 1986; Sales & Mirvis, 1984). Culture has been defined as "the set of important assumptions (often unstated) that members of a community share in common" (Sathe, 1985a). Every group, top management team or otherwise, has a unique culture that is shaped by its members' shared history and experiences (Schein, 1985). The contact between two top management teams may lead to cultural changes that are usually drastic for the managers of the acquired firm, who are often expected to adapt to the culture of the acquiring firm (e.g., Jemison & Sitkin, 1986; Marks, 1994; Sales & Mirvis, 1984).

In spite of the lack of empirical evidence from large samples on the effects of cultural differences in M&As, the reports from many separate cases can help provide a clearer picture. According to those reports, cultural differences between the parties have produced misunderstandings, fueled emotional reactions, and escalated conflicts. Such conflicts and the related negative attitudes of key top managers of the acquired organization toward the merger and the acquiring top management may be major obstacles to the successful integration of the two firms (Weber & Schweiger, 1992). In a survey of European CEOs, "the ability to integrate the company was ranked as the most important factor in acquisition success, ahead of financial and strategic factors" (Booz, Allen, & Hamilton, as quoted in Cartwright & Cooper, 1993b). The key to managing the integration process is "obtaining the participation of the people and creating an atmosphere that can support [capability transfer] is the real challenge" (Haspeslagh & Jemison, 1991, pp. 106-107).

Cultural differences appear to be a critical factor in creating such an atmosphere and obtaining people's participation. Thus the degree of cultural differences between the two organizations may determine the effectiveness of the integration process and eventually the financial performance of the merger.

## Unit of Analysis

This chapter focuses on top management teams as a unit of analysis for five reasons. First, many organizations select their TMTs from the ranks of individuals who appear to best represent the value system of the majority. As such, a TMT's subculture may be a reasonable manifestation of the organization's culture. Second, senior managers play the most significant role in shaping and transmitting corporate culture signals to the broader membership (Schein, 1985). The beliefs and values of these managers are expected to permeate and influence other levels of the organization. Third, some researchers have argued that cultural differences at the top management level are most likely to influence merging organizations' ability to realize the potential synergy of the merger (Davis, 1968; Kitching, 1967; Sales & Mirvis, 1984). The importance of TMT culture is also evidenced by a number of recent studies conducted in a nonmerger context that have found significant relationships between the cultures of TMTs and their firms' financial performance (Covin & Slevin, 1988; Denison, 1990). Fourth, in order to study the effects of cultural differences, one must be able to look at contact between the members of the two cultures. The likelihood of such contact in mergers, in terms of amount and intensity, is greatest at the top management level (Weber & Schweiger, 1992). This is because top managers of the merging firms are in frequent contact throughout the negotiation and transitional stages, whereas middle and lower managers may not have contact with their counterparts in the other organization until later in the transitional stage, if at all. Finally, top managers are involved in and have a wide knowledge of major integration efforts and effectiveness of the integration process.

## Cultural Differences, Performances, and Turnover

The differences in organizational cultures that may have important impacts on the financial success of a merger may also have impacts on the value of the acquiring firm's common equity. It may be instructive to note that the predicted relationship between perceptions of cultural differences and shareholder value is based on a central tenet of financial economics: that the capital asset market is efficient. That is, security prices reflect all publicly available information (Fama, 1976). Accordingly, any change in the value of an acquiring firm's common equity due to merging is brought about by a change in the market's estimate of the firm's future financial performance.

Of course, some may argue that the capital asset market does not concern itself with possible cultural problems in mergers, but instead considers only issues of strategic fit when estimating the financial impact. However, with the continual flow of anecdotal evidence from the business world and the popular business press about the adverse effects of "cultural collisions," it is difficult to believe that the capital asset market does not also factor in the human side of a merger. Clearly, the costs of cultural differences are difficult to quantify a priori, and the capital market may not be omniscient enough to predict actual earnings with complete accuracy. However, the market, on average, uses all information available when setting a price to a firm's security (Fama, 1976), and those investors in the market who are familiar with the top management teams of the combining firms are at least able to form opinions about consolidation costs. To do otherwise would be to overestimate systematically the value of a merger. There is no theoretical or empirical evidence to suggest that the capital market follows this or any other observable and inefficient trading pattern.

Many M&As are characterized by high levels of top management turnover (Gill & Foulder, 1978; Hambrick & Cannella, 1993; Levinson, 1970; Marks, 1994; Pritchett, 1985; Walsh, 1988b, 1989). Recent empirical investigations, however, have not been able to explain acquired TMT turnover effectively through examination of either the degree of relatedness between merging firms (Walsh, 1988b) or the nature of the negotiation process (Walsh, 1989). Nor could Walsh and Ellwood (1991) explain turnover by relating it to the target company's reacquisition performance—that is, through the replacement of an acquired incompetent TMT. Weber and Schweiger (1992) suggest that cultural differences may be positively related to acquired TMT turnover. Furthermore, they suggest that culture clash may be negatively related to acquired TMT commitment. Previous studies in the field of organizational behavior have found that low levels of commitment are associated with high rates of turnover (Mathieu & Zajac, 1990; Porter, Steers, Mowday, & Boulian, 1974).

Nahavandi and Malekzadeh (1988) suggest that cultural differences will be less of a problem when the buying firm "values cultural diversity and is willing to tolerate and encourage it" (p. 83). Conversely, a buying firm that does not tolerate an acquired firm's culture may use a variety of control mechanisms to establish its own culture in the acquired firm, thereby raising the potential for conflict between the two top management teams (Walter, 1985). Put another way, the more the buyer tolerates multiculturalism, the less likely the buyer is to expect the acquired firm to conform to its own goals, strategies, and administrative practices.

The foregoing discussion suggests that the predicted relationships between cultural fit and financial performance and turnover are likely to be moderated by the degree of cultural tolerance. However, it is not clear whether cultural tolerance (a) is independently related to shareholder value and turnover, (b) moderates the relationship between cultural fit and value and turnover, or (c) represents some combination of the two. Regarding possible independent effects, firms can expect to differ according to their cultural tolerance, and some firms may be able to minimize the adverse impacts of cultural differences between the two organizations. To the extent that capital market investors hold opinions about this information, they will factor it in along with other points of information when estimating the value of a merger. Regarding possible moderating influences, it is also likely that, in addition to the two independent effects, investors may consider cultural fit in light of cultural tolerance. Accordingly, there may be a greater probability of value creation when cultural difference is low and cultural tolerance is high.

## Cultural Differences, Tension, and Attitudes

Scholars of organizational conflict regard conflict as a process that includes antecedent conditions, affective states (e.g., tension, stress), negative attitudes on the part of one group toward the other, and conflictual behavior that ranges from passive resistance to overt aggression (Katz & Kahn, 1978; Thomas, 1976). In this subsection, I discuss cultural differences as the antecedents of these affective states and negative attitudes.

Prior to a merger or an acquisition, each firm's TMT usually achieves some degree of equilibrium in understanding its external and internal environment. Over time, and with shared experience among members, each TMT assimilates beliefs and values that greatly influence its decision making (Donaldson & Lorsch, 1983; Shrivastava, 1986; Wilkins & Ouchi, 1983). In M&As, when one TMT culture is exposed to another, as happens in the process of acculturation, the state of equilibrium is disturbed, possibly leading to communication problems between the cultures (Mirvis, 1985; Sales & Mirvis, 1984). The shared beliefs and values that are unique to each TMT culture and that originally functioned to facilitate communication among a team's members (Sathe, 1985a; Wilkins & Ouchi, 1983) become sources of communication problems between members of different TMTs.

These communication problems can lead to ill feelings and to polarization and ethnocentrism (Blake & Mouton, 1985; Sales & Mirvis, 1984), which in turn may "increase the tendency for misunderstanding and conflicts" (Gregory, 1983, pp. 359-360). For example, in studying the contact between the two top management groups following what is known as a "white knight" acquisition of a small manufacturing firm by a multibillion-dollar conglomerate, Sales and Mirvis (1984) found that the cultural differences between the parties produced misunderstandings, fueled emotional reactions, and escalated conflicts.

The conflict that results from cultural differences in M&As is characterized by the following:

1. Tension, distrust, and annoyance on the part of the acquired TMT in working with the acquiring TMT (e.g., Buono et al., 1985; Ivancevich, Schweiger, & Power, 1987; Schweiger & DeNisi, 1991; Sinetar, 1981)
2. Negative attitudes on the part of the acquired TMT toward both the acquiring organization and its TMT in general (e.g., Blake & Mouton, 1985; Buono et al., 1985; Perry, 1986; Sales & Mirvis, 1984)
3. Negative attitudes on the part of the acquired TMT toward cooperating with the acquiring TMT in particular (e.g., Blake & Mouton, 1985; Sales & Mirvis, 1984)

## Commitment and Cooperation of the Acquired TMT

The success or failure of a merger or acquisition depends not only on how much synergy is potentially available from the combination but, more important, on whether the synergy can actually be realized through effective integration (Porter, 1985; Schweiger & Csiszar, in press). Realizing synergies in M&As can be an arduous and difficult task, and its success depends to a large extent on the commitment and cooperation of the acquired TMT (Barrett, 1973; Mace & Montgomery, 1962; Porter, 1985; Shrivastava, 1986).

Commitment may be defined as the willingness to exert on behalf of the organization and the desire to maintain membership in it (Porter et al., 1974; Steers, 1977). Level of commitment is affected by the acquired TMT's attitude toward the new organization (Buchanan, 1974; Steers, 1977) and its level of tension (Argyris, 1970). Therefore, tension and negative attitudes of the acquired TMT toward the new organization will lower the acquired TMT's commitment to the success of the merger.

Cooperative behavior, according to Fishbein's theory (Ajzen & Fishbein, 1973; Fishbein & Ajzen, 1975), is influenced by two sets of attitudes: attitudes toward an action and attitudes toward an object. With regard to the first, noncooperative behavior in M&As may result in top managers' negative attitudes toward the act of cooperating with the acquiring TMT (e.g., Blake & Mouton, 1985; Perry, 1986; Pritchett, 1985). With regard to the second, attitudes toward an object can also be good predictors of behavior associated with that object (Rokeach & Kliejunas, 1972; Wicker, 1969, 1971). In M&As, a negative attitude toward the new organization (the object) can lead to noncooperative behavior on the part of the acquired TMT (e.g., Blake & Mouton, 1985; Perry, 1986).

## Cultural Differences and Intended Integration

As discussed earlier, the degree of contact (intensity and frequency) between cultures may moderate the relationship between the degrees of cultural differences and conflict. More specifically, it suggests that the more members of two cultures come into contact and/or the more contacts they have per a given period of time, the greater the ability of the dominant culture to expose the weaker one to its own features or to impose those features on the other party, and the greater the subsequent potential for conflict. In this subsection, I contend that in M&As the degree of contact between the acquired and the acquiring TMT cultures and the extent to which the weaker culture is dominated by the stronger are determined by the intended level of integration of the two TMTs.

Merging firms achieve synergy by integrating similar departments and functions, such as marketing, inventory, and production. To achieve integration, the acquiring TMT typically intervenes in the decision-making processes of the acquired TMT and imposes standards, rules, and expectations (e.g., Cray, 1984; Goehle, 1980; Vancil, 1979).

M&As vary in their intended level of integration. The higher the intended integration, the more effort the acquiring firm must make to control and coordinate decisions and activities, not only by determining goals for the acquired company, but by generating alternative solutions to strategic problems and making crucial choices. The intended level of integration influences the emotions and attitudes that affect acquired top managers' commitment to and cooperation with the acquiring TMT. This can be expected to happen in two ways. One is through a main effect that could occur even where the beliefs of two TMTs are relatively similar. To many top executives who had previously managed independent operations, superimposed authority following an acquisition or merger is bound to be objectionable. The loss of autonomy through the intervention of the acquiring TMT in the acquired TMT's decision making can be expected to evoke tension and negative attitudes toward the merger (Blake & Mouton, 1985; Levinson, 1970; Marks, 1982; Mirvis, 1985; Perry, 1986; Schweiger, Ivancevich, & Power, 1987).

In addition to its main effect, the intended level of integration may have an interaction effect with belief differences. The integration of two firms requires contact (not necessarily physical) in the decision-making process between the two TMTs (Nahavandi & Malekzadeh, 1988). This contact may elicit conflict because it exposes the belief systems of the two teams to each other and makes the differences salient (Weber, 1988). Furthermore, at higher levels of integration, the acquiring firm imposes more of its beliefs on the acquired TMT (Walter, 1985). This imposition may also contribute to the salience of any belief differences and to the TMT's ability to deal with conflict and tension, and hence may lessen commitment and cooperation (Weber, 1988).

The interaction effect can also be explained by Haspeslagh and Jemison's (1991) presentation of different types of integration approaches, as determined by the needs of the companies for strategic interdependence (low and high) and organizational autonomy. The effects of cultural differences will vary in M&As of different types. The impacts will be felt most strongly in absorption (high interdependence, low autonomy), in which integration brings consolidation of the two cultures. It will be felt least in "preservation types," in which "the source of the acquired [company] benefits [remain] intact" (p. 148).

## Cultural Differences and Nature of Contact

The nature of contact—that is, whether it is friendly or hostile—is determined by the extent to which top management has free choice (prior to the merger or acquisition) in having the other company as a partner. The mergers and acquisitions literature recognizes that whether an acquisition is friendly or hostile may influence the amount of conflict between acquiring and acquired executives (e.g., Mirvis, 1985; Nahavandi & Malekzadeh, 1988; Perry, 1986; Pritchett, 1985; Sales & Mirvis, 1984; Weber, 1988). For example, Mirvis (1985), in his model of premerger negotiations, suggests that the friendliness of the negotiations affects the motivation, commitment, and cooperation of the acquired top management team after the merger or acquisition is effected. Unfriendly takeovers "are likely to promote more conflict than voluntary mergers or acquisitions as the unfriendliness of the purchase poses an immediate threat and presages a battlefield mentality" (p. 81).

Although cultural differences are a source of conflict even in friendly M&As, their effects are likely to be much worse in unfriendly takeovers. An unfriendly takeover is likely to provoke resistance on the part of the acquired TMT to the dominant firm's culture, especially if the two are very different, and the concomitant hostility may prevent friendly exploration of cultural similarities and resolution of cultural differences (e.g., Blake & Mouton, 1985; Sales & Mirvis, 1984), which may further undermine integration in M&As.

## Other Influences

*Industry effect.* The industry context in which M&As take place may also influence the roles and effects of cultural differences, autonomy removal, and commitment on the success of the integration process and a firm's performance. Culture is often thought of as a social control system (O'Reilly, 1989). Unlike formal control systems that typically assess outcomes or behaviors in relatively highly predictable situations, social control systems are more useful when the activities to be controlled are nonroutine and unpredictable, and exist in settings that require initia-

tive and flexibility. Consequently, manufacturing is conducive to formal control systems because processes and products are more tractable. In contrast, service sector firms rely more heavily on social control mechanisms to direct members' actions (Pablo, 1994) because of the high frequency of off-site work, multiple engagements, and the high proportion of professional staff members (Margnet, 1993). The shared beliefs and assumptions that constitute a social control system are internalized and can be especially helpful in the service sector because they can be applied to produce a broad range of appropriate behavioral responses that are difficult for managers to anticipate or formalize in highly uncertain, and largely uncontrollable, situations.

Hence cultural differences in the service sector may be more critical to the effectiveness of the integration process. For the acquiring top management in the service sector, the control of any deviation from original intention will be very difficult. This is because the new management cannot use its accustomed social control system, due to differences in culture and lack of shared beliefs and assumptions with the acquired top managers. This can generate conflict, and, as noted earlier, higher conflict may be associated with more intense effects of autonomy removal due to low cultural tolerance in the service sector compared to that in manufacturing firms.

*Relative size.* The size of the acquired firm relative to its buyer may influence the attitudes, motivation, and turnover of top managers (Kitching, 1967; Walsh, 1989). The acquired top managers in a relatively small firm may feel unimportant, and their human needs may be overlooked or trivialized by the buyer. Alienation may breed discontent, which can prevent a merger from realizing its financial potential.

*Merger type.* Walsh (1989) has found that merger type (related or unrelated) explains turnover. Merger type might influence performance of the combination, because mergers have a greater potential for synergy due to similar departments and functions. However, Nahavandi and Malekzadeh (1988) have pointed out that the strategy underlying a merger determines the extent to which the cultures of two firms come into contact. In related mergers, contact between the members of the two cultures is usually higher than in unrelated mergers and elicits conflict. As I will explain below, the sample for the study described in this chapter was constructed to be relatively homogeneous in terms of merger type. Each merger in our sample, therefore, involved firms that were tangibly "related."

## EMPIRICAL STUDIES: CULTURAL DIMENSIONS

In this section I describe an empirical study based on a questionnaire survey of TMTs. Because of the subjective and perceptual nature of culture, there may be an infinite variety of cultural dimensions. Starting with the work of Kurt Lewin, however, laboratory research and industrial studies have isolated several important dimensions of culture. Although there is no general agreement on what the most important dimensions are (e.g., Trice & Beyer, 1993; see also Ashkanasy, Broadfoot, & Falkus, Chapter 8, this volume), an effort has been made to include those most relevant to this study based on the literature dealing with both mergers and acquisitions and top management culture. Thus the dimensions and items in the questionnaire were derived from measures of culture used successfully in other studies with high levels of reliability and validity. Nevertheless, the identification of specific items and dimensions for this study was based on the need to have a measurement tool that can capture specific characteristics of culture at the strategic level of top management in the context of M&As. For example, Gordon and Cummins's (1979) questionnaire does not in-

clude a dimension that captures the risk-taking philosophy that is an important characteristic of top management culture (e.g., Deal & Kennedy, 1982; Donaldson & Lorsch, 1983). The questionnaire used in the study described below includes the following seven dimensions (for a more complete description and development of these dimensions, see Lubatkin et al., 1999; Weber, 1996; Weber et al., 1996):

1. *Innovation and action orientation:* Top managers who are action oriented value and encourage innovation and rapid response to changes and competitive developments in their environments.
2. *Risk taking:* The propensity to take risks affects many important decisions, such as investment in new ventures, purchase of manufacturing equipment, proportion of the research budget directed to new areas of business, and even the handling of employee pension funds.
3. *Integration—lateral interdependence:* Top management teams differ in regard to their beliefs about the importance of cooperation and communication between various organizational subunits in achieving overall organizational goals.
4. *Top management contact:* This dimension relates to the beliefs of top management in regard to whether subordinates should receive managerial support, warmth, and consideration. This dimension also relates to top managers' beliefs about other individuals and about human nature, such as Theory X and Theory Y, which lead to different managerial cultures in organizations.
5. *Autonomy and decision making:* A fundamental characteristic of top management groups is the value and importance they attach to the degree of autonomy and responsibility they should delegate for important decisions.
6. *Performance orientation:* The nature of the demands that should be placed upon members and the specific focus of performance appraisals constitute another important aspect of the beliefs of top management teams. This dimension also relates to the beliefs held by top managers concerning how much emphasis should be placed on high standards that motivate people to improve their

performance and allow them to feel they will be held accountable for their performance, making performance expectations clear.

7. *Reward orientation:* This dimension relates to the beliefs of top management concerning the extent to which the company should pay competitively and fairly, as well as the degree to which compensation should relate directly to performance.

## Sample

The sample of firms was drawn from exhaustive lists of U.S. mergers published in the *Journal of Mergers and Acquisitions* over a 3-year period. We selected from these lists 198 mergers that met the following criteria: The buying firm gained controlling interest in the acquired firm; the names and addresses of the top managers who were affiliated with the acquired firm immediately before the time of the merger were available, either in the *Directory of Corporate Affiliations* or in *Moody's Manual*; and the core businesses of the merging firms were in the same two-digit standard industrial classification code, to ensure that all of the mergers in the sample would be relatively homogeneous by merger type (i.e., between firms that shared common or related products and/or markets).

From the original 198, we deleted 13 companies from the study upon their request. Of the remaining 185 firms, we received responses from 73, for a response rate of 39%. Of these, 52 firms returned responses from more than one executive. Specifically, 2 firms responded with five completed questionnaires, 2 firms responded with four, 15 firms with three, and 33 firms with two responses. We used these multiple responses to check for interrater reliability.

We checked for potential nonresponse biases using the relative sizes of the merging companies and the time elapsed since the merger announcement, because these variables might have influenced managers' emotions and objectivity (Kitching, 1967; Sales & Mirvis, 1984). The *t* tests of mean differ-

ences were not significant, indicating that there was no nonresponse bias. The questionnaire was mailed directly to each top manager (CEO through senior vice presidential level—the average for the sample was seven top managers per firm) who was in the acquired company prior to and at the time of acquisition.

## SUMMARY OF RESULTS

### Reliability

We conducted a test of survey reliability by examining the responses obtained from the 52 firms with multiple respondents, using Kendall's coefficient of concordance. Interrater reliability was tested for each firm and was found to be significant ($p < 0.05$ or better) in all 52 cases. These results are better than those reported for interrater reliability in recent research (e.g., Finkelstein, 1992). The test, therefore, suggests that each key informant reliably depicted the study's central constructs at the correct unit of analysis. We averaged each item for each of the acquired firms with multiple responses and used the average to represent the views of the firm's top management team.

We further checked the reliability of the perceptions of cultural differences by using a follow-up mailing of the same questionnaire to the top managers of the buying firms, to which 15 companies responded. We found a high level of agreement (i.e., one unit or fewer on the five-point scale) between the responses of the managers of the buying and acquired firms in 12 of the 15 cases, and an acceptable level of agreement (i.e., fewer than two units) in the remaining three cases.

### Construct Validity

Statistical analyses of the original sample showed that all the interrelations among the seven culture difference dimensions were high (at least 0.61), significant ($p < 0.01$), and internally consistent (Cronbach's alpha ranging from a low of 0.82 to a high of 0.94). In keeping with the theory underlying the construction of the culture measures, each dimension demonstrated discriminant validity (Cronbach's alpha for each dimension was higher than the dimension's correlations with any of the other six dimensions).

The data also provide strong evidence of convergent validity, indicating, as expected, that the seven dimensions are part of the same general construct (Buchanan, 1974; Rosenthal & Rosnow, 1989). Although each dimension measures a unique aspect of the phenomenon, all the dimensions refer to the same content domain, making it possible to combine them all in a single index, a procedure for which prior research provides theoretical and statistical support (e.g., Buchanan, 1974; Porter et al., 1974). The combined internal consistency of this single culture differences index was high (Cronbach's alpha = 0.97).

We used factor analysis and a scree test to confirm the unidimensionality of this contrast. The results of the factor analysis provide evidence that the best linear combination was produced when all seven dimensions of the cultural differences construct were aggregated into one factor. The proportion of common variance accounted for by this factor was 0.74. Therefore, we collapsed the seven dimensions into a single cultural difference index by summing the scores for all 29 items and taking their average.

### Predictive Validity

*Shareholder value.* Cultural differences were significantly and negatively correlated with CAR ($r = 0.61$, $p < 0.001$), as expected. Moreover, the regression results indicate that the model was excellent at explaining the variance in the stock market performance of acquiring firms engaged in related mergers. This was found regardless of the time interval used to calculate the CARs, where the $R^2$s for the overall model were high (ranging from 0.28 to 0.38) and the $F$ statistics were significant to at least the 0.05 level. These finding are particularly robust given the small sample sizes. Specifically, the regression results showed that the gains to the shareholders of the buying firm were inversely related to the acquired managers' perceptions of cultural differences ($p < 0.001$).

*Turnover.* Cultural differences were significantly and positively correlated with fourth-year top management turnover ($r = 0.40$, $p < 0.05$), as expected. The regression analysis of the fourth-year turnover revealed that the overall model was strongly significant ($p < 0.001$) and explained a high percentage (42%) of the variance in turnover. Industry seemed to matter, at least in how it interacted with each of the two other measures. The effect of integration on fourth-year turnover was significantly greater for manufacturing firms than for banks ($p < 0.01$), whereas the effect of cultural differences was significantly greater for banks ($p < 0.10$).

## DISCUSSION AND CONCLUSIONS

The literature provides anecdotal evidence that organizational culture may play an important role in the success or failure of merges and acquisitions. In recent years, academicians and practitioners have argued the need for consideration of cultural mismatch between companies involved in M&As in order to avoid, or at least minimize, human resource problems after these deals are consummated. However, there is a shortage of empirical research investigating culture clashes and their consequences in M&As. One crucial reason for this problem is the lack of an instrument that can reliably measure the degree of culture clash during

M&As. In this chapter I have described a new measurement tool, developed to measure cultural fit, that shows high reliability and validity.

I have presented the findings of a study that used this tool, and these findings provide systematic evidence, based on a relatively large sample of M&As, of the relationship between culture clash and the turnover of acquired top executives and the performance of the acquirer. Specifically, acquired top management turnover has been shown to be positively associated with the degree of cultural differences between the acquired top management team and the acquiring firm. Cultural differences have been shown to be negatively associated with shareholder gains. These findings not only explain executive turnover and performance after the merger, they may also predict it. The findings are particularly robust given the small ratio of causes to predictors for which they were tested.

The findings also have practical implications. The existing failure rate of M&As suggests that practitioners have an incomplete understanding of the variables involved in planning and implementing a successful merger. The results of the study described here show that cultural fit is an important factor that should be considered in all stages of M&As. The findings have practical importance because they show that investors are generally skeptical about mergers of firms in which the cultures of the two top management teams are perceived to be incompatible, whereas they are supportive of mergers where the firms' cultures appear to be compatible. The implication is clear: Top managers of the buying firm should pay at least as much attention to issues of cultural fit during the premerger search process as they do to issues of strategic fit and financial and operational analysis.

Of course, one should keep in mind that the above conclusions are based on mergers that have taken place in the United States, and some results, and thus conclusions, may be somewhat different for mergers in other nations. Boyacigiller and Adler (1991) note that U.S. cultural values have imbued organizational science with implicit yet inappropriate universalism. The instrument discussed here, however, affords researchers the opportunity to investigate both the effects of culture clashes within international mergers and acquisitions and the relationship between organizational cultures and national cultures.

There are other opportunities for further research as well. For example, the present findings warrant replication using other forms of measurement, such as anthropological and other nonsurvey approaches, expanded samples, and samples containing unrelated as well as related mergers. In particular, unrelated mergers have fewer operational synergies and therefore can be expected to show different types of contacts between the combining top management teams, which may attenuate or accentuate the findings presented here. Replication studies should also try to measure management's and investors' perceptions during comparable time frames so as to establish other causal links between cultural fit and shareholder value. Of course, it may be very difficult for researchers to gain access to such data. However, any attempt at triangulation would be useful for supporting both the internal and external validities of the present design.

Other research efforts could be directed toward understanding how cultural differences manifest themselves. For example, do they become apparent during negotiations and due diligence or only after closing? Do they manifest themselves in dysfunctional ways, such as in losses in job commitment and increases in intergroup conflict? Can the severity of the conflict explain high management turnover? Finally, can cultural differences be effectively managed to minimize their negative impacts?

# PART IV

# Culture, Climate, Commitment, and Careers

The chapters in Part IV deal with human resource management issues related to organizational culture and climate: attachment, commitment, socialization, and careers. The focus of these chapters is essentially on the role of individuals in organizations. The contributors deal with how organizational members find their way in modern organizations and how they become identified with and loyal to their organizations. Surprisingly, these are topics that have not received a great deal of specific attention in the literature to date, despite the obvious connection between attachment and culture. Nevertheless, they are topics that have immediate interest for practicing managers and for researchers. Indeed, it is difficult to see how the concepts of culture and climate can have relevance without reflection in the individual-level phenomena discussed in the four chapters that follow.

The first two chapters in this part deal with the relationship between organizational culture and climate and various forms of organizational attachment. In Chapter 20, Beyer, Hannah, and Milton provide a broad overview of various types of group and organizational attachment, with a focus on organizational culture rather than climate. In particular, they address the bewildering array of confusing terms and definitions that have tended to obfuscate this area of research in past literature. In Chapter 21, Virtanen focuses more specifically on organizational commitment, but he does so from an interesting perspective that puts a new light on the culture-climate debate. Virtanen asserts in particular that "commitments are instruments of climate but constituents of culture." He goes on to describe a model in which culture is associated with emotionally driven desires and climate is associated with utilitarian strategies. Together, Beyer and her colleagues and Virtanen present different but complementary perspectives on the role of attachment and commitment in the culture and climate literature and provide a strong foundation for future research in this intriguing area.

The following two chapters address the ways in which individuals enter and progress through organizations and the ways in which they interact with organizations' cultures. In Chapter 22, Major focuses on organizational socialization processes, especially the way that socialization contributes to the maintenance of culture in high-performing organizations. In particular, she posits that the cultures of high-performing organizations require new ways of socializing newcomers, utilizing relational processes that result in mutual growth of both newcomers and existing members. In Chapter 23, Gunz deals with the career paths of members within organizations from an interesting and original perspective, but he comes to similar conclusions. Focusing on the phenomenon of "managerial rationality," he presents a model of careers based on a mutually reinforcing cycle and argues that maintenance of the cycle reinforces and builds organizational cultures, whereas disruption of the cycle can lead to sudden and unexpected changes in culture.

Overall, the four chapters in this part of the *Handbook* cover material that is often neglected in the organizational culture and climate literature. These chapters present different perspectives and ideas, many of which are yet to be tested in empirical research. Nevertheless, each chapter is grounded in a thorough review of the literature, and the ideas expressed present exciting challenges for both management practitioners and scholars.

# 20

## Ties That Bind

### Culture and Attachments in Organizations

-- *Janice M. Beyer, David R. Hannah,*
*and Laurie P. Milton*

ecause humans are social animals, they congregate together in groups. Individuals who choose to live isolated from others as hermits are considered deviant. Individuals who are raised apart from other humans (e.g., feral children) lack the very characteristics that make us human (Malson, 1972; Shattuck, 1980). Becoming and remaining fully human, then, require some attachment to other humans.

In this chapter we will explore how cultures contribute to individuals' attachments to social groups and, conversely, how such attachments contribute to cultures. In the process, we will try to confront the confusion in our literatures created by the myriad ways in which both culture and attachment have been labeled and defined. In particular, there is a marked lack of agreement in the literature regarding what to call people's attachments

to groups and a tendency to formulate a unique definition for each label. But, as Homans (1950) has pointed out: "A chief obstacle to clear thinking in the social sciences is the fact that several different sets of words, or language systems, are available for the expression of a single idea. We must be careful not to think the ideas are different just because the words are different" (p. 137).

One of our aims in this chapter is to explore whether differences in terms and the words used in their definitions correspond to useful and important differences in meaning—that is, whether the different terms used actually refer to different phenomena. To do this, we look at the definitions and discussion of different sets of terms for common, underlying social processes that have been postulated as creating and sustaining attachments. A second aim is to employ the useful differences we find to suggest different pathways through which cultures are related to individuals' attachments to their social groups. Before addressing those issues, we will clarify what we mean by culture.

## DEFINITIONS OF CULTURE

The usefulness of scientific concepts depends to a large degree on whether they help to isolate and describe something distinctive about the phenomena under study. Thus it is important to ask about any construct what it describes or tells us that is not captured by other constructs. In regard to the construct of culture, organizational researchers should therefore confront the question of what is distinctive about the meaning of this term and its use in research. What does it point to in organizations that other constructs miss?

Answering this question is complicated by the fact that both organizational researchers and anthropologists who specialize in studying culture disagree on what culture is and use different sets of words to define the construct. Fortunately, some areas of overlap can be discerned. Most basic is that there seems to be general agreement that organizational cultures are based in sets of meanings *shared* by some groups of people. This focus on what is shared has been neglected by other constructs used to study organizations and thus gives the culture construct a useful distinctiveness for organizational research.

There is less agreement on where such shared cultural meanings reside. Some organizational researchers treat cultural meanings as *cognitive* phenomena because they theorize that the most important location of cultural meaning is in people's minds. Others treat cultural meanings as *symbolic* phenomena that are manifest in behavior, language, and artifacts. For example, the distinguished anthropologist Clifford Geertz (1973), quoting Goodenough, argues against locating culture "in the minds and hearts of men," calling

this the "cognitivist fallacy." Geertz cites the example of a Beethoven quartet as something that is clearly cultural, but "not anybody's knowledge or belief about anything" (pp. 11-12). For Geertz, cultural meanings reside in the concrete and observable things that provide the context for human behavior and thought.

All anthropologists do not agree with Geertz on these points, and obviously neither do many organizational researchers, who center their treatments and definitions of culture on cognitions that are variously labeled values, sets of understandings, patterns of interpretations, knowledge, basic assumptions, or shared meanings (e.g., Hofstede, 1980a; Louis, 1985; Martin, 1992; Reichers & Schneider, 1990; Sackmann, 1991; Schein, 1992) and give lesser importance to such observables as symbolic behaviors, language, and artifacts. Other researchers give equal or greater prominence to shared patterns of behaviors and other public, symbolic manifestations in defining and studying culture (e.g., Barley, 1991; Kilduff, Funk, & Mehra, 1997; Trice & Beyer, 1993; Van Maanen, 1991). In this chapter we take the latter perspective and include both the internal, cognitive and the external, symbolic and behavioral sides of culture as important elements of culture.

There is reasonable agreement among organizational scholars that the elements of culture reflexively influence one another over time. Schein's (1992, p. 17) diagram of the three levels of culture he has identified—basic underlying assumptions, espoused values and norms, and artifacts—uses double-headed arrows between the levels. Brown (1995, p. 9) and others repeat this conceptualization. Denison (1990, p. 5) shows beliefs and values interacting with policies and practices in his framework for studying organizational culture and effectiveness. Kono and Clegg (1998, p. 10) show five elements of culture—values, decision-making patterns, behavior patterns, performances, and rewards—as interacting through feedback loops comprising intrinsic and extrinsic rewards. The *reflexivity* of cultural elements is implicit in Trice and Beyer's (1993, p. 77) definition of cultural forms as both expressing and affirming cultural ideologies, and when they refer to cultural forms as contributing to both the emergence and the persistence of cultural ideologies.

Another important aspect of culture is its role in human *survival*. Various scholars have pointed out that human beings lack the kind of genetic programming that guides other species toward behaviors essential to their survival. They see culture as fulfilling this role for human beings. As Geertz (1964) explains, "Cultural patterns . . . are 'programs'; they provide a template or blueprint for the organization of social and psychological processes, much as genetic systems provide a template for the organization of organic processes" (p. 62). Researchers are now discovering that culture also plays a role in the survival of some animal species. Recent research on genetic patterns in whales suggests that culture, as evidenced in similar vocalizations among maternal relatives, may pass on valuable survival skills, such as the techniques involved in feeding, baby-sitting, and fending off predators (Vogel, 1998). Organizational researchers tend to translate culture's role in survival to culture's role in adaptation or effectiveness (e.g., Brown, 1995; Denison, 1990; Kono & Clegg, 1998). Exceptions are Schein (1992), who discusses both surviving in and adapting to external environments, and Trice and Beyer (1993), who see cultures as guiding managers and others as they act "to ensure their organizations' survival and continued prosperity" (p. 1).

Following such leads, we believe that organizational culture research should therefore concern itself with both shared ideas and symbols that help to guide organizational members to survive, adapt, and achieve collectively in their uncertain and sometimes chaotic worlds. A definition of culture that is congruent with this objective has been provided by Trice and Beyer (1993), who argue that "cultures are collective phenomena that embody people's responses to the uncertainties and chaos that are inevitable in human experience" (p. 2). Trice and Beyer see people's responses to uncertainty as falling into two major categories. The first is the substance of culture, which they call "ideologies" and define as "shared, relatively coherently related sets of emotionally charged beliefs, values, and norms that *bind some people together* and help them to make sense of their worlds" (p. 33; emphasis added). The second is cultural forms—"observable entities, including symbols, language, narratives, and practices through which members of a culture express, affirm, and communicate the substance of their culture to one another" (p. 77). Unlike other definitions of culture (e.g. Schein, 1992), Trice and Beyer's makes no assumptions about the relative importance, accessibility, or persistence of these two elements. In this chapter we draw primarily on this perspective on culture.

It should be noted that this perspective on culture builds on different theoretical foundations and traditions from those of research on organizational climates (Denison, 1996; Trice & Beyer, 1993, pp. 20-21). Recent quantitative research on culture appears to have considerable overlap with that on climate, and this methodological approach is not accepted by many other culture researchers. The emphasis on deeply held shared meaning and symbolism that characterizes distinctive research on culture is missing from quantitative studies of both culture and climate. In this chapter we focus on the connections between culture and attachment; we leave the question of how attachment is related to climate for others to answer.

## DEFINITIONS OF ATTACHMENT

Social scientists within various disciplines who have addressed the question of how individuals become attached to social groups have used somewhat different terminology and theoretical perspectives. As with the concept of culture, it has not been clear whether,

---

**TABLE 20.1**　Social Processes Theorized as Underlying Attachment to Groups

| Author | Affective and Cognitive Processes | Social Interactions | Symbols and Behaviors |
|---|---|---|---|
| Durkheim | Common beliefs, common sense of identity | Interdependence, division of labor | Collective action |
| Tönnies | Mutual attraction, love | Reasonable exchange | |
| Homans | Shared sentiments | Interactions | Shared activities |
| Lawler | Emotions | Repeated social exchange | Repeated social exchange |
| Apter | Ideologies, collective identity | | |
| Geertz | Ideology | Solidarity | Systems of signs |
| Anderson | Imagined communities | Fields of exchange | Shared language |
| Hodder | Systems of beliefs | | Shared symbols |
| Kelman | Identity/identification, ideas and feelings/internalization | Rewards/compliance | Rewards/compliance |
| Sumner | Ethnocentrism, mores | Within-group comradeship, intergroup hostility | Folkways |
| Sherif & Sherif | Group membership, perceived intergroup conflict and competition, preferential attributions | Intergroup conflict and hostility | Public and symbolic hostile behavior toward out-groups |
| Brewer | Self-categorization, in-group biases | | |
| Turner et al. | Other- and self-categorization, in-group biases | Personalized and depersonalized interactions | |
| Tajfel & Turner | Awareness of membership, internalization, social identity | Intergroup competition, comparisons that accentuate differences | |

---

in the process, they are addressing the same or different phenomena. There appear to be both overlaps and differences. Table 20.1 summarizes several prominent theories that have addressed this issue.

We have classified the contents of these theories as addressing three broad categories of social processes that contribute to attachment: affective and cognitive processes, social interactions, and symbolism and behaviors. We have combined affective and cognitive processes into one category because both are internal to individuals and clearly closely interrelated in culture, which we have defined as made up of emotionally charged ideas. Social interactions include all kinds of social and economic exchanges, as well as interdependencies among persons. They are external to specific individuals and require some form of relations between or among persons. Such relations enable the substance and forms of culture to become shared. Symbolism and behaviors include observable entities that are external to individuals, do not require interaction, but carry shared meanings. Cultural forms always involve symbolism and often include behaviors. The three categories in Table 20.1 thus mirror three important elements of culture: cultural substance, the shared nature of culture, and cultural forms. Although the last two categories can be seen as conceptually distinct, in practice there can be some overlap, as interactions involve behaviors that can be construed as symbolic because they can also carry shared meanings.

The social theorists listed in Table 20.1 have used a variety of terms to refer to individuals' attachment to groups and to the mechanisms or processes through which attachment occurs. We will review the perspectives they offer as a basis for identifying generic social processes and mechanisms involved in attachment. Later in the chapter, we will address the various ways that organizational researchers have treated attachment.

## Sociological Theories

Sociologists have addressed the question of attachment when they have theorized about what causes people to form and stay in communities. Perhaps the most well-known of these explanations was advanced by Emile Durkheim (1893/1984), who identified two bases for social cohesion that he called mechanical and organic solidarity. Mechanical solidarity reflects bonds based on common beliefs, participation in collective action, and a common sense of identity, whereas organic solidarity reflects material interdependence based on a division of labor (Morrison, 1995). Similar ideas were advanced by Ferdinand Tönnies (1957) through his concepts of gemeinschaft and gesellschaft, with the former reflecting relationships based in mutual attraction and homogeneous culture and the latter reflecting relationships based on exchange and the division of labor.

In theorizing about social groups rather than whole communities, George Homans (1950) argued that three factors lead to social cohesion: interaction, shared activities, and shared sentiments. Homans saw these factors as emergent and mutually reinforcing in all kinds of social groups, suggesting, for example, that greater interaction among people leads to more shared sentiments and often to more shared activities. He defined interaction broadly to include not just social communication but any actions by one person that somehow affect those of another person. Homans's concept of interactions thus would encompass the interdependencies and the division of labor among people. His concept of shared sentiments is similar to Durkheim's shared beliefs and Tönnies's homogeneous culture. His concept of shared activities resembles Durkheim's ideas about participation in collective action.

A current sociological approach to addressing questions of attachment is relational cohesion theory (E. J. Lawler, 1992; Lawler & Yoon, 1993, 1995, 1996, 1998). Edward J. Lawler and his colleagues have developed and experimentally tested models that emphasize the role of social exchange and emotions in creating cohesion and commitment in social networks. They argue that, even though many exchange relations are instrumentally based, repeated exchanges make the exchange relation "expressively valued" and that "repetitiveness—of behavior, interaction, or exchange—tends to foster and maintain" social groups (Lawler & Yoon, 1998, p. 892). The emphasis in this work on emotions echoes the affective aspects of Homans's shared sentiments, whereas the emphasis on exchange resembles both Homans's concept of interactions and Durkheim's and Tönnies's ideas about division of labor and exchange.

In a different stream of research, David Apter (1964) focused on just the cognitive element of the prior theories when he addressed the role of ideology in creating social solidarity. His analysis emphasized the ways in which ideology binds communities together and provides a sense of a collective identity with those who share the same beliefs. He also saw ideologies as systems of beliefs that help to reconcile facts and ideas, thus providing a sense of coherence in a confusing world and a moral basis for actions by making them meaningful. Apter's focus on beliefs as forming a basis for social bonds parallels the ideas of Durkheim and Homans. His ideas about collective identity also resemble those of Durkheim. His inclusion of coherence and meaningful action, however, offers additional explanations for forming attachments.

## Anthropological and Archaeological Theories

Another scholar who saw ideology as binding social groups together is the anthropologist Clifford Geertz (1964), who argued that ideology is a response to the inevitable and insoluble strains, conflicts, and contradictions in social life. Like Apter, Geertz saw ideology as promoting social solidarity by knitting social groups together and creating a sense of community. Geertz's concept of ideologies resembles the shared beliefs mentioned by Durkheim, Tönnies, and Homans. But unlike the other theorists, Geertz argued that ideologies are symbolic in that they represent public actions and signs.

A second anthropologist who addressed the underlying question of how people are attached to social groups is Benedict Anderson (1983), who saw people as tied together into what he called "imagined communities." By using this term, Anderson intended to emphasize that community is based in cognitions and feelings—that although people may never meet each other, they share an image of their communion in their minds (p. 15). Like Durkheim and Apter, Anderson recognized

that people are bound together by a sense of shared identity. Echoing Durkheim, Tönnies, and Lawler, he also suggested that human communities are fields of exchange. In addition, consistent with Geertz's focus on symbolism, Anderson gave a central role to shared language in enabling community.

Related recent research in archaeology offers new evidence that shared ideas and symbols may have played an important role in the formation of human communities in Neolithic times (Balter, 1998). At the site of a huge, 9,000-year-old settlement in Turkey that may have housed as many as 10,000 people, researchers found figurines of a likely mother goddess and wall murals depicting wild animals and hunting scenes. Ian Hodder, the scientist in charge of the excavations, saw parallels between these and other cave drawings and suggested that the transition to communal life required "the domestication of the wild" by bringing it into the house and thus symbolically controlling it. These findings suggest that even these early societies had shared ideas that they captured in symbols, and that, by creating and communicating shared meaning, their shared symbolic life played a role in inducing hunting and gathering groups to band together into settled communities. These findings thus underline the importance of both shared cognitions and symbolism in attaching people to social groups.

## Psychological Theories

Research by social psychologists has also addressed the question of individuals' attachments to groups. One way social psychologists explain social ties among individuals is in terms of social influence. In his analysis of attitude change, for example, Kelman (1958) suggested that there are three levels of social influence: compliance, based in rewards; identification, based on a valued identity; and internalization, based in attitude agreement. He saw compliance as the weakest form of social influence and internalization as the most powerful because it involves making ideas and feelings part of the self. However, all three processes clearly create some degree of attachment. Kelman's inclusion of rewards and compliance implies interactions and some degree of social exchange. His conceptions of identification parallel the ideas of Durkheim and Apter. His use of the concept of internalization seems to make more explicit ideas that were implicit in the work of earlier theorists.

A second stream of psychological research used to explain attachments to social groups focused on the formation of intergroup attitudes, self-categorization, and identification processes. The basic idea underlying this stream of research is that belonging to a social group confers on members a sense of difference from people not in the group. This sense of difference contributes to ethnocentrism, which is evidenced in inter group conflict and hostility (Sherif & Sherif, 1953; Sumner, 1906). Brewer (1979) argues that "any categorization rule that provides a basis for classifying an individual as belonging to one social grouping as distinct from another can be sufficient to produce differentiation of attitudes toward the two groups" (p. 308).

According to subsequent self-categorization theory, individuals tend to categorize themselves and others as members of social categories depending on how closely their individual characteristics match those of various groups and differ from those of other groups (Turner, Hogg, Oakes, Reicher, & Wetherell, 1987). According to social identity theory, individuals further develop their own group-based self-categorizations by internalizing the social categories or memberships involved and thereby coming to identify with them (Tajfel & Turner, 1985). Although the categorization process is largely cognitive (Turner et al., 1987), the identification process encompasses evaluative and possibly affective components in addition to cognition. Following Tajfel's (1982b) conceptualization, in order for a group-based or social identity to exist, at a minimum, an individual must be aware that he or she is a group member and must have made some value judgments about the group. To the extent that the person has invested emotionally in the awareness and evaluation, the social identity in question may be particularly important to his or her self-concept (Markus & Kunda, 1986; Markus & Wurf, 1987).

Although this latter stream of research builds on a different set of observations— that of intergroup awareness and conflict—it ends up with the social process of identification, already recognized by Durkheim, Apter, and Kelman as underlying attachments. Also, like Homans, this line of theorizing emphasizes similarities among group members and suggests that these similarities become more evident and powerful in their attraction when framed in terms of differences from other groups.

## Summary

Table 20.1 shows that, although they use different terms, there is considerable overlap in how these prominent social theorists conceptualized processes underlying attachment to social groups. It is interesting to note that recent psychological theories have been focused on affective and cognitive processes and on social interactions and have paid relatively little attention to symbols and behaviors as bases for attachment. Because the three sets of social processes used to classify these theories mirror important aspects of culture, it seems likely that these specific processes also provide links between culture and attachment. But before analyzing possible linkages, we will review prominent organizational theories regarding attachment.

## CONCEPTS USED TO STUDY ATTACHMENT IN ORGANIZATIONS

Table 20.2 summarizes the organizational theories reviewed in this section in terms of the same categories used in Table 20.1. Like

**TABLE 20.2** Social Processes Theorized as Underlying Attachment to Organizations

| Conceptual Labels/Authors | Affective and Cognitive Processes | Social Interactions | Symbols and Behaviors |
|---|---|---|---|
| **Involvement** | | | |
| Lodahl & Kejner | Self-concept | | |
| Etzioni | Moral involvement, alienative involvement | Calculative involvement | |
| **Commitment** | | | |
| Becker | Perceptions of costs of leaving | Side bets | Investments, behavioral consistency |
| Porter et al.; Mowday et al. | Beliefs, sense of membership, willingness to exert effort | | Behavior |
| Salancik | | | Behavioral acts |
| Allen & Meyer | Affective commitment, normative commitment | Continuance commitment | Continuance commitment |
| **Loyalty** | | | |
| Hirschman | Attitudes | | Voice, loyalist behavior |
| Adler & Adler | Feelings, trust, readiness to contribute, willingness to follow | Alignment of self with group | Teamwork |
| **Identification** | | | |
| Ashforth & Mael | Self-categorization | | |
| Dutton et al. | Self-definition, attractiveness of organizational image and identity | Increased contact with organization, cooperation | Visible affiliation with organization |
| Kramer | Self-categorization | | |
| **Psychological contract** | | | |
| Rousseau; Robinson et al. | Relational obligations, perceived violations | Transactional obligations | |
| **Citizenship behaviors** | | | |
| Barnard | Willingness to contribute effort, perceived alternatives for satisfaction | Cooperative effort, cohesion | Cooperative effort |
| Bateman & Organ | Perceptions of others' intent, positive affect | Reciprocity | Supra-role behavior |
| Organ | Perceived fairness, mutual trust | Fair economic and social exchanges | Altruism, conscientiousness, sportsmanship, courtesy, civic virtue |
| Van Dyne et al. | Social covenants | | Obedience, loyalty, participation |

other social scientists, organizational researchers have advanced, defined, and studied a variety of concepts to address the question of how individuals become and remain attached to social groups. We cannot review all of the extensive literature that has accumulated and is relevant. Instead, we will discuss what selected research drawing on six of these concepts—involvement, commitment, loyalty, identification, psychological contracts, and citizenship behavior—reveals about the processes underlying attachment. Much of the research to be examined is based in general social theory already discussed; it differs from that theory in that it has been used specifically and repeatedly in research on attachment to organizations or organizationally relevant groups.

## Involvement

The term *involvement* has been used in the literature on organizations to refer to individuals' attachments to both organizations and their jobs. Lodahl and Kejner (1965) define job involvement as "the degree to which a person's work performance affects his self-esteem" (p. 25). They also argue, based on their research findings, that employees who are highly involved in their jobs are also highly involved in their organizations (p. 32). This conceptualization of involvement suggests that individuals form bonds with organizations to the degree that their self-conceptions are engaged in their jobs or organizations. It thus appears to be very similar to the ideas of identity and identification as advanced by Durkheim, Apter, Kelman, and Tajfel and Turner.

Etzioni (1975) has proposed three different types of involvement: moral, calculative, and alienative. Individuals are morally involved if they accept and identify with organizational goals, calculatively involved if they perceive an exchange agreement with their organization, and alienatively involved if they have a negative feelings and attachment to their organizations, but are forced to remain due to a lack of alternatives or a behavioral compliance system that forces them to remain (such as if they were in prison). In common with Durkheim, Apter, Kelman, and Tajfel and Turner, both Lodahl and Kejner's definition of job involvement and Etzioni's concept of moral involvement include identification processes that, as already argued, will make individuals more liable to share ideas, values, and norms with other members of the relevant group, and thus to develop a culture. Etzioni's conceptualization also includes attachments based on exchange and the possibility of a form of attachment that includes negative affect.

## Commitment

The concept of commitment has been studied for more than three decades. It is also a concept that has been investigated relative to a variety of social groups, including employing organizations, unions, and occupations. Given the proliferation of constructs and the redundancy associated with many commitment constructs (Morrow, 1983), we will review only four of the most influential and distinct conceptualizations—those offered by Becker (1960), Porter, Steers, Mowday, and Boulian (1974), Salancik (1977), and Allen and Meyer (1990).

Becker (1960) has argued that commitment to an organization occurs when "a person, by making a side-bet, links extraneous interests with a consistent line of activity" (p. 32). When individuals accumulate side bets—such as pension plans, seniority privileges, and status—in an organization, they are more committed to that organization than are individuals who have not accumulated them, especially if they lack alternative means to satisfy the same interests (Ritzer & Trice, 1969; Stevens, Beyer, & Trice, 1978). Becker's conceptualization of commitment resembles Etzioni's calculative involvement and the exchange-based or interdependence approaches of Durkheim, Tönnies, Lawler, and Anderson as bases for attachment.

The second influential conceptualization of commitment is that of Porter et al. (1974). As originally advanced, it included (a) a belief in and acceptance of the values and goals of the organization, (b) a willingness to exert effort on behalf of the organization to achieve organizational goals, and (c) a strong desire to maintain organizational membership. These ties are largely affective and cognitive. Later, Mowday, Porter, and Steers (1982) expanded their conceptualization by suggesting that behaviors can also lead to commitments. Like Kelman and Homans, they posited a cyclical relationship between commitment as an attitude and commitment as a behavior, so that commitment attitudes could lead to commitment behaviors, which would, in turn, reinforce commitment attitudes (Reichers, 1985).

Salancik (1977) has offered a third perspective, defining commitment in terms of a binding of individuals to their behavioral acts. He identifies four characteristics of action as influencing the extent of commitment. According to Salancik, an act that is highly explicit, irrevocable, done by one's own volition, and public will result in strong commitment of the individual to that act, and thus result in likely repetition of it. Clearly, Salancik sees people's attachments as formed primarily through their behaviors, but it seems likely that it is not the mere fact of having performed those behaviors alone that creates commitment, but also the symbolic significance of those behaviors to both the actors and the audience. People will try to behave consistently with their principles (see Virtanen, Chapter 21, this volume). In a sense, then, the meanings of the actions taken will create attachment to groups who share and value those meanings, especially if those actions are taken with or in the presence of those groups. Salancik's approach to commitment uses behavior itself rather than a social group as the referent. In this sense it stands alone relative to others displayed in Tables 20.1 and 20.2.

In a recent attempt to clarify and structure the various approaches to commitment, Allen and Meyer (1990) distinguished among three different types of commitment: affective commitment, continuance commitment, and normative commitment. They define affective commitment as "an affective or emotional attachment to the organization such that the strongly committed individual identifies with, is involved in, and enjoys membership in the organization" (p. 2). This form of commitment echoes the ideas not only of Durkheim, Tönnies, Lawler, Apter, Kelman, and Tajfel and Turner, but of Lodahl and Kejner and of Etzioni. "Cost-induced" or "continuance" commitment resembles Becker's ideas about side bets and individuals' perceptions of alternatives to their current employment (Farrell & Rusbult, 1981). This form of commitment incorporates ideas based in exchange and rewards. It seems to imply continued interaction and shared behavior with others in the employing organization. Allen and Meyer add a third type of commitment they call normative commitment, conceptualized as beliefs about responsibilities or obligations to the employing organization. This conceptualization offers a new set of cognitive and affective processes and complements that of the psychological contract, to be discussed later.

Using various of these approaches, other researchers have investigated commitment to social groups other than organizations (Virtanen, Chapter 21, this volume), including unions (Angle & Perry, 1986) and occupations (Meyer, Allen, & Smith, 1993; Ritzer & Trice, 1969). The results of Ritzer and Trice's (1969) study of organizational and occupational commitment among personnel managers led them to argue that "organizational commitment seems to arise only when the occupation has no really meaningful base to which one may commit [oneself]" (p. 478). However, research by Angle and Perry (1986) found that unionized employees of municipal bus companies could be committed to both their union and their employing organization, provided a cooperative labor relations climate existed. The question of whether commitment to one group precludes commitment to another or whether individuals can have dual commitments to more than one social group is clearly relevant to the role of culture in producing attachment, because individuals in all societies belong to multiple cultures.

## Loyalty

One of the difficulties involved in summarizing the small amount of empirical and theoretical work on loyalty in organizations is that the research done has taken many different and widely divergent conceptual approaches (Adler & Adler, 1988; Withey & Cooper, 1989). For example, scholars have argued that loyalty includes silence in the face of problems (Kolarska & Aldrich, 1980; Withey & Cooper, 1989), constructive behaviors (Ali, Krishnan, & Azim, 1997; Rusbult, Farrell, Rogers, & Mainous, 1988), emotional attachments (Adler & Adler, 1988; Ali et al., 1997), and a willingness to follow leadership and directives of organizations (Adler & Adler, 1988). Many of these conceptualizations overlap with others described here.

Hirschman's (1970) conceptualization of loyalty as a possible response of members to organizational decline is probably the most well-known work on the topic. Hirschman discusses loyalty in two ways: as an attitude that decreases the likelihood that employees will exit from an organization and increases the likelihood that they will use voice (p. 78), and in terms of "loyalist behavior" (p. 86), which involves employees' maintaining a relationship with an organization in the face of organizational decline. Thus Hirschman's conception of loyalty appears to include both attitudes and behaviors (Withey & Cooper, 1989).

In other research treating loyalty in terms of both attitudes and behaviors, Adler and Adler (1988) studied U.S. college basketball players over a 5-year span. They found that a form of intense loyalty to their college developed among some of the players—loyalty that encompassed "feelings of attachment, or belonging, of strongly wanting to be part of something; involving the readiness to contribute part of one's self; it incorporates trust, the voluntary alignment of self with the group, and a willingness to follow faithfully the leadership or guidelines of the organization" (p. 401). Adler and Adler observed that some players, whom they and other players considered loyal, sacrificed potential personal scoring records in favor of doing what was best for team performance. Disloyal players "cared more about bolstering their own playing statistics to enhance their pro chances" (p. 412). Loyalty, according to this conceptualization—and the conceptualizations of Hirschman (1970) and other scholars (Rusbult et al., 1988; Withey & Cooper, 1989)—is a form of attachment that includes both affective and behavioral components.

## Social Identities and Identification

Like other social identification, identification with an organization (Ashforth & Mael, 1989) results from individuals' categorizing themselves as members of organizations or organizational groups and internalizing these social categories or memberships (Tajfel & Turner, 1985). Extending these arguments, Dutton, Dukerich, and Harquail (1994) have suggested that the strength of a person's identification with an organization reflects the extent to which that person's self-concept includes the same characteristics he or she perceives to be distinctive, central, and enduring to the organization.

It is important not to confuse Albert and Whetten's (e.g., 1985) work on organizational identity with work by other scholars on identification with an organization. Albert and Whetten used the organization as their unit of analysis and argued that an organization has an identity to the extent that there is a shared understanding of the central, distinctive, and enduring characteristics of the organization among its members. Their concept of organizational identity is thus quite similar to that of organizational climate.

Elaborating further on the implications of multiple group memberships, Kramer (1991) notes that individuals may belong to and may identify with various work and social groups that are within or associated with their organizations. They may identify, for instance, with immediate work groups, with organizational professional groups, with collegial or friendship groups, or with the whole organization as a group that includes all of its members. To the extent that individuals categorize themselves as members or identify with these groups, they become attached to them. Kramer's insight parallels that of those who have addressed the issue of multiple commitments.

Individuals may also become attached to organizations to the extent that they can enact or express other elements of their self-concepts that are important to them within organizations or to the extent that organizations themselves or the activities of organizations are congruent with aspects of individuals' self-definitions. Beyer and Hannah (1999) found that the extent to which experienced professionals find they can enact their personal identities in new work roles helps to explain the newcomers' adjustment to their new jobs in a new organization.

### Psychological Contracts

The concept of the psychological contract (Argyris, 1960; Levinson, 1962; Rousseau, 1989, 1995; Rousseau & Parks, 1993; Schein, 1965) has been developed around the core idea that employees perceive mutual obligations between themselves and their employing organizations. These obligations have been conceptualized as falling into two broad categories: relational and transactional (Robinson, Kraatz, & Rousseau, 1994; Robinson & Morrison, 1995; Rousseau, 1990b). Relational obligations involve

relatively long time frames and the social elements of relationships; transactional obligations involve monetizable, short-term considerations. These two sets of obligations echo two of the types of attachment already discussed—those based in affect and exchange. An important aspect of psychological contracts is that if employees perceive that their employers have failed to meet their obligations under psychological contracts, the employees feel that their psychological contracts have been violated (Morrison & Robinson, 1997), and their attachments to their organizations lessen. This line of research has not yet addressed the other side of obligations—that of employees to the organization. These obligations, however, seem to be reflected in Allen and Meyer's concept of normative commitment.

Research into the effects of violations of psychological contracts has found that if individuals perceive that their employers have broken their obligations, they respond by lowering their perceptions of their own obligations (Robinson et al., 1994), are less likely to engage in citizenship behavior (Podsakoff, MacKenzie, Moorman, & Fetter, 1990; Robinson, 1996; Robinson & Morrison, 1995), are less likely to intend to remain with the employer, and are more likely to actually leave (Guzzo, Noonan, & Elron, 1994; Robinson, 1996; Robinson & Rousseau, 1994). Violations clearly encourage behaviors that reduce attachment.

### Citizenship Behavior

Chester Barnard (1938), an early theorist, defined organizations as associations of cooperative effort and underscored the importance of people's willingness to contribute effort to a cooperative system. It seems a logical extension to suggest that individuals' willingness is likely to vary with the extent to which those individuals are attached to a social system. Moreover, when individuals are strongly attached they may be more likely to engage in behaviors that further the interests of the group than they otherwise would. In this connection, Bateman and Organ (1983) noted Katz and Kahn's (1966) observation that on many occasions organizational functioning depends on supra-role behavior that cannot be prescribed or required in advance of the circumstance within which it is important. Bateman and Organ labeled these supra-role behaviors *citizenship behaviors.*

Since then, theorists have widely debated both the substance and the usefulness of this construct. Researchers have used various labels, such as prosocial behavior (Brief & Motowidlo, 1986) and organization spontaneity (George & Brief, 1992), in their efforts to bound the domain of the construct. Focusing largely on extrarole behavior, Organ (1988) has identified five categories of citizenship behavior: altruism (helping others with organization tasks), conscientiousness (role behaviors carried out with diligence above what could be expected), sportsmanship (not complaining or engaging in petty grievances), courtesy (passing information on to others), and civic virtue (participating in the political life of the organization). Such behavior, of course, has considerable symbolic meaning, both to those enacting it and to those observing it.

Van Dyne, Graham, and Dienesch (1994) have argued theoretically and empirically for an alternative, somewhat expanded view of organizational citizenship behavior. In a concept they call civic citizenship, they include all positive community-relevant behavior, including obedience, loyalty, and various forms of participation. They also see such social exchange relationships as psychological contracts affecting citizenship behavior. This expanded view of citizenship behavior has considerable overlap with other conceptualizations of attachment.

### Summary

A comparison of Tables 20.1 and 20.2 reveals that there is considerable overlap in the ways organizational researchers and general social theorists have conceptualized people's attachments to collectivities of various kinds. The conceptualizations differ primarily in the social theorists' greater attention to symbolism. The cognitive and affective processes identified by organizational researchers deal with three themes: positive affect, issues of equity, and how self-concepts are tied to group membership. Organizational researchers address social interactions in terms of either exchanges or cooperation, both of which can be seen to rest on the universal norm of reciprocity. These researchers have been especially diligent in identifying a range of behaviors that they usually consider as being consequences of attachment. We include these in Table 20.2 to take advantage of Salancik's (1977) insight that people can become attached to their own behaviors, especially if those behaviors are public and volitional. Thus, we suggest, the repetition of many of the behaviors listed in Table 20.2, which are often public, volitional, and performed only in work settings, will tend to create and reinforce people's attachments to their work, their work groups, and their organizations.

### CULTURE AND ATTACHMENT PROCESSES

In order to explore how cultures may contribute to creating and maintaining people's attachments to social groups and organizations, we must consider exactly what kinds of social processes are implicated in the inclusive definition of culture discussed earlier. Using this definition, we will then consider how the relatively generic social processes listed in Tables 20.1 and 20.2 parallel the initial three characteristics of culture identified—cultural ideologies, sharing, and cultural forms—and thus how they link culture and attachment.

## Ideologies and Attachments

As defined by Trice and Beyer (1993), ideologies are systems of ideas that include three kinds of cognitions: beliefs, values, and norms. Culturally shared beliefs tell members of a culture how things work and why they are the way they are. Shared values indicate what's good or bad, important or unimportant, and generally what is "worth having or doing" (p. 33). The norms of a culture tell its members what they should and should not do. Cultures tend to bundle sets of beliefs, values, and norms together to form meaningful directions for action. Thus, although they can be separated conceptually, in practice they are intertwined and they interact with one another.

When people experience affective or cognitive processes based in shared beliefs, sentiments, emotions, ideas, or feelings, they develop a sense of a collective identity that attaches them to others who think and feel similarly. In cultural terms, when people come to share ideologies held by others, they identify with and become attached to the cultural group expressing those ideologies. Conversely, when people adopt identities that tie them to a particular group of people, they become more susceptible to the ideas and feelings generated within that group. Or, in cultural terms, when people identify with and attach themselves to a cultural group, they tend to adopt its ideologies. Thus shared cognitive or affective processes and cultures are mutually reinforcing—both grow from people coming to think, believe, and feel similarly.

The analyses of various organizational scholars reflect these ideas. For example, Kunda (1992) has suggested that the culture of an organization he studied was "a gloss for an extensive definition of membership in the corporate community that includes rules for behavior, thought, and feeling, all adding up to what appears to be a well-defined and widely shared 'member role'" (p. 7). Schein (1992) gives an example of how French and Italian managers were excluded from the in-

ternal board of directors of their multinational company because the U.S. managers in the company, who assumed that good management requires being unemotional, considered them to be too emotional. Milton (1998) found that diverse members of emergency response groups, who otherwise had little in common and in many cases did not even like each other personally, overcame their differences when working together and stayed in their jobs because they shared a belief that their work is critically important. In the first case, shared ideologies about what it means to be a member created attachment; in the second, a lack of shared ideologies about how good managers should act blocked more intensive attachment and inclusion; in the third, a common belief in the importance of individual performance for their shared critical task attached individuals to their work organization.

## Sharing and Attachments

When people interact repeatedly, they are in a position to learn and be influenced by the cultural ideas, values, and norms of those with whom they interact. Interactions can occur for a variety of reasons, but one situation likely to produce repeated interactions is when people are interdependent with one another for valued resources. Division of labor ordinarily produces such interdependence, but it may not produce repeated interactions unless the social structure allows them to occur. In relatively simple societies and organic organizations, such interactions may be the norm. Social and economic exchanges provide a likely pattern for many of these interactions.

Lawler and Yoon (1998) found that greater frequency of resource exchange among subjects interacting in networks produced more pleasure and satisfaction, and that pleasure and satisfaction, in turn, yielded "positive effects on the perceived cohesiveness of the relation" (p. 885). Their findings suggest that even economic exchanges can, over time, produce attachments that can, in turn, give rise to cultures that inform and socially control those exchanges. Kono and Clegg (1998) suggest that cultures arise as members interact while "living in the same internal environment; sharing the same corporate philosophy; having the same leaders; doing the same job; sharing the same experiences; and being rewarded by the same personnel management system" (p. 111). These analyses echo Homans's insights that increased interaction tends to produce social cohesion. They also illustrate how interactions are likely to be accompanied by shared behavior in organizational settings.

### Cultural Forms and Attachments

Cultural forms foster commitment because they communicate shared meanings and encourage behavioral interaction among members of a group. These meanings are expressed through symbols of various kinds and through symbolic, often scripted behaviors. Using the example of rituals, Kunda (1992) points out that they "are collectively produced, structured, and dramatic occasions that create a 'frame,' a shared definition of the situation within which participants are expected to express and confirm sanctioned ways of experiencing social reality" (p. 93). He quotes Turner (1974) as saying that when ritual works, the reality portrayed assumes emotional significance for participants and produces "a symbiotic interpenetration of individual and society" (p. 56). Also, to the extent that cultural forms support identities that individuals value, individuals are likely to become more cognitively and affectively attached to the organizations that employ them (Milton, 1998).

Cultural forms, including symbols, language, narratives, and practices, remind individuals of what they believe in and value about various shared activities and thus reinforce their attachment to the cultural group with which they are engaging in those activities. Shared activities also provide opportunities for collective sensemaking (Berger & Luckmann, 1967). The potency of such shared activities and the beliefs, feelings, and symbols associated with them can be seen, for instance, in college athletics. Both fans and players bond together in their enthusiasm for and loyalty to "their" teams. One case involving a southwestern university in the United States provides an example of the surprisingly strong sentiments that can be associated with sports-related symbols. When it became necessary for the college to move the graves of the school's former mascot dogs to allow for expansion of the football stadium, university administrators, under pressure from alumni and students, were forced to provide a scoreboard near the new graves because the old graves had been located so that the deceased mascots could "see" the scoreboard in the stadium and thus follow the games (Beyer & Hannah, 2000)!

## CONCLUSIONS

As the preceding discussion shows, the processes that have been theorized as underlying attachment to social groups are cultural as well as social. The stronger the attachment, the more likely it is to be based in or reinforced by shared ideas, interactions, symbolism, and behavior. In addition, the stronger the attachment, the more likely it is to reflect a sense of belonging to and identification with a particular cultural group. Furthermore, as Homans (1950, pp. 99-103) has pointed out, each process delineated in Tables 20.1 and 20.2 is somewhat dependent on the others. As he would put it, shared sentiments depend on repeated social interactions and behaviors. In turn, interactions and shared behaviors depend to some degree on shared sentiments. This reflexivity and interconnectedness are, of course, two of the hallmarks of culture.

It seems likely that the interconnectedness and reflexivity of the social processes theorized as underlying attachment have contributed to the overlap in constructs evident in Tables 20.1 and 20.2. Thus when organizational researchers have tried to delimit their concepts, the better to study them empirically, they have soon found that they needed to expand their definitions to take account of the additional processes listed in Tables 20.1 and 20.2. Such expansions have tended to confuse further rather than to clarify this literature by creating many different sets of terms for the same phenomena. There have been some studies that have incorporated more than one of these constructs to assess their relationships—studies of commitment and citizenship behavior are an example—but these have been relatively rare and have seldom recognized the likely reflexivity of the concepts studied. Meanwhile, readers and students of this literature are confronted by a bewildering array of increasingly overlapping concepts and definitions. If researchers believe that their constructs have independent merit or are in some sense superior to others, they should be expected to delineate those benefits theoretically and empirically relative to the many other constructs cited here. They should explain, as we have done here for culture, how the new constructs they advance focus on phenomena that prior conceptualizations have failed to capture. Also, it would be helpful if future researchers would ground their theoretical approaches in the well-established classical theories reviewed here. If future editors and reviewers will weigh these issues in deciding the contributions of submitted papers, some of the apparent overlaps could be eliminated.

This review of the two areas of research documents that culture begets attachments and attachments beget culture. A few researchers have investigated this connection, but much more work can and should be done. In particular, research on organizational cultures should go beyond the assumption that this connection is obvious and instead observe and describe the social processes involved.

# 21

# Commitment and the Study of Organizational Climate and Culture

## —— Turo Virtanen

The term *commitment* is widely used in sociology, psychology, and organization studies. Definitions and usage of the term emphasizing values, norms, affects, attachments, identification, and so on imply that it shares some of its referents with those of *organizational climate* and *organizational culture*. Wiener (1982) contends that the existing models of commitment do not satisfy the requirements of definitional precision, theoretical integration, and predictive power. Morrow's (1983) analysis reveals that different concepts related to commitment are partially redundant and insufficiently distinct. Allen and Meyer (1990) state that the "use of the term 'commitment' to describe very different constructs has led to considerable confusion in the literature" (p. 14). My purposes in this chapter are (a) to integrate different conceptual constructs of organizational commitment and (b) to specify how organizational commitment can be related to organizational climate and culture

(for analysis of commitment as part of theories of attachment, see Beyer, Hannah, & Milton, Chapter 20, this volume).

I will argue, first, that the study of organizational commitment needs a more multidimensional framework than is currently available. I will then develop a suggestion for a framework using current literature as a starting point, and then show how that framework contributes to the analysis of strength of commitment. I will argue that the concept of commitment can be best connected to those of organizational climate and culture when commitments are seen as instruments of climate but constituents of culture. Finally, I will contend that the strength of an organizational culture can be fruitfully analyzed as the strength of commitment to an organization.

In the context of organizations, commitment is normally understood as different ways to commit oneself to an organization of which one is a member (see Table 21.1 for

**TABLE 21.1    Definitions of Commitment in the Context of Organizations**

Becker (1960): "The committed person has acted in such a way as to involve other interests of his, originally extraneous to the action he is engaged in, directly in that action" (p. 35).

Kanter (1968): "Commitment . . . refers to the willingness of social actors to give their energy and loyalty to social systems, the attachment of personality systems to social relations which are seen as self-expressive" (p. 499).

Porter et al. (1974): Organizational commitment is defined "in terms of the strength of an individual's identification with and involvement in a particular organization. Such commitment can be characterized by at least three factors: (a) a strong belief in and acceptance of the organization's goals and values; (b) a willingness to exert considerable effort on behalf of the organization; (c) a definitive desire to maintain organizational membership" (p. 604).

Wiener (1982): "Organizational commitment is viewed as the totality of internalized normative pressures to act in a way that meets organizational goals and interests" (p. 421).

Reichers (1985): "Commitment is a process of identification with the goals of an organization's multiple constituencies. These constituencies may include top management, customers, unions, and/or the public at large" (p. 465).

O'Reilly and Chatman (1986): "Organizational commitment is conceived of as the psychological attachment felt by the person for the organization; it will reflect the degree to which the individual internalizes or adopts characteristics or perspectives of the organization" (p. 493).

Penley and Gould (1988): "A moral commitment is characterized by the acceptance of and identification with organizational goals." Calculative commitment "is based on the employee's receiving inducements to match contributions." Alienative commitment "may be conceived to represent the kind of organizational attachment which results when an employee no longer perceives that there are rewards commensurate with investments; yet, he or she remains due to environmental pressure" (p. 46, 48).

Jaros et al. (1993): Continuance commitment "reflects the degree to which an individual experiences a sense of being locked in place because of the high costs of leaving." Affective commitment is "the degree to which an individual is psychologically attached to an employing organization through feelings such as loyalty, affection, warmth, belongingness, fondness, happiness, pleasure, and so on." Moral commitment is "the degree to which an individual is psychologically attached to an employing organization through internalization of its goals, values, and missions" (p. 953-955).

Meyer and Allen (1997): "Affective commitment refers to the employee's emotional attachment to, identification with, and involvement in the organization. Employees with a strong affective commitment continue employment with the organization because they *want* to do so. Continuance commitment refers to an awareness of the costs associated with leaving the organization. Employees whose primary link to the organization is based on continuance commitment remain because they *need* to do so. Finally, normative commitment reflects a feeling of obligation to continue employment. Employees with a high level of normative commitment feel that they *ought* to remain within the organization" (p. 11).

major definitions). According to Becker's (1960) side-bet theory of commitment, the committed person's involvement in an organization can make side bets for him or her and constrain his or her future behavior. When these constraints lead to behavior that is consistent with the goals and values of the organization, the individual is committed to the organization. This definition represents an instrumental conception of commitment. Organizational commitment has also been defined as an individual's identification with and involvement in an organization (Porter, Steers, Mowday, & Boulian, 1974). In this view, commitment is characterized by a strong belief in and acceptance of the organization's goals and values, a willingness to exert considerable effort on behalf of the organization, and a strong desire to maintain membership in the organization. This exemplifies a more value-based conception of commitment.

Organizational commitment may be but one of the multiple commitments of the members of an organization, other commitments being, for example, to top management, to profession, to external funding agencies, to union, and to client (Becker, 1992; Gordon, Philpot, Burt, Thompson, & Spiller, 1980; Hunt & Morgan, 1994; Reichers, 1985, 1986). Morrow (1993) has suggested five universal forms of work commitment, of which two are oriented to an entire organization:

1. Work ethic endorsement (the importance of work itself)
2. Career or professional commitment (the importance to the individual of his or her occupation)
3. Job involvement (the degree of daily absorption the individual experiences in work activity)
4. Continuance organizational commitment (cost-based employee dedication to an organization)
5. Affective organizational commitment (emotional employee dedication to an organization)

Other authors have specified three types or components of organizational commitment in somewhat divergent ways (see Table 21.1). The major trichotomies are (a) moral, calculative, and alienative; (b) affective, continuance, and normative; and (c) continuance, affective, and moral. Calculative and continuance forms of commitment involve inducements, rewards, and costs of leaving. Moral, affective, and normative commitment involve acceptance and internalization of or

identification with the values and goals of the organization, as well as emotional attachment and loyalty to an organization, quite in the same way as defined in many studies on organizational climate and culture (Schneider, 1990b).

Tagiuri and Litwin (1968) define organizational climate as the relatively enduring quality of an organization that is experienced by employees, influences their behavior, and can be described as values. According to Payne and Pugh (1976), organizational climate helps to identify how the organization is psychologically meaningful for individual organization members. Also, organizational commitment is commonly understood as a psychological state of an individual (Meyer & Allen, 1997). Definitions of organizational culture, in turn, refer to the following entities:

1. The unique configuration of norms, values, beliefs, ways of behaving, and so on that characterizes the manner in which groups and individuals combine to get things done (Eldridge & Crombie, 1974)
2. A set of largely tacit meanings shared by a group of people (Louis, 1980)
3. A pattern of basic shared assumptions that the group has learned in solving its problems of external adaptation and internal integration (Schein, 1985)
4. The implicit, invisible, intrinsic, and informal consciousness of the organization that guides the behavior of individuals (Scholz, 1987)
5. The commonly held and relatively stable beliefs, attitudes, and values that exist within the organization (Williams, Dobson, & Walters, 1993)

The term *commitment* is not used in definitions of climate and culture, but it is obvious that part of the idea of sharing values, goals, and assumptions includes being committed to them. Commitment as internalization or emotional attachment is not far from implicit and informal consciousness or tacit meanings important in culture studies.

Definitions of organizational commitment, climate, and culture reveal that there is some overlap. Before I present an analysis of the links between commitment and organizational climate and culture, I will discuss the concept of commitment. In the next section, I develop a conceptual framework for organizational commitment and apply it in addressing the strength of commitment. Following that, I will relate organizational commitment to organizational climate and culture, and then analyze strength of culture as strength of commitment.

## COMMITMENT

For analytic purposes, it is useful to differentiate among locus of commitment, object of commitment, base of commitment, focus of commitment, source of commitment, antecedents of commitment, and consequences of commitment. This terminology deviates from the vocabulary common in commitment studies, but I use it here to make the approach sufficiently multidimensional. *Locus of commitment* refers to where we can find different objects to which commitment is oriented. Brown (1996) distinguishes among a person, a group of persons, an entity made up of people (as in organization), and an idea or cause as an object of commitment, but he does not develop these distinctions further. There are basically two loci of commitment. One may be committed to an idea as such—for example, gender equality—or one may be committed to an agent. The agent can be personal, such as the deputy chief of the department of human resource management, or impersonal, such as an organization. An individual forms a commitment to an agent because he or she believes the agent to "carry" appealing ideas—for example, gender equality. The locus of commitment has implications for the measurement of commitment. The "carrier approach" relies more on behavior, whereas the "idea approach" relies

more on intentions or meanings in the formation of knowledge about commitments.

The *object of commitment* is an entity to which commitment is oriented, whether an idea or an agent. In an organizational context, ideational objects of commitment are values, goals, principles, and policies, but so are artifacts like myths and heroes. Agents are entire organizations or different levels of organizational structures: organizational units, managers, professions, and coworkers as individuals or groups. Traditionally, organizational commitment is understood as a commitment to an entire organization (global commitment), but organizational commitment can be understood also as a function of multiple commitments to organizational ideas and agents in an organization. Commitment to agents can be upheld even if the ideas that the agents are seen to carry may be shifting or obscure. One may be committed to obey a deputy chief, for example, although one is not sure about his or her human resources management policies. Organizations very often expect commitment to agents without giving members any opportunity to check the coherence of the values, goals, principles, and policies the agents may actually advocate. Individuals are also often committed to somebody or to something, even though they can describe only in very broad terms the ideas they share with that something or somebody.

The distinction between an idea and the carrier of an idea comes close to the traditional distinction between "attitudinal" and "behavioral" approach to commitment (Brown, 1996; Mowday, Steers, & Porter, 1979). This distinction assumes, however, something about bases and foci of commitment. For example, attitudinal commitment is sometimes called affective commitment, whereas behavioral commitment is called continuance commitment (Aven, Parker, & McEvoy, 1993). This exemplifies the need for careful conceptual analysis.

O'Reilly and Chatman (1986) understand organizational commitment as psychological attachment to organization. Following Kelman (1958), they differentiate among three *bases of commitment:* (a) compliance, or "instrumental involvement for specific, extrinsic rewards"; (b) identification, or "involvement based on a desire for affiliation"; and (c) internalization, or "involvement predicated on congruence between individual and organizational values." I prefer a trichotomy of obligations, utilities, and emotions. These concepts refer more directly to rational and arational bases of commitment that make people bind themselves to objects of commitment. Emotions as bases of commitment constitute mostly arational bindings through the process of identification. They are "beyond reason," not irrational (as the opposite of rational). Obligations and utilities as bases of commitment constitute mostly rational bindings through the mechanisms of compliance and internalization. Obligations may be part of internalization as well as part of compliance, because both internalized value congruence and compliance-related exchange rules create obligations. The same applies for utilities: Value congruence enables acceptable rewards, and exchange rules provide the means for balancing mutual benefits. The binding force is not always transparent to one who is committed. Rational bases are more transparent than arational ones.

Meyer and Allen (1997) differentiate among affective, normative, and continuance components of commitment (see Table 21.1). This resembles the trichotomy of emotion, obligation, and utility. Meyer and Allen understand, however, both affective and normative commitment as emotional commitment, perhaps arational, and continuance commitment as awareness of costs (people need to remain with the organization), probably rational. Contrary to their implication, I hold that the nature of obligations, related to normative commitment in Meyer and Allen's view, is rational rather than arational, because people have rational arguments about norms. Obligations generated by socialization are often only partly transparent, but this does not make them emotional, only deficiently understood. Jaros, Jermier, Koehler, and Sincich (1993), in turn, come closer to my trichotomy, because they relate emotion only to affective commitment but costs to continuance commitment and "a sense of duty, an obligation, or calling" (p. 955) to moral commitment (see Table 21.1). In this way, continuance commitment and moral commitment can probably be understood as rational commitment, and affective commitment as arational commitment. But, contrary to Jaros et al.'s view, obligations can be also other than moral obligations, and even costs have connections to emotions. For analytic clarity, we should not mix bases of commitment with foci of commitment.

The *focus of commitment* tells us about the content of commitment in the same way frameworks reveal the angle from which we see what we see. The focus of commitment can be, for example, moral, legal, economic, and political—in some cases even aesthetic. The foci of commitment are in many ways related to societal institutions, because they have a profound affect on how we see the world. Together with the bases of commitment, foci provide the motive of commitment as it is experienced. This is a perspective that previous research on commitment has not addressed directly. For example, in Reichers's (1985) multiple-constituency model of organizational commitment, the foci of employees' commitment are the goals and values of different groups inside and outside of the organization. In the language I am applying here, values and goals as well as groups are objects of commitment. For every object of commitment there are many foci of commitment, in the same way as there are many frameworks for any object. One may be committed to the idea of gender equality legally and politically but not morally, for instance. Multidimensionality of psychological contracts (Rousseau, 1995) comes closer to my view in the sense that these contracts seem to include all kinds of mutual expectations about rewards, power, emotions, and the like.

The *source of commitment* tells us about the background from which different objects, loci, bases, and foci of commitment are generated. There are many alternatives: education, training, leadership styles and management systems, institutions, socioeconomic class, national culture, and civilizations. These are all responsible for diverse contents of commitments, such as the occurrence of gender equality as a potential object of commitment.

*Antecedents of commitment* (Mathieu, 1991; Mathieu & Zajac, 1990)—age, tenure, task autonomy, and role ambiguity, for example—can be understood as intervening variables that channel the occurrence and strength of different commitments. In order to "manage commitments," we have to know which constellations of different objects, loci, bases, and foci of commitment are related to which antecedents and, further, which antecedents are related to which sources of commitment and how tangible their interrelations are. In this way we can create different commitments for different organizational purposes. These purposes can be refined as the *consequences of commitment,* such as turnover, job performance, and different normative characteristics of organizational behavior (Wiener, 1982).

The framework of organizational commitment that I have laid out broadens the approach to commitments, restructures the terminology used in commitment studies, and enables multidimensional analysis of organizational commitment without losing connections to previous research (Table 21.2). Previous research has not addressed sources and foci of commitment as they are understood here, but some of the objects of commitment have been covered even by traditional quantitative measures of organizational commitment. To embrace all the suggested elements of organizational commitment, qualitative studies are also needed. I will now use the framework developed above to analyze the strength of organizational commitment.

## The Strength of Organizational Commitment

Brown (1996) defines the strength of commitment as "its significance or importance in the life of a person who owns the commitment relative to other commitments and pursuits" (p. 234). He is right, in that relative strength must be linked to effort. The results of committed behavior depend partly on factors that are beyond the control of the one who is committed. Another way to understand the strength of commitment is through the idea that the more commitment constrains future behavior, the stronger commitment is (Salancik, 1977). But because both effort and constraint depend on bases, foci, and objects of commitment, a better understanding of the strength of commitment requires the analysis of their relation to the binding force of commitment.

Brown (1996) analyzes the binding force in terms of the attitudinal-behavioral distinction, not directly in terms of the bases or foci of commitment indicated above. From the behavioral perspective, he differentiates two ways to make a pledge or commitment: overt statements of agreement and actions and behaviors that indicate where one stands. This kind of commitment is seen to be stronger than commitment that is purely internal because "the costs of backing out would be primarily self-imposed" (p. 237). Also, Salancik (1977) contends that commitment becomes stronger according to the extent to which committing behavior is explicit, irreversible, voluntary, and public. From the attitudinal perspective, "a person can become committed without making an overt pledge: if a person develops sufficient positive attitudes or sense of goal congruence, then at some point that person is committed" (Brown, 1996, p. 237). This approach stresses the importance of positive work experiences and role factors.

Brickman (1987, p. 10) has differentiated between positive and negative elements of commitment that lead to "two faces" of each

**TABLE 21.2**   Basic Elements of Organizational Commitment

| Source of Commitment | Antecedent of Commitment | Locus of Commitment | Object of Commitment | Base of Commitment | Focus of Commitment | Consequence of Commitment |
|---|---|---|---|---|---|---|
| Upbringing | Age | Idea | Value | | | Turnover |
| Class | Sex | | Goal | | | Job performance |
| Education | Tenure | | Principle | Obligation | Moral | Sacrifice |
| Institution | Ability | | Policy | Utility | Legal | Preoccupation |
| Training | Salary | | Artifact (myth, | Emotion | Economic | Persistence |
| Leadership | Task autonomy | | hero, etc.) | | Political | Efforts |
| National culture | Job scope | Agent | Organization | | | Attendance |
| Civilization | | | Unit | | | Grievances |
| | | | Team | | | Legitimacy |
| | | | Manager | | | |
| | | | Coworker | | | |
| | | | Profession | | | |

commitment. The dominance of positive elements makes the person's orientation enthusiastic ("want to"—beyond the call of duty), and the dominance of negative elements makes it persistent ("have to"—the call of duty). Brown (1996) sees that persistent attitudes make the commitment weaker, perhaps only to meet the "letter" of the term. Enthusiastic attitudes represent stronger commitment because the terms are interpreted in an expansive way. One may ask whether "have to" commitment is commitment at all, at least if it is only behavioral consistency under the fear of sanctions. Brickman's idea is, however, that even though "have to" and "want to" are logically independent, they are psychologically dependent, and actually their relationship is what commitment is all about. He further sees commitment as "the transition rule, the point at which people switch from rational processing to something else" (p. 18), referring to "nonrational" aspects of commitment (probably the same as arational aspects in my analysis).

It seems that there are both rational and arational elements in the contemplation of commitment as well as both internal (or private) and external (or public) elements in the affirmation of commitment. Rational elements include voluntary obligations, explicit promises, and costs of keeping them, covering both "want to" and "have to." Arational elements include emotional experiences of liking, attraction, attachment, implicit value congruence, and so on. Public elements are overt behavioral expressions, such as making a pledge or declaring one's commitment. Such communication makes social commitment, hence organizational commitment, possible. Private elements are those hidden or obscure ways of committing oneself without another's full knowledge of either the act of commitment or the content of the commitment. The resulting four quadrants, presented in Figure 21.1, create a field where the three bases of commitment—obligations, utilities, and emotions—find their major location.

The binding force coming from *emotions* is beyond the individual's rational control, hence arational, but the emergence of emotions is not necessarily beyond the rational control of either the individual or someone else. One can predict part of their emergence by controlling the individual's access to communication with the objects of commitment. Emotions can be expressed overtly, or self-control may repress them for one reason or another, but their suppression does not make them inefficient in terms of the individual's experiencing the binding force of commitment. For example, at the level of behavior, admiration of a leader who appeals charismatically to an organizational policy of gender equality (PGE) is not expressed similarly by an introverted person and an extroverted person, but both feel the charisma anyway. The stronger the positive experience, the stronger the commitment to the object of emotion. The strength of positivity is partly determined by the qualities of the process of affirmation. "Emotion work" directs socially constructed rules about both what one should feel and how one should express it (Hochschild, 1979). This is the rational part of emotional orientation, whereas the emotional experience of commitment is itself arational. The psychological state that includes rational and arational orientation of positive emotional bindings, as well as the ways they are expressed, can be called *desire*. Desire regulates the contemplation and affirmation of the individual's emotions of commitment, because it constitutes the forms of emotional orientation and abstention.

The binding force of *utilities* comes mainly from rational analysis of the pros and cons of each move in making a pledge. Even though the promises are overt in themselves, it is often against the individual's self-interest to reveal their "price" and the circumstances under which they would contribute to his or her profit. In a bargaining situation, the deepest commitments are mostly hidden. They remain individual commitments. Only the public parts generate potentially social commit-

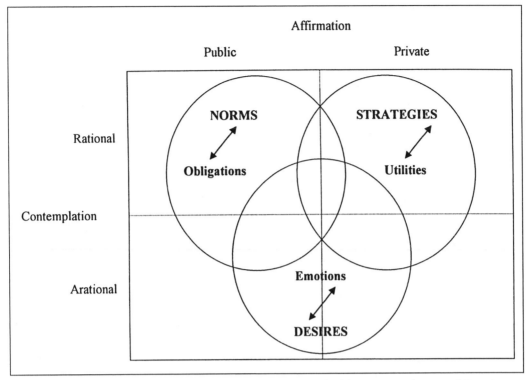

**Figure 21.1.** Norms, Strategies, and Desires as Determinants of Obligations, Utilities, and Emotions

ments needed for organizational commitment. The greater the benefit of keeping a promise, the stronger the commitment to the content of the promise. Part of the benefit results from the rational and successful concealment of commitments. The benefit is related to the prediction of the change in circumstances. This is why it is the situation-based *strategy* that regulates the contemplation and affirmation of the utilities of commitments.

The binding force of *obligation* comes also from rational analysis. It is not related to the consequences of behavior as much as in the case of utilities, but is related mostly to rules that a person consents to or is not able to avoid. Following or acting against these rules presupposes rational contemplation, because otherwise their existence is not recognized. Part of the rules is given only fuzzy approval

or disapproval, which also links obligations to arational consideration. Approval creates the binding force of obligations. Disapproval leads the individual to think in terms of utilities. Approval is mostly overt, because the acceptance of prevailing rules is normal (conformity). The stronger the acceptance, the stronger the commitment to the contents of the rules. The strength is partly determined by the process of affirmation, as, for example, when a person undergoes conversion from one system of obligations to another. Prevailing rules constitute the system of *norms* that regulate the contemplation and affirmation of the obligations of commitments.

Taking all this together, we can conclude that *the strength of commitment is the function of norms, strategies, and desires* that determine interactively the roles of obligations, utilities, and emotions in each situation. Norms as determinants of obligations embrace moral, legal, economic, and political obligations. They belong to different norms with a variety of institutional sources that govern individual commitment. Strategies as determinants of utilities cover moral, legal, economic, and political utilities. They are part of different strategies governing individual commitment. Also, moral strategies are acceptable if we approve of the doctrine of morality as prudentialism (Gauthier, 1986). Desire as a determinant of emotions covers not only legal, economic, and political emotions but also moral emotions. Although morality is not based on emotions, desires affect the emergence of morally relevant emotions. But what types of norms, strategies, and desires are responsible for the strongest commitments—moral, legal, economic, or political ones? This crucial question cannot be addressed here.

Although the concepts of this framework are useful for analyzing the structure of commitment, more empirical research along the lines of the framework is needed to reveal which structure is strong and which is weak. Theoretically, one could expect that commitment to both idea and its carrier is stronger than commitment to only one of them. The more objects of commitment belong to an organization, the stronger the commitment to that particular organization. Commitment with all the three bases—obligation, utility, and emotion—is probably stronger than commitment with fewer bases. The same applies to foci of commitment: The strongest commitment includes moral, legal, economic, and political foci in concert. Commitment to a value is probably weaker than commitment to a (legitimate) policy, because policy needs communication and formal acceptance. Commitment to a person is probably stronger than commitment to an organization, for communication between two persons is more intensive than that between a person and an organization. But all of this needs more empirical research.

## COMMITMENT, CLIMATE, AND CULTURE

Organizational commitment is often understood as an attribute of individual thinking and behavior toward an organization. However, organizational commitment is *social* commitment in the sense that organizations need to influence and control the commitments of their members toward objects relevant for organizational success. This creates the need to make commitments visible and understandable to other people. It also creates a need for sufficiently homogeneous commitments. Organizational commitment presupposes that individual commitments become social commitments that are sufficiently symmetrical in terms of objects, bases, foci, and consequences of commitment. The social asymmetry of commitment is a challenge for the management of commitment. In principle, the same requirement of symmetry is set for organizational climate, culture, and their management. To proceed further, we have to analyze the differences between organizational climate and culture.

According to Rentsch (1990), climate theory assumes that organizational members perceive and make sense of organizational events, but the interpretations of those events are not directly measured, whereas in culture theory there is explicit respect for qualitative variance in meanings. Schneider, Gunnarson, and Niles-Jolly (1994) say that climate is the atmosphere that employees perceive and that is created by practices, procedures, and rewards, whereas culture is the broader pattern of an organization's mores, values, and beliefs that stem from employees' interpretations of the assumptions, values, and philosophies that produce the climate they experience. According to Rousseau (1988), climate is "an individual description of the social setting or context of which a person is part" (p. 140), whereas a key element in culture is "consensus or shared values or beliefs" (p. 149). In the conceptual analysis of Verbeke, Volkering, and Hessels (1998), organizational climate is understood as "a reflection of the way people perceive and come to describe the characteristics of their environment," whereas organizational culture "reflects the way things are done in an organization" (pp. 319-320). Denison's (1996) overview of the literature ends up with the following distinction, which he considers to be most widely accepted: Culture refers to the deep structure of organizations, rooted in the relatively stable values, beliefs, and assumptions held by organizational members, whereas climate is rooted in the organization's value system, subject to direct control, and largely limited to those aspects of the social environment that are consciously perceived by members of the organization.

Denison's analysis shows that there is considerable overlap between studies of organizational climate and studies of organizational culture in the sense that they examine the same organizational phenomena, albeit from different perspectives. One could say that climate is mostly understood to be more manifest than culture, and culture more latent than climate. Climate is based on individual perceptions that are transparent to individuals themselves, but that they do not necessarily share with or reveal to other members of the organization. Culture is based on inherently social meanings that are latently shared with other members of the organization, leading to the holistic nature of culture. The sharing grows through organizational socialization, which is defined as a "process by which an individual comes to appreciate the values, abilities, expected behaviors, and social knowledge essential for assuming an organizational role and for participating as an organizational member" (Louis, 1980, pp. 229-230; see also Chao, O'Leary-Kelly, Wolf, Klein, & Gardner, 1994; Major, Chapter 22, this volume). Even if organizational socialization is something other than learning organizational culture, it cannot exclude culture either.

Denison's (1996) main conclusion is that the central difference lies in the theoretical background: Climate studies have their roots in Lewin's field theory, whereas culture studies are grounded in the symbolic interaction and social construction perspectives developed by Mead and by Berger and Luckmann. The former background leads to the conception that a person is distinct from his or her environment or social context. Consequently, climate is created by the managers, and employees "work within a climate, but they do not create it" (p. 634). The latter theoretical background does not separate the individual from the social environment. Therefore, culture is both the medium and the outcome of social interaction.

When climate is seen to be more controllable than culture, and culture more autonomous than climate and even constitutive of organization, it is logical that the relationship of climate and commitment is seen as external and the relationship of culture and commitment as internal. In this sense, *commitments are instruments of climate but constituents of culture*. Some instruments may in the long run eventually become constituents when their original purposes are forgotten and their signification has become routine in nature. Before constitution can take place, the management of commitment has to lead to symmetrical commitments in which the parties of social relations share objects, bases, and foci of commitment. This assumption gives us an opportunity to see an interaction between climate and culture and to preserve the widely accepted distinctions of climate and culture. However, if commitments are constituents of culture, there is no room for culture of noncommitment, only culture of heterogeneous commitment. Climate of noncommitment can exist if climate can originate without commitments.

Whether the relationship of climate and culture to commitment is internal or external, commitments cannot be created directly, as they are psychosocial states of mind. Creation and change of commitments take place

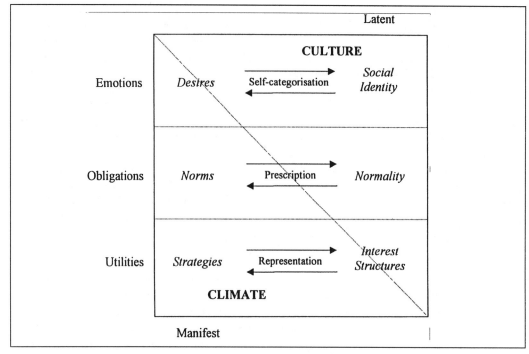

**Figure 21.2.** Organizational Climate and Culture in Relation to Manifest and Latent Determinants of Emotions, Obligations, and Utilities

through determinants of commitments that are related to interaction of all the basic elements of commitment presented in Table 21.2. The determinants of bases of commitments, specified in Figure 21.1, are helpful for presenting the argument that rational and arational contemplation, and public and private affirmation of commitment, can be related to the distinction between manifest and latent, which is relevant for climate and culture (see Figure 21.2).

*Strategies—interest structure.* Strategies as determinants of rational and mostly privately affirmed commitments are the most manifest elements, and hence are instruments of climate rather than of culture. The transparency of utility-based individual commitments makes it relatively easy to use them in the management of climate—for example, as part of a reward system. A sexist climate can be partly influenced if commitment to a PGE

is beneficial for the members of an organization. The latent counterpart of strategies is the *interest structure,* a constituent of culture represented by individual strategies of an organizational commitment. The interest structure of an organizational patriarchy leads to differences in the utility structures between typically female and male commitment. Articulation of more or less stable interest structures keeps organizations together even if their members behave like rational egoists. A new strategy—imposed, for example, by a formal PGE—may eventually become a new latent interest structure.

*Desires—social identity.* Desires as determinants of arational but partly publicly and partly privately affirmed commitments are the least manifest elements, because emotions are mostly autonomous. Desires are partly latent because their origins are obscure for their carrier, which makes them constituents of commitment rather than instruments. The latent counterpart of desires is *social identity*, which is produced by the process of self-categorization (Tajfel, 1982a; Turner, 1985). The attractiveness of a group induces one to categorize oneself as the member of the group, and the value of group membership is increased by the defaming of out-group members. Group becomes part of the self-concept of an individual. Even though the process of self-categorization is cognitive or even rational, the binding force behind identification is understood here to be emotional. Desires of organizational commitment are articulations of preferred social identity, which is inherently fuzzy and imagelike, hence latent. Desires that lead to commitment to a PGE are articulations of the history of intergroup comparisons in which the attractiveness of the supporters of gender equality is strengthened by the denigration of male and female chauvinists. The self-categorization expressed in these comparisons creates both the desires and the social identity and results in commitments that constitute the gender contents of an organization culture.

*Norms—normality.* Norms as determinants of rational and mostly publicly affirmed commitments are less manifest than strategies but more manifest than desires. Acceptable manifest norms lead to commitments based on obligations, which make it possible to manage climate through norms—for example, through a PGE. Norms are partly latent because their origins are very often unknown to individuals, even though the individuals consider their obligations normal. The latent prescription of norms is understood in many ways by the classics of social theory: for example, as collective mind (Durkheim, 1976) or discursive practice that expresses itself as expert knowledge (Foucault, 1972a). Here I call the latent counterpart of norms *normality*. It refers to taken-for-granted beliefs that are nearly impossible to question but create normative pressures for both thinking and behavior. In

some organizations, gender equality may be part of normality. Under these circumstances, obligations to follow this norm are efficient without formal policies exemplifying commitment as a constituent of organizational culture.

Figure 21.2 shows how organizational climate can be understood to cover strategies, norms, and part of interest structures and desires, whereas for organizational culture there remain social identity, normality, and part of interest structures and desires. This division is, of course, imprecise and made only for heuristic purposes. It only suggests how the bases of commitment can be integrated with theory of organizational climate and culture through their manifest and latent determinants. This tentative model can be developed further through the inclusion of foci of commitment. For example, political desires, norms, and strategies, as well as politically understood social identity, normality, and interest structures, are all related to a formal PGE as an object of commitment. These concepts could offer a framework for the analysis of commitment to the PGE as an instrument of organizational climate and as a constituent of organizational culture.

## Strength of Culture as Strength of Commitment

A strong culture is usually understood as a synonym for consistency: Beliefs and values are "shared relatively consistently throughout an organization" (Brown, 1995, p. 183). In the language of commitment, consistency of culture is the social symmetry of objects, bases, foci, and consequences of commitment. Without social symmetry, strong individual commitment is not the same as strong organizational culture. A strong culture is often seen to enable an organization to achieve excellent performance, a hypothesis that has been made by Deal and Kennedy (1982). Brown (1995) discerns three main arguments about strength of culture and performance, all of which can easily be translated into the language of commitment.

First, strong organizational culture is said to facilitate goal alignment, understood as agreement on goals and means. Commitment to goals and means creates social symmetry, which makes coordination of social relations easy. Commitment to agents, such as managers, carrying those goals and means is an alternative way to create coordination, and for some employees it is an even more efficient way. But even if the objects of commitment (goals and means, managers) are the same, the bases, foci, and consequences may differ. The agreement may be asymmetrical; for example, one party might agree on the basis of moral obligation, whereas the other might agree on the basis of economic utilities. The consequences of this difference may be more than harmful for performance.

Second, strong culture is said to lead to high levels of employee motivation. This refines the previous argument. Motives of commitment may differ in terms of bases and foci of commitment. In some cultures, morally strong motives may support performance best; in other cultures, politically strong motives may do so. The strength of motivation contributes to performance only if the motives of commitment are compatible, not necessarily the same. Subcultures with diverse but compatible motivations are often a resource, not a constraint.

Third, strong culture is said to be better able to learn from its past, because it has agreed-upon norms, integrative rituals and ceremonies, and well-known stories. The learning of the same thing is possible if all members are committed to the same standards of "doing it better." However, it may be necessary to challenge the standards to learn new things needed for the adaptation to environment. Commitment to more than one standard may create dissent and yet may be fruitful for survival and innovation. Alternative standards may be external to an organization, but organizations often need this kind

of disloyalty and flexibility to cope with dynamic changes.

Strength of culture can easily be conceptualized as strength of commitments and the optimal degree of their social symmetry. This points out that even though the culture is holistic, it exists only in social relations, which, in turn, can be strengthened by commitments. The framework of commitment (see Table 21.2 and Figures 21.1 and 21.2) provides concepts not only for more multidimensional analysis of the role of commitment in organizational climate and culture, but also for their management. Brown (1995) differentiates between two kinds of mechanisms for managing culture: those relying on various human resource instruments and those involving leader action and inaction. Among the former, we can find recruitment and selection procedures, induction, socialization and training, performance appraisal systems, and reward systems. Among the latter are management by symbols (use of time, language, meetings, agendas and minutes, physical settings) and management by rites of passage, enhancement, degradation, conflict resolution, integration, and renewal. All of these can be understood as targets for management of commitment. Management of commitment is also management of climate and culture, because it is commitment that binds people to organizational ideas and agents.

Managers can affect organizational commitment by learning to use antecedents of organizational commitment. Company tenure, union satisfaction, job satisfaction, job involvement, job equity, and supervisor support have been shown to be significant predictors of company commitment (Johnson & Jones-Johnson, 1992). Team cohesion, task challenge, supervisory behavior, and organizational climate can also be predictors, but in different ways in different career stages (Brooks & Seers, 1991; see also Cohen, 1991). Role strain (role ambiguity, role conflict, role overload), training characteristics, and achievement motivation are also important antecedents of commitment (Mathieu, 1991). The specifically designed fit between individuals' preferences and organizational cultures can be seen as a goal of management of commitment, because both job satisfaction and organizational commitment can be predicted with this fit (O'Reilly, Chatman, & Caldwell, 1991). These regularities are not structured to support management of climate and culture directly, but there is no obstacle preventing researchers from doing quantitative and qualitative research and reconceptualizing the antecedents and consequences of commitment. For this purpose, we need to have a sufficiently multidimensional conception of the content of commitment that is refined to embrace the most important elements of organizational climate and culture, not only organization as a global entity.

For example, the application of a commitment perspective to recruitment and selection procedures, induction, socialization and training, performance appraisal systems, and reward systems would probably reveal something new about these elements as cultural phenomena. The same could apply to management by symbols (use of time, language, meetings, agendas and minutes, physical settings) and management by rites (of passage, enhancement, degradation, conflict resolution, integration, and renewal). This would increase our knowledge of organizational culture not as an attribute of global organization, but as an attribute of the social relations constituting culture. Concentration on the multiple commitments of constituent parts of organization would also contribute to the development of new instruments for managing culture. Brickman (1987) relates the concept of commitment to cognitive processes that either are "nonrational" or take place outside of awareness: Commitment is a device both "for automating things, simplifying them, and putting them out of awareness" and "for keeping things within focal awareness" (p. 17). This surely refers to the value of commitment as both a managerial instrument and an organizational constituent.

## CONCLUSIONS

Commitment is mostly understood to comprise only the base of commitment and "focus" (here object) of commitment. The content of these concepts is too simple to cover culturally relevant issues in organization studies. One reason for this is probably the predominantly quantitative techniques of commitment studies. The conceptual reasoning has been oriented to develop better survey measures of commitment, not to broaden theoretical instruments. These are needed to make the nature of the binding force of commitment more evident. I suggest especially that the concepts of object, base, and focus of commitment be enriched in connection with the dimensions of rational-arational and public-private.

The distinction between commitment to idea and commitment to agent, along with the ensuing distinctions in objects of commitment, would broaden the scope of studies of organizational commitment. Bases of commitment (obligation, utility, and emotion) combined with foci of commitment (moral, legal, economic, and political) would provide better understanding of the motives of commitment to be found in organizations. This would build up connections to societal institutions that structure commitment in organizations. Institutions provide information about the concrete pledges people are expected to make. They affect also the strength of commitment, especially with their latent binding force related to strategies, norms, and desires as determinants of commitment.

The inherently social nature of organizational commitment is often forgotten when commitment is understood as the psychological state of mind of an individual. Research on organizational culture has challenged this by emphasizing social relations as determinants of individual meanings. The formation and demonstration of multiple and sufficiently symmetrical commitments presuppose organizational communication. Aggregation of individual perceptions of an entire organization is not enough. A more multidimensional analysis of commitments in organization opens up a research field where commitments can be approached more qualitatively, both as instruments of organizational climate and as constituents of organizational culture. Also, the strength of culture can be better understood if it is analyzed as strength of multiple commitments.

This conception of commitment comes close to that of Weick (1995), who asserts that commitment has not only motivational but also epistemological consequences for individuals' making sense of organizational phenomena: Commitment "focuses the social construction of reality on those actions that are high in choice, visibility, and irrevocability" (p. 162). As I understand this, commitment is created through the formation of meanings related to manifest actions with high choice, visibility, and irrevocability. In this way, commitments are instruments in the management of organizational climate. Once the meanings become persistent and latent, they construct the organizational reality and are, therefore, constituents of organizational culture. The concepts of object, base, and foci of commitment aid in the analysis of how commitments affect sensemaking and function as sources of order and value.

# 22

# Effective Newcomer Socialization Into High-Performance Organizational Cultures

-- *Debra A. Major*

There appears to be little doubt that the nature of work is changing (Howard, 1995). As we move into the 21st century, predictions are that at least one-third of work organizations will become flatter and increasingly characterized by high-performance cultures (Lengermann, 1988). Such cultures will require high employee involvement in information-rich environments that are dynamic and often unpredictable (E. E. Lawler, 1992; Lawler, Mohrman, & Leford, 1992, 1995). Organizations' competitive advantages will be largely a function of the extent to which they can effectively manage human resources, ensuring that both the organizations' and individuals' expectations are met (Pfeffer, 1995; Rousseau, 1995).

Organizational socialization practices can be key in both transmitting and perpetuating organizational culture (Louis, 1990; Trice & Beyer, 1993). Socialization is typically defined as a learning activity, focusing on what and how newcomers learn as they make the transition from organizational outsiders to insiders (Fisher, 1986). Although there is no single accepted definition of culture (Reichers & Schneider, 1990), it is generally viewed as a common understanding of an organization's values, goals, and practices (Schein, 1985). Thus socialization is considered effective when newcomers come to understand and accept the organization's key values, goals, and practices (Schneider & Rentsch, 1988). Moreover, socialization helps ensure that both the organization's and

AUTHOR'S NOTE: I would like to thank Neal Ashkanasy and Alexis Fink for their helpful comments on earlier drafts of this chapter.

newcomers' expectations are met. The central theme of this chapter is that high-performance cultures will need to conceptualize and implement socialization in a new way, as a relational process that fosters the mutual growth of organizational newcomers and insiders.

In this chapter, I examine how organizational socialization can be reconceptualized as a relational process that helps to ensure that the functional expectations of employers and employees in high-performance cultures are met. I begin with descriptions of the changing nature of work and the organizational culture of the high-performance workplace. These descriptions are followed by a discussion of the limitations of current perspectives for understanding socialization needs in high-performance cultures. Finally, I discuss relational socialization in detail and advocate its use as an effective strategy for encouraging growth in and maintaining high-performance organizational cultures.

## THE ORGANIZATIONAL CULTURE OF THE HIGH-PERFORMANCE WORKPLACE

### The Changing Nature of Work

Our industrial-age notions of a "job" as a prepackaged set of work activities are quickly disappearing (Howard, 1995). As continuous change becomes the norm, the rigidity of the traditional job description is becoming increasingly inconsistent with the fluidity of work. Growth in knowledge, advances in information technology, and globalization are just a few of the factors driving the changing nature of work (Davis, 1995). Likewise, the "line and box" organizational structures depicted in traditional organizational charts are becoming obsolete because they fail to provide the requisite adaptability and flexibility that organizations need to cope with turbulent environments (Mohrman & Cohen, 1995). The key cultural feature of organizations that are able to survive and to thrive in dynamic, unpredictable, and information-rich environments is "high involvement" (E. E. Lawler, 1992; Lawler et al., 1992, 1995).

Given the turbulent environments that they will soon face, organizations will need to utilize a number of employment strategies to meet fluctuating work needs. Organizations are expected to make substantial use of outsourcing, "pooled" workers (i.e., call-ins, substitutes, and periodic part-timers), independent contractors, and temporary workers (Rousseau, 1995; Rousseau & Wade-Benzoni, 1995). These types of employees can be contrasted with long-term core employees whose expertise and critical skills are key to the organization's competitive advantage. It is also the core employees who drive the organization's culture and are, in turn, most affected by it. Thus, although organizations will demand substantial investment and high involvement from core employees, the same cannot be said of more peripheral employees. Compared with core employees, these peripheral types of employees may experience relatively limited socialization into the organization (Bauer, Morrison, & Callister, 1998). Therefore, I limit my discussion here to core employees.

Even for core employees, the changing nature of work is expected to have considerable impacts on psychological contracts between employers and employees (Rousseau, 1995; Rousseau & Wade-Benzoni, 1995). The "traditional" employment arrangement, in which an employer offers a lifetime career in the same organization in exchange for continued loyal service, is essentially nonexistent today and is not likely to make a comeback (Hall & Mirvis, 1995, 1996). The new employment contract is characterized by the recognition that the employment relationship is likely to be transitory and that both the employer and employee share responsibility for maintaining the relationship as long as it is mutually beneficial (Altman & Post, 1996). Compared to traditional contracting, the employee is likely to experience more "self-determination" in setting the terms of the employment contract of the future (Rousseau, 1995). The employer-employee relationship may still reflect "mutual loyalty," but it is much more likely to be based on satisfactory performance than on length of service (Hall & Mirvis, 1996). Changes in the nature of work and the meaning of "career" drive alterations in organizational culture through the expectations that employers and employees have of each other. (For a thorough treatment of the relationship between organizational culture and careers, see Gunz, Chapter 23, this volume.)

## Organizational Expectations of Core Employees

In order to compete in a dynamic and unpredictable global marketplace, organizations will need employees who are flexible and adaptable. To anticipate and to cope with changing demands, organizations will expect these employees to engage in continuous learning and self-development activities. Moreover, given the complexity accompanying the knowledge explosion and advances in technology, employees will be expected to work interdependently, sharing information and participating in teams.

### Flexibility and Adaptability

Because static job descriptions are dysfunctional in high-performance organizations, employers will be interested in employees who demonstrate flexibility and adaptability. In the high-performance culture, "That's not my job" is an unacceptable stance. Confronted with complex tasks to complete and a rapidly changing environment, organizations will expect employees to respond with flexibility, which may mean coping with changes in work schedules, processes, procedures, and coworkers. Adaptability means being open to change, manag-

ing new work relationships, and developing the skills required to get up to speed quickly in order to meet changing demands (Hall & Mirvis, 1995).

### Continuous Learning and Self-Development

The need for flexibility and adaptability points directly to the importance of continuous learning and self-development. For an organization to create a flexible workforce, its core employees must "have an appetite for continuous learning and the capacity to cope with the ambiguity and challenge of shifting job assignments" (Mirvis & Hall, 1996, p. 79). Employees who are multiskilled and comfortable operating in novel situations will be in high demand.

Continuous learning in a high-performance culture requires that employees take responsibility for identifying their own learning needs and seeking out ways to have them met (Hall & Mirvis, 1995). In other words, self-development in this context places heavy emphasis on "the self." To use Mirvis and Hall's expression, engaging in continuous learning can be thought of as taking responsibility for "learning a living," where "learning how to learn" represents a core career competency. In the traditional organization, the employer takes the initiative in identifying training needs and providing learning opportunities at specified intervals. In the high-performance organization, learning will have to be both continuous and largely self-motivated.

The ability to engage in self-development successfully depends to a great extent on prerequisite skills in identity exploration and self-assessment (Hall & Mirvis, 1996). Loosely translated, this means that employees will need to discover who they are, who they want to be, and what they need in order to get there. Of course, employees may also receive assessment assistance from the organization. For instance, popular trends such as 360-degree feedback systems in which peers, subordinates, and superiors provide evaluations in addition to an employee's own self-assessment will contribute greatly to individuals' self-understanding efforts.

Career development experts contend that learning from the experiences provided by one's job assignment is one of the best developmental tools (e.g., Hall & Mirvis, 1995; Seibert, 1996). In high-performance organizations, employees will be expected to tackle a wide variety of assignments as a matter of course. For such assignments to be developmental, however, some thought must be put into their nature and sequencing. Both the organization and the individual should have an a priori understanding of what the employee is expected to gain from the experience. Moreover, it is important to keep in mind that, to a great extent, the notion that we "learn from experience" is a myth. As Seibert (1996) argues, in reality people learn from reflecting on their experiences. Reflection need not wait until the conclusion of experience, however. Although a structured debriefing period is often very functional, Seibert suggests that reflection during experience, "inbriefing," is equally important.

### Information Sharing and Teamwork

The complex and information-rich environments of high-performance organizations will demand that employees be skilled at effective information sharing and teamwork. Indeed, team structures are endemic to the high-performance organization (Mohrman & Cohen, 1995). Complex work precludes individuals from being able to do it alone, and interdependence heightens the need for information sharing. Fletcher (1996) argues that current trends indicate that work accomplishment will require "understanding oneself as increasingly connected to others in more complex and sophisticated ways" (p. 114).

Information sharing can be a delicate matter. Given the overwhelming amount of infor-

mation available in a high-performance workplace, sharing everything with everyone will undoubtedly result in information overload and the ill effects associated with it (Miller, 1960; O'Reilly, 1980). Effective information sharing requires that workers have an understanding of what information is needed and where to get it, as well as an appreciation of what information others require from them and when they need it.

This sensitivity in information sharing contributes greatly to effective team process behavior. The teamwork literature points to a consistent core of activities indicative of team effectiveness, including information exchange, monitoring, feedback, and backup behavior (e.g., Cannon-Bowers, Oser, & Flanagan, 1992; Cannon-Bowers, Tannenbaum, Salas, & Volpe, 1995; Fleishman & Zaccaro, 1992; McIntyre & Salas, 1995; Salas, Dickinson, Converse, & Tannenbaum, 1992). In the context of teamwork, monitoring is described as observing the activities of other team members in order to be prepared to provide feedback and assistance as necessary (McIntyre & Salas, 1995). McIntyre and Salas (1995) are quick to point out that monitoring does not mean "spying" on one's coworkers. Instead, monitoring is part of an implicit contract among work group members in which they agree to look out for one another in order to maintain effective group performance. Feedback often results from monitoring as team members share their observations and evaluations with one another. Backup consists of actually providing needed functional assistance to coworkers in the completion of their job tasks (McIntyre & Salas, 1995).

### Summary

The high-performance organizational culture is characterized by expectations that employees will be flexible and adaptable, will participate in continuous learning and self-development activities, and will be effective information sharers and team players. In exchange for meeting these expectations, core employees will come to high-performance organizations with their own sets of expectations. Fortunately, employer and employee expectations appear to be mutually compatible.

## Core Employees' Expectations of the Organization

Individual careers are becoming more self-directed (D. T. Hall, 1996a, 1996b; Hall & Mirvis, 1996). Changes in the nature of work, coupled with the resultant demise of tenure-based job security, are leading employees to take more responsibility for managing their own careers. As discussed above, a high-performance culture is characterized by some demanding organizational expectations. In exchange for meeting these demands, employees will want their own expectations to be met. More specifically, employees will expect their workplaces to recognize the need for work that is personally and socially meaningful, to provide opportunities for growth and development, and to respect the interpenetration of work, family, and leisure. Both the organization's and employees' expectations contribute to the unique nature of the high-performance culture.

### Personal and Social Meaningfulness

In discussing changes in the nature of work and resultant expectations, D. T. Hall (1996a) asserts, "Now more than ever, people are seeking to base their careers on doing work that has meaning and produces value for the world and to do it in an organization whose purpose and values they can respect" (p. 5). Of course, what specific individuals consider "meaningful" will vary. It is fairly common for people to be interested in engaging work that is challenging and stimulating (Hall & Mirvis, 1995). However, individuals can also find meaning through work that is consistent with their own values, work with

which they can personally identify (D. T. Hall, 1996a; Huntley, 1997). This may mean that individuals seek work that permits them to be socially responsible through supporting important causes (e.g., care of the environment) and making tangible contributions (e.g., time and money) to social welfare (Hall & Mirvis, 1995). Others argue that the type of work an individual does is not as important as the opportunity to serve others in a way that contributes to the individual's own sense of worth and "spirituality" (Rayburn, 1997; Richmond, 1997). Regardless of how "meaningfulness" is defined, it appears that an individual's commitment to work is a result of the personal meaning he or she derives from work (Mohrman & Cohen, 1995).

### Opportunity for Growth and Development

Although psychological contracts in the high-performance workplace are much more likely to be based on performance than on tenure (Hall & Mirvis, 1995, 1996), both the organization and the employee realize that even exemplary performance does not guarantee job security (Altman & Post, 1996). Therefore, "employability" will be the goal of individual employees who must increasingly bear the burden of looking out for their own futures (Altman & Post, 1996; Mirvis & Hall, 1996). This means that employees will expect organizations to offer them opportunities to develop a portfolio of skills that enhances their marketability. Thus organizations will have to provide work assignments and learning opportunities that allow for challenge and growth. Research shows that an organizational environment that emphasizes learning and development is the most consistent predictor of employee self-development activity (Maurer & Tarulli, 1994). The organization serves as an important personal development resource by providing information about various opportunities, supporting individual developmental activities (e.g., providing the time off and funds for educational pursuits), and structuring work assignments in ways that encourage employee growth.

*Recognition of and Respect
for the Interpenetration of
Work, Family, and Leisure*

Although employees' expectations for meaningful work and development opportunities will certainly be fundamental facets of the high-performance organizational culture, employees subjected to such intense demands will also want to achieve greater balance between their work and personal lives. As Mirvis and Hall (1996) point out, there is an increasing recognition among employees that "interesting and challenging work is simply not the end-all and be-all" on the path to self-fulfillment (p. 93). Instead, employees aspire to have more time with their families and greater opportunities for leisure. Moreover, they expect their employers to recognize, respect, and even facilitate the accomplishment of these personal goals (Plas, 1996).

Given the demands of the high-performance workplace and changes in family structure, it is increasingly difficult for employees to maintain clear boundaries, both physical and temporal, separating their work, family, and leisure roles (Hage, 1995). For instance, employees routinely have to work some nights and weekends and take work home. Similarly, family demands associated with single-parent and dual-career households produce strain and create the need for flexible work arrangements. Thus women—and, to an increasing extent, men—are looking for "idiosyncratic" employment situations designed to help them deal with unique family circumstances and demands (Rousseau, 1995).

Young (1996) makes clear that it is not just married people with children who have work-life balance issues and benefit from organizational sensitivity. She explains that single adults without dependent children are often taken advantage of by employers who assume they are available to work longer hours and to do more traveling because of their family status. This attitude fails to recognize the other kinds of family roles (e.g., caregiver to an elderly parent) and individual pursuits (e.g., dating, community involvement) that may be important to unmarried employees.

For employees who must cope with the complex demands of family life and the high-performance workplace, leisure time and the opportunity for emotional rejuvenation are more important than ever. As Hage (1995) notes, attempting to define and comply with the prescriptions of work and family roles drains employees' emotional energy. He also contends that many of the demands of the high-performance workplace, such as teamwork, are in themselves emotionally draining. It is becoming increasingly clear that organizations whose practices, structures, and policies are sensitive to work-life integration are not only meeting employee expectations but helping to ensure productivity and business effectiveness (Fletcher, 1996). Regardless of their family status, it appears that all core employees appreciate an organization's efforts to be sensitive to individual needs through flexible career paths, work arrangements, and work-family programs (Altman & Post, 1996; Grover & Crooker, 1995; Honeycutt & Rosen, 1997).

*Summary*

Perhaps the most obvious compatibility between organizational and employee expectations is found in organizations' expectations for continuous learning and individuals' expectations for growth and development opportunities. Mutual interest in these activities may help ensure that both take responsibility for making them happen. Organizations' desire to have employees who are flexible and adaptable seems consistent with employees' desire that organizations recognize the interpenetration of work, family, and leisure. These two expectations present the opportunity for a transactional exchange "in kind." Employees may be more willing to be flexible in order to meet organizational needs if they perceive that the organization is willing to help them accommodate family and leisure needs, and vice versa. For some individuals, finding meaningful work in a high-performance organization will be quite easy. Those who find meaning in working with others, for instance, will have ample opportunity. For employees interested in pursuing valued social causes, the extent to which they will find meaning in the organization will depend on the compatibility of the organization's mission with their values and the extent to which the organization will support individual employees' efforts to pursue social causes (Hall & Mirvis, 1995).

## NEW STRATEGIES FOR ORGANIZATIONAL SOCIALIZATION

The compatibility of employer and employee expectations in the high-performance organization offers no assurance that the expectations of either will be met. Although newcomer socialization may be an effective tool for meeting expectations and perpetuating organizational culture, current perspectives have limited applicability to high-performance organizations. To be compatible with a high-performance culture, socialization needs to be approached as a process of establishing a relational network that facilitates continuous learning in order to understand and meet changing organizational demands. Moreover, socialization has to be viewed as a reciprocal process that facilitates the growth of both newcomers and insiders.

### Limitations of Current Perspectives on Socialization

Although various researchers have labeled the content of learning during socialization

somewhat differently, there is general agreement regarding the relative importance of different types of information to newcomers. Research has consistently shown that learning related to task mastery is the newcomer's top priority (Chao, O'Leary-Kelly, Wolf, Klein, & Gardner, 1994; Morrison, 1993b; Ostroff & Kozlowski, 1992). Learning related to the newcomer's role and "fit" with others in the work environment appears to be the second most important area of concentration (Chao et al., 1994; Morrison, 1993b; Ostroff & Kozlowski, 1992). More remote topics that have less bearing on the newcomer's immediate success (e.g., organizational goals and values, company history) are lower in priority (Chao et al., 1994).

Although such content-focused research has certainly been important, its applicability to socialization into high-performance cultures is somewhat limited. In the high-performance organization, individual task and role demands will change frequently. Thus in this context socialization is not so much a matter of learning specific content as it is an issue of developing networks and strategies that will help the worker understand and meet changing demands. Although existing socialization research shows that newcomer information seeking facilitates content learning (Morrison, 1993a, 1993b; Ostroff & Kozlowski, 1992), information alone will not be sufficient to assist newcomers in the development of adaptation strategies that will serve them in the high-performance culture.

Another limitation of the existing socialization literature is its one-sided emphasis on how newcomers are influenced by organizational insiders during socialization. With relatively few exceptions (see Jackson, Stone, & Alvarez, 1993; Sutton & Louis, 1987), there has been little attention devoted to how organizational insiders might be affected as a result of their experiences with newcomers. Given the high level of interdependence found in the high-performance workplace, mutual influence between insiders and newcomers is inevitable and desirable.

## Relational Socialization

An interactionist framework has dominated contemporary views on the organizational socialization process (e.g., Chatman, 1991; Jones, 1983a; Reichers, 1987). The interactionist perspective encourages the simultaneous consideration of contextual influences and individual-difference variables in the study of socialization processes. The interactionist model also looks at learning during socialization as the result of interactions initiated by organizational insiders and newcomers (Reichers, 1987).

In addition to facilitating learning (e.g., Ashford & Black, 1996; Morrison, 1993b), newcomers' interactions with organizational insiders also contribute to the development of important interpersonal relationships between newcomers and insiders (Graen & Uhl-Bien, 1995; Katz, 1985; Moreland & Levine, 1989). Effective relationship development lies at the heart of the socialization strategies advocated here. The relational view requires conceptualizing socialization as an individual growth process that occurs through a person's experiences and connections with others. Thus the relational socialization perspective moves a step beyond interactionist models by recognizing that interaction has many important ramifications in addition to newcomer learning. (For additional discussion of the effects of interaction, see Beyer, Hannah, & Milton, Chapter 20, this volume.) In particular, interaction facilitates the development of interpersonal relationships, which are critical to effectiveness in the high-performance culture. Moreover, the relational approach stresses mutuality. According to Fletcher (1996), "Relational growth depends on both parties approaching the interaction expecting to grow and benefit from it" (p. 115). Relational socialization corresponds with current perspectives on career development that emphasize the criticality of human relationships in the workplace (e.g., D. T. Hall, 1996a, 1996b; Hall & Mirvis, 1996; Kahn, 1996; Kram, 1996; Rousseau & Wade-Benzoni, 1995).

## Mutual Interpersonal Influence

Kahn (1996) has eloquently expressed the importance of relationships in the workplace: "It is in the context of relationships with others that people may experience themselves as anchored in organizational contexts and situations that are, like high seas, turbulent and frightening. Work relationships have the potential to help people feel connected rather than disconnected, held fast rather than floundering, soothed rather than disquieted" (p. 163). It is not surprising that newcomers explicitly acknowledge the importance of organizational insiders to their own adjustment processes (Gundry & Rousseau, 1994; Louis, Posner, & Powell, 1983). Not only do organizational insiders provide newcomers with information (Morrison, 1993a, 1993b; Ostroff & Kozlowski, 1992), they also offer social support (e.g., Feldman & Brett, 1983; Fisher, 1985; Nelson & Quick, 1991). Newcomers with stronger systems of support report fewer adverse psychological outcomes related to job performance than do those with less support (Ruben, 1986). Research shows that quality relationships with organizational insiders can even help newcomers overcome the negative effects of unmet expectations (Major, Kozlowski, Chao, & Gardner, 1995).

Although the existing socialization literature acknowledges the importance of insiders to newcomers, there is little consideration of the ways in which newcomers may influence insiders. To be relational, socialization strategies must emphasize reciprocity, mutuality, and interdependence (Kram, 1996). This means that relationships between newcomers and insiders serve as a platform for the personal learning and development of both parties.

Although the impact of newcomers on organizational insiders has not been empirically investigated in the socialization literature, some theorists have considered the issue (Jackson et al., 1993; Sutton & Louis, 1987). Brought in as "competitive resources," it seems likely that newcomers may bring with them new skills and fresh ideas that can be shared with organizational insiders. Newcomers' talents may enhance both the innovation and the power of the work teams they join. Environmental information is another valuable commodity that newcomers could possess, especially if they have been employed by competitors. In addition, newcomers may have positive impacts on insiders' attitudes. Interacting with enthusiastic newcomers may be good for insiders' morale. Moreover, feeling that they have made a valuable contribution to someone's development may enhance insiders' sense of self-worth. As Fletcher (1996) contends, "The teacher grows either because of enhanced self-esteem at using her relational skills to enable another's achievement or through the learning that takes place in listening to, identifying with, or adopting the student's perspective" (p. 115).

The goal of relational socialization is for newcomers and insiders to view themselves as playing both the "student" and "teacher" roles. Fletcher (1996) refers to the importance of the "expectation of fluid expertise," in which each partner comes to expect reciprocity in the teaching and learning that occurs in the relationship. Although this type of relationship may begin to develop during newcomer socialization, its functionality is indefinite. In the turbulent environment of the high-performance organization, developmental relationships serve as an anchor. These liaisons, which Kahn (1996) calls "secure base relationships," provide a major means through which organizational and individual expectations are met.

Consider the organizational expectations discussed previously: flexibility and adaptability, continuous learning and self-development, information sharing and teamwork. For both newcomers and insiders, each of these activities is more likely to occur when growth-fostering relationships provide opportunities for reciprocal learning. Individual expectations for meaning, growth and development, and balance can also be realized through such relationships. For instance, in

his ethnographic research, Kahn (1990) found that interpersonal relationships at work were related to personal engagement and deriving a sense of meaning from work. There is also preliminary evidence that receiving practical accommodation to facilitate balance between one's work and personal life may be contingent upon one's having effective working relationships, especially with one's immediate supervisor (Bernas & Major, 2000).

## Role Flexibility and Innovation

Given its focus on growth and development, relational socialization is likely to result in greater newcomer role flexibility and innovation. This contention is consistent with the existing socialization literature, which provides useful information on structuring newcomer socialization to maximize role innovation. Van Maanen and Schein (1979) identified different sets of socialization tactics and distinguished them based on whether their use was likely to result in newcomers' adopting more custodial or more innovative role orientations. The researchers hypothesized that the following tactics would lead to more custodial responses: formal (isolated from other organizational members), collective (socialized in a group), sequential (socialization follows clearly identified steps), fixed (socialization follows a set timetable), serial (newcomers are trained by a predecessor), and investiture (newcomers are encouraged to keep their prior identity). Each tactic's "opposite" was expected to result in a more innovative newcomer role orientation. Thus Van Maanen and Schein proposed that newcomers would be more likely to initiate change when socialization was characterized as informal (takes place in the presence of other organizational members), individual (new members are socialized singly), random (socialization follows no preestablished path), variable (socialization follows no specific timetable), disjunctive (newcomers are not trained by a predecessor), and divestiture (newcomers are encouraged to reject previous identities).

Empirical research that has attempted to measure these tactics has found them to be highly correlated (e.g., Ashforth & Saks, 1996; Baker & Feldman, 1990; Jones, 1986). Thus Jones (1986) has proposed a more simplified continuum of tactics, ranging from highly institutionalized to highly individualized. Institutionalized tactics are described as more formal in terms of setting, timing, and information provided, whereas individualized tactics are less formal along the same dimensions.

Engaging in relational socialization can certainly be characterized as an individualized process. It appears that institutionalized tactics are likely to be ineffective in encouraging personal growth and development and may even be dysfunctional when newcomer flexibility and adaptability are important goals. Socialization processes that support the development of individual relationships in which more personalized attention can be provided are more compatible with high-performance cultures than "one size fits all" approaches to newcomer socialization.

### Strategic Personal Development

Individualized attention regarding self-development is important because to succeed in the high-performance workplace an individual must employ a strategy with regard to organizational and individual goals. By developing relationships with organizational insiders, the newcomer comes to understand current organizational needs and how his or her individual talents might be used to meet them. Moreover, the individual begins to get a sense of the knowledge, skills, and abilities that he or she will need to develop to achieve personal goals (e.g., desired work assignments) in the organizational setting. Empirical research shows that social support from coworkers and supervisors encourages employee development activity (Noe & Wilk, 1993). Within the dynamic environment of

the high-performance workplace, solid relationships will provide a stable context for the continuous reevaluation of both organizational and individual goals and needs.

Growth-fostering relationships also provide safe places for individuals to let their weaknesses and developmental needs be known. When their weaknesses are out in the open, they have opportunities to overcome them through any variety of means, including individual development, task restructuring, and strategic use of human resources (Plas, 1996). Perfectionism will be dysfunctional in the high-performance workplace. The need for flexibility and adaptability will often demand experimentation. Research shows that newcomers who have strong systems of social support are allowed the freedom to fail (Nelson, Quick, & Joplin, 1991). Such newcomers are sustained as they experiment and engage in continuous learning to keep up with organizational demands. Ashford and Taylor (1990) note that the greater the social support available to newcomers, the greater the potential for problem-focused coping to be effective.

Research on leader-member exchange (LMX) also supports the notion that development opportunities are more likely to occur in the context of an effective relationship. In the organizational literature, LMX is one of the most widely accepted indicators of relationship quality between supervisors and subordinates (Graen & Uhl-Bien, 1995). A basic premise of LMX theory is that leaders (i.e., supervisors) do not treat all subordinates the same way, but instead develop unique relationships with individual subordinates (Dansereau, Graen, & Haga, 1975). Research has demonstrated that LMX is established quickly and has a lasting impact on career development (Liden, Wayne, & Stillwell, 1993). Subordinates in low-LMX relationships are referred to as members of the supervisor's "out-group," whereas those in high-LMX relationships are considered the "in-group." In general, leaders have greater positive affect and professional respect for in-group members, viewing them as more loyal and responsible than out-group members (Liden & Maslyn, 1998). As a result, in-group members are given more challenging assignments, are relied upon more heavily, and enjoy greater autonomy than out-group members. In essence, in-group members receive greater opportunities for growth and advancement than do newcomers in the out-group (Wakabayashi & Graen, 1984; Wakabayashi, Graen, Graen, & Graen, 1988).

Although not all LMX research is based specifically on the experiences of newcomers, the implications seem clear. The developmental opportunities so critical to an individual's success in the high-performance workplace are more likely to be forthcoming when the person has developed effective working relationships as a newcomer. In a study of organizational newcomers, Ashford and Black (1996) found that newcomers who reported actively attempting to build relationships with their bosses demonstrated better job performance.

## Agents of Socialization

The opportunities for personal growth and the realization of organizational and individual expectations are amplified when individuals pursue multiple relationships in the organization (Kram, 1996). Although in the preceding discussion I have alluded to the roles of various agents in relationship development and the socialization of newcomers, this subsection is devoted to a more specific consideration of the unique ways in which different agents may contribute. The socialization literature has established that supervisors, coworkers, and newcomers themselves play important roles in the process (e.g., Major et al., 1995; Morrison, 1993b; Ostroff & Kozlowski, 1992). I consider below the potential growth-fostering activities of each of these agents and their impacts on newcomer socialization.

### Supervisors

Supervisors are in an excellent position to analyze newcomers' skills and abilities and to provide appropriate developmental experiences through coaching, counseling, and feedback (House, 1995). Supervisors also can delegate activities that facilitate newcomer growth. Moreover, supervisors are likely to have the formal authority necessary to provide important resources and eliminate obstacles to task completion. Research shows that adequate performance on delegated assignments has beneficial effects on newcomers' relationships with their supervisors (Bauer & Green, 1996).

As a primary purveyor of organizational expectations, supervisory feedback is critical. Throughout the socialization process, newcomers need to be aware of how well they are meeting task and role demands (Ashford & Cummings, 1983; Nelson, 1990). Feedback accounts for a significant portion of the variance in socialization outcomes, such as job performance, satisfaction, and organizational commitment (Colarelli, Dean, & Konstans, 1987). Feedback has the added benefit of making newcomers feel that the supervisor and the organization are concerned about their progress and adjustment (Leibowitz, Schlossberg, & Shore, 1992; Nelson, 1990).

Through feedback, supervisors also let newcomers know what behaviors and activities are likely to be rewarded (House, 1995). According to Chatman (1991), clear rewards are a hallmark of organizations that effectively socialize newcomers. In addition to their readily apparent value, the rewards that supervisors provide, such as challenging assignments, promotions, and salary increases, may have additional meaning for newcomers. Nelson et al. (1991) suggest that newcomers may interpret such rewards as signs of organizational and supervisory acceptance.

Finally, supervisors serve as important role models. Socialization research shows that newcomers observe supervisors, men-tors, and coworkers in an effort to acquire information and to learn (Ostroff & Kozlowski, 1993). Perhaps one of the most critical things that supervisors can model is the importance of building mutually developmental relationships with others.

### Coworkers

Research shows that coworkers are valuable informational resources (Comer, 1991; Louis et al., 1983). Newcomers consider coworkers a better source of information about work groups (Ostroff & Kozlowski, 1992) and a less risky source than supervisors in terms of potential impression management costs (Miller & Jablin, 1991). Information exchange with coworkers appears to be vital in newcomers' assimilation into the work group, providing newcomers with a sense of acceptance and establishing cohesiveness (Moreland & Levine, 1989). In a high-performance organization, one's coworkers are also likely to be one's teammates. Thus, in terms of team task performance, coworkers are in an excellent position to provide feedback, monitoring, and backup (McIntyre & Salas, 1995).

Although positive job-related feedback may be beneficial to newcomers regardless of the source, negative performance feedback is likely to be less threatening when provided by coworkers instead of by a supervisor (Miller & Jablin, 1991). As a new member of the work group, the newcomer requires constructive criticism and advice for improvement. Furthermore, a newcomer may require personal feedback as well as job-related feedback. According to Kram and Isabella (1985), personal feedback can help the newcomer to develop self-insight and greater awareness of how he or she affects others. Morrison (1993b) found that newcomers were more likely to seek such normative information and social feedback from coworkers than from supervisors.

Peers are not only important because they provide information and feedback; they are also strong sources of emotional social support (Kram & Isabella, 1985). As Kahn (1996) points out, "Work groups offer the most effective locus of caregiving among members as well as a primary source of continuous learning" (p. 168). He contends that, under growth-fostering conditions, coworkers are able to rely on one another for empathy and nurturing.

### Newcomers

The role of newcomers as active information seekers during organizational socialization has substantial empirical support (Morrison, 1993a, 1993b; Ostroff & Kozlowski, 1992). However, recent research has examined other ways in which newcomers may take a proactive role in their own socialization. Ashford and Black (1996) used multiple operationalizations of newcomer proactivity, including information and feedback seeking, relationship building, generating social interactions, negotiating job changes, and framing situations positively. Some of the more relational activities seemed to have positive effects on socialization. For instance, socializing was positively related to job satisfaction. And, as previously noted, newcomers who reported actively attempting to establish relationships with their supervisors demonstrated better job performance.

Information seeking and relationship building are two outwardly demonstrable ways in which newcomers may attempt to facilitate growth. However, more internally directed processes are likely to be equally important. Seibert (1996) defines reflection as "deciding what is happening in an experience, what it means, and what to do about it" (p. 248). For newcomers, this may involve self-reflection regarding their own strengths, weaknesses, and goals. It also means attempting to make sense out of what they perceive to be happening in the organizational context (Louis, 1980; Weick, 1995). From a relational perspective, reflection may also mean maintaining an awareness of the needs of others in the organizational context and developing an understanding of how one might help fulfill those needs (Seibert, 1996).

*Summary*

Socialization processes based on current interactionist views will have limited success in high-performance organizational cultures. Relational socialization moves the focus from content learning to an emphasis on the development of growth-fostering systems that encourage the flexibility and innovation required for high involvement. Through cultivating mutually beneficial relationships with organizational insiders, newcomers are better able to achieve strategic personal development, whereas insiders gain exposure to fresh ideas, different talents, and enthusiastic new team members.

## IMPLICATIONS FOR RESEARCH AND PRACTICE

Although I have focused in this chapter on delineating socialization processes that are most effective in transmitting and perpetuating a high-performance organizational culture, my underlying assumption is more general. The basic tenet is that there must be some compatibility between an organization's socialization practices and its culture. Although the existence of this compatibility seems to be a generally accepted explanation for cultural continuity (e.g., Louis, 1990; Schneider & Rentsch, 1988; Trice & Beyer, 1993), there has been little empirical organizational research to support this thesis. Perhaps more important, the obvious corollary that organizational culture change could be accomplished through "discordant" socialization efforts remains untested. Developing a better understanding of organizational socialization's impact on cultural continuity and change is a fundamental issue for future research.

Examination of the particular relationship between high-performance culture and relational socialization will require careful attention to methodology. Given the interactive interpersonal basis of relational socialization, traditional survey methods are likely to prove inadequate. The participant observation methods of some classic socialization research (e.g., Van Maanen, 1975) may be appropriate for examinations of relationship development and growth. Social network analysis, a technique specifically designed for use in the study of patterns of social relationships, may also be a viable methodological approach. Social network analysis is especially promising because it has also been described as useful for analyzing organizational culture. (For a review of social network analysis and its application to culture, see Kilduff & Corley, Chapter 13, this volume.)

From a practical perspective, relational socialization is proposed to be functionally compatible with the aims of a high-performance organizational culture. Furthermore, stressing interpersonal relationships may have positive implications for organizational outcomes. Sheridan (1992) found that newcomer turnover was significantly lower in a culture emphasizing interpersonal relationship values than in a culture emphasizing work tasks. After 12 months, individuals voluntarily quit their jobs at a much faster rate in the culture emphasizing work task values than in the culture emphasizing interpersonal relationship values, where new employees voluntarily stayed 14 months longer. In determining the financial impact of turnover on organizations, Sheridan estimated the opportunity cost per employee to be $44,000. Based on this figure, he estimated that firms emphasizing work task values incurred opportunity losses of approximately $6 to $9 million more than firms emphasizing interpersonal relationship values. Thus, in addition to its positive implications for sustaining a high-involvement culture, promoting relationship building during socialization and beyond may have a concrete impact on an organization's "bottom line."

## CONCLUSION

Newcomer socialization is a key process in the development and maintenance of organizational culture. The thesis of this chapter is that high-performance cultures need to conceptualize and implement socialization in a new way, as a relational process that fosters the mutual growth of organizational newcomers and insiders. Emphasizing mutual interpersonal influence, role flexibility and innovation, and strategic personal development, relational socialization encourages continuous learning through the development of relationships between newcomers and insiders. Through these relationships, newcomers develop tools and receive the support necessary to thrive in the turbulent and unpredictable high-performance culture and, as a result, contribute to the maintenance of that culture.

# 23

# Organizational Cultures and Careers

## -- *Hugh Gunz*

In many ways, the link between careers and organizational cultures is not a new idea. Students of organizational culture have long been interested in socialization, which focuses attention on the individual's neophyte phase in an organization, an important career stage in anyone's life. But it also introduces a longitudinal dimension into the discussion: the "intergenerational" transfer of organizational belief systems. It is this longitudinal dimension on which I focus in this chapter.

To most people, *career* means a biography, or a life history. In the organizational literature, typically, use of the term is more specific; it refers to that part of the biography that is about someone's working life, if only because it is work organizations that probably have the greatest impact on the greatest number of lives in Western-style economies. Indeed, work careers form the focus of this chapter, and I shall take *career* here to mean work career. So it would not be unreasonable to expect that a chapter about organizational cultures and careers should be about the im-

pacts of different kinds of organizational cultures on the working careers of the people who make their careers within and between these organizations. This would naturally lead to a discussion of the potential impact of changing organizational forms on careers, and in particular on those forms that are the result of changing working arrangements. For example, the term *boundaryless career* is increasingly used to describe careers that are a consequence of the more fluid contractual arrangements that typify many new industries, careers that are much less constrained by single organizations (Arthur & Rousseau, 1996).

This one-way causality—the impact of organizational cultures on careers—provides, however, a very partial view of the relationship between the two phenomena. The starting point I have selected, that of the impact of a collective-level concept (culture) on an individual-level phenomenon (biography), in a sense treats organizational culture as part of the environment in which careers take place. But individual careers are the elements of a

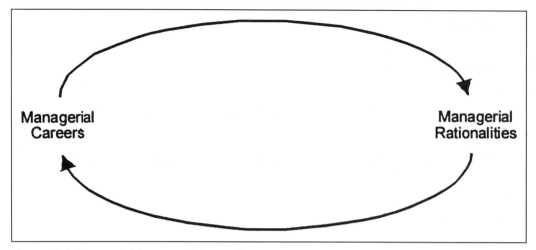

**Figure 23.1.** Managerial Careers and Rationalities

broader picture that encompasses the production and reproduction of social structures. Organizations can be viewed as open systems that need a steady supply of people to replace those lost to retirement, voluntary and involuntary departures, and deaths, as well as to feed the organizations' growth. So just as a pervasive phenomenon such as organizational culture can be expected to affect the pattern of careers within an organization (and between organizations), it seems reasonable to expect that this pattern of people flow should have some kind of impact on a number of organizational phenomena, such as organizational culture. But here we are talking about careers in a very different sense from simply as biographies; by talking in terms of flows of people, and patterns in these flows, we are dealing at the *organizational* level of analysis, a concept I shall explore further below.

For clarity, and because career systems in organizations are so closely linked to the reproduction of management structures, I shall focus on managerial careers. Similarly, in my treatment of culture I will draw heavily on notions of what I shall call *managerial rationality*—in brief, the set of assumptions and beliefs that render certain actions and possibilities "sensible" and "rational" whereas others are ignored or considered "unrealistic" (Whitley, 1987). I do not adopt this managerial focus because nobody else's career matters, but because my objective in this chapter is to build linkages between careers and organizational cultures, and it is helpful, at least in tracing first-order effects, to focus on that part of the social structure that, to paraphrase Schein (1985), is most influential in the creation, maintenance, and change of culture. Furthermore, the perspective on culture that I adopt here is that of Schein's pattern of basic assumptions, the taken-for-granted beliefs that are transmitted to new organizational members as the "correct" way to think about the organization.

In this chapter I will address both halves of the causal loop: the impact of careers on cultures and the impact of cultures on careers (see Figure 23.1). In broad outline, the structure of the chapter is as follows. First, I shall introduce the central concept of managerial rationalities in more depth and explain why it has risen to prominence, particularly in the strategy literature. Next, I shall expand the conceptual scheme in Figure 23.1 to a model that shows the intervening linkages in greater detail. In order to explore the linkages properly, I will need to introduce the concept of careers at the organizational, as opposed to the individual, level of analysis. This will lead to a review of the empirical evidence for a link between careers and organizational outcomes that will form the basis for a discussion of the role of managerial rationalities in shaping these organizational outcomes. Next, I shall examine the predictions the model has for the stability and fragility of organizational culture, and finally I shall consider the implications of these ideas for research on organizational culture.

## MANAGERIAL RATIONALITY

The phenomena that are central to this chapter—organizational careers and organizational culture—are both complex and multifaceted. As explained above, I shall be focusing here on one kind of organizational career, that of managers, with a bias toward the careers of those managers involved at the strategic decision-making level of the organization. I have introduced managerial rationality in passing as that aspect of organizational culture most obviously linked to managerial careers. In this section I explain what is meant by the term, why it is important, and the sense in which it is a form of organizational culture.

Managerial rationalities (which, for simplicity, I will refer to often just as rationalities) have emerged in various guises from a number of influential threads in the strategy literature. As we shall see, there are good reasons to expect them to be influenced by, and to influence, the shapes of organizational careers. They are invoked to explain why different organizations in similar situations may make strategic decisions distinctive to those organizations. Because managers at several different levels, potentially with diverse backgrounds and differing personal characteristics, may contribute to the strategy formulation and execution process, we need a framework for understanding how these individual characteristics are translated into what appears as purposeful organizational action. This problem is typically defined as one of understanding the processes by means of which managers agree on ends and means. In the earlier bureaucratic tradition, shared goals were seen as drivers of action. Subsequent writing stressed the fragmented nature of organizational experience, the bounded rationality of strategic choices, and bias in search behavior (Cyert & March, 1963; March & Simon, 1958; Simon, 1976). More recently, the literature on consensus has sought to identify the circumstances that contribute to shared understandings and the relationship between consensus and performance (Bourgeois, 1980; Dess & Origer, 1987). This has led to a view of organizations with competing logics and evolving "paradigms" (Johnson, 1988), resulting in differences in perceptions among organizations, for example, of threats and opportunities, and thus the adoption of different courses of action (Whitley, 1987).

Thus a number of writers, searching for means of accounting for the ways organizations develop distinctive strategies, have identified a phenomenon variously called, for example, "dominant logics" (Prahalad & Bettis, 1986), "logics of action" (Karpik, 1978), "conceptions of control" (Fligstein, 1990), and "rationalities" (Whitley, 1987). Different writers have their own particular versions of the idea, but a common thread runs through all: that of a set of meanings, shared by the top managers of the enterprise, that shape the way they run their enterprise.

Fligstein (1990) describes conceptions of control as "totalizing world views that cause actors to interpret every situation from a given perspective. They are forms of analysis used by actors to find solutions to the current problems of the organization" (p. 10). He traces the history of American business during the greater part of the 20th century in terms of a series of shifts of conceptions of control, setting them in the context of the success of the strategies they generated and the actions of government in response. Whitley's (1987) rationalities are the ways managers make sense of their business world. A particular rationality renders certain actions and possibilities "sensible" and "rational," whereas others are ignored or considered "unrealistic." Prahalad and Bettis (1986) have a complex definition for their dominant logic. They see it as the way managers conceptualize their business and make critical resource allocation decisions, stored via schemas as "both a knowledge structure and a set of elicited management processes" (p. 490).

Where do these rationalities come from? Fligstein (1990, p. 17) takes a political view, which has echoes of Ginsberg's (1990, p. 521) account of the way in which top management teams (TMTs) adopt a "negotiated belief structure" (Walsh & Fahey, 1986), focusing on the power struggle within the firm to determine which conception of control will dominate and how that conception will be translated into concrete strategies. Prahalad and Bettis (1986, p. 490) take an organizational and individual learning-based approach: managers' experiences, they argue, shape the dominant general management logic(s) that emerge in a firm. The two classes of explanation—political and learning based—are complementary. Fligstein's and Ginsberg's political models may account for *how* the rationalities take shape, and Prahalad and Bettis's reference to managerial experiences may begin to explain *what form* the rationalities might take.

Many writers, then, have identified managerial rationalities (as I shall call them here, after Whitley) as central to the emergence of business strategies. There is a strong implication, especially in Fligstein's and Prahalad and Bettis's formulations, that the rationality of interest to us here is that shared by the upper echelon or TMT. The link with Schein's (1985) concept of organizational culture—the system of shared meanings that are taken as "true" and to be passed on to new members of the organization—is clear. Rationalities are the shared, taken-for-granted assumptions of managers who are involved in decisions of any consequence to the organization about the ways these decisions should be made and about the kinds of decisions that are "good" and "bad."

## CAREERS AND MANAGERIAL RATIONALITIES

At present, the main route available to developing an understanding of the link between careers and organizational culture expressed as managerial rationalities is by drawing inferences from a much more established field of inquiry, namely, that into one of the more intriguing questions in the organizational literature: What impacts do people's career backgrounds have on the ways in which they run their organizations? The quest for an understanding of this link has been a long and frustrating one (Gunz & Jalland, 1996). By *run,* I refer to the strategies chosen by a firm's management and the success with which they are realized (Mintzberg & Waters, 1985). As we have seen, rationalities are widely believed to be important factors in the selection and realization of strategies, but thus far it is the case that their role in mediating between careers and organizational outcomes (strategies) has been inferred rather than directly observed.

Figure 23.1 summarizes the basic argument of this chapter, namely, that rationalities and careers are mutually constitutive. It is elaborated on in Figure 23.2, which is based on work by Gunz and Jalland (1996) linking careers, rationalities, and organizational outcomes in the form of the choice and implementation of strategies. The model is intended to be episodic in nature. For example, a change in an organization's career streams (the shape of the flow of people

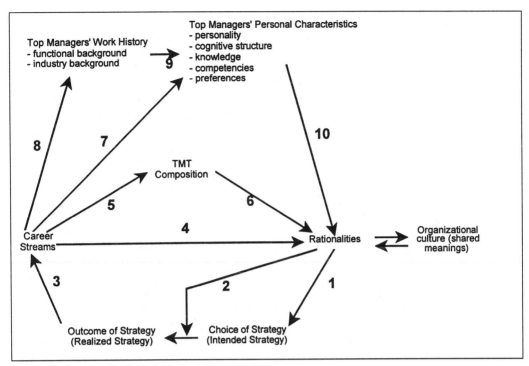

**Figure 23.2.** Integrated Model of Careers, Rationalities, and Organizational Outcomes

through the organization; see below for more detail) will affect the organization's rationalities directly (arrow 4 in Figure 23.2), but will also do so indirectly by, perhaps, affecting TMT composition (arrow 5), top managers' personal characteristics (arrow 7), and top managers' work histories (arrow 8). Similarly, a change in rationalities may affect the way strategies are chosen in the organization (arrow 1) and the success with which they are implemented (arrow 2). The outcome of the strategic choice and implementation process in turn affects the career streams (arrow 3).

The model thus proposes a mutually reinforcing loop in which careers affect rationalities (cultures) and rationalities affect careers. This, as we shall see, has interesting consequences. To anticipate two conclusions that will be explored later, it helps explain both the durability of organizational cultures and their fragility. The durability comes from the mutually constitutive nature of the closed loop: Career streams can be very hard to

change, so the cultures they produce are likely to be hard to change, too. On the other hand, career streams are not completely unchangeable; certain kinds of exogenous shock can produce sudden and dramatic change to career streams, which in turn may produce different cultures.

The model does not claim to account for every factor that affects the careers-rationality link. There are many forces at work other than those shown, acting from "outside" the loop in the figure (Guth, 1993), for example, the extent to which external labor markets are affected both by the cosmopolitan careers of professionals (Gouldner, 1957, 1958) and by economic growth or recession, and organizational structure (Gunz, 1989a; Martin & Strauss, 1956; Vardi & Hammer, 1977). Within the loop, certain aspects of career systems such as top management compensation will have impacts on strategy choices and implementation independent of career streams, and top managers' personal characteristics are likely to influence the ways in which chosen strategies are implemented (Glick et al., 1993; Waller, Huber, & Glick, 1995; Walsh, 1988a).

Before turning to Figure 23.2 in detail, I need to explain the term *career stream,* which in turn requires understanding that careers can be seen at two distinct levels of analysis: the individual and the organizational.

## CAREERS AT THE INDIVIDUAL AND ORGANIZATIONAL LEVELS OF ANALYSIS

The careers literature is complicated by the multiplicity of levels of analysis from which the study of careers can be approached (Gunz, 1989b; Lawrence, 1990). Most research has dealt with the *individual* level of analysis, in which the object of interest is the person and his or her career—the person's work history and the choices he or she makes in navigating through that history. Organizations are not the object of interest, except insofar as they provide the context for the jobs in question. The organizational level, in which the object of study is the flow of people through the organization seen as an open system (von Bertalanffy, 1968), is a more elusive concept. Many writers have pointed out over the years that the individual and the organization are really two sides of the same coin: The study of one informs understanding of the other, and vice versa (Grandjean, 1981; Hughes, 1937; Mills, 1959).

Examples of organizational-level writing include work on the ways reward systems motivate managers (Whitley, 1987), on internal and external labor market theory and demography (DiPrete, 1987; Doeringer & Piore, 1971; Hachen, 1992; Osterman, 1984; Pfeffer, 1985), on organizational ecology (Haveman & Cohen, 1994), and on the use of labor market theory to link career systems with the strategic behavior of companies (Sonnenfeld & Peiperl, 1988).

At the organizational level of analysis, *career* refers to the flows of people through and between organizations, rather than to the individuals themselves. The patterns of these flows have been called "career streams" (Gunz & Jalland, 1996); they differ from the broader concept of "career systems" (Sonnenfeld & Peiperl, 1988), which tends to encompass the human resource management practices that drive the flows (for example, the ways in which people are recruited, compensated, chosen for advancement, developed by lateral moves, or sidelined).

The flows may be in many different directions. Traditionally, they have been thought of as vertical ladders: systems of progression in which one advances by moving to the next rung up as it falls vacant. But there are many possible kinds of moves in organizations other than straight up. The patterns may be straightforward, such as when the predominant move is upward through clearly defined hierarchies, or more complex, as in companies in which different kinds of lateral moves can be found at all levels.

Several kinds of streams have been identified. Perhaps the most well-known is the fast track (Cawsey, Nicholson, & Alban-Metcalfe, 1985; Hall, 1986; Kovach, 1986; Stewman & Konda, 1983), presumably because its occupants provide the future upper echelons of companies. Other widely studied streams include plateaued managers (Evans & Gilbert, 1984; Ference, Stoner, & Warren, 1977; Hall & Isabella, 1985; Near, 1984; Slocum, Cron, Hansen, & Rawlings, 1985) and technical specialists (Dalton, Thompson, & Price, 1977; Goldberg & Shenhav, 1984; Gunz, 1980; Mainiero, 1986; Raelin, 1987; Sofer, 1970). Managers in different career streams within the organization are rewarded in different ways and have differing kinds of access to the firm's power structure. In any organization, certain streams typically lead to top positions and others do not. In some companies it is the accountants who succeed at the expense of their more product-oriented colleagues, whereas in others it is the engineers who succeed.

## Career Streams and Career Logics

Career streams, then, are the patterns in the flows of people through and between organizations. A useful analytic framework for linking career streams to organizational cultures is the *organizational career logic* (OCL; Gunz, 1989a), which descends from Karpik's (1978) concept of "logics of action." OCL is defined as the logic that an observer infers to lie behind the pattern of moves he or she sees managers making in a given organization. Metaphorically, OCLs can be thought of as organizational "jungle gyms" or climbing frames in which the rungs are the managerial posts; managers make their careers by scrambling over the jungle gym.

An OCL represents an observer's subjective interpretation of the career moves he or she sees taking place, and the framework draws attention to the socially constructed nature of these interpretations. It is particularly useful as a tool for distinguishing between the structure of careers in and between different kinds of organizations. For example, three distinct OCLs emerged from a study I conducted of four large industrial firms (Gunz, 1989a). The first, the *command-centered*, is found in firms based on repeating units (e.g., retail banks or chain stores), that support managerial labor markets for the specialists needed to head the units. A successful career in this kind of organization typically involves moving from one unit to the next, where each succeeding unit is successively larger or more prestigious than the previous ones. This contrasts strikingly with the *constructional* OCL, in which managers move constantly between different kinds of jobs, getting as great a variety of experience as possible. This is found in firms with complex structures in which the variety of kinds of positions is high. Finally, the *evolutionary* OCL is found in firms that typically grow by setting up new ventures. Successful careers in these firms involve growing with ventures rather than moving steadily across

the organization. In practice, more than one OCL can be found within a given organization.

Focusing on the logic underlying the way people are recruited to and promoted within firms, Sonnenfeld and Peiperl (1988) have argued that there are four archetypes of career systems, which they call the Baseball Team, the Academy, the Fortress, and the Club. These are based on two dimensions: the entry ports to senior management posts (whether an individual must join the firm at the bottom or may join at any level) and the basis for the assignment of individuals to positions (whether people are rewarded as individual "stars" or as team players). Sonnenfeld and Peiperl use the term *career system* to describe these archetypes because they are interested in the selection and promotion mechanisms that they describe as driving the differences. However it is easy to view the archetypes in terms of the OCL framework, provided one focuses on the intentionality underlying the two dimensions rather than accepting the dimensions as objective descriptions of a labor market structure.

These "logics" foreshadow the direction to be taken later in this chapter. They suggest a link between careers at the organizational level of analysis and organizational culture as a system of shared meanings, the link being the OCL as an interpretative phenomenon. OCLs are an attempt to uncover the taken-for-granted side of career structures in organizations. But this interest in the taken for granted is not limited to careers. As we have seen, a flourishing school of strategy analysis is based on the notion that organizational cultures are central to understanding how strategies are chosen and with what success they are implemented, placing culture at the center of any model linking career backgrounds to organizational outcomes and, in a sense, the "missing link" that builds the bridge between individual and organizational levels of analysis. This is why I have described the approach to be taken in this chapter as inferential, because rationalities are *inferred*, rather than directly observed, to be an important link between careers and organizational outcomes.

The outcomes I focus on here are strategies. There is mounting evidence that there is indeed a link of this nature (Gunz & Jalland, 1996), although space does not allow me to explore it here. When careers are examined at the individual level of analysis the evidence is mixed, but upper-echelon theory, which focuses on the role of the TMT in determining strategy (Hambrick & Mason, 1984), suggests promising leads. For example, diversity of TMT experience is related to diversification strategies (Bouchet, 1976) and reorientation (Lant, Milliken, & Batra, 1992), a preponderance of a particular functional experience with strategies linked to that function (Michel & Hambrick, 1992), levels of education with innovativeness (Wiersema & Bantel, 1992), and long tenure with persisting with strategies that fit the norm for the industry (Finkelstein & Hambrick, 1990). Finally, some limited case-based organizational-level research points to the effects career systems have on, for example, the innovative behavior of firms (see, e.g., Kanter, 1984, pp. 93-96, 149-150; Peters & Waterman, 1982, p. 227).

We can now return to the model in Figure 23.2, to trace the mediating mechanisms that link careers with organizational culture in the form of rationalities.

### Career Streams and Rationalities (Arrows 4-10 in Figure 23.2)

Most directly, rationalities are likely to be shaped directly by the career streams followed by the managers sharing them (arrow 4). We can expect each career stream to generate its own shared definitions of good management and sound business practice—that is, its own rationality—based on the criteria that seem to govern career success within the stream. If it is evident that the best engineers get promoted within an engineering stream, members are likely to believe that high professional standards are the key to success. On the other hand, if success seems to go to engineers who manage to shake off their specialist labels, perhaps by proving that they are versatile enough to function effectively in various nonengineering roles, then members will be anxious to show that there is a great deal more to them than "merely" being a good engineer. In their famous polemic, for example, Hayes and Abernathy (1980) criticize career streams that reward so-called professional managers, whose rationalities result in what the authors describe as myopic, risk-averse corporate behavior.

A second path by means of which career streams can influence rationalities goes via the TMT (arrows 5 and 6). As arrow 5 in Figure 23.2 indicates, the composition of the TMT is, by definition, determined to a considerable extent by the structure of the firm's career streams. Implicitly, therefore, the model suggests a link between career streams and rationalities mediated by TMT composition. And if rationalities are the precursors of intended strategies, as their proponents argue, we expect the relationships identified in a number of studies between TMT composition and strategic choice (see above) to be mediated by rationalities. For example, heterogeneous TMTs, which Lant et al. (1992) found were more likely to reorient, presumably do so because this heterogeneity produces a dominant rationality that is more accepting of alternative viewpoints and new ideas, as opposed to a homogeneous TMT, which is less receptive to anything other than corporate orthodoxy.

Finally, it is possible to identify ways in which careers at the individual level of analysis can influence rationalities. The work histories of individual top managers are, by definition, a function of the firm's career streams (arrow 8). Furthermore, it seems reasonable to assume that executives' career backgrounds will influence the rationality of the group of which they are members (arrow 10). For example, managers who have backgrounds in R&D will probably have a number of characteristics in common, one of which is likely to be a preference for developing innovative technical products. They will probably reinforce each other in the belief—the rationality—that new product development is "good" management, and cost containment and concentration on marketing existing product lines is "bad" (Helmich, 1974; Miller, 1990). Starting from the notion, then, that a set of shared meanings will be affected by the beliefs individual members bring to the group, we can expect rationalities to be affected by the personal characteristics of senior managers.

There was, however, a "reasonable to assume" in this last linkage; it is not axiomatic that personal characteristics are affected by work histories (arrow 9). It has not proven easy to uncover the characteristics that are affected by career background. There have been a number of studies of the ways work history affects personality (e.g., Brousseau, 1983; Kohn & Schooler, 1982; Lueptow, McClendon, & McKeon, 1979) and considerable controversy about whether it affects cognitive structures and decision-making styles (e.g., Glick et al., 1993; March & Simon, 1958; Waller et al., 1995; Walsh, 1988a). Most people would regard the link between career background and personal characteristics as self-evident: Particular kinds of work histories are bound to develop certain characteristics in the people who have gone through them. Someone who has spent a lifetime in marketing must, surely, know a lot more about marketing than someone who has not, and similarly someone who has spent many years in the fast-food industry is likely to know a great deal more about fast food than someone who has not. As Hall (1987) has suggested: "There is probably a socialization process at work . . . the longer a person stays in a certain field, the more he or she will be socialized to fit the occupation better" (p. 307).

It is possible, however, that the characteristics of top managers may be affected by career streams in a second way, which might be called a "selection effect" (arrow 7). It may be that the reason top managers have a given set of characteristics has nothing to do with

their background, but arises simply because the career stream they have followed has selected for people with those characteristics. For example, if a firm's modal OCL (i.e., that leading to top jobs) is command centered, perhaps a retail chain in which retail store management provides the route to the TMT, then it may simply be that managers with those skills get promoted over those who do not.

Career streams, then, can influence rationalities in three ways: directly (arrow 4), via the TMT (arrows 5 and 6), and by affecting the kinds of managers in senior positions (arrows 8-10).

### Rationalities and Strategy Implementation (Arrows 1 and 2 in Figure 23.2)

Career streams are channeled by reward systems that reward certain kinds of behavior over others (Sonnenfeld & Peiperl, 1988; Whitley, 1987), and this has further implications for the relationship between rationalities and strategies. Reward-seeking behavior, together with processes of anticipatory socialization, spreads the rationality of the dominant coalition throughout the organization in a kind of "trickle-down" effect, and particularly among those whose careers are being built within the firm's modal OCL. Evidence for the trickle-down impact of rationalities on strategic choice comes from Bower's (1970; see also Dutton & Ashford, 1987; Schilit & Locke, 1982) study that showed how lower-level managers' assumptions about what their TMT was looking for in its capital budgeting plans affected the nature of the proposals they submitted to the TMT. Not surprisingly, the managers in Bower's sample were reluctant to put forward any proposals that did not fit the general view of what the board was looking for, which led to a high acceptance rate. We can expect such a trickle-down effect to influence both strategy selection and strategy implementation.

Strategy selection is likely to be affected by the trickle-down effect because a multiplier effect is at work: Middle managers' beliefs about the dominant rationality causes them to constrain the TMT's strategic choices yet further. In other words, it is not just the impact of the TMT's dominant rationality on its own collective decision-making processes that matters (arrow 1), but also its impact on the way strategies are presented for selection by lower-level managers.

In addition, we can expect the trickle-down effect to modify the implementation of strategies (arrow 2). Suppose a TMT has decided to implement a strategy that represents a new departure for the firm; using Miles and Snow's (1978) typology, for example, an analyzer might wish to become a prospector. The firm's career system has been rewarding its managers by promoting them on their abilities to make an analyzer strategy work (arrow 7). It may simply not have a managerial cadre capable of working as prospectors—the abilities and mind-sets are just too different. But in addition, given the inertia of organizational systems such as those associated with performance appraisal, it may well be that—despite the stated desires of the TMT—it is evident to middle managers that the old behaviors are still being rewarded. Alternatively, skepticism and cynicism about the new order may have the same effect. So regardless of whether or not those in the managerial cadre are capable of working as prospectors, they may well see no point in trying to do so. The trickle-down effect of managerial rationalities, in other words, has many ways of working through the realpolitik of organizational life to have a major impact on the ways in which intended strategies are implemented.

### Strategies and Career Streams (Arrow 3 in Figure 23.2)

The impact of strategies on career streams has been studied at both individual and orga-

nizational levels of analysis. At the individual level, Smith and White (1987) found evidence that incoming CEOs have backgrounds similar to those of their predecessors and that there is a relationship between firms' previous strategies and successor CEOs' specializations. *Specialization* in this study was operationalized in terms of both functional specialism (production, sales, management, finance, and law) and "institutional" specialism (company, industry, and generalist). A single and vertically integrated strategy (Rumelt, 1974), for instance, tends to be associated with CEOs with single-company and production or sales experience, whereas an unrelated and conglomerate strategy tends to be associated with a generalist and financial or legal background. Although Smith and White are careful not to infer too much about the direction of causality of their findings and argue for further work, the evidence is highly supportive of the conclusion that firms select CEOs whose backgrounds are compatible with the strategies currently in place.

At the organizational level of analysis, my study of four large industrial firms found that the distinctiveness of each firm's OCL could be traced to the firm's structure and its growth strategy (Gunz, 1989a). Two types of strategies were distinguished: growth into territory that was unfamiliar to the firm and growth into territory familiar to the firm (Abell, 1980, chaps. 7-8; Miller & Friesen, 1984, chap. 4; Quinn, 1980). The evolutionary OCL (see above) was associated with firms that have typically grown by starting new ventures (growth into the unfamiliar), because it is likely that they have a series of local labor markets as the various ventures' founders build their own businesses. By contrast, firms that have tended to have grown into the familiar would have one of the other two kinds of OCL (constructional or command centered), depending on their structure.

We have now closed the loop. We have seen how careers can affect cultures (in the form of rationalities) in a number of ways, and rationalities, in turn, can affect the shape of organizations' career streams. I now turn to a consideration of some of the implications of this model for organizational learning and change.

## CULTURAL STABILITY AND CHANGE

The model we have been exploring in this chapter, connecting careers and organizational cultures in the form of rationalities, has moved us a considerable distance from simply looking on cultures as providing some kind of organizational environment within which people make their careers. It is based on the twin precepts that cultures produce careers and careers produce cultures. By reframing the issue as one of social reproduction, we raise the question of the implications the model might have for the stability and fragility of organizational cultures. It is almost a truism that organizational cultures are very durable and hard to change, which is of course the basis of Schein's (1985) dictum about the role of the leader as cultural change agent. The model suggests reasons for expecting that this may not always be so.

It is easy to see why the model suggests that cultures should be so enduring and hard to shift. Given the mutual causality between careers and rationalities, and provided that the two are compatible, the cycle of reproduction is likely to be very hard to break. For example, suppose that the firm has an evolutionary OCL. The career stream associated with this OCL is supportive of Miles and Snow's (1978) prospector strategy (Gunz, Jalland, & Evans, 1998) because it rewards people for concentrating on developing their business, as opposed to the constructional OCL, which, in a sense, punishes people for doing this because of the stigma associated in such a career stream with staying in one place for too long. The culture that develops is highly supportive of continuing with the prospector strategy, which embeds the evolutionary OCL in the organization yet more firmly because of the models that become evident to everyone aspiring to managerial success. It is not just that a given career stream has produced a cadre of managers who believe that prospecting is the right way of doing business and who have both been selected for and developed the skills to do so successfully. The career stream is part of the organization's reward system because it is the means by which people receive the rewards of recognition, power, and influence, and it provides a powerful signaling mechanism to everyone aspiring to these rewards about the behaviors that are necessary to get them. So not only are people shaped by their career backgrounds, but the belief systems—the rationalities—sustained by career streams can be expected to be remarkably durable because they are driven by existing success models in the organization, which have a powerful influence on the beliefs people hold about what they have to do to get ahead.

Paradoxically, and perhaps surprisingly, the cyclic nature of the model also suggests reasons for expecting cultures to shift suddenly and drastically. It is a common complaint that cultures are hard to change, in part because it takes so long to change the people. Indeed, if the only mechanism were the individual-level path (arrows 8-10 in Figure 23.2), the model would predict extremely slow change. But the direct link between career streams and rationalities and the indirect link via TMT composition both suggest mechanisms for rapid change in cultures.

Suppose the career stream experiences a shock, as can happen when an atypical appointment is made to the position of CEO in response to a financial crisis. For example, the financial markets tend to be reassured by an outsider appointment when a company is in trouble (Trifts & Winkler, 1987). What does the model have to say about such a situation?

It depends, of course, on whether the shock is significant enough to have an impact on the career streams. The situation that is probably most familiar is that of an outsider CEO, appointed in an attempt to bring about change, finding the situation too intractable for him or her to have any kind of impact. The existing management cadres watch the new CEO's performance with some skepticism, few take his or her exhortations to move to a brave new world seriously, and little significant change results. But this is by no means always the outcome.

Careers are an exercise in deferred gratification (Stinchcombe, 1983; Wilensky, 1960); much of the reward for present contributions is assumed to come in the future as one moves to positions of centrality in the organization (Schein, 1971). So those making their careers within a given stream look for signals about what they should be doing to make sure that their chances of reaping the reward are as good as possible. One of the characteristics of a well-established career stream is that there is little uncertainty on this score. People in constructional OCLs know that the important thing is to keep on the move, continue to acquire new experiences, and to avoid like the plague getting labeled as an expert. Such a label results in one's becoming "stuck" in one's area of expertise and missing out on opportunities for real advancement. People in command-centered OCLs, by contrast, know that the rewards go eventually to those who have demonstrated real competence at running the basic operating units of the business; in other words, expertise is rewarded, not punished. A good store manager is qualified, not disqualified, for choice as CEO.

Sometimes it can happen that an outsider is appointed to a senior position and is sufficiently different and effective in his or her role for the established assumptions about career streams to be seriously called into question. For example, a multinational textiles firm that was included in my study of four large firms was a classic example of a command-centered OCL (Gunz, 1989a): Plant managers spent their lives managing plants, and their promotion to successively larger plants was an index of their career success. However, not long before I undertook the study, the company had hired a retired military officer with remarkable leadership skills as an internal turnaround specialist. His job was to rescue underperforming units, and his success in so doing had clearly created something of a stir among the plant managers, who were beginning to question their basic assumptions about what they should be doing to get ahead in the company. Louis Gerstner's impact on IBM has been similar.

In such a situation, the taken-for-granted assumptions that underpin the OCL are called into question because it looks to those making their careers within the existing OCL as if the success model may have changed. The stronger the signal that this is the case, the more likely it is that people will take it that there has indeed been a change to their career stream, typically generating shock waves within the company that lead people to wonder whether the rules of the game have changed and whether they need to reassess their views about what it takes to get ahead. If they do, and depending on the nature of the change, this may have a direct and immediate impact on the firm's managerial rationality (arrow 4 in Figure 23.2). Furthermore, it is by no means uncommon that the appointment of an outsider CEO is followed by significant changes in the composition of the TMT. The model suggests potential for this, too, to have a direct impact on the managerial rationality of the firm (arrows 5 and 6 in Figure 23.2). If these changes lead, as the model suggests, to a shift in the strategic direction of the firm, the cyclic nature of the model suggests that the change could well take root as (arrows 1-3) the change in rationality reinforces the change to the career stream.

For example, suppose that the arrival of the outsider CEO sends the signal to a command-centered OCL that the dominant OCL in future will be constructional (the OCL that punishes expertise and rewards people who acquire novel experiences). The CEO underscores this message by appointing to the TMT people (perhaps former colleagues; Gouldner, 1954) who fit the new mold. The rationality that best matches the constructional OCL is that of Miles and Snow's (1978) analyzer, whereas the command-centered OCL is a good match with the defender strategy (Gunz et al., 1998); it would be little surprise if these changes in top management were not accompanied by announcements about changes in strategy away from that of the defender. So the signals to ambitious executives now seem clear: Not only has the career success model changed such that expertise no longer seems to be rewarded in the way that it was, but this has led to a change in the organization's business strategy. Everything points to the constructional OCL as the way of the future. Human resources processes may well be adapted to the new order—for example, placing greater emphasis on cross-functional experience in the profile of senior management development. People look for career moves that will give them the breadth of experience that seems to be needed now, and start looking down on the in-depth expertise of the command-centered manager. So a shift in culture happens, not because *people* have changed, but because their *beliefs about what they have to do to get ahead* have changed.

This view of cultural change raises an important question, because it suggests that there is a point of bifurcation below which change does not happen and above which it does. Is there any way of predicting what is necessary for an outsider CEO to produce the shift in culture outlined in the preceding paragraphs, instead of being swallowed by the system, so to speak? I turn to the research implications of these ideas in the final section.

## CONCLUSION

The starting point of this chapter was my assertion that a reasonable expectation of any discussion of organizational careers and cultures would be that it would deal with the impact of cultures on careers. But that, I argued, would neglect the question of where cultures come from. Because culture is an organizational-level concept, it is necessary to think about careers at the organizational level of analysis, and as soon as we do this we realize that it is not enough simply to think about organizational culture as part of the environment in which careers are pursued. Cultures produce careers, and—because careers at the organizational level of analysis are an account of the way in which the organization produces and reproduces itself—careers, in turn, produce cultures.

The organizational-level analytic construct I have used to conceptualize careers is the career "stream," the pattern in the flows of people through the organization. Career streams come in many different shapes, and the logic that can be inferred to lie behind them, the so-called organizational career logic, provides a helpful way of linking careers and cultures because of the way it directs attention to the thinking that appears to underpin the career moves that take place in the organization as people develop as organizational members.

Because organizational careers are so closely linked with reproducing managerial hierarchies, the aspect of organizational culture on which I have focused in this chapter has a strongly managerial slant. Managerial rationalities, also variously called in the literature dominant logics, logics of action, and conceptions of control, can be thought of as a specialized form of organizational culture, but an extremely influential form in the sense that they are central to the process of determining strategic direction and the effectiveness with which this strategic direction is realized. But although the focus of the model shown in Figure 23.2 appears to be on top management, there are a number of ways in which rationalities have a trickle-down effect, so that, in practice, their influence is pervasive throughout the organization.

The model I have described linking careers (i.e., career streams) and cultures (i.e., managerial rationalities) can be thought of as having three mediating phenomena: strategies, top management team composition, and the nature of the people running the organization. Rationalities influence the strategic behavior of the organization (the strategies it chooses and the ways in which these chosen strategies are realized), which, in turn, has an impact on the shape of the organization's career streams. Career streams affect rationalities directly, by influencing the composition of the top management team and by influencing the nature of the people running the organization.

## Implications for Research

The model in Figure 23.2 is, in many ways, an agenda for research (Gunz & Jalland, 1996). Each of the arrows is a proposition that needs considerably more empirical study than it has had to date. Indeed, it is one of the great puzzles of management and organizational research that issues as fundamental as how career backgrounds affect the ways people manage are still largely unaddressed.

From an organizational culture perspective, the interesting questions lie around the arrows pointing to and from "rationalities." How can rationalities be characterized empirically? How dependent are they on the "shape" of career streams, and how does the strength of this effect compare with the impacts of TMT composition and top managers' personal characteristics? Indeed, what are the mechanisms by means of which rationalities are adjusted by these three sources of influence?

Similarly, how do rationalities affect the choice and implementation of strategy? I have explained above that rationalities have been invoked to provide part of the explanation for the strategic behavior of organizations, and indeed these invocations sound reasonable, but are they right? What actually goes on in the executive suites of our corporate world as belief systems are developed and turned into action?

Perhaps the most interesting research question of all was raised in the preceding section: Is it the case that there is a point of bifurcation in career processes such that change of a certain magnitude can result in a rapid and, perhaps, dramatic, flip in organizational culture? If so, is it possible to predict what is necessary for this flip to occur? Not only is this a matter of considerable theoretical interest, given the conventional belief that organizational cultures are remarkably durable, but it is of very great practical interest as well. It is at the heart of the problem faced by every board of directors and CEO trying to bring about organizational change: Do we have to change the top management to succeed, and if we do, what is necessary for them to have an impact? Is it possible, in other words, to predict the differential impacts of John Sculley at Apple and Louis Gerstner at IBM?

Many of these questions might—and should—be explored in cross-sectional data. But we can anticipate that this may generate yet more hypotheses, because of the closed-loop nature of the causality. So there is also a need for more ethnographic approaches, which are time-consuming, expensive, and not overly rewarded under the publish-in-"top-tier" journals hegemony that seems to be spreading from North America to so many corners of the world of organizational research.

There is still a great deal that we do not know about the relationship between careers and cultures, and in many ways the model described in this chapter sets out an extensive research agenda. Its central idea—that careers and cultures are mutually constitutive —is not new; those who approach careers from a sociological perspective are very familiar with it. As Hughes (1937) has pointed out, for example, "A study of careers—of the moving perspective in which persons orient themselves with reference to the social order, and of the typical sequences and concatenations of office—may be expected to reveal the nature and 'working constitution' of a society" (p. 413). The part of the "working constitution" on which this chapter has focused is organizational culture, and I have, in essence, argued that in the concept of career we have a powerful means for investigating the production and reproduction of organizations in general and organizational cultures in particular. It is time that this means was better exploited.

# PART V

# International Perspectives on Culture

The seven chapters that make up Part V provide insights from national culture research for understanding organizational culture. In Chapter 24, Brannen and Kleinberg review and critique the stimulus that analyses of Japanese national and organizational cultures provided for North American organizational culture theory. They describe ways in which anthropological analysis can add needed complexity and dynamism to overly simple models and provide a base for the analysis of intercultural dynamics.

Analyses of the implications of national culture proliferated following the publication of Hofstede's *Culture's Consequences* in 1980. In Chapter 25, Hofstede and Peterson clarify misunderstood issues in this often-cited but often-misused basic reference. They also note instances in which culture dimensions are overused in international research. Hofstede and Peterson note that national culture and organizational culture are fundamentally different—the former is about values and the latter is about practices.

Beginning from the Rokeach Value Survey and informed by many other ways of viewing values, Sagiv and Schwartz present in Chapter 26 data on national values from schoolteachers (key socializing agents in societies) and their students. They show the relationship of values to national differences in role stress and manager values. Unlike Hofstede, these authors argue that national culture directly affects organizational culture and individual behavior.

In Chapter 27, Rose, Kahle, and Shoham examine national differences in conformity through the lens of role relaxation. National cultures differ in the prevalence of role-relaxed individuals such that organizations will vary in how much culture management should be used to control them.

The Global Leadership and Organizational Behavior Effectiveness (GLOBE) Research Project is the most extensive international organizational research project to date. In Chapter 28, Dickson, Aditya, and Chhokar provide an overview of the project, discuss some methodological insights, and offer some preliminary conclusions. They address the challenges in predicting culture-related variables from nation, organization, and industry. Results of the GLOBE Project to date suggest that national culture tends to reflect values, whereas organizational culture tends to reflect practices.

Social entities other than organizations and nations can be cultural. In Chapter 29, Soeters analyzes a distinctive group of occupational cultures—the uniformed cultures of military and quasi-military organizations. Uniformed cultures have distinctive ways of handling communal life, hierarchy, and discipline, and they operate differently when in action than when under routine conditions. Soeters uses an international database to provide examples of values held by uniformed people that are distinctive to their national cultures.

Granrose, Huang, and Reigadas conclude Part V with a consideration of whether the study of organizational culture has been so shaped by issues in the Japan-U.S. relationship that stimulated it that attempts to understand organizations in other countries have been impeded. As an example, they analyze the cultural dynamics surrounding leadership in China based in the traditional dynamic between the more active Confucian and more passive Taoist approaches to proactive leadership and the recent influence of Maoist and post-Maoist political systems. Although the basic idea and theories of organizational culture make sense, we should expect some quite substantial amendments to be needed when these concepts are transplanted to new locales.

# 24

# Images of Japanese Management and the Development of Organizational Culture Theory

*-- Mary Yoko Brannen and Jill Kleinberg*

Much of the interest in organizational culture in the late 1970s and early 1980s emanated from the perceived link between Japanese management techniques and Japan's superlative economic prowess at that time. In this chapter we frame the development of organizational culture theory in view of perceptions of Japanese management then and now. First, we examine how Western notions of Japanese management have influenced both popular and scholarly conceptualizations of organizations as cultures—including our understanding of what organizational culture is, how it comes into being, its implications for organization, and how it can be managed and changed. We then discuss the limitations of this model of organizational culture and show how current ethnographic research on Japanese management abroad contributes toward the construction of a new iteration of culture theory.

This chapter complements the theorizing of organizational culture as dynamic, contingent, pluralist, and changing put forth by others in this *Handbook* (see, e.g., Hatch, Chapter 15; Rafaeli & Worline, Chapter 4; Tyrrell, Chapter 5). Our particular conceptualization of culture largely grows out of our personal experience, in which we, individually, have analyzed the impacts of cross-national, cross-cultural interaction on organizational culture formation and change in binational (Japanese-American, Japanese-German) organizations. It addresses such issues as how, in today's global organizational context, national culture affects a firm's organizational culture both from the outside, through the filter of the firm's external cultural environment, and from the inside, through ongoing cross-cultural interactions among multinational employees. Our emerging framework, which we characterize as a model of negotiated culture, benefits from an interdisciplinary approach. Recent ethnographic and interpretative research that examines "domestic" organizational settings from a multiple-cultures perspective combines with comparative cross-national research in mixed-cultural "foreign" settings to further our understanding of the process of cultural evolution in today's complex cultural organizations.

## THE PARAGON OF JAPANESE MANAGEMENT: A PARADIGM OF CORPORATE CULTURE

Japan's rapid recovery after World War II and its consequent emergence as a world industrial power sparked keen interest in Japanese management practices among business practitioners as well as among scholars of organization and management. This interest emerged first in North America, then in Europe, and more recently in other parts of Asia. It was fueled by a zeal to increase organizational effectiveness, which in turn would increase country competitiveness. A variety of perspectives have motivated this interest. Depending on local political and economic climates, Japan has been viewed as exemplar, potential market, competitor, or strategic ally. In the United States, the oil crisis of the early 1970s and the consequent economic recession moved practitioners and scholars to consider the reasons for Japan's economic success and to contemplate what they could borrow from Japanese practice in order to strengthen domestic organizations. Books such as *Japan as Number One* (Vogel, 1979), *The Art of Japanese Management* (Pascale & Athos, 1981), and *Theory Z* (Ouchi, 1981) became commonplace items on the shelves of managers. Popular scholarship of this sort promoted a highly idealized image of Japanese management, but, nevertheless, one that

exerted considerable influence on the nascent notion of "corporate culture."

### Early Models of Japanese Organization

These early popularized conceptualizations of Japanese management articulated with the functionalist and management-centric construct then termed *organizational climate* (see Tagiuri & Litwin, 1968) and later termed *corporate culture* (see Enz, 1988; Kilmann, Saxton, Serpa, et al., 1985). (For a thorough review of the interconnections between organizational climate and culture, see Denison, 1990.) This literature emphasized a research agenda seeking to identify aspects of organizational structure and practices (what anthropologists tend to call cultural "behaviors") that managers could influence or control in order to reap positive firm-level outcomes—generally financial in nature. For the most part, the organizational variables identified were tangible or explicit.

Likewise, the early scholarly work on Japanese organizations was comparative in nature, outlining explicit techniques and practices employed by successful Japanese firms and not employed in North America. These findings were often presented as panaceas for North American firms' failing productivity.

The model of Japanese firms commonly presented was that of a tightly knit familial system (much like Likert's system 4) characterized by a long-term orientation toward both human resource management and business strategy and close, cooperative ties with the Japanese government ministries that determined national economic policy. Japanese organizations were depicted as having a cohesive culture that was widely and strongly shared among organizational members. The organizational culture portrayed emphasized loyalty and hard work—even self-sacrifice— as well as consensus decision making and harmonious personal relationships among coworkers and between employees and managers. These normative patterns of social interaction, along with lifetime employment, seniority-based pay and promotion schedules, and the enterprise-based union employment practices that constituted the three pillars supporting the Japanese management system, were considered to be natural outgrowths of Japanese societal culture (Ouchi, 1981; Pascale & Athos, 1981). Thus the view of Japanese organizational culture put forth resonated with the elite, frozen-in-time, mythologized view of Japanese national culture embodied in such archetypes as the "rice-paddy community," the "samurai," and Zen Buddhism.

## Origins of the Early Models: Contrasting Views of Japanese Culture

Although the popular image reflected an overly simplified, idealized view of Japanese organization and management, it drew from a body of social science scholarship that, in fact, offered more refined interpretations of Japanese organization and society. Scholars of Japan have differed in their epistemological frames, however. The early literature on Japanese management can be divided into roughly two distinct views of culture process: the culturalist and the convergence perspectives. The tension between the two perspectives is relevant to the negotiated organizational culture framework we present here. Therefore, we provide a brief characterization of each perspective below.

The culturalist perspective stems from work that is primarily comparative (mostly comparing Japan and the United States) and that seeks to understand differences between Japanese and U.S. organization and management primarily within the context of the two distinct social realities. Since the publication of Ruth Benedict's *The Chrysanthemum and the Sword* (1946), there has been considerable interest in contrasting Japanese and Western value systems, especially as they relate to work organization. Japan's rapid industrialization and modernization after

World War II, despite its resource-poor circumstances (with the exception of human capital), make it a particularly interesting country for comparison. Equally intriguing is Japan's consistent tendency to emerge as an "outlier" nation in surveys of work-related values geared to reveal patterns of country clusters (Haire, Ghiselli, & Porter, 1966; Hofstede, 1980a). Culture, from a culturalist perspective, is viewed broadly as dynamic and changing; nevertheless it is also seen as a persistent and, in the extreme view, conservative force.

A few carefully detailed, fieldwork-based case studies give sociological, anthropological, and historical insight into various aspects of Japanese organizational experience (Abegglen, 1958; Clark, 1979; Cole, 1971; Fruin, 1983; Rohlen, 1974; Yoshino, 1971). Along with more general analyses of Japanese society (Lebra, 1976; Nakane, 1970), these studies have increased our understanding of the intimate link between societal culture and the behavior of people in organizations. For example, the strong bonds tying individuals to work organizations in Japan may be seen as one manifestation of a more general pattern of close relationship between persons in particular group contexts (Lincoln & Kalleberg, 1990). Although today the company is the main corporate unit in Japanese society, in the past the family, village, feudal domain, and nation-state served as similarly strong locales for the integration and identification of group values. The Japanese worker's psychological dependence on and identification with the company, therefore, lie within a set of values that run deep in Japan's cultural tradition.

The earliest among these studies of Japanese organization are notable for having informed, after passing through a significant simplifying filter, the popularized notion of Japanese management that heavily influenced the "corporate culture" model of organizational culture (see Deal & Kennedy, 1982; Ouchi, 1981; Peters & Waterman, 1982). Thus these popular models of Japanese management became the basis for a plethora of widely read "how-to" books on culture.

By focusing more on content (the tangible techniques and practices) than on embedded social processes, these books resulted in a "culture-bound" image of Japanese organization.

The practice of so-called lifetime employment provides a good example. Lifetime employment, even in Japan, has been a cultural ideal rather than a practical reality. Most Japanese recognize lifetime employment as a core organization cultural attribute; nevertheless, it is attainable only by roughly 20% of the Japanese workforce—limited to male employees of large, successful, and well-established organizations (see, e.g., Beck & Beck, 1994). It can be explained as a phenomenon that is compatible with Japanese societal culture, but that is rooted in particular historical circumstances and, from the beginning, has been consciously incorporated into a modern management ideology (Kondo, 1990; Yoshino, 1971).

The convergence perspective downplays the culture-bound or conservative effect of societal culture in favor of what might be termed more of a "culture-free" view. This view generally argues that, rather than societal culture, the limitations of technology and economic efficiency narrowly circumscribe the industrial forms that a society can adopt (Kerr, Dunlop, Harbison, & Myers, 1960). Conventionally stated, the perspective assumes that as Japan industrializes, its organizational mechanisms and structures will become increasingly similar to those in other industrial nations, as with any other country in a like economic phase of development. Likewise, Japan's workers will come to share the outlooks, habits, values, and beliefs of workers in other industrial countries.

Ronald Dore (1973), an early scholar of Japanese management, has nevertheless given the convergence perspective a somewhat different spin. Dore argues that the distinctive management style of modern Japanese work organizations is due less to the conservative force of traditions such as the "samurai ethic" and the "feudal rice farmer mentality," both frequently invoked as cultural explanations for a continuing group orientation, than to Japan's experience as a late-developing economy. He has coined the term *welfare corporatism* to describe a set of institutions that has reached its highest level of deployment in Japan and toward which future organizations will evolve on a global basis.

Certain other comparative research treats the convergence issue somewhat differently. Rather than advancing a convergence perspective by pointing to an evolved transnational organizational form, this research focuses on cross-cultural similarities in Japanese and U.S. work organizations, values, and attitudes. Marsh and Mannari (1971), for example, examined lifetime commitment in Japan after introducing the conceptual difference between commitment based on status enhancement and commitment based on moral loyalty. Data on interfirm mobility indicated that commitment to the organization in both countries is contingent upon the expectancy of status enhancement, not upon moral loyalty to the firm. These researchers conclude that Western scholars have exaggerated the role of cultural variables in the prediction of lifetime employment.

Survey-based comparisons of Japan and the United States frequently point to both similarities and differences (Cole, 1971; Kagono, Nonaka, Sakakibara, & Okumura, 1985; Lincoln & Kalleberg, 1990), and the finding of similarity often leads to critiques of cultural interpretations of Japan. Lincoln and Kalleberg (1990), for instance, suggest that the penchant for mythologizing Japanese management techniques that is so common in the United States arises at least partly from a crisis in work commitment in the United States. Corporations, once content to allow a limited, minimally functional attachment on the part of rank-and-file workers, now are demanding more.

It is important to note, however, that the positivistic research paradigm on which survey research is based is less suited to uncovering the multifaceted "meaning" that work has for people than is anthropological, ethnographic research (Sackmann, Phillips, Kleinberg, & Boyacigiller, 1997). Dore's (1973) treatise on convergence, which integrates a variety of research techniques and approaches, serves as a reminder that cross-national comparison of organizations benefits from showing cognizance of culture as one analytic construct. Dore's discussion of relational contracting and the community model of the company, for example, is anchored in traditional Confucian values.

Whereas portions of research from the culturalist perspective show up in the early corporate culture literature in truncated, superficial form, the research from the convergence perspective has a more obvious link. The prediction of convergence toward a Japanese model put forth by Dore and others writing in this vein anticipates the incorporation of certain "Japanese" techniques into U.S. (or European) management practice, including mechanisms for building an emotional attachment of mutual concern between company and employee. Ouchi's (1981) notion of the "Theory Z" organization, for example, identifies an organizational design and concomitant culture that reflect convergence between Japanese and U.S. ideal types. Ouchi associates the Z-type organization, as exemplified by IBM and Hewlett Packard, with high performance, just as Deal and Kennedy (1982) and Peters and Waterman (1982) appropriate certain Japanese-like characteristics for their criteria for a successful company. The empirical question of whether cultural constraints might inhibit successful cross-national, cross-cultural borrowing (as suggested by the culturalist view) troubled few proponents of the convergence perspective at the time.

## LIMITATIONS OF THE EARLY MODELS OF JAPANESE MANAGEMENT FOR ORGANIZATION CULTURE THEORY

In the early euphoria of borrowing elements of Japanese organizational climate—the much-lauded management techniques and practices—the question of transferability seldom arose. This is ironic given that the prevailing conceptualizaton of culture at that time conformed to what the anthropologist Eric Wolf (1982) describes as a "two billiard ball" understanding, in which societal cultures are depicted as monolithic entities that either collide or roll side by side, remaining intact in their original forms when cross-cultural contact occurs—thus precluding culture transfer.

The research on Japanese society and organizations was amenable to such monolithic interpretations. Particular techniques and practices comprised by the popular model of Japanese management reflected Schein's (1985) observable artifact level (Level I) of organizational culture. Therefore, the model provided practitioners with only a superficial understanding of Japanese management practice. As a consequence, there was little theoretical substance to inform practitioners of the pitfalls they might encounter when elements of one culture are transferred to another.

Among the early culturalist representations of Japanese organization and management, explanatory sociocultural context often was provided, thus giving insight into cultural dynamics (see Hatch, 1993). However, their relative lack of cross-cultural experience inhibited business scholars' and practitioners' awareness of the culture process. Moreover, at the time, organizational effectiveness in domestic firms was falling, and a "quick fix" was needed. At any rate, neither the culturalist nor the convergence perspective offered a theoretical/conceptual framework for understanding intercultural interaction.

We therefore identify four general theoretical limitations of the early Japanese management literature in providing an adequate framework for understanding the cultural dynamics:

1. The concept of culture is parochial.
2. Culture (organizational or national) is assumed to be consistent in thought and behavioral manifestations across a specified cultural grouping of individuals.

3. There is no understanding of the interface between national culture and organizational culture.

4. Cultures are seen as static; there is no allowance for the reinterpretation of original culture over time.

## JAPANESE MANAGEMENT OUTSIDE JAPAN: FROM THE STATIC, MONOLITHIC MODEL TOWARD A DYNAMIC, COMPLEX CULTURE PERSPECTIVE

The organizational context has changed dramatically, however, since the heyday of the corporate culture literature. Most notably, organizations, both domestic and foreign, have become increasingly culturally complex with the dramatic increase in internationalization in the late 1980s and the 1990s. Much of the internationalization reflects direct foreign investment and frequently takes the form of joint ventures, foreign-owned subsidiaries, and multinational corporations in which whole or partial organizational systems are transferred. Whether in the realm of bilateral business negotiation or of binational or multinational organizations, management scholars and practitioners became keenly interested in the impact of national culture on successful outcomes.

From the North American perspective, Japan once again loomed large. A host of articles and books examined how to negotiate with the Japanese (e.g., Black & Mendenhall, 1993; Graham & Sano, 1984). The proliferating Japanese "transplant" firms also were scrutinized (see Liker, Ettlie, & Campbell, 1995). Initial optimism about the smooth transfer of Japanese ideologies and organizational practices from Japanese managers to American employees (Johnson & Ouchi, 1974) nevertheless gave way to recognition that intercultural processes are exceedingly complex (Kleinberg, 1989).

Initially, the lion's share of the literature on Japanese-owned organizations in North America came from a disciplinary orientation in strategic operations management and looked at predominantly practical issues in technology transfer from Japan to North America. Some of this work falls into the convergence perspective and assumes that there is nothing inherently "Japanese" about the management techniques that would curtail the successful implementation of Japan-based transfers of technology. Other work in this area takes up the culturalist position, arguing that without a Japanese workforce the results of technology transfer from Japan to U.S. workplaces will always fall short of the Japanese standard.

But, as more and more reports of friction around work organization, superior and subordinate relations, and other behavioral issues began to emerge in Japanese-owned firms, the research became more focused on the dynamics of cultural interaction (Boyacigiller, 1990; Brannen, 1995; Kleinberg, 1989; Peterson, Peng, & Smith, 1999; Yeh & Latib, 1990). Practitioners as well as researchers began to question whether, indeed, a smooth transference of Japanese management practice to North America was possible. How do North American employees react? What can binational firms tell us about the process of intercultural interaction and its implications for organization? Reports from the workplace pointed to frictions and the complexity of organizational process.

With these questions came a shift in research focus from identifying techniques and practices as key aspects of favorable organizational climates to looking more deeply at the accompanying social and cultural infrastructures. Through U.S. organizations' attempts to borrow and implement the artifacts of Japanese management and organization, it became clear that these were supported by deep cultural infrastructure (see Liker, Fruin, & Adler, 1999). This realization led to rereadings of the earlier in-depth studies of Japanese management with an eye toward understanding Japanese organizational culture as socially constructed. Also, a series of ethnographic studies were conducted in a line of inquiry more akin to the interpretivist/social

constructivist method to gain deeper understandings of the intercultural dynamics at play
in today's complex cultural organizations.

## EMERGENT ORGANIZATIONAL CULTURE: THE NEGOTIATED CULTURE PERSPECTIVE

We present here a broad framework for conceptualizing interrelationships among variables rather than a predictive model. The
schematic nature of the framework can be explained partly by the fact that each ethnographer who has done research in this kind of
setting has had his or her own unique fieldwork experience. It is characteristic of an
ethnographic approach that the research trajectory is shaped by the expressed (or observed) concerns of those who are being studied. Variations in the location, business
focus, and size of a firm, therefore, influence
the particular issues that are salient to the organization at the time of fieldwork. The negotiated culture perspective offered here
draws on data gathered in subsidiaries, joint
ventures, and a Japanese takeover, where expatriate Japanese managers and staff work
together with nationals or residents of the
host country to distribute consumer products, produce paper, and work together to design new products.

In each case, the broad objective has been
to understand the processes and consequences
of cross-national, cross-cultural interaction.
Work attitudes and organizational arrangements, the foci of certain research on binational firms mentioned earlier, are of interest.
In the ethnographic scholarship, however,
these concerns tend to be viewed from a cultural perspective.

### A Concept of Culture

Ethnography, in fact, has been described
by anthropologists as "the science—and
art—of cultural description" (Frake, 1983,
p. 60), and there is widespread agreement

among anthropologists that *culture* refers to
the ideational dimension of human experience (e.g., Frake, 1983; Geertz, 1973;
Goodenough, 1981; Spradley, 1980). Culture can be conceptualized as, variously
stated, the shared meanings, sensemaking,
assumptions, understandings, or knowledge
by which a group of people give order to their
social world. Such cultural knowledge, be it
explicit or tacit, influences both the ways
people behave and the ways they interpret
events, people, and objects in their social and
physical environment (Spradley, 1980). The
ethnographer infers a group's system of
meanings by observing and analyzing group
members' cultural (or patterned) behavior,
cultural artifacts, and speech utterances
(Spradley, 1980).

Although this concept of culture, with its
focus on the ideational or cognitive, has some
similarity to the (also anthropological) definition proposed by Tyrrell in Chapter 5 of
this volume, it differs from our reading in an
important respect. Tyrrell seems to emphasize the adaptive nature of culture; that is,
culture's role in answering particular needs,
problems, and desires. His conceptualization
evokes Schein's (1985) emphasis on the problem-solving function, and malleability, of organizational culture. In contrast, the shared
understandings or sensemaking with which
we are concerned resonates with the interpretative perspective on organization, which
grew, in part, as a response to a management-
centric corporate culture perspective (Alvesson, 1995; Gregory, 1983; Smircich, 1983;
Smircich & Calás, 1987; Sypher, Applegate,
& Sypher, 1985). Czarniawska-Joerges
(1992) describes organizations as "nets of
collective action" in which "the contents of
the collective action are meanings and things
(artifacts)" (p. 37). The collective meanings
may or may not relate directly to an organization's problems or needs as recognized by
management.

Some analyses of the research data from
which the negotiated culture perspective
evolves elucidate shared sensemaking holistically, at the level of various cultural groupings. For example, in her study of a sales sub-

sidiary, Kleinberg (1994a, 1994b, 1994c) arrived at representations of cultural knowledge shared across the organization—reflecting the assumptions or understandings of both Japanese and Americans, cultural knowledge within Japanese and American subgroups, and cultural knowledge within one particular work group. Other ethnographic research illuminates cultural knowledge that concerns more focused arenas of organizational life. Sumihara (1992, 1994), for instance, devotes much of his analysis to shared assumptions that guide decision making, performance appraisal, and compensation practices in the sales subsidiary he studied. Similarly, in her study of a production facility taken over by a Japanese company, Brannen (1994) documents the understandings regarding the transfer and implementation of a new technology and other labor-related issues arrived at by the Japanese management team and local employees.

The body of ethnographic research gains coherence, despite its diverse foci, by virtue of its struggling with certain critical, interconnected conceptual issues. One concerns the construct of national culture: how to surface and represent it and what its implications are for organization. A second issue relates to nature of the link between culture and individual behavior. A third centers on the implications of multiple cultural identities for any individual. And a fourth issue concerns what is created, and the process of that creation, when persons representing different national cultures work together.

### National Culture

The assumption that national culture is a viable social construct underlies the research on binational firms, as does the assumption that linkages exist between national culture and organizational behavior (Child, 1981). Nevertheless, as our earlier discussion indicates, the failure to "operationalize" this unwieldy construct so that it is analytically useful remains a continuing weakness of comparative and cross-cultural management research (Sackmann et al., 1997). Research that contributes to the negotiated culture perspective posits a generalized work culture as a subset of national culture, although it does so with varying degrees of explicitness and relies on various means for determining the content of a national group's work culture. (For systematic efforts to surface such generalized work-related assumptions, see Brannen & Salk, 2000; Kleinberg, 1989.) Thus the linkages between national culture and behavior in organizations can be seen more clearly.

The analyses exhibit notable commonality in what were discovered to be cultural themes and assumptions for any nationality. With regard to Japan, there is obvious resonance with familiar representations of Japanese societal culture (Lebra, 1976; Nakane, 1970; Rohlen, 1974). Emphasis is placed on conforming, on showing the appropriate *taido* (attitude), *kangaekata* (way of thinking), and *ishiki* (spirit) (Brannen, 1994; Sumihara, 1992). American assumptions about work, with their emphasis on the individual (Kleinberg, 1989), also are consonant with anthropological depictions of American society (Stewart & Bennett, 1991). Nonetheless, each ethnographic study constructs only a partial picture of a national work culture. Assumptions concerning the way people conceptualize their formal position or the process of accomplishing work reveal themselves primarily through the fears and criticisms repeatedly voiced by Japanese or Americans about cultural others' transgression of particular work expectations (Kleinberg, 1989). Moreover, we gain greatest insight into work assumptions whose salience is triggered by key events and issues specific to the organization being studied (Brannen, 1994).

### Individual Cultural Expression

Ethnographic research on binational firms highlights the tension between conceptualizing culture as a group-level phenomenon and recognizing that, within any cultural grouping, a range of individual interpretations is expressed (Agar, 1982). Brannen (1994) and Sumihara (1994) draw on Giddens's (1979) theory of structuration to explain the apparent anomaly. In a society, we are able to reproduce familiar social structures because individual social actors have both "discursive knowledge," knowledge that can be expressed at the level of discourse, and tacit or "practical knowledge" about the "rules" that both constrain and enable action. Giddens's notion of structuration allows for individuals to act more than one way within the framework of the rules. Similarly, cognitive anthropology, on which Kleinberg (1994b) draws, views culture as a nonprescriptive "resource in terms of which things get done, given the historical contingencies and human purposes of the moment" (Agar, 1982, p. 83).

Interspersed throughout the "thick description" (Geertz, 1973) contained in the ethnographic accounts, one finds instances of an individual, on different occasions, acting more, or less, as the representation of his or her national culture would anticipate. In Brannen's (1994) terminology, the individual acts in ways that can be placed somewhere along a three-zone continuum from culturally "hypernormal" to "normal" to "marginally normal." For example, an American working for one Japanese boss might not mind if his job is diffuse and lacks clarity, whereas under another Japanese manager he might decry this violation of American assumptions about how a person's job should be ordered (Kleinberg, 1989). The difference can lie in the degree of mutual trust between superior and subordinate and how that trust affects the American's opportunities to perform desirable tasks (Kleinberg, 1994a).

Part of the anomaly, also, is that researchers assume that national cultural identity remains separate and distinct throughout an individual's tenure in the binational, while recognizing that a person's thinking and behavior, in some areas, may be temporarily or enduringly altered by the intercultural experience. The overseas Japanese manager is especially susceptible to cultural ambiguity or change as he undergoes the intense culture shock and, hopefully, the subsequent cultural adaptation typically experienced by Japanese nationals who live and work outside of Japan.

## Traversing Multiple Cultures

Ethnographic research on binational firms or joint ventures has contributed to the current multiple-cultures perspective on organization (Martin, 1992; Sackmann et al., 1997). Individuals bring to the work setting "cultures of origin" (Brannen, 1994) that reflect their particular ongoing histories in various cultural contexts, such as national, regional, ethnic, familial, and occupational. Japanese expatriates, for example, bring with them a generalized Japanese work culture as well as cultures specific to their home organizations and, very likely, the cultures of their business subunits within those organizations. Upon arriving at binational firms, they are caught up in the daily interactions by which work is accomplished and through which cultural meanings specific to those organizations are constructed. Even when they believe they are instituting American-style managerial practices, unconsciously their enactment of these practices reflects their own Japanese cultural logic (Kleinberg, 1994b).

## Negotiating Culture

A view of culture as "emergent" underpins the ethnographic research reported here. Moreover, a broadly conceived notion of "negotiation" threads through the descriptions of the process by which culture emerges (Brannen, 1994; Brannen & Salk, 2000; Kleinberg, 1998; Sumihara, 1992). This view of culture is distinct from many of the traditional anthropological views of culture because it focuses on understanding culture as an output (albeit emergent and shifting) of ongoing interactions between peoples of distinct national cultures.

This emphasis in part reflects the influence that Strauss's concept of "negotiated order" has had on organization scholarship. To quote Strauss (1978): "The negotiated order on any given day could be conceived of as the sum total of the organization's rules and policies, along with whatever agreements, understandings, pacts, contracts, and other working arrangement currently obtained" (p. 5). But our emphasis is also concomitant with more recent accounts in anthropology that reflect a view of culture as created and reproduced through interactions both between and within cultures. The current practice in anthropology reflects this view by accounting for the interactions in the writing up of ethnographic accounts. For example, the notions of reflexivity and ethnographic authority (see, e.g., Clifford, 1988; Clifford & Marcus, 1986; Marcus & Fisher, 1986) are heuristics for understanding the relationship between the culture of the researcher and that of the researched. Critical to this view is an understanding of the political and historical relationship between these cultures (Dwyer, 1982; Ong, 1987; Roseberry, 1989). Ong (1987) summarizes this view:

"Culture" is taken as historically situated and emergent, shifting and incomplete meanings and practices generated in webs of agency and power. Cultural change is not understood as unfolding according to some predetermined logic (of development, modernization or capitalism) but as the disrupted, contradictory, and differential outcomes which involve changes in identity, relations of struggle and dependence, including the experience of reality itself . . . in situations wherein groups and classes struggle to produce and interpret culture within the industrializing milieu. (pp. 2-3)

As important as the theoretical underpinnings of the negotiated culture perspective is the very nature of the fieldwork experience. While conducting the long-term participant observation on which much of the ethnographic research rests, researchers became acutely aware of the stream of communica-

tive acts by Japanese expatriates and local personnel aimed at reaching agreements, understandings, pacts, and so forth. Some of the observed communication conformed to the conventional billiard-ball model of intercultural communication described earlier. Even when it did, however, the responses of persons who experienced culture clash frequently fed into emergent sensemaking. This fact is illustrated by two of the cultural themes that Kleinberg (1994b) has found at the organizationwide level: "We are unique" and "We are a company divided." Both themes reflect Japanese and American cognizance of a cultural gap in concepts of work.

Space limitations prevent us from elaborating on the complexity of the negotiation process at the interpersonal level that is revealed in the ethnographic accounts. We will mention, however, two constructs that have promise for the development of organization culture theory: (a) cultural "cross-knowledge" (Sumihara, 1992, 1998) and (b) "negotiated cultural outcomes" (Brannen & Salk, 2000). In his analysis of performance appraisals, Sumihara shows how both the text and the tangible outcomes of an appraisal are affected by (a) respective Japanese and American stocks of cultural knowledge about performance appraisal and (b) cross-knowledge, or Japanese interpretations of Americans' cultural knowledge about performance appraisal, and vice versa. Furthermore, through the appraisal process, new expectations with regard to this activity are generated. Cultural cross-knowledge derives from interpretations of the cultural other formed prior to participation in the binational organization, in combination with modifications or additions stemming from contact with the cultural other within the binational.

Sumihara concludes that new cultural understandings that are generated may emerge as compromises, as when the norm for pay increases is settled somewhere between Japanese and American expectations. Or they may emerge as previously unknown practices. In addition, they may reflect misapplication of (or the application of incomplete) cross-knowledge, as in one case in which Japanese managers, "understanding" that Americans expect to be commended for their good work, initiated a policy of openly praising American subordinates. Unfortunately, they tended to give praise for abstract personal qualities valued by the Japanese rather than for measurable achievements valued by Americans.

Brannen and Salk (2000) have expanded the theoretical research on negotiated culture by testing basic assumptions in the context of a German-Japanese joint venture. Using data collected through semistructured interviews and analyzed using textual analysis software, they traced the processes that led to distinct negotiated cultural outcomes. In doing so, they discovered there were certain key organizational issues that became catalysts for negotiation. Cultural attributes suggested by aggregate models of cultural difference (e.g., the billiard-ball model) that were not salient to the particular issue at hand were insignificant determinants of the trajectory the negotiated outcome would take. This study shows that structural/contextual influences together with individuals' culturally determined sensemaking in regard to specific organizational events are more useful determinants of negotiated outcomes.

Brannen and Salk (2000) depict a number of negotiated possibilities. For example, over time a type of synchronization began to occur in terms of conflicting decision-making styles whereby Germans began tolerating a slower and more participative process and their Japanese colleagues began allowing for meetings to be shortened and pared down in attendance. Moreover, Brannen and Salk found that the negotiated outcomes did not always reflect one or the other or both cultural parent groups as the terms *cultural hybrid* and *cultural blend*—often used to describe binational organizations—suggest. In fact, the negotiated outcomes in some cases were more like "cultural mutants" in which new cultural knowledge or "know-how" was generated in cases where neither group had a preexisting repertoire for handling certain situations.

This kind of analysis directs us away from a simplistic billiard-ball model and toward a perspective that focuses on what is created through cross-national, cross-cultural interaction.

## Explaining Emergent Organizational Culture

Explanation in anthropological ethnography necessarily takes into account a host of factors. Some, such as stocks of "native" cultural knowledge and cultural cross-knowledge, are immediate to the sorts of communicative acts just described. In order to explain more fully the emergence of site-specific cultural understandings, however, we need to consider wider contextual factors as well.

Binational organizations in which the Japanese are both owners and expatriate managers constitute settings in which asymmetrical power relations temper the negotiated order. The American subgroup culture in the company studied by Kleinberg (1994b), for example, primarily reflected the way members made sense of their relative disadvantages vis-à-vis the Japanese. The particular relationship between the subsidiary and the parent company in Japan also exerted a strong influence on local sensemaking in this company and in others where Japanese managers dominated. The same can be said for joint-venture organizations where power might be distributed more equally, as illustrated by the work of Brannen and Salk (2000). Other critical explanatory contextual factors include the industry in which the organization operates and the global and local political and economic environments.

In Figure 24.1, we offer a schematic representation of the process by which negotiated understandings emerge, noting the influence of individuals' cultures of origin as well as structural/contextual influences in the organization's external and internal environment. Emergent cultural foci, such as subgroups

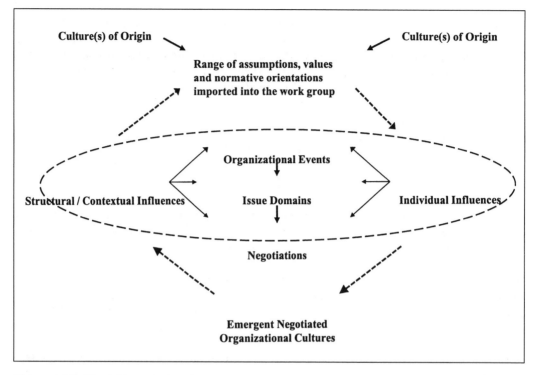

**Figure 24.1.** The Negotiated Cultures Perspective
SOURCE: Adapted from Brannen and Salk (2000).

that distinguish expatriate and local personnel, become part of the internal environment.

The figure shows that negotiation occurs around "issue domains" that are triggered by particular organizational events. An event could be something that is dramatic and engages the entire organization, such as the labor negotiations described by Brannen (1994), or it could involve a comparatively unremarkable ongoing occurrence, such as the arrivals and leave-takings of Japanese expatriate managers, that on any one occasion normally affects sensemaking in select work groups but over time contributes to organizationwide and, possibly, national subgroup cultural knowledge (Kleinberg, 1994b). Depending on the perceived criticality of the event, organizational members may or may not be aware that negotiation is taking place.

In sum, the ethnographic perspective on negotiated organizational cultures gives a view of cultural process and outcomes that is notably different from that offered in what might be considered mainstream organizational culture research. The influence of the "leader" in shaping culture (Schein, 1985), although acknowledged as being critical in certain circumstances (e.g., Kleinberg, 1994a), generally becomes only one explanatory variable among many. The perspective reinforces a line of thought developed by Kunda (1992) that, even where top management might attempt to engineer culture, emergent culture cannot be controlled. Conscious efforts to shape understandings have many unintended consequences. Furthermore, many of the "events" around which shared understandings arise fall outside management's consciousness. Rather than the adaptive function of organizational culture, the negotiated culture perspective emphasizes its sensemaking function.

## DISCUSSION

Whereas through the 1980s and early 1990s there existed a commonly recognized image of Japanese management, albeit an overly simplified, stereotypical one, this image is weakening. Japan's well-documented economic problems, beginning with the burst of the economic bubble in 1991 and the subsequent recession, encourage popular interpretations of Japanese management as being in a state of crisis—old models of management are no longer adequate. Ample commentary, such as that found in the Japan Survey section of the *Economist* in July 1994, titled "Death of a Role Model," proclaims that the Japanese now have more to learn from the West than the other way around.

Scholars of Japanese management and organization indeed observe that Japanese companies are in a period of "deinstitutionalization," and the value of previously taken-for-granted patterns is being questioned (Westney, 1998). To give just one example, pressures on the seniority-based human resource management system intensify in Japan's elite companies as the long domestic recession continues. Companies face the dilemma of how to adjust pay and promotion practices in order to maintain morale and motivation among young employees in an increasingly graying workforce. Forces favoring deinstitutionalization coincide with the growing pressure on Japanese firms to become more global in both strategy and organization (Westney, 1998). The image of the "shadow" Japanese manager who undercuts the power of "token" host-country managers, an image that reflects cognizance of Japanese hegemony in the binational organizations discussed in this chapter, could be altered significantly. The effective integration of non-Japanese employees into the management structures of Japanese multinational companies, both at home and abroad, could have profound effects on management practice.

The predominantly tacit assumptions that make up a nation-specific work culture are resistant to change. Current ethnographic studies of Japanese organizations reveal notable persistence in widely shared assumptions regarding such things as how to get a job done and what it means to be a manager. Time and again, as participant observers in binational work settings, we see Japanese expatriates behaving in accordance with a Japanese cultural logic. Their behavior resembles patterns portrayed by scholars 20 or more years ago as being integral to managing both at home in Japan and in overseas subsidiary operations. These include the following:

- Decision making that involves careful building of agreement among an organization's members, as much through informal networking as through formal procedures
- Managerial roles defined in broad terms and dependent on the initiatives of the individual manager for effectiveness
- Heavy reliance on experience-based tacit know-how and learning by doing
- Emotional commitment to the organization and a tendency to give work priority over other sectors of life (Westney, 1998)

Nonetheless, as Japanese expatriates increasingly participate in a "transnational, deterritorialized ethnoscape" (Appadurai, 1991), it may become more and more problematic to define Japanese work culture according to national boundaries. The globalization of business brings experience to individuals that enlarges the portfolios of cognitive sketch maps they may draw on to guide behavior. Already many large Japanese companies, and Japan itself, recognize the reentry difficulties of *chuzaiin* and their families and are responding with reacculturation programs.

When we recognize that Japanese companies outside of Japan (or within Japan) do not enact a homogeneous set of formal management practices, and when we recognize that a national work culture, although persistent, is still dynamic, a negotiated organizational culture framework makes sense. The framework applies as well to many, if not all, complex organizational settings.

The negotiated organizational culture framework that we propose leads to careful consideration of the issue of cultural representation (Clifford & Marcus, 1986). Representations of culture as a social construct found in much of the organizational culture literature tend to overlook existing variation and inconsistency. This is especially likely if the researcher is targeting a management-oriented academic and practitioner audience that favors a clear, systematic, economical representation. Yet the growing complexity of the global organizational landscape may require representations that are not bound by a logic of cultural coherence.

Certainly within the complex cultural arenas typical of today's global organizations—the multinational companies or international joint ventures characterized by multinational top management teams and special project groups—culture is contested, temporal, and emergent (Clifford, 1986). The binational organizational research reviewed here gives a sense of this dynamism, and the negotiated culture perspective begins to address ways to represent it adequately.

# 25

# Culture

## *National Values and Organizational Practices*

*-- Geert Hofstede and Mark F. Peterson*

In 1980, the first author of the present chapter reacted to the presumed universality of management theory by raising the question of whether American theories apply abroad (Hofstede, 1980b). Almost simultaneously, the world began wondering whether Japanese management theories apply abroad, a discussion in which the second author became involved (Peterson, 1988). The puzzle of whether managers and scholars can learn something from the analysis of national culture that can promote effective management led to the emergence of a new area of consultancy, management practice, and scholarship: organizational culture. Efforts to draw analogies between national and organizational culture have encouraged both creative thought and considerable confusion.

In the present chapter, we consider the core questions of the conceptual distinction between national and organizational culture and the conceptual relationship between the two. We argue here that the concept of national culture differs in important ways from that of organizational culture, although there is some analogy between the two. Rather than repeat extensive reviews of research about culture dimensions (e.g., Hofstede, 1991, 1997b), we will pay most attention to underemphasized and frequently misunderstood aspects. On the one hand, nuances in meanings of the national culture dimensions have sometimes been missed. On the other, directions remain for new and revised uses. We will conclude by reconsidering whether the solution some have offered of applying an

AUTHORS' NOTE: This chapter was drafted by Mark Peterson and approved, with comments and revisions, by Geert Hofstede.

American, Japanese, or other theory of management practice abroad is facilitated by attempts to make the practice part of what others would refer to as an "American organizational culture" or a "Japanese organizational culture."

Culture, the collective programming of the mind, is manifested in four basic ways (Hofstede, 1997, p. 195):

- *Symbols* carry particular meanings for culture members.
- *Heroes* are a culture's role models.
- *Rituals* are technically superfluous but socially necessary for a culture.
- *Values* are feeling-reflecting preferences for certain states of affairs over others.

Together, symbols, heroes, and rituals constitute *practices*.

## NATIONAL CULTURE

Having come to use the idea of culture, analysts face questions of how to divide a historically and contemporaneously integrated world into parts, from humankind in general into cultures, plural. The need to identify cultural boundaries is not unique to businesspeople and management authors. In fact, those who are interested comprise a much wider group that includes philosophers, doctors, social workers, husbands and wives in culturally mixed marriages, psychologists, journalists, and any interested laypersons. Culture is not specific to management—it belongs to the total society of which management is just a part. In the past few centuries, societies have taken actions that help clarify what groups share common cultural identities. Many societies have found their own centers of gravity and, in interaction with neighboring societies through peace and war, have drawn political lines, forming nation-states.

However, lines drawn around some nations reflect internal levels of heterogeneity that participants in the nations' political processes have not found tolerable. Cultural multiplicities formed into nations through coercion by third parties have proven other than helpful for defining cultural self-identity. Societies find lines drawn by former colonial powers and lines drawn by victors in world wars less appealing than lines they draw around themselves. Dissatisfaction with boundary lines drawn by others is sometimes resolved by the relatively peaceful dissolution of a nation, as in the case of the former Soviet Union and the split between the Czech Republic and Slovakia. Other times, it is reflected in continuing civil disturbances, as we have seen in many parts of the world.

Occasionally, participants in a politically stable nation have defined themselves as a multiplicity of groups unified, paradoxically, by a common commitment to diversity. The Swiss share a bond among language groups—German, French, Italian, Romanche—each one finding its identity supported through alliance with the other rather than with some larger nation-state sharing its same language. To say that these language groups share a common bond is not necessarily to say that they share a common culture (Hofstede, 1980a, pp. 335-339). The bond in Switzerland is as though the attraction of speaking German, French, Italian, or Romanche is enhanced rather than diminished by *not* being part of a larger country having the same language.

Still, most of the 200-odd nations throughout the world have achieved some stable cultural coherence that is likely to endure for the foreseeable future. There is some basis for expecting a certain level of cultural coherence within the majority of nations. This is in fact what Hofstede found in the international study of the IBM Corporation that led to *Culture's Consequences* (1980a) and what others have found in a growing number of subsequent projects that have documented clear differences between nations together with identifiable, but more modest, differences among regions or groups within nations (e.g., Lundberg & Peterson, 1994).

Given that we find the idea of culture helpful at the level of a nation despite the paradoxes of societal diversity within national boundaries, what concepts are available for describing a nation's culture? On the basis of a quantitative study across 40 nations, Hofstede (1980a, 1991) empirically derived the following four value dimensions:

- *Power distance:* the extent to which the less powerful members of organizations and institutions (like the family) accept and expect that power is distributed unequally

- *Individualism versus collectivism:* the extent to which individuals are integrated into groups

- *Masculinity versus femininity:* assertiveness and competitiveness versus modesty and caring

- *Uncertainty avoidance:* intolerance for uncertainty and ambiguity

Later on, based on research by Bond among students in 23 countries, Hofstede added a fifth dimension:

- *Long-term versus short-term orientation:* (long-term) thrift and perseverance versus (short-term) respect for tradition, fulfillment of social obligations, and protection of one's "face" (Hofstede & Bond, 1988)

These five dimensions are statistically largely independent, and every country studied could be given a numerical score indicating its relative position on the dimension.

Inkeles and Levinson (1969) provided the theoretical base for the first four dimensions. They reviewed the literatures of anthropology, comparative sociology, and comparative psychology on national culture (then called "national character") through the first half of the century. Their conclusion was that all societies throughout the world faced three kinds of problems: (a) relation to authority, (b) conception of self, and (c) primary dilemmas or conflicts and ways of dealing with them. Power distance has to do with relation to authority and uncertainty avoidance with handling primary dilemmas. Inkeles and Levinson indicated that conception of self has two components: an individual's place relative to society (hence individualism/collectivism) and the concept of masculinity and femininity (Hofstede, 1980a, pp. 14, 44, 313). The conception of each dimension was further shaped by particular literatures discussed in depth elsewhere. However, the theoretical base for the dimensions Hofstede proposed in *Culture's Consequences* is found in the fundamental structure of anthropology through the time of that volume's publication.

We do not claim that the five dimensions are complete, but they have shown their practical and theoretical usefulness across a variety of applications, from training of expatriates to explaining national differences in corruption levels. Other useful dimensions may present themselves; however, those offered so far either are not clearly enough defined to actually be measured or, if they are, they correlate so strongly with one of these five that they represent a facet of it and do not substantially add to the list.

## BEYOND NATIONAL CULTURE AND CULTURE DIMENSIONS

The availability of national culture scores on the four dimensions presents a temptation to look for cultural explanations for many things that happen in organizations. However, common sense dictates that one should rule out simpler explanations—such as levels of national income—before bringing in culture as an explanation. For example, the newspaper press in 1994 mentioned that strong correlations had been found between the relative number of airline crashes in a country and the country's power distance and collectivism scores. Should we suppose that airplanes crash because large power distance makes lower-ranking cockpit members reluctant to raise issues with pilots? This was the explanation suggested. However, when levels of GNP/capita were included in the analysis, it appeared that national poverty offered a better explanation, and that after GNP/capita was controlled for, the correlations between airline crashes and power distance plus collectivism disappeared. Airlines in less wealthy countries tend to buy used airplanes, use them longer, spend less money on maintenance, and have less money to attract and train the most competent flying and ground personnel—is it a surprise that they are likely to experience more accidents?

Locating a country's culture on the five dimensions is like locating its geographic position on a map. The geographic coordinates provide useful, even essential information, but a map only provides limited detail, and more extensive knowledge of a culture calls for broader personal exposure. So the dimension approach does not replace in-depth studies of country cultures; on the contrary, it invites them. An example is a study by d'Iribarne (1989) conducted in three aluminum plants belonging to a French company: one in France, one in the United States, and one in the Netherlands. D'Iribarne connects extensive interviews and observations in these facilities with a historical analysis of the nations within which they are located to describe three quite different philosophies of practice. As an example, his analysis of the French facility suggests that it reflects a strongly hierarchical, almost a caste, society. Not only are there levels of managers and professionals, first-line supervisors, and "non-cadres" of workers, but these levels permeate life and relationships to a degree not paralleled in the other societies studied. Yet each level has its own status, its own *honneur*, that provides a basis for self-respect and respect by other levels.

Are culture dimensions helpful in understanding the *logique de l'honneur*? Yes. The concept includes an element of large power distance—the less powerful parties recognize that substantial power differences in the sys-

tem are legitimate, yet they seem successful in maintaining quite a substantial sense of self-worth and respect for the overall system. It also provides a unique way of managing uncertainty with an element of uncertainty avoidance. It focuses one's responsibilities not on the entirety of society, but on a relatively familiar set of problems peculiar to a manageable portion of it. But could one adequately understand the *logique de l'honneur* simply as an intersection of culture dimensions? No. Culture dimensions were never intended to provide a complete basis for analyzing a culture.

## ORGANIZATIONAL CULTURES AS PRACTICES

In addition to nations, the culture concept has been extended to organizations. Impressionistic studies of organizations have described them as microcosms having some of the same cultural qualities as societies. Using an idea originally framed for large collectives such as nations to think about organizations has generated a new set of controversies. These controversies are quite similar to other kinds of level-of-analysis controversies discussed elsewhere in the present *Handbook*. Some of these controversies in international and organizational culture theory have stimulated creative thought. Are organizations also societies? Can they really be characterized as having or being cultures? We believe they can in some sense. Nations have qualities that transcend the qualities of individuals within them. The same holds for organizations. A collective programming of the mind occurs at both levels.

Organization and nation cultures, however, are certainly quite different things in many central features. A person's socialization, for example, is more fundamentally and deeply shaped by a society's culture than by the culture of an organization for which the person works. The collective programming of the mind at the level of nation principally

| TABLE 25.1 | Organizing in Its Contexts and Environments | |
| --- | --- | --- |
| | *Level of Culture* | *Place of Socialization* |
| | Gender and nation | Family |
| | Class | |
| | Occupation | School |
| | Business | |
| | Organization | Workplace |

SOURCE: Adapted from Hofstede (1997, p. 197).

involves values, which are acquired early in people's lives, generally before age 12. Hofstede, Neuijen, Ohayv, and Sanders (1990) conducted a combined qualitative and quantitative study across 20 Danish and Dutch organizational units and found that programming at the level of organizations principally involves practices (that is, symbols, heroes, and rituals). The idea of culture can also be applied at other levels, such as gender, class, occupation, and business or industry. As indicated in Table 25.1, the relative balance of values compared to practices varies by cultural level. However difficult one might find it to leave one's current employer and join another, immigrants find it far more difficult to leave their nations of birth and join another society. Specific cultural constructs that are meaningful for nations are likely to be less meaningful for organizations, and vice versa.

Do national culture dimensions tell us anything about the cultures of organizations that have tended to spring up in a nation, or about the organizational cultures that a multinational firm is likely to be able to introduce readily into a nation? This question brings us back to some of the others noted above. The culture dimensions developed for understanding nations simply do not work when applied to organizations. Instead, the following six dimensions have been empirically found to distinguish organizational cultures (Hofstede et al., 1990):

- *Process-oriented versus results-oriented cultures:* dominated by technical and bureaucratic routines versus concern for outcomes
- *Job-oriented versus employee-oriented cultures:* responsibility for job performance versus responsibility for members' well-being
- *Professional versus parochial cultures:* identification of members with profession versus identification with organization
- *Open-system versus closed-system cultures:* openness versus closedness to internal and external communication and ease of admission to outsiders and newcomers
- *Tightly controlled versus loosely controlled cultures:* formal and punctual versus informal and casual
- *Pragmatic versus normative cultures:* flexible versus rigid ways of dealing with the environment, particularly customers

In some instances, research to date indicates that national culture and organizational culture will have some relationship (Hofstede et al., 1990). For example, high levels on the national culture dimension of uncertainty avoidance are likely to correspond to closed-system rather than open-system organizational cultures. High levels of power distance are likely to be associated with process-oriented rather than results-oriented organizational cultures. However, these relationships are not particularly strong, and implications of other aspects of national culture for organizational culture dimensions are negligible.

## NATIONAL CULTURE AND ORGANIZATIONS

A great deal of discussion about the implications of national cultures for organizations has been provided elsewhere. Relevant publications include empirical papers (e.g., Hofstede et al., 1990) and a chapter-length review (Hofstede, 1997). Hofstede discusses links between national culture dimensions and management practice at length in *Cultures and Organizations* (1991). Tables summarizing these links are provided there for power distance (p. 37), individualism and collectivism (p. 67), masculinity and femininity (p. 96), and uncertainty avoidance (p. 125). Key elements from these are summarized in Table 25.2.

Rather than repeat this prior literature, we will devote the remainder of this chapter to some of the most controversial issues that continue to arise about the implications of national culture for organizations and to issues that provide the best basis for further research and application. Most are issues of intercultural relations, particularly those faced by multinational corporations that try to operate in national cultures quite different from their home cultures. We particularly have in mind multinationals that come from our own home countries, the Netherlands and the United States, but similar issues are evident in other multinationals.

### Power Distance

A main theme in organizational culture work has been the way that an organization's founders and its subsequent senior leaders shape an organization's culture. Large power distance reflects a generalized acceptance throughout a society, particularly among less powerful members, that power differentials are normal and legitimate together with institutionalized practices supporting separation, compliance, and deference between parties who have different levels of power. The simple conclusion that some have reached is that superiors will have more influence over employees' attitudes and beliefs and over an organization's culture in high power distance cultures than in others. This conclusion is a partial truth: Superiors are indeed likely to have great effects over observable behavior in high power distance countries. However, it also reflects a misunderstanding of the dependence/counterdependence dynamic central to high power distance societies.

For example, senior managers of multinationals headquartered in low power distance countries who seek to establish and use what some would call a "strong organizational culture" are likely to be in for quite a surprise when working in high power distance cultures. Compliance may not mean what they expect it to mean. True, compliance is likely to be rooted in heartfelt respect for power holders by many people in a high power distance society. However, overt compliance is equally likely to be of the very most superficial sort for many others in the same society. An organizational leader's ability to influence an employee's behavior may not extend to influence on that employee's attitudes or opinions in a high power distance context.

What are the implications for organizations? Managers from low power distance countries working in high power distance ones need to be alert to potential counterdependent tensions under the surface of deferential behavior. The kinds of fixes—participation, Theory Y management, management by objectives—considered in an earlier age of U.S. management scholarship have been replaced by others such as transformational leadership, but these others may be equally problematic. A number of books and articles have advocated the universality of strong cul-

TABLE 25.2  Consequences for the Workplace of Differences in National Cultures

| *Small Power Distance Societies* | *Large Power Distance Societies* |
|---|---|
| Hierarchy means an inequality of roles, established for convenience | Hierarchy means an existential inequality |
| Subordinates expect to be consulted | Subordinates expect to be told what to do |
| Ideal boss is resourceful democrat | Ideal boss is benevolent autocrat (good father) |

| *Collectivist Societies* | *Individualist Societies* |
|---|---|
| Value standards differ for in-group and out-groups: particularism | Same value standards apply to all: universalism |
| Other people seen as members of their groups | Other people seen as potential resources |
| Relationship prevails over task | Task prevails over relationship |
| Moral model of employer-employee relationship | Calculative model of employer-employee relationship |

| *Feminine Societies* | *Masculine Societies* |
|---|---|
| Assertiveness ridiculed | Assertiveness appreciated |
| Undersell yourself | Oversell yourself |
| Stress on life quality | Stress on careers |
| Intuition | Decisiveness |

| *Weak Uncertainty Avoidance Societies* | *Strong Uncertainty Avoidance Societies* |
|---|---|
| Dislike of rules—written or unwritten | Emotional need for rules—written or unwritten |
| Less formalization and standardization | More formalization and standardization |
| Tolerance of deviant persons and ideas | Intolerance of deviant persons and ideas |

SOURCE: Adapted from Hofstede (1997).

tures or of visionary leadership for shaping organizational culture. A simple interpretation of power distance, that senior managers are very influential in high power distance countries, is sometimes evoked to suggest that visioning is even more appropriate in high power distance societies than in the moderate power distance culture of the United States, where such practices first became popular. However, a careful analysis of power distance, in particular the dependence/counterdependence dynamic, suggests caution. Practices like visioning that have a particular meaning in the United States will be reinterpreted with respect to the values of any other national culture into which they are introduced. The key questionnaire item defining power distance in *Culture's Consequences* (Hofstede, 1980a) is: "How frequently, in your experience, does the following problem occur: Employees being afraid to express disagreement with their managers?" Superiors' ability to use specific directions to shape compliance by employees who are reluctant to express disagreement is quite different from their ability to shape attitudes and beliefs. Of course, to expect that superiors' influence ever in any culture extends to influence over the *values* of employees is to substantially underestimate the influence of people's early socialization and to overestimate the influence of organizations.

## Individualism/Collectivism

The idea of organizational culture has been stimulated as authors in individualistic cultures have looked at collective cultures. Hence it has come to evoke images of a collective. The basic idea behind individualism and collectivism at the national level appears on the surface to be immediately relevant—collectivism implies a link between the individual's self-identity and a collective, whereas individualism implies that the two are more fully distinct. In discussions of how to manage organizational culture, some have drawn an analogy with collectivism in national culture. Their argument is that whereas a strong, unitary organizational culture is a natural experience of a collectivist society, through appropriate management it can be imitated by an organization in an individualist society. However, this belief underestimates the significance of childhood socialization in shaping people's values and overestimates the role an organization's managers have in shaping values. Inkeles and Levinson (1969), when presenting the theoretical basis for the culture dimensions used in *Culture's Consequences,* also reviewed the anthropological and psychological literature on childhood socialization. Their review and a great deal of subsequent social science research supports a position that individualist or collectivist values are linked to personal socialization and to a complex nexus of social forces in a larger society. The idea that managers can compete with this socialization and these forces to engineer a "strong culture" analogous to collectivism is not realistic.

This misunderstanding is a natural one given the historical development of the organizational culture literature. The view of collectivism that has entered into that literature is based on the very unique and often romanticized model of Japanese collectivism and Japanese organizations. The in-group in Japan can sometimes extend to an entire organization or even a family of interrelated organizations. Japan, in fact, is quite an exception, and even within Japan only some groups show the stereotypical Japanese employee commitment. Other sorts of social identities are equally possible in a collectivist culture and more typical in other collectivist nations. Commitment may be to an occupation or social stratum rather than to an organization. Occupational or departmental distinctions can be challenging for managers to integrate even in an individualist society. The challenge could conceivably become even more politicized in a hypothetical collectivist society where organization members identify quite strongly with one faction and view other factions as out-groups. Collectivism at the national level does not imply strong organizational culture in the sense of value-based commitment to an organization, and it does not imply the potential to readily create and manage through strong organizational cultures. Depending on the specific nature of collectivism in a particular society, it may contribute to either organizational coherence or fragmentation among subgroups.

Another misunderstanding of the distinction between individualism and collectivism can easily occur when the distinction is viewed from an individualist standpoint. The misunderstanding is about the nature of the collective. Does collectivism mean that the sense of self is linked somehow to the social world in general? In an individualist society, the fundamental distinction in social life is between self and other. Self and other are experienced as quite distinct and are only bound together at all by a world of universal principles. In a collectivist society, the fundamental distinction is different—it is between in-group and out-groups. Rules and principles that apply to the self in relation to the in-group are quite different from those that apply to out-groups. Collectivist societies were romanticized by some in individualist societies as being comprehensively open to the social world in general. However, out-groups in a collectivist society are quite distinct, and they may be treated with compassion, competition, or hostility. Regardless of which way of dealing with out-groups prevails, out-groups are clearly and fundamentally other in a collectivist society. The misunderstanding that collectivism means identity with all other people on the planet is natural from an individualist mindset. It contributed to what some now speak of as a fad of collectivism that prevailed for a time in cross-cultural psychology and it has contributed to inappropriate analogies between collectivism and strong organizational cultures.

## Uncertainty Avoidance

Uncertainty avoidance at the national level has to do with reactions by a society and its members to the different and unfamiliar. Uncertainty is handled at the level of national societies primarily through *technology, law,* and *religion.* In nations where uncertainty avoidance predominates, some combination of these will be central elements in societal institutions, including organizations.

Some ways of looking at why organizations exist tie closely to the value of reducing uncertainty. Organizations are contrived to alleviate uncertainties in social relationships at work and, as emphasized in the U.S. literature on organizational economics, in markets (Hofstede, 1993). As uncertainty-limiting devices, organizations offer internal management practices that either complement or compete with societal institutions that provide alternative ways to reduce uncertainty. Organizational analogies to technology and law are part of the literatures on rational management programs such as scientific and administrative management. Organizational culture theory, focusing as it does on symbols, heroes, and rituals, contributes to management theory by directing attention to the analogy with some of the distinguishing qualities of religions. Religious symbols, heroes, and rituals draw attention to truths. Their organizational counterparts are described elsewhere in this volume as having a similar func-

tion. Religious figures are among Carlyle's (1841) exemplars in the analysis of societal heroes. Formal organization leaders are similarly romanticized to provide certainties for an organization's cultural practices (Meindl, Ehrlich, & Dukerich, 1985).

The most extensive development of the organizational culture literature has occurred in low to moderate uncertainty avoidance societies. We would speculate that these are national cultures in which organizations have more discretionary room than in other societies to create their own cultures. Throughout history, societal institutions have competed in ways of handling uncertainty. Today, the latitude for creating a distinctive organizational culture may be more limited in high uncertainty avoidance cultures than in other societies. The uncertainty of how to do work may already be resolved in other ways. In an uncertainty avoidant culture with a high gross national product, technologically based systems of rules, scientific and other rational management devices, may well limit the role of a distinctive organizational culture in governing organizational behavior. In an uncertainty avoidant culture with a low GNP, local traditions, perhaps linked to religion or to local national heroes, may compete with managers' attempts to use organizational culture to manage.

As in the case of power distance, we anticipate that efforts to shape organization behavior through shaping organizational culture are likely to be less successful in high uncertainty avoidant cultures than has been found in the United States and northern Europe. At minimum, efforts to manage organizational culture would do well to consider carefully the specifics of not only nationally shared laws, but especially unwritten codes, heroic examples, and religious values shaping behavior in high uncertainty avoidant cultures.

## Masculinity/Femininity

The masculinity/femininity dimension of national culture has been taboo even among social scientists, particularly in those societies scoring toward the masculine side of the dimension. Taboos reflect values that have great emotive significance in a society, sometimes to the extent that the values cannot be discussed openly. Taboos can impede scientific discussion. In order to complement the extensive attention others have provided to individualism/collectivism, uncertainty avoidance, and power distance, Hofstede has recently published *Masculinity and Femininity: The Taboo Dimension of National Cultures* (1998). In keeping with this chapter's focus on the more controversial aspects of culture dimensions, we will discuss this dimension more thoroughly than we have the others.

Some of the misapprehensions about this dimension seem to be based on a sense that the label is rooted in ideology or prejudice. Values traditionally linked to one gender or another have long been part of various social science literatures, and studies of gender relationships recently have increased with the literature on gender diversity. Discussions of gender have often been infused with particular political agendas, so the concern that a gender-related culture dimension may be ideologically biased is not at all surprising. Scholars, including us, are certainly affected by the values of their cultures. It may well be that taboos surrounding the discussion of gender would mean that a scholar from a masculine society would have picked a different label, or that this dimension would have received more support from scholars and managers in such societies were it to appear in a different guise. Indeed, the two Americans, Inkeles and Levinson (1969), whose work influenced the theory underlying Hofstede's four culture dimensions describe gender identity as a key element in the conception of self. Rather than speculating about the effects of culture on labeling choices and the popularization of concepts, another route to clearing up some of the controversies surrounding this dimension is to highlight some particulars about its origin and implications.

The dimension is empirically derived from questions about work goals. Respondents were asked about the importance of 14 work goals. In order to control for the propensity of people in some countries to score all goals higher than would people in other countries, responses were standardized for each country so that the importance of one goal was scored relative to the importance of all the others.

A factor analysis of these standardized goals items, aggregated to the country level, provided two factors. Scores on the first factor were used to create the individualism/collectivism measure noted above. Those on the second were used to create what eventually became the concept of masculinity/femininity. The masculine side of the measure includes what were originally called *ego* goals of earnings, recognition, advancement, challenge, and an opportunity to use one's skills. The feminine side includes what were first identified as *social* goals such as relationship with the manager, cooperation, living in a desirable area, and security.

As the data were more fully analyzed, gender differences within countries on ego and social goal preferences also became evident. Although goal preferences of women showed some cross-society tendency to be closer to the social goal side than those of men, this gender difference in goal preference was more pronounced in some societies—the ones scoring overall more to the ego side—than in others. Gender differences within societies became apparent on goal items that fit distinctions that are traditional in many societies between male and female roles. At the point in the research where gender differences in goal preferences became evident, the similarity between this dimension and Inkeles and Levinson's (1969) concept of gender and self became clear as well.

Recognizing that using taboo labels constitutes a social intervention that may not be appropriate on some occasions or for some audiences, trainers in masculine cultures have sometimes introduced alternative labels. The original label that was given to the masculinity/femininity factor was ego versus social goals. This label, or some other like it, perhaps "assertive versus nurturant," may serve well in training. Entirely leaving out the dimension, either in research or training, however, omits something quite important about national cultures in general and about the American culture in particular, something important enough to be taboo. However, given the accumulation of research using the masculinity/femininity label and the evident empirical link between this dimension and other gender-related issues, masculinity/femininity is the label, with all its controversies, likely to communicate best in the scholarly world.

The results for the work goals items in the IBM study directed attention to a basic concept. In two replications, researchers have found that the work goals that cohere in other samples to reflect this concept differ in some ways from those in the IBM study. Hoppe (1990), in his study of elites using the IBM work goals items, found that "earnings" as a work goal did not correlate with the other items representing masculinity as it did at IBM. Apparently at IBM, earnings corresponded to recognition, advancement, challenge, and opportunity to use one's skills. In Hoppe's broader sample of elites, respondents' work domain—government, business, professions, academic—varied more widely in the extent to which earnings corresponded to other aspects of success. For example, among a society's elites, movement from business to an influential position in government, consulting, or academe would be an advancement in influence, but would result in a reduced salary. Preliminary results from a second ongoing study among upmarket consumers in 15 European countries replicate the earlier results and show that masculinity/femininity predicts national consumption patterns. In both studies, once adjustments were made in measurement structure, the new country-level data from the masculinity/femininity measures correlated quite highly with country-level data from the earlier IBM study.

For organizations, this dimension has implications for typical work goal preferences

and for gender relations. The most basic implication is due to the link of societal masculinity/femininity to overall trends in values. For example, national tendencies on this dimension are likely to affect the purposes of organizational culture analysis by authors in different parts of the world. Martin and Frost (1996) note that different factions among organizational culture authors have competing agendas. Is the aim of those who analyze culture to understand organizations, to promote effective social relationships, or to make it possible for organizations to manipulate and control employees? Culture management programs developed during the 1980s reflect the last of these three—clearly a culturally masculine performance ethos. To the extent that organizational culture is analyzed to gain information that can be used to promote organizational performance, culture management programs are likely to be most popular in masculine countries.

In gender relationships, the finding that work goal preferences vary more by gender in masculine than in feminine societies has implications for how openly gender issues can be discussed and addressed within organizations. For example, the struggle to manage gender equity is likely to prove challenging in masculine societies, where gender most affects typical preferences for work relationships, rewards, and work-nonwork relationships. In the United States, programs designed to promote organizational cultural practices that support gender diversity fit the society's moderately high masculinity. The society shows some openness to dealing with gender differences, but explicit programs are needed to deal with the strains created by the values of individual equality and ego combined with the taboo against open discussion of gender relations. Such programs are likely to be considered less necessary in societies toward the femininity pole. Multinationals based in the United States would need to move with the same caution in transferring programs to promote gender relations as they do in transferring other aspects of their management practice that have a particular meaning at home due to the cultural values of the home country.

## IMPLICATIONS

### Can Organizational Culture Be Shaped to Make One Country's Management Theories Apply Abroad?

This last issue of the effect that cultural masculinity or femininity has had for the analysis of organizational culture brings us back to a main reason for a chapter about national and organizational culture. Can a company headquartered in one country somehow re-create a microcosm of that country's national culture in its foreign operations in a way that provides a basis to replicate the headquarters' practices around the world? Alternatively, should a company operating in one country try to create something like the national culture of another country so that desirable management practices discovered in that other country can be transferred back home? Ouchi (1981) stimulated the analysis of organizational culture by arguing that managers are able to establish strong organizational cultures, perhaps even cultures that reflect values different from those of the larger national culture. Can an organization engage in socialization that competes with societal socialization to produce values in its members?

Such suggestions coming out of organizational culture analysis were an advance over prior management theory in some respects, but they created confusion as well. They recognized the significance of national culture to an extent not well recognized earlier. They also recognized that an organizational intervention cannot focus on just one single management practice, but needs to consider a whole integrated set of symbols, heroes, and rituals—an organizational culture. Still, advocates of using an organization's culture

to help transfer management practices from one country to another often have underappreciated the force of a nation's culture. Using phrases like *Dutch organizational culture* and *American organizational culture* encourages confusion between values and practices. The nationality of the mother company clearly shows in a multinational's organizational culture. However, organizational cultural practices that originally reflected a particular set of values in the home country will be reinterpreted in light of local values when these practices are transferred abroad. A company's national heritage is nothing to be ashamed of. The age of the "geocentric" company ideal is past—ethnocentrism is functional. A manager need not be ashamed of a company's Americanness or Japaneseness, but should not expect foreign employees to adopt the underlying values that a company's practices express in the home country. Employees will just comply with the practices for their own purposes in ways reflecting their own country's values. National culture affects values, whereas organizational culture affects practices. For managers to believe that they can create a microcosm of a nation's culture would be also to mistake the difference between values and practices. Maintaining coherence in a multinational firm requires transferring a configuration of practices, where practices more than values lie at the root of organizational culture.

### Old Data? Older Cultures!

What about the current status of the dimensions introduced in *Culture's Consequences* (Hofstede, 1980a)? We have indicated throughout this chapter ways in which culture dimensions are overused, misused, and underused. A logically prior issue is whether these dimensions have any current relevance at all. Are the country scores for culture dimensions first presented in 1980 from data collected in the late 1960s and early 1970s any longer relevant as the world has changed? This issue is an important one for scholars who are doing research with only a handful of countries and who want to use culture dimensions to provide part of the national value context for interpreting their results. It is also an important one for managers who are unable to validate the culture dimensions against a database of operations throughout the world.

Whether in a study or a multinational corporation, the experience of working with only a small number of countries provides little basis for evaluating the continuing relevance of the 1980 dimensions. The alternative of replicating them at the individual level makes no sense, because they are national culture dimensions based on country-level data structures. For quite some time, the best base for confidence that the scores have value beyond the world situation when they were collected was provided in the original documentation of the measures. The original research evaluated stability by replicating over a 4-year interval. The measures were also validated against data from 38 prior studies from up to several decades before they were collected, as well as up to about a decade after they were collected.

Subsequent to that initial report, several broad-scope projects have indicated that the dimensions remain meaningful. Among the more complete replications, Hoppe's (1990) study of elites in 19 countries, noted above as supporting the masculinity/femininity construct, showed support for the other dimensions as well. Inter/View, a market research agency, has replicated all dimensions except power distance across 15 European countries. Another broad-scope project using the same items surveyed more than 10,000 airline pilots from 22 countries (Helmreich & Merritt, 1998). Relatively recent studies validating the measures against other comparative cross-national data from large numbers of countries are provided by Hofstede and Bond (1988) for students from 23 countries answering a Chinese-made values questionnaire; by Franke, Hofstede, and Bond (1991) for national GDP and related indexes; and by Peterson et al. (1995) for role stress. A complete update of this validating work is provided in a book currently being prepared, a revised edition of *Culture's Consequences* (Hofstede, in press). The data from which country dimensions were developed are old, but national cultures are even older and appear from recent research to be relatively persistent. Those who wish to use culture to frame studies of just a few countries can generally make use of the country dimensions. They also would benefit by considering any evidence that there has been unusual social change in the countries they are studying, and by supplementing an analysis based on culture dimensions alone with a more complete analysis of national cultures. As in the example above, like France, countries are only partially captured by their positions on four or five culture dimensions. However, as d'Iribarne (1989) makes abundantly clear in his analysis of historical cultural roots shaping institutionalized business practices, the values of nations reflect patterns apparent for periods exceeding 200 years.

## Avoiding Misinterpretations

Although the national culture dimensions continue to have value, they are easily misunderstood and misapplied in the organizational culture literature. Developing scientifically useful concepts and making up labels for them is hard work. The concept of culture itself has proven a difficult one. Using the same label for something at the national and organizational levels has been awkward. Labeling the national and organizational culture dimensions was also hard. Labeling becomes challenging when we need to describe things at levels of abstraction outside the direct physical experience of individuals. We share with many other scholars in many fields the struggle to avoid using labels that tempt application at inappropriate levels. It is a struggle shared even with the abstractions in physics. Using the naive experience labels of *particles* and *waves* to try to describe the properties of light is problematic

(Frank, 1957; Peterson, 1998). What is the solution? Use labels for what they are—conveniences that help link an idea with experience. Provide sufficient description in defining them to shape the naive meanings of the labels themselves. Continue to watch and manage their use. When labels interfere with communication, keeping the content and revising the label for a particular application, especially for a nonscientific use (as in training about cultural masculinity and femininity), is better than dropping the content.

We have sought here to clarify some common misconceptions that creep into the literature on national and organizational culture due in part to the inherent limitation of simple labels. Power distance implies recognition that power differences are normal and also a generalized societal preference for institutions and practices to accommodate power differences. However, the dynamic between emotionally charged dependence and counterdependence is central to high power distance cultures such that compliance and heartfelt dedication need to be distinguished carefully. Collectivism implies a close link between self and other. However, the particular other in view will be a specific in-group; it does not encompass all human beings. The implications of uncertainty avoidance for an organization are affected by the history of technology, law, and religion in the larger society. The result for an organization is likely to be reliance on rules and experts, but the particulars about what kinds of rules and what kinds of experts—those rooted in technology or those rooted in tradition—are likely to vary widely. Societal masculinity and femininity are likely to affect the goals of people and organizations. Issues of gender and goals are likely to be most challenging to manage in masculine societies where they are most taboo, where managers are least likely to want to discuss them. Quite a bit of room remains for research about the challenges that the values central to national cultures pose for using the practices that constitute organizational cultures.

## Applications of Culture Dimensions Beyond the Realm of Management and Organizational Culture

In keeping with the focus of this *Handbook,* our discussion here has been about the implications national culture has for organizational culture. However, in business, does national culture have its strongest implications for organizational culture? The idea of culture dimensions was first applied to the problem of management practices likely to be found most comfortable or normal in different parts of the world. However, other business implications may be at least as consequential.

For example, people who for some purposes are organization members are for other purposes consumers. Recent events in Europe have produced an economic convergence that has greatly contributed to the well-being of poorer countries by improving the efficiency of their business and economic systems while also expanding the pie so that the benefits contribute to the prosperity of Europe as a whole. Gross domestic product thus is reduced as a factor affecting consumption patterns. Relative to economics, then, culture matters more in Europe. For example, differences in cosmetics and clothing choices among countries are made for reasons of societal masculinity/femininity (De Mooij, 1998).

## CONCLUSION: RESEARCH DIRECTIONS

We have noted a number of research implications as we have discussed the theme of national values and organizational practices. Some highlights:

- Research needs to avoid focusing inappropriately on culture dimensions to the neglect of other aspects of national difference. Gross national product often matters more than national culture.

- Research needs to avoid ending with culture dimensions as the basis for forming hypotheses and should instead use them as a helpful, but incomplete, beginning.

- Hypotheses about culture dimensions should go beyond a simplistic first look and consider carefully their nuances. Collectivism is not universalism. Power distance may or may not mean psychological as well as behavioral conformity. Uncertainty avoidance may mean that there is little societal flexibility for managers to shape organizational cultures.

Finally, although national culture has enough influence on management theory that we can speak of "Japanese" or "American" theories, the relationships of national cultures, based mainly in values, to organizational cultures, based mainly in practices, are loose ones. Careful controls will be needed to limit the effects of industry, organization history, and international corporate culture heritage when research is undertaken to tease out the implications of national cultural values for organizational cultural practices.

# 26

# A New Look at National Culture

## Illustrative Applications to Role Stress and Managerial Behavior

—— *Lilach Sagiv and Shalom H. Schwartz*

Cultures provide organizational members with more or less articulated sets of ideas that help them individually and collectively to cope with . . . uncertainties and ambiguities. (Trice & Beyer, 1993, p. 2)

Although the specific ideologies that form the substance of an organization's culture are developed within it, their content is heavily influenced and framed by the surrounding culture. (Trice & Beyer, 1993, p. 46)

The surrounding national or transnational culture is potentially important as an external source of influence on organizational culture. The surrounding culture may affect the behavior of organizational members through its impact on the culture of the organization itself. It may also affect behavior through its impact on the beliefs, norms, and values that individual members bring into the organization.

Qualitative studies have spelled out in rich detail effects of national culture on the substance of organizational culture and on the practices through which organizational culture is manifest. Studies of managerial ideology in the United States and Russia (Bendix, 1956), of managers' and workers' behavior

AUTHORS' NOTE: Preparation of this chapter was supported by a grant from the Recanati Fund of the School of Business Administration at the Hebrew University of Jerusalem to the first author, by Grant 94-00063 from the United States–Israel Binational Science Foundation and a grant from the Israel Foundations Trustees to the second author, and by the Leon and Clara Sznajderman Chair in Psychology. We gratefully acknowledge the contribution of the 74 researchers who collected the data used in this study. Please contact the first author for a full list of those involved.

in France (Crozier, 1964), and of authority patterns in organizations across several non-Western nations (Kakar, 1971) exemplify this approach. Qualitative studies are limited to analyses of single nations or to comparisons among a few nations at most, however. This limitation reflects not only the costs of in-depth research but the conviction that each culture is best understood in its own unique terms. Granting some validity to this conviction, we nonetheless ask whether quantitative studies across large numbers of nations may not yield insights into the effects of national culture as well.

The assumption that national culture influences behavior in organizations underlies the numerous applications of Hofstede's (1980a, 1991; Hofstede, Neuijen, Ohayv, & Sanders, 1990) theory of dimensions of national culture. In this chapter we present another theory of dimensions of national culture. This theory may offer an even more powerful tool for understanding differences in behavior in organizations across national boundaries. Empirical work based on this theory has identified systematic national differences in culture as well as meaningful transnational cultures (e.g., sub-Saharan African, West European, East Asian; Munene, Schwartz, & Smith, 2000; Schwartz, 1999; Schwartz & Bardi, 1997; Schwartz & Ros, 1995).

At the outset, we note that national culture is only one of many influences on the symbols, ideologies, and practices that constitute organizational culture and affect members' perceptions, understandings, and behavior. Trice and Beyer (1993) identify additional sources of influence, such as regional and community cultures, industry ideologies, and occupational ideologies. Particular technologies, competitive conditions, worker pools, relations to government, and other influences pose problems whose ongoing resolutions also contribute to the unique cultures of different organizations within and across nations. Even within organizations, diverse subcultures emerge and change as subsets of organizational members cope with different types of problems.

These many sources of influence contribute to variation in ideologies and practices across organizations within each nation. To the extent that the surrounding national culture influences what goes on in organizations, however, we may expect to find systematic national variation over and above within-nation differences. That is, managers and workers from different organizations within each nation may exhibit some commonality of beliefs, norms, values, and practices that distinguishes them from members of organizations in other nations.

We agree with Hofstede (1991) that *values* are the heart of culture. Cultural values are implicitly or explicitly shared abstract ideas about what is good, right, and desirable in a society (e.g., success, justice, freedom, tradition, social order; Williams, 1970). Cultural values are expressed in widely shared norms, symbols, rituals, practices, and ways of thinking. They are the vocabulary of socially approved goals used to motivate action and to express and justify the preferred solutions to societal problems. Societal institutions (economic, political, family, educational, and so on) express these values in their modes of operation, in their goals, and in the justifications and explanations their members invoke for policies and behavior (for an explication, see Schwartz, 1999).

In this chapter we examine the impact of national variations along dimensions of culture—manifest as differences in cultural values—on two aspects of managers' perceptions, experiences, and preferences. We first present our theory of cultural dimensions (Schwartz, 1997, 1999; Schwartz & Ros, 1995) and note some implications of the theory for understanding organizational culture. Using these dimensions, we provide an empirically grounded overview of the cultural profiles of nations around the world. We then illustrate the application of our approach to findings from two published studies of national differences.

Available theories suggest numerous dimensions of culture (e.g., Hofstede, 1980a; Inglehart, 1990; Triandis, 1989). Hofstede (1980a) has provided the most comprehensive set of dimensions in his study of IBM workers in 53 countries. The theory we explicate seeks to capture a fuller range of potentially relevant cultural dimensions. After presenting these dimensions, we will compare them to those developed by Hofstede. The research growing out of our theory provides data from regions of the world not well covered in the Hofstede research, and, unlike earlier studies, it uses an instrument validated for cross-cultural equivalence of meaning.

## A THEORY OF CULTURAL VALUE DIMENSIONS

We define values as conceptions of the desirable that guide the ways social actors (e.g., organizational leaders, individual persons) select actions, evaluate people and events, and explain their actions and evaluations (see Kluckhohn, 1951; Rokeach, 1973; Schwartz, 1992). Values are trans-situational criteria or goals (e.g. security, hedonism) ordered by importance as guiding principles in life. Cultural dimensions of values reflect the basic issues or problems that societies confront in order to regulate activity. Societal members recognize and communicate about these problems, plan responses to them, and motivate one another to cope with them.

By considering three issues that confront all societies, we have derived dimensions of values for comparing cultures. The first issue is the nature of the relation or the boundaries between the individual and the group. A large literature suggests that resolutions of this issue give rise to the most critical cultural dimension. Variants of this dimension include individualism/collectivism, independence/interdependence, and the like (Kagitcibasi, 1997). Two questions are often associated

with this dimension: (a) Should individual or group interests take precedence? (b) To what extent are people autonomous versus embedded in their groups? We believe the second theme is more fundamental.[1] We therefore label the polar locations on the cultural dimension we have derived *embeddedness versus autonomy.*

In *embedded* cultures, people are viewed as entities embedded in the collectivity who find meaning in life largely through social relationships, through identifying with the group, participating in its shared way of life, and striving toward its shared goals. Such values as social order, respect for tradition, security, and wisdom are especially important. Embedded cultures emphasize maintaining the status quo and restraining actions or inclinations that might disrupt the solidary group or the traditional order. Organizations in such cultures function as extended families. They are likely to take responsibility for their members in all domains of life and to expect members to identify with and work dutifully toward shared goals.

In *autonomy* cultures, people are viewed as autonomous, bounded entities who find meaning in their own uniqueness and who are encouraged to express their internal attributes (preferences, traits, feelings, motives). We distinguish two types of autonomy: *Intellectual* autonomy encourages individuals to pursue their own ideas and intellectual directions independently (important values include curiosity, broad-mindedness, creativity); *affective* autonomy encourages individuals to pursue affectively positive experience for themselves (values include pleasure, exciting life, varied life). Organizations in such cultures may be relatively open to change and diversity. They are likely to treat their members as independent actors with their own interests, preferences, abilities, and allegiances.

The second societal problem is to guarantee responsible behavior that preserves the social fabric. People must be induced to consider the welfare of others, coordinate with them, and thereby manage their unavoidable social interdependencies. The polar solution that we label cultural *hierarchy* relies on hierarchical systems of ascribed roles to ensure responsible behavior. It defines the unequal distribution of power, roles, and resources as legitimate (values include social power, authority, humility, wealth). People are socialized and sanctioned to comply with the obligations and rules attached to their roles. In hierarchical cultures, organizations are likely to emphasize the chain of authority, to assign well-defined roles in a hierarchical structure, and to demand compliance in the service of goals set from the top.

The polar alternative of hierarchy, labeled cultural *egalitarianism,* seeks to induce people to recognize one another as moral equals who share basic interests as human beings. It emphasizes transcendence of selfish interests in favor of voluntary behavior that promotes the welfare of others (values include equality, social justice, responsibility, honesty). People are socialized to internalize a commitment to voluntary cooperation with others and to feel concern for everyone's welfare. Organizations are likely to express egalitarianism by acknowledging the legitimacy of cooperative negotiation among members who flexibly enact their roles and try to affect organizational goals. These goals may include the welfare of group members and of the larger society, not only profitability. Leaders are likely to motivate others by enabling them to share in goal setting and by appealing to the joint welfare of all.

The third societal problem is to regulate the relation of humankind to the natural and social world. The cultural orientation that we label *mastery* encourages active self-assertion in order to master, change, and exploit the natural and social environment to attain personal or group goals (values include ambition, success, daring, competence). Organizations in cultures that emphasize mastery are likely to be dynamic, competitive, and strongly oriented toward achievement and success.

The polar response to this problem is to accept the world as it is, trying to compre-hend and fit in rather than to change or exploit. In this view, applying technology to manipulate the environment is problematic and may even be seen as illegitimate. This cultural orientation, labeled *harmony,* emphasizes fitting harmoniously into the environment (values include unity with nature, protecting the environment, world at peace). Where harmony is important, organizations are likely to be viewed holistically as systems to be integrated with the larger society, which should minimize competition. Leaders are likely to try to understand the social and environmental implications of organizational actions and to seek nonexploitative ways to work toward organizational goals.

In sum, the theory specifies three bipolar dimensions of culture that represent alternate resolutions to each of the three problems that confront all societies: embeddedness versus autonomy, hierarchy versus egalitarianism, and mastery versus harmony. A societal emphasis on the cultural type at one pole of a dimension typically accompanies a deemphasis on the opposite. Pairs of cultural value types share basic assumptions that yield the following coherent circular order of types: embeddedness, hierarchy, mastery, autonomy, egalitarianism, harmony, and back to embeddedness (see Figure 26.1). (See Schwartz, 1999, for a presentation of the shared assumptions.)

## COMPARISON WITH THE HOFSTEDE DIMENSIONS

Hofstede (1980a) has proposed four dimensions of national work culture:

1. *Individualism versus collectivism:* the degree of preference for acting as individuals rather than as group members
2. *Power distance:* the degree of inequality among people considered as normal
3. *Uncertainty avoidance:* the degree of preference for structured over unstructured situations

4. *Masculinity versus femininity:* the relative prevalence of values such as assertiveness, performance, success, and competition versus values such as quality of life, warm personal relations, service, care for the weak, and solidarity

In this section we briefly note some of the differences between these cultural dimensions and those proposed by the theory just presented.

The dimension of autonomy/embeddedness overlaps conceptually to some degree with Hofstede's individualism/collectivism dimension. Both concern the relationship between the individual and the collective, and both contrast an autonomous view of people with an interdependent view. However, the dimensions also differ. Autonomy/embeddedness strongly contrasts openness to change with maintaining the status quo; individualism/collectivism does not. Moreover, many theorists associate individualism with the self-interested pursuit of personal goals (Kagitcibasi, 1997; Triandis, 1995), whereas Schwartz rejects selfishness as an inherent quality of autonomy.

The hierarchy pole of the hierarchy/egalitarianism dimension overlaps somewhat with Hofstede's power distance (Schwartz, 1994, 1996a). Both concern legitimating social inequality. Power distance refers to the acceptance of inequality by less powerful people. It also expresses their fear of authority. Hofstede sees it as a response to the inevitability of social inequality. The bipolar hierarchy/egalitarian dimension addresses a different issue—assurance of responsible behavior that preserves the social fabric. Their capacity to assure responsible behavior gives hierarchical systems of ascribed roles their legitimacy. Hierarchy does not necessarily entail a preference for distance from authority. Egalitarianism emphasizes the moral equality of individuals, their capacity to internalize commitments to the welfare of others and to cooperate voluntarily with them. These key elements of egalitarianism are absent from low power distance.

The mastery pole of mastery/harmony overlaps somewhat with masculinity. Both emphasize assertiveness and ambition. Hofstede contrasts masculinity to femininity (tenderness, care, and concern for others). This implies that masculinity neglects or rejects the interests of others. Schwartz contrasts mastery to harmony (being in tune with others and the environment). Mastery calls for an active, even disruptive stance, but it does not imply selfishness. Harmony might seem to overlap conceptually with uncertainty avoidance, because both idealize a harmonious order. However, harmony stresses that people and nature can exist comfortably together without assertion of control. In contrast, uncertainty avoidance emphasizes controlling ambiguity and unpredictability through institutions and beliefs that provide certainty.[2]

## EVALUATING THE THEORY EMPIRICALLY

Our theory of cultural dimensions has been tested mainly through the examination of the cultures of national groups. However, it applies equally to subgroups within nations and to clusters of culturally related nations. With regard to heterogeneous nations, the descriptions of national culture presented here refer largely to the value culture of the dominant, majority group.

We infer the cultural values that characterize a society by aggregating the value priorities of individuals (see Hofstede, 1980a; Inkeles & Smith, 1974; Morris, 1956). Individual value priorities are a product of both shared culture and unique personal experience. Shared cultural values in a society help to shape the contingencies to which people must adapt in their daily interactions. As a result, members of each cultural group share many value-relevant experiences, and they are socialized to accept shared social values. Of course, within cultural groups, individuals' unique experiences, personalities, and genetic heritages give rise to differences in their value priorities. Critically, however, the *average* importance that societal members attribute to different values is unaffected by these individual differences. It reflects the shared aspects of enculturation. Hence average societal priorities point to the underlying, common cultural values.

To operationalize the values theory, we developed a survey intended to include all the motivationally distinct goals likely to be recognized across cultures. The survey includes 56 (57) single values.[3] Respondents rate their importance "as a guiding principle in MY life" on a 9-point scale. Respondents from 63 nations on every inhabited continent have completed the survey anonymously in their native languages ($N > 60,000$). For cross-cultural comparison, only values that have reasonably equivalent meanings across cultures may legitimately be used. Examination of separate multidimensional scaling analyses of the values within each of the 63 nations has established such equivalence for 45 of the values (Schwartz, 1992, 1994, and unpublished data). We included only these 45 values in the analyses to validate the cultural dimensions.

We assessed the validity of the three cultural dimensions and the relations among them with data gathered in the period 1988-1997 (details in Schwartz, 1999). A multidimensional scaling analysis (SSA; Borg & Lingoes, 1987; Guttman, 1968) was performed on the correlations between the mean ratings of each of the 45 values in each of 185 samples from 63 nations. Because the analysis uses means of samples that represent cultures, the analysis yields dimensions that are unaffected by individual differences in values within cultures (Hofstede, 1980a; Schwartz, 1999). This analysis clearly discriminated the seven value types, related as expected, as the poles of the three cultural dimensions. Thus there is empirical justification for using the cultural value dimensions to compare national cultures.

To compare nations, we, like Hofstede (1980a), obtained samples that were matched on critical characteristics from the dominant cultural group in each nation. The focal type of sample we studied was urban schoolteachers who teach the full range of subjects in grades 3-12 of the most common type of school system. No single occupational group represents a culture, but schoolteachers constitute a particularly suitable group for such comparison. They make up the largest occupational group, with similar educational and socioeconomic status relative to the wider population, in almost all nations. They also play an explicit role in value socialization.

We compared the value hierarchies of teacher samples from 55 nations with those of college students from 55 nations and of representative or near-representative samples from 12 nations on 5 continents. These comparisons confirmed the assumption that, although representative samples, students, and teachers in the various nations differ in their value priorities, the *order* of nations on the value means, using the different kinds of samples, is quite similar (mean intercorrelation .89, range .74 to .98).

## THE CULTURAL PROFILES OF NATIONS: AN OVERVIEW

In this section we summarize the cultural value priorities of 57 national cultures, based on teacher samples. We compare national cultures on the whole profile of their seven value priorities. The score for each value type is the average rating in the sample of the single values that index that type (see Schwartz, 1999). For cross-cultural comparisons, we eliminated sample differences in scale use by standardizing the mean importance of all seven value types within each sample.

We compare cultural profiles with a technique (coplot; Goldreich & Raveh, 1993)

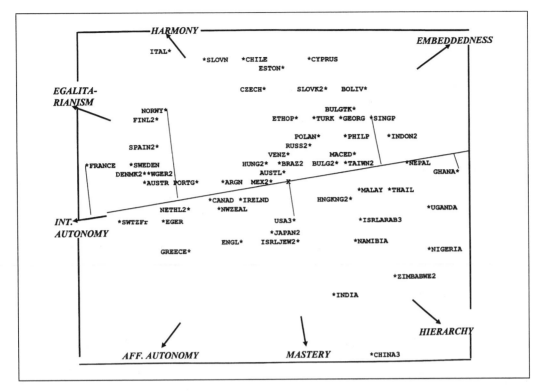

**Figure 26.1.** Coplot: Teacher Samples, 57 National Cultures

NOTE: Multiple samples from national cultures are indicated by a number following the label.

that constructs a matrix of profile differences between all pairs of samples. It sums the absolute differences between the standardized ratings that each sample gave to each of the seven value types. It then uses this matrix to generate a two-dimensional spatial representation of the similarities and differences among samples on all seven cultural value types simultaneously (see Figure 26.1). Vectors placed in the space indicate the order of the samples on each of the seven value types. Locations of the samples along these vectors relative to one another reveal, graphically, the specific ways in which any national sample resembles or differs from any other.

Each cultural value type is labeled in Figure 26.1 to show the direction of its increasing importance relative to the center of the two-dimensional space (the X just below Australia). Imagine a directional line drawn

through the center to the small arrow adjacent to the name of each type. Such a line is drawn for intellectual autonomy. It extends from right to left. The vector for each of the value types is the regression line that optimally represents the order of the samples on the importance they attribute to that cultural value type.

For example, the farther toward the left that a national sample is located, the greater the importance the sample, relative to all other samples, attributes to intellectual autonomy. And the farther toward the right, the less importance the sample attributes to intellectual autonomy. To locate a sample on a cultural value type, we draw a perpendicular line from the position of the sample to the vector for that type. The perpendiculars drawn to the intellectual autonomy vector show that this cultural type is very important in France and less important in Norway, then India, then Singapore, and, finally, very unimportant in Nigeria.

Now consider how the full cultural profile of a single sample is represented on all seven cultural values. For example, the set of two Finnish samples (upper left)[4] attributed high importance to egalitarianism, harmony, and intellectual autonomy and moderate importance to affective autonomy. Their location suggests that Finnish culture gives little emphasis to embeddedness and very low emphasis to mastery and hierarchy. In contrast, the set of two samples from Zimbabwe (lower right) attributed high importance to hierarchy and mastery, moderate importance to embeddedness and affective autonomy, and very low importance to egalitarianism, intellectual autonomy, and harmony.

The coplot summarizes the positions of samples on seven different cultural value types in only two spatial dimensions. Consequently, the location of each sample in the graphic representation cannot be perfect. Nonetheless, the locations of the vast majority of samples do provide quite an accurate picture.[5] This is because cultures usually exhibit profiles that reflect the coherence of the theoretical structure of cultural dimensions. In cultures where the cultural value type at one pole of a cultural dimension is important, the polar opposite type is typically unimportant. Moreover, in each culture, adjacent cultural value types usually have similar levels of importance.[6]

The set of profiles for the 57 nations and subcultures points to the existence of transnational cultural groupings. All the samples from Western Europe are grouped together in a region (on the left-hand side of the figure) characterized by the high importance of egalitarianism and intellectual autonomy and the low importance of hierarchy and embeddedness. A second region, encompassing the samples from Eastern Europe (upper center), reveals a shared culture that emphasizes harmony and embeddedness rather than mastery and both types of autonomy. Samples from the English-speaking nations (lower center)

share a culture that tends to emphasize mastery rather than harmony and affective autonomy rather than embeddedness.

The far right of the coplot map groups the samples from sub-Saharan Africa. This location reflects strong cultural emphases on embeddedness and hierarchy, little importance for affective autonomy and harmony, and very little importance for intellectual autonomy and egalitarianism. The samples from East Asia also give little emphasis to egalitarianism and intellectual autonomy. However, they vary substantially in their emphases on mastery and harmony. The samples from China and India (lower right) attribute especially high importance to mastery and low importance to harmony; other samples from East Asia are more moderate on these values. The wealthier and more Europeanized Latin American nations (center) and, perhaps, the Islamic nations (center right) may also constitute transnational cultures.

Many of these groupings are related to geographic proximity. However, they are based on shared histories, religion, level of development, culture contact, and other factors. To buttress these quantitative cultural profiles, it is necessary to ground them in broad social and historical analyses of specific nations and transnational regions. Schwartz and Ros (1995), Schwartz and Bardi (1997), and Schwartz, Bardi, and Bianchi (in press) have taken first steps in this direction.

A coplot based on college student samples from 40 nations (only 31 overlapping those for the teachers) virtually replicated the findings in Figure 26.1 (Schwartz, 1999). That is, the comparative positions of national cultures are similar when two different types of matched samples are used to measure the cultural value profiles. Recall, too, that the order of nations on cultural value types was quite similar for random samples from 12 nations. This provides substantial support for the robustness of the cross-national structure of cultural profiles. The observed national cultural profiles may therefore be useful for examining the influence of national culture on managers' perceptions, experiences, and preferences across nations.

## ILLUSTRATIVE APPLICATIONS OF THE THEORY OF CULTURE

We will now illustrate how applying the theory of cultural value dimensions can increase understanding of what goes on in organizations. As noted earlier, national and transnational cultures may influence the ideologies, symbols, and practices that constitute organizational culture and that affect members' perceptions, understandings, and behavior. To the extent that this occurs, the organizational cultures and the practices of managers and workers from all organizations within each nation will exhibit some shared aspects. These shared aspects should, in turn, discriminate among organizations from different nations. Hence the experiences and preferences of managers should vary systematically across nations in ways that are predictable from the cultural profiles of the nations. We assess this proposition below by reexamining findings from two earlier cross-national studies in light of the theory of cultural value dimensions.

### Role Stress in Organizations: Conflict, Ambiguity, and Overload

We first illustrate the relations of national culture to differences across nations in managers' experiences of role stress. Organizational culture and practices are likely to influence the psychological environment perceived by managers. One component of this environment is role stress. National cultures, through their influence on organizational cultures and practices, are also likely to influence levels of role stress. We can therefore derive hypotheses regarding the impacts of

national culture on levels of role stress in organizations.

Peterson et al. (1995) studied variation in three types of role stress reported by middle managers from 21 nations: role conflict, ambiguity, and overload. National differences in role stress were greater than differences due to personal characteristics (e.g., gender) and organizational features (e.g., ownership form). Peterson et al. sought to explain these national differences by using Hofstede's (1994) four dimensions of national work culture—individualism, power distance, uncertainty avoidance, and masculinity. They hypothesized that managers experience more of each type of stress in nations with work cultures high on uncertainty avoidance and masculinity. Regarding individualism and power distance, they offered hypotheses in *both* directions for all three types of stress. Only 2 of the 12 hypothesized correlations (3 types of stress × 4 dimensions) were even marginally significant. Do our new dimensions of culture explain national variation in organizational stress more effectively? We present hypotheses for these dimensions for each type of stress in turn.

### Role Overload

When managers lack the personal resources to fulfill their role obligations, requirements, or commitments, they experience role overload (Kahn, Wolfe, Quinn, Snoek, & Rosenthal, 1964). We hypothesize that role overload is more likely in nations where the prevailing national culture emphasizes mastery and hierarchy and attributes little importance to harmony.

A prevailing emphasis on mastery encourages and legitimates active striving to get ahead through self-assertion. Within organizations, this is likely to translate into continued pressure from managers, on themselves and on their subordinates, to achieve and to succeed. This is likely to confront managers with open-ended obligations and an unlimited stream of demands that place a constant strain on their personal resources. A cultural emphasis on hierarchy calls for regulating interdependencies by enforcing role obligations in a hierarchical structure. It demands commitment to organizational goals even at the expense of personal needs and interests. Consequently, those in positions of authority can legitimately overlook their subordinates' capacities and overload them with demands.

A national emphasis on harmony should have the opposite influence. Cultural harmony encourages and justifies acceptance of the world as it is, fitting in rather than trying to change or improve it. Efforts intended to mold the environment and to exploit it are illegitimate. Management compatible with this cultural orientation would find it neither necessary nor legitimate to pressure people beyond their limits. Hence role overload would be unlikely.

### Role Ambiguity

Role ambiguity involves uncertainty about what is required to fulfill a role (Kahn et al., 1964). We hypothesize that role ambiguity is greater the more emphasis in a national culture on egalitarianism and intellectual autonomy and the less on embeddedness.

Egalitarianism is based on a conception of people as moral equals who should negotiate their interests guided by an internalized commitment to voluntary cooperation. Diversity is recognized as acceptable and potentially productive. If managers import this conception into organizations, they will view formal role obligations more as guidelines and less as definitions of required behavior. Individuals may introduce new expectations into their role relationships, drop others, and redefine still others as part of the ongoing legitimate negotiation of new options and mutual commitments. This would create role ambiguity.

Intellectual autonomy reflects an expectation of and tolerance for unpredictability in behavior, as indicated by the values that mea-

sure it—creativity, curiosity, broad-mindedness. Within organizations, this too should lead to looser, changing specifications of role obligations and hence to role ambiguity. In contrast, in embedded cultures, traditional, relatively unchanging expectations and modes of behavior prevail, so members of collectivities know clearly what is expected of them. Cultural embeddedness downplays the expression of individual uniqueness in favor of maintenance of the status quo in relations among members of an all-embracing collectivity. Managers guided by this national cultural orientation will follow well-established procedures and rules and communicate stable expectations. This should minimize role ambiguity.

### Role Conflict

Role conflict is incompatibility between the expectations of multiple role partners or between aspects of a single role (Kahn et al., 1964). We hypothesize greater role conflict in nations where hierarchy and mastery prevail and less role conflict in nations whose national cultures emphasize harmony.

A hierarchical culture legitimates the unequal, hierarchical distribution of power, roles, and resources. In organizations consistent with such a culture, exercising control over others is critical to the accomplishment of tasks and attainment of goals. Organization members are therefore likely to make many and frequent demands on one another. This produces multiple sources of demands from above and expectations from below. At least some of these demands and expectations are likely to be incompatible and hence to generate role conflict.

Mastery emphasizes control and exploitation of the environment in the service of group or personal interests. Organizations that import a mastery orientation into their cultures will promote ambition and pursuit of success, encouraging members to take on multiple roles and even to overreach themselves. As members strive for their goals, their attempts to control and influence one another are likely to produce conflicting expectations. Moreover, mastery justifies a degree of manipulativeness in the pursuit of objectives. Conflict is likely to arise as actors seek to attain personal objectives while presenting themselves as pursuing group goals.

In contrast, in harmony cultures, motivation for change and influence is relatively low, and success does not require setting ever-higher goals and striving for them. In organizations, this national cultural orientation should translate into managers' setting goals that are attainable without extraordinary efforts and demanding little beyond standard role obligations. Thus there are few grounds for conflicts to arise. Moreover, because harmony is important in such organizations, members are likely to avoid conflictual situations.

To test the hypotheses noted above, we reanalyzed the data presented by Peterson et al. (1995).[7] They reported role stress scores from middle managers in 21 nations: Australia, Brazil, Finland, France, Germany, Hong Kong, India, Indonesia, Iran, Japan, Korea, Mexico, the Netherlands, Nigeria, Portugal, Singapore, South Africa, Spain, Uganda, the United Kingdom, and the United States. They adjusted the stress scores for variation between nations in personal and organizational characteristics. Each score was based on several agree/disagree items rated on 5-point scales (e.g., for overload, "I feel overburdened in my role"; for ambiguity, "I [do not] know exactly what is expected of me"; for conflict, "I receive incompatible requests from two or more people").

We tested the hypotheses by correlating nation scores on each of the seven cultural values with scores on each of the three types of role stress. Cultural value scores were available for 18 of the 21 nations (excluding Iran, Korea, and South Africa). In cases where we hypothesized a correlation with role stress for one polar value of a cultural dimension but not for the other, we introduced a control. We wished to predict only with the variance in the cultural value that was not

shared with its polar opposite. We therefore partialed on the opposite; for example, we partialed on egalitarianism when examining the correlation of hierarchy with role overload. Table 26.1 presents the findings.

*Role overload.* The correlations in the first row of the table support all three hypotheses. Managers in nations high on mastery and hierarchy but low on harmony are more likely to report experiencing role overload. There is also an unexpected negative correlation with intellectual autonomy. When the correlation with hierarchy is partialed for egalitarianism, the other pole of the dimension, it is slightly strengthened.

*Role ambiguity.* The correlations in the second row of Table 26.1 provide little support for our hypotheses. We expected positive associations with egalitarianism and intellectual autonomy and negative with embeddedness. The correlations are all weak. However, when the correlation with egalitarianism is partialed for hierarchy values, the other pole of the dimension, the predicted association becomes significant.

*Role conflict.* The correlations in the third row of the table support two of the three hypotheses. Managers in nations with cultures high on hierarchy and low harmony report greater role conflict. Although the correlation with mastery is in the expected direction, it is not significant. When the correlation with hierarchy is partialed for egalitarianism, the predicted association is slightly lower, and insignificant.

A brief comparison of these findings with those that Peterson et al. (1995) report for the Hofstede dimensions highlights some advantages of the new cultural dimensions. As noted above, Hofstede's and Schwartz's cultural dimensions overlap conceptually and empirically to some degree, although they also differ in important ways. Mastery (Schwartz) and masculinity (Hofstede) share emphases on assertiveness. On this basis, both we and Peterson et al. predicted positive

**TABLE 26.1**  Correlations of Role Overload, Ambiguity, and Conflict With Cultural Value Dimensions

| Type of Role Stress | Cultural Value Dimensions | | | | | | |
|---|---|---|---|---|---|---|---|
| | Harmony | Embeddedness | Hierarchy | Mastery | Affective Autonomy | Intellectual Autonomy | Egalitarianism |
| Overload | -.54** | .27 | .47** (.55**) | .47** | -.17 | -.49 | -.16 |
| Ambiguity | -.20 | -.20 | .03 | .05 | .15 | -.04 | .38 (.65**) |
| Conflict | -.40* | .16 | .41*(37) | .23 | -.01 | -.21 | -.24 |

NOTE: Hypothesized associations appear in boldface. Partial correlations appear in parentheses.
*$p < .10$; **$p < .05$.

correlations with role overload and role conflict. Observed correlations were more consistent with hypotheses for mastery (.47 and .23, respectively) than with those for masculinity (–.12 and .19).

Another empirical overlap is between harmony (Schwartz) and uncertainty avoidance (Hofstede). Conceptual differences between these dimensions led, however, to opposing hypotheses for role overload and conflict (see Peterson et al., 1995). Observed correlations were consistent with our hypotheses based on harmony (–.40, –.54) but opposite to those Peterson et al. derived for uncertainty avoidance (–.34, –.25).

Egalitarianism versus hierarchy (Schwartz) overlaps partially with power distance (Hofstede). We offered differential hypotheses for egalitarianism and hierarchy. Findings were fully consistent with our hypotheses for hierarchy but inconsistent with the Peterson et al. hypotheses for power distance. As for egalitarianism, its one hypothesized association with role ambiguity was weakly supported (.38), but it was clearly supported after hierarchy was controlled for (.65).

Finally, embeddedness versus autonomy (Schwartz) partially overlaps with individualism versus collectivism (Hofstede). Peterson et al. postulated that relations of individualism/collectivism with stress are identical to those of power distance. Observed correlations were indeed very similar, although weaker than for power distance and not significant. Controlling for power distance did not increase any of these correlations to an acceptable level of reliability. Hence Peterson et al. concluded that these two dimensions have redundant effects with regard to role stress, at least in their sample. The redundancy of power distance and individualism/collectivism is a common critique of the Hofstede dimensions (Schwartz, 1997; Smith & Schwartz, 1997). The autonomy versus embeddedness cultural dimension performed poorly as a predictor of stress. Neither autonomy nor embeddedness predicted role ambiguity reliably, contrary to the hypotheses.

In sum, national differences in role stress correlated more consistently with the new set of cultural dimensions than with those from Hofstede. Even in instances where related cultural dimensions yielded parallel hypotheses, correlations with the new dimensions were stronger and received better support. This set of dimensions was not fully supported, of course. But correlations were in the predicted direction for eight of the nine hypotheses, and six correlations were significant. Moreover, the findings suggest that the seven value types, although related, are not redundant with regard to role stress.

## Managers' Choices in Organizational Dilemmas

We next illustrate the impact of national culture on the understandings and preferences of managers from different nations. Hampden-Turner and Trompenaars (1993) studied organizational dilemmas that organizations in different nations may face. They explicated each dilemma, describing the meanings of the choices and the values likely to underlie each. Managers' decisions in those dilemmas reflect and express the substance of their organizational cultures, cultures that are influenced by the surrounding national culture. Hence we expect managers from different nations to vary in their choices in those dilemmas.

We apply the new theory of cultural dimensions to generate hypotheses regarding national differences in managers' choices in three of Hampden-Turner and Trompenaars's dilemmas. Tests of these hypotheses evaluate the usefulness of the theory for understanding what goes on in organizations.

### Analyzing Versus Integrating

Hampden-Turner and Trompenaars (1993) differentiate managers who "analyze phenomena into parts (i.e., items, tasks, numbers, units, points, specifics)" from those who "integrate and configure such details into whole patterns, relationships and wider contexts" (pp. 10-11). Analyzing is based on the notion that the whole is the sum of its parts. To understand the whole, one studies its parts. Managers who analyze prefer to focus on organizational tasks and employee qualifications, to use quantitative measures to set goals and evaluate achievements. Integrating reflects a view of the whole as more than the sum of its parts. To understand organizations, integrating managers are likely to focus on organizational relationships and interaction among individuals and groups and on complex qualitative as well as quantitative measures of success.

Hampden-Turner and Trompenaars measured the preference for an analyzing versus an integrating orientation by asking managers to choose between two ways to describe a company:

1. As a system designed to perform functions and tasks in an efficient way: People are hired to fulfill these functions with the help of machines and other equipment. They are paid for the tasks they perform.
2. As a group of people working together: The people have social relations with other people and with the organization. The functioning is dependent on these relations.

We hypothesize that a cultural emphasis on harmony induces managers to adopt an integrating rather than an analyzing orientation. Cultural harmony encourages people to try to comprehend and accept the social and physical world in all its complexity, to fit harmoniously into the wider environment. Managers influenced by this perspective are more likely to view the organization holistically, to focus on the complex relations among its parts, and to see employees as mutually interdependent in ways not easily reduced to individual elements. In low-harmony cultures, managers are more likely to adopt an analyzing orientation, seeing individual tasks, qualifications, profits, and so on as constituting the organization.

Embeddedness might also be conducive to viewing relationships as the essence of a company, whereas autonomy might lead to rejection of this view. However, we expect no associations of these two cultural orientations with this choice of Hampden-Turner and Trompenaars. Both choices treat people as functional parts of the organization whose unique interests and aspirations do not matter. Consequently, both choices are compatible with a cultural emphasis on embeddedness, and both clash with a cultural emphasis on autonomy.

Hampden-Turner and Trompenaars gathered data from managers in 12 nations: Australia, Belgium, Canada, France, Germany, Italy, Japan, the Netherlands, Singapore, Sweden, the United Kingdom, and the United States. For all but Belgium there are cultural values scores. Table 26.2 presents the percentages of managers in each national sample who chose one option rather than the other in each dilemma. We split the nations into subgroups at the "natural" breaks in the percentages of managers who endorsed one option. That is, we formed subgroups of nations discriminated by large gaps in the ordered array of percentages. Table 26.2 also presents national scores on the cultural value dimensions, based on teacher data from each nation. To test our hypotheses, we compared the relevant mean cultural value scores of the subgroups of nations discriminated by the managers' choices in the dilemmas.[8]

Panel A of Table 26.2 presents the percentages of managers who chose the analyzing rather than the integrating conception of a company and the ratings of the importance of cultural harmony. As hypothesized, managers in nations with cultures that emphasize harmony tended to choose the integrating option: The mean rating of harmony was higher in the five nations where managers preferred the integrating option (4.17, $sd = .41$) than in the six nations where most managers chose the analyzing option (3.82, $sd = .22$). Overall, harmony was more important in nations where most managers chose the integrating option in 24 of the 30 pairwise comparisons of values between nations across the

**TABLE 26.2** Percentages of Managers Making Particular Organizational Choices and Cultural Value Means in Various Nations

**Panel A**

| | United States | Canada | Netherlands | Australia | Sweden | United Kingdom | Mean (6) | Italy | Germany | Singapore | France | Japan | Mean (5) | t (df) |
|---|---|---|---|---|---|---|---|---|---|---|---|---|---|---|
| Analyzing vs. integrating (%) | 74 | 69 | 61 | 59 | 56 | 55 | 62 | 46 | 41 | 39 | 35 | 29 | 38 | |
| Harmony | 3.56 | 3.92 | 3.85 | 3.93 | 4.08 | 3.55 | 3.82 | 4.67 | 4.34 | 3.60 | 4.30 | 3.94 | 4.17 | 1.71 (9) |

**Panel B**

| | Japan | Singapore | Italy | Mean (3) | Sweden | France | Germany | Netherlands | Australia | Canada | United States | United Kingdom | Mean (8) | t (df) |
|---|---|---|---|---|---|---|---|---|---|---|---|---|---|---|
| Pay: work only vs. family size (%) | 32 | 65 | 67 | 55 | 89 | 88 | 91 | 91 | 92 | 94 | 95 | 96 | 92 | |
| Embeddedness | 3.74 | 4.25 | 3.70 | 3.90 | 3.45 | 3.23 | 3.29 | 3.56 | 3.94 | 3.72 | 3.77 | 3.68 | 3.58 | 1.61 (9) |
| Affective autonomy | 3.41 | 2.91 | 2.81 | 3.04 | 4.02 | 4.29 | 3.90 | 3.38 | 3.37 | 4.15 | 3.56 | 3.84 | 3.82 | 3.47 (9) |
| Intellectual autonomy | 4.55 | 3.56 | 4.46 | 4.19 | 4.83 | 5.03 | 4.62 | 4.31 | 4.00 | 3.93 | 3.97 | 4.19 | 4.36 | .49 (9) |

**Panel C**

| | Japan | Germany | United States | United Kingdom | Mean (4) | Netherlands | France | Sweden | Italy | Singapore | Mean (5) | t (df) |
|---|---|---|---|---|---|---|---|---|---|---|---|---|
| Organization vs. friend (%) | 86 | 76 | 75 | 72 | 77 | 60 | 54 | 49 | 48 | 46 | 51 | |
| Mastery | 4.14 | 3.88 | 4.14 | 4.01 | 4.04 | 3.85 | 3.77 | 3.85 | 3.95 | 3.80 | 3.84 | 2.97 (7) |
| Hierarchy | 2.73 | 2.15 | 2.25 | 2.43 | 2.39 | 2.13 | 2.04 | 1.94 | 1.55 | 2.63 | 2.06 | 1.53 (7) |
| Egalitarianism | 4.57 | 5.25 | 4.90 | 4.94 | 4.91 | 5.27 | 5.32 | 5.24 | 5.44 | 4.67 | 5.19 | 1.45 (7) |

two subgroups (6 nations × 5 nations × 1 value). Thus the harmony hypothesis gained support. The subgroups did not differ on the other six cultural values.

### Work Versus Family Size in Setting Pay

A second dilemma that Hampden-Turner and Trompenaars studied is whether companies should set pay levels exclusively based on their employees' work productivity or whether they should also take account of the employees' family situations. Managers chose between two ways a company might fix the level of its employees' income:

1. Some people think a company should take into account the size of the employee's family. In their eyes, the company is responsible for the extra compensation per child.
2. Other people believe that an employee should be paid on the basis of the work he is doing for the company. Therefore, the company does not have to take into account the employee's family.

Hampden-Turner and Trompenaars suggest that the first statement should appeal more to managers from what they call "communitarian" cultures, where the community is more important than the individual and individuals find self-fulfillment in serving their social group. These are what we have described as national cultures high in embeddedness. As noted above, we theorize that organizations in embedded cultures function as extended families that take responsibility for the welfare of their members in all domains of life and expect their members to identify with and work dutifully toward shared goals. We therefore hypothesize that cultural embeddedness induces managers to be more willing to take account of their employees' family situations in setting pay.

In autonomous cultures, in contrast, managers are likely to reject this choice in favor of setting pay exclusively according to workers' contributions. In such cultures, people are viewed as autonomous, bounded entities who are encouraged to pursue their own ideas (intellectual autonomy) and emotional experiences (affective autonomy) independently. Organizations in autonomous cultures are likely to treat their members as independent actors with their own preferences, abilities, and allegiances. Specific contractual arrangements of work bind employers and employees. Their mutual obligations do not extend beyond the workplace. Hence employers are unlikely to view the worker's family status as relevant in setting compensation.

Panel B of Table 26.2 presents the percentage of managers in each of the 11 nations studied who preferred to base payment on individual work. Also shown are the ratings of the importance of embeddedness and intellectual and affective autonomy. We compared the culture scores of the subsets of nations in which 67% or less versus 88% or more of the managers chose payment exclusively by work. As hypothesized, managers in nations where embeddedness is emphasized tended to choose this option *less* often: The mean rating of embeddedness is lower in the nations where the large majority of managers chose payment exclusively by work (3.58, $sd = .25$) than in nations where a third or more favored taking account of the size of the worker's family (3.90, $sd = .31$). Also as hypothesized, managers in nations where autonomy is highly important tended *more* to choose the work-only option: Affective autonomy is higher where the large majority of managers chose this option (3.81 [$sd = .35$] versus 3.04 [$sd = .32$]). The overall results supported the hypotheses for embeddedness and affective autonomy: 41/48 pairwise culture comparisons between the nations in the two subgroups (3 nations × 8 nations × 2 values) were as predicted.

Results for intellectual autonomy did not support the hypothesis, although they were in the expected direction. Nations in which the vast majority of managers chose compensation based only on work are slightly, but not significantly, higher on intellectual autonomy (4.36, $sd = .42$) than nations in which fewer managers chose this option

(4.19, *sd* = .55). Moreover, only 14/24 pairwise comparisons are consistent with the hypothesis. The two subgroups of nations do not differ on any of the other cultural dimensions.

### Organization Versus Friend

Hampden-Turner and Trompenaars contrasted managers' commitment to their companies' interests with their commitment to the crucial interests of a friend. They asked: "You have just come from a secret meeting of a board of directors of a certain company. You have a close friend who will be ruined unless he can get out of the market before the board's decision becomes known. You happen to be having dinner at your friend's home this evening. What right does your friend have to expect you to tip him off?" Commitment to the organization prohibits exposing confidential information; commitment to the friend demands sharing this knowledge.

We hypothesize that cultural hierarchy and mastery are conducive to the choice of maintaining organizational interests, whereas cultural egalitarianism is conducive to ignoring organizational obligations in favor of a friend. Where hierarchy is high, people are socialized to view compliance with role obligations and rules as a legitimate demand and to expect sanctions for failure to comply. As incumbents of organizational roles, managers are therefore likely to honor their formal commitments to the organization over any informal commitments to a friend. Cultural mastery encourages self-assertive pursuit of success. It justifies self-interested behavior in order to further group and personal goals. If managers import this orientation into their work, they will avoid risk to the success of their organization and to their own personal interests (if caught revealing confidential information), even at the expense of a friend.

Cultural egalitarianism calls for internalized, voluntary commitment to the welfare of other individuals and groups. People are expected to find mutually satisfactory modes of exchange through give-and-take, rather than to build their relations on rigid or ascribed role expectations. Managers influenced by this national cultural emphasis would therefore tend to view their role obligations as more open to negotiation and situational revision. The value of concern for others would incline them to help a friend and to such action, whereas their more complex conception of role commitments would weaken organizational restraints. Hence they might be more ready to weigh harm to organization against harm to friend and decide in favor of the latter.

We expect no association between embeddedness and choice in this dilemma, despite the emphasis of embeddedness on obligations to members of the in-group. This is because such obligations apply both to the collectivity at large (here, the organization) and to friends. We also expect no association of the choice with either affective or intellectual autonomy. The emphasis of these cultural orientations on following one's own feelings and ideas independently reduces obligations both to a friend and to the organization.

Panel C of Table 26.2 presents the percentages of managers who chose organization over friend and the ratings of the importance of hierarchy, mastery, and egalitarianism in the nine nations in which Hampden-Turner and Trompenaars posed this dilemma. We compared the importance of these cultural orientations in nations in which 72% or more versus 60% or less of the managers made this choice. As hypothesized, nations in which more than 72% of the managers favor the organization emphasize mastery more strongly in their cultures: Mastery is more important in the nations where the large majority of managers favor this option (4.04, *sd* = .12) than in those where a substantial number favor the friend (3.84, *sd* = .07). Results for hierarchy are similar (2.39 [*sd* = .25] versus 2.06 [*sd* = .39]). Also as expected, egalitarianism values are less important where the large majority of managers favor the organization (4.91 [*sd* = .28] versus 5.19 [*sd* =.30]). The two subgroups of nations do not differ on any of the other cultural value dimensions. Overall, 52 of the 60 pairwise comparisons of cultural values between nations across the two subgroups (4 nations × 5 nations × 3 values) were consistent with the hypotheses.

## DISCUSSION

Using data from published studies, we have illustrated how the Schwartz theory of cultural dimensions can explain cross-national variation in some aspects of what goes on in organizations. The set of cultural values helped to account for national levels of role stress in organizations and for managers' choices and preferences. No single cultural value type or dimension explained variation in all the variables studied. However, every one of the seven explained variance in at least one aspect of role stress or managers' choices. Thus the entire set of cultural dimensions is useful for illuminating national differences in perceptions and preferences within organizations.

A comparison of the current findings for role stress with those using Hofstede's dimensions suggests an advantage for the Schwartz dimensions. Correlations were generally stronger with the latter dimensions, and a larger proportion of hypotheses was confirmed. Moreover, the Hofstede dimensions of individualism/collectivism and power distance were redundant in the Peterson et al. analyses. In contrast, none of the parallel pairs of value types (embeddedness and autonomy, hierarchy and egalitarianism) was redundant. Each yielded unique hypotheses, most of which were confirmed. In cases where conceptually related dimensions from Hofstede (e.g., masculinity) and Schwartz (e.g., mastery) were hypothesized to have similar associations, the empirical findings supported the Schwartz dimensions more strongly.

The stronger findings for the Schwartz cultural dimensions may reflect the particular set of data studied here, or more reliable or more recent measurement. On the other hand, one might expect the IBM employees Hofstede sampled to be more suitable for the study of organizations than the teacher and student samples used by Schwartz. Perhaps, however, the most important reasons for the differences in outcomes are the conceptual differences between the two sets of dimensions that we elaborated in the section on pages 421-422.

In addition to the impact of national cultures, expressed in cultural values, values from other sources influence the culture of the organization as well. These include values characteristic of groups in the surrounding society (e.g., ethnic and religious groups), of the professions prevalent in the organization (e.g., engineering, marketing, administration), and of the industry (e.g., textiles, high-tech) or sector (private or public) to which the organization belongs (e.g., Thompson, Stradling, Murphy, & O'Neill, 1996; Trice & Beyer, 1993). The unique value priorities held by individual organizational members are an additional source of influence on organizational culture that is often overlooked. Each member brings the value priorities that serve as guiding principles in his or her life into the organization and is influenced by them in his or her work behavior. As individuals communicate their values and express them in action, they contribute to the ongoing process of shaping and reshaping the ideologies, norms, and values of the organization.

In this chapter we have analyzed relations of *national* culture to perceptions, behaviors, and choices of organizational managers. Neither of the studies we have discussed (i.e., Hampden-Turner & Trompenaars, 1993; Peterson et al., 1995) examined individual differences in value priorities among managers. Undoubtedly, the personal values of the individual managers also influenced them. Neither we nor other researchers have investigated the joint influences on behavior in organizations of individual differences in value priorities and the other sources of values identified here. Multilevel studies that simultaneously examine national cultures, individual value priorities, and some of the other sources of values discussed here would yield greater insight into what goes on in organizations.

## NOTES

1. Societies cannot legitimate the selfish pursuit of interests, either by individuals or by groups, if they are to run smoothly. Regulating interests is a concern of the dimension discussed next.

2. Based on analyses of 33 overlapping nations, the shared variance of the four Hofstede and three Schwartz dimensions ranges from 38% down to near zero. Hence it makes a real difference which approach one uses to order nations when studying culture.

3. We have discussed evidence for comprehensiveness in previous work (Schwartz, 1992; Schwartz & Sagiv, 1995). These same values are used to operationalize our theory of basic individual values (Schwartz, 1992). The cultural theory should not be confused with that individual theory from which it is conceptually independent.

4. Multiple samples from single nations are combined in the graphic presentation. They consistently emerged in close proximity on the coplot map, reflecting their highly similar cultural profiles.

5. The correlations between the scores of national cultures on each of the seven cultural values and their graphic locations along the vectors representing that value range from .78 for egalitarianism and harmony to .97 for embeddedness.

6. Japan presents a striking exception. Six samples from around Japan reveal strong cultural emphases on hierarchy and harmony but not on embeddedness, which is adjacent to them, and a strong emphasis on intellectual autonomy but not on the adjacent egalitarianism. Thus the location of Japan in the coplot is necessarily misleading. The findings suggest that Japanese culture has evolved in a manner different from most others and/or that it is in a period of transition.

7. We did not include data from countries added later (Peterson & Smith, 1997) because the researchers changed the measures of role stress, excluding many items and providing no measure of role conflict.

8. Given the small number of nations, we set a .10 level for statistical significance.

# 27

# Role Relaxation and Organizational Culture

## A Social Values Perspective

-- *Gregory M. Rose, Lynn R. Kahle, and Aviv Shoham*

In many ways, role theory is central to the field of organizational culture. Role theory antedates organizational culture theory, although formal roles (see Peterson & Smith, Chapter 6, this volume) are generally not thought of as central to organizational culture. The entire literature on organizational culture, especially the normative part of that literature, can be viewed as emphasizing how to use programs and practices such as transformational leadership, vision creation, and various team programs to deal with societies more heavily populated by certain types of role conflicts than are most societies in the world.

In this chapter, we emphasize role-relaxed behavior in an organizational and cultural context. Role-relaxed individuals decide how to act based primarily on personal considerations (Kahle, 1995; Kahle & Shoham, 1995; Shoham, Rose, & Kahle, 1998). They emphasize individually oriented values, are less affected by the opinions of others than are more role-rigid individuals, and place little importance on conforming to minor social conventions. Thus role relaxation is an individual trait that evaluates the degree to which an individual adheres to and conforms to perceived social norms. Most previous research has examined role relaxation within a consumer context (Kahle, 1995; Kahle & Shoham, 1995; Shoham et al., 1998). Role-relaxed consumers are often intentionally oblivious to social considerations. They assign a low level of importance to style, brand names, fashion, and the prestige of producers when making purchases (Kahle & Shoham, 1995). As a whole, role-relaxed consumers tend to construct and define the consumer role rather broadly, perceiving choices within a relatively large set of individually defined options, relatively unconstrained by social pressures and conventions. The broad construction of interpersonal roles is a defining quality of role-relaxed behavior.

Although previous research has focused mostly on consumption, role relaxation likely also influences a number of different organizational behaviors. For example, non-role-relaxed individuals should conform with, perpetuate, and adhere to perceived cultural and organizational norms of behavior. Organizations operating primarily in less role-relaxed cultures should require less direct control over reward systems than more role-relaxed cultures and organizations. These organizations should also require less immediate and individually based reward systems. Role-relaxed employees should tend to construct and define the employee role rather broadly, perceiving choices within a relatively large set of individually defined options, relatively unconstrained by social pressures and conventions.

One major difference in how role-relaxed and role-rigid people relate to an organizational culture is in how thorough or value based their socialization needs to be in order to effect change. Role-rigid people should be more willing to conform superficially based on norms communicated by other people, particularly authorities. Role-relaxed people will need to be wooed to accept organizational values, but once they have integrated these values with their self-images, they should have strong effects on behavior.

Role relaxation should be accepted as a central theme in the international organizational culture literature. Japan did not need an organizational culture literature, but the United States did. The normative literature on organizational culture seems to have come about as scholars sought ways of understanding how to have some influence on those people who are not inclined to accept social influence in the way it is exercised in, for example, Japan. At least one main theme, if not *the* main theme, in organizational culture research is how to get people to somehow link their self-images with those of their employers. Because role-relaxed individuals are not likely to accept influence unless they genuinely buy into the values offered, managers need to go to great lengths to try to get them to buy in. The idea of organizational culture management, with all its rhetoric of values, visions, and missions, is to accomplish just that change. Such programs can be viewed as intended especially to influence role-relaxed people who have resisted other forms of influence.

In this chapter we will address individual differences in role relaxation within an international and organizational context. Initially, we will discuss role theory. We will then describe role relaxation theoretically and incorporate it into a network of existing constructs about roles, values, and interpersonal relations. Finally, we present a discussion of the implications of role relaxation for organizational behavior and organizational culture

## ROLE THEORY

Role theory begins from a drama metaphor. Just as actors have expectations from playwrights, directors, audiences, and other actors that guide what they do on a certain stage at a certain time, likewise other humans in other contexts must also respond to expectations by following certain scripts appropriate for certain positions in the social structure (Fisher, 1982). Role theory's usefulness derives from its ability to integrate behavior from the individual level and the social organization level, from a wide range of phenomena (interpersonal attraction, leadership, group dynamics, socialization), and from several disciplines (psychology, sociology, anthropology) (Sarbin & Allen, 1968).

Several mechanisms in role theory define how social behavior proceeds. People have role *positions* that define groups of focal people with similar attributes and with similar likely reactions from others. The ways these focal people ought to behave are called role *expectations;* these include rights, rewards, obligations, and common behaviors. Focal people normally occupy whole sets of roles that sometimes conflict with each other, creating tensions that must be reduced somehow.

Merton (1957b) notes that individuals have various role sets because they occupy groups of roles simultaneously. One person may occupy the roles of Republican, woman, mother, executive vice president, and Red Cross volunteer. People interact in given roles with role partners, who also have expectancies in specific situations and multiple role sets. Role tensions may emerge because individuals must interact with role partners who have different values, statuses, and expectancies regarding some specific roles.

Merton identifies at least five social mechanisms for the articulation of roles in the role set, which helps to reduce role tension:

1. The mechanism of *differing intensity of role involvement* implies that expectations are not maintained with the same intensity or inherent commitment by all occupants of the role set. Sometimes one role is not of sufficient importance for the individual to worry about violating its norms.

2. The mechanism of *differences in power* implies that some people have a greater capacity to impose their own will in social action. Responding to power allows the target person to accept performance of certain types of undesired behaviors gracefully.

3. The mechanism of *insulating role activities from observation by members of the role set* is important because the social consequences of unobservable behaviors are greatly diminished.

4. The mechanism of *social support by others in similar social statuses with similar difficulties of coping with an unintegrated role set* is frequently evident in occupational and professional associations. People experiencing similar role-set tensions convey how to reduce stress.

5. The mechanism of *abridgement of the role set through the disruption of role relationships* generally results, according to Merton, in the individual's being removed from the status part of the role set related to that abridgement. The role remains, but the role participant departs.

Role theory has long served as an important influence in organizational research, especially in Western cultures. Indeed, one popular definition of organizations is "open systems of roles" (Katz & Kahn, 1978, p. 187). Kahn, Wolfe, Quinn, Snoek, and Rosenthal (1964), for another example, believe one of the major, dominant trends of the times is that large-scale organizations shape people's lives by defining role expectations. Organizations direct individuals to behave, dress, and talk in prescribed manners with persistence, selectivity, and restrictiveness that would not occur outside of the organizational context.

The changing times have changed the importance of role performance. In agricultural harvesting of a century ago, one failure in an individual's role fulfillment reduced production by a magnitude of the efforts of one person, a relatively modest amount. In a contemporary assembly-line context, one failed role fulfillment may render an entire product defective or inoperative (Kahn et al., 1964). The contemporary pace of change has created a situation in which conflict and ambiguity often thwart even the most loyal members of organizations in their attempts to comply with role expectations.

Kahn et al. (1964) observe, "The behavior of any organizational performer is the product of members of his role set, because they constantly bring influence to bear upon him which serves to regulate his behavior in accordance with the *role expectations* they hold for him" (p. 35). Two positions in a role set are those of the focal person and the role senders. Role senders communicate role expectations to the focal person, including instructions on role behavior, evaluation, policies, structures, technology, and rewards and punishments. The focal person receives a role, but this reception depends upon communication, personal attributes, and interpersonal factors. Transmission is not always accurate, but the process of sending and receiving role information is how organizations socialize new role occupants and negotiate role expectancies with long-term role occupants. Role expectations facilitate organizational stability and allow needed change because they are both perceptible and somewhat arbitrary. Individuals may arrive or leave, but their organizational roles can remain relatively stable after being corrected for personal attributes and interpersonal styles of individuals. Likewise, individuals within roles can be directed to adapt their roles as organizational needs transform.

Role theory also helps us to understand international and cross-cultural issues. The importance of maintaining face in Eastern cultures, for example, introduces new complexity into role theory (Earley, 1997) by modifying relevant norms. In another example, the class superiority implied with the title of shop steward increases the authority role in decision making more in Britain than in the United States (Locke & Latham, 1990).

These theories have not always been applied successfully in practice because different individuals respond to organizational pressures differently. The organizational culture literature has sought to find ways to get past the social influence envisioned in early role theory (e.g., Kahn et al., 1964) and to find powerful new ways to get at the values of people inclined to be, for example, role relaxed. Let us turn now to a consideration of role-relaxed behavior.

## ROLE RELAXATION

Role-relaxed individuals interpret their roles within a social community in broad and flexible terms (Kahle, 1995; Kahle & Shoham, 1995). Although everyone is influenced by

the social environment, people differ in their perceptions of their obligations and duties as well as what constitutes proper behavior within a social context. Some people allow themselves a high degree of flexibility and individuality in interpreting their roles; we refer to these individuals as *role relaxed.* Other people interpret and construct their roles in a more narrow, circumscribed manner. We refer to these individuals as *role rigid,* because they tend to have relatively tightly bounded and constricted interpretations of individual roles and expectancies.

In a sense, role relaxation is similar to nonconformity. Both involve an individual's reactions to perceived group pressures or norms. More precisely, conformity involves an individual's internalization of group norms because of a shared sense of values, a desire to avoid punishment or gain rewards through compliance, or a desire to be identified or to seek a relationship with a desirable individual or group (Kelman, 1958). Thus conformity involves similarity in attitudes, values, or behaviors. Role relaxation, in contrast, focuses on the bounds, implementation, or perceived flexibility of an individual in constructing and responding to group responsibility and roles. Role-relaxed individuals may exhibit membership in and attraction to a group but interpret their roles within a wide range of acceptable behaviors. Greater conformity, however, would be expected among role-rigid individuals, because role rigidity stems from a perceived, implicit understanding of the duties, obligations, and responsibilities of being a group member. Thus role relaxation, in contrast with conformity, focuses on an individual's perceptions of the bounds of acceptable behavior rather than on actual similarity. In short, nonconformity and role relaxation are conceptualized as correlates, because role relaxation examines the degree of the boundaries an individual imposes on him- or herself in conforming to group expectations and norms. The value-based influence facet of Kelman's influence model, the facet most relevant to organizational culture theory, is the most relevant to role-relaxed people, and the other facets, consistent with influence in role theory, are less relevant to such people and more relevant to role-rigid people.

Role relaxation is also conceptually linked to susceptibility to interpersonal influence (Bearden, Netemeyer, & Teel, 1989; Kahle, 1995; Lennox & Wolfe, 1984; McGuire, 1968). Role-relaxed individuals exhibit a relatively low degree of acquiescence and compliance to interpersonal influence attempts across groups. Highly role-relaxed individuals, moreover, personalize, interpret, and react to interpersonal influence within a relatively wide range of perceived acceptable responses. Thus role relaxation should be negatively correlated to susceptibility to interpersonal influence.

The role-relaxed person tends to display a high degree of creativity and originality. The role-relaxed person is not rebelling for the sake of rebelling—rather, he or she sees a more compelling way to behave. Rationality overrides norms. As consumers, role-relaxed people often become trendsetters, because they devise more efficient ways to consume.

Role-relaxed people tend to approach roles with less intensity than do non-role-relaxed individuals. They pay less attention to role senders and sending. They may tolerate more tension-producing activity because they do not find themselves drawn into the game quite as completely. They may have slightly less concern about the formal rights and rewards associated with the role, but they may also expect more indirect benefits from roles than would others. Role-relaxed individuals probably communicate more than others about their motivations in order to prevent others from viewing them as outright deviants.

Role-relaxed individuals experience less desire than do others to utilize the social mechanisms for the articulation of roles in the role set described by Merton. The mechanism of differing intensity of role involvement for role-relaxed individuals implies that role-relaxed persons do not observe expectations as intensely or literally as do others. The

mechanism of differences in power by role-relaxed individuals implies that they have a greater capacity to impose their own will in social action than do others who fear power more. Role-relaxed people use the mechanism of insulating role activities from observation by members of the role set less often than others because the social consequences of observable behaviors mean less for them. The mechanism of seeking social support by others in similar social statuses may be attractive to some role-relaxed individuals because it allows them to select behaviors from a variety of potential sources. The mechanism of abridgement of the role set through disruption of role relationships may be used more often by role-relaxed members of an organization, but abridgement is not their primary goal. They may develop unique mechanisms to preserve their organizational status in spite of deviance because their deviance is not antisocial. This effect has been demonstrated empirically (Shoham, 1999).

One critical issue for the understanding of role-relaxed behavior is that it emanates primarily from social values. Role expectancies are generally attitudes about behaviors, which occupy a middle ground in cognitions about adaptation. As we have articulated in our work on social adaptation theory (Kahle 1983, 1984, 1996; Kahle, Homer, O'Brien, & Boush, 1997; Kahle, Kulka, & Klingel, 1980), people will generally try to function in their social environments by developing social cognitions such as attitudes and values that optimize adaptation. Values guide attitude formation and behaviors. Social comparison values, such as beauty and being well respected, have been found to be related (negatively) to role relaxation in the United States (Kahle & Shoham, 1995), and independence-oriented values, such as self-respect and equality, are related to role relaxation in North America. These values provide the criteria that individuals use in determining when to approach a role in a relaxed fashion and when to approach it rigidly. To explain this relationship more fully, we turn now to a more general consideration of values.

## SOCIAL VALUES

Values serve as guiding principles (Kahle, 1983) or desirable and enduring end states (Rokeach, 1973) that influence both attitudes and behaviors. As stable, abstract cognitions, values provide structure, organization, and purpose to individuals' interactions with their environments (Kahle, 1996). People develop values from life experiences. They utilize values to incorporate new information with existing knowledge structures and to interact successfully with their environments. Values provide a purpose or underlying motivation for people's actions. What is deemed acceptable or desirable for one person may be undesirable or even strongly antithetical to another. Thus values provide a means of assessing what is important or desirable.

Numerous studies have documented the link between personal or social values and specific attitudes and behaviors, including leadership, sports participation, smoking, gift giving, and conformity in dress (see Kahle, 1996). Values also relate to a number of activities in organizational behavior, ranging from commitment to effectiveness of sales management efforts (Kahle & Eisert, 1986; Weeks & Kahle, 1990a, 1990b). Although values have been related to a number of behaviors, the direct link between specific values and behaviors remains complex. Values are more usefully regarded as part of a larger cognitive network than as single predictors in their own right. Homer and Kahle (1988), for example, utilized structural equations to link personal values empirically to specific food-shopping behaviors of 831 consumers. This empirical pattern has been replicated several times (e.g., Kahle et al., 1997; Madrigal & Kahle, 1994; Rose, Shoham, Kahle, & Batra, 1994). For example, Rose et al. (1994) demonstrated a sequence from values to group identification and need for affiliation to attitudes toward conformity. Overall, Rokeach (1973) is correct in describing values as enduring end states, but values can change even in a short period of time, and they exist in the context of other social cognitions and phenomena. In the context of the organizational culture theme, this line of research is consistent with the idea that we should analyze organizational cultures as analogous to national cultures.

The link between values and culture remains a primary concern among scholars such as Rokeach (1973), Hofstede (1980a), Kahle (1983), Triandis (1989), and Schwartz (1992). Rokeach (1973) stimulated much of the modern work on social values. He divided social values into terminal, or desirable end states, and instrumental, or actions needed to achieve those desirable end states. Subsequent studies have applied Rokeach's Value Survey (RVS) in a variety of contexts, including cross-cultural contexts. The Rokeach work is enormously important, but it has at least three drawbacks. First, the RVS involves several societal values that transcend individuals, such as world of peace and national security, which may therefore have minimal applicability in an applied setting (Beatty, Kahle, Homer, & Misra, 1985). Although people may believe that world peace is a good thing, they may not regularly formulate decisions in their daily lives based on that belief. Second, others have failed to replicate the distinction between instrumental and terminal values when using methods other than the RVS (e.g., Schwartz, 1992). Third, the RVS instrument is relatively long and cumbersome when used in conjunction with other instruments.

In response to these and other difficulties, we have used the List of Values (LOV) in our research (see Kahle, 1983, 1996). The LOV offers a succinct 9-item scale that focuses on action-oriented terminal values. Specifically, the LOV includes the following items: sense of accomplishment, security, self-respect, warm relationships with others, sense of belonging, being well respected, self-fulfillment, excitement, and fun and enjoyment in life. These specific values are not intended to be an exhaustive list of all possible human values. They were selected because of their potential theoretical uses and their potential applicability to life's major roles: work, leisure, marriage, and parenting.

One way to conceptualize differences in role-relaxed behaviors would be to begin with the epidemiology of social values. As mentioned above, social comparison values, such as beauty and being well respected, have been found to be related (negatively) to role relaxation in the United States (Kahle & Shoham, 1995), and independence-oriented values, such as self-respect and equality, are related to role relaxation in North America. We have found self-respect to be especially strong in the United States and in Latin America. We have also found being well respected to be strong in Arab countries and in Scandinavia. These data would suggest that the nations of the Americas may be places where one might observe more role-relaxed behavior.

Schwartz (1992) proposes a system of values that focuses on motivational domains. Each is composed of specific values from various sources (e.g., Chinese Culture Connection, 1987; Hofstede, 1980a; Rokeach, 1973) conceptually similar to LOV although more cumbersome to measure, and each is contained within an overall cross-culturally validated structure of human values. Each motivational domain is conceptualized as having compatible (adjacent) and conflicting (opposite) motivational domains. Thus, Schwartz provides an important empirical description of the structure of human values (see Sagiv & Schwartz, Chapter 26, this volume).

One way in which an organization might influence role-relaxed individuals is to try to find ways to link their values to the organization's values. Once that is done, there can be a lot of self-control at the level of attitudes and behaviors, and everyone remains satisfied.

In the next section, we discuss potential cultural and value differences in role relaxation based on additional important conceptualizations and comparisons of personal and cultural values. Our focus is on central issues in role implementation.

## EXPECTED CULTURAL DIFFERENCES IN ROLE RELAXATION

Values research has produced a rich conceptual and empirical tradition of classifying and understanding individual and cultural differences in personal values (Hofstede, 1980a; Kahle, 1983; Kahle, Rose, & Shoham, in press; Rose, 1997; Schwartz, 1992; Triandis, 1989). Although several important frameworks have been proposed (e.g., Chinese Culture Connection, 1987; Kahle, 1983, 1996; Rokeach, 1973; Schwartz, 1992), we begin our discussion with individualism/collectivism because it has been widely accepted as a dimension describing fundamental differences in basic values (Hofstede, 1980a; Rose, 1997; Triandis, 1989; Schwartz, 1992). Although individualism and collectivism constitute a subset of research on social values, the concepts have been well articulated and widely discussed.

### Individualism/Collectivism

Triandis (1989) has examined extensively the difference between individualism and collectivism. Collectivist societies emphasize group goals and naturally subjugate individual needs to the needs of the group. Individualists, in contrast, are emotionally independent from "groups, organizations, and/or other collectives" (Hofstede, 1980a, p. 224). Although some groups, such as the family, are accorded fundamental importance, individualists view the self as inherently detached and separate from others.

For collectivists the values of duty and obligation are paramount, along with the reciprocation of favors, respect for tradition, and the primary importance of in-group success (Liu, 1997; Schwartz, 1992). Individualists emphasize values such as self-actualization, self-expression, individual development, and personal goals.

Value derivation also differs between collectivists and individualists. Collectivists tend to derive values from the culture and society to a larger extent, whereas individualists tend to formulate their own values with greater individual reflection.

Collectivists have stronger associations with fewer in-groups than do members of more individualist societies. Markus and

Kitayama (1991) describe the interdependent self as inherently interpersonal and defined primarily by group membership and the individual's relationship to others. Collectivists are highly committed to a few in-groups. Social norms, roles, and duty shape actions to a larger extent in collectivist societies than in individualist societies.

Individualists, in contrast, perceive themselves as inherently autonomous and independent from others (Rose, 1997). They define themselves almost entirely in individual terms (Triandis, 1989), value self-oriented outcomes, such as self-fulfillment, and have weak associations with many in-groups (Kahle et al., in press). Group membership is generally regarded as fluid and changeable in individualist societies, and individuals in these societies often define in-groups as those groups that agree with them on important issues and values (Rokeach, 1960).

Collectivists generally perceive personal goals within the confines of the collectives to which they belong. No inherent conflict is perceived between personal and group interests, and conformity is perceived as a natural part of the individual's duty. Individualists are taught to resist group pressure, and in individualist societies conformity generally carries a negative connotation (Triandis, 1989).

Role relaxation is more likely to be found among individualists than among collectivists. Individualists regard self-interests as primary, value autonomy, and regard independent thinking and actions as desirable. As we have noted, independence-oriented values, such as self-respect and equality, are related to role relaxation in North America (Kahle & Shoham, 1995). In contrast, low levels of role relaxation are likely to be found among collectivists. As noted, social comparison values, such as beauty and being well respected, have been found to be related (negatively) to role relaxation in the United States (Kahle & Shoham, 1995), and collectivism is based on a tendency to subjugate self-interests to the needs of the group.

Schwartz (1992) provides an insightful critique of the individualist/collectivist distinction. Although he recognizes the fundamental importance of this distinction in explaining differences in behaviors and perceptions across cultures, he argues that it fails to account for the full complexity of human values, as one might expect from the structure of values in his theory. Triandis (1989) also recognizes the limitations of a monolithic view of individualism/collectivism in that he has written extensively about different expressions of individualism and collectivism across societies, including recent work on vertical and horizontal forms of individualism and collectivism (Triandis, 1995). Recently, Triandis and his colleagues have described individualism and collectivism as independent constructs. Individualism consists of "separation from in-groups" and "self-reliance with hedonism." Collectivism consists of "family integrity" and "interdependence with sociability."

Collectivists perceive themselves as similar to others, and they regard excessive individuality as undesirable. Individualists perceive themselves as autonomous, unique, and distinct from others. Thus collectivist cultures are generally more homogeneous than individualist cultures (Triandis, 1989), which leads to differences in communication such as high versus low context.

## High Versus Low Context

Hall (1976) describes two distinct patterns of communication across societies. Low-context cultures focus on the specific words spoken, whereas high-context cultures often communicate implicitly through presumed understanding among speakers. High-context cultures tend to be more homogeneous than low-context cultures. In Japan, for example, most people share a common heritage, language, and history (Nakane, 1970), which facilitates nonverbal, intuitive, high-context communication (Iwata, 1999). The United States, in contrast, is a low-context culture, with greater variety in racial backgrounds, ethnicities, social classes, incomes, and levels of education. As Kato and Kato (1992) note, "Living in a heterogeneous society, Americans must speak loudly and clearly with their tongue, in order to communicate with each other" (p. 47). Thus communication in the United States tends to be more direct, verbal, and explicit than communication in Japan. Heterogeneity among group members should also lead to a high degree of role relaxation. Individuals should incorporate their own meanings, interpretations, and connotations to group membership and role identities. More homogeneous cultures, in contrast, should produce more tightly defined, mutually understood roles. The duties, responsibilities, and meanings of group membership should be implicitly understood and observed, much as communication is assumed and contextual, based on similar frames of reference (Hall, 1976).

### Hofstede's Dimensions

Four of Hofstede's (1980a) dimensions of human values are expected to be associated with role relaxation. The first, individualism/collectivism, has already been discussed. The second, power distance, refers to the extent to which people accept or reject unequal distributions of power and espouse egalitarian ideals. Power distance is generally associated with a high degree of formality and deference to power, which should be associated with a low degree of role relaxation, because role-relaxed individuals tend to be less respecting of power and less conforming than role-rigid individuals.

The third Hofstede dimension, uncertainty avoidance, examines "the extent to which people feel threatened by ambiguous situations, and have created beliefs and institutions that try to avoid these" (Hofstede & Bond, 1984, pp. 419-420). Uncertainty avoiding cultures and individuals exhibit a preference for unambiguous, clearly defined situations, which should be associated with a preference for highly defined unambiguous roles and a low degree of role relaxation. Thus power distance and uncertainty avoidance should be associated with relatively high levels of role rigidity.

Hofstede's fourth dimension, masculinity/femininity, concerns the extent to which the dominant values in society are instrumental, focusing on success, money, and things (masculinity), or relational, focusing on interpersonal relationships and caring for others (femininity) (Hofstede & Bond, 1984, pp. 419-420). Feminine individuals and societies should exhibit lower degrees of role relaxation, because of their desire to maintain harmonious relationships with others.

In summary, role relaxation examines personal variations in the implementation or actualization of interpersonal roles. Role-relaxed individuals are expected to be anti-conforming, non-power distant, and individualistic. Role rigidity, in contrast, is expected to be associated with collectivism, uncertainty avoidance, and a relatively homogeneous, high-context culture. Thus role relaxation is an individual trait that should vary across cultures. Individuals from high-context, collectivist cultures should perceive and construct interpersonal roles in relatively constrained and normatively similar terms. Individualists should exhibit greater variance in their perceptions and implementation of group responsibilities and norms. We now turn to the managerial and organizational implications of these expectations.

### IMPLICATIONS OF ROLE RELAXATION FOR ORGANIZATIONAL BEHAVIOR

Role-relaxed employees may experience less tension or stress from roles, leading to potentially higher satisfaction among these individuals when they are given amenable working conditions. Although they may not achieve the low levels of absenteeism desired by some managers, they will probably manifest higher productivity when given amenable working conditions. Their creativity and need to demonstrate loyalty in spite of their independence will most likely manifest itself in intangible, off-diagonal benefits to the organization, especially if the responsibilities require creativity and independence. Role-relaxed individuals are more likely than others to dissent or to become whistle-blowers. Role-relaxed employees probably will respond more to opportunity rewards and less to strictly economic ones than some other employees. Because role-relaxed people are less susceptible to social influence, the functions of senders and managers become one notch more difficult. Role-relaxed employees should be especially positive contributors to efforts to develop and live by visions, missions, team-based programs, and transformational leadership, for example.

When role-relaxed behavior is not recognized or appreciated, the consequences will depend on who occupies which status position. A manager intolerant of role-relaxed behavior with role-relaxed employees will experience frustration that will likely result in unpleasant outcomes, such as dissatisfaction, absenteeism, and turnover. A role-relaxed manager with role-rigid employees, on the other hand, may create an effective and interesting environment.

Because different countries and organizations differ in their cultures' central tendency toward role relaxation, and because this variable is often absent from the vocabulary of managers, the potential for cross-cultural conflict related to role rigidity is very real. One could imagine a situation in which role-relaxed but loyal behavior is perceived as disobedient, disloyal, and deviant. Western organizational culture management programs may need to be different or may not be relevant in countries where role relaxation is likely to be more rare, for example. Recognizing this potential problem and exploring ways of dealing with it are important issues for managers in cross-cultural situations.

## CONCLUSION

The conceptualization of and research on role-relaxed behaviors have numerous implications for cross-cultural research in organizational behavior. Role-relaxed employees exercise creativity and independence even as they fail to respond as quickly as other employees to role-sender and other social influences. Their core values motivate them to march to a different drummer at times. When cultures allow this marching, organizations may be better off for it. When the marching is misunderstood or punished, organizations will often suffer.

This line of thinking has many implications for international culture research on organizations and role-relaxed behavior (see Shoham, 1999). Do the predicted country differences in role relaxation manifest themselves empirically and translate into the effects predicted above? How does role relaxation relate to employee and employer motivation, effort, autonomy, and specialization? Do managers as consumers and managers as workplace employees behave at similar levels of role relaxation, implying greater utility in cross-fertilization of the organizational behavior and the consumer behavior literatures? Do mismatches among employees of different cultures or nationalities impede vision creation, team functioning, and efforts at transformational leadership? The potential research agenda for understanding the full cross-cultural implications of role-relaxed behavior in organizations seems limitless.

# 28

## Definition and Interpretation in Cross-Cultural Organizational Culture Research

### Some Pointers From the GLOBE Research Program

-- *Marcus W. Dickson, Ram N. Aditya, and Jagdeep S. Chhokar*

Understanding culture as it is manifested *across societies* is a difficult undertaking, as is reflected in the wealth of literature on the topic. Understanding culture as it is manifested across organizations *within a single society* is also a difficult undertaking, as is reflected in the wealth of literature on that topic. Understanding culture as it is manifested *across organizations from different societies*—cross-cultural organizational culture analysis—is an extraordinarily difficult undertaking, as is reflected by the relative *lack* of literature on the topic.

AUTHORS' NOTE: We would like to thank Mark Peterson, Paul Hanges (GLOBE co-principal investigator), Fred Dansereau, and Katherine Klein for their helpful comments in the preparation of this chapter. We would also like to recognize GLOBE principal investigator Robert J. House, the GLOBE Coordinating Team, and all the members of the GLOBE Project for the work they have done on leadership and culture, and for allowing us to present our perspective on and learnings from the GLOBE Project in this chapter. The opinions expressed in this chapter are those of the authors, and not necessarily those of the GLOBE Project or any of its other members.

In fact, examining organizational culture in a cross-cultural context raises the question, What precisely *is* organizational culture? If the differences among organizations from different countries are largely attributable to differences among the countries themselves, is this a question of organizational culture at all? Further, if the differences are attributable to differences among industries, or among regions within a country, to what extent are these issues of *organizational* culture?

In this chapter, we address several issues of interpretation of cross-cultural organizational culture data. We provide some suggestions on how to deal with these data (and how not to deal with them) and also raise some questions for researchers to ask themselves about the data they have, the goals of their research, and what they consider to be part of the construct called *organizational culture.*

We bring to this chapter our experiences in working with the Global Leadership and Organizational Behavior Effectiveness (GLOBE) Research Project, which is a currently ongoing study of the interrelationships of leadership, societal culture, and organizational culture (Den Hartog et al., 1999; Hanges & Dickson, in press; House et al., 1999). The GLOBE Project's 180 members have, to date, collected data from 64 cultures, more than 800 organizations, and more than 20,000 individuals. GLOBE has developed, validated, and cross-validated scales measuring societal culture, organizational culture, and preferences for leader behaviors and attributes, and has demonstrated the construct validity of these scales. Many of our recommendations come from our experiences in dealing with these multilevel data, although other experiences in cross-cultural research have shaped our thinking as well.

We first briefly describe the GLOBE Research Program in order to lay the groundwork for many of the arguments that follow. We then discuss the evolution of the culture construct, highlighting culture as a phenomenon that is enacted at multiple levels of analysis. Next, we highlight several difficulties researchers face in conducting cross-cultural organizational culture analyses. We conclude with questions and recommendations for researchers engaged in such analyses.

## THE GLOBE RESEARCH PROGRAM

The essence of the GLOBE Research Project (Hanges & Dickson, in press; House et al., 1999), originally conceived by Robert J. House in 1991, is exploration of organizational leadership and its impact on organizational effectiveness. A primary goal from the beginning of the project was to reach a better understanding of the phenomenon of leadership as it is enacted in different contexts; societal culture and organizational culture were both seen as important influences on the nature of the leadership relationship. From its very inception, therefore, GLOBE has been focused on the study of the interrelationships among societal culture, organizational culture, and effective leadership in organizations. Details of the project are available in several recent and forthcoming publications, and conference presentations, chapters, and other findings are available on the project's Web site (http://www.bsos.umd.edu/psyc/hanges/globepag.htm).

One of the strengths of GLOBE is that the project started afresh in terms of defining and operationalizing the phenomena of interest. The project has defined culture, for example, as "shared motives, values, beliefs, identities, and interpretations or meanings of significant events that result from common experiences of members of collectivities and are transmitted across age generations" (House et al., 1999). This definition of culture, which has been adopted for both societal and organizational levels, was arrived at consensually at a meeting of many of the participating researchers of GLOBE in 1994. A similar approach was followed for operationalization of other leadership and culture constructs. Starting with an initial pool of more than

**TABLE 28.1    GLOBE's Dimensions of Organizational Culture**

| Dimension | Focus of the Dimension at the Organizational Level |
| --- | --- |
| Power distance | The degree to which members of an organization (should) accept distinctions between members on the basis of organizational position; includes such things as perquisites, status, and decision-making power |
| Uncertainty avoidance | The degree to which members of an organization (should) actively attempt to reduce ambiguity in organizational life by relying on norms, rules, and policies |
| Humane orientation | The degree to which members of an organization (should) encourage and reward individuals for being fair and kind to other organization members |
| Assertiveness | The degree to which members of an organization are (should be) assertive, dominant, and demanding in their interactions with other organization members |
| Gender egalitarianism | The degree to which men and women are (should be) treated equally in the organization in terms of tasks assigned and opportunities for training and advancement |
| Future orientation | The degree to which an organization (should) encourages and rewards long-term versus short-term planning and projects |
| Performance orientation | The degree to which an organization (should) focuses on and rewards high performance and efforts to improve quality |
| Individualism/collectivism | The degree to which an organization (should) focuses on individual accomplishment versus group accomplishment |
| Organizational collectivism | The degree to which organizational members (should) take pride in being associated with the organization |

800 items, the GLOBE researchers developed 16 unidimensional leadership scales and 9 unidimensional culture scales, all of which exhibited satisfactory psychometric properties. Details of the scale development and validation are reported in Hanges and Dickson (in press).

## Operationalization of Culture

Culture being one of the major phenomena of interest to GLOBE, its operationalization was done at several levels. First, nine attributes of culture were identified and selected based on existing theoretical and empirical literature on measurement of culture:

uncertainty avoidance, power distance, the individualism/collectivism continuum, family/organizational collectivism, gender egalitarianism, assertiveness, future orientation, performance orientation, and humane orientation. These are based on the works of Hofstede (1980a), Hofstede and Bond (1988), Kluckhohn and Strodtbeck (1961), McClelland (1961, 1985), and Putnam (1993), among others. Detailed definitions of these nine dimensions can be found in House et al. (1999), and brief descriptions of the dimensions are provided in Table 28.1.

The second level of operationalization of culture was in terms of what may be called the *content* and *process* of culture. Culture is often manifested in two distinct ways. The

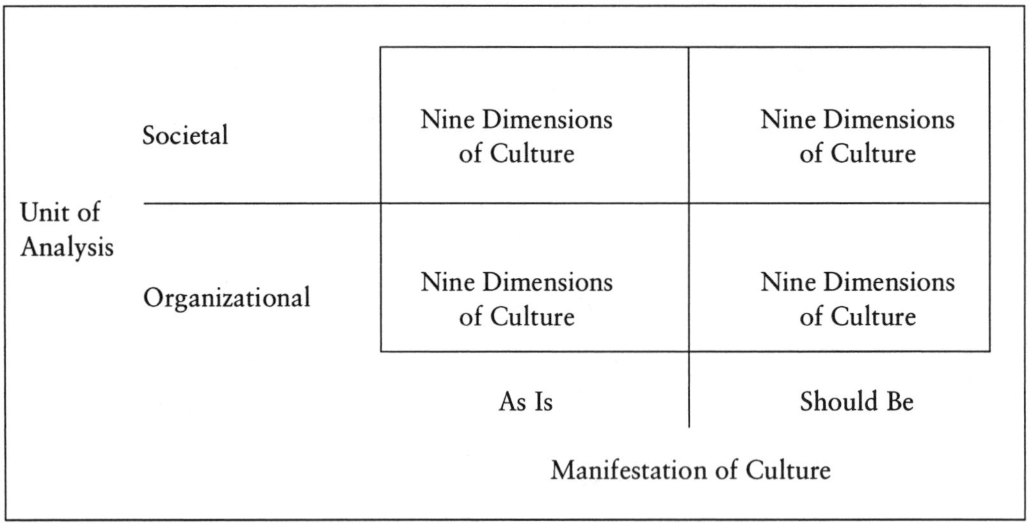

| | | As Is | Should Be |
|---|---|---|---|
| Unit of Analysis | Societal | Nine Dimensions of Culture | Nine Dimensions of Culture |
| | Organizational | Nine Dimensions of Culture | Nine Dimensions of Culture |
| | | As Is | Should Be |
| | | Manifestation of Culture | |

**Figure 28.1.** GLOBE's Approach to Culture

first is as values, beliefs, schemas, and implicit theories commonly held among members of a collectivity (society or organization); these are variously called the *attributes* or *content* of culture. The second way culture is manifested is as commonly observed and reported *practices* of entities such as families, schools, work organizations, economic and legal systems, and political institutions; these are often referred to as the *process* of culture. The GLOBE Project measures all of the nine dimensions of culture in both these manifestations. The former are expressed as responses to questionnaire items in the form of judgments of what *should be* and the latter as assessments of what *is* with regard to common behaviors, institutional practices, prescriptions, and proscriptions.

The third and final level of operationalization focused on the unit of analysis. Because the GLOBE Project was designed to assess the impact of societal culture *and* organizational culture on perceptions of effective leadership, society and organizations within society were considered as separate units of analysis. Therefore, culture has been measured in GLOBE at *both* these levels. (We discuss culture as a phenomenon at multiple lev-

els of analysis in more detail below.) Accordingly, items were written for all nine dimensions of culture as "quartets" having isomorphic structures across two units of analysis (societal and organizational) and across two manifestations of culture (*as is* and *should be*), as shown in Figure 28.1. Although the four items in a quartet are similar in terms of their structure, they differ in the frames of reference respondents are cued to use while responding to them. The frame of reference is changed according to the particular manifestation of culture and the unit of analysis. An example of such a quartet is shown in Figure 28.2, which contains essentially the same statement in four forms: "Society *as is*," "Society *should be*," "Organization *as is*," and "Organization *should be*." Items representing the nine dimensions of culture were derived from (a) a review of literature on societal and organizational culture and (b) interviews and focus groups conducted in several of the participating countries. Appropriate psychometric analyses showed that grouping the items into nine scales, each corresponding to one of the dimensions of culture, was amply justified (Hanges & Dickson, in press).

| | | |
|---|---|---|
| **Society** | The economic system in this society is designed to maximize:<br><br>1  2  3  4  5  6  7<br><br>Individual   ·   Collective<br>Interests      Interests<br><br>(Societal Practices) | The economic system in this society *should* be designed to maximize:<br><br>1  2  3  4  5  6  7<br><br>Individual      Collective<br>Interests      Interests<br><br>(Societal Values) |
| **Organization** | The pay and bonus system in this organization is designed to maximize:<br><br>1  2  3  4  5  6  7<br><br>Individual      Collective<br>Interests      Interests<br><br>(Organizational Practices) | In this organization, the pay and bonus system *should* be designed to maximize:<br><br>1  2  3  4  5  6  7<br><br>Individual      Collective<br>Interests      Interests<br><br>(Organizational Values) |

**Figure 28.2.** Example of a GLOBE Item Quartet Addressing Societal and Organizational Culture

The intention with this design was to take into account varying perspectives on culture and its measurement—in the earliest days of GLOBE's discussions about measure development, the more anthropologically oriented members advocated measures of values, whereas the more psychologically oriented members advocated measures of practices. (One may also argue that the measures of common practices are actually measures of organizational and societal *climate,* whereas the measures of shared values are the measures of organizational and societal culture.)

GLOBE is also a multiphase project. Phase 1, consisting of two pilot studies, psychometric analyses (such as item analysis, factor analysis, and generalizability analysis), double-blind translation of items to the languages of participating countries, and review of items by country co-investigators of participating countries, resulted in the development of valid and reliable scales for assessing societal culture, organizational culture, and perceptions of effective leadership. Phase 2 consisted of data collection and assessment of the core societal and organizational *as is* and *should be* dimensions, assessment of culturally endorsed implicit leadership theories (CLTs) based on the leadership scales, organizational contingencies in firms included in the sample in various countries, and respondent demographic variables. In addition, two independent sets of scales (unobtrusive measurement scales and participant observation scales) were developed to assess societal-level culture dimensions *qualitatively.* Some of the qualitative methods used were focus groups, ethnographic interviews, nonreactive measures, and media analysis. (Details of future phases and a more complete description of the leadership aspects of GLOBE are available in House et al., 1999, and at the GLOBE Web site.)

GLOBE is therefore a multiphase, multimethod, and multiculture project in which multiple investigators are cooperating to study societal culture, organizational culture, and leadership, and their interactions, over a number of years. It provides multilevel data that can be analyzed and interpreted in a variety of ways depending on the objective of the investigation, and thus is an excellent source of data for multiple levels of analysis in the study of organizational culture across societies.

## CULTURE: A PHENOMENON ENACTED AT MULTIPLE LEVELS

In our various cross-cultural research efforts, we have become keenly aware of the truth of Barley's (1995) assertion that culture is an exceptionally difficult concept to define. Indeed, Kroeber and Kluckhohn (1952) identified no fewer than 164 definitions of the term by anthropologists. Hofstede (1980a) has defined culture rather simplistically as "the collective programming of the mind which distinguishes members of one human group from another" (p. 25). This is distinguished from the "universal" level of mental programming that is common to all humankind: The collective level is shared with some but not all other humans. In Hofstede's study, the collective was defined by national borders.

Culture at the organizational level has been addressed by a number of scholars since the 1960s (e.g., Blake & Mouton, 1964; Deal & Kennedy, 1982; Hofstede, Neuijen, Ohayv, & Sanders, 1990; Ott, 1989). Interest in this topic gathered momentum with the intensification of international competition in the late 1970s (see Brannen & Kleinberg, Chapter 24, this volume) and with Hofstede's (1980a) seminal work on national cultures.

How do we isolate the elements of mental programming at one level of collective from those at the other level? Often, the elegance of science lies in parsimony of explanation, and Hofstede's definition of culture provides the means to draw a distinction between organizational and national culture. Societal culture may be seen as the collective programming of the mind with the collective defined as a society, whereas organizational culture may be defined as the collective programming of the mind with the collective in this case being the organization. However, the simplicity of the definition belies the complexity of the constructs; the definition sounds more precise than it is. In a subsequent study, Hofstede et al. (1990) arrived at a distinction by focusing on national culture as values and organizational culture as practices.

House, Wright, and Aditya (1997) adopted a more specific definition of cultures as "distinctive normative systems consisting of modal patterns of shared psychological properties among members of collectivities that result in compelling common affective, attitudinal, and behavioral orientations that are transmitted across generations and that differentiate collectivities from each other" (pp. 539-540). Further, they proposed an experiential definition of culture as "distinctive environments of collectivities about which members share meaning and values" (p. 540), resulting in the modal patterns referred to in the earlier definition. These definitions taken together allow us to distinguish the operational elements of national culture from those of organizational culture by identifying the experiential components, or environmental events, at the organizational and national levels. Ott (1989), after reviewing 38 prominent definitions of organizational culture from various sources, held that organizational culture is "a socially constructed, unseen, and unobservable force behind organizational activities." But perhaps the one depiction of organizational culture that best captures the experiential component mentioned above is Lawson and Shen's (1998) description of the culture of an organization as "the shared and unifying thoughts, feelings, values, and actions of organizational members *in response to organizational issues and challenges*" (p. 42; emphasis added).

Organizational culture clearly revolves around organizational issues and challenges, whereas national culture does not. This suggests to us that the appropriate approach in developing survey questions or other measures regarding organizational culture is to focus on organizational events and values central to and shared by members of an organization, and that the appropriate approach in developing questions about societal culture is to focus on societal events and values central to and shared by members of a society. For example, Cameron and Freeman (1988; cited in Meschi & Roger, 1994), in their typology of organizational culture, focus on such organization-level considerations as participation, teamwork, and sense of family; leader characteristics such as entrepreneurship, facilitative disposition, risk-taking behavior, and innovativeness; bonding factors such as tradition and sense of loyalty; and strategic emphases such as development of human resources, growth, commitment, and long-term stability versus competitive advantage.

As noted above, GLOBE takes this approach of assessing organizational culture using an organizationally focused frame of reference and assessing societal culture using a societally focused frame of reference. In contrast, Hofstede's (1980a) study of national culture used items relevant to the workplace rather than items directly assessing societal phenomena and aggregated these to the societal level.

## DIMENSIONS OF ORGANIZATIONAL CULTURE

There have been several conceptualizations of the dimensions that constitute organizational culture. Ashkanasy, Broadfoot, and Falkus ably review measures based on many of these conceptualizations in Chapter 8 of this volume, so we will not review them here. Instead, we present GLOBE's conceptualization of organizational culture dimensions.

### GLOBE's Organizational Culture Dimensions

GLOBE works from the perspective that societal and organizational cultures can be described using the same dimensions, recognizing that these dimensions can have somewhat different psychological meanings at the different levels of analysis. This approach makes sense when the primary goal is to understand the direct influence of societal-level variables on organizational-level variables, and when one presumes that societal culture will have a main effect on organizational culture—what Lytle, Brett, Barsness, Tinsley, and Janssens (1995) refer to as "Type I hypotheses." This does indeed describe a major goal and assumption of GLOBE.

In doing organizational culture analyses with GLOBE data, however, GLOBE researchers have taken care to demonstrate that factors developed at the societal level, which are then assumed a priori to be meaningful at the organizational level, are in fact conceptually distinct, unidimensional, and meaningful at the organizational level of analysis. It is recognized that the factors GLOBE has used at the organizational level of analysis do not necessarily span the entire constructual domain of organizational culture and that these dimensions are not necessarily those that would emerge from an exploratory factor analysis of the data.

The GLOBE a priori measures of organizational culture have been shown through Q-sort to be conceptually distinct from one another, and through factor analysis have been shown to be unidimensional, although many of them are intercorrelated (Hanges & Dickson, in press). The dimensions and their meanings at the organizational level of analysis are shown in Table 28.1.

### Exploratory Analysis of GLOBE Data

As noted above, the GLOBE organizational culture dimensions were designed to be analogous to societal dimensions of culture, to facilitate investigation of cross-level influences. However, it is possible that a researcher may be more interested in variance that is purely at the organizational level of analysis, and in such a case there is no need to constrain the dimensions of organizational culture to map onto the dimensions of societal culture.

To this end, we have also done exploratory factor analyses of the GLOBE questionnaire items at the organizational level, after first standardizing all items within culture to eliminate linear and nonlinear effects of societal culture. Perhaps not surprisingly, given the intercorrelations between the a priori dimensions described above, we have found a smaller number of factors. However, these factors do conceptually replicate many of the dimensions identified at the societal level. Specifically, the first factor to emerge in these exploratory organization-level analyses would be labeled *organizational collectivism/commitment*; the second, *humane orientation*; the third, *assertiveness*; the fourth, a combination of *uncertainty avoidance* and *future orientation*; the fifth, *gender egalitarianism*; and the sixth and final factor, *individualism/collectivism*. These dimensions show acceptable psychometric properties, and preliminary tests suggest that they relate in meaningful ways to other organizational phenomena, such as leadership styles endorsed by organizational members.

Thus we propose that some of the broad dimensions of culture at the societal level of analysis are in fact meaningful at the organizational level of analysis, even when variance attributable to society is removed. Again, we do *not* argue that these dimensions span the entire constructual domain of organizational culture, but we do find them to be conceptually, theoretically, and empirically meaningful.

## SOURCES OF INFLUENCE ON ORGANIZATIONAL CULTURE

Three sources of influence are widely believed to interact to create organizational culture: the values and beliefs held by the founding leaders of the organization and the organization's subsequent history (e.g., Schein,

1983), the particular characteristics of the industry of which the organization is a part (e.g., Chatman & Jehn, 1994; Deal & Kennedy, 1982), and the broader society in which the organization is located (e.g., Hofstede et al., 1990). Of these three, the first two are more easily discerned.

### Influence of the Organizational Founders and Organizational History

The values and beliefs held by an organization's founders on such broad issues as human nature, attitude toward work, the value of time, and interpersonal relationships influence the culture of the organization through the initial selection of staff and staff members' self-selection out of the organization if they feel they do not "fit," leading to a self-perpetuating sharing of beliefs and values among organizational members (Kristof, 1996; Schneider, 1987; Schneider, Goldstein, & Smith, 1995; Schneider, Smith, Taylor, & Fleenor, 1998). These beliefs and values may be detected in some of the questions asked of job applicants in interviews, in conversations among members, and in the stories, legends, rites, and rituals that attend events in the organization (e.g., Deal & Kennedy, 1982).

A great deal has been written on this topic—indeed, most writings on sources of organizational culture are limited to issues related to organizational founders and history, because most organizational culture analyses examine organizations within a single industry within a single society. In such cases, industry and societal effects are presumed to be affecting the organizations of interest in equivalent ways, and so are essentially ignored.

### Influence of the Industry

The nature of the industry influences organizational culture through the constraints it places on the behavior of all persons in the organization (Gordon, 1991), including founding members (Schein, 1992). Certain organizational practices become necessary for the organization to survive in the industry (e.g., Lawrence & Lorsch, 1967; Burns & Stalker, 1961), and these cannot be ignored even by the founders. These practices are shaped by the economic conditions faced by the industry as well as by the role the industry plays in the national economy. Certain organizational practices may be forged, for instance, by the existence of a strong labor union that enjoys nationwide subscription. These practices, in turn, may determine organizational members' values relating to work, perhaps creating subcultures within the corporation. Their influence, although not as easily detected, will soon become apparent to any newcomer in the process of settling into the work routine.

It is important to note, however, that even in an industry that is common across societies, industry-level constraints and the effects of those constraints may differ widely from society to society. Governmental regulation, development of the industry within a society, status as a national monopoly, and national economic system are just a few of the factors that can affect the ways in which a given industry is enacted in a given society. This was made especially clear to one of us during a summer working in a village on one of the islands in the Caribbean, where the only telephone available in each village was at a central office. Clearly, the telecommunications industry was enacted very differently there relative to the pager- and cellular-phone-infested United States. Of course, the influence that societal culture may exert on economic/industrial variables of a country (e.g., McClelland, 1961) only serves to make the situation more complicated.

## Influence of the Societal Culture

The third source, societal culture, has the least easily discernible influence on the ways things move in organizations nested within that culture. Its link to organizational culture may be, ironically enough, less apparent to a member of the nesting society than to an individual outside it. Indeed, because researchers often examine organizational culture within the context of a single society, they frequently overlook society as a potentially major source of influence on organizational culture because it is not salient to them.

Further, the question of the extent to which societal culture has an impact upon organizational culture is one of considerable debate. The literature addressing this question has been inconclusive, and even within this section of this *Handbook,* the various chapters addressing international issues in organizational culture analysis take different positions with regard to this relationship.

Because national culture is an integral part of the environment in which organizations function, organizational culture by implication should be influenced by the broader societal culture. Lee and Barnett (1997), following earlier theorizing such as that by Emery and Trist (1965), view organizations as "open systems influenced by the environment" (p. 398). They operationalized organizational culture in terms of perceived distances between pairs of concepts such as happiness, seniority, success, the self, one's job, supervisor, money, and the names of the countries. They observed significant differences between organizational cultures of a Taiwanese, a Japanese, and an American bank located in their respective countries, but found little difference between the Taiwanese bank and an American bank located in Taiwan. These findings highlight the influence of national culture, more than that of leaders' values, in determining organizational culture. Additionally, Meschi and Roger (1994) report a strong linear relationship between perceived distance separating national cultures and that separating organizational cultures ($r = .71$).

GLOBE's own analyses provide some support for this perspective as well—although with some clarifications. Using GLOBE's societal culture scales to predict the analogous organizational culture scales (e.g., societal uncertainty avoidance predicting organizational uncertainty avoidance), we find that *values* shared at the societal level account for as much as 50% of the variance in values shared at the organizational level. However, values shared at the societal level typically account for very little of the variance (5-10%) in organizational *practices,* presumably because organizational practices are constrained by so many other things, including industry-level demands (Hanges & House, 1998).

Additionally, the same societal values can lead to different practices at the organizational level, as in the case when a high level of uncertainty avoidance in one society leads organization members to adopt many strict policies, whereas a high level of uncertainty avoidance in another society leads organization members to develop very few policies, but rather to meet and discuss each situation at length to come to clear consensus as to what to do. This would, of course, lead to a reduced level of variance explained when cross-cultural analysis is employed, because the meaning of the dependent variable changes from condition to condition.

A further difficulty in determining the extent to which societal culture will influence the organizational culture of organizations within a given society is the fact that researchers have typically assumed (and thus looked for) direct linear relationships between the two constructs. We propose, however, that the influence of national culture on organizational culture is not uniform across dimensions or across societies. Rather, for dimensions of societal culture for which members of a given society are in strong agreement, there is likely to be little variation at the organizational level of analysis *within that culture* on related organization-level dimensions. However, members of a different society, when asked about the same dimension of societal culture, may show significantly less agreement regarding the appropriate level of that dimension, and thus one may expect significantly greater variation at the organizational level of analysis on related dimensions of organizational culture, compared to the first case.

Indeed, our preliminary analyses of data from the GLOBE Project provide evidence for this assertion. We find that measures of societal-level agreement (specifically, $r_{wg}$; James, Demaree, & Wolf, 1984, 1993) correlate negatively with within-society between-organization standard deviation for items with absolute anchors (e.g., "20%," "once a week"), with an average correlation of approximately $-.25$. This suggests that the higher the level of agreement on the appropriate level of a dimension of societal culture within a given society, the less the variation between organizations on the analogous organization-level dimension. (This finding does not hold with items using relative anchors, e.g., "to a great extent"; we explain this pattern of responses below, in discussing "frame-of-reference effects.")

Thus analyses predicting organization-level values from societal values would lead us to conclude that societal culture has a significant direct effect on organizational culture, accounting for as much as 50% of the organizational variance. On the other hand, analyses predicting organization-level practices from societal values would lead us to conclude that societal culture has a very small direct effect on organizational culture, accounting for as little as 5% of the organizational variance. In other words, the strength of the direct effect of societal culture on organizational culture appears to us to be largely determined by the process through which items are constructed, how culture is defined and operationalized at each level of analysis, and how the analyses are done. Changes in any one of these can lead to significantly different results, and the current lack of consistency in the literature on this issue is thus understandable.

## ISSUES TO CONSIDER IN CROSS-NATIONAL STUDIES OF ORGANIZATIONAL CULTURE

Having discussed several different approaches to organizational culture, and the various sources of influence on organizational culture, we are now faced with the most perplexing of our problems: how to compare organizational culture dimension scores for organizations from different societal cultures. Practically speaking, the question is, Can we make sense of organizational culture data from organizations in different countries?

Addressing this question reminds us of the well-known blind-men-and-elephant problem described by Hofstede, Bond, and Luk (1993), only with several more complications thrown in. In this case, there are two types of elephants, representing societal and organizational cultures. Further, the relationship between the two types of elephants is of interest. Moreover, data on the elephants have been collected from several groups of blind men, the groups representing countries in this case. Additionally, the equivalence of calibration between groups of blind men (i.e., respondents from different countries) is not known. Under these circumstances, a number of considerations become critical in any attempt to interpret the data.

## Frame-of-Reference Effects

Respondents on organizational culture measures tend to make their ratings against the backdrop of other organizations within their own countries. The idea is not new— Katz and Kahn (1966), for instance, have suggested that people within an organization develop systems by which they filter outside information, which leads them to be most attuned to events that occur and data generated within the boundaries of their system (pp. 60-61). Thus, for example, an English electrical engineer is likely to compare her workplace with other workplaces employing electrical engineers in Great Britain, rather than with organizations in Saudi Arabia or Canada. This will be especially true for employees who do not work for multinational corporations.

Further, when responding to scale items with relative anchors (e.g., *to a greater degree* or *more future oriented than most*), respondents will use organizations within their own societies as their high-end and low-end comparators and will respond accordingly. For example, an organization perceived by its members as being much more future oriented than most other organizations *within its society* will be rated by its members as quite high on a future-orientation scale, even though that organization may be less future oriented than the vast majority of other organizations in the world. This is because organization members do not consider organizations in other countries as comparators when they make their evaluations about their own organizations.

Even where respondents are familiar with organizations in other cultures, perceived similarity of organizations within the national borders may influence the choice of comparators (Adams, 1965; Festinger, 1954). This suggests a need to "align" organizational scores across societies before meaningful comparisons can be made. In other words, we argue that interpreting raw scale scores of organizations from different societal cultures can lead to significant errors of interpretation, and that standardization of organizational scores within country is one means of providing this "alignment." (For examples of this approach, see Bajdo & Dickson, 1999; Dickson, 1998.)

## Culture-Based Response Biases

Culture, being a construct deeply embedded at multiple levels of a society, often strongly influences how subjects respond to research instruments. The most common research instrument in cross-cultural research has been the questionnaire, and it is likely to continue to be used extensively (Bhagat, Kedia, Crawford, & Kaplan, 1990; Peng, Peterson, & Shyi, 1991). People respond to questionnaires on the basis of their response sets. In cross-cultural organizational culture research, therefore, some problems arise because societal cultures often differ in their response sets on the basis of which people respond to questionnaires (Hui & Triandis, 1989; Triandis, 1994). This results in a number of response biases that are culturally based. For example, two organizations from different cultures may show similar scores and yet be different from each other, or show different scores and yet be similar to each other, because of society-level response sets. Further, when industry-level effects are examined cross-culturally, differences in enactment of the industry between cultures and differences in culture-based response sets will be difficult to tease apart.

The well-known response bias of social desirability also plays a role in cross-cultural organizational culture research, only here the issue is compounded by the fact that what is socially desirable in one culture may not be so in another. For example, d'Iribarne (1997) mentions the U.S. model of "fair contract," the French "logic of honor," and the Dutch "consensus," which guide organizational functioning in these three countries, thus influencing what is considered socially desirable. Organizational members' responses to organizational culture items will be conditioned by such influences, rendering direct comparisons of organizational culture scores from these three countries erroneous.

Another culture-based response bias arises from differing use of the response format or scale. This can take varied forms, such as the excessive use of the end points of the scale, called extreme response set bias (Hui & Triandis, 1989), and the failure to use the extreme ends. Although the latter is often considered to be associated with Eastern cultures, Stening and Everett (1984) found differences even within Asian cultures, with the Japanese most likely and the Thai least likely to give midpoint responses. Varying response patterns can sometimes result from respondents' lack of familiarity with graded response formats. This could explain why Adler, Campbell, and Laurent (1989) found that more than 50% of their respondents from the People's Republic of China chose entirely bimodal answers on the 5-point Likert scale. Lack of consistency in the use of the scale across countries also creates problems in direct comparison of organizational culture scores across countries.

## Society-Level Agreement and Organization-Level Variability

Culture-based response sets and frame-of-reference effects are not the only difficulties with direct comparison of organizational culture scores for organizations from different countries. An additional difficulty arises from the fact that the within-country between-organization variance on any given organizational culture dimension may vary significantly across countries, according to the degree to which the members of the society are in agreement about the appropriate level of analogous society-level dimensions. Thus, for a societal culture dimension on which society members are in strong agreement, the true range within which organizations vary on a given dimension may be quite small, although organizational respondents may show significant variability in their organizational culture responses.

This discrepancy occurs because minute differences in expression of a deeply embedded concept may be quite noticeable to respondents, given that the concept is highly agreed upon within the society, thus leading to a small "just noticeable difference." Alternately, on the same dimension of societal culture but in a country where there is less agreement about the dimension, there may be significant absolute variation on analogous organizational culture dimensions, and organizational respondents may still report significant relative variability in their organizational culture responses. In this case, minute differences in the enactment of the concept may be less noticeable to respondents because the appropriate level of the concept is not highly agreed upon within the society.

The end result is that in both cases there is likely to be variability in organizations' descriptions of their own cultures. The meanings of these reports are different, however, and one cannot understand and interpret them without understanding the degree to which the society is in agreement about the appropriate level of the construct in question.

Variability in the data should be examined at both societal and organizational levels. Especially when societal and organizational culture items are constructed in parallel, as in the GLOBE study, responses to societal culture items may exhibit low variability whereas organizational culture items show high variability across cultures. This is likely to occur in "entrenched" value systems, or when there are highly agreed-upon societal values at extreme ends of a dimension. Such entrenched values sensitize respondents to minute deviations from the societal norm, hence the variability in analogous organizational culture responses.

On the other hand, sometimes a dimension may actually be less *salient* for respondents in countries where the values on that dimension are more deeply entrenched—Schein (1992) and Lord and Maher (1991) both note that some values and beliefs are so deeply held that people are not aware of the fact that they hold those values and beliefs. Such beliefs are seen simply as reflecting "the way the world is" rather than as values on which individuals may differ. (Values that are consciously chosen and adopted, however, are likely to be quite salient.) The end result of this is that organization scores from two such countries may appear to be similar in their distributions when in fact the underlying reasons for the distributions may be quite different.

### Scale Equivalence in Items

The overall cultural context tends to have significant influence on responses to the same item in different cultures. For instance, taking the expression "to break a rule" as an example based on an ethnographic study of metallurgical factories in three countries,

d'Iribarne (1997) observes, "It is not unreasonable to assume that, whereas an American will tend to speak of 'breaking a rule,' a Frenchman might tend to speak rather of 'interpreting the spirit of the rule intelligently'" (p. 44). The difference in scores between French and U.S. respondents on a question relating to rules, therefore, may not necessarily mean significantly different levels of formalization in their organizations. Statistical processes exist for evaluating different types of equivalence for both constructs and measures (Brett, Tinsley, Janssens, Barsness, & Lytle, 1997; Hulin, 1987; Peng et al., 1991). Equivalence can often be improved through the deletion of problematic items identified in factor comparisons. Caution, however, is necessary to ensure that such deletion does not (a) render the resulting scale unusable or (b) lose some key concepts from the instrument.

### Summary of Problems

We have identified several major roadblocks in the direct comparison of organizational culture dimension scores for organizations from different societal cultures, including the problem of the comparator, culture-based response biases, the problem of level of societal agreement on related dimensions, and scale equivalence in items. Each of these serves to prevent meaningful interpretation of raw organizational culture dimension scores cross-culturally. We next turn to some useful and not-so-useful statistical approaches to this type of data.

## METHODOLOGICAL CONSIDERATIONS

The issues discussed above raise several methodological considerations that researchers must address in attempting to understand organizational cultures in cross-national context. In this section we briefly describe several of these considerations.

## Factor Analysis

If researchers exercise sufficient care concerning the aspects listed above, then the data are more likely to lend themselves to answering a number of research questions. Currently, our understanding of organizational culture on a global scale is still at a nascent stage, and thus an initial objective might be to unearth universal dimensions of organizational culture. Under these circumstances, factor analysis can be meaningfully applied at various levels of analysis and the findings taken together for a better understanding of organizational culture. There exists extensive documentation of the theoretical and practical considerations involved (e.g., Chinese Culture Connection, 1987; Hofstede, 1980a; Hofstede et al., 1993; Leung & Bond, 1989), and we will not elaborate on them here, except to note the additional consideration of industry as a level of analysis. If data are obtained across several industries, then the influence of industry must be weeded out also, along with the influence of the societal culture. The same overall philosophy and procedure apply in this case: Factor analyses within industry are called for, and industry scores may also have to be taken into account in the overall exploratory factor analysis. Of course, to apply these procedures, researchers need multiple organizations in the sample from each industry.

## Sample Sizes

There are several approaches that can be used in the analysis of cross-cultural organizational culture data, including the multiple-relationships analysis component of within-and-between analysis (Dansereau et al., 1986; see also Dansereau & Alutto, 1990, for an example of this in their discussion of psychological and organizational climate) and

hierarchical linear modeling (Bryk & Raudenbush, 1992). However, each of these approaches requires several cases from each hypothesized nested level. In other words, a researcher who is truly interested in understanding organizational culture in a cross-cultural context would have to have data from several cultures, data from several industries within each culture, data from several organizations within each industry, and data from several individuals within each organization. Such data sets are extremely difficult and time-consuming to gather, making individual research efforts very difficult. Without such data sets, however, interpretation of the source of variation is ambiguous at best—variation that appears to represent organizational culture could in fact be due to differences in societal cultures, differences in industries as they are enacted in different societies, or other sources of variation. Thus researchers should not attempt cross-cultural organizational culture analysis, in our opinion, unless they can secure in advance significant resources, time, and access to necessary data. This is one of the reasons we advocate the large research team approach for this type of research.

## Level of Analysis and Unit of Analysis

Level of analysis and unit of analysis errors are all too common in the study of multilevel phenomena (Klein, Dansereau, & Hall, 1994). (The level of theory problem is a related but separate, and equally important, issue about which researchers must be clear to avoid significant errors of interpretation; see Brett et al., 1997.) In the "figure-ground" terminology of the study of perception, the appropriate unit of analysis becomes the figure and all the other levels of analysis become the background. When the purpose of analysis is to understand organizational culture across different countries, the researcher must be extremely alert to and control for the effects of other levels, such as societal culture and industry. This alertness needs to inform all of the researchers' decisions, including choice of instruments, if existing instruments are to be used. If new instruments are developed, the desired units of analysis should guide decisions at every stage, including item generation, response format, and the wording of items. In the case of organizational culture, the researcher should recognize the influence of both industry and societal cultures in constructing items. Further, simple aggregation of individual scores to the organizational or societal level is not meaningful (Sego, Hui, & Law, 1997) unless items have been constructed specifically for that level.

## TOWARD A BETTER UNDERSTANDING OF CROSS-CULTURAL ORGANIZATIONAL CULTURE: LESSONS FROM GLOBE

The GLOBE study, as detailed earlier, has taken a fresh perspective on the study and operationalization of organizational culture. GLOBE attempted to operationalize organizational culture by mapping theoretically established dimensions of societal culture. This approach has both strengths and weaknesses, and both are instructive about organizational culture in a cross-national context in their own ways. We present our major observations below.

### Practices Versus Values

One useful contribution of the GLOBE study is the operationalization of culture items through both practices and values. The data show that practices and values responses on the organizational culture items differ. This might be predicted from previous research. Hofstede and his associates (1990) had surmised from their study that national

culture is represented by values and organizational culture by practices. However, the GLOBE data reveal that the issue may not be as simple as that: Although differences between values and practices are observed across levels (organizational and societal), there is no consistent correspondence across dimensions between organizational and societal levels in the responses to values or practices items. These findings support the GLOBE perspective on culture, which includes both practices and values at any given level of analysis.

### Society and Industry Influences

To interpret cross-cultural organizational culture analyses accurately, one must understand both absolute and relative aspects of organizational functioning. For instance, for organization A, "long-range planning" may mean the development of a 2-year plan, whereas for organization B it may refer to a 10-year plan. These absolute differences are important for predicting and understanding conflict between organizations and which organizations are likely to integrate well with each other. However, whether an organization will see 2-year plans or 10-year plans as "long-term" is a function not only of organizational culture, but of industrial characteristics as well. For instance, power utilities have to plan 10 years ahead at the very least—for them, "long-range" may mean two or more decades. In contrast, 2 years would be a very long time for the computer industry, and 20 years in that industry is much too far in the future to plan with any degree of certainty.

The above case may be seen as an example of industry influence on organizational culture, and should be distinguished from the frame-of-reference effects discussed as an artifact earlier. The issue is how to extract this effect appropriately from the data. The problem is analogous to the acquiescence bias discussed by Hofstede (1980a, pp. 77-80), only in this case we do not want to rid the data of the influence of industry; rather, we study it as an influence on organizational culture. The methods of standardization suggested by Hofstede (1980a) and others are not appropriate to handle this problem. For these reasons, we cannot pool organizational culture data across societies statistically, even in an exploratory factor analysis procedure, unless we can make a reasonable assumption of invariance of reference frames in item responses across cultures. The solution, as we see it in retrospect, is in prevention rather than cure—it lies in the item construction stage. Questions intended for direct cross-cultural comparison should be constructed with rating scale anchors that are objectively defined (e.g., *four times a week* instead of *very frequently*). Separate items will be needed to address the issue of what, in the example above, constitutes "long-range planning" for the organization.

On the other hand, it is also important to know how an organization is perceived as ranking relative to other organizations in the same country. For instance, suppose that the organizations in cultures X and Y both scored the same moderately low score on uncertainty avoidance. One may conclude that these two companies are relatively low on their risk-taking propensity. However, it may turn out that the company in culture X is very high in risk taking *relative to other organizations in its own culture,* whereas the company in culture Y is very low in risk taking relative to other organizations in *its* culture. Thus company X is likely to face problems securing bank loans within its country, whereas company Y will probably breeze through. Researchers, of course, have no means of understanding such differences unless they look at *within-culture* standings of the organizations.

### Banding Versus Mean Scores and Rankings

A common fallacy in cross-cultural research involves the treatment of mean scores as representing an absolute value on a dimension or attribute, when only the relative positions of observations can be meaningfully interpreted. Even a ranking can prove tricky for interpretation when there is little variation in country mean scores. In GLOBE, a statistical "banding" procedure has been borrowed from the personnel selection literature to differentiate countries from each other on dimensions of societal culture. To construct a band, one determines how large a difference must be to be statistically significant and then calculates a range from the top score. Thus countries falling within that band are not statistically different from the top score, but the first country outside of the band *is* statistically significantly different from the top score. This procedure, although not perfect, does at least provide some basic understanding of how much of a difference in mean scores is necessary to be meaningful. (For a more detailed description of the banding process, see Cascio, Outtz, Zedeck, & Goldstein, 1991.)

This same procedure can be applied to organization scores (assuming a sufficient number of organizations), with the added benefit that it enables the researcher to determine if organizations from one country cluster together within a single band (as might be expected for deeply embedded concepts) or range across several bands.

### Use of Qualitative Measures to Confirm Construct Meanings

As we have noted, similar values can lead to different organizational practices, and the same construct can have different meanings in different cultures. Standardized questionnaires are not likely to uncover these phenomena, regardless of how well they are constructed. GLOBE has also developed and collected data using unobtrusive measures, media analysis, participant observation, and other methodologies (analyses on these measures is currently under way). Such a multiple-measures approach is critical to our gaining a thorough understanding of organizational culture in a cross-cultural context. Questionnaires by themselves provide useful information, but they are subject to the wide range of flaws and errors of interpretation already listed. For these reasons, other types of measures, especially more qualitative measures such as media analysis, unobtrusive measures, and interviews, will be invaluable for identifying differences in origins of practices and in meanings of constructs. (For details on GLOBE's unobtrusive measures, see House et al., 1999.)

## Corrections for Response Biases: A Cautionary Note

As noted above, the difference between some Eastern and Western cultures in the tendency to utilize the extreme points of rating scales has been documented in the literature. This issue should be examined in any cross-cultural data; usually it will reflect in a consistent difference in variance across all items in a questionnaire. Triandis (1994) has developed a technique for correcting for response biases by standardizing each individual's responses on *all* items, but GLOBE analyses suggest that results from data thus corrected correlate highly ($r > .90$) with results from uncorrected items (Hanges & Dickson, in press). Thus GLOBE's results suggest that cultural response sets may not be as serious a problem as others have suggested, although there is evidence to the contrary from other research (alluded to above). Exploration with newer approaches, such as item response theory, and with innovative combinations of existing approaches such as item analysis, LISREL, and multidimensional scaling is likely to help in resolving this difficult issue. (For an example of such an attempt, see Peterson, Smith, & Tayeb, 1993.)

Understanding differences among the cultures of organizations from different societies is a difficult undertaking, as we have learned at GLOBE. It requires recognition of the differential influences on organizations

of societal culture, of the industry nested within societies, and of the history, structure, leadership, and other aspects of organizations. It is clearly a more complex undertaking than the analysis of cultural differences at the societal level, and the wealth of literature on that topic shows how difficult that task has proven over the years.

We conclude by listing for researchers in this area a number of basic questions they might ask themselves before embarking on a study. Their answers could save them a great deal of effort later on and could make a difference in whether their results are interpretable or hopelessly confounded.

- What phenomena are you interested in? Are you interested only in organization-level differences, or are you interested in differences among organizations in different countries that are attributable to societal culture? Your choice will determine how you approach the data, whether you eliminate society-level variance or focus on it, whether you control for industry effects or attend to them, and how you describe what you find.

- Do you have measures available that have already been validated and for which norms are available for the societies in which you have gathered organizational culture data? If so, you will be able to make some comparisons between your findings and the norms of the society. If not, you may need to collect enough data to be able to determine norms.

- Which society-level dimensions are likely to be related (or, in the case of GLOBE data, are analogous) to the organizational culture dimensions of interest? Determine if such data as means and degree of agreement within the society about the appropriate level of the dimension are available.

- Are you interested in organizational practices, values, or both? GLOBE data suggest that societal values are strongly related to organizational values, but not so strongly related to organizational practices.

- Are you bound to a single method? Because any single method is subject to biases, multiple methods are useful. Indeed, monomethod research may suggest linear relationships among variables where multimethod research reveals nonlinear relationships (Baltes et al., 1999). It is thus a good idea to team up with experts in different methodologies of data collection as well as analysis. Triangulation is especially important in this area.

- Do you have firsthand knowledge and experience with at least several of the cultures from which you are gathering data? In GLOBE we have had the advantage of a cooperative enterprise. Others before GLOBE have also realized the fruits of cross-cultural cooperation (e.g., Chinese Culture Connection, 1987; Peterson et al., 1995), whereas some of the cross-cultural research efforts of researchers from single cultures have encountered difficulties of interpretation. (For a discussion of the importance of cross-cultural research teams, see Graen, Hui, Wakabayashi, & Wang, 1997.)

Having worked with the GLOBE Project for more than 5 years, and having tried to condense what we have learned about cross-cultural organizational culture analysis into a few pages, we conclude that to understand organizational culture cross-culturally, we may need to move beyond the data-analytic techniques with which people are most familiar and comfortable. We will need to employ quantitatively complex analytic processes such as confirmatory multilevel hierarchical linear modeling (e.g., Hanges & House, 1998), but these will provide only part of the answer. We need to use multiple measures from multiple perspectives to assess both absolute and relative standings on dimensions. We need to employ qualitative methodologies to gain an understanding of the variations in meanings that exist across societies. In our experience, no one person is likely to have all of the skills necessary to acquire a full understanding of organizational culture in a cross-cultural context. We have seen the large research team model work in GLOBE, and we encourage others to develop similar collaborative teams as we wrestle with this complex issue.

# 29

## Culture in Uniformed Organizations

_-- Joseph L. Soeters_

Although many organizations require their employees to wear company clothing, most of these are not known as _uniformed organizations_. Not even hospitals, with their prescribed clothing for all work situations, are known as such. The label seems to apply only to organizations that represent state authority: the military, the police, fire departments, and various hybrid organizations such as coast guards, forest services, and gendarmerie. In these organizations uniforms are symbols of the organizational culture (see Rafaeli & Worline, Chapter 4, this volume).

The uniforms that the men and women of these organizations wear signify something that is highly unique to the public and their colleagues. To the general public, the uniform indicates state authority, which encompasses the power to forbid, to instruct, to authorize, and to punish people. To colleagues, the uniform signifies hierarchical importance, specific qualifications, and sometimes special achievements of the wearer. In uniformed organizations one simply has to look at the shoulder or the collar of a person in order to know how to approach him or her (Heffron, 1989). Uniforms are a highly specific form of organizational dress that demonstrates both organizational uniqueness and stratification within the organization (Rafaeli & Pratt, 1993).

Uniformed organizations are peculiar. They represent specific occupational cultures

AUTHOR'S NOTE: During the preparation of this chapter I profited from discussions with Professor van Rheenen (University of Utrecht) and Police Commissioner Broer, who introduced me to the latest developments in policing. Aart Bontekoning of the Dutch Fire Department Academy revealed some of the cultural secrets of firefighting brigades. Charles Moskos (Evanston, Illinois) and Cornelius Lammers (University of Leiden)—fellow sociologists with an interest in military affairs—commented on a previous draft. Charles's son, Peter Moskos, a Harvard student of police affairs, and Richard Bullis of the U.S. Center of Army Leadership made some additional remarks. Ricardo Recht helped to polish my English and provided some relevant references, as did Lieutenant Colonel Eric Linssen and Jack Rovers. On behalf of the editorial board, Mark Peterson made critical but stimulating comments.

that are relatively isolated from society, although the extent of isolation varies depending on national cultural characteristics. Higher-ranking personnel in these organizations, for instance, are normally trained and educated in specific institutions, usually called (military, police, fireguard) academies. Although there is a tendency in many countries to have officer candidates come from civilian universities, these candidates undergo an additional (military, police, fireguard) training program in special institutes, such as the aforementioned academies. Apparently, civilian schools and universities do not fully qualify for the education and training of the future leaders of uniformed organizations.

Uniformed organizations share some basic characteristics that distinguish them from other organizations. They are "greedy institutions" because they require a lot from their employees: During active duty, personnel are on permanent, 24-hour call with rather idiosyncratic working shifts; their leave is subject to cancellation (Druckman, Singer, & van Cott, 1997). The jobs in these organizations may be dangerous and potentially life threatening. For this reason, the employees of uniformed organizations are usually armed or at least equipped with protective instruments and materials. If necessary, the employees can make use of legitimated violence (Hunt, 1985/1995). Uniformed organizations, furthermore, require their employees to perform their duties without making any non-work-related distinctions among (groups of) people. Hence these employees have to be fundamentally nondiscriminatory in their organizational behavior. Finally, these organizations are state funded (i.e., noncommercial) because they fulfill the state's core tasks, the risks of which are not likely to be insured by or delegated to private companies (Wilson, 1989).

All of these peculiarities justify the special attention of researchers to the culture and identity of these specific organizations. But there is an even more fundamental reason to pay attention to these specific organizations: Uniformed organizations may influence the political order of societies. The 1981 attack by a few Guardia Civil officers on the Spanish parliament was the last incident in this respect to occur up to now in Western Europe, but in many other parts of the world such threats are still present. The political developments in Indonesia and Nigeria in 1998 underline the impacts that police and military forces may have on political situations. This reason alone vindicates the expenditure of special attention on uniformed organizations.

In this chapter, I aim to deal with the world of uniformed organizations. In doing so, I focus on a specific occupational culture that is a cultural level between organizational culture and national culture (Hofstede, 1991, p. 182). There is no such thing as one single occupational culture of uniformed organizations. I will show that the cultures of uniformed organizations vary from country to country; hence I will address the levels of both occupational culture and national culture. I will also acknowledge the multiple cultures that occur in the various types of uniformed organizations, such as the police, the military, and fire departments.

Not to complicate matters, but to enhance our understanding of uniformed organizations, I will also make a distinction between the two sides of these organizations, which I will describe as Janusian (from the two faces of the Roman god Janus; Hunt & Phillips, 1991). This is the distinction between the world of the street cop and the world of the police manager, the distinction between the soldier on the battlefield and the soldier in garrison, and the distinction between the organization of firefighters suppressing a fire and the organization of the fire squad waiting and preparing for an alarm. Uniformed organizations are really two-sided: They have one side for prevention, facilitation, and preparation, and one side for the real action. Finally, I will address the question of how an individual becomes a "uniformed" person, and then close the chapter with a sketch of avenues for further research.

## CULTURE IN UNIFORMED ORGANIZATIONS

Among uniformed organizations, military organizations, as some of the oldest and traditionally most prominent examples of formal organization, have attracted considerable attention from social scientists. In an extensive review, Lang (1965) points to various specific aspects of military organizations that seem to apply to other uniformed organizations as well (see also van Doorn, 1975; Wilson, 1968). First, there is the "communal" character of life in uniform. This specific character relates to the degree to which the control of the organization extends to various aspects and stages of personal life, much more than in ordinary organizations. Second, there is a heavy emphasis in military and other uniformed organizations on hierarchy, which may even lead to a certain authoritarian ideology. And third, but closely corresponding to the second point, there is a chain of command postulating a downward flow of directives. This chain of command simply aims at the execution of orders, hence introducing discipline and control.

These features of military life seem to apply to all uniformed organizations' cultures, obviously in varying degrees and forms. In the following subsections I address each of these three features in turn, distinguishing uniformed organizations from other organizations. In each discussion I will account for national variations and differences among the various types of uniformed organizations.

### Communal Life

In connection to Lang's (1965) first observation as to the communal character of military life, the so-called institutional/occupational distinction has become an important model in military sociology (Moskos & Wood, 1988). This model discerns between two extremes with regard to the normative orientation of employees working in the military. On one side, the employees are fully oriented toward the military institution (or military organization). If this institutional orientation dominates, such matters as leisure time, family matters, living conditions, (high) salary, and career prospects on the external labor market are relatively insignificant. The only thing that matters in life is the military and the values for which the military stands: the nation or constitution, the king or queen. In this situation, military life and personal life tend to overlap, transforming the job into a part of communal life. If the occupational orientation prevails, however, neither military personnel nor their families will focus all their attention solely on military life and the military labor market. On the contrary, they will aim to live outside of the direct military environment, they will strive for market wages, and they will prefer to acquire educational qualifications that can also be utilized outside the internal military labor market. In this case, working in the military is "just another job" (Moskos & Wood, 1988).

In a comparative Hofstede-based study among military academies in 18 (mostly Western) countries, it was found that military cultures differ substantially in this respect (Soeters, 1997; Soeters & Recht, 1998). The cultures in the armed forces in countries such as Belgium, Italy, and Germany, but to a lesser degree also in the Netherlands, France, and Spain, appeared to be rather institution oriented, which implies that military personnel are less inclined toward private life and material gains. Military officers in these countries normally stay within the military during their whole working lives, periods of up to 40 years. This is what the student-officers have in mind when starting their careers at the age of 20 or younger. Obviously, military existence in these armed forces (at least for the officers) is something more than "just another job"; it certainly tends to be something like a communal life.

However, in countries such as Denmark, Norway, the United States, and Canada, officers are more inclined to value leisure time, an attractive living environment, high salaries, and promotion opportunities. In their view, military life certainly is not something that stands out above everything else in importance. In the United States and Canada, this may be related to the fact that student-officers in these countries generally embark on 20-year careers (Druckman et al., 1997). This situation provides them with the opportunity (and sometimes makes it necessary) to be and remain oriented toward careers in the civilian sector. Hence the differences between the two groups of countries.

In general, however—and this may be an even more important result—military cultures were found to be far more institutional when compared with business organizations' cultures (Soeters, 1997). In this respect, there appears to be something like an overarching international and homogeneous military culture. Business organizations' cultures tend to emphasize leisure time, private life, and performance-based material gains. Military cultures, on the contrary, are indeed more "greedy" and institutional, requiring commitment from their personnel 24 hours a day and offering fixed pay structures only. Given these differences, it may come as no surprise that organizational conflict in the peacekeeping force sent to Cyprus was found between military personnel and civilians and not among the different national military contingents (Moskos, 1976).

More or less the same cultural characteristic has been observed in police organizations. Hofstede, Neuijen, Ohayv, and Sanders (1990) found organizational cultures in Dutch police organizations to be relatively more parochial (or local) compared to more professional (or cosmopolitan) business organizations. With this distinction, they showed that members of police forces feel the organization's norms cover their behavior at home as well as on the job. Apparently, there is no sharp division between work life and private life in police organizations, although there may be national variations in this respect.[1] In addition, police employees feel that in hiring, police organizations take applicants' social and family backgrounds into account as much as their job competence (it helps to have a father who is a police officer). Finally, employees in these organizations do not look far into the future, probably assuming that their organizations will do that for them (see also Hofstede, 1991, pp. 190-191). Even more explicitly, traditional police force members see themselves as cops for the rest of their careers (Reuss-Ianni & Ianni, 1983, p. 270). All these features indicate that police and military employees share more or less the same communal (i.e., institutional or parochial) orientation toward working life.

## Hierarchy

Lang's (1965) second observation, dealing with hierarchy, can be related to the bureaucratic character of military life. As James Wilson (1989, pp. 163-164) has pointed out, uniformed organizations—at least during peacetime conditions—are bureaucracies "par excellence." However, there may be variations. Mintzberg (1979) has distinguished between machine and professional bureaucracies. Machine bureaucracies (e.g., McDonald's-like service organizations, social security agencies, Ford-like production plants) have steep hierarchies as well as elaborated sets of rules and regulations formulated by specialists and imposed on the rest of the organization by the managing elite. Professional bureaucracies, such as hospitals and schools, on the other hand, rely more on the specialized knowledge of the operating core; this specialized operating core consists of educated professionals whose activities are embedded in a more general bureaucratic framework and are steered by a small hierarchy of (professional) leaders only.

In a similar vein, Adler and Borys (1996) make an interesting distinction between "coercive" and "enabling" bureaucracies. Whereas coercive logic leads to the machine form of bureaucracies, enabling logic provides employees with frames of reference— that is, contextual information designed to help employees do their jobs more effectively and to reinforce their commitment. In the enabling bureaucracy, procedures are designed to afford employees an understanding of where their own tasks fit into the whole. Hierarchies and rules exist in both types of bureaucracies, but in the coercive form "bad," noncontributing rules dominate, whereas in the enabling bureaucracy "good" rules—that is, rules that are taken for granted and are rarely noticed—are predominant (Perrow, 1986). Coercive logic is often considered to be an inevitable, even necessary, evil. This is especially advocated in organizations where (a) a high degree of asymmetry of power exists between managers and employees and (b) on an everyday basis no or only few "reality checks" are provided by external influences (Adler & Borys, 1996, pp. 82-83).

With this in mind, it may come as no surprise that military cultures are more coercive than the cultures of business organizations. This has been shown in a comparative study among military academies (Soeters, 1997; Soeters & Recht, 1998). The level of power distance (i.e., hierarchy) in military academies is much larger than that in the business sector. The same applies, although somewhat less clearly, to the degree of rule orientation in the military. This result is hardly surprising given that military organizations traditionally have a strong social order ("grid") based on vertical, power-related classifications and regulations (Douglas, 1973). In addition, military organizations do not frequently face reality checks that would urge them to make changes.

Concerning country differences among military organizations, the coercive orientation is fairly strong in Latin countries such as Belgium, France, Italy, Spain, and Brazil, but the exact opposite of this Latin cluster is to be found in two countries where the level of power distance and the degree of rule orientation are relatively small: Norway and Canada. The military cultures in these countries are clearly more "enabling." In these countries people are enabled by the organizations' rules and hierarchies to do their jobs properly.

What is true of the military seems to apply to the police as well. Although police forces face far more reality checks in their everyday operations than do military organizations— hence making the police culture in principle more enabling than military culture—there are ingrained national differences in the police sector as well. A limited comparative study among police forces in three countries—the Netherlands, Belgium, and Germany—has made this perfectly clear (Soeters, Hofstede, & van Twuyver, 1995). All the police forces showed cultural characteristics— or policing "styles," as Wilson (1968) would put it—that reflect the specific features of their national cultures.

In Belgium, the police organization is a vertical pyramid, with large power distances between the various layers leading to fairly opaque behavior of the organizational elite; consequently, distrust between the public and the police organization is rather normal in Belgium. In Germany, a strong emphasis is put on a machinelike compliance with the rules and procedurally correct behavior based on technical and legal competence (so-called *Legalitätsprinzip*). In the Netherlands, the police culture is nonconfrontational and strongly directed toward helping people (see also van Rheenen, 1997). In addition, the Dutch police culture is oriented toward the achievement of consensus among police employees, and it allows for a somewhat loose or relaxed performance during duty—here, rules provide only frames of reference, certainly not deterministic instructions as to what to do.

On the basis of all these results, one can observe various expressions of the coercive versus enabling bureaucratic dimension in both the military and the police.

## Discipline

Lang's (1965) third and final observation concerns discipline, which is the extent of compliance with rules, the acceptance of orders and authority, and the way the organization deals with disobedience through overt punishment (Shalit, 1988). Obviously, this relates to the characteristic of hierarchy and may even be considered as an extension of it. Organizations may differ as to the amount and character of the discipline they impose on employees. These differences can be related to formal or ceremonial discipline (e.g., salutes, outward appearance, uniform) and to functional discipline (e.g., acting in accordance with the rules and the commander's intentions). Functional discipline is intended as a specific means of enabling employees to perform better in certain specific circumstances. Formal discipline can be looked upon as an aim in itself, a generalized behavioral pattern that can be considered appropriate to a wide range of situations (Shalit, 1988, pp. 122-126).

In the previously mentioned survey among military academies (Soeters & Recht, 1998), it became clear that student-officers in Western European countries such as Germany, the Netherlands, Belgium, Sweden, Denmark, and Norway attached below-average importance to most aspects of military discipline. In only a few, exceptional cases did the student-officers in these countries ascribe a great deal of importance to certain aspects of discipline, and these virtually never concerned formal or ceremonial discipline. Dutch cadets, for instance, considered the uniform, salutes, polished shoes, and so forth less important than did virtually all other foreign cadets. In this they closely resemble their compatriots in the police (Soeters et al., 1995).

The "Latin" cluster, with the exception of Belgium, yielded scores that could indeed be expected from relatively (machine) bureaucratic and institutional academy or military cultures. In the academies of France, Italy, Spain, Argentina, and Brazil, the various aspects of discipline were generally considered to be of above-average importance. Interestingly, the British student-officers considered virtually all aspects of military discipline to be of above-average importance. This must be related to the extremely high level of power distance in the British academy that was also found in the survey. Military life in the United Kingdom apparently is steeped in military discipline.

Another interesting finding relates to the importance attached to acting in accord with informal group norms. In those countries where importance is attached to the various aspects of military discipline and, specifically, ceremonial discipline, informal group norms are not deemed very important. Conversely, where virtually no aspect of military discipline is relatively highly valued, this one aspect is considered to be of significant importance. It may be assumed on the basis of these findings that self-steering with the influence of informal group norms is an alternative to the imposition of general military discipline.

Compared to the armed forces, the police, in principle, exhibit the same aspects of discipline. It seems, however, that in police organizations the semi- or quasi-military model of leadership, characterized by impersonal, highly directive, authoritarian leadership and routinized tasks, receives little support. As long ago as the 1960s, the semimilitary model of organizing police activities was criticized and said to bring new uncertainties into the organization while attempting to rule out others (McNamara, 1967). A later study found that subordinates in police organizations indicated less job satisfaction and organizational commitment when confronted with a quasi-military type of leadership (Jermier & Berkes, 1979). In contrast, leader participativeness and task variability were found to be highly significant predictors of both job satisfaction and organizational commitment. Apparently, leaders in police organizations should not act out the role of military commander. An example of such a situation occurred in the Netherlands in 1997, when a highly successful two-star general from the infantry took up the lead position in the Rotterdam police force. Even before and more vehemently very soon after his appointment, friction arose between him and the police unions regarding his style of leadership and organizational change. Within a year of his taking over the police force, this friction became unmanageable and forced him into early retirement.

Police forces have good reasons to be less inclined toward (authoritarian) discipline, although national differences undoubtedly will occur in this regard to the same extent as in the military. In general, the police face more reality checks in their everyday operations. They are continuously confronted with situations that require immediate decisions and actions. In these situations commanders are not always present, and ordinary police officers have to make their own decisions, relatively independent of others (Wilson, 1968). In this way they have to act on a more or less self-steering basis. It is understandable that rank-and-file police officers, who are used to independence and autonomy on the street, are not very pleased when leaders behave in authoritarian ways in situations when they are present (e.g., McNamara, 1967, p. 183).

There is one more striking difference in this regard between the military and the police. Police officers continuously receive feedback from the general public in the communities in which they operate (Nordholt & Straver, 1983); this makes them relatively more customer and quality oriented, or pragmatic, as Hofstede et al. (1990) have named this aspect of organizational culture. In the military, the idea of customer orientation is, for understandable reasons, much less well conceived. The implementation of inviolable rules and keeping up a unit's standards of ethics and aesthetics are more important than customer orientation in the military. Hence these organizational cultures are more normative (Hofstede et al., 1990). The relationship of this aspect of organizational culture to (formal and functional) discipline is obvious and requires no further explanation.

## Developments

It is tempting—although methodologically precarious—to put the various characteristics of culture in uniformed organizations in a time perspective. It could be hypothesized that there is a traditional uniformed culture that is institutional, hierarchical, and discipline oriented. This traditional type of uniformed culture still occurs abundantly in the military (and presumably also in the police) organizations of various countries; this type will occur especially in the less Western parts of the world, starting with Latin European countries such as Italy.

However, there seem to be developments in the Western world that point toward the emergence of a more "businesslike" attitude among police and military personnel, which will also affect the organization of work activities. For reasons of efficiency, uniformity, and standardization, uniformed organizations will be bureaucratic forever (see Wilson, 1989). However, the character of that bureaucracy is likely to change gradually from coercive toward more enabling; in the latter case, the organization's rules and standard operating procedures provide frames of reference that are designed to enable employees to do their work properly. Within the framework of "good" bureaucratic rules, which are hardly noticed, people can behave fairly autonomously and in a self-steering way, although always in accordance with the group's informal norms. Coercive rules and commands, in contrast, are becoming more and more obsolete. As far as leadership is concerned, one can clearly observe that acting according to the "commander's intent" (mission-oriented command)—implying freedom of action among the rank and file and mutual trust between leader and followers—is replacing traditional, coercive styles of leadership (Vogelaar & Kramer, 1997). The introduction of team-based organizing will be inevitable to keep up with the increasing complexity of the work, although the pace and extent of application will vary according to national cultural characteristics (Kirkman

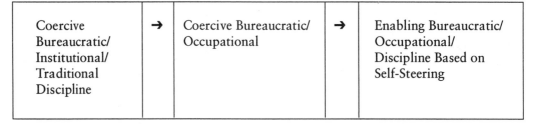

**Figure 29.1.** The Presumed Process of Development of Uniformed Organizations' Cultures

& Shapiro, 1997). One could assume that in the long run this development will bridge the gap between uniformed and other organizations in many ways.

This presumed development is most likely related to several general developments: the continuous Westernization and individualization of national cultures, the expansion of information and communication technologies, the improving educational qualifications of the work population ("smarter soldiers and police officers"), and, finally, comparable tendencies in the business sector (Adler & Borys, 1996). For the military specifically, the end of conscription in increasingly more Western countries will contribute to this development as well. This development is depicted in Figure 29.1.

Although there will inevitably be national variations in policing as much as there are national variations in the military (e.g., Soeters et al., 1995), it can be argued that the police on average will be further along in this presumed development than the armed forces. This may be illustrated by the mere fact that police officers rarely wear their uniforms when they are off duty, in contrast to many members of the military. Social bonds among police officers are increasingly being restricted to work time and are diminishing in out-of-work settings. What once was a family culture in police organizations seems to be turning gradually into a business culture. Furthermore, many leading officers whose education and mobility make them eligible for alternate careers outside the police have entered police forces already (Reuss-Ianni &

Ianni, 1983, pp. 254, 256, 270). In addition, police organizations—at least in the Netherlands—have for quite some time been moving toward more decentralization and self-steering in order to meet the increasing complexities in the work (Nordholt & Straver, 1983; van Rheenen, 1979). This trend may have something to do with the reality checks with which police forces are constantly confronted. This peculiarity is even more important when one considers the divided character of culture in uniformed organizations.

## A JANUSIAN CULTURE

As mentioned previously, uniformed organizations in fact have two sides: (a) the side of the organization that tries to prevent the occurrence of problems and provides the preconditions for the core task, which is performed by (b) the side of the organization on the street, in a crisis or on a battlefield, or responding to a fire (e.g., van Doorn, 1975; Wilson, 1989). Uniformed organizations apparently have two faces, like the Roman god Janus (Hunt & Philips, 1991). In fact, however, this seemingly simple Janusian peculiarity is a bit more complicated. Specifying the distinction between the two faces, one can see various dimensions of organizational activities to be relevant: the personal risk, the turbulence of critical events, and the time dimension. Using these dimensions, one can distinguish four exemplary general situations in uniformed organizations:

1. Headquarters or staff departments
2. The garrison of the army, the barracks of firefighters, the navy vessel on a peacetime sailing mission and routine peacekeeping operations
3. The activities of cops on the street and the operations on an aircraft carrier
4. The uniformed organization in battle, crisis, or disaster

In this list, the personal risks to those in uniformed organizations and the turbulence of critical events progressively increase, whereas the time spans of activities become increasingly shorter. For the sake of simplicity, the first two situations may be taken together, as may the last two; for reasons to be explained later, situations 1 and 2 may be said to constitute the *cold* side of the uniformed organization, and situations 3 and 4 may be said to be the *hot* side. Each side or face has its own (sub)cultural content and dynamics. I deal with these two sides or faces of the uniformed organization in the next two subsections.

## *The Subculture of the Cold Organization*

The managing organization at headquarters or the staff of the uniformed organization closely resembles an ordinary office organization. It is a real bureaucracy, with specialization, rational decision making, (strategic) planning, paperwork, quality and cost control, and hierarchies. Like many bureaucracies, it is process rather than goal oriented. It knows all aspects of bureau politics as well: emotional meetings, power struggles, negotiations on targets and budgets, and contacts with the media and other external, mostly political, influences. In this organization one could say the white-collar work (although in uniform) is being done. In police organizations there is mention of the world of the "management cops" (Reuss-Ianni & Ianni, 1983). In the world of firefighters, which is dominated by volunteers (Thompson & Bono, 1993), one speaks of the "cold organization"—obviously the part of the

organization that does not face the heat of fires. In this world traditionally there are only a few managers, which makes the fire department "only as bureaucratic as it has to be to satisfy legal requirements" (Benoit & Perkins, 1997, p. 25).

But for "real" firefighters as well, the organization may be rather "cold" in many circumstances, as it usually is for the larger parts of the armed forces. These are the times where there is no need for real action. The "only" thing one has to do in the garrison, in the barracks, and on routine navy sailing missions is constantly make preparations for the worst case: train, exercise, maintain the force, and simply be there. Leadership in these circumstances is traditional and disciplinary, rational and linear, and based on cognitive and analytic skills (Hunt & Phillips, 1991, p. 423).

Not only in garrison but also in low-intensity operations such as those on Cyprus and in the Sinai, military operations may be predominantly fairly cold. In these situations the main tasks are observation and presence. The subculture or organizational climate, consequently, is dominated by boredom, perceptions of underutilization, stimulus deprivation, and concerns for privacy. If boredom in such a situation is a recurrent theme, many negative experiences are expressed and internal conflicts are likely to occur (Harris & Segal, 1985). Commanders in these situations should therefore make every effort to strengthen the unit's cohesion. This is important because cohesion is a prerequisite of the satisfactory performance of uniformed organizations, not only under cold but certainly also under hot conditions. The dynamics of working in uniformed organizations make temperature shifts quite common.

## *The Subculture of the Hot Organization*

Some segments of uniformed organizations face "hot" conditions quasi-permanently; these are the frontline parts of uniformed or-

---

**TABLE 29.1**   Elements of the Cop's Code

Watch out for your partner first and then the rest of the guys.

Don't give up another cop.

Show balls.

Be aggressive when you have to be, but don't be too eager.

Don't trust a new guy until you've checked him out.

Don't talk too much or too little.

Don't leave work for the next tours.

Don't give them too much activity.

Don't seek favors just for yourself.

Know your bosses.

SOURCE: Derived from Reuss-Ianni and Ianni (1983, pp. 266-269).

---

ganizations, such as street police squads and units of air operations personnel. As such they are comparable to frontline organizations in other sectors, such as street-level bureaucracies in social services and emergency rooms in health care (Smith, 1979). Some parts of uniformed organizations, however, face hot conditions only incidentally, when they are on the battlefield, in crisis, or in disaster—in sum, when they are in conditions that are turbulent and potentially life threatening. Hot conditions occur when the heat is on, when members have to perform in critical, dangerous, violent, ambiguous, and hence stressful circumstances (Vogelaar & Kramer, 1997).

Whereas the cold organization is a real, classical organization of the bureaucracy type, the hot organization is built around flexible groups having all the characteristics of either the ("one leader") simple structure or—when explicitly based on self-managing—the adhocracy (Druckman et al., 1997; Mintzberg, 1979). Leadership in the hot organization should definitely be something more than conventional linear and cognitive behavior. It should contain emotional aspects

as well, such as courage, fear control, and compassion (Hunt & Phillips, 1991). In hot circumstances the uniformed organization is rather frequently dominated by a "can-do" mentality, and its culture is generally perceived to be virile and competitive. In addition, under hot conditions the uniformed organization is often full of "us" and "them" classifications: "them" being the enemy, the criminals, the general public, the media—but also the managers in the cold organization as well as the politicians (e.g., Harris, 1973, p. 99). Personnel in the hot organization generally are critical toward outsiders.

For the police, this division and its corresponding split of organizational culture has been described insightfully in a study on the New York Police Department by Reuss-Ianni and Ianni (1983). These researchers make an explicit distinction between street cops and management cops. Street cops have their own culture that includes codes of shared understanding (jokes, prejudices) as well as conventions of behavior that are binding for all officers in their precinct. Table 29.1 presents a summary of the elements of this code.

| TABLE 29.2 | Elements of the Flight Deck Code |
|---|---|

If it is not written down, you can do it.

Look for clouds in every silver lining.

Most positions on this deck were bought in blood.

Never get into something you can't get out of.

SOURCE: Derived from Weick and Roberts (1993).

Street-cop culture sees local response and flexibility as more important than pre-planned and "packaged" solutions to problems. Central to the street cops' culture is a sense of territoriality: "This space belongs to our precinct, to our team." This orientation is more limited (parochial, one could perhaps say) than the systemwide or citywide way of thinking in the management cops' organization. Street-cop culture (as well as the cultures of battlefield troops and of firefighters suppressing a fire) is a manifestation of what Jane Jacobs (1992) has called the "guardian morale syndrome": a public organization's way of thinking that wants members to be courageous, obedient, loyal, and traditional, but also to be exclusive, vengeful, and ostentatious. Central to the street cops' culture above all is group orientation and commitment to fellow officers (Harris, 1973).

The same orientation can be found among members of the military-in-action, although firsthand studies on the performance of military teams in crisis and war operations are not abundantly available. Probably these operations occur too seldom or are too dangerous for civilian researchers to be involved. However, Weick and Roberts (1993) have produced an in-depth study on group performance on the flight decks of aircraft carriers of the U.S. Navy. Operations on such a carrier, even under peacetime conditions, may resemble crisis and wartime operations to a large extent. The work is dangerous to a life-threatening degree and necessitates quick, immediate responses to changing conditions.

Weick and Roberts have made it perfectly clear that in such circumstances there is a strong need for a so-called collective mind. Every individual plays his or her own role, but in doing so each person (in the tower, on the deck, in the aircraft) has to interrelate heedfully with the others. For instance, a pilot does not land his aircraft, he is "recovered" by the people on board. On a flight deck there are no solitary acts. Hence solitarily acting "strong" individuals or commanders are not welcome there. As among street cops, on the flight deck there are common action patterns and shared meanings as well as a common language or cultural code. Elements of this code are listed in Table 29.2. The enemy being at a safe distance, the culture codes predominantly stress safety aspects of the work on the deck.

If in such circumstances the collective mind deteriorates and people's actions become less interconnected, there is less comprehension of the implications of unfolding events, slower correction of errors, and more opportunities for small errors to combine and amplify. If heedful interrelating fails, there is a greater chance of small lapses leading to failure or even to fatal disasters.

In crises or crisislike situations, organizational members form a strong, cohesive group with a collective mind—a "mechanical solidarity," so to speak (Winslow, 1998)—that as an organizational form and cultural entity differs greatly from the cold uniformed organization. Compared to the latter, the organization-in-action is more organic, flexible, and independent of other organizational units, but it knows a high level of interdependency within in its own boundaries. Although there is less emphasis on rules and regulations, rules and conventions are certainly not absent; they have been internalized into the minds of people and are less the product of paperwork. In general, the organization-in-action is characterized by "swift trust," which is a manifestation of bonding among team members. Swift trust is more likely to occur when uncertainty is high and the situation is unfamiliar and dangerous (Meyerson, Weick, & Kramer, 1995).

This bonding may even lead to the development of subcultural patterns with rules and codes that are not considered legitimate or appropriate in the "official" world. Often these subjects and their discussion are considered taboo (Heffron, 1989). Only if outsiders (e.g., the media) or critical insiders remark on this inappropriate behavior might the taboo dissolve. Among police, organized graft, corruption, and "police lying" are regularly mentioned (Manning, 1974; Reuss-Ianni & Ianni, 1983, p. 256), as is the questionable use of violence (Hunt, 1985/1995). For undercover units this danger is even more prevalent, because in the "guardian morale syndrome" one is allowed "to deceive for the sake of the task" (Jacobs, 1992, p. 215). In the Netherlands during the 1990s, the (alleged) misbehavior of undercover agents led to a real crisis in the legal system. In the military, excessive violence is a continuing point of attention, in real war as much as in peace-enforcing missions (e.g., van Doorn & Hendrix, 1970; Winslow, 1998). For the cold organization the only way to control these manifestations of deviant behavior is to issue more specific rules, such as rules of engagement as well as disciplinary correction measures. Obviously, this may intensify the always-existing tensions and antagonism between the two sides of the uniformed organization (Reuss-Ianni & Ianni, 1983, p. 263).

As mentioned earlier, not all manifestations of the hot uniformed organization occur on a quasi-permanent basis. For the larger parts of uniformed organizations, hot conditions occur only incidentally. But even then there may be variations: Hot conditions may be well-known to such an extent that everybody is fully prepared to do his or her task. If parts of the uniformed organization, however, enter battle, crisis, or disaster conditions they have never experienced before, the culture or collective mind of the group is likely to disintegrate. As Weick (1993) has shown in his analysis of "smokejumpers" fighting a forest fire, general patterns of action and shared codes of understanding may fall apart in the face of life-threatening events that have always been considered improbable. In such a case people are likely to stop thinking and panic. They no longer listen to the orders of their superiors, their mutual ties cease to exist, and fear is set free (Weick, 1993, p. 637). Due to the panic, there are more casualties than would have been inevitable in the given situation. Only by stressing the importance of improvisation, simulation, wisdom, and respectful ("heedful") interrelating in a unit's way of behaving may an organization prevent such "unnecessary" casualties (see also Hutchins, 1991). Through the uniformed organization's culture, personnel should be prepared for the unthinkable. Obviously, this should be accomplished in the stages of socialization, training, and preparation—in sum, in the process of developing uniformed persons.

## BECOMING A UNIFORMED PERSON

The integration of individual employees into an existing organizational culture obviously is a key issue in cultural management. Figure 29.2 illustrates four general ways in which this integration takes place. These vary to the extent that employees are attracted to or—in contrast—distanced from the organizational culture. If a person's individual and organizational values overlap

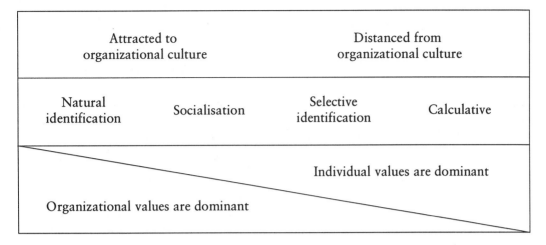

**Figure 29.2.** Ways of Integrating Personnel Into the Organizational Culture
SOURCE: Based on Heinen (1987).

fully, organizational values will be dominant. In this situation the individual employee shows a natural identification with the existing culture. This type of cultural integration frequently occurs in organizations with strong missions, such as churches, political parties, business organizations with outspoken histories (e.g., Shell or IBM), and, of course, uniformed organizations.

In uniformed organizations, "endo-recruitment" (recruitment of new employees whose parents are police officers or serve in the military) is a fairly common phenomenon. Through this mechanism, uniformed organizations add new recruits who have learned as children to value the importance of working in such organizations. This so-called anticipatory socialization has been found in all uniformed organizations (Heffron, 1989). For instance, during a seminar for fire brigade officers, a high-ranking commander proudly explained how his 4-year-old son loves to wear his father's helmet and uniform, pretending to be a fire brigade commander himself. Obviously, father and son reinforce each other in the boy's adoption of the fire department's organizational values at a very early stage of his life. In the United States, many fire departments explicitly try to exploit this form of "presocialization" by selling replicas of uniforms and helmets to the general public. This form of cultural integration definitely coincides with the institutional or parochial character of uniformed cultures, a feature discussed earlier in this chapter. Also, the U.S. Forest Service is known for screening employee candidates carefully in order to select only individuals with a public service orientation (Kaufman, 1967).

However, natural identification or anticipatory socialization does not suffice fully and in all cases. For that reason, new employees need to be socialized in training and educational institutes. One of the arguments for uniformed organizations to have their own academies and training institutes is that the new recruits are interned, which makes them available to the organization on a 24-hour basis. This is the situation of Goffman's (1961) "total institution." Basic military, police, and firefighting training in such institutions facilitates the recruits' transition into new social roles and statuses. A special element in this training is a process that at West Point is called the plebe system and that is known as the "degreening" program in European (military) academies. Shortly after entering the training institute, the new recruits go through a process of degradation or "mortification"—that is, a process of deconstruction of their civilian status. Subsequently, having become receptive to new values, the cadet officers are "rebuilt"—given a new identity. This means that they are exposed intensively to the norms, authority relations, and disciplinary codes of the organization, which are expressed to them by all senior cadets.

Although perhaps somewhat old-fashioned to most observers, this practice is still vivid and highly valued in most uniformed training institutes. This is understandable given that "formal training settings (such as academies) concentrate more upon attitude than act" (Van Maanen, 1975, p. 225; see also Druckman et al., 1997). This harsh system survives because its cruelty and humiliation imply a reward: "If full membership were too easily attained it would not be worth having" (Heffron, 1989, p. 217). Because, as indicated earlier, many recruits in uniformed organizations already tend to have a natural identification with the organization's values, the socialization in training institutes only seems to provide the finishing touch to the new recruits' integration into the organizational culture (Lammers, 1963).

Socialization in training and educational institutes, however, is only the first and not always a very satisfying (Van Maanen, 1975, p. 222) stage in the total socialization process. When the posttraining recruit is confronted with real circumstances, an additional step follows to complete or, some would say, redirect the socialization process. Outside the academy, the recruit moves from idealizations to the practicalities of real life (Hunt, 1985/1995). As mentioned before, in this stage the new recruit learns to adopt team-based working, to adapt to the informal norms of the group, to deal with difficult and ambiguous circumstances, and—perhaps most of all—to stay out of trouble.

One additional and interesting point is that job motivation and commitment of employees in police and probably all uniformed organizations seem to decline swiftly after those employees face real-life situations (Van Maanen, 1975). This may be the result of a certain disenchantment originating from the confrontation with the "real thing." New police officers and firefighters often expect their jobs to be exciting, glamorous, and full of adventure. These expectations are usually not completely fulfilled; often they experience boredom, anger, anxiety, and dislike instead of the anticipated excitement, enjoyment, and pleasure (Heffron, 1989). In addition, there may be a certain degree of routinization that inevitably leads to more realistic and hence more sober attitudes toward the organization. However, expressed commitment to the organization, although dropping after the first periods of socialization, seems to stay relatively high in uniformed organizations compared to several other occupational and organizational settings in business, banking, health care, and public utilities (Van Maanen, 1975, pp. 217-218). This may come as no surprise given that employees in uniformed organizations, on average, display a greater tendency toward natural identification, institutionalism, and parochialism than employees in other organizations.

For that reason, it may be clear that selective and especially calculative identification—the latter two integrating mechanisms mentioned in Figure 29.2—are not likely to be the most self-evident ways of integrating employees into uniformed organizations' cultures. However, as occupationalism tends to grow in police as well as in military organizations (see Figure 29.1) and a certain convergence between uniformed and business cultures seems to develop, calculation too will be an aspect for people to consider before they become motivated to join a uniformed organization. Uniformed organizations therefore will increasingly have to compete in the labor market on the basis of material conditions (salaries, work hours, promotion opportunities). This is merely a matter of time. Obviously, such a development will have strong impacts on their cultures.

## TO CONCLUDE:
## FUTURE DEVELOPMENTS AND
## AVENUES FOR FURTHER RESEARCH

In summary, one can say that uniformed cultures traditionally are fairly idiosyncratic, with an emphasis on institutionalism and parochialism and on rules, hierarchy, and disciplinary control. However, there are developments pointing toward the introduction of a more contemporary civilian or businesslike culture, consisting of occupationalism and team-based, self-steering practices relying on general, enabling frameworks of rules and operating procedures. Obviously, there are national culture-related variations on this axis and the police (and probably fire departments as well), facing reality checks on an everyday basis, may be more ahead in this respect than the military.

In these developments the Janusian character of uniformed organizations plays a role as well. It looks like the organization-in-action—the hot organization—becomes more dominant in the design and command philosophies of military organizations, at least compared to earlier Cold War times, when the cold military organization provided the model for organizing activities (Vogelaar & Kramer, 1997). This must be due to the experiences Western armed forces had in various out-of-area operations in the 1990s. For fire departments, however, the opposite development may occur, because fire prevention is advocated to be more effective than responding to fire alarms (Osborne & Gaebler, 1992, pp. 223-226). Hence developments in this specific respect may go both ways. The general developments will induce changes in the uniformed organizations' cultures, which may create avenues for further research in this area.

First, with respect to the Janusian character of uniformed organizations, there is and will be a certain amount of tension between the cold and the hot organizations, or—if one

wishes—between the hierarchy and the team in the uniformed organization. Uniformed organizations will have to prepare their personnel for both sides of their working environment. More specifically, they must prepare personnel to handle (sudden) temperature shifts from cold to hot and then back to cold again. It remains to be seen how successful uniformed organizations will be in dealing with this. To mention just one particular issue: Which people will be promoted to top positions—those who have best performed in the hot organization, or those who have best performed in the cold?

Second, if more new recruits enter the uniformed organization without any prior developed identification with the organization, and if more recruits enter the organization without aiming to stay for a lifelong career, occupationalism undoubtedly will grow. This is an obvious and overriding tendency. The question, however, is how this will affect uniformed organizations' performance. Will performance worsen or will it improve? One hypothesis could be that with the recruitment of employees with more occupational attitudes—that is, people who are more independent of the organization—in general more "internally controlled" people will enter the organization. These are people who attribute the results of their work to their own abilities and efforts and not to matters outside their own spheres of influence, such as the system, the procedures, the mandate, bad luck, or mere coincidence (Rotter, Seeman, & Liverant, 1962). A further hypothesis would be that such internally controlled persons will do a better job, because they have no excuses such as waiting for orders from above, hiding within the group, or blaming rules and regulations. There is some evidence that cultures that include more internally controlled people perform better in terms of the prevention of military aircraft accidents (Soeters & Boer, 2000). A further question would be how the traditional core of the uniformed culture will react to this development: Will there be a conservative backlash among core personnel within uniformed organizations, or will they gradually accept the unavoidable developments?

Third, the uniformed organization's culture has traditionally been male dominated; it has been described as a masculine, warrior-like culture (Dunivin, 1994). There are at least two developments that may affect this phenomenon. The performance of uniformed organizations is increasingly becoming less oriented toward violence and aggressive behavior. Military organizations are becoming more and more involved in humanitarian actions, civil military collaborations, and distant violence based on smart technology. The traditional aggressive, warriorlike culture will gradually have to be balanced with these new developments in task requirements. The same applies to police and fire departments, with, as noted above, the latter organizations expecting to elaborate their work more toward the prevention of fire risks (Osborne & Gaebler, 1992). Furthermore, new categories of personnel will enter the world of uniformed organizations. Women and cultural minorities are entering uniformed organizations increasingly, as they are entering all other organizations. The management of demographic diversity (Cox, 1993) will therefore become a priority on the agenda of uniformed organizations, especially because the very entrance of women and ethnic minorities may influence the ways uniformed organizations perceive and perform their work, as some research conducted during the Somalia operations in 1993 has indicated (Moskos & Miller, 1995).

Fourth, it has been shown that national variations exist among uniformed organizations. For instance, Belgian armed and police forces bear specific national characteristics that make them unique and distinguishable from German or British armed and police forces. In times of increasing internationalization, national forces have to work together in peacekeeping operations, crime fighting and firefighting across borders, and humanitarian actions. Commanders of such international operations should be aware of the intercultural variations that exist within

their (temporary) organizations. It remains to be seen how these international organizations will succeed in overcoming intercultural difficulties.

Finally, the behavior of uniformed organizations toward their stakeholders requires attention. Mintzberg (1996) has shown that government organizations have to deal with at least four types of stakeholders among the general public: subjects, citizens, clients, and customers. Traditionally, uniformed organizations have been used to emphasize the subject role of the public. But currently, increased attention to human rights stresses the need for such organizations to be aware of the citizenship aspects or their work (van Rheenen, 1997), and an orientation toward clients is increasingly valued as well, at least in Western countries. Finally, attention should be paid to the way uniformed organizations deal with another important set of stakeholders: their superiors, the politicians. As we know, this relationship is always somewhat precarious (Harris, 1973), but especially in emerging democratic countries, such as in Eastern Europe, it may be put under strain.

Due to all these shifts in emphasis, it is only logical that uniformed organizations are searching for new directions. In these processes uniformed organizations will have to introduce new ways of structuring work activities, developing new human resources management policies, preparing for new forms of leadership, and creating a greater transparency (media!) and awareness of accountability and quality. This permanent search for new directions may cause difficulties. Public and uniformed organizations value stability (Heffron, 1989), and for good reason: In times of trouble the general public must be able to rely on these organizations. Not surprisingly, the well-known "liability of reorganization" poses serious threats to uniformed organizations. There have been various recent examples of uniformed organizations-in-action that were not able to cope with situations in ways the general public would expected them to. Consequently, uniformed organizations have to balance their attempts to introduce new ways of working, and hence new cultures, with the necessity of preserving the traditional basics. Changing uniformed cultures, therefore, requires patience and wisdom.

## NOTE

1. Although Hofstede et al. (1990) found that Dutch police forces are more parochial than Dutch business organizations, Peter Moskos (personal communication) observed in his study of the Amsterdam and Boston police that the Dutch police officers made a relatively sharp division between work and private life compared to the Bostonians, who were much more cop focused. This surely is a nice example of the complicated interaction between national and occupational cultural influences.

# 30

# Changing Organizational Cultures in Chinese Firms

—— *Cherlyn Skromme Granrose, Qiang Huang, and Elena Reigadas*

Can insights gained from Western organizational culture theory aid our understanding of organizational culture change in China? In particular, what is the role of transformational leadership in creating and changing Chinese organizational culture? These are the questions addressed in this chapter.

Trice and Beyer (1993) define organizational culture as "collective phenomena that embody people's responses to the uncertainties and chaos that are inevitable in human experience" (p. 2). Several authors have tried to explain organizational cultural change. Schein (1992) asserts that organizational cultures continually change because of changes in the environment, critical incidents, structural changes, membership changes, and internal leadership. Others claim that transformational leadership is the key to describing how organizational cultures are created

and maintained (Bass & Aviolo, 1994; Conger & Kanungo, 1987). This claim has been disputed as attributing too much power to the leader or as not relevant for non-Western developed countries (Hunt & Peterson, 1997; Meindl, 1990).

Trice and Beyer (1993) use strain between competing ideologies and the actions of charismatic leaders who found organizations, transformational leaders who change organizations, institutional leaders who embody organizational cultures, and consensus and transactional leaders who integrate cultures to describe how organizational cultures originate and change. Weber (1978) asserts that charismatic leadership is the primary source of *societal* cultural change, but he also gives cultural members or followers some influence in the change process. This follower process, which Weber calls routinization, softens the revolutionizing impact of leader-inspired new meaning to a level of change that can be tolerated by culture members.

One of the best examples of recent models of organizational change has been proposed by Hatch (1993; see also Chapter 15, this volume), who integrates some aspects of the work of Trice and Beyer, Schein, and Weber by claiming that cultural change can occur from both internal processes and exposure to new ideas from external sources. In her cultural dynamics model, Hatch presents organizational cultural change as two counteracting forces, one focused on the production of artifacts and the other on the production of meaning. She identifies four processes linking these phenomena: manifestation (values and norms evoked into consciousness), realization (manifestations acted upon to create artifacts), symbolization (artifacts used to create meaning), and interpretation (location of symbols in the broad cultural context of collective meaning). In this perspective, when a powerful leader redefines meaning and presents new artifacts, cultural change may occur. However, followers may alter the ideas leaders introduce to suit their everyday lives and to fit the historical-political context as they include leader acts into the collective meaning making. New cultural meanings persist when materials favoring these new assumptions and values outnumber those favoring any other view. Thus, in Hatch's view, not only leaders but also followers (organization members) have greater roles to play in the continuous process of changing organizational culture than the roles advocated by Trice and Beyer, Schein, and Weber.

In this chapter, we will examine the broader cultural heritage of leadership in China as well as leadership in the context of current changes in Chinese organizational structure and culture. In this process we will use the Hatch model of organizational culture change and the Trice and Beyer identification of ideologies and different types of cultural leadership to analyze the Chinese situation. We concentrate on Chinese organizations and leave the complexities of the cultures of Chinese joint ventures to other discussions.

## SOCIETAL HERITAGE OF ASSUMPTIONS ABOUT LEADERSHIP AND CHANGE

Although there is controversy about the relationship between national culture and organizational cultures, we adopt the position that cultural values as expressed in measures of national culture reside in the minds of organizational employees and influence the collective minds of organizations as well. In Western discussions, different organizational cultures arise from different ideologies of entrepreneurial founders, from industrial constraints, and from societal differences. Trice and Beyer (1993) assert that ideologies have the functions of catharsis of emotional tension, legitimation of tension by moral claims, and creation of group solidarity. Competing ideologies make clear and advocate differing resolutions of contradictory cultural issues. A key issue in the Chinese situation is that there are competing ideologies: traditional ones from the ancient past, ideologies from the Communist/socialist era of the mid-20th century, and the new ideology of market socialism. The ideologies of founders and industrial differences have been strongly constrained by national political ideology in China, leaving organizational differences in culture to reside primarily in differentiated emphasis of national cultural values and in different adaptations to market principles. Without some knowledge of a few central beliefs prevalent in Chinese history, it is impossible to fathom the collective mind-set of members constructing current Chinese organizational culture.

### Traditional Ideologies

The family was the basic unit of organization of the ancient Chinese agrarian society. Kong Fu Zhi (551-479 B.C.) codified many Chinese family values into a structured set of beliefs. A central principle of Confucian thought values hierarchical interpersonal relationships, including obligation of the superior to protect, sustain, and guide the subordinate in exchange for loyalty and obedience from the subordinate. The Confucian gentleman (leader) seeks constant self-improvement, educates others, exhibits patriotic loyalty to the ruler, supports reverence for those older or higher in the hierarchy, and is a generalist with high moral principles rather than a technological expert (Stockwell, 1993). According to Confucianism, change occurs through moral and educational actions of rulers and elite leaders and is implemented by loyal followers.

Although Confucianism is often described as the core philosophy defining Chinese leadership, other philosophies also have made a contribution to contemporary culture. Lao Zhi (552-497 B.C.) codified the animistic principle of emphasizing harmony with the natural order into the more formal religious system of Taoism. This perspective emphasized "active not doing" as a way of engaging the world that was quite contrary to the Confucian emphasis on hard work and self-improvement. The norm that all relationships, including leader-follower relationships, should be harmonious arises from this perspective. The Taoists believe that change should occur in a gradual, harmonious way in the internal experience of each individual, with little action from a leader.

In the traditional Chinese philosophies, the characteristics of a good leader do not sound like those of a transformational leader; rather, they sound more like institutional forms of leadership. Leaders support tradition, care for their followers, exhibit morality, and live in harmony with the natural way. Followers, on the other hand, are socialized to do as the leader bids, to exhibit loyalty, and to conform to tradition as upheld by the leaders. Their ostensible role as culture shapers is expected to be passive.

## Socialist Ideology

More recent influences on Chinese culture are the political philosophies of socialism and communism. The socialist system was instituted through the revolutionary, charismatic leadership of Mao Ze Dong and his colleagues, who actively suppressed expression of traditional Confucian and Taoist philosophies. During the anti-Japanese and civil wars, basic values and forms of social organization were established that would persist into the time of the establishment of the People's Republic of China (PRC). These include advocating the principle of egalitarianism rather than elitism; combining military, production, education, and economy in each social subunit; elevating the status of women; and initiating some forms of worker participation in decision making. With the influence of the Soviet Union during the first formative decade of the new republic, the idea that the central government should be the instrument of control for this social arrangement also became a guiding principle of the PRC. The ideology of egalitarianism and the political realities of uprooting traditional Chinese fiefdoms resulted in strong political requirements that homogenized organizational cultures to fit the politically correct dogma. Under socialism, followers theoretically have a more important role than they did under the previous ideologies, but as it is currently implemented followers are expected to follow the decisions of the leadership. This contemporary ideology calls for more transactional or consensus forms of leadership; different stakeholder groups need to be fused into an organizational whole. To obtain organizational resources from centralized bureaucracies, one must placate various stakeholders.

According to Chinese cultural history, there is no agreement about how cultural change occurs. Change occurs through revolution in the Communist way and through gradual reform in the traditional ways. Leaders play an important role in change in Communist and Confucian ideas but play a less important role in the Taoist tradition. The question is, How are these ideas expressed inside contemporary Chinese organizations? To answer this question, we need to understand the external pressures for change being exerted on Chinese organizations.

## THE CURRENT
## ORGANIZATIONAL CONTEXT

Current organizational change in China has been stimulated by an important shift in ideology and economic policy that began in 1978. Comparing the lagging economic development of China to the boom of other emerging Asian economies, and observing contemporary government-influenced capitalism with more central limits than the robber-baron capitalism of past Chinese experience, Deng Xiao-Ping used pragmatism to justify a major shift from concentration on class struggle to implementation of four modernizations. Current political thought in China has evolved to advocate three basic principles of "socialism with market characteristics." The country (a) must have modernization of its economy (including limited market mechanisms), (b) must retain some socialist characteristics (some centralized planning or industrial coordination), and (c) must reject capitalist exploitation of workers and democratic political reform (Kurtenbach, 1998; Lockett, 1983; Wang, 1993).

At the ninth National People's Congress meeting in March 1998, Jiang Ze-Min, Zhu Rong Ji, and Li Peng, exhibiting institutional and transactional political leadership, consolidated many ideological changes by initiating a reduction in the number of ministries and the number of personnel working for the central and regional government. They also promoted more rapid implementation of social changes that have been introduced gradually over the past decade: greater autonomy of organizational leaders, greater risks that organizational leaders could be replaced, loss of guaranteed employment, individual ownership of housing, and implementation of social welfare insurance policies to replace work-unit provision of services. Each of these societal-level changes has great implications for the core ways organizations conduct themselves and could be expected to trigger large-scale organizational change. Traditional socialist organizations met almost every sustenance need of each member according to centralized plans. Market organizations will be free to create their own plans and to shift the responsibility of each person to meet his or her own needs onto the shoulders of the individual. This structural shift requires a shift in worldview with profound implications for the psychological definition of an organization and the accompanying definition of each organization's culture.

These political changes have the potential to permit more variation in organizational culture in China in the future, but the potential has not yet been formally realized. Implementation of these new policies has been carried out in an erratic and piecemeal fashion, in part due to the shear volume of new changes but also in part due to ideological differences and perceived differences in self-interest (Cooper, Wehrly, & Bao, 1997; Jackson, 1992). There is resistance to change from many forces: Central government bureaucrats don't want to lose authority, employees don't want to lose their "iron rice bowl" job security, and conservative party leaders don't want to lose the ideology of socialism and communism (Shenkar, 1991). In addition, empirical examination of national cultural values confirms the persistence of Confucian values (Cragin, 1986; Ralston, Gustafon, Elsass, Cheung, & Terpstra, 1992; Ralston, Kai-Cheng, Wang, Terpstra, & Wei, 1994). In this ambiguous national environment, according to many views, the situation could be ripe for a charismatic leader to show the way to solve these organizational problems and to create new market-oriented organizational cultures.

## THE CHANGING STRUCTURE
## OF ORGANIZATIONS

The cultures of Chinese organizations are influenced primarily by the organizations' structures and the economic sectors in which they operate. Traditional state-owned enterprises (SOEs) and collectives include organizations in which human resources and raw materials, production, and sales were directly or indirectly controlled through a government ministry or institution. Market changes introduced enterprise-direct sales SOEs and collectives, in which central control exists but sales are permitted to enterprises other than the central government, and free market organizations, where market forces directly determine production and sales (Wang, Wang, & Gong, 1991). In the changing reality of the PRC organizational system at the end of the 1990s, most SOEs are a hybrid of all of these organizational types, and non-SOE private organizations are common (Boisot & Child, 1996). Thus the organizational cultures may also be undergoing change.

The structure of Chinese organizations has a profound impact on the way Chinese organizational cultures differ from most organizational cultures found in U.S. organizations. A traditional SOE is composed of three intertwined systems. First, the life-support system includes the institutions needed to support the daily life of the members of the unit: the housing, goods, schools, and security force, which provide basic life necessities to all organization members. The business system includes the managers and workers who operate the core systems for achieving the economic purposes of the organization. The sociopolitical system includes the Chinese Communist Party (CCP) groups that assure that work is done according to the central plan and performs a social control function through control of job appointments and personnel files (*dang an;* Nyaw, 1991). This traditional structure both constrains a single leader's ability to change the organizational culture (because the leader must collaborate with leaders of the other two systems) and enlarges the scope of cultural change possible (because the organization controls almost every facet of the lives of its members). The structure and therefore the organizational culture includes social functions within the organization that most U.S. social scientists would include in the national

cultural domain rather than within organizational culture.

Recent policies grant more autonomy to organizational leaders of the business system and diminish the need for the other two systems, but the basic three-part system still exists in most SOE work units and may exist in attenuated form in market organizations. The question of change in current Chinese organizational cultures concerns how organizations are transforming themselves from the traditional SOE form to the market form. The roles of leaders and followers in this process are somewhat different from those roles in Western firms, and the role of top managers in leadership positions is enacted in a uniquely Chinese manner.

## LEADERSHIP IN CHINESE ORGANIZATIONS

Given this background of national ideologies and organizational structure influencing Chinese organizational cultures, we can now use information from Trice and Beyer's (1993) work about different forms of leadership and Hatch's (1993) model of organizational culture change to analyze the effects of leadership on changing organizational cultures in Chinese organizations. To analyze the role of leaders in the process of organizational culture change, we organize the following subsections according to the broad categories of the Hatch model: manifestation, realization, symbolization, and interpretation.

### Organizational Culture Manifestation of Leadership: Formal Norms

The CCP-sanctioned norms about how leaders should influence and motivate subordinates include reasoning, affection, setting a good example, recreational education (using propaganda media or educational recreational events), and monitoring subordinates' behavior (Mao, 1943/1960b, 1957/1960a; Martinko & Yan, 1990). According to the principles of political ideological work (Li, 1984), managers have the responsibility to arouse worker motivation and enthusiasm for work, and workers have the responsibility to confront managers if they appear ideologically unsound. Moral encouragement can take the form of leaders' setting a good example, giving mobilization speeches, and instituting group discussions or heart-to-heart talks with peers or superiors. A meritorious manager should follow CCP ideology, develop close ties, and consult with the masses, as well as act independently, unselfishly, and energetically (Mao, 1957/1960a). Current party ideology emphasizes that to be a leader one should have *nian qing hua* (youth), *ji shu hua* (technical or scientific expertise), and *quan mian hua* (managerial and broad comprehensive knowledge). In addition, one must have politically correct ideology. Western assessment of Chinese leadership style reveals that Chinese leaders are expected to exhibit moral character, a Confucian value also included in Maoist thought, as well as contribute task and maintenance leadership roles (Ling, Chen, & Wang, 1987; Peterson, 1988; Tan, 1995). Although the norms do include giving mobilization speeches to motivate workers, the norms promoted in these descriptions of the role of leader make explicit cultural values of stability and security rather than change and revolution. They do not include many characteristics of charismatic or transformational leaders. They do resemble the norms for a person consolidating a particular organizational vision or culture, that is, institutional leadership.

## Realization:
## Leader Role Enactment

When we examine the enactment of culture through behavior in organizational leadership roles, we see that the cultural real-ization of the managerial role in China has some characteristics distinctly different from enactment of the managerial role in Western firms and different from the leadership norms outlined above. In Chinese organizations, managers are by definition top organizational leaders. Leadership is didactic and controlling, but leaders are also caught in many obligations of obedience to their superiors and government agents (Pegels, 1987; Redding & Wong, 1986). In practice, leaders motivate workers through distribution of material rewards and privileges more than through moral encouragement. For example, Boisot and Liang (1992) studied managerial work by conducting a week of qualitative observation of six male organizational directors using methods similar to those employed by Mintzberg (1973). The picture this research paints resembles consensus and transactional leaders, not transformational leaders. In many instances managers were spending increasing amounts of time negotiating for resources previously provided by state planning and seeking informal ways to circumvent conflicting or impossible-to-meet regulations. Advance planning and appointments were rare as managers darted from one obligation to another and constantly needed to be available to meet the needs of those with higher authority. All employees expected the managers to personally guarantee his solution to their problems, making delegation impossible.

A qualitative picture of managers in a market-oriented organization emerges from Kane's (1995) insider interviews with 15 EMBA students who were middle managers in an SOE in charge of foreign trade that had recently moved one subsidiary to Hong Kong. This picture confirms the transactional leader behavior even in organizations in the midst of great demands for change. Respondents stated that the biggest problem for the organization was the requirement that the organization must make a profit and must represent the PRC to the outside world, yet older managers in higher positions did not have a profit orientation. Younger managers were more familiar with a profit orientation but felt they could not insult, criticize, or disagree openly with older managers. This report presents one example of a situation in which those in positions of leadership hindered change rather than using transformational leadership to institute needed organizational cultural change.

When Smith, Peterson, and Wang (1996) compared U.S., British, and Chinese managers' responses to nine common managerial events, they found that Chinese managers were more likely to use rules and procedures or to use their own experience to guide their actions and were less likely to use advice from peers or superiors. However, for particular events, Chinese managers found that it was not helpful to rely on their own experience or peers to handle changes in work procedures or to rely on their own experience in rewarding good work. This reliance on rules and procedures rather than on unique individual judgment in dealing with change is the antithesis of transformational leadership.

The vertical dyad relationship between superior and subordinate in all types of Chinese organizations is formal and sometimes suspicious, and it carries large mutual obligations. These characteristics of Chinese leadership do not fit any Western typology, but they help us to understand how organizational cultural change does not rest in the hands of either leaders or followers as independent entities. From the leader's point of view, the subordinate may be perceived as presenting loyalty and *guanxi* (a reciprocal obligation to help when needed) but may also represent the threat of loss of support or of taking over the leader's position. From the subordinate's position, the superior may be perceived as a beneficent patron available to help in times of need, but the subordinate may also maintain a constant fear of misperceiving the superior's wishes and a desire to gain the superior's approval, because the subordinate needs the superior's support in order to access most organizational resources. Trust may be more highly developed if there are family connections, but even within families these dyadic interactions are often filled with anxiety.

In traditional SOEs, leaders often use shame to get conformity and, in response, usually get pragmatic feigned compliance. Feigned compliance often is countered by inspection tours designed to catch unrealistic reports to central government as well as to top firm officials (Pye, 1988). This feigned compliance is a legacy of traditional Chinese obedience to authority as well as a result of the post-Cultural Revolution period, when mortal enemies were required to work side by side. In this context many individuals were required to separate their private emotions from their public actions. The result of the struggles of organizational leaders to protect their face or reputation, and to enhance their *guanxi* (both essential to their ability to perform leadership roles effectively), is the creation of an organizational culture that appears on the surface to consist of polite, positive relationships. However, underneath this facade is a "seething hostility of cliques and tense interpersonal relationships based on differences between obligation networks. The relationships between competing obligation networks may consist of deceit, obfuscation, collusion, and selective performance of assigned tasks" (Wang, 1990, p. 203). Another consequence of feigned compliance and surface politeness is that individuality in the realization of many aspects of organizational culture may be suppressed or at least invisible to any outside observer and to many internal members as well.

The change to a market orientation has enlarged rather than reduced the reliance on face and networks of *guanxi* relationships to accomplish organizational tasks. Whereas in the traditional socialist organizational system, the central government and its representatives set goals, distributed raw materials, and distributed finished products, in the market economy, with few institutions of a true market system, each of these tasks must be accomplished through personal exchange relationships. Thus one of the key characteristics of the collective mind-set as organizations move to a market economy is constant concentration on how leaders can develop these relationships outside of the organizations and how followers can do the same with those inside the organization. Thus, rather than supporting organizational individuality of cultures through transformational leadership, societal structures strongly reinforce leaders skilled in consensus and transactional leadership.

## Symbolization: Expressions of Leadership

According to Hatch, Schein, and other scholars of organizational culture, if symbols are the creation of the collective mind-set, we can examine the symbols of leadership and explicate the meanings behind these symbols to identify how leadership is conceptualized in a Chinese organizational culture. Top-level managers may have their own offices, furnished with their own desks and padded chairs. Decorations include symbols used to legitimate power from each of the competing ideologies of Chinese cultural heritage. Walls may be decorated with calligraphy (Confucianism) or with depictions of traditionally lucky zodiac animals (Taoism) or powerful dragons (symbol of the emperor). If the organization is headquarters for a large SOE, offices may contain pictures of the offices' occupants posing with a top government official or may have political icons such as pictures of the premier or an idealized model worker (Communist). The collective meaning of these symbols is that the people who occupy the offices deserve loyalty because of their legitimate power as well as because they are admirable people with aesthetic appreciation and good moral character.

Access to telephone, computer, fax, and other telecommunications technology depends upon the nature of the business and sensitivity to market forces. People at higher levels and working in more market-oriented organizations in coastal urban areas have access to more technological office equipment, more sophisticated cars, and more opportunities to travel. Also, they are certain to be seen wearing Western business attire rather than the factory uniform more common among lower-level supervisory and worker personnel. The symbols of technology, automobiles, and clothing may indicate acceptance into the global business world to outsiders and may represent signs of power, status, face, and modernization to those inside the organization.

According to Trice and Beyer (1993), one of the ways leaders create and consolidate organizational culture is through the use of rites and rituals. Top leaders often serve as hosts at ritualistic banquets where they shower delicacies on guests in displays of conspicuous consumption and as insurance of future obligation. The symbolic meaning of such rituals is tied in with the building of an ongoing long-term business relationship (*guanxi*). This indicates that the firm is in good financial shape and says, "I have the capacity and generosity to take care of you; I expect you to reciprocate when I need help." This ritual cements relationships with those outside of the firm.

To cement relationships with those inside the firm, the banquet ritual is elevated to a high art, primarily during the organizational Spring Festival celebration (based on a Taoist belief following the rhythms of nature as the lunar New Year begins). Usually the ceremony is held in an organizational hall or large meeting room in the style of a general meeting. Following a state-of-the-organization speech by the president, leaders reward the model or good (*xian-jin*) work subunit and model workers and distribute year-end bonuses. During the meeting, some of the managers informally talk to conflicting groups or individuals about their problems. Supervisors and top-level managers visit senior and retired workers and give them gifts to honor their seniority and hard work.

The symbolic meaning of Spring Festival rituals is to create harmony and reward loyalty and seniority. Another meaning is to encourage and publicly reward high performance, thus giving prestige to those honored as well as to the leader. By choosing who to reward and how much of the reward to base on performance, leaders have one of their best opportunities to indicate important shifts toward or away from market values in the organizational culture.

Market-oriented organizations have an additional type of ritual, usually performed when an organization opens a new retail outlet, secures an important contract, or is first listed on a stock exchange. At such an event, the leader is showered with congratulatory plaques, bouquets, baskets of artificial flowers, and testimonials from those in the leader's obligation network. Again, these acts represent the extension of the obligation network that the leader may bring to bear to solve problems as well as an indication of the leader's status or reputation. The importance or status of each individual is indicated by his or her position in receiving lines, on platforms, and at dinner tables and by the size of the crowd of following subordinates ready to use their ubiquitous cell phones to solve any problem or meet any request. Individuality in organizational cultures may be signified by the people who are present and by the organizations they represent.

## Interpretation and Pseudosymbols in Chinese Organizational Culture

According to Hatch, the interpretation of organizational symbols is key in integrating the meaning of cultural symbols into "the broader context of a history of cultural meanings and a geography of cultural artifacts" (Chapter 15, this volume). However, great caution must be used in interpreting Chinese leadership symbols. The world of public symbolization—including titles, clothing, physical possessions, and public displays of loyalty—may not represent the actual scope of any individual's power. To preserve face, or appearance of status, however, the formal positions will be honored in official public interactions. Members of the organization know these symbols to be pseudosymbols. The power of real leaders in an organization rests primarily in the networks of relationships they possess as a result of their access to organizational and nonorganiza-

tional resources. For example, some individuals who have low official rank in an organization may also have harmonious, influential relationships with a wide network of managerial and nonmanagerial organizational members (i.e., they are willing to spend private time playing mah-jongg or going fishing with them). Such people may in fact be very powerful in the organization because of their ability to use the obligations in their networks of relationships to make things happen. Or a person may have a strong relationship with a pivotal person in a key government agency capable of providing many benefits that are very effective in solving a wide array of organizational problems. It is common for some obligation relationships such as these to be very private or even secret, and they are certainly never revealed by external symbols. Thus the real symbol of power and leadership is the ability to solve a problem, not the external trappings of status artifacts.

Real symbols of leadership as interpreted in the entire cultural context reveal a mixture of a few symbols of Communist egalitarian patriotism and many symbols of Taoist harmony and Confucian hierarchy. The religious aspects of this mixture were forbidden when Mao and the Gang of Four were concerned about wiping out signs of ancient beliefs and imposing a common culture of national unity based upon areligious Communist thought. The presence of these symbols today reveals the extent to which ancient ways persist in the cultural mind-set and perhaps indicate a weakening of the ideological tenets of pure Communist doctrine as the market economy changes are introduced.

## TRANSFORMATIONAL LEADERS AND CHANGE IN ORGANIZATIONAL CULTURE IN CHINA

Most discussions of the role of transformational leadership in creating organizational culture change are based on a body of cultural literature written from a Western perspective (Allaire & Firsirotu, 1984; Bass & Aviolo, 1994; Burns, 1978; Hatch, 1993; Rohner, 1984; Triandis, 1980; Trice & Beyer, 1993). Western theories of transformational leadership and organizational change emphasize that change is accomplished through the leader's implementation of a unique vision of the organization through powerful persuasive personal characteristics and actions designed to change internal organizational cultural forms and substance (Bass & Aviolo, 1994; Porras & Robertson, 1992; Hatch, 1993). In contrast, the Chinese government has made many plans for economic change, and these changes have created an ongoing series of critical incidents and external circumstances that require Chinese organizations to change. But organizational leaders have limited autonomy in how to enact the organizational change needed to bring organizations into line with national policies and few norms or models that might cause them to act in transformational leadership ways.

Organizational culture change is mind-set change. The mind-set change typically needed in Western organizations is a change related to the focus and implementation of the strategic vision of the organization. In contrast, the organizational cultural change (mind-set change) in China today demands moving from the socialist way of thinking to the market way of thinking. The socialist mind-set requires belief in contribution to the common good and loyalty to the state in exchange for individual or family security. The market mind-set encourages belief in self-sufficiency by attaining organizational profit as a means to obtain individual or family security. Given this difference in mind-set, the typical recommendations that transformational leaders should motivate followers by making them more aware of important task outcomes and should encourage them to transcend their own self-interests for the sake of the organization may be inappropriate for the Chinese situation.

The source of change initiatives envisioned in the Western theory of transformational leadership is one of a leader looking at market conditions in a regulated capitalist system to articulate a vision of the way his or her organization should respond to environmental threats and opportunities. If we examine how Chinese market change initiatives have occurred, we observe that in most cases, change is initiated by central government policy, proposed either by a powerful government leader or by central political meetings and institutionalized by political and bureaucratic government followers. The government documents (*wen jian*) that carry the essential philosophy or guidelines of the new policy are produced at the meetings and passed through the central, provincial, and local government agencies. The agency members attend meetings to learn the meaning of the documents (*Xue-xi hui-yi jin-sheng*) and to discuss the practical strategies for and potential difficulties in implementing the policies. The organizational leaders may attend these meetings and also receive the *wen jian* by mail. This is not the transformational leadership suggested by Bennis and Nanus and exemplified by the likes of Lee Iacocca. Rather, institutional leadership used in consolidating organizational cultures seems to describe this situation.

Participation and empowerment are certainly elements in normative models of organizational culture change, but these correspond only roughly to the sort of participation and empowerment enacted by senior leaders in China. In SOEs, the business leaders convene meetings with relevant department heads to discuss policy implementation. Leaders may accept feedback from managers with special expertise in constructing the actual strategy for implementing the new policy. The organizational leaders usually do not want to damage their relationships with the government officials charged with implementing the new policy. Thus a new organizational policy consistent with the national political policy changes usually is proclaimed by top organizational business leaders in consultation with the top leaders of the maintenance and party systems of the organization. The middle-level managers implement the policy and report on follow-up to the organizational leaders and government agencies. If the new government policy seems impossible to implement or is in conflict with the wishes of the organizational leaders, the organizational leaders will reconstruct the policy into an internal strategy that appears to follow the government guidelines. The strategy will be implemented in a way that enables the organization to survive and is consistent with the organizational leaders' opinions. In this way, as Weber has stated, the culture is protected from drastic changes by organizational leaders and members, even if such a drastic change is advocated by the central government.

In market-oriented organizations, and especially in organizations led by individuals or stockholders, the business leaders or the stockholder representative committee may be sufficiently more powerful than the leaders of the maintenance and party systems that the consultation with these individuals is *pro forma*. If there are policy changes responsive to new government regulations, such as changes in housing or social welfare insurance, the process may be very similar to that of an SOE. For other internal policy changes concerning market matters, such as opening a new branch office or retail outlet, the process is more streamlined and may be more strongly influenced by the leaders or stockholder committee, with little consultation with the life-support and sociopolitical organizational unit heads.

As outlined by Schein (1992), to reinforce these changes and embed them into the organizational culture, organizational leaders could use direction of attention, reaction to crises, role modeling, allocation of rewards, and criteria for selection and dismissal to reinforce their priorities. Of these, Chinese leaders most often use allocation of rewards, selection and dismissal, and direction of attention to implement cultural change. Chinese organizational leaders have always had the power to direct attention and to allocate rewards and punishment within loose organizational structures, and this power has in-

creased since market reforms began. Leaders may give better jobs, travel opportunities, free coupons for holiday goods, bonuses, better housing, and other fringe benefits (*fu-li dai-yu*) to reinforce new policies. Although the ability to control entry and exit across organizational boundaries was limited before market reforms, organizational leaders could always arrange for members to get better or worse jobs in the organization. Now hiring and firing have also come into their domain (Wang, 1990). However, this system differs from those of Western transformational leaders in that these strategies are most often used not to initiate novelty within a unique organizational culture but to reinforce new ideas suggested from above and applied in many organizations.

The Hatch model of organizational culture change emphasizes the roles of both leaders and followers in creating organizational culture and the role of followers in creating leadership. The role of organizational members in Chinese organizational culture change is complex. On one hand, leaders need to maintain good relationships with followers and so are reluctant to initiate unpopular change. On the other hand, followers also need good relationships with the leader, who now is more likely to hold power over their employment than was possible in the past (especially in a market organization). The consequences of this interdependence are that leaders initiate change (a) when they are certain that there will be some level of compliance because the followers agree, (b) when followers are afraid of the consequences of noncompliance, or (c) when leaders and followers both know that officially the new policy must be announced for political reasons but also realize implicitly that no consequences will occur for noncompliance.

The power of the followers rests in large part in their ability to give real or feigned compliance. Centuries of oppression have raised the art of surface compliance and subsurface noncompliance to a high art in China. Communist doctrine that gives workers rights to confront unpopular leadership decisions conflict with centuries of obedience to leaders powerful enough to make life-or-death decisions over the fates of employees. The result is almost always the appearance of compliance with differing levels of subjective agreement with surface reality. The practice of adopting feigned compliance rather than attempting to change or influence the policy with which one disagrees is an indicator that Chinese followers may be more passive than active in their ability to shape organizational culture. This occurs because of the overwhelming imposition of politics into Chinese daily organizational life. People develop a passive pragmatic strategy to appear to go along with the political situation while seeking opportunities to pursue a better life.

In order for new policies (cultural artifacts) to become incorporated into the collective mind-set and be infused with symbolic meaning, some group agreement with the policy must occur. This is accomplished through work group meetings where work unit supervisors and department managers discuss the new policies with workers. If real adoption of the changes into the collective mind-set is to occur as a group phenomenon, this is where the perception of collective agreement is realized. If collective agreement does not occur, feigned obedience or pseudo-compliance at all levels results. If the feigned obedience is discovered, swift and severe punishment may result.

The incorporation of new market changes into existing cultural subjectivity by the process of interpretation has evoked not only a reinterpretation of socialism, but a renewed expression of traditional cultural values. That is, in the current rethinking of what socialism with market characteristics means, relaxation of the obligations of the state to provide for each citizen seems to be accompanied by increases in realization of ancient values venerating leaders. These values give a great deal of power to leaders but constrain that power in complex networks of mutual obligation that no leader can afford to ignore.

## EVALUATION OF THE APPLICABILITY OF TRANSFORMATIONAL LEADERSHIP TO THE CHINESE SITUATION

This discussion of leadership and organizational change in China is one example of issues raised in extended application of organizational culture theory to new global issues. The Hatch (1993; see also Chapter 15, this volume) model is a particularly current, sophisticated development in transformational leadership theory. This model and other discussions of the role of transformational leadership in organizational change are in some ways compatible, in other ways incompatible, and in some ways incomplete for analyzing China. Examples of leader-follower systems adopting new market ways fit many aspects of Hatch's description of the ongoing cycle of production of artifacts and production of meaning as organizational cultures change. In addition, the reappearance of ancient values seems congruent with her discussion of sources of change coming from outside of the organization and from those other than the leader.

The image of Chinese leaders does not fit the traditional view of transformational leader and is more likely to fit the view of institutional and transactional leaders used for consolidating existing cultures. The Chinese leader does not include the dramatic alternative vision and strategy so central to the description of charismatic leaders initiating change in Western organizational literature (Bennis & Nanus, 1985). Only a few Chinese market organization leaders initiate novelty in their organizations, and these individuals still have obligations to do so within the political framework set out by higher government officials and by obligations to their own *guanxi* networks.

Most writing on transformational leaders gives the leader large responsibility for shaping organizational culture. Hatch treats the leader as both creator and product of the social context. We have many examples of leaders creating artifacts, such as new internal policies, that *appear to be* symbolized through obedience or feigned compliance. These examples clearly illustrate the power of followers to appear to comply on the surface without really adopting change at the level of shared cultural meaning. In this instance the followers are constructing the meaningful reality of the organization according to their own interpretation, as Hatch suggests, but do not seem to be creating the meaning of leader as artifact in the Hatch perspective. The use of pseudosymbols that have little organizational shared meaning might need to be more explicitly addressed in future discussions of leaders as artifacts in the Hatch model.

There are several characteristics of Chinese organizations that seem to have no clear expression in many discussions of transformational leadership or in the Hatch model. The first is the great power a Chinese leader has over the lives of organizational members. Leaders gain power from their position in the political structure, from social norms supporting obedience, and from the societal system that espouses market freedoms but lacks social institutions to support individual career choice. In current Chinese society it is still difficult to be fired from an SOE, but so many SOEs have excess workers that it is common to lose a position and be placed on a roll of excess workers, with barely enough income to survive. In market organizations there is still a norm making firing difficult, but it does occur. Individuals who become unemployed or underemployed as a consequence of noncompliance with a leader's wishes may lose their entire social lives, jobs, homes, medical care, and their children's schooling in a society with few market mechanisms to help them to enter another work unit. Their alternatives are to use family network resources to avoid the penalties of noncompliance with a leader's wishes or to start their own businesses with these resources—both high-risk choices.

Second, Western theory assumes that a transformational organizational leader might initiate and confirm organizational change through several mechanism (Hatch, 1993, Chapter 15, this volume; Schein, 1992; Trice & Beyer, 1993). But these perspectives do not adequately take into account the leader as a person embedded in a network of obligations to many others inside and outside the organization. Even the top leaders of market organizations must conform to ideological guidelines set down by political superiors. In addition, all organizational leaders must develop extended business networks to accomplish the goals of their organizations. The individuals in these networks constrain leaders' actions as much as any superior. These social constraints on what leaders do and how leaders might initiate or implement change are currently outside of Western models of organizational change and require new conceptualizations.

Third, Western models contain fundamental assumptions that individuals have the freedom to actively construct and interpret the meaning systems of organizational culture. In the Chinese situation, where political conformity is required, some democratic aspects of market reform as potential ingredients of new cultural meaning may not even reach the level of manifestation, let alone the level of realization. The passivity of organizational members under these constraints limits the possibilities for organizational culture change in ways not accounted for by the simple process of routinization as described by Weber and Hatch.

Although most models of organizational culture clearly include subjective and emotional experiences as central to their conceptualizations, the processes of symbolization and interpretation as described by Hatch remain as basically rational or self-oriented processes. In China, organizational members embedded in obligation networks do not always think or act in utilitarian ways. Personal trust and network obligations (*guanxi*) rather than assessment of costs and benefits are often the standard for evaluating beliefs and actions within organizational cultures and in decisions about new cultural content.

Finally, China has a rapidly changing and ambiguous economic environment, with internal organizational leadership accustomed to relying on direction from the government and limited organizational experience with capitalist, market organizations. In these circumstances, Chinese organizational culture is strongly influenced by another available ideology or a collective mind-set, the traditional societal cultural values that have persisted in cultural beliefs even when they were condemned in public. Lack of familiarity with Western market practices make it less likely that assumptions of Western capitalism will be adopted, even though the macro-organizational structure assumes some characteristics of a market economy. Western models of transformational leadership may need to be refined to take into account the process of old, unexpressed cultural values reappearing within organizational cultures in times of great change.

In summary, when we apply Western models of transformational leadership in organizational change, such as the one proposed by Hatch, to the changes currently occurring in Chinese organizations, we find that the basic outlines fit many aspects of the Chinese situation. But we also find aspects of organizational cultural change that are not accounted for by these models, such as secrecy and pseudosymbols, leader power over life space, leaders as followers, and violations as assumptions of freedom and individual rationality. As all Western models of organizational behavior are applied to other societal contexts in the future, we must consider that the suggestions indicated by the Chinese context may warrant permanent changes in these models if they are to be applied globally.

# References

Aaker, D. A. (1994). Building a brand: The Saturn story. *California Management Review, 36*(2), 114-133.

Aaker, D. A., & Meyers, J. G. (1987). *Advertising management.* Englewood Cliffs, NJ: Prentice Hall.

Aaltio-Marjosola, I. (1994). Gender stereotypes as cultural products of the organisation. *Scandinavian Journal of Management, 10*(2), 147-162.

Aaltio-Marjosola, I., & Lehtinen, J. (1998). Male managers as fathers? Contrasting management, fatherhood and masculinity. *Human Relations, 51,* 121-136.

Aaltio-Marjosola, I., & Sevøn, G. (1997). Gendering organization topics. *Hallinnon Tutkimus* [Finnish Journal of Administrative Studies], *4,* 269-271.

Abbott, A. (1988). *The system of the professions.* Chicago: University of Chicago Press.

Abegglen, J. (1958). *The Japanese factory.* Glencoe, IL: Free Press.

Abell, D. F. (1980). *Defining the business.* Hemel Hempstead, England: Prentice Hall.

Abella, R. S. (1984). *Equity in employment: A Royal Commission report.* Ottawa: Canadian Ministry of Supply and Services.

Abolafia, M. Y., & Kilduff, M. (1988). Enacting market crisis: The social construction of a speculative bubble. *Administrative Science Quarterly, 33,* 177-193.

Acker, J. (1992). Gendering organizational theory. In A. J. Mills & P. Tancred (Eds.), *Gendering organizational analysis* (pp. 248-260). Newbury Park, CA: Sage.

Adams, J. S. (1965). Inequity in social exchange. In L. Berkowitz (Ed.), *Advances in experimental social psychology.* New York: Academic Press.

Adkins, C. L., Ravlin, E. C., & Meglino, B. M. (1992, August). *Value congruence between co-workers and its relationship to work-related outcomes.* Paper presented at the annual meeting of the Academy of Management, Las Vegas.

Adler, N. J. (1997). *International dimensions of organizational behavior* (3rd ed.). Cincinnati, OH: South-Western.

Adler, N. J., Campbell, N., & Laurent, A. (1989). In search of appropriate methodology: From outside the People's Republic of China looking in. *Journal of International Business Studies, 20,* 61-74.

Adler, P., & Adler, P. A. (1988). Intense loyalty in organizations: A case study of college athletics. *Administrative Science Quarterly, 33,* 401-417.

Adler, P. S., & Borys, B. (1996). Two types of bureaucracy: Enabling and coercive. *Administrative Science Quarterly, 41,* 61-89.

Agar, M. H. (1982). Whatever happened to cognitive anthropology: A partial review. *Human Organization, 41,* 82-86.

Agger, B. (1991). Critical theory, poststructuralism, postmodernism: Their sociological relevance. *Annual Review of Sociology, 17,* 105-131.

Agocs, C., Burr, C., & Somerset, F. (1992). *Employment equity: Cooperative strategies for organisational change.* Scarborough, ON: Prentice Hall.

Agre, P. (1994). *Networking on the network.* Available Internet: message to request@weber.ucsd.edu and subject line "archive send network."

Ajzen, I., & Fishbein, M. (1973). Attitudinal and normative variables as predictors of specific behaviors. *Journal of Personality and Social Psychology, 27,* 41-57.

Ajzen, I., & Fishbein, M. (1980). *Understanding attitudes and predicting social behavior.* Englewood Cliffs, NJ: Prentice Hall.

Albert, S., & Whetten, D. A. (1985). Organizational identity. In L. L. Cummings & B. M. Staw (Eds.), *Research in organizational behavior* (Vol. 7, pp. 263-295). Greenwich, CT: JAI.

Alchian, A. A., & Demsetz, H. (1972). Production, information costs, and economic organization. *American Economic Review, 62,* 777-795.

Alexander, C. P. (1985). The theories of Likert and Gibb: New tools for determining management readiness for quality circles and similar OD interventions. *Organization Development Journal, 3*(1), 15-20.

Ali, A. J., Krishnan, K., & Azim, A. (1997). Expatriate and indigenous managers' work loyalty and attitude towards risk. *Journal of Psychology, 131,* 260-271.

Allaire, Y., & Firsirotu, M. (1984). Theories of organizational culture. *Organization Studies, 5,* 193-226.

Allen, N. J., & Meyer, J. P. (1990). The measurement and antecedents of affective, continuance and normative commitment to the organization. *Journal of Occupational Psychology, 63,* 1-18.

Allen, R. F. (1985). Four phases for bringing about cultural change. In R. H. Kilmann, M. J. Saxton, R. Serpa, & Associates (Eds.), *Gaining control of the corporate culture* (pp. 332-350). San Francisco: Jossey-Bass.

Allen, R. F., & Dyer, F. J. (1980). A tool for tapping the organizational unconscious. *Personnel Journal, 59,* 192-198.

Altman, B. W., & Post, J. E. (1996). Beyond the social contract: An analysis of the executive view at twenty-five large companies. In D. T. Hall (Ed.), *The career is dead—long live the career: A relational approach to careers* (pp. 46-71). San Francisco: Jossey-Bass.

Alvesson, M. (1995). *Cultural perspectives on organizations*. New York: Cambridge University Press.

Alvesson, M., & Berg, P. O. (1992). *Corporate culture and organizational symbolism: An overview*. New York: Walter de Gruyter.

Alvesson, M., & Billing, Y. D. (1997). *Understanding gender and organizations*. Thousand Oaks, CA: Sage.

Alvesson, M., & Deetz, S. (1996). Critical theory and postmodern approaches to organizational studies. In S. R. Clegg, C. Hardy, & W. R. Nord (Eds.), *Handbook of organization studies* (pp. 191-217). Thousand Oaks, CA: Sage.

Amabile, T. M. (1988). A model of creativity and innovation in organizations. In B. M. Staw & L. L. Cummings (Eds.), *Research in organizational behavior* (Vol. 10, pp. 123-167). Greenwich, CT: JAI.

Amabile, T. M. (1998). How to kill creativity. *Harvard Business Review*, 76(5), 76-87.

Ancona, D. G. (1988). Groups in organizations: Extending laboratory models. In C. Hendrick (Ed.), *Annual review of personality and social psychology: Group and intergroup processes*. Newbury Park, CA: Sage.

Ancona, D. G., & Chong, C.-L. (1996). Entrainment: Pace, cycle, and rhythm in organizational behavior. In B. M. Staw & L. L. Cummings (Eds.), *Research in organizational behavior* (Vol. 18, pp. 251-284). Greenwich, CT: JAI.

Anderson, B. (1983). *Imagined communities: Reflections on the origin and spread of nationalism*. London: Verso/NLB.

Anderson, J. C., Rungtusanatham, M., & Schroeder, R. G. (1994). A theory of quality management underlying the Deming management method. *Academy of Management Review, 19*, 472-509.

Anderson, N., Hardy, G., & West, M. (1990). Innovative teams at work. *Personnel Management, 22*(9), 48-53.

Anderson, N., & King, N. (1993). Innovation in organizations. In C. L. Cooper & I. T. Robertson (Eds.), *International review of industrial and organizational psychology* (Vol. 8, pp. 1-34). New York: John Wiley.

Angle, H. L., & Perry, J. L. (1986). Dual commitment and labor-management relationship climates. *Academy of Management Journal, 29*, 31-50.

Appadurai, A. (1991). Global ethnoscapes: Notes and queries for a transnational anthropology. In R. G. Fox (Ed.), *Recapturing anthropology: Working in the present* (pp. 191-210). Santa Fe, NM: School of American Research Press.

Apter, D. E. (1964). Introduction: Ideology and discontent. In D. E. Apter (Ed.), *Ideology and discontent* (pp. 15-46). London: Free Press.

Argote, L. A., & McGrath, J. E. (1993). Group processes in organizations: Continuity and change. In C. L. Cooper & I. T. Robertson (Eds.), *International review of industrial and organizational psychology* (Vol. 8). New York: John Wiley.

Argyris, C. (1957). Some problems in conceptualizing organizational climate: A case study of a bank. *Administrative Science Quarterly, 2*, 501-520.

Argyris, C. (1960). *Understanding organizational behavior.* Homewood, IL: Dorsey.

Argyris, C. (1970). *Intervention theory and method.* Reading, MA: Addison-Wesley.

Argyris, C. (1982). *Reasoning, learning, and action.* San Francisco: Jossey-Bass.

Argyris, C. (1993). *Knowledge for action: A guide to overcoming barriers to organizational change.* San Francisco: Jossey-Bass.

Armon, C. (1993). Developmental conceptions of good work: A longitudinal study. In J. Demick & P. M. Miller (Eds.), *Development in the workplace.* Hillsdale, NJ: Lawrence Erlbaum.

Armstrong, P., & Armstrong, H. (1990). *Theorizing women's work.* Toronto: Garamond.

Arthur, M. B., & Rousseau, D. M. (Eds.). (1996). *The boundaryless career: A new employment principle for a new organizational era.* New York: Oxford University Press.

Ashford, S. J., & Black, J. S. (1996). Proactivity during organizational entry: The role of desire for control. *Journal of Applied Psychology, 81,* 199-214.

Ashford, S. J., & Cummings, L. L. (1983). Feedback as an individual resource: Personal strategies of creating information. *Organizational Behavior and Human Performance, 32,* 370-398.

Ashford, S. J., & Taylor, M. S. (1990). Adaptation to work transitions: An integrative approach. In G. R. Ferris & K. M. Rowland (Eds.), *Research in personnel and human resources management* (Vol. 8, pp. 1-39). Greenwich, CT: JAI.

Ashforth, B. E., & Humphrey, R. H. (1995). Emotion in the workplace: A reappraisal. *Human Relations, 48,* 97-125.

Ashforth, B. E., & Mael, F. (1989). Social identity theory and the organization. *Academy of Management Review, 14,* 20-39.

Ashforth, B. E., & Saks, A. M. (1996). Socialization tactics: Longitudinal effects on newcomer adjustment. *Academy of Management Journal, 39,* 149-178.

Ashkanasy, N. M., & Holmes, S. (1995). Perceptions of organizational ideology following merger: A longitudinal study of merging accounting firms. *Accounting, Organizations, and Society, 20,* 19-34.

Ashmos, D. P., & Huber, G. P. (1987). The systems paradigm in organization theory: Correcting the record and suggesting the future. *Academy of Management Review, 12,* 607-622.

Atkinson, A. A., Waterhouse, J. H., & Wells, R. B. (1997). A stakeholder approach to strategic performance measurement. *Sloan Management Review, 38*(3), 25-38.

Aubrey, R. (1998, July 7). Toy time: Child's playthings help relieve tension at work. *Ann Arbor News,* p. A8.

St. Augustine. (1912). *Confessions* (Vol. 2, W. Watts, Trans.). New York: Macmillan.

Aven, F. A., Jr., Parker, P., & McEvoy, G. M. (1993). Gender and attitudinal commitment to organizations: A meta-analysis. *Journal of Business Research, 26,* 63-73.

Babin, B. J., & Darden, W. R. (1995). Consumer self-regulation in a retail environment. *Journal of Retailing, 71,* 47-70.

Badaracco, J. L., Jr., & Ellsworth, R. R. (1989). *Leadership and the quest for integrity.* Boston: Harvard Business School Press.

Bajdo, L., & Dickson, M. W. (1999, August). *The impact of organizational culture on women's advancement in organizations.* Paper presented at the annual meeting of the Academy of Management, Chicago.

Baker, H. E., III, & Feldman, D. C. (1990). Strategies of organizational socialization and their impact on newcomer adjustment. *Journal of Managerial Issues, 2,* 198-212.

Baker, T., & Jones, R. (1967). *Coffee, tea or me? The uninhibited memoirs of two airline stewardesses.* New York: Bartholomew House.

Bakhtin, M. M. (1981). *The dialogic imagination: Four essays by M. M. Bakhtin* (M. Holquist, Ed.; M. Holquist & C. Emerson, Trans.). Austin: University of Texas Press.

Balazs, A. L. (1990). Value congruency: The case of the "socially responsible" firm. *Journal of Business Research, 20,* 171-181.

Balter, M. (1998, November 20). Why settle down? The mystery of communities. *Science, 282,* 1442-1445.

Baltes, B. B., Lacost, H., Parker, C. P., Altmann, R., Huff, J., & Young, S. (1999, April). *A multitrait-multimethod examination of hierarchical models of psychological climate.* Poster session presented at the 14th Annual Meeting of the Society for Industrial and Organizational Psychology, Atlanta, GA.

Bandura, A. (1977). *Social learning theory.* Englewood Cliffs, NJ: Prentice Hall.

Bandura, A. (1997). *Self-efficacy: The exercise of control.* New York: W. H. Freeman.

Bargh, J. (1990). Auto-motives: Preconscious determinants of social interaction. In E. T. Higgins & R. M. Sorrentino (Eds.), *Handbook of motivation and cognition: Foundations of social behavior* (Vol. 2, pp. 93-130). New York: Guilford.

Bargh, J., Chen, M., & Burrows, L. (1996). Automaticity of social behavior: Direct effects of tacit construction and stereotype activation on action. *Journal of Personality and Social Psychology, 71,* 230-244.

Barkow, J. H., Cosmides, L., & Tooby, J. (Eds.). (1992). *The adapted mind: Evolutionary psychology and the generation of culture.* New York: Oxford University Press.

Barley, S. R. (1983). Semiotics and the study of occupational and organizational cultures. *Administrative Science Quarterly, 28,* 393-413.

Barley, S. R. (1990). The alignment of technology and structure through roles and networks. *Administrative Science Quarterly, 35,* 61-103.

Barley, S. R. (1991). Semiotics and the study of occupational and organizational culture. In P. J. Frost, L. F. Moore, M. R. Louis, C. C. Lundberg, & J. Martin (Eds.), *Reframing organizational culture* (pp. 39-54). Newbury Park, CA: Sage.

Barley, S. R. (1995). Culture. In N. Nicholson (Ed.), *The Blackwell encyclopedic dictionary of organizational behavior.* Cambridge, MA: Blackwell.

Barley, S. R., & Kunda, G. (1992). Design and devotion: Surges of rational and normative ideologies of control in managerial discourse. *Administrative Science Quarterly, 37,* 363-399.

Barley, S. R., Meyer, G. W., & Gash, D. C. (1988). Cultures of culture: Academics, practitioners and the pragmatics of normative control. *Administrative Science Quarterly, 33,* 24-60.

Barnard, C. I. (1938). *Functions of the executive.* Cambridge, MA: Harvard University Press.

Barney, J. B. (1986). Organizational culture: Can it be a source of sustained competitive advantage? *Academy of Management Review, 11,* 656-665.

Barney, J. B. (1991). Firm resources and sustained competitive advantage. *Journal of Management, 17,* 99-120.

Barney, J. B. (1997). *Gaining and sustaining competitive advantage.* Reading, MA: Addison-Wesley.

Barney, J. B., & Hesterly, W. (1996). Organizational economics: Understanding the relationship between organizations and economic analysis. In S. R. Clegg, C. Hardy, & W. R. Nord (Eds.), *Handbook of organization studies* (pp. 115-147). Thousand Oaks, CA: Sage.

Baron, R. A. (1994). The physical environment of work settings: Effects on task performance, interpersonal relations, and job satisfaction. In B. M. Staw & L. L. Cummings (Eds.), *Research in organizational behavior* (Vol. 16, pp. 1-46). Greenwich, CT: JAI.

Barrett, P. E. (1973). *The human implications of mergers and takeovers.* London: Institute of Personnel Management.

Barry, D. (1996). Artful inquiry: A symbolic constructivist approach to social science research. *Qualitative Inquiry, 2,* 411-438.

Bartunek, J. M. (1993). The multiple cognition and conflicts associated with second order organizational change. In J. K. Murnighan (Ed.), *Social psychology in organizations: Advances in theory and research* (pp. 322-349). Englewood Cliffs, NJ: Prentice Hall.

Bass, B. M. (1985). *Leadership and performance beyond expectations.* New York: Free Press.

Bass, B. M. (1998). *Transformational leadership: Industrial, military, and educational impact.* Mahwah, NJ: Lawrence Erlbaum.

Bass, B. M., & Aviolo, B. J. (Eds.). (1994). *Improving organizational effectiveness through transformational leadership.* Thousand Oaks, CA: Sage.

Bateman, T. S., & Organ, D. W. (1983). Job satisfaction and the good soldier: The relationship between affect and employee "citizenship." *Academy of Management Journal, 26,* 587-595.

Bauer, T. N., & Green, S. G. (1996). The development of leader-member exchange: A longitudinal test. *Academy of Management Journal, 39,* 1538-1567.

Bauer, T. N., Morrison, E. W., & Callister, R. R. (1998). Organizational socialization: A review and directions for future research. In G. R. Ferris (Ed.), *Research in personnel and human resources management* (Vol. 16, pp. 149-214). Greenwich, CT: JAI.

Bearden, W. O., Netemeyer, R. G., & Teel, J. E. (1989). Measurement of consumer susceptibility to interpersonal influence. *Journal of Consumer Research, 15,* 473-481.

Beatty, S. E., Kahle, L. R., Homer, P. M., & Misra, S. (1985, Fall). Alternative measurement approaches to consumer values: The list of values and the Rokeach Value Survey. *Psychology and Marketing, 2,* 181-200.

Beck, J. C., & Beck, M. N. (1994). *The change of a lifetime: Employment patterns among Japan's managerial elite.* Honolulu: University of Hawaii Press.

Beck, N. (1992). *Shifting gears: Thriving in the new economy.* Toronto: HarperCollins.

Becker, B. W., & Connor, P. E. (1986). On the status and promise of values research. *Management Bibliographies and Reviews, 12,* 3-17.

Becker, H. S. (1960). Notes on the concept of commitment. *American Journal of Sociology, 66,* 32-40.

Becker, H. S., Geer, B., Hughes, E. C., & Strauss, A. L. (1961). *Boys in white: Student culture in medical school.* Chicago: University of Chicago Press.

Becker, T. E. (1992). Foci and bases of commitment: Are they distinctions worth making? *Academy of Management Journal, 35,* 232-244.

Beecroft, G. D. (1995). *Implementing total quality management.* Waterloo, ON: University of Waterloo, Institute for Improvement of Quality and Productivity.

Beer, M. (1987). Revitalizing organizations: Change process and emergent model. *Academy of Management Executive, 1*(1), 51-55.

Beer, M., Eisenstat, R. A., & Spector, B. (1990). Why change programs don't produce change. *Harvard Business Review, 69*(2), 158-166.

Bendix, R. (1956). *Work and authority in industry.* New York: John Wiley.

Benedict, R. (1946). *The chrysanthemum and the sword.* Boston: Houghton Mifflin.

Bennett, A. (1990). *The death of the organization man.* New York: William Morrow.

Bennis, W. G., & Nanus, B. (1985). *Leaders: The strategies for taking charge.* New York: Harper & Row.

Benoit, J., & Perkins, K. (1997). Volunteer fire-fighting activity in North America as serious leisure. *World Leisure and Recreation, 39*(3), 23-29.

Berger, P. L., & Luckmann, T. (1967). *The social construction of reality: A treatise in the sociology of knowledge.* Garden City, NY: Doubleday.

Berkowitz, L. (1993). *Aggression: Its causes, consequences, and control.* New York: McGraw-Hill.

Bernas, K. L., & Major, D. A. (2000). Contributors to stress resistance: Testing a model of women's work-family conflict. *Psychology of Women Quarterly, 24,* 170-178.

Bernstein, W. M., & Burke, W. W. (1989). Modeling organizational meaning systems. In R. W. Woodman & W. A. Pasmore (Eds.), *Research in organizational change and development* (Vol. 3, pp. 117-159). Greenwich, CT: JAI.

Berry, L. L. (1995). Relationship marketing of services: Growing interest, emerging perspectives. *Journal of the Academy of Marketing Science, 23,* 236-245.

Beyer, J. M. (1981). Ideologies, values, and decision making in organizations. In P. C. Nystrom & W. H. Starbuck (Eds.), *Handbook of organizational design* (Vol. 2, pp. 166-202). New York: Oxford University Press.

Beyer, J. M., & Hannah, D. R. (1999). *Building on the past: The role of personal identities in the adjustment of experienced workers to a new setting.* Manuscript submitted for publication.

Beyer, J. M., & Hannah, D. R. (2000). The cultural significance of athletics in U.S. higher education. *Journal of Sport Management, 14,* 105-132.

Bhagat, R. S., Kedia, B. L., Crawford, S. E., & Kaplan, M. (1990). Cross-cultural and cross-national research in organizational psychology: Emergent trends and directions for research in the 1990s. In C. L. Cooper & I. T. Robertson (Eds.), *International review of industrial and organizational psychology* (Vol. 5, pp. 59-99). New York: John Wiley.

Bigley, G. A., & Pearce, J. L. (1998). Straining for shared meaning in organization science: Problems of trust and distrust. *Academy of Management Review, 23,* 405-421.

Binder, D. (Chair). (1998, April). *The challenge of making change happen: A case study.* Practitioner forum conducted at the 13th Annual Meeting of the Society for Industrial and Organizational Psychology, Dallas.

Bitner, M. J. (1992). Servicescapes: The impact of physical surroundings on customers and employees. *Journal of Marketing, 56*(2), 57-71.

Black, S., & Mendenhall, M. (1993). Resolving conflicts with the Japanese mission impossible? *Sloan Management Review, 34*(3), 49-59.

Blackler, F. (1992). Formative contexts and activity systems: Postmodern approaches to the management of change. In M. Reed & M. Hughes (Eds.), *Rethinking organization: New directions in organization theory and analysis.* Newbury Park, CA: Sage.

Blackler, F. (1993). Knowledge and the theory of organizations: Organizations as activity systems and the reframing of management. *Journal of Management Studies, 30,* 863-884.

Blake, R. R., & Mouton, J. S. (1964). *The managerial grid: Key orientations for achieving production through people.* Houston, TX: Gulf.

Blake, R. R., & Mouton, J. S. (1985). How to achieve integration on the human side of the merger. *Organizational Dynamics, 13*(3), 41-56.

Blau, J. R. (1982). Structural sociology and network analysis: An overview. In P. V. Marsden & N. Lin (Eds.), *Social structure and network analysis* (pp. 273-279). Beverly Hills, CA: Sage.

Blood, M. R. (1969). Work values and job satisfaction. *Journal of Applied Psychology, 53,* 456-459.

Bluedorn, A. C. (1997). Primary rhythms, information processing, and planning: Toward a strategic temporal technology. *Technology Studies, 4,* 1-36.

Bluedorn, A. C. (1998a). An interview with anthropologist Edward T. Hall. *Journal of Management Inquiry, 7,* 109-115.

Bluedorn, A. C. (1998b). [Psychometric properties of the individual values version of the Inventory of Polychronic Values]. Unpublished raw data.

Bluedorn, A. C. (1998c, June). *A taste for change: An investigation of the correlates of individuals' orientation to change.* Paper presented at the conference "The 21st Century Change Imperative: Evolving Organizations and Emerging Networks," Columbia, MO.

Bluedorn, A. C., & Denhardt, R. B. (1988). Time and organizations. *Journal of Management, 14,* 299-320.

Bluedorn, A. C., Kalliath, T. J., Strube, M. J., & Martin, G. D. (1999). Polychronicity and the Inventory of Polychronic Values (IPV): The development of an instrument to measure a fundamental dimension of organizational culture. *Journal of Managerial Psychology, 14,* 205-230.

Bluedorn, A. C., Kaufman, C. F., & Lane, P. M. (1992). How many things do you like to do at once? An introduction to monochronic and polychronic time. *Academy of Management Executive, 6*(4), 17-26.

Blumberg, A., & Wiener, W. (1971). One from two: Facilitating an organizational merger. *Journal of Applied Behavioral Science, 7,* 87-102.

Boisot, M., & Child, J. (1996). From fiefs to clans and network capitalism: Explaining China's emerging economic order. *Administrative Science Quarterly, 41,* 600-628.

Boisot, M., & Liang, X. G. (1992). The nature of managerial work in the Chinese enterprise reforms: A study of six directors. *Organization Studies, 13,* 161-184.

Bolles, R. N. (1993). *What color is your parachute?* Berkeley, CA: Ten Speed.

Bolman, L. G., & Deal, T. E. (1991). *Reframing organizations: Artistry, choice, and leadership.* San Francisco: Jossey-Bass.

Borg, I., & Lingoes, J. C. (1987). *Multidimensional similarity structure analysis.* New York: Springer-Verlag.

Borgatti, S. P., Everett, M. G., & Freeman, L. C. (1992). *UCINET IV.* Columbia, SC: Analytic Technologies.

Bouchet, J.-L. (1976). *Diversification: Composition of the top management team and performance of the firm.* Paper presented at the EGOS Conference on the Sociology of the Business Enterprise, Oxford.

Bourdieu, P. (1977). *Outline of a theory of practice* (R. Nice, Trans.). Cambridge: Cambridge University Press. (Original work published 1972)

Bourdieu, P. (1991). *Language and symbolic power* (J. B. Thompson, Ed.; G. Raymond & M. Adamson, Trans.). Cambridge, MA: Harvard University Press.

Bourgeois, L. J., III. (1980). Performance and consensus. *Strategic Management Journal, 1,* 227-248.

Bourgeois, V. W., & Pinder, C. C. (1983). Contrasting philosophical perspectives in administrative science: A reply to Morgan. *Administrative Science Quarterly, 28,* 608-613.

Bowen, D. E. (1983). *Customers as substitutes for leadership in service organizations.* Unpublished doctoral dissertation, Michigan State University.

Bowen, D. E., & Schneider, B. (1988). Services marketing and management: Implications for organizational behavior. In B. M. Staw & L. L. Cummings (Eds.), *Research in organizational behavior* (Vol. 10, pp. 43-80). Greenwich, CT: JAI.

Bower, J. L. (1970). *Managing the resource allocation process.* Boston: Harvard Business School, Division of Research.

Boyacigiller, N. (1990, August). *Staffing in a foreign land: A multi-level study of Japanese multinationals with operations in the United States.* Paper presented at the annual meeting of the Academy of Management, San Francisco.

Boyacigiller, N., & Adler, N. J. (1991). The parochial dinosaur: Organizational sciences in a global context. *Academy of Management Review, 16,* 262-290.

Bradshaw, P., & Wicks, D. (1997). Women in the academy: Cycles of resistance and compliance. In P. Prasad, A. J. Mills, M. Elmes, & A. Prasad (Eds.), *Managing the organizational melting pot: Dilemmas of workplace diversity* (pp. 199-225). Thousand Oaks, CA: Sage.

Brannen, M. Y. (1992). "Bwana Mickey": Constructing cultural consumption at Tokyo Disneyland. In J. Tobin (Ed.), *Remade in Japan: Everyday life and consumer taste in a changing society* (pp. 216-234). New Haven, CT: Yale University Press.

Brannen, M. Y. (1994). *Your next boss is Japanese: Negotiating cultural change at a Western Massachusetts paper plant.* Unpublished doctoral dissertation, University of Massachusetts, Amherst.

Brannen, M. Y. (1995). Does culture matter? Negotiating a complementary culture to successfully support technological innovation. In J. K. Liker, J. Ettlie, & J. Campbell (Eds.), *Engineered in Japan: Japanese technology management practices.* Oxford: Oxford University Press.

Brannen, M. Y., Liker, J. K., & Fruin, W. M. (1999). Recontextualization and factory-to-factory knowledge transfer from Japan to the U.S.: The case of NSK. In J. K. Liker, W. M. Fruin, & P. S. Adler (Eds.), *Remade in America: Transplanting and transforming Japanese management systems.* New York: Oxford University Press.

Brannen, M. Y., & Salk, J. (2000). Partnering across borders: Negotiating organizational culture in a German-Japanese joint venture. *Human Relations, 53*(4).

Braverman, H. (1974). *Labor and monopoly capital.* New York: Monthly Review Press.

Brayfield, A. H., & Crockett, W. H. (1955). Employee attitudes and employee performance. *Psychological Bulletin, 52,* 396-424.

Breiger, R. L., Boorman, S. A., & Arabie, P. (1975). An algorithm for clustering relational data with applications to network analysis and comparison with multidimensional scaling. *Journal of Mathematical Psychology, 12,* 323-383.

Brett, J. M., Tinsley, C. H., Janssens, M., Barsness, Z. I., & Lytle, A. L. (1997). New approaches to the study of culture in industrial/organizational psychology. In P. C. Earley & M. Erez (Eds.), *New perspectives on international industrial/organizational psychology* (pp. 75-129). San Francisco: New Lexington.

Brewer, M. B. (1979). In-group bias in the minimal intergroup situation: A cognitive-motivational analysis. *Psychological Bulletin, 86,* 307-324.

Brickman, P. (1987). *Commitment, conflict and caring.* Englewood Cliffs, NJ: Prentice Hall.

Bridges, W. (1994). *Jobshift: How to prosper in a workplace without jobs.* Reading, MA: Addison-Wesley.

Brief, A. P., & Motowidlo, S. J. (1986). Prosocial organizational behaviors. *Academy of Management Review, 11,* 710-725.

Brinkman, R. L., & Brinkman, J. E. (1997). Cultural lag: Conception and theory. *International Journal of Social Economics 24,* 609-627.

Brissett, D., & Edgley, C. (1990). *Life as theater: A dramaturgical sourcebook* (2nd ed.). New York: Aldine de Gruyter.

Broadfoot, L. E., & Ashkanasy, N. (1994). *The dimensions of survey instruments used in the measurement of organizational culture: An analysis and exploratory test.* Paper presented at the annual meeting of Australasian Social Psychologists, Cairns, Queensland, Australia.

Bromley, D. (1993). *Reputation, image, and impression management.* New York: John Wiley.

Brooks, J. L., & Seers, A. (1991). Predictors of organizational commitment: Variations across career stages. *Journal of Vocational Behavior, 38,* 53-64.

Brooks, S. M., & Guth, T. (1999, April). *When service support means more: Its impact on customer opinions across work environments.* Paper presented at the 14th Annual Meeting of the Society for Industrial and Organizational Psychology, Atlanta, GA.

Brooks, S. M., & Kam, S. M. (1998, April). *Linking employee opinions with customer satisfaction and organizational outcomes.* Paper presented at the 13th Annual Meeting of the Society for Industrial and Organizational Psychology, Dallas.

Brousseau, K. R. (1983). Towards a dynamic model of job-person relationships: Findings, research questions, and implications for work system design. *Academy of Management Review, 8,* 33-45.

Brown, A. (1995). *Organisational culture.* London: Pitman.

Brown, A. (1998). *Organisational culture.* London: Financial Times/Pitman.

Brown, A., & Greenberg, J. (1990). *Behavior in organizations: Understanding and managing the human side of work* (3rd ed.). Boston: Allyn & Bacon.

Brown, D. M., & Laverick, S. (1994). Measuring corporate performance. *Long Range Planning, 27,* 89-98.

Brown, K. A., & Mitchell, T. R. (1993). Organizational obstacles: Links with financial performance, customer satisfaction, and job satisfaction in a service environment. *Human Relations, 46,* 725-757.

Brown, M. A. (1976). Values: A necessary but neglected ingredient of motivation on the job. *Academy of Management Review, 1,* 15-23.

Brown, R. B. (1996). Organizational commitment: Clarifying the concept and simplifying the existing construct typology. *Journal of Vocational Behavior, 49,* 230-251.

Bryk, A. S., & Raudenbush, S. W. (1992). *Hierarchical linear models: Applications and data analysis methods.* Newbury Park, CA: Sage.

Buchanan, B., II. (1974). Building organizational commitment: The socialization of managers in work organizations. *Administrative Science Quarterly, 19,* 533-546.

Buenger, V., Daft, R. L., Conlon, E. J., & Austin, J. (1996). Competing values in organizations: Contextual influences and structural consequences. *Organization Science, 7, 557-576.*

Buono, A. F., Bowditch, J. L., & Lewis, J. W. (1985). When cultures collide: The anatomy of a merger. *Human Relations, 38,* 477-500.

Burke, M., Borucki, C., & Hurley, A. (1992). Reconceptualizing psychological climate in a retail service environment: A multiple stakeholder perspective. *Journal of Applied Psychology, 77,* 717-729.

Burke, W. W. (1982). *Organization development: Principles and practices.* Boston: Little, Brown.

Burke, W. W. (1994). *Organization development: A process of learning and changing* (2nd ed.). Reading, MA: Addison-Wesley.

Burke, W. W. (1997). The new agenda for organization development. *Organizational Dynamics, 26*(1), 7-20.

Burke, W. W., & Litwin, G. H. (1992). A causal model of organizational performance and change. *Journal of Management, 18,* 523-545.

Burningham, C., & West, M. (1995). Individual, climate, and group interaction processes as predictors of work team innovation. *Small Group Research, 26,* 106-117.

Burns, J. M. (1978). *Leadership.* New York: Harper & Row.

Burns, T., & Stalker, G. M. (1961). *The management of innovation.* London: Tavistock.

Burrell, G. (1992). Sex and organizational analysis. In A. J. Mills & P. Tancred (Eds.), *Gendering organizational analysis* (pp. 71-92). Newbury Park, CA: Sage.

Burt, R. S. (1992). *Structural holes: The social structure of competition.* Cambridge, MA: Harvard University Press.

Burt, R. S., & Ronchi, D. (1990). Contested control in a large manufacturing plant. In J. Wessie & H. Flap (Eds.), *Social networks through time* (pp. 121-157). Utrecht: University of Holland.

Burton, M. L., Moore, C. C., Whiting, J. W. M., & Romney, A. K. (1996). Regions based on social structure. *Current Anthropology, 37,* 87-123.

Bushe, G. R. (1988). Cultural contradictions of statistical process control in American manufacturing organizations. *Journal of Management, 14,* 19-31.

Cadogan, M. (1992). *Women with wings.* London: Macmillan.

Calás, M. B., & Smircich, L. (1987). *Post-culture: Is the organizational culture literature dominant but dead?* Paper presented at the Third International Conference on Organizational Symbolism and Corporate Culture, Milan.

Calás, M. B., & Smircich, L. (1992). Using the "F" word: Feminist theories and the social consequences of organizational research. In A. J. Mills & P. Tancred (Eds.), *Gendering organizational analysis* (pp. 222-234). Newbury Park, CA: Sage.

Calás, M. B., & Smircich, L. (1996). From "the woman's" point of view: Feminist approaches to organization studies. In S. R. Clegg, C. Hardy, & W. R. Nord (Eds.), *Handbook of organization studies* (pp. 218-257). Thousand Oaks, CA: Sage.

Calori, R., Lubatkin, M., Very, P., & Veiga, J. F. (1997). Modeling the origins of nationally-bound administrative heritages: A historical institutional analysis of French and British firms. *Organization Science, 8,* 681-696.

Calori, R., & Sarnin, P. (1991). Corporate culture and economic performance: A French study. *Organization Studies, 12,* 49-74.

Cameron, K., & Freeman, S. (1988). *Cultural congruence, strength, and type: Relationship to effectiveness* (Working paper). Ann Arbor: University of Michigan, Graduate School of Business Administration.

Cameron, K. S., & Quinn, R. E. (1999). *Diagnosing and changing organizational culture: The competing values framework.* Reading, MA: Addison-Wesley.

Camisón, C. (1998). Total quality management and cultural change: A model of organizational development. *International Journal of Technology Management, 16,* 479-493.

Campbell, D. E. (1979). Interior office design and visitor response. *Journal of Applied Psychology, 64,* 648-653.

Campbell, J. P., Dunnette, M. D., Lawler, E. E., III, & Weick, K. E. (1970). *Managerial behavior, performance, and effectiveness.* New York: McGraw-Hill.

Cannon-Bowers, J. A., Oser, R., & Flanagan, D. L. (1992). Work teams in industry: A selected review and proposed framework. In R. W. Swezey & E. Salas (Eds.), *Teams: Their training and performance* (pp. 355-377). Norwood, NJ: Ablex.

Cannon-Bowers, J. A., Tannenbaum, S. I., Salas, E., & Volpe, C. E. (1995). Defining competencies and establishing team training requirements. In R. A. Guzzo & E. Salas (Eds.), *Team effectiveness and decision making in organizations* (pp. 333-380). San Francisco: Jossey-Bass.

Canter, D. (1997). The facets of place. In G. T. Moore & R. W. Marans (Eds.), *Advances in environment, behavior, and design* (Vol. 4, pp. 109-147). New York: Plenum.

Carley, K. (1991). A theory of group stability. *American Sociological Review, 56,* 331-354.

Carlyle, T. (1841). *On heroes, hero-worship and the heroic in history.* New York: Appleton.

Carroll, D. T. (1983). A disappointing search for excellence. *Harvard Business Review, 61*(6), 78-88.

Cartwright, S., & Cooper, C. L. (1993a). The psychological impact of merger and acquisition on the individual: A study of building society managers. *Human Relations, 46,* 327-347.

Cartwright, S., & Cooper, C. L. (1993b). The role of culture compatibility in successful organizational marriage. *Academy of Management Executive, 7*(2), 57-70.

Carver, C. S. (1989). How should multifaceted personality constructs be tested? Issues illustrated by self-monitoring, attributional style, and hardiness. *Journal of Personality and Social Psychology, 56,* 577-585.

Carver, C. S., & Scheier, M. F. (1985). Aspects of self and the control of behavior. In B. R. Schlenker (Ed.), *The self and social life*. New York: McGraw-Hill.

Cascio, W. F., Outtz, J., Zedeck, S., & Goldstein, I. L. (1991). Statistical implications of six methods of test score use in personnel selection. *Human Performance, 4,* 233-264.

Cawsey, T. F., Nicholson, N., & Alban-Metcalfe, B. (1985). Who's on the fast track? The relationship between career mobility, individual and task characteristics. In *Proceedings of the annual meeting of the Academy of Management Proceedings, 1985* (pp. 51-55). Briarcliff Manor, NJ: Academy of Management.

Champy, J. (1995). *Reengineering management: The mandate for new leadership*. New York: HarperCollins.

Chang, F. S., & Wiebe, H. A. (1996). The ideal culture profile for total quality management: A competing values perspective. *Engineering Management Journal, 8*(2), 19-26.

Changing a corporate culture. (1984, May 14). *Business Week,* pp. 130-138.

Chao, G. T., O'Leary-Kelly, A. M., Wolf, S., Klein, H. J. K., & Gardner, P. D. (1994). Organizational socialization: Its content and consequences. *Journal of Applied Psychology, 79,* 730-743.

Chase, R. B. (1981). The customer contact approach to services: Theoretical bases and practical extensions. *Operations Research, 29,* 698-706.

Chatman, J. A. (1991). Matching people and organizations: Selection and socialization in public accounting firms. *Administrative Science Quarterly, 36,* 459-484.

Chatman, J. A., & Jehn, K. A. (1994). Assessing the relationship between industry characteristics and organizational culture: How different can you be? *Academy of Management Journal, 37,* 522-553.

Chen, H.-T. (1991). *Theory-driven evaluations*. Newbury Park, CA: Sage.

Chen, M., & Bargh, J. A. (1997). Nonconscious behavioral confirmation processes: The self-fulfilling consequences of automatic stereotype activation. *Journal of Experimental Social Psychology, 33,* 541-560.

Chevalier, J., & Cheerbrant, A. (1994). *A dictionary of symbols*. Cambridge, MA: Blackwell.

Child, J. (1981). Culture, contingency and capitalism in the cross-national study of organizations. In B. M. Staw & L. L. Cummings (Eds.), *Research in organizational behavior* (Vol. 3, pp. 303-356). Greenwich, CT: JAI.

Chinese Culture Connection. (1987). Chinese values and the search for culture-free dimensions of culture. *Journal of Cross-Cultural Psychology, 18,* 143-174.

Christopher, M., Payne, A., & Ballantyne, D. (1991). *Relationship marketing: Bringing quality, customer service and marketing together*. London: Butterworth-Heinemann.

Chung, B. G. (1996). *Focusing HRM strategies toward service market segments: A three-factor model*. Unpublished doctoral dissertation, University of Maryland.

Chusmir, L. H., & Parker, B. (1991). Gender and situational differences in managers' values: A look at work and home lives. *Journal of Business Research, 23,* 325-335.

Clarckson, M. B. E. (1995). A stakeholder framework for analyzing and evaluating corporate social performance. *Academy of Management Review, 20,* 92-117.

Clark, P. (1978). Temporal inventories and time structuring in large organizations. In J. T. Fraser, N. Lawrence, & D. Park (Eds.), *The study of time III* (pp. 391-418). New York: Springer-Verlag.

Clark, P. (1985). A review of the theories of time and structure for organizational sociology. *Research in the Sociology of Organizations, 4,* 35-80.

Clark, R. (1979). *The Japanese company.* New Haven, CT: Yale University Press.

Clegg, S. R. (1981). Organization and control. *Administrative Science Quarterly, 26,* 532-545.

Clegg, S. R., Hardy, C., & Nord, W. R. (Eds.). (1996). *Handbook of organization studies.* Thousand Oaks, CA: Sage.

Clifford, J. (1986). Introduction: Partial truths. In J. Clifford & G. E. Marcus (Eds.), *Writing culture: The poetics and politics of ethnography* (pp. 1-26). Berkeley: University of California Press.

Clifford, J. (1988). *The predicament of culture: Twentieth-century ethnography, literature, and art.* Cambridge: Harvard University Press.

Clifford, J., & Marcus, G. E. (Eds.). (1986). *Writing culture: The poetics and politics of ethnography.* Berkeley: University of California Press.

Cockburn, C. (1991). *Brothers: Male dominance and technological change.* London: Pluto.

Cohen, A. (1976). *Two-dimensional man.* Berkeley: University of California Press.

Cohen, A. (1991). Career stage as a moderator of the relationships between organizational commitment and its outcomes: A meta-analysis. *Journal of Occupational Psychology, 64,* 253-268.

Colarelli, S. M., Dean, R. A., & Konstans, C. (1987). Comparative effects of personal and situational influences on job outcomes of new professionals. *Journal of Applied Psychology, 72,* 558-566.

Cole, R. (1971). *Japanese blue collar: The changing tradition.* Berkeley: University of California Press.

Collard, R. (1989). *Total quality: Success through people.* London: Institute of Personnel Management.

Collins, R. (1994). *Four sociological traditions.* Oxford: Oxford University Press.

Collinson, D. L. (1988). Engineering humor: Masculinity, joking and conflict in shopfloor relations. *Organization Studies, 9,* 181-199.

Comer, D. R. (1991). Organizational newcomers' acquisition of information from peers. *Management Communication Quarterly, 5,* 64-89.

Conger, J. A., & Kanungo, R. N. (1987). Toward a behavioral theory of charismatic leadership. *Academy of Management Review, 12,* 637-647.

Connolly, T., Conlon, E. M., & Deutsch, S. J. (1980). Organizational effectiveness: A multiple constituency approach. *Academy of Management Review, 5,* 211-218.

Connor, P. E., & Becker, B. W. (1975). Values and the organization: Suggestions for research. *Academy of Management Journal, 18,* 550-561.

Connor, P. E., & Becker, B. W. (1994). Personal values and management: What do we know and why don't we know more? *Journal of Management Inquiry, 3,* 67-73.

Connor, P. E., & Becker, B. W. (1995). *Personal value systems and decision styles of public managers* (Working paper). Salem, OR: Willamette University, Atkinson Graduate School of Management.

Connor, P. E., & Lake, L. K. (1994). *Managing organizational change* (2nd ed.). New York: Praeger.

Conte, J. M., Rizzuto, T. E., & Steiner, D. D. (1999). A construct-oriented analysis of individual-level polychronicity. *Journal of Managerial Psychology, 14,* 269-287.

Cooke, R. A. (1997). *Organizational Effectiveness Inventory.* Arlington Heights, IL: Human Synergistics/Center for Applied Research.

Cooke, R. A., & Lafferty, J. C. (1986). *Organizational Culture Inventory (Form III).* Plymouth, MI: Human Synergistics.

Cooke, R. A., & Lafferty, J. C. (1983). *Level V: Organizational Culture Inventory (Form 1).* Plymouth, MI: Human Synergistics.

Cooke, R. A., & Lafferty, J. C. (1987). *Organizational Culture Inventory.* Plymouth, MI: Human Synergistics.

Cooke, R. A., & Lafferty, J. C. (1994). *Organizational Culture Inventory—Ideal.* Plymouth, MI: Human Synergistics.

Cooke, R. A., & Rousseau, D. M. (1988). Behavioral norms and expectations: A quantitative approach to the assessment of organizational culture. *Group & Organization Studies, 13,* 245-273.

Cooke, R. A., & Szumal, J. L. (1993). Measuring normative beliefs and shared behavioral expectations in organizations: The reliability and validity of the Organizational Culture Inventory. *Psychological Reports, 72,* 1299-1330.

Cooper, R. B. (1994). The inertial impact of culture on IT implementation. *Information and Management, 27,* 17-31.

Cooper, R. B., & Quinn, R. E. (1993). Implications of the competing values framework for management information systems. *Human Resource Management, 32,* 175-201.

Cooper, T. L., Wehrly, M., & Bao, Y. (1997). Organizational loyalty and personal ethics: The moral priorities of Chinese cadres. *International Journal of Public Administration, 20,* 1791-1820.

Cooperrider, D. L. (1990). Positive image, positive action: The affirmative basis of organizing. In S. Srivastva & D. L. Cooperrider (Eds.), *Appreciative management and leadership: The power of positive thought and action in organizations* (pp. 91-125). San Francisco: Jossey-Bass.

Cooperrider, D. L., & Srivastva, S. (1987). Appreciative inquiry into organizational life. In R. W. Woodman & W. A. Pasmore (Eds.), *Research in organizational change and development* (Vol. 1, pp. 129-169). Greenwich, CT: JAI.

Cosmides, L., & Tooby, J. (1992). Cognitive adaptations for social change. In J. H. Barkow, L. Cosmides, & J. Tooby (Eds.), *The adapted mind: Evolutionary psychology and the generation of culture*. New York: Oxford University Press.

Cosmides, L., & Tooby, J. (1997). *Evolutionary psychology: A primer.* Available Internet: http://www.psych.ucsb.edu/research/cep/primer.htm

Cotte, J., & Ratneshwar, S. (1999). Juggling and hopping: What does it mean to work polychronically? *Journal of Managerial Psychology, 14,* 184-204.

Cotter, J. J. (1995). *The 20% solution: Using rapid redesign to create tomorrow's organizations today.* New York: John Wiley.

Covin, J. G., & Slevin, D. P. (1988). The influence of organizational structure on the utility of an entrepreneurial top management style. *Journal of Management Studies, 25,* 217-234.

Cox, T., Jr. (1993). *Cultural diversity in organizations: Theory, research and practice.* San Francisco: Berrett-Koehler.

Cragin, J. P. (1986). Management technology absorption in China. In S. R. Clegg, D. C. Dunphey, & S. G. Redding (Eds.), *Enterprise and management in East Asia.* Hong Kong: University of Hong Kong, Centre of Asian Studies.

Craig, S. B., & Gustafson, S. B. (1998). Perceived leader integrity scale: An instrument for assessing employee perceptions of leader integrity. *Leadership Quarterly, 9,* 127-146.

Cray, D. (1984). Control and coordination in multinational corporations. *Journal of International Business Studies, 15,* 85-98.

Crompton, R., & Jones, G. (1984). *White-collar proletariat: Deskilling and gender in clerical work.* London: Macmillan.

Cronbach, L. J., & Meehl, P. E. (1955). Construct validity in psychological tests. *Psychological Bulletin, 52,* 281-302.

Crozier, M. (1964). *The bureaucratic phenomenon.* Chicago: University of Chicago Press.

Csikszentmihalyi, M., & Rochberg-Halton, E. (1981). *The meaning of things: Domestic symbols and the self.* Cambridge: Cambridge University Press.

Cummings, T. G., & Worley, C. G. (1998). *Organization development and change* (5th ed.). St. Paul, MN: West.

Cunningham, M., & Schumer, F. (1984). *Powerplay: What really happened at Bendix.* New York: Ballantine.

Cyert, R. M., & March, J. (1963). *A behavioral theory of the firm.* Englewood Cliffs, NJ: Prentice Hall.

Czarniawska-Joerges, B., & Joerges, B. (1990). Organizational change as materialization of ideas. In *The study of power and democracy in Sweden.* Stockholm: Stockholm School of Economics, Economic Research Institute.

Daft, R. L. (1992). *Organization theory and design.* St. Paul, MN: West.

Dale, M. (1997, July/August). Connecting performance with culture: A case example of change within Procurement at British Aerospace

Airbus. *Focus on Change Management* [On-line]. Available Internet: http://www.mwdale.demon.co.uk/cpwc.htm

Dalton, G. W., Thompson, P. H., & Price, R. L. (1977). Four stages of professional careers: A new look at performance by professionals. *Organizational Dynamics, 6*(1), 19-42.

Dalton, M. (1959). *Men who manage.* New York: John Wiley.

D'Andrade, R. G. (1984). Cultural meaning systems. In R. A. Shweder & R. A. LeVine (Eds.), *Culture theory: Essays on mind, self, and emotion* (pp. 88-119). Cambridge: Cambridge University Press.

D'Andrade, R. G. (1992). Schemas and motivation. In R. G. D'Andrade & C. Strauss (Eds.), *Human motives and cultural models* (pp. 23-44). Cambridge: Cambridge University Press.

Dandridge, T. C. (1983). Symbol's function and use. In L. R. Pondy, P. J. Frost, G. Morgan, & T. C. Dandridge (Eds.), *Organizational symbolism* (pp. 69-79). Greenwich, CT: JAI.

Dandridge, T. C., Mitroff, I., & Joyce, W. F. (1980). Organizational symbolism: A topic to expand organizational analysis. *Academy of Management Review, 5,* 77-82.

Dansereau, F., & Alutto, J. A. (1990). Level-of-analysis issues in climate and culture research. In B. Schneider (Ed.), *Organizational climate and culture* (pp. 193-236). San Francisco: Jossey-Bass.

Dansereau, F., Chandrasekaran, G., Dumas, M., Coleman, D., Ehrlich, S., & Bagchi, D. (1986). *Data enquiry that tests entity and correlational/causal theories.* Williamsville, NY: Institute for Theory Testing.

Dansereau, F., Graen, G. B., & Haga, W. J. (1975). A vertical dyad approach to leadership within formal organizations. *Organizational Behavior and Human Performance, 13,* 46-78.

Das, T. K. (1986). *The subjective side of strategy making: Future orientations and perceptions of executives.* New York: Praeger.

Davidow, W. H., & Utall, B. (1989). *Total customer service.* New York: Harper & Row.

Davies, P. (1995). *About time: Einstein's unfinished revolution.* New York: Simon & Schuster.

Davies, R. (1996). Telecommuting: Culture, social roles and managing telecommuters. *International Journal of Career Management, 8,* 1-9. Available Internet: http://www.mcb.co.uk/literati/articles/telecom.htm

Davis, D. D. (1995). Form, function, and strategy in boundaryless organizations. In A. Howard (Ed.), *The changing nature of work* (pp. 112-138). San Francisco: Jossey-Bass.

Davis, J. A. (1979). The Davis/Holland/Leinhardt studies: An overview. In P. W. Holland & S. Leinhardt (Eds.), *Perspectives on social network research* (pp. 51-62). New York: Academic Press.

Davis, R. E. (1968). Compatibility in corporate marriages. *Harvard Business Review, 46*(6), 86-93.

Davis, T. R. V. (1984). The influence of the physical environment in offices. *Academy of Management Review, 9,* 271-283.

Dawson, S., Bloch, P., & Ridgway, N. (1990). Shopping motives, emotional states, and retail outcomes. *Journal of Retailing, 66,* 408-427.

Deal, T. E., & Kennedy, A. A. (1982). *Corporate cultures: The rites and rituals of corporate life.* Reading, MA: Addison-Wesley.

Dean, J. W., Ramirez, R., & Ottensmeyer, E. (1997). An aesthetic perspective on organizations. In C. L. Cooper & S. E. Jackson (Eds.), *Creating tomorrow's organizations: A handbook for future research in organizational behavior* (pp. 419-437). New York: John Wiley.

Deci, E. L., & Ryan, R. M. (1980). The empirical exploration of intrinsic motivational processes. In L. Berkowitz (Ed.), *Advances in experimental social psychology* (Vol. 13, pp. 39-80). New York: Academic Press.

de Geus, A. (1997). *The living company: Habits for survival in a turbulent business environment.* Boston: Harvard Business School Press.

deGraef, P., deTroy, A., & D'Ydewalle, G. (1992). Local and global contextual constraints on the identification of objects in scenes. *Canadian Journal of Psychology, 46,* 489-501.

DeKerckhove, D. (1995). *The skin of culture.* Toronto: Patrick Crean.

De Lima, K. J. (1999). *Organisational "C4Q" (the culture and climate for total quality): Consequences and antecedents.* Unpublished doctoral dissertation, Lincoln University, Canterbury, New Zealand.

Dellheim, C. (1986). Business in time: The historian and corporate culture. *Public Historian, 8*(2), 9-22.

de Man, P. (1983). *Blindness and insight.* Minneapolis: University of Minnesota Press.

Deming, W. E. (1986). *Out of the crisis.* Cambridge: Massachusetts Institute of Technology, Center for Advanced Engineering.

De Mooij, M. (1998). Masculinity/femininity and consumer behavior. In G. Hofstede & Associates, *Masculinity and femininity: The taboo dimension of national cultures.* Thousand Oaks, CA: Sage.

Den Hartog, D. N., House, R. J., Hanges, P. J., Ruiz-Quintanilla, S. A., Dorfman, P. W., et al. (1999). Culture-specific and cross-culturally generalizable implicit leadership theories: Are attributes of charismatic/transformational leadership universally endorsed? *Leadership Quarterly, 10,* 219-256.

Den Hartog, D. N., & Verburg, R. M. (1998). Charisma and rhetoric: Communicative techniques of international business leaders. *Leadership Quarterly, 8,* 355-391.

Denison, D. R. (1984). Bringing corporate culture to the bottom line. *Organizational Dynamics, 13*(2), 59-76.

Denison, D. R. (1990). *Corporate culture and organizational effectiveness.* New York: John Wiley.

Denison, D. R. (1996). What *is* the difference between organizational culture and organizational climate? A native's point of view on a decade of paradigm wars. *Academy of Management Review, 21,* 619-654.

Denison, D. R., Hooijberg, R., & Quinn, R. E. (1995). Paradox and performance: Toward a theory of behavioral complexity in managerial leadership. *Organization Science, 6,* 524-540.

Denison, D. R., & Mishra, A. K. (1995). Toward a theory of organizational culture and effectiveness. *Organization Science, 6,* 204-223.

Denzin, N. K. (1978). *The research act: A theoretical introduction to sociological methods* (2nd ed.). New York: McGraw-Hill.

Derrida, J. (1978). Structure, sign, and play in the discourse of the human sciences. In J. Derrida, *Writing and difference* (A. Bass, Trans., pp. 278-293). Chicago: University of Chicago Press.

Derrida, J. (1988). *Limited Inc.* Evanston, IL: Northwestern University Press.

DeShon, R. P., & Landis, R. S. (1997). The dimensionality of the Hollenbeck, Williams and Klein (1989) measure of goal commitment on complex tasks. *Organizational Behavior and Human Decision Processes, 70,* 105-116.

Dess, G. G., & Origer, N. K. (1987). Environment, structure and consensus in strategy formulation: A conceptual integration. *Academy of Management Review, 12,* 313-330.

Dickson, M. W. (1998, April). *Differences in within-organization agreement when describing the organization—and implications of those differences.* Paper presented at the 13th Annual Meeting of the Society for Industrial and Organizational Psychology, Dallas.

Digman, J. M. (1990). Personality structure: Emergence of the five-factor model. *Annual Review of Psychology, 41,* 417-440.

DiMaggio, P. J., & Powell, W. W. (1991). The iron cage revisited: Institutional isomorphism and collective rationality in organization fields. In W. W. Powell & P. J. DiMaggio (Eds.), *The new institutionalism in organizational analysis* (pp. 63-82). Chicago: University of Chicago Press.

DiPrete, T. A. (1987). Horizontal and vertical mobility in organizations. *Administrative Science Quarterly, 32,* 422-444.

d'Iribarne, P. (1989). *La logique de l'honneur: Gestion des entreprises et traditions nationales.* Paris: Seuil.

d'Iribarne, P. (1997). The usefulness of an ethnographic approach to the international comparison of organizations. *International Studies of Management & Organization, 26*(4), 30-47.

Ditton, J. (1979). Baking time. *Sociological Review, 27,* 157-167.

Doeringer, P. B., & Piore, M. J. (1971). *Internal labor markets and manpower analysis.* Lexington, MA: D. C. Heath.

Donaldson, G., & Lorsch, J. W. (1983). *Decision making at the top.* New York: Basic Books.

Donaldson, L. (1996). The normal science of structural contingency theory. In S. R. Clegg, C. Hardy, & W. R. Nord (Eds.), *Handbook of organization studies* (pp. 57-76). Thousand Oaks, CA: Sage.

Donaldson, T., & Preston, L. E. (1995). The stakeholder theory of the corporation: Concepts, evidence and implications. *Academy of Management Review, 20,* 65-91.

Donovan, R. J., & Rossiter, J. R. (1982). Store atmosphere: An environmental psychology approach. *Journal of Retailing, 58,* 34-57.

Donthu, N., Bernhardt, K. L., & Kennet, P. A. (in press). A longitudinal analysis of satisfaction and profitability. *Journal of Business Research.*

Dore, R. (1973). *British factory–Japanese factory: The origins of national diversity in industrial relations.* Berkeley: University of California Press.

Doty, D. H., Glick, W. H., & Huber, G. P. (1993). Fit, equifinality, and organization effectiveness: A test of two configurational theories. *Academy of Management Journal, 36,* 1196-1250.

Douglas, M. (1973). *Natural symbols.* Baltimore: Penguin.

Doyle, P. (1994). Setting business objectives and measuring performance. *Journal of General Management, 20,* 1-19.

Drucker, P. F. (1985). *Management: Tasks, responsibilities, practices.* New York: Harper.

Druckman, D., Singer, J. E., & van Cott, H. (Eds.). (1997). *Enhancing organizational performance.* Washington, DC: National Academy Press.

Dubinskas, F. A. (Ed.). (1988). *Making time: Ethnographies of high technology organizations.* Philadelphia: Temple University Press.

Dummett, M. (1978). *Truth and other enigmas.* Cambridge, MA: Harvard University Press.

Duncan, W. J. (1989). Organizational culture: "Getting a fix" on an elusive concept. *Academy of Management Executive, 3*(3), 229-238.

Dunivin, K. O. (1994). Military culture: Change and continuity. *Armed Forces and Society, 20,* 531-547.

Durkheim, E. (1976). *The elementary forms of the religious life* (2nd ed.). London: Allen & Unwin.

Durkheim, E. (1984). *The division of labor in society* (W. D. Halls, Trans.). New York: Free Press. (Original work published 1893)

Dutton, J. E., & Ashford, S. J. (1987). Selling issues to top management. *Academy of Management Review, 12,* 76-90.

Dutton, J. E., & Dukerich, J. M. (1991). Keeping an eye on the mirror: Image and identity in organizational adaptation. *Academy of Management Journal, 34,* 517-554.

Dutton, J. E., Dukerich, J. M., & Harquail, C. B. (1994). Organization images and member identification. *Administrative Science Quarterly, 39,* 239-263.

Dwyer, K. (1982). *Moroccan dialogues: Anthropology in question.* Baltimore: Johns Hopkins University Press.

Earley, P. C. (1997). *Face, harmony, and social structure: An analysis of organizational behaviors across cultures.* New York: Oxford University Press.

Eastman, W., & Bailey, J. R. (1998). Mediating the fact-value antimony: Patterns in managerial and legal rhetoric, 1890-1990. *Administrative Science Quarterly, 9,* 232-245.

Ebert, R. J., & Piehl, D. (1973). Time horizon: A concept for management. *California Management Review, 15*(4), 35-41.

Eccles, T. (1993). The deceptive allure of empowerment. *Long Range Planning, 26*(6), 13-21.

Eco, U. (1976). *A theory of semiotics.* Bloomington: University of Indiana Press.

Edwards, J. R. (1994). The study of congruence in organizational behavior research: Critique and a proposed alternative. *Organizational Behavior and Human Decision Processes, 58,* 51-100. (See also erratum in Vol. 58, 1994, 323-325)

Edwards, J. R., & Parry, M. E. (1993). On the use of polynomial regression equations as an alternative to difference scores in organizational research. *Academy of Management Journal, 36,* 1577-1613.

Efron, B. (1979). Bootstrap methods: Another look at the jackknife. *Annals of Statistics, 7,* 1-26.

Eisenhardt, K. (1989). Agency theory: An assessment and review. *Academy of Management Review, 14,* 57-74.

Eldridge, J. E. T., & Crombie, A. D. (1974). *A sociology of organisations.* London: Allen & Unwin.

El Sawy, O. (1983). Temporal perspective and managerial attention: A study of chief executive strategic behavior. *Dissertation Abstracts International, 44*(05A), 1556-1557. (University Microfilms No. AAI83-20705)

Emery, F. E., & Trist, E. L. (1965). The causal texture of organizational environments. *Human Relations, 18,* 21-32.

Emirbayer, M., & Goodwin, J. (1994). Network analysis, culture, and the problem of agency. *American Journal of Sociology, 99,* 1411-1154.

England, G. W. (1975). *The manager and his values.* New York: Ballinger.

England, G. W., & Lee, R. (1974). The relationship between managerial values and managerial success in the United States, Japan, India, and Australia. *Journal of Applied Psychology, 59,* 411-419.

Enteman, W. F. (1993). *Managerialism: The emergence of a new ideology.* Madison: University of Wisconsin Press.

Enz, C. A. (1986). *Power and shared values in corporate culture.* Ann Arbor, MI: UMI Research.

Enz, C. A. (1988). The role of value congruity in intraorganizational power. *Administrative Science Quarterly, 33,* 284-304.

Epstein, S. (1986). Does aggregation produce spuriously high estimates of behavior stability? *Journal of Personality and Social Psychology, 50,* 1199-1210.

Erez, M., & Earley, P. C. (1993). *Culture, self-identity and work.* Oxford: Oxford University Press.

Estes, R. (1996). *Tyranny and the bottom line: Why corporations make good people do bad things.* San Francisco: Berrett-Koehler.

Etzioni, A. (1961). *A comparative analysis of complex organizations.* New York: Free Press.

Etzioni, A. (1975). *An evaluation of complex organizations: On power, involvement, and their correlates* (Rev. ed.). New York: Free Press.

Evans, M., & Gilbert, E. (1984). Plateaued managers: Their need gratifications and their effort performance expectations. *Journal of Management Studies, 21,* 99-108.

Exterbille, K. (1996). TQM can be DOA without a proper communications plan. *Journal for Quality and Participation, 19*(2), 32-35.

Falkus, S. A. (1998). *An assessment of a new organizational culture measure.* Unpublished master's thesis, University of Queensland.

Fama, E. F. (1976). *Foundations of finance*. New York: Basic Books.

Farrell, D., & Rusbult, C. E. (1981). Exchange variables as predictors of job satisfaction, job commitment, and turnover: The impact of rewards, costs, alternatives, and investments. *Organizational Behavior and Human Performance, 28,* 79-95.

Fayol, H. (1949). *General and industrial management*. London: Pitman.

Feather, N. T. (1992). Values, valences, expectation, and actions. *Journal of Social Issues, 48,* 109-124.

Feather, N. T. (1995). Values, valences, and choice: The influence of values on perceived attractiveness and choice of alternatives. *Journal of Personality and Social Psychology, 68,* 1135-1151.

Feinberg, R. A. (1986). Credit cards as spending facilitating stimuli: A conditioning interpretation. *Consumer Research, 13,* 348-356.

Feldman, D. C., & Brett, J. N. (1983). Coping with new jobs: A comparative study of new hires and job changers. *Academy of Management Journal, 26,* 258-272.

Feldman, M. (1997). *The budgetary process in a university housing authority*. Unpublished manuscript, University of Michigan, School of Public Policy.

Feldman, M. S., & March, J. G. (1981). Information in organization as signal and symbol. *Administrative Science Quarterly, 26,* 171-186.

Ference, T. P., Stoner, J. A. F., & Warren, E. K. (1977). Managing the career plateau. *Academy of Management Review, 2,* 602-612.

Ferguson, I. (1998). *Sacred realms and icons of the damned: The ethnography of an Internet-based child pornography trading ring*. Unpublished master's thesis, Carleton University. Available Internet: http://www.trytel.com/~iferguso

Ferguson, K. E. (1984). *The feminist case against bureaucracy*. Philadelphia: Temple University Press.

Festinger, L. (1954). A theory of social comparison processes. *Human Relations, 7,* 117-140.

Festinger, L. (1957). *A theory of cognitive dissonance*. Evanston, IL: Row Peterson.

Festinger, L., & Hutte, H. A. (1954). An experimental investigation of the effect of unstable interpersonal relations in a group. *Journal of Abnormal and Social Psychology, 49,* 513-523.

Finkelstein, S. (1992). Power in top management teams: Dimensions, measurement, and validation. *Academy of Management Journal, 35,* 505-538.

Finkelstein, S., & Hambrick, D. C. (1990). Top-management team tenure and organizational outcomes: The moderating role of managerial discretion. *Administrative Science Quarterly, 35,* 484-503.

Firth, R. (Ed.). (1957). *Man and culture*. New York: Routledge & Kegan Paul.

Fishbein, M., & Ajzen, I. (1975). *Belief, attitude, intention, and behavior: An introduction to theory and research*. Reading, MA: Addison-Wesley.

Fisher, C. D. (1985). Social support and adjustment to work: A longitudinal study. *Journal of Management, 11,* 39-53.

Fisher, C. D. (1986). Organizational socialization: An integrative review. In G. R. Ferris & K. M. Rowland (Eds.), *Research in personnel and human resources management* (Vol. 4, pp. 101-145). Greenwich, CT: JAI.

Fisher, R. J. (1982). *Social psychology: An applied approach.* New York: St. Martin's.

Fishman, N., & Kavanaugh, L. (1989, December). Searching for your missing quality link. *Journal for Quality and Participation, 12,* 28-32.

Fiske, A. P. (1992). The four elementary forms of sociality: Framework for a unified theory of social relations. *Psychological Review, 99,* 689-723.

Fiske, S. T., & Taylor, S. E. (1991). *Social cognition* (2nd ed.). New York: McGraw-Hill.

Fitzgerald, L. F., Drasgow, F., Hulin, C. L., Gelfand, M. J., & Magley, V. J. (1997). Antecedents and consequences of sexual harassment in organizations: A test of an integrated model. *Journal of Applied Psychology, 82,* 578-589.

Fleishman, E. A., & Zaccaro, S. J. (1992). Toward a taxonomy of team performance functions. In R. W. Swezey & E. Salas (Eds.), *Teams: Their training and performance* (pp. 31-56). Norwood, NJ: Ablex.

Fletcher, J. K. (1996). A relational approach to the protean worker. In D. T. Hall (Ed.), *The career is dead—long live the career: A relational approach to careers* (pp. 101-131). San Francisco: Jossey-Bass.

Fligstein, N. (1990). *The transformation of corporate control.* Cambridge, MA: Harvard University Press.

Flynn, B. (1998, February). *Quality now and direction for the 21st century.* Keynote presentation at the Conference on Quality and Management, sponsored by the Academy of Management, Arizona State College of Business, and Arizona State University Department of Management, Tempe, AZ.

Fombrun, C. J. (1996). *Reputation: Realizing the value from corporate image.* Boston: Harvard Business School Press.

Fombrun, C. J., & Shanley, M. (1990). What's in a name: Reputation building and corporate strategy. *Academy of Management Journal, 33,* 233-258.

Fondas, N. (1997). Feminization unveiled: Management qualities in contemporary writings. *Academy of Management Review, 22,* 257-282.

Foucault, M. (1972a). *The archaeology of knowledge.* London: Tavistock. (Original work published 1969)

Foucault, M. (1972b). *The archaeology of knowledge and the discourse on language* (A. M. S. Smith, Trans.). New York: Pantheon. (Original works published 1969 & 1971)

Foucault, M. (1975). *The birth of the clinic* (A. M. S. Smith, Trans.). New York: Random House. (Original work published 1963)

Frake, C. O. (1983). Ethnography. In R. E. Emerson (Ed.), *Contemporary field research* (pp. 60-67). Prospect Heights, IL: Waveland.

Frank, P. (1957). *Philosophy of science: The link between science and philosophy.* Englewood Cliffs, NJ: Prentice Hall.

Franke, R. H., Hofstede, G., & Bond, M. H. (1991). Cultural roots of economic performance: A research note. *Strategic Management Journal, 12*, 165-173.

Fraser, J. T. (1975). *Of time, passion, and knowledge.* New York: George Braziller.

Fraser, J. T. (1978a). The individual and society. In J. T. Fraser, N. Lawrence, & D. Park (Eds.), *The study of time III* (pp. 419-442). New York: Springer-Verlag.

Fraser, J. T. (1978b). Temporal levels: Sociobiological aspects of a fundamental synthesis. *Journal of Social and Biological Structures, 1*, 339-355.

Fraser, J. T. (1987). *Time, the familiar stranger.* Redmond, WA: Tempus.

Fraser, J. T. (1994). Hierarchical theory of time. In S. L. Macey (Ed.), *Encyclopedia of time* (pp. 262-264). New York: Garland.

Frederiksen, N., Jensen, O., & Beaton, A. E. (1972). *Prediction of organizational behavior.* Elmsford, NY: Pergamon.

Freeman, L. C. (1979). Centrality in social networks: I. Conceptual clarification. *Social Networks, 1*, 215-239.

Freeman, L. C. (1992). Filling in the blanks: A theory of cognitive categories and the structure of social affiliation. *Social Psychology Quarterly, 55*, 118-127.

Freeman, L. C., Romney, A. K., & Freeman, S. C. (1987). Cognitive structure and informant accuracy. *American Anthropologist, 89*, 311-325.

Freeman, R. E. (1984). *Strategic management: A stakeholder approach.* Boston: Pitman.

Freud, S. (1989). The interpretation of dreams. In P. Gay (Ed.), *The Freud reader.* New York: W. W. Norton.

Frost, P. J., Moore, L. F., Louis, M. R., Lundberg, C. C., & Martin, J. (Eds.). (1991). *Reframing organizational culture.* Newbury Park, CA: Sage.

Fruin, W. M. (1983). *Kikkoman.* Cambridge, MA: Harvard University Press.

Furnham, A. (1997). *The psychology of behavior at work: The individual in the organization.* East Sussex: Psychological Press.

Furnham, A., & Gunter, B. (1993). Corporate culture: Definition, diagnosis and change. In C. L. Cooper & I. T. Robertson (Eds.), *International Review of Industrial and Organizational Psychology* (Vol. 8, 233-261). New York: John Wiley.

Gabarro, J. J. (1987). *The dynamics of taking charge.* Boston: Harvard Business School Press.

Gagliardi, P. (1986). The creation and change of organizational cultures: A conceptual framework. *Organization Studies, 7*, 117-134.

Gagliardi, P. (1990a). Artifacts as pathways and remains of organizational life. In P. Gagliardi (Ed.), *Symbols and artifacts: Views of the corporate landscape.* New York: Walter de Gruyter.

Gagliardi, P. (Ed.). (1990b). *Symbols and artifacts: Views of the corporate landscape.* New York: Walter de Gruyter.

Gagliardi, P. (1996). Exploring the aesthetic side of organizational life. In S. R. Clegg, C. Hardy, & W. R. Nord (Eds.), *Handbook of organization studies* (pp. 565-580). Thousand Oaks, CA: Sage.

Galbraith, J. (1973). *Designing complex organizations.* Reading, MA: Addison-Wesley.

Gardner, H. (1995). *Leading minds: An anatomy of leadership.* New York: Basic Books.

Garson, B. (1988). *The electronic sweatshop.* Toronto: Penguin.

Garvin, D. A. (1988). *Managing quality: The strategic and competitive edge.* New York: Free Press.

Gaucher, E., & Kratochwill, E. (1993). The leader's role in implementing total quality management. *Quality Management in Health Care, 1*(3), 10-18.

Gauthier, D. (1986). *Morals by agreement.* Oxford: Oxford University Press.

Geertz, C. (1964). Ideology as a cultural system. In D. E. Apter (Ed.), *Ideology and discontent* (pp. 47-76). London: Free Press.

Geertz, C. (1973). *The interpretation of cultures: Selected essays.* New York: Basic Books.

Geertz, C. (1983). *Local knowledge: Further essays in interpretive anthropology.* New York: Basic Books.

George, J. M. (1990). Personality, affect, and behavior in groups. *Journal of Applied Psychology, 75,* 107-116.

George, J. M., & Brief, A. P. (1992). Feeling good–doing good: A conceptual analysis of the mood at work-organization spontaneity relationship. *Psychological Bulletin, 112,* 310-329.

George, J. M., & James, L. R. (1993). Personality, affect, and behavior in groups revisited: Comment on aggregation, levels of analysis, and a recent application of within and between analysis. *Journal of Applied Psychology, 78,* 798-804.

Georgopoulos, B. S. (1986). *Organizational structure, problem solving, and effectiveness.* San Francisco: Jossey-Bass.

Gersick, C. J. G. (1988). Time and transition in work teams: Toward a new model of group development. *Academy of Management Journal, 31,* 9-41.

Gersick, C. J. G. (1989). Marking time: Predictable transitions in task groups. *Academy of Management Journal, 32,* 274-309.

Gersick, C. J. G. (1994). Pacing strategic change: The case of a new venture. *Academy of Management Journal, 37,* 9-45.

Gherardi, S. (1995). *Gender, symbolism, and organizational cultures.* Thousand Oaks, CA: Sage.

Ghoshal, S., & Bartlett, C. A. (1996). Rebuilding behavioral context: A blueprint for corporate renewal. *Sloan Management Review, 37*(2), 23-36.

Giddens, A. (1979). *Central problems in social theory: Action, structure and contradiction in social analysis.* Berkeley: University of California Press.

Giddens, A. (1987). Structuralism, post-structuralism and the production of culture. In A. Giddens, *Social theory and modern sociology* (pp. 73-108). Stanford, CA: Stanford University Press.

Gifford, B. E., Gallagher, K., & Zammuto, R. F. (1997). *Evaluating efforts to improve the accessibility of prenatal care services for teens.* Tempe, AZ: Center for Health Management Research.

Gill, J., & Foulder, I. (1978, January). Managing a merger: The accession and the aftermath. *Personnel Management, 10,* 14-17.

Ginsberg, A. (1990). Connecting diversification to performance: A socio-cognitive approach. *Academy of Management Review, 15,* 514-535.

Ginsburg, F., & Tsing, A. L. (Eds.). (1990). *Uncertain terms: Negotiating gender in American culture.* Boston: Beacon.

Gioia, D. A. (1986). Symbols, scripts, and sensemaking: Creating meaning in organizational experience. In H. P. Sims & D. A. Gioia (Eds), *The thinking organization* (pp. 49-74). San Francisco: Jossey-Bass.

Glaser, R. (1983). *The corporate culture survey.* Bryn Mawr, PA: Organizational Design and Development.

Glick, W. H., Beyer, J. M., Chattopadhyay, P., George, E., Knoll, K., Ogilvie, D. T., Pugliese, D., & Saxena, S. (1993, August). *The selective perception of managers revisited.* Paper presented at the 53rd Annual Meeting of the Academy of Management, Atlanta, GA.

Goehle, D. G. (1980). *Decision making in multinational corporations.* Ann Arbor, MI: UMI Research.

Goffman, E. (1959). *The presentation of self in everyday life.* Garden City, NY: Doubleday.

Goffman, E. (1961). *Asylums: Essays on the social situation of mental patients and other inmates.* Garden City, NY: Doubleday.

Goffman, E. (1974). *Frame analysis: An essay on the organization of experience.* Cambridge, MA: Harvard University Press.

Goldberg, A. I., & Shenhav, Y. A. (1984). R&D career paths: Their relation to work goals and productivity. *IEEE Transactions on Engineering Management, 31,* 111-117.

Goldreich, Y., & Raveh, A. (1993). Coplot display technique as an aid to climatic classification. *Geographical Annals, 25,* 337-353.

Goldstein, H. (1995). *Multilevel statistical models.* London: Edward Arnold.

Goodenough, W. H. (1981). *Culture, language, and society.* Menlo Park, CA: Benjamin-Cummings.

Goodrich, R. (1982). Seven office evaluations. *Environment and Behavior, 14,* 353-378.

Goodstein, L. D., & Burke, W. W. (1991). Creating successful organizational change. *Organizational Dynamics, 19*(4), 5-17.

Gordon, G. G. (1991). Industry determinants of organizational culture. *Academy of Management Review, 16,* 396-415.

Gordon, G. G., & Cummins, W. W. (1979). *Managing management climate.* Lexington, MA: Lexington.

Gordon, G. G., & DiTomaso, N. (1992). Predicting corporate performance from organizational culture. *Journal of Management Studies, 29,* 783-798.

Gordon, M. E., Philpot, J. W., Burt, R. E., Thompson, C. A., & Spiller, W. E. (1980). Commitment to union: Development of a measure and an examination of its correlates. *Journal of Applied Psychology Monograph, 65,* 479-499.

Goss, T., Pascale, R., & Athos, A. (1993). The reinvention rollercoaster: Risking the present for a powerful future. *Harvard Business Review, 72*(2), 97-108.

Gouldner, A. W. (1954). *Patterns of industrial bureaucracy*. New York: Free Press.

Gouldner, A. W. (1957). Cosmopolitans and locals: Toward an analysis of latent social roles I. *Administrative Science Quarterly, 2*, 281-306.

Gouldner, A. W. (1958). Cosmopolitans and locals: Toward an analysis of latent social roles II. *Administrative Science Quarterly, 2*, 444-480.

Graen, G. B., Hui, C., Wakabayashi, M., & Wang, Z.-M. (1997). Cross-cultural research alliances in organizational research: Cross-cultural partnership-making in action. In P. C. Earley & M. Erez (Eds.), *New perspectives on international industrial/organizational psychology* (pp. 160-190). San Francisco: New Lexington.

Graen, G. B., & Scandura, T. (1987). Toward a psychology of dyadic organizing. In L. L. Cummings & B. M. Staw (Eds.), *Research in organizational behavior* (Vol. 9). Greenwich, CT: JAI.

Graen, G. B., & Uhl-Bien, M. (1995). Relationship-based approach to leadership: Development of leader-member exchange (LMX) theory of leadership over 25 years: Applying a multi-level multi-domain perspective. *Leadership Quarterly, 6*, 219-247.

Graham, J. (1986). Principled organizational dissent: A theoretical essay. In B. M. Staw & L. L. Cummings (Eds.), *Research in organizational behavior* (Vol. 8, pp. 1-52). Greenwich, CT: JAI.

Graham, J. L., & Sano, Y. (1984). *Smart bargaining: Doing business with the Japanese*. Cambridge, MA: Ballinger.

Grandjean, B. D. (1981). History and career in a bureaucratic labor market. *American Journal of Sociology, 86*, 1057-1092.

Granick, D. (1960). *The red executive*. Garden City, NY: Anchor.

Granovetter, M. S. (1985). Economic action and social structure: The problem of embeddedness. *American Journal of Sociology, 91*, 481-510.

Graves, D. (1981). Individual reactions to a merger of two small firms of brokers in the reinsurance industry: A total population survey. *Journal of Management Studies, 18*, 89-113.

Greenwood, R., Hinings, C. R., & Brown, J. (1994). Merging professional service firms. *Organization Science, 5*, 239-257.

Gregory, K. L. (1983). Native-view paradigms: Multiple cultures and culture conflicts in organizations. *Administrative Science Quarterly, 28*, 359-376.

Gronroos, C. (1990). *Service management and marketing: Managing the moments of truth in service competition*. Lexington, MA: Lexington.

Grossman, B. A. (1988). *Corporate loyalty: A trust betrayed*. Toronto: Penguin.

Grover, S. L., & Crooker, K. J. (1995). Who appreciates family-responsive human resource policies: The impact of family-friendly policies on the organizational attachment of parents and non-parents. *Personnel Psychology, 48*, 271-288.

Grundy, L. K., & Rousseau, D. M. (1994). Critical incidents in communicating culture to newcomers: The meaning is in the message. *Human Relations, 47*, 1063-1088.

Guiltinan, J. P. (1987). The price bundling of services: A normative framework. *Journal of Marketing, 51*, 74-85.

Guion, R. M. (1973). A note on organizational climate. *Organizational Behavior and Human Performance, 9,* 120-125.

Guion, R. M. (1976). *Personnel testing.* New York: McGraw-Hill.

Gundry, L. K., & Rousseau, D. M. (1994). Critical incidents in communicating culture to newcomers: The meaning is the message. *Human Relations, 47,* 1063-1088.

Gunz, H. P. (1980). Dual ladders in research: A paradoxical organizational fix. *R&D Management, 9,* 29-32.

Gunz, H. P. (1989a). *Careers and corporate cultures: Managerial mobility in large corporations.* Oxford: Blackwell.

Gunz, H. P. (1989b). The dual meaning of managerial careers: Organizational and individual levels of analysis. *Journal of Management Studies, 26,* 225-250.

Gunz, H. P., & Jalland, R. M. (1996). Managerial careers and business strategies. *Academy of Management Review, 21,* 718-756.

Gunz, H. P., Jalland, R. M., & Evans, M. G. (1998). New strategy, wrong managers? What you need to know about career streams. *Academy of Management Executive, 12*(2), 21-37.

Gutek, B. A. (1985). *Sex and the workplace.* San Francisco: Jossey-Bass.

Guth, W. D. (1993). Commentary on "Strategies, organizational learning, and careers: The fallout from restructuring." In P. Shrivastava, A. Huff, & J. Dutton (Eds.), *Advances in strategic management* (Vol. 9, pp. 217-222). Greenwich, CT: JAI.

Gutting, G. (1996). Michel Foucault: A user's manual. In G. Gutting (Ed.), *The Cambridge companion to Foucault* (pp. 1-27). Cambridge: Cambridge University Press.

Guttman, L. (1954). A new approach to factor analysis: The radex. In P. F. Lazarsfeld (Ed.), *Mathematical thinking in the social sciences* (pp. 258-348). Glencoe, IL: Free Press.

Guttman, L. (1968). A general nonmetric technique for finding the smallest coordinate space for a configuration of points. *Psychometrica, 33,* 469-506.

Guzzo, R. A., Noonan, K. A., & Elron, E. (1994). Expatriate managers and the psychological contract. *Journal of Applied Psychology, 79,* 617-626.

Haber, S. B., O'Brien, J. N., Metlay, D. S., & Crouch, D. A. (1991). *Influence of organizational factors on performance reliability* (Report to the U.S. Nuclear Regulatory Commission, Division of Systems Research). Upton, NY: Brookhaven National Laboratory.

Hachen, D. S., Jr. (1992). Industrial characteristics and job mobility rates. *American Sociological Review, 57,* 39-55.

Hackman, J. R., & Oldham, G. R. (1974). *The Job Diagnostic Survey: An instrument for the diagnosis of jobs and evaluation of job redesign projects* (Tech. Rep. No. 4). New Haven, CT: Yale University, Department of Administrative Science.

Hackman, J. R., & Oldham, G. R. (1980). *Work redesign.* Reading, MA: Addison-Wesley.

Hackman, J. R., & Wageman, R. (1995). Total quality management: Empirical, conceptual, and practical issues. *Administrative Science Quarterly, 40,* 309-342.

Hage, J. (1995). Post-industrial lives: New demands, new prescriptions. In A. Howard (Ed.), *The changing nature of work* (pp. 485-512). San Francisco: Jossey-Bass.

Hage, J., & Dewar, R. (1973). Elite values versus organizational structure in predicting innovation. *Administrative Science Quarterly, 18*, 279-290.

Haire, M., Ghiselli, E. E., & Porter, L. W. (1966). *Managerial thinking: An international study.* New York: John Wiley.

Haley, B. R. (1998). *The relationship of unit culture and RN and client outcomes.* Unpublished doctoral dissertation, University of Illinois at Chicago.

Hall, D. T. (1986). Dilemmas in linking succession planning to individual executive learning. *Human Resource Management, 25*, 235-265.

Hall, D. T. (1987). Careers and socialization. *Journal of Management, 13*, 301-321.

Hall, D. T. (1996a). Introduction: Long live the career—a relational approach. In D. T. Hall (Ed.), *The career is dead—long live the career: A relational approach to careers* (pp. 1-12). San Francisco: Jossey-Bass.

Hall, D. T. (1996b). Protean careers of the 21st century. *Academy of Management Executive, 10*(4), 8-16.

Hall, D. T., & Isabella, L. A. (1985). Downward movement and career development. *Organizational Dynamics, 14*(1), 5-23.

Hall, D. T., & Mirvis, P. H. (1995). Careers as lifelong learning. In A. Howard (Ed.), *The changing nature of work* (pp. 323-361). San Francisco: Jossey-Bass.

Hall, D. T., & Mirvis, P. H. (1996). The new protean career. In D. T. Hall (Ed.), *The career is dead—long live the career: A relational approach to careers* (pp. 15-45). San Francisco: Jossey-Bass.

Hall, E. T. (1959). *The silent language.* Garden City, NY: Anchor.

Hall, E. T. (1966). *The hidden dimension.* Garden City, NY: Anchor.

Hall, E. T. (1976). *Beyond culture.* Garden City, NY: Anchor.

Hall, E. T. (1983). *The dance of life: The other dimension of time.* Garden City, NY: Anchor.

Hall, E. T., & Hall, M. R. (1990). *Understanding cultural differences.* Yarmouth, ME: Intercultural Press.

Hall, S. (1996). Introduction: Who needs identity? In S. Hall & P. du Gay (Eds.), *Questions of cultural identity* (pp. 1-17). Thousand Oaks, CA: Sage.

Hambrick, D. C., & Cannella, B. (1993). Relative standing: A framework for understanding departures of acquired executives. *Academy of Management Journal, 36*, 733-762.

Hambrick, D. C., & Mason, P. M. (1984). Upper echelons: The organization as a reflection of its top managers. *Academy of Management Review, 9*, 193-206.

Hambrick, D. C., Nadler, D. A., & Tushman, M. L. (Eds.). (1998). *Navigating change: How CEOs, top teams, and boards steer transformation.* Boston: Harvard Business School Press.

Hampden-Turner, C., & Trompenaars, A. (1993). *The seven cultures of capitalism.* Garden City, NY: Doubleday.

Handy, C. (1979). *Gods of management.* London: Pan.

Hanges, P. J., & Dickson, M. W. (in press). Scale development and validation. In R. J. House, P. J. Hanges, M. Javidan, & P. Dorfman (Eds.), *Cultural influences on leadership and organizations: A 62-nation study.* Thousand Oaks, CA: Sage.

Hanges, P. J., & House, R. J. (1998, October). *The relationship between societal cultures and organizational practices and values.* Invited address presented at the annual meeting of the Society for Organizational Behavior, Washington, DC.

Hardy, C., Lawrence, T. B., & Phillips, N. (1998). Talk and action: Conversations and narrative in interorganizational collaboration. In D. Grant, T. Keenoy, & C. Oswick (Eds.), *Discourse and organization* (pp. 65-83). Thousand Oaks, CA: Sage.

Harris, D. H. (Ed.). (1994). *Organizational linkages: Understanding the productivity paradox.* Washington, DC: National Academy Press.

Harris, J. J., & Segal, D. R. (1985). Observations from the Sinai: The boredom factor. *Armed Forces and Society, 11,* 235-248.

Harris, M. (1979). *Cultural materialism: The struggle for a science of culture.* New York: Vintage.

Harris, P. R., & Moran, R. T. (1984). *Managing cultural differences.* Houston, TX: Gulf.

Harris, R. N. (1973). *The police academy: An inside view.* New York: John Wiley.

Harris, S. G., & Mossholder, K. W. (1996). The affective implications of perceived congruence with culture dimensions during organizational transformation. *Journal of Management, 22,* 527-547.

Harrison, R. (1975). Diagnosing organization ideology. In J. Jones & P. Pfeiffer (Eds.), *The 1975 annual handbook for group facilitators* (pp. 101-107). La Jolla, CA: University Associates.

Harrison, R. (1979). Understanding your organization's character. *Harvard Business Review, 57*(5), 119-128.

Harrison, R. (1995). *The collected papers of Roger Harrison.* San Francisco: Jossey-Bass.

Haspeslagh, P. C., & Jemison, D. B. (1991). *Managing acquisitions: Creating value through corporate renewal.* New York: Free Press.

Hatch, M. J. (1993). The dynamics of organizational culture. *Academy of Management Review, 18,* 657-693.

Hatch, M. J. (1997). *Organization theory and theorizing: Modern, symbolic-interpretive and postmodern perspectives.* Oxford: Oxford University Press.

Haveman, H. A., & Cohen, L. E. (1994). The ecological dynamics of careers: The impact of organizational founding, dissolution, and merger on job mobility. *American Journal of Sociology, 100,* 104-152.

Hawkins, P. (1997). Organizational culture: Sailing between evangelism and complexity. *Human Relations, 50,* 417-440.

Hayes, R., & Abernathy, W. (1980). Managing our way to economic decline. *Harvard Business Review, 58*(6), 67-77.

Headland, T. N., Pike, K. L., & Harris, M. (Eds.). (1990). *Emics and etics: The insider/outsider debate.* Newbury Park, CA: Sage.

Hearn, J., & Parkin, P. W. (1987). *"Sex" at "work": The power and paradox of organisational sexuality.* Brighton, England: Wheatsheaf.

Hearn, J., Sheppard, D., Tancred-Sheriff, P., & Burrell, G. (Eds.). (1989). *The sexuality of organisation.* London: Sage.

Heckscher, C. C. (1988). *The new unionism.* New York: Basic Books.

Heffron, F. (1989). *Organization theory and public organizations: The political connection.* Englewood Cliffs, NJ: Prentice Hall.

Heider, F. (1958). *The psychology of interpersonal relations.* New York: John Wiley.

Hellriegel, D., & Slocum, J. W., Jr. (1974). Organizational climate: Measures, research, and contingencies. *Academy of Management Journal, 17,* 255-280.

Helmich, D. L. (1974). Organizational growth and succession patterns. *Academy of Management Journal, 17,* 771-775.

Helmreich, R. L. (1994). Anatomy of a system accident: The crash of Avianca Flight 052. *International Journal of Aviation Psychology, 4,* 265-284.

Helmreich, R. L., & Merritt, A. C. (1998). *Culture at work in aviation and medicine: National, organizational and professional influences.* Aldershot, England: Ashgate.

Helms Hatfield, J. C. (1994). Implementation and results of a planned culture change in a public utility. *Proceedings of the Annual Conference of the Administrative Sciences of Canada, 15,* 102-111.

Helms Hatfield, J. C. (1996). A case study of organisational change in a Canadian electrical company. *Case Study Proceedings of Administrative Sciences Association of Canada Conference, 1,* 1-20.

Helms Hatfield, J. C. (1997). *Framing the space: Making sense of organisational change programmes.* Paper presented at the 13th International Colloquium of the Standing Conference on Organisational Symbolism, Warsaw, Poland.

Helms Hatfield, J. C. (1998, July). *Competition as a sensemaking device in the management of meaning: A case study.* Paper presented at the 14th International Colloquium of the Standing Conference on Organisational Symbolism.

Helms Hatfield, J. C., & Mills, A. J. (1997). *Guiding lights and power sources: Consultants plug into the management of meaning in an electrical company.* Paper presented at the 15th International Colloquium of the European Group on Organisational Studies, Budapest.

Heskett, J. L., Sasser, W. E., Jr., & Schlesinger, L. A. (1997). *The service profit chain.* New York: Free Press.

Hildebrandt, E. (1988). Work, participation, and co-determination in computer-based manufacturing. In D. Knights & H. Willmott (Eds.), *New technology and the labour process* (pp. 50-65). London: Macmillan.

Hirschman, A. O. (1970). *Exit, voice, and loyalty: Responses to decline in firms, organizations, and states.* Cambridge, MA: Harvard University Press.

Hitt, M. A., & Ireland, R. D. (1987). Peters and Waterman revisited: The unended quest for excellence. *Academy of Management Executive, 1*(2), 91-98.

Hochschild, A. R. (1979). Emotion work, feeling rules, and social structure. *American Journal of Sociology, 85,* 551-575.

Hochschild, A. R. (1983). *The managed heart: Commercialization of human feeling.* Berkeley: University of California Press.

Hofstadter, D. R. (1979). *Godel, Escher, Bach: An eternal golden braid.* New York: Vintage.

Hofstadter, D. R., & Dennett, D. C. (1981). *The mind's I: Fantasies and reflections on self and soul.* Toronto: Bantam.

Hofstede, G. (1980a). *Culture's consequences: International differences in work-related values.* Beverly Hills, CA: Sage.

Hofstede, G. (1980b). Motivation, leadership and organization: Do American theories apply abroad? *Organizational Dynamics, 8*(3), 42-63.

Hofstede, G. (1991). *Cultures and organizations: Software of the mind.* London: McGraw-Hill.

Hofstede, G. (1993). Cultural constraints in management theories. *Academy of Management Executive, 7*(1), 81-94.

Hofstede, G. (1994). Management scientists are human. *Management Science, 40,* 4-13.

Hofstede, G. (1997a). *Cultures and organizations: Software of the mind* (Rev. ed.). New York: McGraw-Hill.

Hofstede, G. (1997b). Organization culture. In A. Sorge & M. Warner (Eds.), *The IEBM handbook of organizational behavior* (pp. 193-210). London: International Thomson Business Press.

Hofstede, G. (in press). *Culture's consequences: International differences in work-related values* (2nd ed.). Thousand Oaks, CA: Sage.

Hofstede, G., & Associates. (1998). *Masculinity and femininity: The taboo dimension of national cultures.* Thousand Oaks, CA: Sage.

Hofstede, G., & Bond, M. H. (1984). Hofstede's culture dimensions: An independent validation using Rokeach's value survey. *Journal of Cross-Cultural Psychology, 15,* 417-433.

Hofstede, G., & Bond, M. H. (1988). The Confucius connection: From cultural roots to economic growth. *Organizational Dynamics, 16*(4), 4-21.

Hofstede, G., Bond, M. H., & Luk, C. (1993). Individual perceptions of organizational cultures: A methodological treatise on levels of analysis. *Organization Studies, 14,* 483-503.

Hofstede, G., Neuijen, B., Ohayv, D. D., & Sanders, G. (1990). Measuring organizational cultures: A qualitative and quantitative study across twenty cases. *Administrative Science Quarterly, 35,* 286-316.

Holland, P. W., & Leinhardt, S. (1977). Transitivity in structural models of small groups. In S. Leinhardt (Ed.), *Social networks: A developing paradigm* (pp. 49-66). New York: Academic Press.

Homans, G. C. (1950). *The human group.* New York: Harcourt, Brace & World.

Homer, P. M., & Kahle, L. R. (1988). A structural equation test of the value-attitude-behavior hierarchy. *Journal of Personality and Social Psychology, 54,* 638-646.

Honeycutt, T. L., & Rosen, B. (1997). Family friendly human resource policies, salary levels, and salient identity as predictors of organizational attraction. *Journal of Vocational Behavior, 50,* 271-290.

Hope, T., & Hope, J. (1996). *Transforming the bottom line: Managing performance with the real numbers.* Boston: Harvard Business School Press.

Hoppe, M. H. (1990). *A comparative study of country elites.* Unpublished doctoral dissertation, University of North Carolina.

House, R. J. (1977). A 1976 theory of charismatic leadership. In J. G. Hunt, B. R. Baliga, H. P. Dachler, & C. A. Schriesheim (Eds.), *Emerging leadership vistas* (pp. 189-207). Lexington, MA: Lexington.

House, R. J. (1995). Leadership in the twenty-first century: A speculative inquiry. In A. Howard (Ed.), *The changing nature of work* (pp. 411-450). San Francisco: Jossey-Bass.

House, R. J., Hanges, P. J., Ruiz-Quintanilla, S. A., Dorfman, P. W., Javidan, M., Dickson, M. W., Gupta, V., & GLOBE. (1999). Cultural influences on leadership: Project GLOBE. In W. Mobley, J. Gessner, & V. Arnold (Eds.), *Advances in global leadership* (Vol. 1, pp. 171-233). Greenwich, CT: JAI.

House, R. J., Schuler, R. S., & Levanoni, E. (1983). Role conflict and ambiguity scales: Reality or artifacts? *Journal of Applied Psychology, 68,* 334-337.

House, R. J., Wright, N., & Aditya, R. N. (1997). Cross-cultural research on organizational leadership: A critical analysis and a proposed theory. In P. C. Earley & M. Erez (Eds.), *New perspectives on international industrial/organizational psychology* (pp. 535-625). San Francisco: New Lexington.

Howard, A. (Ed.). (1995). *The changing nature of work.* San Francisco: Jossey-Bass.

Hsieh, P. (1998). *The relationship between nursing unit characteristics and nurses' interaction processes in an acute care medical center in Taiwan.* Unpublished doctoral dissertation, University of Texas at Austin.

Hughes, E. C. (1937). Institutional office and the person. *American Journal of Sociology, 43,* 404-413.

Hui, C. H., & Triandis, H. C. (1989). Effects of culture and response format on extreme response styles. *Journal of Cross-Cultural Psychology, 20,* 296-309.

Hulin, C. L. (1987). A psychometric theory of evaluations of item and scale translations: Fidelity across languages. *Journal of Cross-Cultural Psychology, 18,* 115-142.

Hulin, C. L., & Blood, M. R. (1968). Job enlargement, individual differences, and worker responses. *Psychological Bulletin, 69,* 41-55.

Human Synergistics. (1986). *Improving store management effectiveness.* Atlanta, GA: Coca-Cola Retailing Research Council.

Human Synergistics/New Zealand. (1998). *Developing a sales culture in retail banking.* Auckland: Author.

Hunt, J. (1995). Police accounts of normal force. In J. M. Henslin (Ed.), *Down to earth sociology: Introductory readings* (8th ed.). New York: Free Press. (Reprinted from *Urban Life, 13,* 1985)

Hunt, J. G. (1991). *Leadership: A new synthesis.* Newbury Park, CA: Sage.

Hunt, J. G., & Philips, R. L. (1991). Leadership in battle and garrison: A framework for understanding the differences and preparing for both. In R. Gal & A. D. Mangelsdorff (Eds.), *Handbook of military psychology* (pp. 411-429). Chichester: John Wiley.

Hunt, J. L., & Peterson, M. F. (1997). International perspectives on international leadership. *Leadership Quarterly, 8,* 203-231.

Hunt, S. D. (1994). On the rhetoric of qualitative methods: Toward historically informed argumentation in management inquiry. *Journal of Management Inquiry, 3,* 221-234.

Hunt, S. D., & Morgan, R. M. (1994). Organizational commitment: One of many or key mediating construct? *Academy of Management Journal, 37,* 1568-1587.

Huntley, H. L., Jr. (1997). How does "God-talk" speak to the workplace? An essay on the theology of work. In D. P. Bloch & L. J. Richmond (Eds.), *Connections between spirit and work in career development: New approaches and practical perspectives* (pp. 115-136). Palo Alto, CA: Davies-Black.

Hurley, M. E., Scandura, T. A., Schriesheim, C. A., Brannick, M. T., Seers, A., Vandenbreg, R. J., & Williams, L. J. (1997). Exploratory and confirmatory factor analysis: Guidelines, issues and alternatives. *Journal of Organizational Behavior, 18,* 667-683.

Hurst, D. K. (1995). *Crisis and renewal: Meeting the challenge of organizational change.* Boston: Harvard Business School Press.

Hutchins, E. (1991). Organizing work by adaptation. *Organization Science, 2,* 14-39.

IBM division reborn to motivated productivity. (1998, December). *Workforce,* p. 74.

Inglehart, R. (1990). *Culture shift in advanced industrial society.* Princeton, NJ: Princeton University Press.

Inkeles, A., & Levinson, D. J. (1969). National character: The study of modal personality and sociocultural systems. In G. Lindzey & E. Aronson (Eds.), *The handbook of social psychology* (2nd ed., Vol. 4, pp. 418-506). Reading, MA: Addison-Wesley.

Inkeles, A., & Smith, D. (1974). *Becoming modern.* Cambridge, MA: Harvard University Press.

Innis, H. A. (1964). *The bias of communications.* Toronto: University of Toronto Press.

Isaacs, W. (1993). Taking flight: Dialogue, collective thinking, and organizational learning. *Organizational Dynamics, 21*(3), 24-39.

Isaacs, W. (1999). *Dialogue and the art of thinking together: A pioneering approach to communicating in business and in life.* Garden City, NY: Doubleday.

Isabella, L. A. (1988). Career stage as a frame of reference for interpreting key organizational events. *Journal of Organizational Behavior, 9,* 345-358.

Isabella, L. A. (1990). Evolving interpretations as a change unfolds: How managers construe key organizational events. *Academy of Management Journal, 33,* 7-41.

Ivancevich, J. M., Schweiger, D. M., & Power, F. R. (1987). Strategies for managing human resources during mergers and acquisitions. *Human Resource Planning, 10,* 19-35.

Iwata, Y. (1999). *Difference in business communication between the U.S. and Japan.* Unpublished doctoral dissertation, University of Mississippi.

Jackofsky, E. F., & Slocum, J. W., Jr. (1988). A longitudinal study of climate. *Journal of Organizational Behavior, 9,* 319-334.

Jackson, S. (1992). *Chinese enterprise management reforms in economic perspective.* Berlin: Walter de Gruyter.

Jackson, S. E., & Schuler, R. S. (1985). A meta-analysis and conceptual critique of research on role ambiguity and role conflict in work settings. *Organizational Behavior and Human Decision Processes, 33,* 1-21.

Jackson, S. E., Stone, V. K., & Alvarez, E. B. (1993). Socialization amidst diversity: The impact of demographics on work team oldtimers and newcomers. In L. L. Cummings & B. M. Staw (Eds.), *Research in organizational behavior* (Vol. 15, pp. 45-109). Greenwich, CT: JAI.

Jacobs, J. (1992). *Systems of survival: A dialogue on the moral foundations of commerce and politics.* New York: Vintage.

James, L. R. (1982). Aggregation bias in estimates of perceptual agreement. *Journal of Applied Psychology, 67,* 219-229.

James, L. R., Demaree, R. G., & Wolf, G. (1984). Estimating within-group interrater reliability with and without response bias. *Journal of Applied Psychology, 69,* 85-98.

James, L. R., Demaree, R. G., & Wolf, G. (1993). $r_{wg}$: An assessment of within-group interrater agreement. *Journal of Applied Psychology, 78,* 306-309.

James, L. R., James, L. A., & Ashe, D. K. (1990). The meaning of organizations: The role of cognition and values. In B. Schneider (Ed.), *Organizational climate and culture* (pp. 40-84). San Francisco: Jossey-Bass.

James, L. R., & Jones, A. P. (1974). Organizational climate: A review of theory and research. *Psychological Bulletin, 81,* 1096-1112.

Jaques, E. (1951). *The changing culture of a factory.* London: Tavistock.

Jaques, E. (1976). *A general theory of bureaucracy.* London: Heinemann.

Jaques, E. (1982). *The form of time.* New York: Crane Russak.

Jaros, S. J., Jermier, J. M., Koehler, J. W., & Sinich, T. (1993). Effects of continuance, affective, and moral commitment on the withdrawal process: An evaluation of eight structural equation models. *Academy of Management Journal, 36,* 951-995.

Jemison, D. B., & Sitkin, S. B. (1986). Corporate acquisitions: A process perspective. *Academy of Management Review, 11,* 145-163.

Jensen, M. C., & Meckling, W. H. (1976). Theory of the firm: Managerial behavior, agency costs and ownership structure. *Journal of Financial Economics, 3,* 305-360.

Jermier, J. M., & Berkes, L. J. (1979). Leader behavior in a police command bureaucracy: A closer look at the quasi-military model. *Administrative Science Quarterly, 24,* 1-23.

Jha, S. J., Michela, J. L., & Noori, H. (1996). The dynamics of continuous improvement: Aligning organizational attributes and activities for quality and productivity. *International Journal of Quality Science, 1,* 19-47.

Jick, T. D. (1979). Mixing qualitative and quantitative methods: Triangulation in action. *Administrative Science Quarterly, 24,* 602-611.

Johannesson, R. E. (1973). Some problems in the measurement of organizational climate. *Organizational Behavior and Human Performance, 10,* 118-144.

Johnson, G. N. (1988). Rethinking incrementalism. *Strategic Management Journal, 9,* 75-92.

Johnson, J. C. (1994). Anthropological contributions to the study of social networks: A review. In S. Wasserman & J. Galaskiewicz (Eds.), *Advances in social network analysis* (pp. 113-151). Thousand Oaks, CA: Sage.

Johnson, J. W. (1996). Linking employee perceptions of service climate to customer satisfaction. *Personnel Psychology, 49,* 831-852.

Johnson, R. T., & Ouchi, W. G. (1974). Made in America (under Japanese management). *Harvard Business Review, 53*(1), 61-69.

Johnson, W. R., & Jones-Johnson, G. (1992). Differential predictors of union and company commitment: Parallel and divergent models. *Psychology, 29,* 1-12.

Johnston, H. R. (1976). A new conceptualization of source of organizational climate. *Administrative Science Quarterly, 21,* 95-103.

Jones, A. P., & James, L. R. (1979). Psychological climate: Dimensions and relationships of individual and aggregated work environment perceptions. *Organizational Behavior and Human Performance, 23,* 201-250.

Jones, G. R. (1983a). Psychological orientation and the process of organizational socialization: An interactionist perspective. *Academy of Management Review, 8,* 464-474.

Jones, G. R. (1983b). Transaction costs, property rights, and organizational culture: An exchange perspective. *Administrative Science Quarterly, 28,* 454-467.

Jones, G. R. (1986). Socialization tactics, self-efficacy, and newcomers' adjustments to organizations. *Academy of Management Journal, 29,* 262-279.

Jones, M. O. (1993). *Studying organizational symbolism: What, how, why?* Newbury Park, CA: Sage.

Jordan, A. T. (1994). Organizational culture: The anthropological approach. In A. T. Jordan (Ed.), *Practicing anthropology in corporate America: Consulting on organizational culture* (pp. 3-16). Arlington, VA: American Anthropological Association.

Judge, T. A., & Bretz, R. D., Jr. (1992). Effects of work values on job choice decisions. *Journal of Applied Psychology, 77,* 261-271.

Judge, W. Q., & Spitzfaden, M. (1995). The management of strategic time horizons within biotechnology firms. *Journal of Management Inquiry, 4,* 179-196.

Jung, C. G. (1923). *Psychological types*. New York: Harcourt, Brace.

Jung, C. G. (1959). The archetypes and the collective unconscious. In *The collected works of C. G. Jung* (Vol. 9, Pt. 1). Princeton, NJ: Princeton University Press.

Kagitcibasi, C. (1997). Individualism and collectivism. In J. W. Berry, M. H. Segall, & C. Kagitcibasi (Eds.), *Handbook of cross-cultural psychology* (2nd ed., Vol. 3, pp. 1-50). Boston: Allyn & Bacon.

Kagono, T., Nonaka, I., Sakakibara, K., & Okumura, A. (1985). *Strategic vs. evolutionary management*. Amsterdam: North Holland.

Kahle, L. R. (Ed.). (1983). *Social values and social change: Adaptation to life in America*. New York: Praeger.

Kahle, L. R. (1984). *Attitudes and social adaptation: A person-situation interaction approach*. Oxford: Pergamon.

Kahle, L. R. (1995). Role relaxed consumer: A trend for the nineties. *Journal of Advertising Research, 35*(2), 66-71.

Kahle, L. R. (1996). Social values and consumer behavior: Research from the list of values. In C. Seligman, J. M. Olson, & M. P. Zanna (Eds.), *The Ontario Symposium: Vol. 8. The psychology of values* (pp. 135-151). Mahwah, NJ: Lawrence Erlbaum.

Kahle, L. R., & Eisert, D. C. (1986). Social values and adaptation in the American workplace. In E. G. Flamholtz, Y. Randle, & S. A. Sackmann (Eds.), *Future directions in human resource management* (pp. 203-223). Los Angeles: University of California.

Kahle, L. R., Homer, P. M., O'Brien, R. M., & Boush, D. M. (1997). Maslow's hierarchy and social adaptation as alternative accounts of value structures. In L. R. Kahle & L. Chiagouris (Eds.), *Values, lifestyles, and psychographics* (pp. 111-137). Mahwah, NJ: Lawrence Erlbaum.

Kahle, L. R., Kulka, R. A., & Klingel, D. M. (1980). Low adolescent self-esteem leads to multiple interpersonal problems: A test of social adaptation theory. *Journal of Personality and Social Psychology, 39*, 492-502.

Kahle, L. R., Rose, G. M., & Shoham, A. (in press). Value differences around the world. *Journal of International Consumer Marketing*.

Kahle, L. R., & Shoham, A. (1995). Role relaxed consumers: Empirical evidence. *Journal of Advertising Research, 35*(3), 59-62.

Kahn, R. L., Wolfe, D. M., Quinn, R. P., Snoek, J. D., & Rosenthal, R. A. (1964). *Occupational stress: Studies in role conflict and role ambiguity*. New York: John Wiley.

Kahn, W. A. (1990). Psychological conditions of personal engagement and disengagement at work. *Academy of Management Journal, 33*, 692-724.

Kahn, W. A. (1996). Secure base relationships at work. In D. T. Hall (Ed.), *The career is dead—long live the career: A relational approach to careers* (pp. 158-179). San Francisco: Jossey-Bass.

Kakar, S. (1971). Authority patterns and subordinate behavior in Indian organizations. *Administrative Science Quarterly, 16*, 298-307.

Kalleberg, A., Knoke, D., & Marsden, P. V. (1995, July). *Interorganizational networks and the changing employment contract*. Paper presented at the International Social Network Conference, London. Available Internet: http://www.soc.umn.edu/~knoke/pages/nos96.htm

Kam, S. M., & Brooks, S. M. (1998). Touching the customer by understanding employees: Preliminary linkage research results from four regions of Kaiser Permanente. *Permanente Journal, 2,* 47-54.

Kane, K. (1995). An inside view of management in a People's Republic of China global enterprise. *Journal of Management Inquiry, 4,* 381-387.

Kane, P. (1974). *Sex objects in the sky.* Chicago: Follett.

Kanter, R. M. (1968). Commitment and social organization: A study of commitment mechanisms in utopian communities. *American Sociological Review, 33,* 499-517.

Kanter, R. M. (1977). *Men and women of the corporation.* New York: Basic Books.

Kanter, R. M. (1984). *The change masters: Corporate entrepreneurs at work.* London: George Allen & Unwin.

Kanter, R. M. (1988). When a thousand flowers bloom: Structural, collective, and social conditions for innovation in organizations. In B. M. Staw & L. L. Cummings (Eds.), *Research in organizational behavior* (Vol. 10, pp. 169-211). Greenwich, CT: JAI.

Kanter, R. M., Stein, B. A., & Jick, T. D. (1992). *The challenge of organizational change: How companies experience it and leaders guide it.* New York: Free Press.

Kaplan, R. S., & Norton, D. P. (1992). The balanced scorecard: Measures that drive performance. *Harvard Business Review, 70*(3), 71-79.

Kaplan, R. S., & Norton, D. P. (1996). *Translating strategy into action: The balanced scorecard.* Boston: Harvard Business School Press.

Kaplan, S. (1992). Environmental preference in a knowledge-seeking, knowledge-using organism. In J. H. Barkow, L. Cosmides, & J. Tooby (Eds.), *The adapted mind: Evolutionary psychology and the generation of culture.* New York: Oxford University Press.

Kaplan, S., & Kaplan, R. (1983). *Cognition and environment: Functioning in an uncertain world.* Ann Arbor, MI: Ulrich's.

Karpik, L. (1978). Organizations, institutions and history. In L. Karpik (Ed.), *Organization and environment: Theory, issues and reality* (pp. 15-68). Beverly Hills, CA: Sage.

Kasl, S. V. (1994). Stress and health. In L. Breslow, J. E. Fielding, & L. B. Lave (Eds.), *Annual review of public health* (Vol. 5, pp. 319-341). Palo Alto, CA: Annual Reviews.

Kato, H., & Kato, S. (1992). *Understanding and working with the Japanese business world.* Englewood Cliffs, NJ: Prentice Hall.

Katz, D., & Kahn, R. L. (1966). *The social psychology of organizations.* New York: John Wiley.

Katz, D., & Kahn, R. L. (1978). *The social psychology of organizations* (2nd ed.). New York: John Wiley.

Katz, R. (1985). Organizational stress and early socialization experiences. In T. A. Beehr & R. S. Bhagat (Eds.), *Human stress and cognition in organizations* (pp. 117-139). New York: John Wiley.

Kaufman, C. F., Lane, P. M., & Lindquist, J. D. (1991). Exploring more than 24 hours a day: A preliminary investigation of polychronic time use. *Journal of Consumer Research, 18,* 392-401.

Kaufman, H. (1967). *The forest ranger.* Baltimore: Johns Hopkins University Press.

Keeley, M. 1980. Organizational analogy: A comparison of organismic and social contract models. *Administrative Science Quarterly, 25,* 337-362.

Keenan, G. M., Cooke, R. A., & Hillis, S. L. (1998). Norms and nurse management of conflicts: Keys to understanding nurse-physician collaboration. *Research in Nursing and Health, 21,* 59-72.

Kekele, T. (1998). The effects of organizational culture on success and failures in implementation of some total quality management approaches: Towards a theory of selecting a culturally matching quality approach. *Acta Wasaensia, 65.*

Kelman, H. C. (1958). Compliance, identification, and internalization: Three processes of attitude change. *Journal of Conflict Resolution, 2,* 51-60.

Kenny, D. A., Bond, C. F., Mohr, C. D., & Horn, E. M. (1996). Do we know how much people like one another? *Journal of Personality and Social Psychology, 71,* 928-936.

Kenny, D. A., & DePaulo, B. M. (1993). Do people know how others view them? An empirical and theoretical account. *Psychological Bulletin, 114,* 145-161.

Kerfoot, D., & Knights, D. (1993). Management, masculinity and manipulation: From paternalism to corporate strategy in financial service in Britain. *Journal of Management Studies, 30,* 659-677.

Kerr, C., Dunlop, J. T., Harbison, F., & Myers, C. A. (1960). *Industrialism and industrial man.* Cambridge, MA: Harvard University Press.

Kerr, J., & Slocum, J. W. (1987). Managing corporate culture through reward systems. *Academy of Management Executive, 1*(2), 99-108.

Kerr, S. (1995). An academy classic: On the folly of rewarding A, while hoping for B. *Academy of Management Executive, 9*(1), 7-16.

Kets de Vries, M. F. R. (1989). The leader as mirror: Clinical reflections. *Human Relations, 42,* 607-623.

Kieser, A. (1989). Organizational, institutional, and societal evolution: Medieval craft guilds and the genesis of formal organizations. *Administrative Science Quarterly, 34,* 540-564.

Kilduff, M., & Funk, J. L. (1998). *Enactment and social networks in a Japanese factory* (Working paper). University Park: Pennsylvania State University.

Kilduff, M., Funk, J. L., & Mehra, A. (1997). Engineering identity in a Japanese factory. *Organization Science, 8,* 1-14.

Kilduff, M., & Krackhardt, D. (1994). Bringing the individual back in: A structural analysis of the internal market for reputation in organizations. *Academy of Management Journal, 37,* 87-108.

Kilduff, M., & Mehra, A. (1997). Postmodernism and organizational research. *Academy of Management Review, 22,* 453-481.

Kilmann, R. H. (1981). Toward a unique/useful concept of values for interpersonal behavior: A critical review of the literature on value. *Psychological Reports, 48,* 939-959.

Kilmann, R. H. (1995). A holistic program and critical success factors of corporate transformation. *European Management Journal, 13,* 175-186.

Kilmann, R. H. (1998, August). *Achieving corporate transformation: Integrating TQM, reengineering, and learning organizations.* Paper presented at the annual meeting of the Academy of Management, San Diego, CA.

Kilmann, R. H., & Saxton, M. J. (1983). *The Kilmann-Saxton Culture-Gap Survey.* Pittsburgh: PA Organizational Design Consultants.

Kilmann, R. H., Saxton, M. J., Serpa, R., & Associates. (Eds.). (1985). *Gaining control of the corporate culture.* San Francisco: Jossey-Bass.

Kim, U., & Berry, J. W. (Eds.). (1993). *Indigenous psychologies: Research and experience in cultural context.* Newbury Park, CA: Sage.

Kipnis, D. (1996). Trust and technology. In R. M. Kramer & T. R. Tyler (Eds.), *Trust in organizations: Frontiers of theory and research* (pp. 39-50). Thousand Oaks, CA: Sage.

Kirkman, B. L., & Shapiro, D. L. (1997). The impact of cultural values on employee resistance to teams: Toward a model of globalized self-managing work team-effectiveness. *Academy of Management Review, 22,* 730-757.

Kitching, J. (1967). Why do mergers miscarry? *Harvard Business Review, 45*(4), 84-101.

Klein, A. S., Masi, R. J., & Weidner, C. K. (1995). Organizational culture, distribution and amount of control, and perceptions of quality. *Group and Organization Management, 20,* 122-148.

Klein, K. J., Dansereau, F., & Hall, R. J. (1994). Levels issues in theory development, data collection, and analysis. *Academy of Management Review, 19,* 195-229.

Klein, K. J., & Sorra, J. S. (1996). The challenge of innovation implementation. *Academy of Management Review, 21,* 1055-1080.

Klein, M. I. (1992). *Corporate culture and store performance: Differences among high performance and low performance stores.* Unpublished doctoral dissertation, Temple University.

Klein, R. L., Bigley, G. A., & Roberts, K. H. (1995). Organizational culture in high reliability organizations: An extension. *Human Relations, 48,* 771-793.

Kleinberg, J. (1989). Cultural clash between managers: America's Japanese firms. In S. B. Prasad (Ed.), *Advances in international comparative management* (Vol. 4, pp. 221-244). Greenwich, CT: JAI.

Kleinberg, J. (1994a). "The crazy group": Emergent culture in a Japanese-American bi-national work group. In M. G. Serapio, Jr., S. Beechler, & A. Bird (Eds.), *Research in international business and international relations: Vol. 6. Emerging trends in Japanese management* (pp. 1-45). Greenwich, CT: JAI.

Kleinberg, J. (1994b). Practical implications of organizational culture where Americans and Japanese work together. *National Association for the Practice of Anthropology Bulletin, 14,* 48-65.

Kleinberg, J. (1994c). Working here is like walking blindly into a dense forest. In T. Hamada & W. E. Sibley (Eds.), *Anthropological perspectives on organizational culture* (pp. 153-191). New York: University Press of America.

Kleinberg, J. (1998). An ethnographic perspective on cross-cultural negotiation and cultural production. In J. A. Wagner III (Ed.), *Advances in
qualitative organization research* (Vol. 1, pp. 201-249). Greenwich,
CT: JAI.

Kluckhohn, C. (1942). Myths and rituals: A general theory. *Harvard
Theological Review, 35,* 45-79.

Kluckhohn, C. (1951). Value and value orientations in the theory of action.
In T. Parsons & E. Shils (Eds.), *Toward a general theory of action.*
Cambridge, MA: Harvard University Press.

Kluckhohn, F. R., & Strodtbeck, F. L. (1961). *Variations in value orientations.* Evanston, IL: Row, Peterson.

Kober, K., & Knowles, R. (1996). Measurement in self-organizing systems. *Journal for Quality and Participation, 19*(1), 38-41.

Koene, B. A. S. (1996). *Organizational culture, leadership and performance in context: Trust and rationality in organizations.* Unpublished
doctoral dissertation, Rijksuniversiteit Limburg.

Kohlberg, L. (1969). Stage and sequence: The cognitive-developmental
approach to socialization. In D. Goslin (Ed.), *Handbook of socialization: Theory and research.* Chicago: Rand McNally.

Kohn, M. L., & Schooler, C. (1982). Job conditions and personality: A
longitudinal assessment of their reciprocal effects. *American Journal of
Sociology, 87,* 1257-1286.

Kohn, M. L., & Schooler, C. (1983). *Work and personality.* Norwood,
NJ: Ablex.

Kolarska, L., & Aldrich, H. (1980). Exit, voice, and silence: Consumers'
and managers' responses to organizational decline. *Organization
Studies, 1,* 41-58.

Kondo, D. K. (1990). *Crafting selves: Power, gender, and discourses
of identity in a Japanese workplace.* Chicago: University of Chicago
Press.

Kono, T., & Clegg, S. R. (1998). *Transformations of corporate culture:
Experiences of Japanese enterprises.* New York: Walter de Gruyter.

Kopelman, R. E., Brief, A. P., & Guzzo, R. A. (1990). The role of climate
and culture in productivity. In B. Schneider (Ed.), *Organizational climate and culture* (pp. 282-318). San Francisco: Jossey-Bass.

Korten, D. C. (1995). *When corporations rule the world.* West Hartford,
CT: Kumarian.

Korvajarvi, P. (1998). *Gendering dynamics in white-collar work organisations.* Tampere, Finland: University of Tampere.

Kosmoski-Goepfert, K. (1994). *Effects of registered nurses' work design
on hospital culture, quality, and cost of patient care.* Unpublished doctoral dissertation, University of Illinois at Chicago.

Kotter, J. P. (1995). Leading change: Why transformation efforts fail.
*Harvard Business Review, 73*(4), 59-67.

Kotter, J. P. (1996, August 5). Kill complacency. *Fortune, 134,* 168-170.

Kotter, J. P., & Heskett, J. L. (1992). *Corporate culture and performance.*
New York: Free Press.

Kovach, B. E. (1986). The derailment of fast-track managers. *Organizational Dynamics, 15*(2), 41-48.

Kozlowski, S. W. J., & Hattrup, K. (1992). A disagreement about within-group agreement: Disentangling issues of consistency versus consensus. *Journal of Applied Psychology, 77,* 161-167.

Krackhardt, D., & Kilduff, M. (1990). Friendship patterns and culture: The control of organizational diversity. *American Anthropologist, 92,* 142-154.

Kram, K. E. (1996). A relational approach to career development. In D. T. Hall (Ed.), *The career is dead—long live the career: A relational approach to careers* (pp. 132-157). San Francisco: Jossey-Bass.

Kram, K. E., & Isabella, L. A. (1985). Mentoring alternatives: The role of peer relationships in career development. *Academy of Management Journal, 28,* 110-132.

Kramer, R. M. (1991). Intergroup relations and organization dilemmas: The role of categorization processes. In L. L. Cummings & B. M. Staw (Eds.), *Research in organizational behavior* (Vol. 13, pp. 191-228). Greenwich, CT: JAI.

Kraut, A. I., & Saari, L. M. (1999). Organization surveys: Coming of age for a new era. In A. I. Kraut & A. K. Korman (Eds.), *Evolving practices in human resource management* (pp. 302-327). San Francisco: Jossey-Bass.

Kristof, A. L. (1996). Person-organization fit: An integrative review of its conceptualizations, measurement, and implications. *Personnel Psychology, 49,* 1-50.

Kroeber, A. L., & Kluckhohn, C. (1951). *The concept of culture: A critical review of definitions.* Cambridge, MA: Harvard University, Peabody Museum of American Archeology and Ethnology.

Kroeber, A. L., & Kluckhohn, C. (1952). *Culture: A critical review of concepts and definitions.* Cambridge, MA: Harvard University, Peabody Museum of American Archeology and Ethnology.

Kroeck, K. G. (1994). Corporate reorganization and transformations in human resource management. In B. M. Bass & B. J. Aviolo (Eds.), *Improving organizational effectiveness through transformational leadership* (pp. 193-201). Thousand Oaks, CA: Sage.

Kumbasar, E. A., Romney, K., & Batchelder, W. H. (1994). Systematic biases in social perception. *American Journal of Sociology, 100,* 477-505.

Kunda, G. (1992). *Engineering culture: Control and commitment in a high-tech corporation.* Philadelphia: Temple University Press.

Kurtenbach, E. (1998, December 18). *China vows to continue reforms.* Associated Press report to InfoBeat on-line news service.

LaFollette, W. R., & Sims, H. P., Jr. (1975). Is satisfaction redundant with climate? *Organizational Behavior and Human Performance, 10,* 118-144.

Lahiry, S. (1994). Building commitment through organizational culture. *Training and Development Journal, 48*(4), 50-52.

Lakoff, G., & Johnson, M. (1980). *Metaphors we live by.* Chicago: University of Chicago Press.

Lammers, C. J. (1963). *Het Koninklijk Instituut voor de Marine. Een sociologische analyse van de inlijving van groepen adspirant-officieren in de zeemacht* (The Netherlands Naval College: A sociological analysis of the integration of groups of prospective officers in the navy). Assen, Netherlands: van Gorcum.

Lang, K. (1965). Military organizations. In J. G. March (Ed.), *Handbook of organizations* (pp. 838-878). Chicago: Rand McNally.

Langeler, G. H. (1992). The vision trap. *Harvard Business Review, 70*(4), 46-55.

Lant, T. K., Milliken, F. J., & Batra, B. (1992). The role of managerial learning and interpretation in strategic persistence and reorientation: An empirical exploration. *Strategic Management Journal, 13,* 585-608.

Larwood, L., Falbe, C. M., Kriger, M. P., & Meising, P. (1995). Structure and meaning of organizational vision. *Academy of Management Journal, 38,* 740-769.

Laughlin, C. D. (1996, May). *The evolution of cyborg consciousness.* Paper presented at the annual meeting of the Canadian Anthropology Society. Available Internet: http://www.carleton.ca/~claughli

Laughlin, C. D., & d'Aquili, E. G. (1974). *Biogenetic structuralism.* New York: Columbia University Press.

Lawler, E. E., III (1992). *The ultimate advantage: Creating the high-involvement organization.* San Francisco: Jossey-Bass.

Lawler, E. E., III. (1996). *From the ground up: Six principles for building the new logic corporation.* San Francisco: Jossey-Bass.

Lawler, E. E., III, Mohrman, S. A., & Leford, G. E., Jr. (1992). *Employee involvement and total quality management.* San Francisco: Jossey-Bass.

Lawler, E. E., III, Mohrman, S. A., & Leford, G. E., Jr. (1995). *Creating high performance organizations: Practices and results of employee involvement and total quality management in* Fortune *1000 companies.* San Francisco: Jossey-Bass.

Lawler, E. J. (1992). Choice processes and affective attachments to nested groups: A theoretical analysis. *American Sociological Review, 57,* 327-339.

Lawler, E. J., & Yoon, J. (1993). Power and the emergence of commitment behavior in negotiated exchange. *American Sociological Review, 58,* 465-481.

Lawler, E. J., & Yoon, J. (1995). Structural power and emotional processes in negotiations: A social exchange approach. In R. Kramer & D. Messick (Eds.), *Negotiation as a social process* (pp. 143-165). Thousand Oaks, CA: Sage.

Lawler, E. J., & Yoon, J. (1996). Commitment in exchange relations: Test of a theory of relational cohesion. *American Sociological Review, 61,* 89-108.

Lawler, E. J., & Yoon, J. (1998). Network structure and emotion in exchange relations. *American Sociological Review, 63,* 871-894.

Lawrence, B. S. (1990). At the crossroads: A multiple-level explanation of individual attainment. *Organization Science, 1,* 65-85.

Lawrence, P. R., & Lorsch, J. W. (1967). *Organization and environment: Managing differentiation and integration.* Boston: Harvard University, Graduate School of Business Administration.

Lawson, R. B., & Shen, Z. (1998). *Organizational psychology.* New York: Oxford University Press.

Lawton, R., Patterson, M., Maitlis, S., Payne, R. L., & West, M. (1997). *Organizational climate: What's the right question?* (Working paper). Sheffield, England: Sheffield University, Institute of Work Psychology.

Leach, E. R. (1976). *Culture and communication, the logic by which symbols are connected: An introduction to the use of structural analysis in social anthropology.* New York: Cambridge University Press.

Lebra, T. (1976). *Japanese patterns of behavior.* Honolulu: University of Hawaii Press.

Lee, M., & Barnett, G. A. (1997). A symbols-and-meaning approach to the organizational cultures of banks in the United States, Japan, and Taiwan. *Communication Research, 24,* 394-412.

Leeds, C. (1999). *The effects of communications training and mentoring on individual communication self-efficacy, job performance, and normative beliefs.* Unpublished doctoral dissertation, University of Illinois at Chicago.

Leibowitz, Z. B., Schlossberg, N. K., & Shore, J. E. (1992). New employees: A career development challenge. In D. H. Montross & C. J. Shinkman (Eds.), *Career development: Theory and practice* (pp. 137-161). Springfield, IL: Charles C Thomas.

Lengermann, J. J. (1988). Compatibility between people needs and organization needs: Projections and cautions on quality of work issues in the future organization. In J. Hage (Ed.), *Futures of organizations* (pp. 227-243). Lexington, MA: Lexington.

Lennox, R. D., & Wolfe, R. N. (1984). Revision of the self-monitoring scale. *Journal of Personality and Social Psychology, 46,* 1349-1363.

Lessem, R. (1990). *Managing corporate culture.* Brookfield, VT: Gower.

Leung, K., & Bond, M. H. (1989). On the empirical identification of dimensions for cross-cultural comparisons. *Journal of Cross-Cultural Psychology, 20,* 133-151.

Levine, R. V., & Bartlett, K. (1984). Pace of life, punctuality, and coronary heart disease in six countries. *Journal of Cross-Cultural Psychology, 15,* 233-255.

Levine, R. V., Lynch, K., Miyake, K., & Lucia, M. (1989). The Type A city: Coronary heart disease and the pace of life. *Journal of Behavioral Medicine, 12,* 509-524.

Levinson, H. A. (1962). *Men, management, and mental health.* Cambridge, MA: Harvard University Press.

Levinson, H. A. (1970). Psychologist diagnoses merger failures. *Harvard Business Review, 48*(4), 139-147.

Levitt, B., & Nass, C. (1989). The lid on the garbage can: Institutional constraints on decision making in the technical core of college text publishers. *Administrative Science Quarterly, 34,* 190-207.

Levy, A., & Merry, U. (1986). *Organizational transformation: Approaches, strategies, theories.* New York: Praeger.

Levy, P. E. (1993). Self-appraisal and attributions: A test of a model. *Journal of Management, 19,* 51-62.

Lewin, K. (1935). *A dynamic theory of personality.* New York: McGraw-Hill.

Lewin, K. (1948). *Resolving social conflicts.* New York: Harper & Row.

Lewin, K. (1951). *Field theory in social science.* New York: Harper & Row.

Lewin, K., Lippitt, R., & White, R. K. (1939). Patterns of aggressive behavior in experimentally created "social climates." *Journal of Social Psychology, 10,* 271-299.

Li, M. (1984). Exploration on some issues of political ideological work in industrial organizations. In M. Li, *Selected readings on political ideological work in industrial organizations.* Beijing: Economic Science Press.

Liden, R. C., & Maslyn, J. M. (1998). Multidimensionality of leader-member exchange: An empirical assessment through scale development. *Journal of Management, 24,* 43-72.

Liden, R. C., Wayne, S. J., & Stillwell, D. (1993). A longitudinal study on the early development of leader-member exchanges. *Journal of Applied Psychology, 78,* 662-674.

Liker, J. K., Ettlie, J., & Campbell, J. (Eds.). (1995). *Engineered in Japan: Japanese technology management practices.* Oxford: Oxford University Press.

Liker, J. K., Fruin, W. M., & Adler, P. S. (Eds.). (1999). *Remade in America: Transplanting and transforming Japanese management systems.* New York: Oxford University Press.

Likert, R. (1961). *New patterns of management.* New York: McGraw-Hill.

Likert, R. (1967). *The human organization.* New York: McGraw-Hill.

Lim, B. (1995). Examining the organizational culture and organizational performance link. *Leadership and Organization Development Journal, 16*(5), 16-21.

Lincoln, J. R., & Kalleberg, A. L. (1990). *Culture, control, and commitment: A study of work organizations and work attitudes in the United States and Japan.* Cambridge: Cambridge University Press.

Ling, W. Q., Chen, L., & Wang, D. (1987). Construction of CPM scale for leadership behavior assessment. *Acta Psychologica Sinica, 3,* 236-242.

Lippitt, G. L., Langseth, P., & Mossop, J. (1985). *Implementing organizational change: A practical guide to managing change efforts.* San Francisco: Jossey-Bass.

Litwin, G. H., Bray, J., & Brooke, K. L. (1996). *Mobilizing the organization: Bringing strategy to life.* Englewood Cliffs, NJ: Prentice Hall.

Litwin, G. H., & Stringer, R. A. (1968). *Motivation and organizational climate.* Boston: Harvard Business School Press.

Liu, L. C. (1997). *The effects of cultural dimensions on ethical decision making in marketing.* Unpublished doctoral dissertation, University of Mississippi.

Locke, E. A. (1969). What is job satisfaction? *Organizational Behavior and Human Performance, 4,* 309-336.

Locke, E. A., & Latham, P. G. (1990). *A theory of goal setting and task performance.* Englewood Cliffs, NJ: Prentice Hall.

Locke, J. (1997). *Essay concerning human understanding.* New York: Penguin. (Original work published 1690)

Lockett, M. (1983). Organizational democracy and politics in China. In C. Crouch & F. Heller (Eds.), *Organizational democracy and political processes* (pp. 591-635). New York: John Wiley.

Lodahl, T. M., & Kejner, M. (1965). The definitions and measurement of job involvement. *Journal of Applied Psychology, 49,* 24-33.

Lord, R. G., & Maher, K. J. (1991). *Leadership and information processing: Linking perceptions and performance.* Boston: Unwin Hyman.

Louis, M. R. (1980). Surprise and sense making: What newcomers experience in entering unfamiliar organizational settings. *Administrative Science Quarterly, 25,* 226-251.

Louis, M. R. (1985). Sourcing workplace cultures: Why, when, and how. In R. H. Kilmann, M. J. Saxton, R. Serpa, & Associates (Eds.), *Gaining control of the corporate culture* (pp. 126-136). San Francisco: Jossey-Bass.

Louis, M. R. (1990). Acculturation in the workplace: Newcomers as lay ethnographers. In B. Schneider (Ed.), *Organizational climate and culture* (pp. 85-129). San Francisco: Jossey-Bass.

Louis, M. R., Posner, B. Z., & Powell, G. N. (1983). The availability and helpfulness of socialization practices. *Personnel Psychology, 36,* 857-866.

Louis, M. R., & Sutton, R. I. (1991). Switching cognitive gears: From habits of mind to active thinking. *Human Relations, 44,* 55-76.

Lubatkin, M. (1983). Mergers and the performance of the acquiring firm. *Academy of Management Review, 8,* 218-225.

Lubatkin, M., Schweiger, D. M., & Weber, Y. (1999). Top management turnover in related M&A's: An additional test of the theory of relative standing following mergers. *Journal of Management, 25,* 55-73.

Lueptow, L. B., McClendon, J., & McKeon, J. W. (1979). Father's occupation and son's personality: Findings and questions for the emerging linkage hypothesis. *Sociological Quarterly, 20,* 463-475.

Lundberg, C. C. (1985). On the feasibility of cultural intervention in organizations. In P. J. Frost, L. F. Moore, M. R. Louis, C. C. Lundberg, & J. Martin (Eds.), *Organizational culture* (pp. 169-185). Beverly Hills, CA: Sage.

Lundberg, C. C., & Peterson, M. F. (1994). The meaning of working in U.S. and Japanese local governments at three hierarchical levels. *Human Relations, 47,* 1459-1487.

Lundby, K. M., Dobbins, G. H., & Kidder, P. J. (1995, April). *Climate for service and productivity in high and low volume jobs: Further evidence for a redefinition of service.* Paper presented at the 10th Annual Meeting of the Society for Industrial and Organizational Psychology, Orlando, FL.

Lurie, A. (1981). *The language of clothes.* New York: Random House.

Lytle, A. L., Brett, J. M., Barsness, Z. I., Tinsley, C. H., & Janssens, M. (1995). A paradigm for confirmatory cross-cultural research in organizational behavior. In L. L. Cummings & B. M. Staw (Eds.), *Research in organizational behavior* (Vol. 17, pp. 167-214). Greenwich, CT: JAI.

Mace, L. M., & Montgomery, G. G. (1962). *Management problems of corporate acquisitions.* Cambridge, MA: Harvard University Press.

Mackie, M. (1987). *Constructing women and men.* Toronto: Holt, Rinehart & Winston.

Madrigal, R., & Kahle, L. R. (1994, Winter). Predicting vacation activity preferences on the basis of value-system segmentation. *Journal of Travel Research, 32,* 22-28.

Magnuson, E. (1986, March 10). A serious deficiency: The Rogers' commission faults NASA's "flawed" decision making. *Time,* pp. 41-42.

Mainiero, L. A. (1986). Early career factors that differentiate technical management careers from technical professional careers. *Journal of Management, 12,* 561-575.

Major, D. A., Kozlowski, S. W. J., Chao, G. T., & Gardner, P. D. (1995). A longitudinal investigation of newcomer expectations, early socialization outcomes, and the moderating effects of role development factors. *Journal of Applied Psychology, 80,* 418-431.

Malinowski, B. (1944). The functional theory. In B. Malinowski (Ed.), *A scientific theory of culture and other essays* (pp. 146-176). Chapel Hill: University of North Carolina Press. (Original work published 1939)

Malinowski, B. (1947). The problem of meaning in primitive languages. In C. K. Ogden & I. A. Richards (Eds.), *The meaning of meaning* (pp. 296-336). New York: Harcourt, Brace. (Original work published 1923)

Malinowski, B. (1960). *A scientific theory of culture.* New York: Oxford University Press. (Original work published 1944)

Malinowski, B. (1961a). *Argonauts of the western Pacific.* New York: E. P. Dutton. (Original work published 1922)

Malinowski, B. (1961b). *The dynamics of culture change.* New Haven, CT: Yale University Press. (Original work published 1945)

Malinowski, B. (1965a). *Coral gardens and their magic.* Bloomington: Indiana University Press. (Original work published 1935)

Malinowski, B. (1965b). *The language of magic and gardening.* Bloomington: Indiana University Press. (Original work published 1935)

Malson, L. (1972). *Wolf children.* London: NLB.

Managing by values: Is Levi-Strauss's approach visionary—or flaky? (1994, August 1). *Business Week,* pp. 45-52.

Manning, P. K. (1974). Police lying. *Urban Life and Culture, 3,* 283-306.

Manning, P. K. (1987). *Semiotics and fieldwork.* Newbury Park, CA: Sage.

Mao T.-T. (1960a). On the correct handling of contradictions among the people. *Selected works of Mao Tse-Tung* (Vol. 5). Beijing: People's Publishing House. (Original work published 1957)

Mao T.-T. (1960b). Some questions concerning methods of leadership. In *Selected works of Mao Tse-Tung* (Vol. 4). Beijing: People's Publishing House. (Original work published 1943)

Marans, R. A., & Spreckelmeyer, K. F. (1982). Evaluating open and conventional office design. *Environment and Behavior, 14,* 333-351.

March, J. G., & Olsen, J. P. (1976). *Ambiguity and choice in organizations.* Bergen, Norway: Universitetsforlaget.

March, J. G., & Simon, H. A. (1958). *Organizations.* New York: John Wiley.

Marcoulides, G. A., & Heck, R. H. (1993). Organizational culture and performance: Proposing and testing a model. *Organization Science, 4,* 209-225.

Marcus, G. E., & Fisher, M. J. (1986). *Anthropology as cultural critique.* Chicago: University of Chicago Press.

Margerison, C. (1979). *How to assess your management style.* New York: McB Human Resources.

Margnet, M. (1993). Good news for the service economy. *Fortune, 127*(9), 46-52.

Marks, M. L. (1994). *From turmoil to triumph.* Lexington, MA: Lexington.

Marks, M. L. (1982, Summer). Merging human resources: A review of current research. *Mergers and Acquisitions,* pp. 38-44.

Markus, H. (1977). Self-schemas and processing information about the self. *Journal of Personality and Social Psychology, 35,* 63-78.

Markus, H., & Kitayama, K. (1991). Culture and the self: Implications for cognition, emotion, and motivation. *Psychological Review, 98,* 224-253.

Markus, H., & Kunda, Z. (1986). Stability and malleability of the self-concept. *Journal of Personality and Social Psychology, 51,* 858-866.

Markus, H., & Wurf, E. (1987). The dynamic self-concept: A social psychological perspective. *Annual Review of Psychology, 38,* 299-337.

Markus, H., & Zajonc, R. B. (1985). The cognitive perspective in social psychology. In G. Lindzey & E. Aronson (Eds.), *Handbook of social psychology: Vol. 1. Theory and method.* New York: Random House.

Markus, K. A. (1997, May). *Discursive processes in organizational membership.* Paper presented at the Fifth A. F. Jacobson Symposium in Communications, Omaha, NB.

Markus, K. A. (1998a). Psychological processes and mental states. *American Psychologist, 53,* 1077-1078.

Markus, K. A. (1998b). Science, measurement, and validity: Is completion of Samuel Messick's synthesis possible? *Social Indicators Research, 45,* 7-34.

Markus, M. L., & Benjamin, R. I. (1997). The magic-bullet theory of IT-enabled transformation. *Sloan Management Review, 38*(2), 55-68.

Marrow, A. J. (1969). *The practical theorist.* New York: Basic Books.

Marsh, R. M., & Mannari, H. (1971). Lifetime commitment in Japan: Roles, norms, and values. *American Journal of Sociology, 76,* 795-813.

Martin, J. (1990a). Breaking up the mono-method monopolies in organizational analysis. In J. Hassard & D. Pym (Eds.), *The theory and philosophy of organizations* (pp. 30-43). London: Routledge.

Martin, J. (1990b, August). *Rethinking Weber: A feminist search for alternatives to bureaucracy.* Paper presented at the annual meeting of the Academy of Management, San Francisco.

Martin, J. (1992). *Cultures in organizations: Three perspectives.* New York: Oxford University Press.

Martin, J. (1995). Organizational culture. In N. Nicholson (Ed.), *The Blackwell encyclopedic dictionary of organizational behavior* (pp. 376-382). Cambridge, MA: Blackwell.

Martin, J., Feldman, M., Hatch, M. J., & Sitkin, S. (1983). The uniqueness paradox in organization studies. *Administrative Science Quarterly, 28,* 438-453.

Martin, J., & Frost, P. (1996). The organizational culture war games: A struggle for intellectual dominance. In S. R. Clegg, C. Hardy, & W. R. Nord (Eds.), *Handbook of organization studies* (pp. 599-621). Thousand Oaks, CA: Sage.

Martin, N., & Strauss, A. (1956). Patterns of mobility within industrial organizations. *Journal of Business, 29,* 101-110.

Martin, R. (1993). Changing the mind of the corporation. *Harvard Business Review, 72*(2), 5-12.

Martinko, M. J., & Yan, F. Z. (1990). A comparison of leadership theory and practices in the People's Republic of China and the United States. In A. Nedd, G. S. Khem, & F. Luthans (Eds.), *International human resource management review* (Vol. 1, pp. 109-122). Singapore: McGraw-Hill.

Maslow, A. H. (1954). *Motivation and personality.* New York: HarperCollins.

Mason, R. O., & Mitroff, I. I. (1981). *Challenging strategic planning assumptions: Theory, cases and techniques.* New York: John Wiley.

Mathieu, J. E. (1991). A cross-level nonrecursive model of the antecedents of organizational commitment and satisfaction. *Journal of Applied Psychology, 76,* 607-618.

Mathieu, J. E., & Zajac, D. M. (1990). A review and meta-analysis of the antecedents, correlates, and consequences of organizational commitment. *Psychological Bulletin, 108,* 171-194.

Maurer, T. J., & Tarulli, B. A. (1994). Investigation of perceived environment, perceived outcome, and person variables in relationship to voluntary development activity by employees. *Journal of Applied Psychology, 79,* 3-14.

Mauss, M. (1990). *The gift* (W. D. Halls, Trans.). New York: W. W. Norton. (Original work published 1950)

Mayhew, B. (1980). Structuralism versus individualism: I. Shadowboxing in the dark. *Social Forces, 59,* 335-375.

Mayo, E. (1945). *The social problems of an industrial civilization.* Boston: Harvard University, Graduate School of Business Administration.

Maznevski, M., & Peterson, M. F. (1997). Societal values, social interpretation, and multinational teams. In C. S. Granrose & S. Oskamp (Eds.), *Cross-cultural work groups* (pp. 61-89). Thousand Oaks, CA: Sage.

McCall, M., & Belmont, H. J. (1996). Credit card insignia and restaurant tipping: Evidence for an associative link. *Journal of Applied Psychology, 81,* 609-613.

McCarrt, A. T., & Rohrbaugh, J. (1995). Managerial openness to change and the introduction of GDSS: Explaining initial success and failure in decision conferencing. *Organization Science, 6,* 569-584.

McClelland, D. C. (1961). *The achieving society.* Princeton, NJ: Van Nostrand.

McClelland, D. C. (1985). *Human motivation.* Glenview, IL: Scott, Foresman.

McDaniel, C., & Stumpf, L. (1995). The organizational culture: Implications for nursing service. *Journal of Nursing Administration, 23,* 54-60.

McDonald, P., & Gandz, J. (1992). Getting value from shared values. *Organizational Dynamics, 20*(3), 64-77.

McGrath, J. E., & Kelly, J. R. (1986). *Time and human interaction: Toward a social psychology of time.* New York: Guilford.

McGrath, J. E., & Rotchford, N. L. (1983). Time and behavior in organizations. In L. L. Cummings & B. M. Staw (Eds.), *Research in organizational behavior* (Vol. 5, pp. 57-101). Greenwich, CT: JAI.

McGregor, D. M. (1960). *The human side of enterprise.* New York: McGraw-Hill.

McGuire, J., Schneeweis, T., & Hill, J. (1986). An analysis of alternative measures of strategic performance. In R. Lamb, P. Shrivastava, H. B. Thorelli, A. Huff, J. Dutton, & C. Stubbart (Eds.), *Advances in strategic management* (Vol. 4, pp. 127-154). Greenwich, CT: JAI.

McGuire, W. J. (1968). Personality and susceptibility to social influence. In E. F. Borgatta & W. W. Lambert (Eds.), *Handbook of personality theory and research* (pp. 1130-1187). Chicago: Rand McNally.

McIntyre, R. M., & Salas, E. (1995). Measuring and managing for team performance: Lessons from complex environments. In R. A. Guzzo & E. Salas (Eds.), *Team effectiveness and decision making in organizations* (pp. 9-45). San Francisco: Jossey-Bass.

McLuhan, M. (1962). *The Gutenberg galaxy: The making of typographic man.* Toronto: University of Toronto Press.

McNamara, J. H. (1967). Uncertainties in police work: The relevance of police recruits' backgrounds and training. In D. J. Bordua (Ed.), *The police: Six sociological essays* (pp. 163-252). New York: John Wiley.

McNeely, B. L., & Meglino, B. M. (1992). Good soldiers or good duty? The role of work values and contextual antecedents in prosocial organizational behavior. In J. L. Wall & L. R. Jauch (Eds.), *Academy of Management best paper proceedings, Las Vegas* (pp. 232-236). Briarcliff Manor, NJ: Academy of Management.

McPherson, J. M., Popielarz, P. A., & Drobnic, S. (1992). Social networks and organizational dynamics. *American Sociological Review, 57,* 153-170.

Mead, M. (1949). *Coming of age in Samoa.* New York: William Morrow. (Original work published 1928)

Meek, V. L. (1988). Organizational culture: Origins and weaknesses. *Organization Studies, 9,* 453-473.

Meglino, B. M., Ravlin, E. C., & Adkins, C. L. (1989). A work values approach to corporate culture: A field test of the value congruence process and its relationship to individual outcomes. *Journal of Applied Psychology, 74,* 424-432.

Meglino, B. M., Ravlin, E. C., & Adkins, C. L. (1991). Value congruence and satisfaction with a leader: An examination of the role of interaction. *Human Relations, 44,* 481-495.

Mehra, A., Kilduff, M., & Brass, B. (1998). At the margins: A distinctiveness approach to the social identity and social networks of underrepresented groups. *Academy of Management Journal, 41,* 441-452.

Meindl, J. R. (1990). On leadership: An alternative to the conventional wisdom. In B. M. Staw & L. L. Cummings (Eds.), *Research in organizational behavior* (Vol. 12, pp. 159-203). Greenwich, CT: JAI.

Meindl, J. R., Ehrlich, S. B., & Dukerich, J.M. (1985). The romance of leadership. *Administrative Science Quarterly, 30,* 78-102.

Merali, Y., & McKiernan, P. (1993). The strategic positioning of information systems in post-acquisition management. *Journal of Strategic Information Systems, 2*(2), 105-124.

Merton, R. K. (1957a). The role set. *British Journal of Sociology, 8,* 106-120.

Merton, R. K. (1957b). *Social theory and social structure* (Rev. ed.). Glencoe, IL: Free Press.

Meschi, P., & Roger, A. (1994). Cultural context and social effectiveness in international joint ventures. *Management International Review, 34,* 197-215.

Meyer, A. D. (1982a). Adapting to environmental jolts. *Administrative Science Quarterly, 27,* 515-537.

Meyer, A. D. (1982b). How ideologies supplant formal structures and shape responses to environments. *Journal of Management Studies, 19,* 45-61.

Meyer, A. D., & Starbuck, W. H. (1993). Interactions between politics and ideologies in strategy formation. In K. Roberts (Ed.), *New challenges to understanding organizations.* New York: Macmillan.

Meyer, J. P., & Allen, N. J. (1991). A three component conceptualization of organizational commitment. *Human Resource Management Review, 108*(2), 61-89.

Meyer, J. P., & Allen, N. J. (1997). *Commitment in the workplace: Theory, research, and application.* Thousand Oaks, CA: Sage.

Meyer, J. P., Allen, N. J., & Smith, C. A. (1993). Commitment to organizations and occupations: Extension and test of a three-component model. *Journal of Applied Psychology, 78,* 538-551.

Meyerson, D. (1990). Uncovering socially undesirable emotions: Experiences of ambiguity in organizations. *American Behavioral Scientist, 33,* 296-307.

Meyerson, D. (1991). Acknowledging and uncovering ambiguities. In P. J. Frost, L. F. Moore, M. R. Louis, C. C. Lundberg, & J. Martin (Eds.), *Reframing organizational culture* (pp. 131-144). Newbury Park, CA: Sage.

Meyerson, D., & Martin, J. (1981). Cultural change: An integration of three different views. *Journal of Management Studies, 18,* 1-26.

Meyerson, D., Weick, K. E., & Kramer, R. M. (1995). Swift trust. In R. M. Kramer & T. R. Tyler (Eds.), *Trust in organizations* (pp. 166-195). Thousand Oaks, CA: Sage.

Michel, J. G., & Hambrick, D. C. (1992). Diversification posture and top management team characteristics. *Academy of Management Journal, 35,* 9-37.

Michela, J. L. (1996). Social psychology and organizations. In G. Semin & K. Fiedler (Eds.), *Applied social psychology* (pp. 227-256). London: Sage.

Michela, J. L., Clark, A., Jha, S., & Noori, H. (1998). *You can get there from here: Mapping one route to a quality culture* (Tech. Rep. No. RR-98-08). Waterloo, ON: University of Waterloo, Institute for Improvement of Quality and Productivity.

Michela, J. L., Jha, S., Noori, H., Weitzman, E. A., & Eickmeier, B. E. (1997, August). *The nature of continuous improvement as revealed by bibliographic citation analysis.* Paper presented at the annual meeting of the Academy of Management, Boston.

Michela, J. L., Lukaszewski, M. P., & Allegrante, J. A. (1995). Organizational climate and work stress: A general model applied to inner-city schoolteachers. In S. L. Sauter & L. R. Murphy (Eds.), *Organizational risk factors for job stress* (pp. 61-80). Washington, DC: American Psychological Association.

Micklethwait, J., & Wooldridge, A. (1996). *The witch doctors.* New York: Times Business.

Migliore, R. H., Conway, A., Martin, R., & Stevens, R. E. (1992). *An analysis of Pan-Pacific Canadian organizational climate.* Paper presented at the Pan-Pacific Conference, Calgary, Alberta.

Miles, R. E., & Creed, W. E. D. (1995). Organizational forms and managerial philosophies: A descriptive analysis and analytical review. In L. L. Cummings & B. M. Staw (Eds.), *Research in organizational behavior* (Vol. 17, pp. 333-372). Greenwich, CT: JAI.

Miles, R. E., & Snow, C. C. (1978). *Organization strategy, structure and process.* New York: McGraw-Hill.

Miles, R. H. (1997a). *Corporate comeback: The story of renewal and transformation at National Semiconductor.* San Francisco: Jossey-Bass.

Miles, R. H. (1997b). *Leading corporate transformation: A blueprint for change.* San Francisco: Jossey-Bass.

Miller, D. (1990). *The Icarus paradox: How exceptional companies bring about their own downfall.* New York: Harper.

Miller, D., & Friesen, P. H. (1984). *Organizations: A quantum view.* Englewood Cliffs, NJ: Prentice Hall.

Miller, E. J., & Rice, A. K. (1967). *Systems of organization.* London: Tavistock.

Miller, J. G. (1960). Information input, overload and psychopathology. *American Journal of Psychiatry, 116,* 367-386.

Miller, V. D., & Jablin, F. M. (1991). Information seeking during organizational entry: Influences, tactics, and a model of the process. *Academy of Management Review, 16,* 92-120.

Mills, A. J. (1988a). Organization, gender and culture. *Organization Studies, 9,* 351-369.

Mills, A. J. (1988b). Organisational acculturation and gender discrimination. In P. K. Kresl (Ed.), *Canadian issues, X1: Women and the workplace* (pp. 1-22). Montreal: Association of Canadian Studies/ International Council for Canadian Studies.

Mills, A. J. (1993). Organisational discourse and the gendering of identity. In M. Parker & J. Hassard (Eds.), *Postmodernity and organisations* (pp. 132-147). London: Sage.

Mills, A. J. (1994). The gendering of organisational culture: Social and organisational discourses in the making of British Airways. In M. DesRosiers (Ed.), *Proceedings of the Administrative Sciences Association of Canada, Women in Management Division* (Vol. 15, pp. 11-20). Halifax, Nova Scotia: Administrative Sciences Association of Canada.

Mills, A. J. (1995). Managing subjectivity, silencing diversity: Organisational imagery in the airline industry—the case of British Airways. *Organisation, 2,* 243-269.

Mills, A. J. (1996). Strategy, sexuality and the stratosphere: Airlines and the gendering of organisation. In E. S. Lyon & L. Morris (Eds.), *Gender relations in public and private: New research perspectives* (pp. 77-94). London: Macmillan.

Mills, A. J. (1997a). Dueling discourses: Desexualization versus eroticism in the corporate framing of female sexuality in the British airline industry, 1945-60. In P. Prasad, A. J. Mills, M. Elmes, & A. Prasad (Eds.), *Managing the organizational melting pot: Dilemmas of workplace diversity* (pp. 171-198). Thousand Oaks, CA: Sage.

Mills, A. J. (1997b). Practice makes perfect: Corporate practices, bureaucratization and the idealized gendered self. *Hallinnon Tutkimus* [Finnish Journal of Administrative Studies], *4,* 272-288.

Mills, A. J. (1998). Cockpits, hangars, boys and galleys: Corporate masculinities and the development of British Airways. *Gender, Work and Organisation, 5*(3), 172-188.

Mills, A. J., & Murgatroyd, S. J. (1991). *Organization rules.* Milton Keynes: Open University Press.

Mills, A. J., & Tancred, P. (Eds.). (1992). *Gendering organizational analysis.* Newbury Park, CA: Sage.

Mills, C. W. (1959). *The sociological imagination.* London: Oxford University Press.

Mills, P. K., & Morris, J. H. (1986). Clients as partial employees of service organizations: Role development in client participation. *Academy of Management Review, 11,* 726-735.

Milton, L. P. (1998). *Managing diversity to improve the bottom-line: Confirming identities to enhance work group dynamics and performance.* Unpublished doctoral dissertation, University of Texas at Austin.

Mink, O. G., Esterhuysen, P. W., Mink, B. P., & Owen, K. Q. (1993). *Change at work: A comprehensive management process for transforming organizations.* San Francisco: Jossey-Bass.

Mintzberg, H. (1973). *The nature of managerial work.* New York: Harper & Row.

Mintzberg, H. (1979). *The structuring of organizations.* Englewood Cliffs, NJ: Prentice Hall.

Mintzberg, H. (1983). *Structure in fives: Designing effective organizations.* Englewood Cliffs, NJ: Prentice Hall.

Mintzberg, H. (1996). Managing government, governing management. *Harvard Business Review, 74*(3), 75-83.

Mintzberg, H., & Waters, J. A. (1985). Of strategies, deliberate and emergent. *Strategic Management Journal, 6,* 257-272.

Mirvis, P. H. (1985). Negotiations after the sale: The roots and ramifications of conflict in an acquisition. *Journal of Occupational Behavior, 6,* 65-84.

Mirvis, P. H., & Hall, D. T. (1996). New organizational forms and the new career. In D. T. Hall (Ed.), *The career is dead—long live the career: A relational approach to careers* (pp. 72-100). San Francisco: Jossey-Bass.

Mitchell, J. C. (1969). *Social networks in urban situations.* Manchester, England: Manchester University Press.

Mitchell, J. C. (1974). Social networks. *Annual Review of Anthropology, 3,* 279-299.

Mitchell, R. K., Agle, B. R., & Wood, D. J. (1997). Toward a theory of stakeholder identification and salience: Defining the principle of who and what really counts. *Academy of Management Review, 22,* 853-886.

Mizruchi, M. S. (1982). *The American corporate network: 1904-1974.* Beverly Hills, CA: Sage.

Mizruchi, M. S. (1994). Social network analysis: Recent achievements and current controversies. *Acta Sociologica, 37,* 329-343.

Mohrman, S. A., & Cohen, S. G. (1995). When people get out of the box: New relationships, new systems. In A. Howard (Ed.), *The changing nature of work* (pp. 365-410). San Francisco: Jossey-Bass.

Monge, P. R., & Eisenberg, E. M. (1987). Emergent communication networks. In F. M. Jablin, L. L. Putnam, & L. W. Porter (Eds.), *Handbook of organizational communication* (pp. 304-342). Newbury Park, CA: Sage.

Moreland, R. L., & Levine, J. M. (1989). Newcomers and oldtimers in small groups. In P. B. Paulus (Ed.), *Psychology of group influence* (2nd ed., pp. 143-186). Hillsdale, NJ: Lawrence Erlbaum.

Morgan, G. (1986). *Images of organization.* Beverly Hills, CA: Sage.

Morgan, G. (1997). *Images of organization* (2nd ed.). Thousand Oaks, CA: Sage.

Morgan, G., Frost, P. J., & Pondy, L. R. (1983). Organizational symbolism. In L. R. Pondy, P. J. Frost, G. Morgan, & T. C. Dandridge (Eds.), *Organizational symbolism.* Greenwich, CT: JAI.

Morgan, N. (1988). *The equality game: Women in the federal public service (1908-1987).* Ottawa: Canadian Advisory Council on the Status of Women.

Morin, W. J. (1991). *Trust me.* New York: Drake Beam Morin.

Morley, I. E., & Hosking, D. M. (1984). Decisionmaking and negotiation. In M. Gruneberg & T. Wall (Eds.), *Social psychology and organizational behaviour* (pp. 71-92). Chichester: John Wiley.

Morris, C. W. (1956). *Varieties of human value.* Chicago: University of Chicago Press.

Morrison, E. W. (1993a). Longitudinal study of the effects of information seeking on newcomer socialization. *Journal of Applied Psychology, 78,* 173-183.

Morrison, E. W. (1993b). Newcomer information seeking: Exploring types, modes, sources, and outcomes. *Academy of Management Journal, 36,* 557-589.

Morrison, E. W., & Robinson, S. L. (1997). When employees feel betrayed: A model of how psychological contract violation develops. *Academy of Management Review, 22,* 226-256.

Morrison, K. (1995). *Marx, Durkheim, Weber: Formations of modern social thought.* London: Sage.

Morrison, K. A. (1997, July). How franchise job satisfaction and personality affects performance, organizational commitment, franchisor relations, and intention to remain. *Journal of Small Business Management,* pp. 39-67.

Morrow, P. C. (1983). Concept redundancy in organizational research: The case of work commitment. *Academy of Management Review, 8,* 486-500.

Morrow, P. C. (1993). *The theory and measurement of work commitment.* Greenwich, CT: JAI.

Morrow, P. C., & McElroy, J. C. (1981). Interior office design and visitor response: A constructive replication. *Journal of Applied Psychology, 66,* 646-650.

Morse, N., & Reimer, E. (1956). The experimental change of a major organizational variable. *Journal of Abnormal and Social Psychology, 52,* 120-129.

Moskos, C. C. (1976). *Peace soldiers: The sociology of a United Nations military force.* Chicago: University of Chicago Press.

Moskos, C. C., & Miller, L. L. (1995). Humanitarians or warriors? Race, gender and combat status in operation Restore Hope. *Armed Forces and Society, 21,* 615-637.

Moskos, C. C., & Wood, F. R. (Eds.). (1988). *The military: More than just a job?* Washington, DC: Pergamon/Brassy.

Mowday, R. T., Porter, L. W., & Steers, R. M. (1982). *Employee-organization linkages.* New York: Academic Press.

Mowday, R. T., Steers, R. M., & Porter, L. W. (1979). The measurement of organizational commitment. *Journal of Vocational Behavior, 28,* 224-247.

Munene, J. C., Schwartz, S. H., & Smith, P. B. (2000). *Development in sub-Saharan Africa: Cultural influences and managers' decision behavior.* Manuscript submitted for publication.

Murdock, G. P. (1940). The cross-cultural survey. *American Sociological Review, 5,* 361-370.

Murnighan, J. K., & Brass, D. J. (1991). Intraorganizational coalitions. In B. Sheppard, R. Lewicki, & M. Bazerman (Eds.), *Research on negotiations in organizations* (pp. 283-307). Greenwich, CT: JAI.

Murray, H. A. (1938). *Explorations in personality.* New York: Oxford University Press.

Musbach, A., & Davis, B. (1980). *Flight attendant.* New York: Crown.

Myers-Briggs, I. (1980). *Gifts differing.* Palo Alto, CA: Consulting Psychologists Press.

Nadler, D. A. (1998). *Champions of change: How CEOs and their companies are mastering the skills of radical change.* San Francisco: Jossey-Bass.

Nadler, D. A., Gerstein, M. S., & Shaw, R. B. (1992). *Organizational architecture: Designs for changing organizations.* San Francisco: Jossey-Bass.

Nadler, D. A., Shaw, R. B., Walton, A. E., & Associates. (1994). *Discontinuous change: Leading organizational transformation.* San Francisco: Jossey-Bass.

Nahavandi, A., & Malekzadeh, A. (1988). Acculturation in mergers and acquisition. *Academy of Management Review, 13,* 79-90.

Nakane, C. (1970). *Japanese society.* Berkeley: University of California Press.

Near, J. P. (1984, July-August). Reactions to the career plateau. *Business Horizons,* pp. 75-79.

Nelson, D. L. (1990). Adjusting to a new organization: Easing the transition from outsider to insider. *Prevention in Human Services, 8,* 61-86.

Nelson, D. L., & Quick, J. C. (1991). Social support and newcomer adjustment in organizations: Attachment theory at work? *Journal of Organizational Behavior, 12,* 543-554.

Nelson, D. L., Quick, J. C., & Joplin, J. R. (1991). Psychological contracting and newcomer socialization: An attachment theory foundation. *Journal of Social Behavior and Personality, 6,* 55-72.

Neuijen, B. (1992). *Diagnosing organizational cultures: Patterns of continuance and change.* Graningdon, Netherlands: Walters-Noordhoff.

Nevis, E. C., Lancourt, J., & Vassallo, H. G. (1996). *Intentional revolutions: A seven-point strategy for transforming organizations.* San Francisco: Jossey-Bass.

Newman, V., & Chaharbaghi, K. (1998). The corporate culture myth. *Long Range Planning, 31,* 514-522.

Niccoli, O. (1990). *Prophecy and people in Renaissance Italy* (L. G. Cochrane, Trans.). Princeton, NJ: Princeton University Press.

Nicholson, N. (1997). Evolutionary psychology: Towards a new view of human nature and organizational society. *Human Relations, 50,* 1053-1078.

Nielsen, G. P. (1982). *From sky girl to flight attendant: Women and the making of a union.* Ithaca, NY: ILR.

Niemeijer, R. (1973). Some applications of the notion of density to network analysis. In J. Boissevain & J. C. Mitchell (Eds.), *Network analysis: Studies in human interaction.* The Hague: Mouton.

Noe, R. A., & Wilk, S. L. (1993). Investigation of the factors that influence employees' participation in development activities. *Journal of Applied Psychology, 78,* 291-302.

Nord, W. R., Brief, A. P., Atieh, J. M., & Doherty, E. M. (1988). Work values and the conduct of organizational behavior. In B. M. Staw & L. L. Cummings (Eds.), *Research in organizational behavior* (Vol. 10, pp. 1-42). Greenwich, CT: JAI.

Nordholt, E., & Straver, R. (1983). The changing police. In M. Punch (Ed.), *Control in the police organization* (pp. 36-46). Cambridge: MIT Press.

Normann, R. (1984). *Service management: Strategy and leadership in service business.* New York: John Wiley.

Novak, T. P., & Hoffman, D. L. (1997). *Measuring the flow experience among Web users.* Unpublished manuscript. Available Internet: http://www.2000.ogsm.vanderbilt.edu

Nyaw, M. K. (1991). The significance of managerial roles of trade unions in joint ventures in China. In O. Shenkar (Ed.), *Organization and management in China 1979-1990* (pp. 109-124). Armonk, NY: M. E. Sharpe.

Nystrom, H. (1990). Organizational innovation. In M. A. West & J. L. Farr (Eds.), *Innovation and creativity at work: Psychological and organizational strategies.* Chichester: John Wiley.

Oakley, A. (1972). *Sex, gender and society.* London: Temple Smith.

O'Connor, E. S. (1998, August). *Plotting the organization: A comprehensive narrative approach to studying organizing.* Paper presented at the annual meeting of the Academy of Management, San Diego, CA.

Ogden, C. K., & Richards, I. A. (Eds.). (1947). *The meaning of meaning.* New York: Harcourt, Brace. (Original work published 1923)

Ogilvy, D. (1985). *Ogilvy on advertising.* New York: Vintage.

Oldham, G. R., Cummings, A., & Zhou, J. (1995). The spatial configuration of organizations: A review of the literature and some new research directions. In G. R. Ferris (Ed.), *Research in personnel and human resources management* (Vol. 13, pp. 1-37). Greenwich, CT: JAI.

Olian, J. D., & Rynes, S. L. (1991). Making total quality work: Aligning organizational processes, performance measures, and stakeholders. *Human Resource Management, 30,* 303-333.

Oliver, R. (1997). *Satisfaction: A behavioral perspective on the consumer.* New York: McGraw-Hill.

Olsen, J. P. (1970). Local budgeting: Decision making or ritual act? *Scandinavian Political Studies, 5,* 85-115.

Ong, A. (1987). *Spirits of resistance and capitalist discipline: Factory women in Malaysia.* Albany: State University of New York Press.

Ong, W. J. (1982). *Orality and literacy: The technologizing of the word.* London: Methuen.

Onken, M. (1999). Temporal elements of organizational culture and impact on firm performance. *Journal of Managerial Psychology, 14,* 231-243.

O'Reilly, C. (1989). Corporation, culture, and commitment: Motivation and social control in organizations. *California Management Review, 31*(4), 9-25.

O'Reilly, C. A., III. (1980). Individuals and information overload in organizations: Is more necessarily better? *Academy of Management Journal, 23,* 684-696.

O'Reilly, C. A., III, Caldwell, D. F., & Mirable, R. (1992). A profile comparison approach to person-job fit: More than a mirage. In J. L. Wall & L. R. Jauch (Eds.), *Academy of Management best paper proceedings, Las Vegas* (pp. 237-241). Briarcliff Manor, NJ: Academy of Management.

O'Reilly, C. A., III, & Chatman, J. A. (1986). Organizational commitment and psychological attachment: The effects of compliance, identification, and internalization on prosocial behavior. *Journal of Applied Psychology, 71,* 492-499.

O'Reilly, C. A., III, Chatman, J. A., & Caldwell, D. F. (1988). *People, jobs and organizational culture* (Working paper). Berkeley: University of California.

O'Reilly, C. A., III, Chatman, J. A., & Caldwell, D. F. (1991). People and organizational culture: A profile comparison approach to assessing person-organization fit. *Academy of Management Journal, 34,* 487-516.

Organ, D. W. (1988). *Organization citizenship behavior: The "good soldier" syndrome.* Lexington, MA: Lexington.

Organization Technology International. (1979). *Management value inventory* [In-house document]. Singapore: Author.

Ornstein, S. (1986). Organizational symbols: A study of their meanings and influences on perceived psychological climate. *Organizational Behavior and Human Decision Processes, 38,* 207-229.

Ortner, S. B. (1973). On key symbols. *American Anthropologist, 75,* 1338-1346.

Osborne, D., & Gaebler, T. (1992). *Reinventing government: How the entrepreneurial spirit is transforming the public sector.* New York: Plume.

Osterman, P. (Ed.). (1984). *Internal labor markets.* Cambridge: MIT Press.

Osterman, P. (1994). How common is workplace transformation and who adopts it? *Industrial and Labor Relations Review, 47,* 173-188.

Ostroff, C. (1992). The relationship between satisfaction, attitudes, and performance: An organizational level analysis. *Journal of Applied Psychology, 77,* 963-974.

Ostroff, C., & Kozlowski, S. W. J. (1992). Organizational socialization as a learning process: The role of information acquisition. *Personnel Psychology, 45,* 849-874.

Ostroff, C., & Kozlowski, S. W. J. (1993). The role of mentoring in the information gathering process of newcomers during early organizational socialization. *Journal of Vocational Behavior, 42,* 170-183.

Ott, J. S. (1989). *The organizational culture perspective.* Pacific Grove, CA: Brooks/Cole.

Ouchi, W. G. (1980). Markets, bureaucracies and clans. *Administrative Science Quarterly, 25,* 129-141.

Ouchi, W. G. (1981). *Theory Z: How American business can meet the Japanese challenge.* Reading, MA: Addison-Wesley.

Ouchi, W. G., & Jaeger, A. M. (1978). Type Z organization: Stability in the midst of mobility. *Academy of Management Review, 3,* 305-314.

Ouchi, W. G., & Johnson, J. B. (1978). Types of organizational control and their relationship to emotional well-being. *Administrative Science Quarterly, 23,* 293-317.

Pablo, A. L. (1994). Determinants of acquisition integration level: A decision-making perspective. *Academy of Management Journal, 37,* 803-826.

Pace, C. R., & Stern, G. G. (1958). An approach to the measurement of psychological characteristics of college environments. *Journal of Educational Psychology, 49,* 269-277.

PA Consulting Group. (1991). *Organizational values and styles questionnaire.* Brisbane, Queensland: Author.

Padmore, J., Gaston, K., & Payne, R. L. (1993). *A pragmatic approach to the problem of aggregation in organizational climate research* (Discussion paper). Sheffield, England: Sheffield University, Management School.

Padmore, J., & Payne, R. L. (1995). *A pragmatic approach to the problem of aggregation in organizational climate research: Part 2* (Discussion paper). Sheffield, England: Sheffield University, Management School.

Parkington, J. P., & Schneider, B. (1979). Some correlates of experienced job stress: A boundary role study. *Academy of Management Journal, 22,* 270-281.

Parsons, T. (1956). Sociological approach to the theory of organizations. *Administrative Science Quarterly, 1,* 63-86, 225-240.

Parsons, T. (1957). Malinowski and the theory of social systems. In R. Firth (Ed.), *Man and culture: An evaluation of the work of Bronislaw Malinowski.* New York: Routledge & Kegan Paul.

Pascale, R. T., & Athos, A. G. (1981). *The art of Japanese management.* New York: Simon & Schuster.

Patterson, M., Payne, R. L., & West, M. (1996). Collective climates: A test of their socio-psychological significance. *Academy of Management Journal, 39,* 1675-1691.

Pawar, B. S., & Eastman, K. K. (1997). The nature and implications of contextual influences on transformational leadership: A conceptual examination. *Academy of Management Review, 22,* 80-109.

Payne, R. L. (1990). Madness in our method: A comment on Jackofsky and Slocum's paper, "A longitudinal study of climates." *Journal of Organizational Behavior, 11,* 77-80.

Payne, R. L. (1996). The characteristics of organizations. In P. B. Warr (Ed.), *Psychology at work* (4th ed.). Harmondsworth: Penguin.

Payne, R. L. (1997). Never mind structure—what about climate? In T. Clark (Ed.), *Advancement in organizational behavior: Essays in honour of D. S. Pugh* (pp. 89-104). Aldershot, England: Ashgate.

Payne, R. L., Brown, A. D., & Gaston, K. (1992). *Reliability and validity of an updated version of the Business Organisation Climate Index (BOCI)* (Discussion paper). Sheffield, England: Sheffield University, Management School.

Payne, R. L., & Pheysey, D. C. (1971). G. G. Stern's Organizational Climate Index: A reconceptualization and application to business organizations. *Organizational Behavior and Human Performance, 6,* 77-98.

Payne, R. L., & Pugh, D. S. (1976). Organizational structure and climate. In M. D. Dunnette (Ed.), *Handbook of industrial and organizational psychology* (pp. 1125-1173). Chicago: Rand McNally.

Pegels, C. C. (1987). *Management and industry in China.* New York: Praeger.

Peng, T. K., Peterson, M. F., & Shyi, Y. (1991). Quantitative methods in cross-national management research: Trends and equivalence issues. *Journal of Organizational Behavior, 12,* 87-107.

Penley, L. E., & Gould, S. (1988). Etzioni's model of organizational involvement: A perspective for understanding commitment to organizations. *Journal of Organizational Behavior, 9,* 43-59.

Pennings, J. M., & Goodman, P. S. (1977). Toward a framework of organizational effectiveness. In P. S. Goodman, J. M. Pennings, & Associates (Eds.), *New perspectives on organizational effectiveness.* San Francisco: Jossey-Bass.

Penrose, H. (1980). *Wings across the world: An illustrated history of British Airways.* London: Cassell.

Perlow, L. A. (1997). *Finding time.* Ithaca, NY: ILR.

Perlow, L. A. (1998). Boundary control: The social ordering of work and family time in a high-tech corporation. *Administrative Science Quarterly, 43,* 328-357.

Perlow, L. A. (1999). The time famine: Towards a sociology of work time. *Administrative Science Quarterly, 44,* 57-81.

Perrow, C. (1970). *Organizational analysis: A sociological view.* Belmont, CA: Wadsworth.

Perrow, C. (1986). *Complex organizations: A critical essay* (3rd ed.). New York: McGraw-Hill.

Perrow, C. A. (1961). The analysis of goals in complex organizations. *American Journal of Sociology, 26,* 854-866.

Perry, T. L. (1986). Merging successfully: Sending the "right" signals. *Sloan Management Review, 27*(3), 47-57.

Persing, D. L. (1991). The effect of effort allocation information on perceptions of intellectual workers and evaluations of their products. *Dissertation Abstracts International, 52*(09A), 3350-3351. (University Microfilms No. DA92-05834)

Peters, T. (1978). Symbols, patterns, and settings: An optimistic case for getting things done. *Organizational Dynamics, 7*(2), 3-22.

Peters, T. J., & Waterman, R. H., Jr. (1982). *In search of excellence: Lessons from America's best-run companies.* New York: Harper & Row.

Peterson, M. F. (1988). PM theory in Japan and China: What's in it for the United States? *Organizational Dynamics, 16*(4), 22-38.

Peterson, M. F. (1998). Embedded organizational events: The units of process in organization science. *Organization Science, 9,* 16-33.

Peterson, M. F., Elliott, J. R., Bliese, P. D., & Radford, M. H. B. (1996). Profile analysis of sources of meaning reported by U.S. and Japanese local government managers. In P. Bamberger, M. Erez, & S. Bacharach (Eds.), *Research in the sociology of organizations* (pp. 91-147). Greenwich, CT: JAI.

Peterson, M. F., Peng, T. K., & Smith, P. B. (1999). Using expatriate supervisors: A longitudinal, intercultural study of leadership style, attitudes and performance. In J. K. Liker, W. M. Fruin, & P. S. Adler (Eds.), *Remade in America: Transplanting and transforming Japanese management systems.* New York: Oxford University Press.

Peterson, M. F., Rodriguez, C. L., & Smith, P. B. (2000). Extending agency theory with event management and foreign direct investment theories: U.S. investments in Brazilian banks. In P. C. Earley & H. Singh (Eds.), *Innovations in international and cross-cultural management.* Thousand Oaks, CA: Sage.

Peterson, M. F., & Smith, P. B. (1997). Does national culture or ambient temperature explain cross-national differences in role stress? No sweat! *Academy of Management Journal, 40,* 930-946.

Peterson, M. F., Smith, P. B., Akande, D., Ayestaran, S., Bochner, S., Callan, V., Cho, N. G., Correia Jesuino, J., D'Amorim, M., Francois, P. H., Hofmann, K., Koopman, P. L., Leung, K., Lim, T. K., Mortazavi, S., Munene, J., Radfort, M., Ropo, A., Savage, G., Setiadi, B., Sinha, T. N., Sorenson, R., & Viedge, C. (1995). Role conflict, ambiguity and overload by national culture: A 21 nation study. *Academy of Management Journal, 38,* 429-452.

Peterson, M. F., Smith, P. B., Bond, M. H., & Misumi, J. (1990). Personal reliance on alternative event-management processes in four countries. *Group & Organization Studies, 15,* 75-91.

Peterson, M. F., Smith, P. B., & Tayeb, M. H. (1993). Development and use of English versions of Japanese PM leadership measures in electronic plants. *Journal of Organizational Behavior, 14,* 261-267.

Peterson, M. F., & Sorenson, R. (1991). Cognitive processes in leadership: Interpreting and handling events in an organizational context. In J. A. Anderson (Ed.), *Communication yearbook 14* (pp. 501-534). Newbury Park, CA: Sage.

Pettigrew, A. M. (1979). On studying organizational cultures. *Administrative Science Quarterly, 24,* 570-581.

Pettigrew, A. M. (1985). *The awakening giant: Continuity and change in imperial chemical industries.* Oxford: Blackwell.

Pettigrew, A. M. (1990). Organizational climate and culture: Two constructs in search of a role. In B. Schneider (Ed.), *Organizational climate and culture* (pp. 413-434). San Francisco: Jossey-Bass.

Petty, M. M., Beadles, N. A., II, Lowery, C. M., Chapman, D. F., & Connell, D. W. (1995). Relationships between organizational culture and organizational performance. *Psychological Reports, 76,* 483-492.

Pfeffer, J. (1981). Management as symbolic action: The creation and maintenance of organizational paradigms. In B. M. Staw & L. L. Cummings (Eds.), *Research in organizational behavior* (Vol. 3, pp. 1-52). Greenwich, CT: JAI.

Pfeffer, J. (1985). Organizational demography: Implications for management. *California Management Review, 28*(1), 67-81.

Pfeffer, J. (1995). Producing sustainable competitive advantage through the effective management of people. *Academy of Management Executive, 9*(1), 55-72.

Pfeffer, J. (1997). *New directions for organization theory: Problems and prospects.* New York: Oxford University Press.

Pfiffner, J. M., & Sherwood, F. P. (1960). *Administrative organization.* Englewood Cliffs, NJ: Prentice Hall.

Pike, K. L. (1960). *Language in relation to a unified theory of the structure of human behavior.* Glendale, CA: Summer Institute of Linguistics. (Original work published 1954)

Pil, F. K., & MacDuffie, J. P. (1996). The adoption of high involvement work practices. *Industrial Relations, 35,* 423-455.

Pinder, C. C. (1998). *Work motivation in organizational behavior.* Upper Saddle River, NJ: Prentice Hall.

Pinder, C. C., & Bourgeois, V. W. (1982). Controlling tropes in administrative science. *Administrative Science Quarterly, 27,* 641-652.

Pine, G. J., & Innis, G. (1987). Cultural and individual work values. *Career Development Quarterly, 35,* 279-287.

Plas, J. M. (1996). *Person-centered leadership: An American approach to participatory management.* Thousand Oaks, CA: Sage.

Plato. (1974). *The republic* (2nd rev. ed., D. Lee, Trans.). New York: Penguin. [Original text published around 375 BC]

Podsakoff, P. M., MacKenzie, S. B., & Ahearne, M. (1997). Moderating effects of goal acceptance on the relationship between group cohesiveness and productivity. *Journal of Applied Psychology, 82,* 374-383.

Podsakoff, P. M., MacKenzie, S. B., Moorman, R. H., & Fetter, R. (1990). Transformational leader behaviors and their effects on followers' trust in leader, satisfaction, and organizational citizenship behaviors. *Leadership Quarterly, 1,* 107-142.

Polanyi, K. (1944). *The great transformation.* New York: Rinehart,

Polanyi, K. (1977). *The livelihood of man* (H. W. Pearson, Ed.). New York: Academic Press.

Polanyi, M. (1962). *Personal knowledge: Towards a post-critical philosophy.* Chicago: University of Chicago Press. (Original work published 1958)

Pollert, A. (1981). *Girls, wives, factory lives.* London: Macmillan.

Pondy, L. R. (1978). Leadership is a language game. In M. W. McCall & M. M. Lombardo (Eds.), *Leadership: Where else can we go?* (pp. 88-99). Durham, NC: Duke University Press.

Pondy, L. R., Frost, P. J., Morgan, G., & Dandridge, T. C. (Eds.). (1983). *Organizational symbolism.* Greenwich, CT: JAI.

Poole, M. S. (1985). Communication and organizational climates. In R. D. McPhee & P. K. Thompson (Eds.), *Organizational communication: Traditional themes and new directions* (pp. 79-108). Beverly Hills, CA: Sage.

Porras, J. I., & Robertson, P. J. (1992). Organizational development, theory, practice, and research. In M. D. Dunnette & L. M. Hough (Eds.), *Handbook of industrial and organizational psychology* (2nd ed., Vol. 3, pp. 719-822). Palo Alto, CA: Consulting Psychologists Press.

Porter, L. W., Allen, R. W., & Angle, H. L. (1981). The politics of upward influence in organizations. In B. M. Staw & L. L. Cummings (Eds.), *Research in organizational behavior* (Vol. 3). Greenwich, CT: JAI.

Porter, L. W., Steers, R. M., Mowday, R. T., & Boulian, P. V. (1974). Organizational commitment, job satisfaction, and turnover among psychiatric technicians. *Journal of Applied Psychology, 59,* 603-609.

Porter, M. E. (1980). *Competitive strategy.* New York: Free Press.

Porter, M. E. (1985). *Competitive analysis.* New York: Free Press.

Posner, B. Z., & Munson, J. M. (1979). The importance of values in understanding organizational behavior. *Human Resource Management, 18,* 9-14.

Powell, W. W., & DiMaggio, P. J. (Eds.). (1991). *The new institutionalism in organization analysis.* Chicago: University of Chicago Press.

Powell, W. W., Koput, K. W., & Smith-Doerr, L. (1996). Interorganizational collaboration and the locus of innovation: Networks of learning in biotechnology. *Administrative Science Quarterly, 41,* 116-145.

Prahalad, C. K., & Bettis, R. A. (1986). The dominant logic: A new linkage between diversity and performance. *Strategic Management Journal, 7,* 485-501.

Prahalad, C. K., & Hamel, G. (1990). The core competence of the corporation. *Harvard Business Review, 68*(5), 79-91.

Pratkanis, A. R., & Greenwald, A. G. (1989). A sociocognitive model of attitude structure and function. In L. Berkowitz (Ed.), *Advances in experimental social psychology* (Vol. 22, pp. 245-285). New York: Academic Press.

Pratt, M. G., & Rafaeli, A. (1997). Organizational dress as a symbol of multilayered social identities. *Academy of Management Journal, 40,* 862-898.

Preston, L. E., & Sapienza, H. J. (1990). Stakeholder management and corporate performance. *Journal of Behavioral Economics, 19,* 361-375.

Prince-Gibson, E., & Schwartz, S. H. (1998). Value priorities and gender. *Social Psychology Quarterly, 61,* 49-67.

Pringle, R. (1989). Bureaucracy, rationality and sexuality: The case of secretaries. In J. Hearn, D. L. Sheppard, P. Tancred-Sheriff, & G. Burrell (Eds.), *The sexuality of organisation* (pp. 158-177). London: Sage.

Pritchett, P. (1985). *After the merger: Managing the shock waves.* New York: Dow Jones-Irwin.

Pugh, M. (1992). *Women and the women's movement in Britain 1914-1959.* London: Macmillan.

Putnam, R. D. (1993). *Making democracy work.* Princeton, NJ: Princeton University Press.

Pye, L. W. (1988). *The Mandarin and the cadre: China's political cultures* (Michigan Monograph in Chinese Studies No. 59). Ann Arbor: University of Michigan, Center for Chinese Studies.

Quinn, J. B. (1980). *Strategies for change and logical incrementalism.* Hemel Hempstead, England: Irwin.

Quinn, R. E. (1988). *Beyond rational management: Mastering the paradoxes and competing demands of high performance.* San Francisco: Jossey-Bass.

Quinn, R. E., & Cameron, K. S. (1988). Paradox and transformation: A framework for viewing organization and management. In R. E. Quinn & K. S. Cameron (Eds.), *Paradox and transformation: Toward a theory of change in organization and management* (pp. 289-308). Cambridge, MA: Ballinger.

Quinn, R. E., Hildebrandt, H. W., Rogers, P. S., & Thompson, M. P. (1991). A competing values framework for analyzing presentational communication in management contexts. *Journal of Business Communication, 28,* 213-232.

Quinn, R. E., & McGrath, M. R. (1985). The transformation of organizational cultures: A competing values perspective. In P. J. Frost, L. F. Moore, M. R. Louis, C. C. Lundberg, & J. Martin (Eds.), *Organizational culture* (pp. 315-334). Beverly Hills, CA: Sage.

Quinn, R. E., & Rohrbaugh, J. (1983). A spatial model of effectiveness criteria: Toward a competing values approach to organizational analysis. *Management Science, 29,* 363-377.

Quinn, R. E., & Spreitzer, G. M. (1991). The psychometrics of the competing values culture instrument and an analysis of the impact of organizational culture on quality of life. *Research in Organizational Change and Development, 5,* 115-142.

Raelin, J. A. (1987). Two-track plans for one-track careers. *Personnel Journal, 66,* 96-101.

Rafaeli, A. (1989). When clerks meet customers: A test of variables related to emotional expressions on the job. *Journal of Applied Psychology, 74,* 385-393.

Rafaeli, A. (1997). What is an organization? Who are the members? In C. L. Cooper & S. E. Jackson (Eds.), *Creating tomorrow's organizations: A handbook for future research in organizational behavior.* New York: John Wiley.

Rafaeli, A., Dutton, J., Harquail, C. V., & Mackie-Lewis, S. (1997). Navigating by attire: The use of dress by female administrative employees. *Academy of Management Journal, 40,* 9-45.

Rafaeli, A., & Kluger, A. (1998). *The cognitive and emotional influence of service context on service quality: A model and initial findings.* Unpublished manuscript, Hebrew University of Jerusalem. Available Internet: http://iew3.technion.ac.il:8080/~anatr/project_webpage.html#model

Rafaeli, A., & Pratt, M. G. (1993). Tailored meanings: On the meaning and impact of organizational dress. *Academy of Management Review, 18,* 32-55.

Rakow, L. F. (1986). Rethinking gender research in communication. *Journal of Communication, 36*(4), 11-24.

Ralston, D. A., Gustafon, D. J., Elsass, P. M., Cheung, F., & Terpstra, R. H. (1992). Eastern values: A comparison of managers in the United States, Hong Kong, and the People's Republic of China. *Journal of Applied Psychology, 77,* 664-671.

Ralston, D. A., Kai-Cheng, Y., Wang, X., Terpstra, R. H., & Wei, H. (1994, August). *An analysis of managerial work values across the six regions of China.* Paper presented at the annual meeting of the Academy of Management, Dallas.

Ramsay, K., & Parker, M. (1992). Gender, bureaucracy and organisational culture. In M. Savage & A. Witz (Eds.), *Gender and bureaucracy* (pp. 252-276). Oxford: Blackwell.

Rappaport, R. A. (1968). *Pigs for the ancestors.* New Haven, CT: Yale University Press.

Ravlin, E. C., & Meglino, B. M. (1987a). Effect of values on perception and decision making: A study of alternative work values measures. *Journal of Applied Psychology, 72,* 666-673.

Ravlin, E. C., & Meglino, B. M. (1987b). Issues in work values measurement. In J. E. Post (Ed.), *Research in corporate social performance and policy* (Vol. 9, pp. 153-183). Greenwich, CT: JAI.

Ravlin, E. C., & Meglino, B. M. (1989). The transitivity of work values: Hierarchical preference ordering of socially desirable stimuli. *Organizational Behavior and Human Decision Processes, 44,* 494-508.

Rayburn, C. A. (1997). Vocation as calling: Affirmative response or "wrong number." In D. P. Bloch & L. J. Richmond (Eds.), *Connections between spirit and work in career development: New approaches and practical perspectives* (pp. 163-183). Palo Alto, CA: Davies-Black.

Razack, S. (1991). *Canadian feminism and the law: The Women's Legal Education and Action Fund and the pursuit of equality.* Toronto: Second Story.

Reason, P. (in press). Integrating action and reflection through cooperative inquiry. *Management Learning.*

Reason, P., & Rowan, J. (Eds.). (1981). *Human inquiry: A sourcebook of new paradigm research.* Chichester: John Wiley.

Redding, G., & Wong, G. Y. Y. (1986). The psychology of Chinese organizational behavior. In M. H. Bond (Ed.), *The psychology of the Chinese people* (pp. 213-266). Hong Kong: Oxford University Press.

Reed, M. (1990). From paradigms to images: The paradigm warrior turns post-modernist guru. *Personnel Review, 19*(3), 35-40.

Reed, M. (1992). *The sociology of organisations: Themes, perspectives and prospects.* London: Harvester Wheatsheaf.

Reed, M. (1998). Organizational analysis as discourse analysis: A critique. In D. Grant, T. Keenoy, & C. Oswick (Eds.), *Discourse and organization* (pp. 193-213). Thousand Oaks, CA: Sage.

Reger, R. K., Gustafson, L. T., DeMarie, S. M., & Mullane, J. V. (1994). Reframing the organization: Why implementing total quality is easier said than done. *Academy of Management Review, 19,* 565-584.

Reichers, A. E. (1985). A review and reconceptualization of organizational commitment. *Academy of Management Review, 10,* 465-476.

Reichers, A. E. (1986). Conflict and organizational commitment. *Journal of Applied Psychology, 71,* 508-514.

Reichers, A. E. (1987). An interactionist perspective on newcomer socialization rates. *Academy of Management Review, 12,* 278-287.

Reichers, A. E., & Schneider, B. (1990). Climate and culture: An evolution of constructs. In B. Schneider (Ed.), *Organizational climate and culture* (pp. 5-39). San Francisco: Jossey-Bass.

Rentsch, J. R. (1990). Climate and culture: Interaction and qualitative differences in organizational meanings. *Journal of Applied Psychology, 75,* 668-681.

Reuss-Ianni, E., & Ianni, F. A. J. (1983). Street cops and management cops: The two cultures of policing. In M. Punch (Ed.), *Control in the police organization* (pp. 251-274). Cambridge: MIT Press.

Reynolds, P. D. (1986). Organizational culture as related to industry, position and performance: A preliminary report. *Journal of Management Studies, 23,* 333-345.

Richmond, L. J. (1997). Spirituality and career assessment: Metaphors and measurement. In D. P. Bloch & L. J. Richmond (Eds.), *Connections between spirit and work in career development: New approaches and practical perspectives* (pp. 209-235). Palo Alto, CA: Davies-Black.

Ricoeur, P. (1976). *Interpretation theory: Discourse and the surplus of meaning.* Fort Worth: Texas Christian University Press.

Rifkin, J. (1994). *The end of work: The decline of the global labor force and the dawn of the post-market era.* New York: Putnam.

Rigby, D. K. (1998, September 7). What's today's special at the consultants' café? *Fortune,* pp. 162-163.

Ritzer, G., & Trice, H. M. (1969). An empirical study of Howard Becker's side bet theory. *Social Forces, 47,* 475-478.

Roberts, K. H., Hulin, C. L., & Rousseau, D. M. (1978). *Developing an interdisciplinary science of organizations.* San Francisco: Jossey-Bass.

Roberts, K. H., Rousseau, D. M., & La Porte, T. R. (1994). The culture of high reliability: Quantitative and qualitative assessment aboard nuclear aircraft carriers. *Journal of High Technology Management Research, 5,* 141-161.

Robinson, S. L. (1996). Trust and breach of the psychological contract. *Administrative Science Quarterly, 41,* 574-599.

Robinson, S. L., Kraatz, M. S., & Rousseau, D. M. (1994). Changing obligations and the psychological contract: A longitudinal study. *Academy of Management Journal, 37,* 137-152.

Robinson, S. L., & Morrison, E. W. (1995). Psychological contracts and OCB: The effect of unfulfilled obligations on civic virtue behavior. *Journal of Organizational Behavior, 16,* 289-298.

Robinson, S. L., & Rousseau, D. M. (1994). Violating the psychological contract: Not the exception but the norm. *Journal of Organizational Behavior, 15,* 245-259.

Roethlisberger, F. J., & Dickson, W. J. (1975). *Management and the worker: An account of a research programme conducted by Western Electric Company, Hawthorne Works Chicago.* Cambridge, MA: Harvard University Press. (Original work published 1939)

Rogers, B. (1988). *Men only: An investigation into men's organisations.* London: Pandora.

Rogers, P. S., & Hildebrandt, H. W. (1993). Competing values instruments for analyzing written and spoken management messages. *Human Resource Management, 32,* 121-142.

Rogers, W., Lee, M., & Fisk, A. (1995). Contextual effects on general learning, feature learning, and attention strengthening in visual search. *Human Factors, 37*(1), 158-172.

Rohlen, T. P. (1974). *For harmony and strength: Japanese white-collar organizations in anthropological perspective.* Berkeley: University of California Press.

Rohner, R. P. (1984). Toward a conception of culture for cross-cultural psychology. *Journal of Cross-Cultural Psychology, 15,* 111-138.

Rokeach, M. (1960). *The open and closed mind.* New York: Basic Books.

Rokeach, M. (1969). *Beliefs, attitudes and values: A theory of organization and change.* San Francisco: Jossey-Bass.

Rokeach, M. (1973). *The nature of human values.* New York: Free Press.

Rokeach, M. (1979). From individual to institutional values: With special reference to values of science. In M. Rokeach (Ed.), *Understanding human values* (pp. 47-70). New York: Free Press.

Rokeach, M., & Ball-Rokeach, S. J. (1989). Stability and change in American value priorities: 1968-1989. *American Psychologist, 44,* 775-785.

Rokeach, M., & Grube, J. W. (1979). Can values be manipulated arbitrarily? In M. Rokeach (Ed.), *Understanding human values.* New York: Free Press.

Rokeach, M., & Kliejunas, P. (1972). Behavior as a function of attitude-toward-object and attitude-toward-situation. *Journal of Personality and Social Psychology, 22,* 194-201.

Romney, A. K., Weller, S. C., & Batchelder, W. H. (1986). Culture as consensus: A theory of culture and informant accuracy. *American Anthropologist, 88,* 313-338.

Rose, G. M. (1997). Cross-cultural values research: Implications for advertising. In L. R. Kahle & L. Chiagouris (Eds.), *Values, lifestyles, and psychographics* (pp. 389-400). Mahwah, NJ: Lawrence Erlbaum.

Rose, G. M., Shoham, A., Kahle, L. R., & Batra, R. (1994). Fashion, dress, and conformity. *Journal of Applied Social Psychology, 24,* 1501-1519.

Rose, M. (1978). *Industrial behaviour.* Harmondsworth: Penguin.

Roseberry, W. (1989). *Anthropologies and histories.* New Brunswick, NJ: Rutgers University Press.

Rosenau, P. M. (1992). *Post-modernism and the social sciences: Insights, inroads, and intrusions.* Princeton, NJ: Princeton University Press.

Rosenberg, M. (1957). *Occupations and values.* Glencoe, IL: Free Press.

Rosenthal, R., & Rosnow, R. L. (1989). *Essentials of behavioral research: Methods and data analysis* (2nd ed.). New York: McGraw-Hill.

Rotter, J., Seeman, M., & Liverant, S. (1962). Internal versus external control of reinforcement: A major variable in behavioral theory. In N. Wahburne (Ed.), *Decisions, values and groups.* Oxford: Pergamon.

Rousseau, D. M. (1985). Issues of level in organizational research: Multilevel and cross-level perspectives. In L. L. Cummings & B. M. Staw (Eds.), *Research in organizational behavior* (Vol. 7, pp. 1-37). Greenwich, CT: JAI.

Rousseau, D. M. (1988). The construction of climate in organizational research. In C. L. Cooper & I. T. Robertson (Eds.), *International review of industrial and organizational psychology* (Vol. 3). New York: John Wiley.

Rousseau, D. M. (1989). Psychological and implied contracts in organizations. *Employee Responsibilities and Rights Journal, 2,* 121-139.

Rousseau, D. M. (1990a). Assessing organizational culture: The case for multiple methods. In B. Schneider (Ed.), *Organizational climate and culture* (pp. 153-192). San Francisco: Jossey-Bass.

Rousseau, D. M. (1990b). New hire perceptions of their own and their employers' obligations: A study of psychological contracts. *Journal of Organizational Behavior, 11,* 389-400.

Rousseau, D. M. (1990c). Normative beliefs in fund-raising organizations: Linking culture to organizational performance and individual responses. *Group & Organization Studies, 15,* 448-460.

Rousseau, D. M. (1995). *Psychological contracts in organizations: Understanding written and unwritten agreements.* Thousand Oaks, CA: Sage.

Rousseau, D. M., & Parks, J. M. (1993). The contracts of individuals and organizations. In L. L. Cummings & B. M. Staw (Eds.), *Research in organizational behavior* (Vol. 15, pp. 1-43). Greenwich, CT: JAI.

Rousseau, D. M., Sitkin, S. B., Burt, R. S., & Camerer, C. (1998). Not so different after all: A cross-discipline view of trust. *Academy of Management Review, 23,* 393-404.

Rousseau, D. M., & Wade-Benzoni, K. A. (1995). Changing individual-organization attachments: A two-way street. In A. Howard (Ed.), *The changing nature of work* (pp. 290-322). San Francisco: Jossey-Bass.

Roy, D. F. (1960). "Banana time": Job satisfaction and informal interaction. *Human Organization, 18,* 158-168.

Ruben, D. H. (1986). The management of role ambiguity in organizations. *Journal of Employment Counseling, 23,* 120-130.

Rubin, I., & Inguagiato, R. (1991). Changing the work culture. *Training and Development Journal, 45*(7), 57-60.

Rucci, A. J., Kirn, S. P., & Quinn, R. T. (1998). The employee-customer-profit chain at Sears. *Harvard Business Review, 76*(3), 83-97.

Ruitenbeek, H. M. (Ed.). (1963). *The dilemma of organizational society.* New York: E. P. Dutton.

Rumelt, R. P. (1974). *Strategy, structure and economic performance.* Boston: Harvard Business School, Division of Research.

Rusbult, C. E., Farrell, D., Rogers, G., & Mainous, A. G., III. (1988). Impact of exchange variables on exit, voice, loyalty, and neglect: An integrative model of responses to declining job satisfaction. *Academy of Management Journal, 31,* 599-627.

Rust, R. T., Zahorik, A. J., & Kenningham, T. L. (1996). *Service marketing.* New York: HarperCollins.

Ryan, A. M., Schmit, M. J., & Johnson, R. (1996). Attitudes and effectiveness: Examining relations at an organizational level. *Personnel Psychology, 49,* 853-882.

Sackmann, S. A. (1991). *Cultural knowledge in organizations: Exploring the collective mind.* Newbury Park, CA: Sage.

Sackmann, S. A. (1992). Culture and subcultures: An analysis of organizational knowledge. *Administrative Science Quarterly, 37,* 140-161.

Sackmann, S. A., Phillips, M., Kleinberg, J., & Boyacigiller, N. (1997). Single and multiple cultures in international cross-cultural management research. In S. A. Sackmann (Ed.), *Cultural complexity in organizations: Inherent contrasts and contradictions* (pp. 14-48). Newbury Park, CA: Sage.

Sadri, G., & Robertson, I. T. (1993). Self-efficacy and work-related behavior: A review and meta-analysis. *Applied Psychology, 42,* 139-152.

Saffold, G. S. (1988). Culture traits, strength, and organizational performance: Moving beyond "strong" culture. *Academy of Management Review, 13,* 546-558.

Sagiv, L., & Schwartz, S. H. (1995). Value priorities and readiness for outgroup social contact. *Journal of Personality and Social Psychology, 69,* 437-448.

Sahlins, M. (1972). *Stone Age economics.* Chicago: Aldine.

Sahlins, M. (1985). *Islands of history.* Chicago: University of Chicago Press.

Salancik, G. R. (1977). Commitment and the control of organizational behavior and belief. In B. M. Staw & G. R. Salancik (Eds.), *New directions in organizational behavior* (pp. 1-54). Chicago: St. Clair.

Salancik, G. R., & Pfeffer, J. (1978). A social information processing approach to job attitudes and task design. *Administrative Science Quarterly, 23,* 224-253.

Salas, E., Dickinson, T. L., Converse, S. A., & Tannenbaum, S. I. (1992). Toward an understanding of team performance and training. In R. W. Swezey & E. Salas (Eds.), *Teams: Their training and performance* (pp. 3-29). Norwood, NJ: Ablex.

Sales, M. S., & Mirvis, P. H. (1984). When culture collides. Issues in acquisition. In J. R. Kimberly & R. E. Quinn (Eds.), *Managing transitions.* Homewood, IL: Irwin.

Sampson, A. (1984). *Empires of the sky: The politics, contests and cartels of world airlines.* New York: Random House.

Sampson, E. E., & Insko, C. A. (1964). Cognitive consistency and conformity in the autokinetic situation. *Journal of Personality and Social Psychology, 68,* 184-192.

Sandelands, L. E. (1998). Feeling and form in groups. *Visual Sociology, 13*(1), 5-23.

Sarbin, T. R., & Allen, V. L. (1968). Role theory. In G. Lindzey & E. Aronson (Eds.), *The handbook of social psychology* (2nd ed., Vol. 1). Reading, MA: Addison-Wesley.

Sarkis, H. D., Sanders, W., & Pattillo, J. (1992, March). *How to ensure success in safety and operating reliability.* Paper presented at the Forest Industries Clinic, Portland, OR.

Sashkin, M., & Fulmer, R. (1985, August). *Measuring organizational excellence culture with a validated questionnaire.* Paper presented at the annual meeting of the Academy of Management.

Sasser, W. E., Jr., Hart, C. W. L., & Heskett, J. L. (1991). *The service management course: Cases and readings.* New York: Free Press.

Sathe, V. (1985a). *Culture and related corporate realities.* Homewood, IL: Irwin.

Sathe, V. (1985b). How to decipher and change corporate culture. In R. H. Kilmann, M. J. Saxton, R. Serpa, & Associates (Eds.), *Gaining control of the corporate culture* (pp. 230-261). San Francisco: Jossey-Bass.

Sathe, V. (1994, October 6). *Phases of corporate transformation.* Paper presented at the Claremont Graduate School, Peter F. Drucker Graduate Management Center.

Sathe, V. (in press). Creating mindset and behavior change. *Ivey Business Journal*.

Sathe, V. (2000). *Top managers as entrepreneurs: Influencing new business creation in a corporate division*. Manuscript in preparation, Claremont Graduate University.

Saunders, G. (1984). *The committed organization*. Brookfield, VT: Gower.

Sawicki, J. (1996). Foucault, feminism and questions of identity. In G. Gutting (Ed.), *The Cambridge companion to Foucault* (pp. 286-313). Cambridge: Cambridge University Press.

Saxenian, A. (1994). *Regional advantage: Culture and competition in Silicon Valley and Route 128*. Cambridge, MA: Harvard University Press.

Scheiberg, S. L. (1990). Emotions on display: The personal decoration of work space. *American Behavioral Scientist, 33,* 330-338.

Schein, E. H. (1961). *Coercive persuasion*. New York: W. W. Norton.

Schein, E. H. (1965). *Organizational psychology*. Englewood Cliffs, NJ: Prentice Hall.

Schein, E. H. (1971). The individual, the organization and the career: A conceptual scheme. *Journal of Applied Behavioral Science, 7,* 401-426.

Schein, E. H. (1981). Does Japanese management style have a message for American managers? *Sloan Management Review, 23*(1), 55-68.

Schein, E. H. (1983). The role of the founder in creating organizational culture. *Organizational Dynamics, 12*(1), 13-28.

Schein, E. H. (1985). *Organizational culture and leadership: A dynamic view*. San Francisco: Jossey-Bass.

Schein, E. H. (1987). *The clinical perspective in fieldwork*. Newbury Park, CA: Sage.

Schein, E. H. (1990). Organizational culture. *American Psychologist, 45,* 109-119.

Schein, E. H. (1991a). Coming to a new awareness of organizational culture. In D. A. Kolb, I. M. Rubin, & J. S. Osland (Eds.), *The organizational behavior reader* (pp. 369-284). Englewood Cliffs, NJ: Prentice Hall.

Schein, E. H. (1991b). What is culture? In P. J. Frost, L. F. Moore, M. R. Louis, C. C. Lundberg, & J. Martin (Eds.), *Reframing organizational culture* (pp. 243-253). Newbury Park, CA: Sage.

Schein, E. H. (1992). *Organizational culture and leadership: A dynamic view* (2nd ed.). San Francisco: Jossey-Bass.

Schein, E. H. (1993a). How can organizations learn faster? The challenge of entering the green room. *Sloan Management Review, 34*(2), 85-92.

Schein, E. H. (1993b). Legitimating clinical research in the study of organizational culture. *Journal of Counseling and Development, 71,* 703-708.

Schein, E. H. (1993c). On dialogue, culture, and organizational learning. *Organizational Dynamics, 22*(2), 40-51.

Schein, E. H. (1996a). Culture: The missing concept in organization studies. *Administrative Science Quarterly, 41,* 229-240.

Schein, E. H. (1996b). *Strategic pragmatism: The culture of Singapore's Economic Development Board*. Cambridge: MIT Press.

Schein, E. H. (1999a). *The corporate culture survival guide*. San Francisco: Jossey-Bass.

Schein, E. H. (1999b). *Process consultation revisited: Building the helping relationship*. Reading, MA: Addison-Wesley.

Schein, V. E. (1994). Managerial sex typing: A persistent and pervasive barrier to women's opportunities. In M. J. Davidson & R. J. Burke (Eds.), *Women in management: Current research issues* (pp. 41-52). London: Paul Chapman.

Schilit, W. K., & Locke, E. A. (1982). A study of upward influence in organizations. *Administrative Science Quarterly, 27*, 304-316.

Schmidt, W. H., & Finnigan, J. P. (1992). *The race without a finish line*. San Francisco: Jossey-Bass.

Schmit, M. J., & Allscheid, S. P. (1995). Employee attitudes and customer satisfaction: Making theoretical and empirical connections. *Personnel Psychology, 48*, 521-536.

Schmitt, B., & Simonson, A. (1997). *Marketing aesthetics: The strategic management of brands, identity, and image*. New York: Free Press.

Schneider, A. (1998, January 23). Frumpy or chic? Tweed or kente? Sometimes clothes make the professor. *Chronicle of Higher Education*, pp. A12-A14.

Schneider, B. (1972). Organizational climate: Individual preferences and organizational realities. *Journal of Applied Psychology, 56*, 211-217.

Schneider, B. (1973). The perception of organizational climate: The customer's view. *Journal of Applied Psychology, 57*, 248-256.

Schneider, B. (1975). Organizational climates: An essay. *Personnel Psychology, 28*, 447-479.

Schneider, B. (1980). The service organization: Climate is crucial. *Organizational Dynamics, 9*(2), 52-65.

Schneider, B. (1985). Organizational behavior. *Annual Review of Psychology, 36*, 573-611.

Schneider, B. (1987). The people make the place. *Personnel Psychology, 40*, 437-454.

Schneider, B. (1990a). The climate for service: An application of the climate construct. In B. Schneider (Ed.), *Organizational climate and culture* (pp. 383-412). San Francisco: Jossey-Bass.

Schneider, B. (Ed.). (1990b). *Organizational climate and culture*. San Francisco: Jossey-Bass.

Schneider, B. (1994). HRM—a service perspective: Toward a customer-focused HRM. *International Journal of Service Industry Management, 5*, 64-76.

Schneider, B., Ashworth, S. D., Higgs, A. C., & Carr, L. (1996). Design, validity, and use of strategically focused employee attitude surveys. *Personnel Psychology, 49*, 695-705.

Schneider, B., & Bartlett, J. (1968). Individual differences and organizational climate I: The research plan and questionnaire development. *Personnel Psychology, 21*, 323-333.

Schneider, B., & Bartlett, J. (1970). Individual differences and organizational climate II: Measurement of organizational climate by the multitrait-multirater matrix. *Personnel Psychology, 23,* 493-512.

Schneider, B., & Bowen, D. E. (1985). Employee and customer perceptions of service in banks: Replication and extension. *Journal of Applied Psychology, 70,* 423-433.

Schneider, B., & Bowen, D. E. (1995). *Winning the service game.* Boston: Harvard Business School Press.

Schneider, B., Brief, A. P., & Guzzo, R. A. (1996). Creating a climate and culture for sustainable organizational change. *Organizational Dynamics, 24*(4), 6-19.

Schneider, B., Goldstein, H. W., & Smith, D. B. (1995). The ASA framework: An update. *Personnel Psychology, 48,* 747-773.

Schneider, B., Gunnarson, S. K., & Niles-Jolly, K. (1994). Creating the climate and culture of success. *Organizational Dynamics 23*(1), 17-29.

Schneider, B., Parkington, J. J., & Buxton, V. M. (1980). Employee and customer perceptions of service in banks. *Administrative Science Quarterly, 25,* 252-267.

Schneider, B., & Rentsch, J. R. (1988). Managing climates and cultures: A futures perspective. In J. Hage (Ed.), *Futures of organizations* (pp. 181-200). Lexington, MA: Lexington.

Schneider, B., Smith, D. B., Taylor, S., & Fleenor, J. (1998). Personality and organizations: A test of the homogeneity of personality hypothesis. *Journal of Applied Psychology, 83,* 462-470.

Schneider, B., & Snyder, R. A. (1975). Some relationships between job satisfaction and organizational climate. *Journal of Applied Psychology, 60,* 318-328.

Schneider, B., Wheeler, J. K., & Cox, J. J. (1992). A passion for service: Using content analysis to explicate service climate themes. *Journal of Applied Psychology, 77,* 705-716.

Schneider, B., White, S., & Paul, M. C. (1997). Relationship marketing: An organization perspective. In T. A. Swartz, D. E. Bowen, & S. W. Brown (Eds.), *Advances in services marketing and management* (Vol. 6, pp. 1-22). Greenwich, CT: JAI.

Schneider, B., White, S., & Paul, M. C. (1998). Linking service climate and customer perceptions of service quality: Test of a causal model. *Journal of Applied Psychology, 83,* 150-163.

Scholtes, P., & Hacquebord, H. (1988, July). Beginning the quality transformation, Parts 1 & 2. *Quality Progress,* pp. 28-33.

Scholz, C. (1987). Corporate culture and strategy: The problem of strategic fit. *Long Range Planning, 20,* 78-87.

Schön, D. A. (1971). *Beyond the stable state.* New York: W. W. Norton.

Schrader, C. B., Lincoln, J. R., & Hoffman, A. N. (1989). The network structures of organizations: Effects of task contingencies and distributional form. *Human Relations, 42,* 43-66.

Schriber, J. B., & Gutek, B. A. (1987). Some time dimensions of work: Measurement of an underlying aspect of organizational culture. *Journal of Applied Psychology, 72,* 642-650.

Schroeder, D. M. (1998, February). *Quality now and direction for the 21st century.* Keynote presentation at the Conference on Quality and Management, sponsored by the Academy of Management, Arizona State College of Business, and Arizona State University Department of Management, Tempe, AZ.

Schroeder, D. M., & Robinson, A. G. (1991). America's most successful export to Japan: Continuous improvement programs. *Sloan Management Review, 32*(3), 67-81.

Schroeder, R. (1992). *Max Weber and the sociology of culture.* London: Sage.

Schultz, M. (1995). *On studying organizational cultures: Diagnosis and understanding.* New York: Aldine de Gruyter.

Schwab, D. P. (1980). Construct validity in organizational behavior. In B. M. Staw & L. L. Cummings (Eds.), *Research in organizational behavior* (Vol. 2, pp. 3-43). Greenwich, CT: JAI.

Schwab, D. P. (1999). *Research methods for organizational studies.* Mahwah, NJ: Lawrence Erlbaum.

Schwartz, S. H. (1992). Universals in the content and structure of values: Theoretical advances and empirical tests in 20 countries. In M. P. Zanna (Ed.), *Advances in experimental social psychology* (Vol. 25, pp. 1-65). San Diego, CA: Academic Press.

Schwartz, S. H. (1994). Are there universal aspects in the structure and contents of human values? *Journal of Social Issues, 50,* 19-45.

Schwartz, S. H. (1996a, August). *New dimensions of culture: East is not East, West is not West.* Paper presented at the 26th Annual International Congress of Psychology, Montreal.

Schwartz, S. H. (1996b). Value priorities and behavior: Applying a theory of integrated value systems. In C. Seligman, J. M. Olson, & M. P. Zanna (Eds.), *The Ontario Symposium: Vol. 8. The psychology of values* (pp. 1-24). Mahwah, NJ: Lawrence Erlbaum.

Schwartz, S. H. (1997). Values and culture. In D. Munro, S. Carr, & J. Schumaker (Eds.), *Motivation and culture* (pp. 69-84). New York: Routledge.

Schwartz, S. H. (1999). Cultural value differences: Some implications for work. *Applied Psychology, 48,* 23-47.

Schwartz, S. H., & Bardi, A. (1997). Influences of adaptation to communist rule on value priorities in Eastern Europe. *Political Psychology, 18,* 385-410.

Schwartz, S. H., Bardi, A., & Bianchi, G. (in press). Value adaptation to the imposition and collapse of communist regimes in Eastern Europe. In S. A. Renshon & J. Duckitt (Eds.), *Political psychology: Cultural and cross-cultural perspectives.* London: Macmillan.

Schwartz, S. H., & Bilsky, W. (1987). Toward a universal psychological structure of human values. *Journal of Personality and Social Psychology, 53,* 550-562.

Schwartz, S. H., & Bilsky, W. (1990). Toward a theory of universal content and structure of values: Extensions and cross-cultural replications. *Journal of Personality and Social Psychology, 58,* 878-891.

Schwartz, S. H., & Ros, M. (1995). Values in the West: A theoretical and empirical challenge to the individualism-collectivism cultural dimension. *World Psychology, 1*, 99-122.

Schwartz, S. H., & Sagiv, L. (1995). Identifying culture specifics in the content and structure of values. *Journal of Cross-Cultural Psychology, 26*, 92-116.

Schweiger, D. M., & Csiszar, E. N. (in press). An integrative framework for creating value through acquisition. In H. E. Glass (Ed), *Handbook of business strategy*. Boston: Warren, Gorham & Lamont.

Schweiger, D. M., & DeNisi, A. S. (1991). Communication with employees following a merger: A longitudinal field experiment. *Academy of Management Journal, 34*, 110-135.

Schweiger, D. M., Ivancevich, J. M., & Power, F. R. (1987). Executive actions for managing human resources before and after acquisition. *Academy of Management Executive, 1*(1), 127-137.

Scott, W. R. (1987). The adolescence of institutional theory: Problems and potential for organizational analysis. *Administrative Science Quarterly, 32*, 493-512.

Scott, W. R. (1990). *Social network analysis*. London: Sage.

Scott, W. R. (1992). *Organizations: Rational, natural, and open systems* (3rd ed.). Englewood Cliffs, NJ: Prentice Hall.

Scott, W. R. (1995). *Institutions and organizations*. Thousand Oaks, CA: Sage.

Scriven, M. (1991). *Evaluation thesaurus* (4th ed.). Newbury Park, CA: Sage.

Searby, F. W. (1969). Control postmergers change. *Harvard Business Review, 48*(1), 4-17.

Sego, D. J., Hui, C., & Law, K. S. (1997). Operationalizing cultural values as the mean of individual values: Problems and suggestions for research. In P. C. Earley & M. Erez (Eds.), *New perspectives on international industrial/organizational psychology* (pp. 148-159). San Francisco: New Lexington.

Seibert, K. W. (1996). Experience is the best teacher, if you can learn from it. In D. T. Hall (Ed.), *The career is dead—long live the career: A relational approach to careers* (pp. 246-264). San Francisco: Jossey-Bass.

Seligman, C., & Katz, A. N. (1996). The dynamics of value systems. In C. Seligman, J. M. Olson, & M. P. Zanna (Eds.), *The Ontario Symposium: Vol. 8. The psychology of values* (pp. 53-75). Mahwah, NJ: Lawrence Erlbaum.

Selznick, P. (1957). *Leadership in administration: A sociological interpretation*. Evanston, IL: Row, Peterson.

Senge, P. M. (1990). *The fifth discipline: The art and practice of the learning organization*. New York: Currency/Doubleday.

Sethia, N. K., & Van Glinow, M. A. (1985). Arriving at four cultures by managing the reward system. In R. H. Kilmann, M. J. Saxton, R. Serpa, & Associates (Eds.), *Gaining control of the corporate culture* (pp. 400-420). San Francisco: Jossey-Bass.

Shalit, B. (1988). *The psychology of conflict and combat*. New York: Praeger.

Shattuck, R. (1980). *The forbidden experiment: The story of the Wild Boy of Aveyron.* New York: Farrar, Straus & Giroux.

Shenkar, O. (Ed.). (1991). *Organization and management in China 1979-1990.* Armonk, NY: M. E. Sharpe.

Sheridan, J. E. (1992). Organizational culture and employee retention. *Academy of Management Journal, 35,* 1036-1056.

Sherif, M., & Sherif, C. (1953). *Groups in harmony and tension: An integration of studies on intergroup relations.* New York: Harper.

Shirley, R. C. (1973). Analysis of employee and physician attitude toward hospital merger. *Academy of Management Journal, 16,* 465-480.

Shirley, R. C. (1977). The human side of merger planning. *Long Range Planning, 10,* 35-39.

Shoham, A. (1999). *Role-relaxed managers: The impact of social values on management style* (Working paper). Haifa: Technion-Israel Institute of Technology.

Shoham, A., Rose, G. M., & Kahle, L. R. (1998). Risky sports participation: From intention to action. *Journal of the Academy of Marketing Science, 26,* 307-321.

Shortell, S. M., O'Brien, J. L., Carman, J. M., Foster, R. W., Hughes, E. F. X., Boerstler, H., & O'Connor, E. J. (1995). Assessing the impact of continuous quality improvement/total quality management: Concept versus implementation. *Health Services Research, 30,* 377-401.

Shortell, S. M., Rousseau, D. M., Morrison, E. M., Gillies, R. R., Devers, K. J., & Simons, T. L. (1991). Organizational assessment in intensive care units (ICUs): Construct development, reliability, and validity of the ICU nurse-physician questionnaire. *Medical Care, 29,* 709-726.

Shrivastava, P. (1986). Postmerger integration. *Journal of Business Strategy, 7*(1), 65-76.

Shrout, P. E., & Fleiss, J. L. (1979). Intraclass correlations: Uses in assessing rater reliability. *Psychological Bulletin, 86,* 420-428.

Shurberg, D. A., & Haber, S. B. (1992). Organizational culture during the accident response process. In American Nuclear Society (Ed.), *Proceedings of the topical meeting on risk management* (pp. 152-155). La Grange Park, IL: American Nuclear Society.

Shweder, R. A., & LeVine, R. A. (Eds.). (1984). *Culture theory: Essays on mind, self, and emotion.* Cambridge: Cambridge University Press.

Siddiqi, K., Tressness, K., & Kinia, B. (1996). Parts of visual form: Psychophysical aspects. *Perception, 25,* 399-424.

Siehl, C., & Martin, J. (1988). Measuring organizational cultures: Mixing quantitative and qualitative methods. In M. O. Jones, M. D. Moore, & R. D. Snyder (Eds), *Inside organizations* (pp. 45-59). Newbury Park, CA: Sage.

Siehl, C., & Martin, J. (1990). Organizational culture: A key to financial performance? In B. Schneider (Ed.), *Organizational climate and culture* (pp. 241-281). San Francisco: Jossey-Bass.

Sikula, A. F. (1971). Values and value systems: Importance and relationship to managerial and organizational behavior. *Journal of Psychology, 78,* 277-286.

Silverzweig, S., & Allen, R. F. (1976). Changing the corporate culture. *Sloan Management Review, 17*(3), 33-49.

Simon, H. A. (1976). *Administrative behavior: A study of decision-making processes in administrative organization* (3rd ed.). New York: Free Press.

Sinetar, M. (1981). Mergers, morale and productivity. *Personnel Journal, 60,* 863-867.

Sitkin, S. B., & Stickel, D. (1996). The road to hell: The dynamics of distrust in an era of quality. In R. M. Kramer & T. R. Tyler (Eds.), *Trust in organizations: Frontiers of theory and research* (pp. 39-50). Thousand Oaks, CA: Sage.

Skeat, W. W. (1958). *An etymological dictionary of the English language.* Oxford: Oxford University Press.

Skinner, B. F. (1971). *Contingencies of reinforcement.* East Norwalk, CT: Appleton-Century-Crofts.

Slater, S. F., & Narver, J. C. (1995). Market orientation and the learning organization. *Journal of Marketing, 59*(3), 63-75.

Slocombe, T. E., & Bluedorn, A. C. (1999). Organizational behavior implications of the congruence between preferred polychronicity and experienced work-unit polychronicity. *Journal of Organizational Behavior, 20,* 75-99.

Slocum, J. W., Cron, W. L., Hansen, R. W., & Rawlings, S. (1985). Business strategy and the management of plateaued employees. *Academy of Management Journal, 28,* 133-154.

Slowinski, G. (1992). The human touch in successful strategic alliances. *Mergers and Acquisitions, 27,* 44-47.

Smircich, L. (1983). Concepts of culture and organizational analysis. *Administrative Science Quarterly, 28,* 339-358.

Smircich, L. (1985). Is the concept of culture a paradigm for understanding organizations and ourselves? In P. J. Frost, L. F. Moore, M. R. Louis, C. C. Lundberg, & J. Martin (Eds.), *Organizational culture* (pp. 55-72). Beverly Hills, CA: Sage.

Smircich, L., & Calás, M. B. (1987). Organizational culture: A critical assessment. In F. M. Jablin, L. L. Putnam, & L. W. Porter (Eds.), *Handbook of organizational communication.* Newbury Park, CA: Sage.

Smircich, L., & Morgan, G. (1982). Leadership: The management of meaning. *Journal of Applied Behavioral Science, 18,* 257-283.

Smith, C. A., Organ, D., & Near, J. P. (1983). Organizational citizenship behavior: Its nature and antecedents. *Journal of Applied Psychology, 68,* 653-663.

Smith, F. J. (1977). Work attitudes as predictors of attendance on a specific day. *Journal of Applied Psychology, 62,* 16-19.

Smith, G. (1979). *Social work and the sociology of organizations.* London: Routledge & Kegan Paul.

Smith, J. A., & Foti, R. J. (1998). A pattern approach to the study of leader emergence. *Leadership Quarterly, 9,* 147-160.

Smith, M., & White, M. C. (1987). Strategy, CEO specialization, and succession. *Administrative Science Quarterly, 32,* 263-280.

Smith, P. B., & Misumi, J. (1989). Japanese management: A sun rising in the West? In C. L. Cooper & I. T. Robertson (Eds.), *International review of industrial and organizational psychology* (Vol. 4, pp. 330-369). New York: John Wiley.

Smith, P. B., & Peterson, M. F. (1988). *Leadership, organisations and culture: An event management model.* London: Sage.

Smith, P. B., & Peterson, M. F. (1995, August). *Beyond value comparisons: Sources used to give meaning to work events in twenty-five countries.* Paper presented at the annual meeting of the Academy of Management, Vancouver.

Smith, P. B., Peterson, M. F., & Misumi, J. (1994). Event management and team effectiveness in Japan, Britain and the U.S.A. *Journal of Occupational and Organizational Psychology, 67,* 33-43.

Smith, P. B., Peterson, M. F., & Wang, Z. M. (1996). The manager as a mediator of alternative meanings: A pilot study from China, the U.S.A., and U.K. *Journal of International Business Studies, 27,* 115-137.

Smith, P. B., & Schwartz, S. H. (1997). Values. In J. W. Berry, M. H. Segall, & C. Kagitcibasi (Eds.), *Handbook of cross-cultural psychology* (2nd ed., Vol. 3, pp. 77-118). Boston: Allyn & Bacon.

Soeters, J. L. (1997). Values in military academies: A thirteen country study. *Armed Forces and Society, 24,* 7-32.

Soeters, J. L., & Boer, P. (2000). Culture and flight safety in military aviation. *International Journal of Aviation Psychology, 10,* 111-133.

Soeters, J. L., Hofstede, G., & van Twuyver, M. (1995). Culture's consequences and the police: Cross-border cooperation between police forces in Germany, Belgium and the Netherlands. *Policing and Society, 5,* 1-14.

Soeters, J. L., & Recht, R. (1998). Culture and discipline in military academies: An international comparison. *Journal of Political and Military Sociology, 26,* 169-189.

Sofer, C. (1970). *Men in mid-career.* Cambridge: Cambridge University Press.

Sonnenfeld, J. A., & Peiperl, M. A. (1988). Staffing policy as a strategic response: A typology of career systems. *Academy of Management Review, 13,* 588-600.

Sparrow, P. R., & Gaston, K. (1996). Generic climate maps: A strategic application of climate survey data? *Journal of Organizational Behavior, 17,* 679-698.

Spencer, B. A. (1994). Models of organization and total quality management: A comparison and critical evaluation. *Academy of Management Review, 19,* 446-471.

Spradley, J. P. (1979). *The ethnographic interview.* New York: Harcourt Brace Jovanovich.

Spradley, J. P. (1980). *Participant observation.* New York: Holt, Rinehart & Winston.

Stajkovic, A. D., & Luthans, F. (1997). A meta-analysis of the effects of organizational behavior modification on task performance, 1975-95. *Academy of Management Journal, 40,* 1122-1149.

Steele, F. I. (1973). *Physical settings and organizational development.* Reading, MA: Addison-Wesley.

Steele, F. I. (1981). *The sense of place.* Boston: CBI.

Steers, R. M. (1977). Antecedents and outcomes of organizational commitment. *Administrative Science Quarterly, 22,* 46-56.

Stening, B. W., & Everett, J. E. (1984). Response styles in a cross-cultural managerial study. *Journal of Social Psychology, 122,* 151-156.

Stern, G. G. (1970). *People in context.* New York: John Wiley.

Stevens, J. M., Beyer, J. M., & Trice, H. M. (1978). Assessing personal, role, and organizational predictors of managerial commitment. *Academy of Management Journal, 21,* 380-396.

Stewart, E. C., & Bennett, M. J. (1991). *American cultural patterns: A cross-cultural perspective.* Yarmouth, ME: Intercultural Press.

Stewart, R. (1982). *Choices for the manager.* Englewood Cliffs, NJ: Prentice Hall.

Stewman, S., & Konda, S. (1983). Careers and organizational labor markets: Demographic models of organizational behavior. *American Journal of Sociology, 88,* 637-685.

Stinchcombe, A. L. (1983). *Economic sociology.* New York: Academic Press.

Stockwell, F. (1993). *Religion in China today.* Beijing: New World.

Strauss, A. (1978). *Negotiations.* San Francisco: Jossey-Bass.

Strebel, P. (1994). Choosing the right change path. *California Management Review, 36*(2), 29-51.

Strebel, P. (1999). *The change pact: Building commitment to ongoing change.* London: Financial Times/Pitman.

Suarez, J. G. (1994). Managing fear in the workplace. *Journal for Quality and Participation, 17*(7), 24-29.

Suchman, L. A. (1983). Office procedure as practical action: Models of work and system design. *Transactions on Office Information Systems, 1,* 320-328.

Sumihara, N. (1992). *A case study of structuration in a bicultural work organization: A study of a Japanese-owned and -managed corporation in the U.S.A.* Ann Arbor, MI: UMI Dissertation Services.

Sumihara, N. (1994). Compensation system and practice at a Japanese owned and managed sales subsidiary in the USA. In N. Campbell & F. Burton (Eds.), *Japanese multinationals: Strategies and management in the global kaisha* (pp. 241-249). New York: Routledge.

Sumihara, N. (1998). Negotiating a third culture: Roles of knowledge and "cross-knowledge." An example of performance appraisal in a Japanese corporation in New York. In A. Bird & S. Beechler (Eds.), *Managing Japanese multinationals abroad.* New York: Oxford University Press.

Sumner, W. G. (1906). *Folkways.* Boston: Ginn.

Sutton, R. I., & Callahan, A. (1988). The stigma of bankruptcy: Spoiled organizational image and its management. In K. S. Cameron, D. A. Whetten, & R. I. Sutton (Eds.), *Readings in organizational decline: Frameworks, research, and prescriptions* (pp. 241-263). New York: Harper & Row.

Sutton, R. I., & Louis, M. R. (1987). How selecting and socializing newcomers influences insiders. *Human Resource Management, 26,* 347-361.

Swartz, M. (1997). *Get wired, get hired.* Scarborough, ON: Prentice Hall.

Sypher, B., Applegate, J. L., & Sypher, H. E. (1985). Culture and communication in organizational contexts. In W. B. Gudykunst, L. P. Stewart, & S. Ting-Toomey (Eds.), *Communication, culture, and organizational processes* (pp. 13-29). Beverly Hills, CA: Sage.

Szumal, J. L. (1998). *Organizational Culture Inventory interpretation and development guide.* Plymouth, MI: Human Synergistics.

Tagiuri, R., & Litwin, G. (Eds.). (1968). *Organizational climate: Explorations of a concept.* Boston: Harvard Business School, Division of Research.

Tajfel, H. (Ed.). (1982a). *Social identity and intergroup relations.* Cambridge: Cambridge University Press.

Tajfel, H. (1982b). Social psychology of intergroup relations. *Annual Review of Psychology, 33,* 1-39.

Tajfel, H., & Turner, J. C. (1985). The social identity theory of intergroup behavior. In S. Worchel & W. G. Austin (Eds.), *Psychology of intergroup relations* (pp. 7-24). Chicago: Nelson-Hall.

Takahashi, S. (1995). Aesthetic properties of pictorial perceptions. *Psychological Review, 102,* 671-683.

Tan, C. K. (1995). *The Chinese employee's view of effective leadership: A test of the CPM model.* Unpublished master's thesis, University of Hong Kong.

Tannen, D. (1994). *Talking 9 to 5.* New York: William Morrow.

Tannenbaum, A. S. (1968). *Control in organizations.* New York: McGraw-Hill.

Taylor, F. W. (1911). *The principles of scientific management.* New York: Harper.

Tetlock, P. E. (1986). A value pluralism model of ideological reasoning. *Journal of Personality and Social Psychology, 50,* 819-827.

Tett, R. P., Jackson, D. N., & Rothstein, M. (1991). Personality measures as predictors of performance: A meta-analytic review. *Personnel Psychology, 44,* 703-742.

Thomas, K. W. (1976). Conflict and conflict management. In M. D. Dunnette (Ed.), *Handbook of industrial and organizational psychology* (pp. 889-935). Chicago: Rand McNally.

Thomas, R. (1994). *What machines can't do.* Berkeley: University of California Press.

Thompson, A., III, & Bono, B. (1993). Work without wages: The motivation for volunteer fire fighters. *American Journal of Economics and Sociology, 52,* 323-343.

Thompson, B., & Daniel, L. G. (1996). Factor analytic evidence for the construct validity of scores: A historical overview and some guidelines. *Educational and Psychological Measurement, 56,* 197-208.

Thompson, J. D. (1967). *Organizations in action.* New York: McGraw-Hill.

Thompson, J. W. (1996). Employee attitudes, organizational performance, and qualitative factors underlying success. *Journal of Business and Psychology, 11,* 171-191.

Thompson, N., Stradling, S., Murphy, M., & O'Neill, P. (1996). Stress and organisational culture. *British Journal of Social Work, 26,* 647-665.

Thornbury, J. E. (1994). *The relationship between behavioural norms, organisational culture and the ability to assimilate change.* London: KPMG Management Consulting.

Timmons, K. (Producer/Director). (1991). *Groupthink* [Video]. Carlsbad, CA: CRM Films.

Tinsley, C. (1998). Models of conflict resolution in Japanese, German, and American cultures. *Journal of Applied Psychology, 83,* 316-323.

Tönnies, F. (1957). *Community and society.* East Lansing, MI: University Press.

Tornow, W. W., & Wiley, J. W. (1991). Service quality and management practices: A look at employee attitudes, customer satisfaction, and bottom-line consequences. *Human Resource Planning, 14,* 105-116.

Trahant, B., & Burke, W. W. (1996, February). Traveling through transitions. *Training and Development Journal, 50,* 37-41.

Triandis, H. C. (1980). Reflections on trends in cross-culture research. *Journal of Cross-Cultural Psychology, 11,* 35-58.

Triandis, H. C. (1989). Cross-cultural studies of individualism and collectivism. In J. Berman (Ed.), *Nebraska Symposium on Motivation: Cross-cultural perspectives* (Vol. 37, pp. 41-134). Lincoln: University of Nebraska Press.

Triandis, H. C. (1994). Cross-cultural industrial and organizational psychology. In H. C. Triandis, M. D. Dunnette, & L. Hough (Eds.), *Handbook of industrial and organizational psychology* (2nd ed., Vol. 4, pp. 103-172). Palo Alto, CA: Consulting Psychologists Press.

Triandis, H. C. (1995). *Individualism and collectivism.* Boulder, CO: Westview.

Trice, H. M. (1993). *Occupational subcultures in the workplace.* Ithaca, NY: ILR.

Trice, H. M., & Beyer, J. M. (1984). Studying organizational culture through rites and ceremonies. *Academy of Management Review, 9,* 653-669.

Trice, H. M., & Beyer, J. M. (1985). Using six organizational rites to change culture. In R. H. Kilmann, M. J. Saxton, R. Serpa, & Associates (Eds.), *Gaining control of the corporate culture* (pp. 370-399). San Francisco: Jossey-Bass.

Trice, H. M., & Beyer, J. M. (1993). *The cultures of work organizations.* Englewood Cliffs, NJ: Prentice Hall.

Trifts, J. W., & Winkler, D. T. (1987). *The value of corporate leadership: The case of CEO successions* (Working Paper in Banking, Finance, Insurance and Real Estate No. DOR C-87-06). Columbia: University of South Carolina.

Trist, E. L., & Bamforth, K. W. (1951). Some social and psychological consequences of the longwall method of coal-getting. *Human Relations, 4,* 3-38.

Trompenaars, F., & Hampden-Turner, C. (1998). *Riding the waves of culture: Understanding diversity in global business* (2nd ed.). New York: McGraw-Hill.

Trumbo, D. A. (1961). Individual and group correlates of attitudes toward work-related change. *Journal of Applied Psychology, 45,* 338-344.

Tsui, A. S. (1990). A multiple constituency model of effectiveness: An empirical examination at the human resource subunit level. *Administrative Science Quarterly, 35,* 458-483.

Tsui, A. S. (1998, August). *Influence of relational demography and "guanxi" in Chinese organizations.* Paper presented at the 24th International Congress of Applied Psychology, San Francisco.

Tuckman, A. (1994). The yellow brick road: Total quality management and the restructuring of organizational culture. *Organization Science, 5,* 727-751.

Tukey, J. U. (1977). *Exploratory data analysis.* Reading, MA: Addison-Wesley.

Turnbull, C. M. (1962). *The forest people: A study of the Pygmies of the Congo.* Garden City, NY: Doubleday.

Turner, B. A. (Ed.). (1990). *Organizational symbolism.* New York: Walter de Gruyter.

Turner, J. C. (1985). Social categorization and the self-concept: A social cognitive theory of group behavior. In E. J. Lawler (Ed.), *Advances in group processes: Theory and research* (Vol. 2, pp. 77-122), Greenwich, CT: JAI.

Turner, J. C., Hogg, M., Oakes, P., Reicher, S., & Wetherell, M. (1987). *Rediscovering the social group: A self-categorization theory.* Oxford: Blackwell.

Turner, V. (1969). *The ritual process: Structure and anti-structure.* Chicago: Aldine de Gruyter.

Turner, V. (1982). *From ritual to theatre: The human seriousness of play.* New York: PAJ.

Turner, V. W. (1974). *Dramas, fields, and metaphors: Symbolic action in human society.* Ithaca, NY: Cornell University Press.

Tushman, M. L., & O'Reilly, C. A., III. (1997). *Winning through innovation: A practical guide to leading organizational change and renewal.* Boston: Harvard Business School Press.

Tyrrell, M. W. D. (1994, April). *"It's not your fault, but . . .": Notes on the ritualization of corporate culture change in firing practices.* Paper presented at the annual meeting of the North Eastern Anthropology Association, Geneseo, NY.

Tyrrell, M. W. D. (1995, October.). *The "gift" of information: Reciprocity in late 20th century job search strategies.* Paper presented at the Third Annual Work in Progress Seminar, Carleton University. Available Internet: http://www.cyberus.ca/~mwtyrrel/index.htm

Tyrrell, M. W. D. (1996a). *Cultural evolution in cyberspace: Notes towards a virtual-world systems theory.* Paper presented at the annual meeting of the American Sociological Association, New York.

Tyrrell, M. W. D. (1996b, May). *From cyberia to cyburbia: An examination of the links between consciousness in cyberspace and the restructuring of the "real world."* Paper presented at the annual meeting of the Canadian Anthropology Society, Brock University, St. Catharines, ON.

Tyrrell, M. W. D. (1998, May). *Surfing, searching and scavenging: Hunting and gathering "communities" on the 'Net.* Paper presented at the annual meeting of the Canadian Anthropology Society, University of Toronto.

Tyrrell, M. W. D., & Ferguson, I. (1998, March). *Contingency and community in cyberspace: Technological and social evolution in cyberspace.* Paper presented at the annual meeting of the North Eastern Anthropology Association, University of Maine, Orono.

Ulrich, D. (1997). *Human resource champions: The next agenda for adding value and delivering results.* Boston: Harvard Business School Press.

Ulrich, D., Halbrook, R., Meder, D., Stuchlik, M., & Thorpe, S. (1991). Employee and customer attachment: Synergies for competitive advantage. *Human Resource Planning, 14,* 89-104.

Unger, R. M. (1987). *Social theory: Its situation and its task.* Cambridge: Cambridge University Press.

United Auto Workers. (Producer). (1990). *The leadership alliance at Hydra-Matic Toledo* [Video]. Detroit, MI: Author.

U.S. Department of Labor. (1991). *Dictionary of occupational titles* (4th ed.). Washington, DC: U.S. Employment Service.

Ussher, J. (1991). *Women's madness: Misogyny or mental illness?* Hertfordshire, England: Harvester Wheatsheaf.

Usunier, J.-C. G., & Valette-Florence, P. (1994). Perceptual time patterns ("time styles"): A psychometric scale. *Time and Society, 3,* 219-241.

Uzzi, B. (1996). The sources and consequences of embeddedness for the economic performance of organizations: The network effect. *American Sociological Review, 61,* 674-698.

Vancil, R. F. (1979). *Decentralization: Managerial ambiguity by design.* Homewood, IL: Dow Jones-Irwin.

van der Velde, M., & Class, M. D. (1995). The relationship of role conflict and ambiguity to organizational culture. In S. L. Sauter & L. R. Murphy (Eds.), *Organizational risk factors for job stress* (pp. 53-59). Washington, DC: American Psychological Association.

Van de Ven, A. H. (1993). Managing the process of organization innovation. In G. P. Huber & W. H. Glick (Eds.), *Organizational change and redesign* (pp. 269-294). New York: Oxford University Press.

Van de Ven, A. H., & Poole, M. S. (1990). Methods for studying innovation development in the Minnesota Innovation research program. *Organization Science, 1,* 313-335.

van Doorn, J. A. A. (1975). *The soldier and social change: Comparative studies in the history and sociology of the military.* Beverly Hills, CA: Sage.

van Doorn, J. A. A., & Hendrix, W. J. (1970). *Ontsporing van geweld. Over het Nederlands-Indisch-Indonesisch conflict* [Derailment of violence: On the Dutch-Indian-Indonesian conflict]. Rotterdam: University Press of Rotterdam.

Van Dyne, L., Graham, J. W., & Dienesch, R. M. (1994). Organization citizenship behavior: Construct redefinition, measurement, and validation. *Academy of Management Journal, 37,* 765-802.

Van Maanen, J. (1973). Observations on the making of policemen. *Human Organization, 32,* 407-418.

Van Maanen, J. (1975). Police socialization: A longitudinal examination of job attitudes in an urban police department. *Administrative Science Quarterly, 20,* 207-228.

Van Maanen, J. (1978). The "asshole." In P. K. Manning & J. Van Maanen (Eds.), *Policing: A view from the street* (pp. 231-238). Santa Monica, CA: Goodyear.

Van Maanen, J. (1988). *Tales of the field: On writing ethnography.* Chicago: University of Chicago Press.

Van Maanen, J. (1991). The smile factory: Work at Disneyland. In P. J. Frost, L. F. Moore, M. R. Louis, C. C. Lundberg, & J. Martin (Eds.), *Reframing organizational culture.* Newbury Park, CA: Sage.

Van Maanen, J., & Barley, S. R. (1985). Cultural organization: Fragments of a theory. In P. J. Frost, L. F. Moore, M. R. Louis, C. C. Lundberg, & J. Martin (Eds.), *Organizational culture* (pp. 31-54). Beverly Hills, CA: Sage.

Van Maanen, J., & Schein, E. H. (1979). Toward a theory of organizational socialization. In B. M. Staw (Ed.), *Research in organizational behavior* (Vol. 1, pp. 209-264). Greenwich, CT: JAI.

van Rheenen, P. (1979). *Overheidsgeweld* [Violence by government]. Samson, Netherlands: Alphen & Rijn.

van Rheenen, P. (1997). The Amnesty adventure: Amnesty International's police group in the Netherlands. *Netherlands Quarterly of Human Rights, 15,* 475-493.

Vardi, I. S., & Hammer, T. H. (1977). Intra-organizational mobility and career perception among rank and file employees. *Academy of Management Journal, 20,* 622-634.

Vaughn, D. (1996). *The* Challenger *launch decision: Risky technology, culture, and deviance at NASA.* Chicago: University of Chicago Press.

Venkatraman, N., & Ramanujam, V. (1986). Measurement of business performance in strategy research: A comparison of approaches. *Academy of Management Review, 11,* 811-814.

Verbeke, W., Volkering, M., & Hessels, M. (1998). Exploring the conceptual expansion within the field of organizational behavior: Organizational climate and organizational culture. *Journal of Management Studies, 35,* 303-329.

Vogel, E. (1979). *Japan as number one: Lessons for America.* Cambridge, MA: Harvard University Press.

Vogel, G. (1998, November 27). DNA suggests cultural traits affect whale's evolution. *Science, 282,* 1616.

Vogelaar, A., & Kramer, F. J. (1997). Mission-oriented command in ambiguous situations. *Netherlands Annual Review of Military Studies, 1,* 174-194.

Vollman, T. E. (1996). *The transformation imperative: Achieving market dominance through radical change.* Boston: Harvard Business School Press.

von Bertalanffy, L. (1968). *General system theory.* New York: George Braziller.

von Meier, A. (1999). Occupational cultures as a challenge to technological innovation. *IEEE Transactions on Engineering Management, 46,* 101-114.

Vroom, V. H. (1964). *Work and motivation.* New York: John Wiley.

Wakabayashi, M., & Graen, G. (1984). The Japanese Career Progress Study: A seven year follow-up. *Journal of Applied Psychology, 69,* 603-614.

Wakabayashi, M., Graen, G., Graen, M., & Graen, M. (1988). Japanese management progress: Mobility into middle management. *Journal of Applied Psychology, 73,* 217-227.

Waldinger, R., Aldrich, H., Ward, R., et al. (1990). *Ethnic entrepreneurs: Immigrant business in industrial societies.* Newbury Park, CA: Sage.

Waldman, D. A., Lituchy, T., Gopalakrishnan, M., Laframboise, K., Galperin, B., & Kaltsounakis, Z. (1998). A qualitative analysis of leadership and quality improvement. *Leadership Quarterly, 9,* 177-201.

Walkerdine, V. (1990). *School girl fictions.* London: Virago.

Waller, M. J., Huber, G. P., & Glick, W. H. (1995). Functional background as a determinant of executives' selective perception. *Academy of Management Journal, 38,* 943-974.

Walsh, J. P. (1988a). Selectivity and selective perception: An investigation of managers' belief structures and information processing. *Academy of Management Journal, 31,* 873-896.

Walsh, J. P. (1988b). Top management turnover following mergers and acquisition. *Strategic Management Journal, 9,* 173-183.

Walsh, J. P. (1989). Doing a deal: Merger and acquisition negotiations and their impact upon target company top management turnover. *Strategic Management Journal, 10,* 307-322.

Walsh, J. P., & Fahey, L. (1986). The role of negotiated belief structures in strategy making. *Journal of Management, 12,* 325-338.

Walsh, J. P., & Ellwood, J. W. (1991). Mergers, acquisitions, and pruning of management deadwood. *Strategic Management Journal, 12,* 201-218.

Walter, G. A. (1985). Culture collisions in mergers and acquisitions. In P. J. Frost, L. F. Moore, M. R. Louis, C. C. Lundberg, & J. Martin (Eds.), *Organizational culture* (pp. 301-314). Beverly Hills, CA: Sage.

Walton, R. E. (1989). *Up and running: Integrating information technology and the organization.* Boston: Harvard Business School Press.

Wang, R. L., Wang, C., & Gong, Y. R. (1991). Enterprise autonomy and market structures in China. In O. Shenkar (Ed.), *Organization and management in China 1979-1990* (pp. 23-34). Armonk, NY: M. E. Sharpe.

Wang, S. (1993). Basic framework and advanced pattern of economic systems of the socialist market economy. *China's Economic Structure Reform, 1,* 16-18.

Wang, Z. M. (1990). Human resource management in China: Recent trends. In R. Pieper (Ed.), *Human resource management: An international comparison.* New York: Walter de Gruyter.

Weatherly, K. A., & Tansik, D. A. (1993). Managing multiple demands: A role-theory examination of the behaviors of customer contact service workers. In T. A. Swartz, D. E. Bowen, & S. W. Brown (Eds.), *Advances in services marketing and management* (Vol. 2, pp. 279-300). Greenwich, CT: JAI.

Webber, R. A. (1972). *Time and management.* New York: Van Nostrand Reinhold.

Weber, M. (1964). *The theory of social and economic organization* (A. M. Henderson & T. Parsons, Trans.). New York: Free Press.

Weber, M. (1978). *Economy and society* (G. Roth & C. Wittich, Eds.). Berkeley: University of California Press.

Weber, Y. (1988). *The effects of top management culture clash on the implementation of mergers and acquisitions.* Unpublished doctoral dissertation, University of South Carolina.

Weber, Y. (1996). Corporate cultural fit and performance in mergers and acquisitions. *Human Relations, 49,* 1181-1202.

Weber, Y., Ganzah, Y., & Ben-Yemini, H. (1995). Integrating and preserving different cultures after acquisition. *International Journal of Conflict Management, 6,* 192-210.

Weber, Y., Lubatkin, M., & Schweiger, D. M. (1994, August). *Top management turnover following mergers: A longitudinal study of perceptual and attitudinal determinants.* Paper presented at the annual meeting of the Academy of Management, Dallas.

Weber, Y., & Pliskin, N. (1996). The effects of information systems, integration and organizational culture on a firm's effectiveness. *Information and Management, 30,* 81-90.

Weber, Y., & Schweiger, D. M. (1992). Top management culture conflict in mergers and acquisitions: A lesson from anthropology. *International Journal of Conflict Management, 3,* 1-17.

Weber, Y., Shenkar, O., & Raveh, A. (1996). National vs. corporate cultural fit in mergers and acquisition: An exploratory study. *Management Science, 42,* 1215-1221.

Webster, J., Michela, J. L., Greenstein, A., King, R., Nolan, J., & Weiss, A. (1998). *Diagnosing the design of a matrixed software development team.* Waterloo, ON: University of Waterloo, Organizational Research and Consulting Group.

Weeks, J. (1994, August). *Dimensions of strength: Strong culture revisited.* Paper presented at the annual meeting of the Academy of Management, Dallas.

Weeks, W. A., & Kahle, L. R. (1990a, February). Salespeople's time use and performance. *Journal of Personal Selling and Sales Management, 10,* 29-37.

Weeks, W. A., & Kahle, L. R. (1990b). Social values and salespeople's effort: Entrepreneurial versus routine selling. *Journal of Business Research, 20,* 183-190.

Wegbreit, R. A. (1992). *The dynamics of culture change: An examination of the process of modification of shared assumptions.* Unpublished doctoral dissertation, Claremont Graduate School.

Wegenr, B. M., & Bargh, J. A. (1988). Control and automaticity in social life. In D. T. Gilbert & S. T. Fiske (Eds.), *The handbook of social psychology* (4th ed., Vol. 2, pp. 446-496). New York: McGraw-Hill.

Weick, K. E. (1969). *The social psychology of organizing*. Reading, MA: Addison-Wesley.

Weick, K. E. (1979). *The social psychology of organizing* (2nd ed.). New York: Random House.

Weick, K. E. (1985). The significance of corporate culture. In P. J. Frost, L. F. Moore, M. R. Louis, C. C. Lundberg, & J. Martin (Eds.), *Organizational culture* (pp. 381-389). Beverly Hills, CA: Sage.

Weick, K. E. (1993). The collapse of sensemaking in organizations: The Mann Gulch disaster. *Administrative Science Quarterly, 38*, 628-652.

Weick, K. E. (1995). *Sensemaking in organizations*. Thousand Oaks, CA: Sage.

Weick, K. E., & Quinn, R. E. (1999). Organizational change and development. *Annual Review of Psychology, 50*, 361-386.

Weick, K. E., & Roberts, K. H. (1993). Collective minds in organizations. Heedful interrelating on flight decks. *Administrative Science Quarterly, 38*, 357-381.

Weidner, C. K., II. (1997). *Trust and distrust at work: Normative and dyad-exchange influences on individual and subunit performance.* Unpublished doctoral dissertation, University of Illinois at Chicago.

Weishut, D. J. N. (1989). *The meaningfulness of the distinction between instrumental and terminal values.* Unpublished master's thesis, Hebrew University of Jerusalem.

Weiss, D., Dawis, R., England, G., & Lofquist, L. (1967). *Manual for the Minnesota Satisfaction Questionnaire.* Minneapolis: University of Minnesota, Industrial Relations Center.

Weiss, H. M., & Cropanzano, R. (1996). Affective events theory: A theoretical discussion of the structure, causes and consequences of affective experiences at work. In B. M. Staw & L. L. Cummings (Eds.), *Research in organizational behavior* (Vol. 18, pp. 1-74). Greenwich, CT: JAI.

Wellman, B. (1998). Introduction. In B. Wellman, *Networks in the global village* [on-line]. Available Internet: http://www.chass.utoronto.ca/~Ewellman/in/in_index.htm

West, M. A. (1990). The social psychology of innovation in groups. In M. A. West & J. L. Farr (Eds.), *Innovation and creativity at work: Psychological and organizational strategies* (pp. 309-333). Chichester: John Wiley.

Westney, D. E. (1998). Changing perspectives on the organization of Japanese multinational companies. In A. Bird & S. Beechler (Eds.), *Managing Japanese multinationals abroad.* New York: Oxford University Press.

White, H. C. (1992). *Identity and control: A structural theory of social action.* Princeton, NJ: Princeton University Press.

White, H. C., Boorman, S. A., & Breiger, R. L. (1976). Social structure from multiple networks I: Blockmodels of roles and positions. *American Journal of Sociology, 81*, 730-780.

Whitley, R. D. (1987). Taking firms seriously as economic actors: Towards a sociology of firm behavior. *Organization Studies, 8*, 125-147.

Whyte, W. F. (1948). *Human relations in the restaurant industry.* New York: McGraw-Hill.

Whyte, W. H. (1956). *The organization man.* Garden City, NY: Doubleday.

Wicker, A. W. (1969). Attitudes vs. actions: The relationship of verbal and overt behavioral responses to attitude objects. *Journal of Social Issues, 25,* 41-78.

Wicker, A. W. (1971). An examination of the "other variables" explanation of attitude-behavior inconsistency. *Journal of Personality and Social Psychology, 19,* 18-30.

Wicks, D. (1998). Organisational structures as recursively constructed systems of agency and constraint: Compliance and resistance in the context of structural conditions. *Canadian Review of Sociology and Anthropology, 35,* 369-390.

Wiener, Y. (1982). Commitment in organizations: A normative view. *Academy of Management Review, 7,* 418-428.

Wiersema, M. F., & Bantel, K. A. (1992). Top management team demography and corporate strategic change. *Academy of Management Journal, 35,* 91-121.

Wilderom, C. P. M., & Van den Berg, P. T. (1998, August). *A test of the leadership-culture-performance model within a large Dutch financial organization.* Paper presented at the annual meeting of the Academy of Management, San Diego, CA. [*Best paper proceedings,* S. Havlovic, ed.]

Wilensky, H. L. (1960). Work, careers, and social integration. *International Social Science Journal, 12,* 543-560.

Wiley, J. W. (1991). Customer satisfaction and employee opinions: A supportive work environment and its financial cost. *Human Resource Planning, 14,* 117-127.

Wiley, J. W. (1996). Linking survey results to customer satisfaction and business performance. In A. I. Kraut (Ed.), *Organizational surveys: Tools for assessment and change* (pp. 330-359). San Francisco: Jossey-Bass.

Wiley, J. W. (1998, April). *Using culture survey results to predict dealership satisfaction and operational performance.* Paper presented at the 13th Annual Meeting of the Society for Industrial and Organizational Psychology, Dallas.

Wilkins, A. L., & Ouchi, W. G. (1983). Efficient cultures: Exploring the relationship between culture and organizational performance. *Administrative Science Quarterly, 28,* 468-481.

Williams, A., Dobson, P., & Walters, M. (1993). *Changing culture: New organizational approaches* (2nd ed.). London: Institute of Personnel Management.

Williams, R. M. (1970). *American society: A sociological interpretation* (3rd ed.). New York: Alfred A. Knopf.

Williamson, O. E. (1975). *Markets and hierarchies: Analysis and antitrust implications.* New York: Free Press.

Wilson, E. M. (1997). Exploring gendered cultures. *Hallinnon Tutkimus* [Finnish Journal of Administrative Studies], *4,* 289-303.

Wilson, J. Q. (1968). *Varieties of police behavior: The management of law and order in eight communities.* Cambridge, MA: Harvard University Press.

Wilson, J. Q. (1989). *Bureaucracy: What government agencies do and why they do it.* New York: Basic Books.

Wind, J. Y., & Main, J. (1998). *Driving change: How the best companies are preparing for the 21st century.* New York: Free Press.

Windsor, C., & Ashkanasy, N. M. (1996). Auditor independence decision-making: The role of organizational culture perceptions. *Behavioral Research in Accounting, 8* (Supplement), 80-97.

Winslow, D. (1998). Misplaced loyalties: The role of military culture in the breakdown of discipline in peace operations. *Canadian Review of Sociology and Anthropology, 35,* 345-367.

Withey, M. J., & Cooper, W. H. (1989). Predicting exit, voice, loyalty, and neglect. *Administrative Science Quarterly, 34,* 521-539.

Wittgenstein, L. (1958). *The blue and brown books.* New York: HarperTorchbooks.

Witz, A., & Savage, M. (1992). The gender of organisations. In M. Savage & A. Witz (Eds.), *Gender and bureaucracy* (pp. 3-62). Oxford: Blackwell.

Wolf, E. (1982). *Europe and the people without history.* Berkeley: University of California Press.

Wolf, N. (1991). *The beauty myth.* Garden City, NY: Doubleday.

Wollack, S., Goodale, G., Wijting, P., & Smith, P. C. (1971). Development of the Survey of Work Values. *Journal of Applied Psychology, 55,* 331-338.

Woodcock, M. (1989). *Clarifying organizational values.* Brookfield, VT: Gower.

Woodman, R. W., & King, D. (1978). Organizational climate: Science or folklore? *Academy of Management Review, 3,* 816-826.

Woodruff, R. B. (1997). Customer value: The next source for competitive advantage. *Journal of the Academy of Marketing Science, 25,* 139-153.

Woods, J. A. (1997). The six values of a quality culture. *National Productivity Review, 16*(2), 49-55.

Woodward, J. (1958). *Management and technology.* London: Her Majesty's Stationery Office.

Xenikou, A., & Furnham, A. (1996). A correlational and factor analytic study of four questionnaire measures of organizational culture. *Human Relations, 49,* 349-371.

Yammarino, F. J., & Markham, S. E. (1992). On the application of within and between analysis: Are absence and affect really group based phenomena? *Journal of Applied Psychology, 77,* 168-176.

Yeh, R., & Latib, M. (1990). *Japanese trust in local subordinates in overseas investments.* Paper presented at the annual meeting of the International Academy of Management, Toronto.

Yoshino, M. Y. (1971). *The Japanese marketing system: Adaptations and innovations.* Cambridge: MIT Press.

Young, M. (1996). Career issues for single adults without dependent children. In D. T. Hall (Ed.), *The career is dead—long live the career: A relational approach to careers* (pp. 196-219). San Francisco: Jossey-Bass.

Zaheer, A., McEvily, B., & Perrone, V. (1998). Does trust matter? Exploring the effects of interorganizational and interpersonal trust on performance. *Organization Science, 9,* 141-160.

Zaltman, G., & Duncan, R. (1977). *Strategies for planned change.* New York: John Wiley.

Zammuto, R. F., & Krakower, J. Y. (1991). Quantitative and qualitative studies of organizational culture. *Research in Organizational Change and Development, 5,* 84-114.

Zammuto, R. F., & O'Connor, E. J. (1992). Gaining advanced manufacturing technology's benefits: The roles of organization design and culture. *Academy of Management Review, 17,* 701-728.

Zeithaml, V. A., & Bitner, M. J. (1996). *Services marketing.* New York: McGraw-Hill.

Zeithaml, V. A., Parasuraman, A., & Berry, L. L. (1990). *Delivering quality service: Balancing customer perceptions and expectations.* New York: Free Press.

Zerubavel, E. (1979). *Patterns of time in hospital life: A sociological perspective.* Chicago: University of Chicago Press.

Zerubavel, E. (1981). *Hidden rhythms: Schedules and calendars in social life.* Chicago: University of Chicago Press.

Zerubavel, E. (1985). *The seven day circle: The history and meaning of the week.* Chicago: University of Chicago Press.

Zohar, D. (1980). Safety climate in industrial organizations: Theoretical and applied implications. *Journal of Applied Psychology, 65,* 96-102.

Zoltners, A. A., Sinha, P. K., & Murphy, S. J. (1997). *The fat firm: The transformation of a firm from fat to fit.* New York: McGraw-Hill.

Zuboff, S. (1988). *In the age of the smart machine.* New York: Basic Books.

Zytkowski, D. G. (1970). The concept of work values. *Vocational Guidance Quarterly, 18,* 176-186.

# Author Index

# Subject Index

# About the Contributors

**Ram N. Aditya** is Assistant Professor and Coordinator of the Industrial and Organizational Psychology Program at Louisiana Tech University. With a bachelor's degree in physics and a master's degree in business administration, he served for several years as a management professional in the corporate sector before obtaining his M.A. and Ph.D. in social and organizational psychology from Temple University. Prior to joining Louisiana Tech University, he was a Senior Research Associate and member of the General Coordinating Team of the Global Leadership and Organizational Behavior Effectiveness (GLOBE) Research Project, a 60-nation study of leadership headquartered at the University of Pennsylvania. He is currently engaged in the creation of an interpersonal acumen scale for use in executive development and training. His research activities include the areas of social intelligence, cross-cultural issues and methodology, leadership, and sequential influence techniques in business negotiations, in addition to his continuing involvement with the GLOBE Project.

**Neal M. Ashkanasy** is Professor of Management in the Graduate School of Management, University of Queensland, in Brisbane, Australia. He has a Ph.D. in psychology from the same university, and has research interests in emotions, organizational culture, leadership, and ethics. He is on the editorial boards of the *Academy of Management Journal* and the *Journal of Management* and has published in such journals as *Organizational Behavior and Human Decision Processes, Journal of Personality and Social Psychology,* and *Accounting, Organizations and Society.* He is also program chair of the Academy of Management Managerial and Organizational Cognitions Division. He is coeditor of a forthcoming book on emotions in working life and is also writing a book on this topic. He is the founder and administrator of two international e-mail discussion groups: Orgcult (the Organizational Culture Caucus) and Emonet (the Network for Emotions in Organizations).

**Janice M. Beyer** is the Harkins and Company Centennial Chair in Business Administration, Professor of Sociology, and Professor of Communication Studies at the University of Texas at Austin. Her publications include two coauthored books titled *Implementing Change* and *The Cultures of Work Organizations* and more than 90 articles and book chapters on such topics as organizational design, interorganizational relations, commitment, ideologies and values, rites and ceremonies in organizations, the sociology of science and universities, human resources policies and practices, total quality management, and the utilization of organizational research. Her current research interests focus on organizational culture, socialization, knowledge management, and cultural leadership. She has served as editor of the *Academy of Management Journal* and as President of the Academy of Management and of the International Federation of Scholarly Associations in Management, and is currently a member of the editorial boards of *Administrative Science Quarterly, Journal of World Business,* and the *Journal of Quality Management.* She is a Fellow of the Academy of Management and holds a Ph.D. in organizational behavior from Cornell University.

**Allen C. Bluedorn** received his Ph.D. in sociology from the University of Iowa, and since then he has taught and studied organizational behavior for 24 years, first at the Pennsylvania State University, then at the University of Missouri–Columbia, where he continues to do so today as a Professor of Management. Articles reporting his research on subjects such as turnover, organizational culture, and time have appeared in many journals, including the *Academy of Management Review, Journal of Applied Psychology, Journal of Organizational Behavior, Journal of Political and Military Sociology, Educational and Psychological Measurement, Research in Organizational Change and Development, Journal of Management, Public Administration Review, Research in the Sociology of Organizations, Human Relations, Academy of Management Executive,* and *Strategic Management Journal.* For many years his research has focused on time and organizational behavior, and a recently completed project in this domain consists of two-plus special issues of the *Journal of Managerial Psychology* (1999, Vol. 14, Nos. 3, 4, and part of 5) devoted to polychronicity for which he served as guest editor. His service has included terms as President of the Midwest Academy of Management, as a member of the Organizational Behavior Teaching Society's Board of Directors, and as a Representative-at-Large to the Academy of Management's Board of Governors.

**David E. Bowen** is Professor of Management, Department of World Business at Thunderbird, the American Graduate School of International Management. He has an M.B.A. (1977) and a Ph.D. in business administration (1983) from Michigan State University. His research, teaching, and consulting interests in the area of service management include the development of high-performance customers, strategic human resource management in service firms, and empowerment of service employees. He is coauthor, with Benjamin Schneider, of *Winning the Service Game* and a coeditor of the book series *Advances in Services Marketing and Management.* His service research has also been published in *Sloan Management Review, Academy of Management Review, Journal of Applied Psychology, Organizational Dynamics,* and *Organization Science.*

**Mary Yoko Brannen** is Associate Professor of International Business at San Jose State University and Associate Professor of Executive Education at the University of Michigan Business School. She received her M.B.A. with emphasis in international business and Ph.D. in organizational behavior with a minor in anthropology from the University of Massachusetts at Amherst, and a B.A. in comparative literature from the University of California at Berkeley. Her research interests include cultural evolution in multinational work arenas, bicultural alienation in Japanese-owned U.S. companies, and the effects of culture on internationalization.

**Lyndelle E. Broadfoot** is a practitioner in the field of human resource management with an active interest in the field of organizational culture. She holds a bachelor's degree with honors from the University of Queensland and a master's degree from the University of Wollongong. Her research focuses on the development of survey measures for organizational culture. As a human resources professional she has worked for several large multinational corporations in the exploration and mining industry and for Australia's leading scientific research organization.

**Scott M. Brooks** is Consultant and Manager of Research and Development for Gantz Wiley Research, a consulting firm specializing in employee opinion and customer satisfaction surveys for international corporate clients. In addition to employee survey consulting, he manages the R&D function, which includes oversight of all projects linking employee surveys to customer or business performance measures. His other work includes developing customized and standard employee and customer survey products based upon these linkages, as well as managing WorkTrends™, Gantz Wiley Research's unique database of employee opinions. He has authored numerous presentations and publications based upon linkage research, surveys in general, and other job attitude and measurement topics. Prior to taking his current position at GWR, he worked for the retailer Mervyn's, a division of Dayton Hudson Corporation. He received his Ph.D. in industrial and organizational psychology from the Ohio State University. He is a member of the Society for Industrial and Organizational Psychology and the American Psychological Association.

**W. Warner Burke,** Ph.D., is Professor of Psychology and Education and Chair of the Department of Organization and Leadership at Teachers College, Columbia University. He is also CEO of W. Warner Burke Associates, Inc., an organizational consulting firm. The author or editor of 13 books, including *Organization Development: A Process of Learning and Changing* (1994), he has also authored or co-authored more than 100 articles and book chapters. He is a Fellow of the Academy of Management, the American Psychological Society, and the Society of Industrial and Organizational Psychology. He is also a Diplomate in Industrial/Organizational Psychology, American Board of Professional Psychology. He is past editor of the American Management Association's quarterly publication, *Organizational Dynamics,* and served as initial editor for the *Academy of Management Executive.* He is the recipient of numerous awards, including the NASA Public Service Medal; the Distinguished Contribution to Human Resource Development Award, presented by the American Society for Training and Development; and the Organization Development Professional Practice Area Award for Excellence, also awarded by ASTD. A former member of the Board of Governors of the Academy of Management and the American Society for Training and Development, he designed and served as faculty director of the Columbia Business School's executive program, "Leading and Managing People," from 1988 to 1995. He recently served on a task force for enhancing organizational performance for the National Research Council of the Academy of Science.

**Jagdeep S. Chhokar** is Professor at the Indian Institute of Management in Ahmedabad. He earned his Ph.D. from Louisiana State University in 1983 and has taught previously in Australia and the United States. He had earlier worked in industry for more than a decade in a variety of managerial and engineering positions. Actively involved in cross-cultural research for the past few years, he has eclectic professional interests ranging from organizational behavior and organization theory to international marketing and management, cross-cultural management, human resource management, and strategic management. His research has appeared in such journals as the *Journal of Applied Psychology, Columbia Journal of World Business, International Labor Review, Industrial Relations,* and *Journal of Safety Research.* He has also contributed chapters to edited books and has written several teaching cases. He is a charter member and a member of the Coordinating Team of the Global Leadership and Organizational Behavior Effectiveness (GLOBE) Research Project.

**Patrick E. Connor** is Professor of Organization Theory and Behavior at the Atkinson Graduate School of Management, Willamette University, in Salem, Oregon. He received his bachelor's degree in electrical engineering from the University of Washington, a master's degree in industrial administration from Purdue University, and his Ph.D. in organization theory from the University of Washington.

He has previously served on the faculties of Oregon State University and the University of British Columbia. He teaches graduate courses in organization design, managing organizational change, and managerial value systems. He has published five books on management in 10 editions, and some 50 articles, chapters, and book reviews in professional journals and books. His research has appeared in the *Academy of Management Journal, Academy of Management Review, IEEE Transactions on Engineering Management, Journal of Management Inquiry,* and *Public Administration Review,* among others. His principal research interests are focused on managerial value systems, especially as they relate to decision making. He is a member of the Academy of International Business, the Academy of Management, the International Society for the Study of Work and Organizational Values, the Organizational Behavior Teaching Society, and the Western Academy of Management (of which he is a past president).

**Robert A. Cooke** is Director of Human Synergistics/Center for Applied Research and Associate Professor of Managerial Studies at the University of Illinois at Chicago. He previously was an Associate Research Scientist at the University of Michigan's Survey Research Center and a Visiting Scholar at Stanford University. He received his Ph.D. in organizational behavior from the Kellogg Graduate School of Management at Northwestern University, where he was a National Defense and Commonwealth Edison Fellow. He has developed numerous survey instruments used for organizational research and development, including the Human Systems Reliability Survey, the Organizational Culture Inventory, the Organizational Effectiveness Inventory, Leadership/Impact, the Group Styles Inventory, and the AMA DISC Survey. His publications on these surveys have appeared in such journals as *Psychological Reports, Journal of Applied Psychology,* and the *Journal of Applied Behavioral Science.* His survey-based research has been selected for the William Davis Memorial Award for outstanding scholarly research and the Douglas McGregor Memorial Award for Excellence in the Applied Social Sciences.

**Kevin G. Corley** is a doctoral student studying organizational theory and organizational behavior at the Smeal College of Business Administration at Pennsylvania State University. His current research interests include organizational culture, organizational reputation and image manager, and how the sensemaking of organizational members is influenced by actions taken at the organizational level. He has forthcoming pieces in the *Academy of Management Review* and the *Academy of Management Journal,* as well as a coauthored paper (with Martin Kilduff) on cultural diaspora in the on-line journal *M@n@gement.*

**E. Jane Davidson** has undergraduate degrees in chemistry and psychology and an M.A. in industrial and organizational psychology. She has several years of experience as both an internal and an external consultant in government and private sector organizations and runs a small, New Zealand-based consulting business. Her areas of specialization are in the evaluation of organizational change, organizational learning, and personnel evaluation. She is currently completing a Ph.D. in organizational behavior and evaluation at Claremont Graduate University.

**Marcus W. Dickson** is Assistant Professor of Industrial/Organizational Psychology at Wayne State University in Detroit, Michigan. He was a charter member of the Global Leadership and Organizational Behavior Effectiveness (GLOBE) Research Project and a member of the GLOBE Coordinating Team for 6 years, and he served as Co-Principal Investigator on that project for 2 years. He received his Ph.D. in industrial/organizational psychology from the University of Maryland in 1997. His current research interests include cross-cultural organizational culture analysis, organizational climate (especially ethical climates in organizations and climates for innovation), and computer-mediated communication in organizations.

**Mark G. Ehrhart** is pursuing a Ph.D. in industrial/organizational psychology from the University of Maryland. His research interests include service quality, leadership, and selection in organizations.

**Sarah Falkus** received her master's degree in organizational psychology from the University of Queensland in 1998. Her research interests at that time focused on organizational culture. She currently has publications forthcoming in the areas of ethical behavior, in the *Journal of Business Ethics,* and leadership, as a part of the Global Leadership and Organizational Behavior Effectiveness (GLOBE) Research Project team led by Robert House at Wharton College. She works at Blackwell Publishers in Oxford, England.

**Blair Gifford** is Assistant Professor of Health Management in the College of Business, University of Colorado at Denver. His research interests include health system reform and consolidation. He is currently conducting research on teen prenatal care, quality of life and cardiac mortality, and antitrust issues for hospital mergers. He has a Ph.D. in sociology from the University of Chicago and more than 10 years' experience in health services research prior to his coming to the University of Colorado in 1993.

**Ursula Glunk** is Assistant Professor in the Management Department at the University of Maastricht in the Netherlands. She received her Ph.D. in organization studies at Tilburg University in the Netherlands and holds a master's degree in organizational psychology from the University of Mannheim, Germany. In her Ph.D. research she studied the link between internal resources and stakeholder performance in professional service firms. Her current research interests include organizational cognition and the management of professionals.

**Eric A. Goodman** received his Ph.D. from the University of Colorado at Boulder and is currently a professor of management at Colorado Technical University. His research interests include burnout, empowerment, turnover, organizational justice, mentoring, and change processes. His work has appeared in several outlets, including *Group and Organization Management, Organization Development Journal, Journal of Vocational Behavior, Journal of Health and Human Resources Administration, Academic Emergency Medicine,* and *Annals of Emergency Medicine.*

**Cherlyn Skromme Granrose** is Professor of Management and OB at Berry College. She received her Ph.D. from Rutgers University in 1981, and from 1981 to 1999 she taught courses in organizational behavior and human resources at Temple University and Claremont Graduate University. She has had a Fulbright summer seminar award to South Korea and Taiwan, a Fulbright research award to Singapore, and a Fulbright teaching award to the People's Republic of China. Her research publications include articles and books on Asian managers' careers, women's work-family choices, and participative decision making. She is an active member of the International Division of the Academy of Management and has also served on the executive boards of the Women in Management Division and the Careers Division of the Academy of Management.

**Hugh Gunz** trained as a chemist in New Zealand and has Ph.D.s in chemistry and organizational behavior. His career started in the petrochemical industry, and he has taught on the faculties of Manchester Business School and the University of Toronto. He has published papers on the careers of managers, professionals and others, the management of technical professionals, and management education. He is the author of *Careers and Corporate Cultures.* His research interests include the structure of managerial careers in and between organizations and their impact on firms' strategic management, the application of complexity science to careers, and ethical dilemmas experienced by employed professionals.

**David R. Hannah** is a doctoral candidate in the Department of Management at the University of Texas at Austin. His dissertation research is on trade secret protection and misappropriation in organizations. His other research interests include psychological contracts, organizational socialization, deviant behavior, and cultural ties between sport and business. He is coauthor of an article forthcoming in the *Journal of Sport Management* and has presented several papers at professional meetings.

**Mary Jo Hatch** (Ph.D., Stanford University) is Professor of Commerce, McIntire School of Commerce, University of Virginia. Her research interests include organizational culture, identity, and image; managerial and organizational humor, irony, and contradiction; and narrative and metaphoric approaches to the study of organizations and organization theory, with particular interests in jazz and theater as metaphors for organizing in the 21st century. She has published articles in the *Academy of Management Review, Organization Studies, Organization Science, Administrative Science Quarterly, Journal of Management Inquiry, European Journal of Marketing,* and *Studies in Cultures, Organizations and Societies.* She is European editor for the *Journal of Management Inquiry* and sits on the editorial boards of *Human Relations, Journal of Organizational Change Management,* and *Corporate Reputation Review.* She is the author of *Organization Theory: Modern, Symbolic, and Postmodern Perspectives* (1997).

**Jean C. Helms Mills** is Assistant Professor of Organizational Behaviour at Mount Allison University in New Brunswick, Canada. Seventeen years with the airline industry instilled in her the need to make sense of the culture of organizations. Her most recent journal article—in *Studies in Cultures, Organizations and Societies*—compares the relationship between culture and strategy in two Canadian airline companies. She is currently involved in a long-term study of culture and discriminatory practices in the airline industry, funded by the Social Science and Humanities Research Council of Canada.

**Geert Hofstede** is a native of the Netherlands and an Honorary Professor at the University of Hong Kong. He was the founder and first director of the Institute for Research on Intercultural Cooperation, now at Tilburg University. He is Emeritus Professor of Organizational Anthropology and International Management at Maastricht University in the Netherlands and a Fellow of the Center for Economic Research at Tilburg University. He holds a master's-level degree in mechanical engineering from Delft Technical University and a doctorate in social psychology from the University of Groningen. He worked in Dutch as well as international business companies in roles varying from production worker to director of human resources. After that he researched and taught at IMD (Lausanne, Switzerland), INSEAD (Fontainebleau, France), EIASM (Brussels, Belgium), and IIASA (Laxenburg Castle, Austria). Some of his books are *Culture's Consequences* (1980) and *Cultures and Organizations: Software of the Mind* (1991). He is among the top 100 most cited authors in the *Social Science Citation Index* and, of these, one of few non-Americans.

**Karen M. Holcombe** is pursuing a Ph.D. in industrial/organizational psychology at the University of Maryland. Her research interests include service quality, leadership, and cross-cultural issues in organizations.

**Qiang Huang,** who is from the People's Republic of China, finished his master's degree in sociology at Oklahoma State University and is working on his MFA at Temple University. In his master's thesis, titled *Ideology and Social Construction of Reality: A Case Study on Music Therapy,* he concludes that ideology has become part of constructed social realities and plays an important role in the process of constructing scientific knowledge. He is a member of Midsouth Sociological Association and has published several sociological articles and poetry in various journals.

**Lynn R. Kahle** is James Warsaw Professor and Department Chair of Marketing at the University of Oregon in Eugene. Topics of his research include social adaptation, values, and sports marketing. His articles have appeared in such outlets as the *Journal of Consumer Research, Journal of Marketing, Sport Marketing Quarterly, Public Opinion Quarterly, Journal of Personality and Social Psychology,* and *Child Development.* His books include *Social Values and Social Change, Marketing Management,* and *Values, Lifestyles, and Psychographics.*

**Martin Kilduff** (Ph.D., Cornell University) is Professor of Organizational Behavior at Pennsylvania State University. His recent publications, with a variety of coauthors, include a social distance approach to perceived networks (in *Journal of Personality and Social Psychology,* May 1999), an examination of the role of cognitive diversity in the performance of top management teams (in *Organization Science,* in press), and a distinctiveness approach to the social identity and social networks of underrepresented groups (in *Academy of Management Journal,* 1998). His current network research is focused in three areas: networks of ethnic entrepreneurs, personality and social networks, and perceived networks. An ongoing interest in approaches from the humanities and their influence on organizational research continues to provide him with creative new research directions in the areas of organizational culture and ethnography, represented in a recent publication on postmodernism (*Academy of Management Review,* 1997) and a forthcoming article on resisting the discourse of modernity (*Human Relations*).

**Jill Kleinberg** is Associate Professor in the University of Kansas School of Business, where she teaches courses on comparative and cross-cultural management, cross-cultural negotiation, business and society in Japan, and organizational ethnography. She has a Ph.D. in cultural anthropology and an M.A. in Japanese studies from the University of Michigan. Her research and publications to date primarily concern emergent culture in Japanese-owned and -managed organizations operating in the United States. She is beginning a research project that is focused on cross-cultural management issues and the negotiation of cultural identity in Japanese firms in Mexico.

**Debra A. Major** received her doctorate in industrial/organizational psychology from Michigan State University in 1992. She is currently Associate Professor in the Psychology Department at Old Dominion University, where she is responsible for training doctoral students in industrial/organizational psychology. Her research interests include several career development issues, including growth-fostering relationships in the workplace, organizational socialization, and the integration of work and family life. She also studies team effectiveness topics, such as decision making, situational awareness, and training. Her work has appeared in the *Journal of Applied Psychology, Human Resource Development Quarterly, International Journal of Selection and Assessment,* and *Training Research Journal,* as well as in several book chapters. She is actively involved in the Society for Industrial and Organizational Psychology and the Academy of Management.

**Keith A. Markus** earned his doctoral degree in industrial and organizational psychology from the City University of New York Graduate School by way of Baruch College. Location continues the narrative: He currently holds the position of Assistant Professor of Psychology at John Jay College of Criminal Justice. Activity statements follow: He teaches undergraduate and graduate courses in research methods. His methodological and substantive research involves the manner in which discursive practices exceed formal structures, as does this biography.

**Ralf Maslowski** is a Research Associate at the Department of Educational Administration, University of Twente, in the Netherlands. His primary research interests are organizational culture and effectiveness. His current Ph.D. research is focused on the development of an instrument for measuring school culture and on investigation of the relationship between organizational culture and performance in secondary schools in the Netherlands. He has published several articles on the nature of organizational culture and its impact on the functioning of schools.

**John L. Michela** holds a tenured faculty position in the Department of Psychology at the University of Waterloo, Ontario, and an adjunct appointment in Waterloo's Department of Management Sciences. His research and teaching concern various topics in organizational behavior (e.g., culture, leadership, identification, stress), organization development and change (as for innovation), and research methods and statistics (e.g., hierarchical linear modeling). At Waterloo, he has undertaken research and training program collaborations with the Institute for Improvement of Quality and Productivity and with the Institute for Innovation Research. He also has served as Head of the Doctoral Program in Industrial/Organizational Psychology and is cofounder of the Waterloo Organizational Research and Consulting Group. He was previously a tenured faculty member in Columbia University's Program in Social and Organizational Psychology, and he received his Ph.D. in psychology from the University of California, Los Angeles. He likes to think of his set of competencies as unusual, involving cutting-edge statistical methods, theoretical analysis, and real-world applications involving OB and OD topics and approaches.

**Albert J. Mills** is Professor of Management at Saint Mary's University in Nova Scotia, Canada. His research activities center on the impacts of organizational realities upon people, focusing on organizational change and human liberation. This concern was formulated on the shop floor of British industry and through involvement in the movements for social change that characterized the 1960s. He left school at 15, and his early images of organization—images of frustration, sexually segregated work, power disparities, and conflict—were experienced through a series of unskilled jobs and given broader meaning through campaigns for peace, women's liberation, environmental survival, and social change. His coauthored/coedited books include *Organizational Rules* (1991), *Gendering Organizational Analysis* (1992), *Reading Organization Theory* (second edition, 1998), and *Managing the Organizational Melting Pot* (1997).

**Laurie P. Milton,** M.Sc., M.B.A., Ph.D., is Visiting Professor in the Faculty of Management at the University of Calgary. Two themes consistently unite her research agenda: cooperation and performance within and between work groups, and corporate governance. She studies identity and identity negotiation, social interaction and relationships within organizations, participation or involvement, diversity, group dynamics, and corporate culture because they inform these two themes. She earned her Ph.D. in management from the University of Texas at Austin, her M.B.A. from the University of Calgary, and her M.Sc. from the University of Alberta.

**Roy L. Payne,** B.A., Ph.D., graduated in psychology at Liverpool University and spent 2 years in postgraduate study in the MRC Unit for Occupational Aspects of Ageing. From there he joined the Aston group at the University of Aston in Birmingham, then followed Derek Pugh to the London Graduate School of Business Studies. Seventeen years after leaving there, he went as Professor of Organizational Behaviour to Manchester Business School, having spent the intervening years at the MRC/ESRC Social and Applied Psychology Unit at Sheffield University. After 5 years at Manchester he returned to Sheffield in 1992 to a chair in Organizational Behaviour at Sheffield University Management School, and since June 1997 has been Professor of Organizational Psychology at Curtin University of Technology, Perth, Western Australia. His work at Aston led to publications in major international journals on organizational structure and climate/culture in particular, and he has also published extensively in the occupational stress area. The latter publications include four books coedited with Cary L. Cooper that are widely cited in the occupational stress literature. These remain active interests as well as his more recent work on trust in organizations. He has done research and consulting for major organizations in both the public and private sectors.

**Mark F. Peterson,** Ph.D., is Professor of Management and International Business at Florida Atlantic University. His principal interests are in the ways managers make sense of work situations and in the implications of culture and international relations for the ways organizations should be managed. He has published more than 60 articles and chapters, a similar number of conference papers, and several books. The articles have appeared in major management and international management journals such as *Administrative Science Quarterly, Academy of Management Journal, Journal of International Business Studies, Leadership Quarterly, Human Relations,* and *Organization Science.* He has also contributed international management themes to the basic social science literature through chapters in such leading annual volumes as the *Annual Review of Psychology, Communication Yearbook,* and *Research in the Sociology of Organizations.* He has written about the roles different parties play in decision making in organizations throughout the world, the effects that culture has on the role stresses that managers experience, the way immigrant entrepreneur communities operate, and the way that intercultural relationships in multicultural teams and across hierarchical levels should function.

**Andrew M. Pettigrew** is Professor of Strategy and Organisation at Warwick Business School in England, where he founded and directed the internationally renowned Centre for Corporate Strategy and Change. He is the author or editor of 16 books and many articles in scholarly journals. His latest books are *The Innovating Organisation* (edited with Evelyn Fenton) and *The Handbook of Strategy and Organisation* (edited with Howard Thomas and Richard Whittington). Both books are scheduled to appear in 2000.

**Craig C. Pinder** received his Ph.D. in organizational behavior in 1975 from Cornell University. He is author of two books on work motivation, most recently *Work Motivation in Organizational Behavior* (1998), and many articles in scholarly periodicals on topics related to work motivation, employee transfers and mobility, and philosophy of administrative science. His current research interests include employee silence behavior, organizational retreats, and injustice in work organizations. He is past president of the Western Academy of Management and is currently a member of the board of directors of the British Columbia Human Resources Management Association. He has recently moved to the Faculty of Business at the University of Victoria, after nearly 25 years at the University of British Columbia.

**Anat Rafaeli** is Associate Professor of Organizational Behavior at the Faculty of Industrial Engineering and Management at the Technion, Israel's Institute of Technology. She is interested in emotional and symbolic self-presentation in organizations, especially as they occur in service interactions.

**Elena Reigadas,** M.A., is a doctoral student at Claremont Graduate University in the Social Psychology Program; her area of specialization is cross-cultural psychology. She is currently Assistant Director of the Center for Learning and Academic Support Services at California State University, Dominguez Hills. She is also a program evaluator and an independent consultant, owner of Multicultural Research Links. She provides research support services to ensure that research instruments are culturally equivalent and reliable. As an independent consultant she has worked for various agencies and research organizations, providing consulting services in the areas of culture, education, and community program evaluation.

**Gregory M. Rose** is Assistant Professor of Marketing at the University of Mississippi. He received his Ph.D. from the University of Oregon. His research has been published in the *Journal of Marketing, Journal of the Academy of Marketing Science, Journal of Advertising, Journal of Applied Social Psychology, Journal of Consumer Research,* and other journals and proceedings.

**Lilach Sagiv** is a Lecturer in the School of Business Administration at the Hebrew University of Jerusalem. She recently received her Ph.D. in social psychology at the Hebrew University, where she studied the role of personal values in the processes and outcomes of career counseling. Her current research focuses on the impacts of congruency between the values of the person and those emphasized in organizational settings (e.g., organizations, occupations). She is also investigating the mechanisms that link personal values to actual behavior.

**Vijay Sathe** is Professor of Management in the Peter F. Drucker Graduate School of Management at the Claremont Graduate University in Claremont, California. He was previously a faculty member at Harvard Business School, at IMD in Switzerland, and at Georgia Institute of Technology. His publications include three books and numerous articles in academic and professional journals. He has taught in a number of M.B.A. and executive education programs in the United States and Europe, and has researched and consulted with organizations of various types around the globe.

**Edgar H. Schein** is the Sloan Fellows Professor of Management Emeritus and Senior Lecturer at the MIT Sloan School of Management, where he has taught since 1956. He has written on career development, process consultation, and organizational culture. His most recent books are *Process Consultation Revisited* (1999) and *The Corporate Culture Survival Guide* (1999).

**Benjamin Schneider** is Professor of Psychology and Chair of the Industrial and Organizational Psychology Program at the University of Maryland. He has also taught at Michigan State University and Yale University and, for shorter periods of time, at Bar-Ilan University (Israel, on a Fulbright), University of Aix-Marseille (France), and Peking University (People's Republic of China). He holds a Ph.D. in psychology (University of Maryland, 1967) and also an M.B.A. (City University of New York, 1964). His academic accomplishments include more than 85 journal articles and book chapters, six books, and appointments to the editorial review boards of the *Journal of Applied Psychology* and other journals. His interests concern service quality, organizational climate and culture, staffing issues, and person-organization fit, especially the role of manager personality in organizational effectiveness. His most recent book (with David E. Bowen) is *Winning the Service Game* (1995). Professional recognition for his accomplishments includes election to Fellowship in the American Psychological Association, the American Psychological Society, and the Academy of Management, as well as election to the post of President of the Organizational Behavior Division of the Academy of Management and of the Society for Industrial and Organizational Psychology. He is also listed in *Who's Who in America* and derivative volumes. In addition to his academic work, he is Vice President, Organizational and Personnel Research, Inc. His recent research consultantships have included the state of Alabama, Allstate Research and Planning Center, the state of Pennsylvania, Sotheby's, the Metropolitan Opera, and American Express.

**Shalom H. Schwartz** is the Leon and Clara Sznajderman Professor of Psychology at the Hebrew University of Jerusalem, where he has been for the past 20 years. He earlier taught at the University of Wisconsin–Madison and received a Ph.D. in social psychology from the University of Michigan. His major current research interests involve studies of human values. He developed a theory of the structure and content of values whose main postulates have been supported in more than 60 countries in an international project he coordinates. This theory has been the focus of work on antecedents and consequences of individual differences in values. He has also generated a theory of dimensions of culture and used the data from the international project to array more than 60 nations around the world on these dimensions. This theory challenges the well-known individualism/collectivism approach. He is currently studying implications of national culture for what goes on within nations and trying to untangle the mutual causal influences of national culture, social structure, demography, psychological experience, and individual behavior.

**Aviv Shoham** (Ph.D., University of Oregon, 1993) is Senior Lecturer of Marketing and Marketing Area Coordinator at the William Davidson Faculty of Industrial Engineering and Management, Technion-Israel Institute of Technology, Haifa. His research focuses on international marketing and marketing strategy and has appeared in such publications as the *Journal of the Academy of Marketing Science, Journal of International Marketing, Journal of Business Research, Journal of Advertising Research, International Business Review,* and *Journal of Global Marketing.*

**Peter B. Smith** is Professor of Social Psychology at the University of Sussex, England. He obtained his Ph.D. from the University of Cambridge in 1962. He is author or coauthor of six books, most recently *Social Psychology Across Cultures* (with M. H. Bond), and more than 90 other publications in the fields of social and organizational psychology. He has spent the past 15 years studying cross-cultural aspects of leadership and management. He is editor of the *Journal of Cross-Cultural Psychology*.

**Joseph L. Soeters** is Professor of Social Sciences at the Faculty of Military Studies of the Royal Netherlands Military Academy in Breda. In addition, he serves as a Professor of Sociology at Tilburg University. His studies focus on the cultural and international dimensions of organizations, and he has published extensively in such journals as *Organization Studies, Policing and Society, Journal of Management Studies, Armed Forces and Society,* and *Accounting, Organizations, and Society.*

**Richard W. Stackman** is Assistant Professor of Business Administration at the University of Washington, Tacoma. He earned his doctorate in business administration from the University of British Columbia in 1995, where his studies focused on organizational behavior. He holds an undergraduate degree in business administration from the University of California, Berkeley, where he graduated with honors and was inducted into Phi Beta Kappa. His scholarly interests include personal work networks, personal values, career and job-search strategies, and organizational sages.

**Janet L. Szumal** is a Senior Research Associate at Human Synergistics/Center for Applied Research. She received both her B.S. degree (1987) in management and her Ph.D. degree (1995) in human resource management from the University of Illinois at Chicago. She is the author of the *Organizational Culture Inventory Interpretation and Development Guide* and the *Cultural Change Situation* (a simulation designed to help people to understand and interpret their OCI results) and has coauthored articles on the reliability and validity of the OCI.

**Marc W. D. Tyrrell** is currently completing a Ph.D. in sociology at Carleton University, examining the outplacement industry in Canada. His primary research area is in symbolic and behavioral adaptation to change, and he has done fieldwork with career counselors, cyberspace communities, and modern neo-pagans. He has an academic background in comparative religion, anthropology, and sociology, and his work tends to be syncretic and to focus on the similarity of adaptations human groups come up with. He has presented papers at the annual meetings of the American Sociological Association and the Canadian Anthropological Society as well as at several regional conferences.

**Turo Virtanen** is Professor and Head of the Department of Political Science at the University of Helsinki, Finland. He teaches courses in theories of leadership and management, theory of public administration and organizations, international administration, and methodology of social science. His research interests have spanned management and leadership of universities and scientific work, philosophy of administration, information management, competencies of civil servants and human resource management in general, theory of policy implementation, international civil service, theory of social action and power, leadership culture, and public management. He is currently doing research on leadership culture and performance management in Finnish state government. He is the author of seven research monographs (published in Finland) and has also published widely in journals and contributed many chapters to books on new public management and human resource management.

**Yaakov Weber** heads the Strategic Management area at the School of Management, Ben-Gurion University of the Negrev in Israel. He has authored numerous articles on mergers and acquisitions that have been published in such journals as *Strategic Management Journal, Management Science, Journal of Management, Human Relations,* and *Information and Management.* His primary research interests involve the study of the effects of national and organizational culture on the behavior of top managers and on integration processes following international and domestic mergers and acquisitions.

**Celeste P. M. Wilderom** is Full Professor of Organization Studies in the Department of Business Administration, Faculty of Economics, at Tilburg University in the Netherlands. After she received her master's degree in the social sciences in the Netherlands, she acquired a Ph.D. from the State University of New York at Buffalo. She continued her academic career working for the Department of Business Administration at the Free University of Amsterdam, prior to her current appointment. Her main research work concerns the impact of culture on organizational bottom line and politicking, leadership, and other predictors of organization performance, particularly in (professional) service-type organizations.

**Jack W. Wiley,** Ph.D., is President of Gantz Wiley Research, a consulting firm specializing in conducting employee and customer satisfaction surveys for international corporate clients. Previously, he was Director of Organizational Research at Control Data Business Advisors. He has also held personnel research positions at National Bank of Detroit and Ford Motor Company. He has internationally recognized expertise in linking employee survey results to measures of customer satisfaction and business performance, and has developed WorkTrends™, a normative database of employee opinions. He has written several articles and book chapters on survey research topics and has made numerous presentations to professional associations. He received his Ph.D. in organizational psychology from the University of Tennessee. He is a licensed consulting psychologist, accredited as a senior professional in human resources, and has several years of graduate/business school teaching experience as an adjunct professor. He is a member of the Society for Industrial and Organizational Psychology, the American Psychological Society, the International Association of Applied Psychology, and the Academy of Management.

**Monica Worline** is a graduate student in organizational psychology at the University of Michigan. She is interested in the social nature of learning and the ways in which narratives and symbols affect learning processes in organizations.

**Raymond F. Zammuto** (Ph.D., University of Illinois) is Professor of Management at the University of Colorado at Denver. He has conducted research and taught in the areas of organization design, strategic management, turnaround management, and organizational culture for 15 years. He has published two books, *Assessing Organizational Effectiveness: Systems Change, Adaptation, and Strategy* and *Organizations: Theory and Design* (with A. Bedeian), as well as numerous articles. Over the past few years, he has consulted on and conducted workshops about organization culture and organization redesign and reengineering for a variety of organizations. Much of this work has focused on helping managers understand why many organizations attempting to redesign themselves fail to achieve their goals and what they can do to reduce organizational barriers to success. His current research focuses on how different organizational cultures and managerial ideologies affect the ability of organizations to adapt to changing environments. He has served on the board of directors of the Organizational Behavior Teaching Society and as Chair of the Organization and Management Theory Division of the Academy of Management. He has been a member of several editorial boards, including those of the *Academy of Management Journal, Administrative Science Quarterly,* and *Organization Science,* and is a past associate editor of the *Academy of Management Executive,* a journal dedicated to translating academic theory and research into practical information for managers.